Carmarthenshire & Beyond: Studies in History and Archaeology in Memory of Terry James

Edited by

HEATHER JAMES & PATRICIA MOORE

*with the assistance of the David Rees bequest
for the preparation of maps and plans*

CARMARTHENSHIRE
ANTIQUARIAN
SOCIETY
2009

Carmarthenshire Antiquarian Society Monograph Series Volume 8

ISBN 978-0-906972-05-2

Cover illustration
Watercolour of Carmarthen Quay, 1899, by Benjamin Archibald Lewis.
(Collection: Carmarthenshire County Museum. Copyright: the artist's estate).

Back cover
Air photograph of Pen-y-Gaer hillfort, Llanybydder, by Terry James.

Printed in Wales by
Dinefwr Press
Rawlings Road, Llandybie
Carmarthenshire, SA18 3YD

Contents

Introduction   *Rev. J. Towyn Jones (President, Carmarthenshire Antiquarian Society)* vii
Terry James: a brief description of his life and work   *Heather James* ix
List of Publications xx

Erasmus and the Scholar-Printers   *Gwyn Walters* 1
Papermaking in West Wales   *Terry Wells* 9
Carmarthen Printing and Ancillary Trades, 1720-1820   *Eiluned Rees* 27
Early Travellers and their Printed Images of the Tywi Valley   *Jill & Conrad Davies* 40
Artists' Depiction of Carmarthen Quay   *Ann Dorsett* 61
Christopher Williams and Carmarthenshire   *Dylan Rees* 67
John Francis Lloyd . . . A Carmarthen Photographer   *Chris Delaney* 81
J. F. Jones's Slides and Photographs of Carmarthenshire Country Houses   *Thomas Lloyd* 87
Nantymwyn, A Carmarthenshire Klondike   *Tina Carr & Annemarie Schöne* 94
The Present and Future of Aerial Archaeology in Carmarthenshire   *Toby Driver* 98
The Joys of Enclosures: Aspects of Aerial Reconnaissance in Devon and Somerset   *Frances Griffith* 107
A Romano-British Cremation at Allt-y-Cnap Road, Carmarthen   *John Purdue, Dee Williams*
    & Ros Coard (edited and with contributions by H. James) 123
Some Preliminary Observations on Sir John Gardner Wilkinson's Survey of the Ogofau Gold Mines,
    Dolaucothi, of 1868   *C. Stephen Briggs* 135
St Peter's and the Men of Old Carmarthen   *William Strange* 150
Pentowyn, Llanstephan – a Pre-conquest Possession of Llanteulyddog (Carmarthen Priory)   *Heather James* ... 155
The Advowson of Abernant Church   *J. Beverley Smith* (with additional notes by H. James) 169
From Chapel to Cloister (A study in continuity and change over seven centuries)   *J. Wyn Evans* 174
'A Plot within the Close of the College Church': Abergwili Bishop's Palace
    and College Revisited   *Neil Ludlow* 192
The Topography of Mediaeval Cardigan   *Seamus Cunnane* 204
Place-names in Early Printed Maps of Carmarthenshire   *D. Huw Owen* 224
Sir John Perrot's Deer Park at Cyffig   *Ken Murphy* 231
The Trenches at Falkland, Fife: a Legacy of Royal Deer-management?   *Simon Taylor* 235
At the Margins: the Dynamics of Post-Mediaeval Land-use and Settlement around the Farm of Sarn Faen
    in the Twrch Valley, Carmarthenshire   *Muriel Bowen-Evans and Anthony Ward* 245
Dinas, Cwm Doethïe: Reflections on a Deserted Upland Farmstead   *Richard Suggett* 259
Toponymy and Land-use in the Uplands of the Doethïe Valley (Cardiganshire)   *Iwan Wmffre* 270
The Pothouse: a Carmarthen Waterfront Building   *Terrence James* 284
A Further Study of the Pothouse and its Surroundings   *Edna Dale-Jones* 298

List of Subscribers 312

Index 314

Introduction

Reverend J. Towyn Jones

(President, Carmarthenshire Antiquarian Society)

As one now contemplates in awe the magnificence of St Paul's Cathedral, restored of late to its original glory both without and within, one realises and acknowledges anew the pertinence of the famous inscription over the interior of the North Door which celebrates its designer Sir Christopher Wren:

Si monumentum requiris, circumspice
[If you would see his monument look around]

It is with similar profound respect that I write these words mindful as I am of Terry James' eminent contribution. My task is as simple as it is honourable. I am unveiling this most excellent epitaph to one beloved as a friend and so highly regarded as a historian, especially of the ancient borough and county of Carmarthen. What memorial would one truly choose for oneself? How would one wish to be remembered in an age when so many statements are transient and ephemeral? The Welsh poet Eifion Wyn avowed:

Caed eraill faen o fynor
A thorch o flodau ffug;
Ond . . .
[Let others have a marble tablet / And a wreath of imitation blooms / But . . .]

Surely this remembrancer surpasses all others? What greater and more worthy tribute than this volume could the Carmarthenshire Antiquarian Society afford one who not only served it so well, but whose entire life-work was so in accordance with its *raison d' être*.

For as long as Carmarthen prevails and people persist in the study of history within and without the borders of its shire, they will often reach for this volume. Every time they do, Terry's name and contribution will be commemorated. During his campaign Barak Obama quoted William Faulkner:

The past is never dead. It's not even past.

Nor will Terry James ever be.

This is a volume of learned and definitive essays by his peers on various aspects of history of particular interest to him. They are dedicated with love and admiration to perpetuate the name of one whose friendship and intellect enriched our lives.

And so, if I may adapt a little of that famous eulogy:

Si monumentum requiris, librum circumspice . . .
[If you would see his monument look in this book]

Terry James: a brief description of his life and work

Heather James

In an obituary written for the CBA Wales Newsletter,[1] Stephen Briggs, a friend and former colleague of Terry's at the Royal Commission on Ancient & Historical Monuments, Wales (RCAHMW) doubted whether the career that Terry had pursued in archaeology would be possible today. This introduction to the volume of papers in Terry's memory gives an outline of his life and attempts to describe and characterise his career and assess his contribution to the history and archaeology of west Wales in particular and archaeological practice in general. It reflects some of the massive changes in archaeological practice which have taken place since the mid 1970s, changes in the main which Terry relished and adapted to rapidly and successfully. A recent survey by the Institute of Field Archaeologists[2] shows that 99% of those working in the profession today have archaeology degrees – that was very far from being the case thirty or so years ago when the needs of 'rescue' archaeology[3] were creating today's profession.

Terry was a Carmarthen boy, born and bred; his home, Rudd's Cottage,[4] lies well within the sound of St Peter's Church bells. He had a happy outdoor sort of childhood, of the kind that today attracts an immense nostalgia. Terry's older brother, Peter, was keener on football – for which his father Emrys, had a lifelong enthusiasm, running junior teams in the town with minimal funds. Terry's passion was fishing; the River Towy, and the Bishop's Pond at Abergwili provided opportunities for he and his friends to be out all day pursuing what subsequent reminiscences portray as an almost legendary pike in the Pond in terms of size and voracity, and there were sewin, salmon, and eels in the river. Money was short but Terry's mother, Audrey, took

the boys for regular walks along Pondside, generally with their dog, Spot. Audrey shared her passion for nature with the boys and generally stimulated their imagination. Rudd's Cottage garden then stretched down the whole length of what is now St Peter's Car Park and next door was the empty and ruinous Norton's Brewery, a paradise for forbidden exploration of its cellars and outbuildings. Lifelong friendships were made. School was less satisfactory and Terry made no secret of the fact that he was a late starter and was deemed to have more practical than intellectual skills. A failure (common at the time) to identify a degree of dyslexia did not help. I turn to his dear friend Sian Morris' funeral address for a reminiscence of his teenage years: 'I remember Terry as a Saturday boy at Edwards the Sports, in Lammas Street. He was a handsome, fun-loving teenager whose life revolved around wheels – first the bicycle, then the motorbike (the Cotton) and then, when he was legally allowed to drive, membership of the Motor Club provided a chance to take part very successfully in car rallies'.[5]

Terry left school in 1963, aged fourteen, to take up a six year letterpress apprenticeship at the local newspaper, *The Carmarthen Journal*. In 2002, he wrote an account of those years for the Society's volume of reminiscences, *Carmarthenshire Memories of the Twentieth Century*.[6] From that distance of time, he could look back on both the Journal years, his work at the Oxford University Press and his own Rampart Press (1981-82 full-time) and realise that he had lived through a revolution in the production and dissemination of the printed word. 'Apart from using a few modern machines, our practices differed little from those of the seventeenth century printers, because I can read the pages of

Fig. 1: *Terry composing the title page for* Camden's Wales
at The Rampart Press.
(Photograph: Heather James).

Moxon's *Mechanick Exercises*[7] and say, "Yes, that is how we did it too".'

These values and skills learned in the printing trade were carried over into his work as an archaeologist and historian to the benefit of both. He would have greatly appreciated the tribute paid by Margaret Faull who wrote a short obituary in the *Society for Landscape Studies Newsletter* recalling her work with Terry on the first few issues of that Society's Journal, which he printed, choosing typefaces, deciding on layout and paper. She emphasised that 'it is only now, nearly thirty years after he helped establish the house style, that . . . the Society is looking to update the appearance of the Journal'.[8] Layout, typography, the use of images, whether plans or photographs or drawings – all these are as important today in communicating archaeological and historical discoveries and research when so much is now possible with computer software and the internet. How many books and websites do we still see where colour overwhelms the text, where founts are too small, where plans and drawings do not relate to the text?

To return for the moment to the *Carmarthen Journal* days – his memoir does not go into details of his grow-

ing engagement in union and left wing politics. He was a member of the NGA (National Graphical Association) and was at a young age elected FoC (Father of Chapel), the trade's term for shop steward. He negotiated a number of improvements in working conditions and rates with the management. I suppose he would qualify as an 'angry young man', and was something of a thorn in the flesh of the Carmarthen Labour Party of which he was a member. But having said that, there was a period when he was considered as a possible future labour candidate for an east Carmarthenshire seat. He had moved to Oxford in 1969 and spent two years working at the Oxford University Press on high quality bookwork as a fully qualified compositor. From there he gained an NGA funded scholarship to Ruskin College to study politics and economic history (1971-73), years when he was also active in left wing and union politics. In 1973 he was awarded a Diploma in Labour Studies by the College. His thesis was entitled 'Socialism and the War: a study of attitudes during World War II amongst the Socialist Left'. It was driven by a Marxist, or more precisely Trotskyist, ideology. It definitely began what was a life-long interest in primary historical research directly from source material.

Terry returned to Carmarthen in 1973 for health and family reasons and was considering embarking on an MA in economic history at Warwick University. Funds however were not forthcoming and he went back to work at the *Journal.* On his return he had plunged into urgent research into the status of Bishop Rudd's charity and the history of Rudd's Cottage itself – one of Rudd's almshouses – since this was a critical period for the family striving to convert their tenancy from the Town Council into ownership and then embark on wholesale improvements. His future direction was uncertain but he joined the Carmarthenshire Antiquarian Society (of which his mother, Audrey, was already a member) and was soon influenced by the unassuming but remarkably persuasive Bill Morris, the then editor of the *Carmarthenshire Antiquary*. He suggested that Terry research the early nineteenth century history of the Carmarthen Tinworks, and this was when he began to seriously develop his photographic skills. The Tinworks were then, in the 1970s, atmospheric ivy-clad ruins whose future was far from assured. He made as full a photographic record as possible and partly for financial reasons, cash being short, but mainly because he liked to get rapid results and control the processes, he set up a dark room at home and taught himself how to develop and print his

Fig. 2: *Duke's Yard, Priory Street, Carmarthen, now demolished and photographed by Terry in 1984.*

own photographs. He continued to take photographs of the rapidly changing Carmarthen townscape and these now form a considerable archive.

And archaeology? The Antiquarian Society and many in Carmarthen were still 'buzzing' from the trail-blazing excavation campaigns between 1969 and 1971 of the late Professor Barri Jones, ably assisted by John Little of Carmarthen Museum, which were the first professional excavations in the Roman town. The large St Peter's Car Park excavation lay just outside the end of Rudd's cottage garden and although he did not take part, being away in Oxford at the time, on his home visits. Terry became very interested in what was being discovered – and how it was done. Barri Jones also pioneered a programme of aerial reconnaissance as well as excavation work at Pumpsaint and Dolaucothi. Bill Morris and John Little were prominent local members of a small committee working with the then Ministry of Public Buildings and Works in Cardiff in the person of Ancient Monuments Inspector Dai Morgan Evans to set up the four Welsh Archaeological Trusts, essentially in place by 1974. Don Benson was appointed Director of the Dyfed Archaeological Trust and shortly afterwards I was

recruited as Assistant Director. We were soon introduced to Terry. There were many evenings (and it has to be said, the occasional afternoon) of intense discussion and exchange of ideas in several of Carmarthen's pubs. Don Benson recognised Terry's potential and he was employed, at first on a short contract, to research and write a Survey of Carmarthen's topography and archaeology.[9] At a personal level, Terry and I found that we had much in common and a developing relationship led to our marriage in March 1978.

At the same time as researching the history, topography, previous archaeological and antiquarian work and finds for the *Survey*, Terry was creating entries for the Trust's newly established *Sites and Monuments Record*. George Williams, the second Field Officer to be recruited, led a small team to create the record for Dyfed from, in the first instance, the Ordnance Survey's archaeology record cards. Don Benson had pioneered Sites and Monuments Records in Oxfordshire and DAT's model was adopted for the other Welsh Trusts. The Carmarthen Survey was intended to establish research priorities before embarking on a series of 'rescue' excavations. Events however intervened and the first Trust excavation took place at Church Street, Carmarthen, which I directed and which lay within the Roman town. Terry took part as site photographer but also to excavate and he learnt very quickly. We were much exercised by trying to improve the speed, quality and objectivity of our data recognition, recording and planning. Developing Don's photographic tower used on his excavations on the Neolithic Chambered Tomb at Ascott-under-Wychwood, Terry built a reduced pyramid and experimented with vertical photographs covering grid squares to build up a photomosaic of different surfaces exposed.[10] Single context recording – the Harris matrix for checking stratigraphic relationships and systematic standardised descriptions of features, soils and artefacts – was soon to be a at the core of the early computerised excavation records databases with software being developed by Jo Jefferies for the then Central Excavation Unit.

Terry's site planning, draughting and photographic skills were developed by working as co-director with George Williams on excavations on Iron Age defended enclosure sites on Pembrey Mountain, Carmarthenshire in Spring in 1977.[11] In 1979 Terry directed his first excavation on part of the site of St John's Priory, Carmarthen, where a sewage pumping station was to be built. Much of the background historical and antiquarian detail was well known to him through the Carmarthen Survey

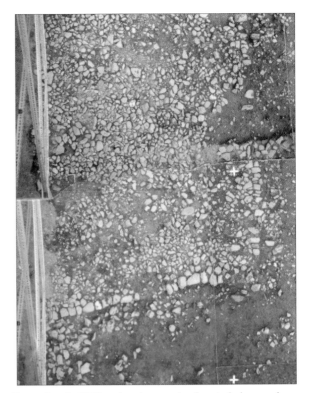

Figs. 3 a & b: *The photographic pyramid in use at Church Street Excavations in 1978 and a photomosaic of vertical photographs.*

Work but the excavation elucidated the position and part of the plan of the Priory Church and we also gained some early mediaeval radiocarbon dates assumed to relate to the pre-conquest native Welsh monastery of St Teulyddog. A deepening interest was developing into the contribution the little studied Carmarthen Cartulary could make to many aspects of mediaeval Carmarthen's history – a theme explored in the three papers in this volume. Most importantly, as it turned out, the St John's Priory excavation gave Terry valuable experience for the much larger Carmarthen Greyfriars excavations which he undertook between 1983 and 1990. But that is to rush ahead.

Both from this account, and Terry's list of publications, it will be apparent that he was simultaneously engaged in many different aspects of the archaeological profession and discipline. To some extent, all of us were at that period and perhaps this is one of the main differences between the profession now and then when there is a greater degree of specialisation. He, however, had a greater range of technical skills than most of us but they were always for him a means to an end. Don Benson, who by now was a friend as well as a boss, had come to Dyfed with an extensive background of aerial reconnaissance in Oxfordshire and the Upper Thames Valley. With his photographic skills and knowledge of the county, Terry required little persuasion to take to the air in 1979 and at first he 'hitched a ride' with Doug Simpson of the County Council, who was photographing caravan sites from the air to check on any infringements. Flight paths to and from such sites were somewhat loosely interpreted and this enabled the trainee flyers to build up sufficient air photographs to publish *Ancient West Wales from the Air* in 1980. This was intended to stimulate interest in air photography and demonstrate its potential for discovery and record in west Wales. In her paper on air photography in Devon, Frances Griffith has covered the trials and tribulations of handling cameras in flight, changing backs and lenses and labelling rolls of film as well as the advantages local flyers had in locating their photographs. Toby Driver has summarised Terry's aerial photographic career in his article and writes of the 2005 flight when he invited Terry to accompany him. I know how much Terry enjoyed the experience and how delighted he was to see brought to fruition the improvements in capturing the images, plotting the flight paths and site locations and rapid sharing of results that digital photography and GPS logging have brought.

Then in 1981 came another career change – Terry left the Trust to set up his own printing business – The Rampart Press. He wanted to be his own master. The idea was to print specialist historical and archaeological journals in high quality letterpress. There was a great deal of redundant hot-metal printing equipment around at that time which could be purchased cheaply. We bought a workshop formerly used by a signwriter, in Penuel Street just up the road from our house and set up the Press there. It was exciting, I must admit, to go up to large printing press works like Bayliss's in Worcester and buy up surplus type and machinery. He equipped himself to smelt type metal, cast type with a fiendishly complex Monotype caster, driven by punched tape instructions from a Monotype keyboard to produce galleys of copy. Printing was done on a superb Heidelberg double cylinder Press. He did print some academic journals and continued to print the *Carmarthenshire Antiquary*, even after returning to archaeology. His major work was a masterwork of letterpress printing, *Camden's Wales* (to which Gwyn Walters alludes in his paper on Erasmus) when the whole of Gibson's edition was recast and reset in hot metal as a facsimile, producing a beautiful book, but in some ways, looking back, a somewhat quixotic enterprise. It is safe to say that no-one will ever do such a thing again! In fact this was not a viable business and some hard lessons on being self employed were learnt. The changes to offset litho and then computer-aided printing came at remarkable speed and letterpress printing was coming to an end. So when the Trust advertised for a Director for what were clearly going to be major excavations at Carmarthen Greyfriars, he applied for the post and (to our great relief) was appointed for the second time to the Trust, against some stiff competition.

Planning permission had been given for a Tesco supermarket on Carmarthen Greyfriars site and with support from the Planning department of the then Carmarthen District Council, developer funding was won for excavation and post-excavation work. Following on information gained from two very long (and in places very deep) trial trenches, large areas of what were identified as the Friary's double cloisters were opened up. Subsequently parts of the church and other claustral buildings were explored. These excavations were on as large a scale as any urban rescue archaeological excava-

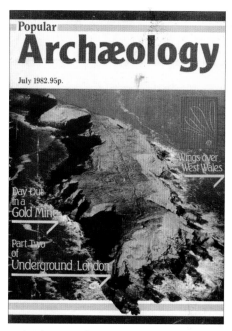

Fig. 4: *The cover of* Popular Archaeology, *July 1982, edited by Barri Jones, showing Terry's photograph of Gateholm Island, Pembrokeshire which won the 1979 Kodak Award to Aerial Archaeology.*

tions in Britain and Carmarthen Greyfriars remains the most extensively investigated urban grey friary in Britain. Excavations in 1990 were directed by Ken Murphy since Terry had sustained a severe head injury but he wrote the main excavation Report. A later phase of excavation was directed by Andrew Manning. These excavations at their peak employed up to fifty people, many on Manpower Service Commission schemes. Considerable managerial and organisational skills were required because, although these job creation schemes did bring able people into archaeology there were, inevitably, others whose skills and interests most definitely lay elsewhere. Thus, like all of us, directing excavations in that era, Terry needed to constantly train and motivate a large and disparate group of people and his own background helped in doing this. Carmarthen Greyfriars, like many urban excavations, were difficult to co-ordinate with large open areas being uncovered in some locations and 'key-hole' trenches in others. Terry made full use of the 'delilah'[12] software for manipulating the site data and its powerful checking facilities for stratigraphic relationships were vital in establishing overall sequences and chronologies on site. An early decision was made to plan the site at a scale of 1:50 – a much

Fig. 5: *Planning and excavation underway at Carmarthen Greyfriars in part of the choir of the Friary church. The robbed out lines of the three ascending sanctuary steps leading to the high altar (outside the excavation are) can be seen across the photograph. This sought after burial area was crowded with a succession of graves of important people.*
(Photograph: Terry James).

more difficult process for site planners than the normal 1:20 scale. The benefit was that little further reduction was needed for the final published plans. The excavations attracted much media and public interest particularly when it became possible to link excavated graves and skeletons with known historical figures buried at the Friary – such as William de Valence, or Tudur Aled, bard to Sir Rhys ap Thomas who ended his days in comfort as a 'corrodian' or pensioner at the Friary.

Don Benson had developed the idea of 'Topic Reports' for the vast amounts of data from the specialist reports on finds, and, for Greyfriars, valuable information from the human remains. The technology of the time – desk-top but pre-internet publishing – enabled Dyfed Archaeological Trust to produce an overview summary report for a national journal[13] that was backed up by the capacity to generate the detailed individual topic reports on demand and at cost. Terry's expertise enabled him to deliver this publication 'package' with enthusiasm.

Unexpected circumstance, as often happens, caused the next major change in Terry's career. Following the tragic death of Charles Stenger, the Trust's Sites and Monuments Record Officer, in a motor accident in 1986, Terry took over the SMR. In Don Benson's words 'this was a key period in the development of electronic techniques for handling and disseminating information in archaeology. Working with Jo Jefferies, by then in England's Ancient Monuments and Historic Buildings Branch, Terry was instrumental in developing and testing programmes which were fundamental to progress in the field and which were subsequently widely utilised in both England and Wales.'[14] He was fast developing his ideas on dynamic and inter-related databases. An up-to-date account of the Dyfed Archaeological Trust's Record, now known as the Historic Environment Record has recently been written by the current HER officer.[15]

Terry had applied for the post of Investigator in Aerial Archaeology at RCAHMW in 1986 but had been pipped at the post by his friend and colleague Chris

Musson. In 1991 another post at the Commission came up – this time directly related to his field of work – that of Computer Manager. Terry shared Don's vision for a national Welsh archaeological record which could be created by linking Welsh Archaeological Trust SMRs with a newly computerised Commission Record strong on the built heritage – ENDEX, or the Extended National Database. This was a goal being promoted at the time in a joint Trusts/Commission/Cadw working party. Terry had hoped that his own Trust background and contacts with colleagues in the other Welsh Archaeological Trusts would help the organisations to come together. It was not to happen in such a straight-forward way. The new post was the last appointment made by the retiring secretary, Peter Smith and in fact Terry started work at the Commission in October 1991 almost at the same time as the new Secretary, Peter White. Major changes in working methods and indeed organisational goals were set in train with all staff being now trained to work with personal computers. Terry was involved in much hands-on work in this and in training as well as creating a network for office, archive and fieldwork. Terry was very proud of being a member of the Royal Commission but it certainly involved for him major changes in ways of working and getting used to the Civil Service way of doing things.

Thus the years from 1991 were devoted to setting up an Information Technology infrastructure for the whole of the Commission's work – and, not surprisingly, it took time. In 1996 he was given managerial responsibility for the National Monument Record's archive which awakened a growing interest in the conservation of photographic records in particular. Evolving databases were at the core not just of recording and storage of material but, most importantly, the ability to retrieve records for users. Much work was done with his colleague Chris Musson on systems for cataloguing air photographs. By 1998 a major restructuring of the Commission was in place and Terry successfully applied for the post of Head of Information Management. Thus Terry's working life in the 1990s at the Royal Commission evolved from a fairly practical hands on role in the early days to a managerial and policy making nature. He began to participate in heritage policy making at much more of a national level, serving for a time on CBA and other committees and gaining a wider perspective through meetings with colleagues in the English and Scottish Commissions, as well as Cadw-Welsh Historic Monuments and English Heritage.

During the 1990s when working at the Royal Commission, he was also able to continue and develop a number of other projects and interests, some of which dovetailed with Commission work and others which were undertaken in his own time. Unfortunately however, the later 1990s were dogged by ill health in the form of persistent lower back pain and to his bitter disappointment, he had finally to leave in 2000 the Royal Commission through early retirement on ill-health grounds. It was a career cut short, but I would like to conclude this brief account of Terry's life and work with some details on the major areas of interest which were pursued throughout the 1980s and 1990s and beyond, many up to his final months.

Although all too conscious of his linguistic short-comings – he was not a Welsh speaker although he had a working knowledge of the language – Terry was very interested in Welsh – and English – place-names. The Carmarthenshire Place-names Survey he instigated was carried out by members of Carmarthenshire Antiquarian Society. It typified in many ways his preference for bottom-up, low cost, practical computer applications and his abilities to motivate volunteers and sustain and bring to fruition an ambitious project. Curated at present by Dyfed Archaeological Trust, the Survey remains a resource awaiting more use and development. From the outset Terry was interested in plotting the distribution of certain common elements and many of us at the early workshops and demonstrations were intrigued by his demonstration on the project's PC of the markedly different locations of common elements like 'cae' and 'parc' (both meaning enclosed field) demonstrable from this data – it still awaits explanation. He continued in retirement to develop his GIS (geographical information systems) skills which were being introduced at the Royal Commission when he was working there.

The Carmarthenshire Survey was one of a small group of other Welsh county-based projects and considerable interest was aroused by Terry's database structure for recording and manipulating place-names. He was invited in 1992 by Professor Bedwyr Lewis Jones of Bangor to assess methods and costs in computerising the late Melville Richards place-name archive then held on paper slips in Bangor. The vision was for this to form the core of a national, Welsh place-names database which could be shared and developed in future years. The growing involvement in promoting computer applications in place-names studies led to an invitation to attend a Symposium on Computers in Place-Names

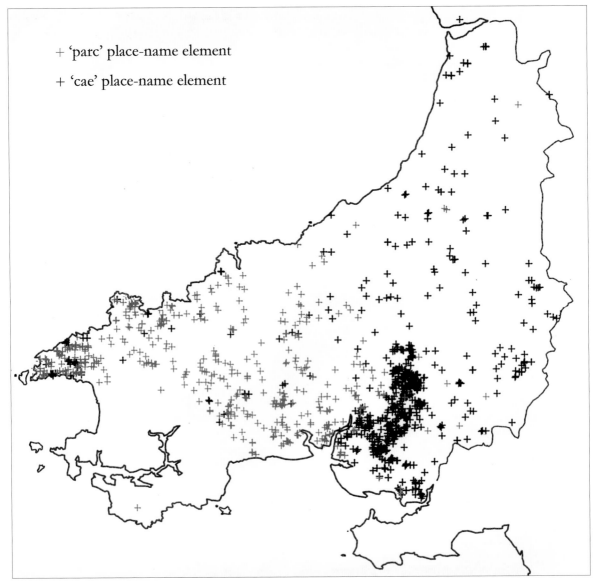

+ 'parc' place-name element

+ 'cae' place-name element

Fig. 6: *An early digitised map of Dyfed with the distribution of place-names with the elements* cae *and* parc
(taken from the Carmarthen place-name survey and DAT's SMR produced by Terry for Survey workshops).

studies held at the Department of Celtic, Queen's University, Belfast in 1993. There he met Simon Taylor who asked Terry to help design a Scottish place-names database. This was partly done in his own time but also dovetailed in with frequent visits to the Scottish Royal Commission to discuss evolving record structures and computer applications. It is fair to say, sadly (for us) that Scotland has progressed at a much faster rate than Wales towards the goal of an interactive computer-based place-names record.

Hill walking was a passion which we both shared throughout the 1980s and 1990s and the three 'uplands' papers in this volume on the Black Mountain and the Doithïe Valley concern themselves with 'deserted rural settlements'. A massive amount of basic survey and recording work by the Royal Commission and the Welsh Archaeological Trusts took place in the Welsh Uplands in the the 1990s.[16] However, when, with friends Anthony Ward, Bill Morris and Muriel Bowen Evans from the Carmarthenshire Antiquarian Society, we first encountered these evocative ruined farmsteads in the late 1980s, clustered in specific locations on the Black Mountain, they were mainly unrecorded and their dates and purpose hardly understood. Anthony Ward went on to study these sites in depth and fortunately the Royal Commission was eventually able to map and plan the whole upland landscape there – way beyond our resources.[17] Then, in the 1990s we discovered the Doithïe valley on the borders of Carmarthenshire and Ceredigion and devoted many winter weekends to finding and planning its ruined farmsteads. Initially the project was driven by the rather naive goal of finding the sites at least of the mediaeval buildings described there as extant in the fourteenth century in the Bishop of St Davids hunting reserve, Fforestyresgob or the Bishop's Forest. Terry was delighted to meet Iwan Wmffre whilst at the Commission then researching Ceredigion's place-names for his doctoral thesis and Iwan's paper on the Doithie in this volume, together with Richard Suggett's on Dinas do much to progress our understanding of historical process in the uplands explaining how and when these structures were built and used and why they are now deserted and ruinous. Anthony and Muriel's paper on Sarn Faen provides a similar Black Mountain case-study. Simply recording and mapping these settlements will not in itself provide these explanations. Our data remains unpublished and I intend to remedy this as soon as practicable.

Although Terry had known the River Towy and estuary since boyhood as a keen fisherman, and had ventured across Carmarthen Bar and out into the Bay in a friend's fishing boat, I am responsible for introducing him to sailing in the early 1980s. It became an abiding passion and he delighted in coastal navigation and pilotage. We graduated from crossing the Bar and venturing to Tenby and Caldey Island in our National Eighteen clinker dinghy to voyages to the West Country, Brittany and Ireland in bigger cruising yachts. But the start or end of any voyage crossing Carmarthen Bar remained a challenge – it is a formidable obstacle, drying out between tides to a vast extent of sandbanks and shifting channels. With the end of commercial shipping to the port of Carmarthen shortly after World War II, Trinity House ceased to maintain buoyage across the Bar and up the river to the port. It was altogether typical of Terry's 'can-do' and self-help mentality and determination to use what techniques and equipment were available that he inspired a group of local yachtsmen and boatowners from the four local clubs to collaborate

and found The Carmarthen Bar Navigation Committee in 1989. He was the co-ordinator until 2000 and I was the Secretary. The Committee sought and raised funds, purchased and made buoys and other sea marks, placing topmarks on nineteenth century barrel posts and checking each year on the ever changing position of channels across the Bar. With so few fixed points however, once out on these vast expanses of sand banks at low water, establishing the latitude and longitude of the edges of channels and marking obstacles was a challenge with the equipment at our disposal. With helpers, Terry produced charts of the Bar and our seamarks and buoys were inspected annually by Trinity House. Terry and the Committee were gratified to have their data adopted by the Hydrographic Office and included in their latest sailing directions. Local Boat Club members still survey

Fig. 7: *Terry (second from left) with members of the Carmarthen Bar Navigation Committee having erected a south cardinal navigation mark on the then dangerously exposed wreck of the* Craigwhinnie *on Carmarthen Bar in 1993. The mark did not survive the winter gales. Today the wreck is once again covered by sand.*
(Photograph: Heather James).

the Bar each spring and circulate a number of waypoints for safe transit.

Terry was eager to use any new navigational aids as soon as they could be afforded and handheld GPS units revolutionised the way the Committee could do its work – and indeed our own coastal pilotage. They have, to a large extent, now made buoyage of these ever-changing channels unnecessary. Methods and equipment which would have been familiar to Captain Cook, or perhaps more prosaically to Lieutenant H. M. Denham surveying the Bar and the Bay in the 1830s with sextant, compass and lead line are now utterly redundant. Terry retained a huge interest in these older techniques and the knowledge helped to inform and indeed inspire his articles on coastal change and shipping.

Coastal change and Intertidal archaeology were shared interests. When the *Carmarthenshire Antiquarian Society* entrusted me with preparing a commemorative volume of essays in memory of both Bill Morris and Mike Evans[18] Terry embarked upon a period of intensive new research for his paper on coastal change entitled 'Where Sea meets Land'. We had first looked at what we only later came to recognise as fishweirs in the estuaries of the Towy and Gwendraeth with Bill Morris in the 1980s. Constant revisits as the sands shifted and then recovered these features over nearly a decade enabled us to finally see them for what they were. Then came the opportunity of a flight over these heavily restricted access military areas when tide and light coincided for good photography. The benefits of better hand held GPS units for more accurate position fixing and planning over a short window of access between tides was equally instrumental in bringing the project to fruition. A glance at the recent overview of coastal archaeological work funded by Cadw-Welsh Historic Monuments and the Royal Commission, and also of course the work carried out by the Welsh University archaeological departments shows how spectacular the results can be from a multi-disciplinary deployment of considerable resources in inter-tidal archaeology.[19] But close acquaintance over a number of years and a detailed regional knowledge is essential and local amateur fieldworkers still have a significant contribution to make.

It is difficult for me to be objective in trying to sum up Terry's work and achievements. There is much I have omitted in perhaps less glamorous work in writing up his many articles, compiling databases, cataloguing and archiving photographs, helping wherever possible the work of local museums and archives and being an active and productive member of many societies and committees. Yet an overemphasis on this would make Terry's life and work appear worthy, but perhaps, merely useful. It was more than that. He did produce work of lasting value. Most important however was his impact on other people – he could inspire and encourage, he was enthusiastic, good humoured and willing and able to help friends and colleagues, and he enjoyed what he did very much. He was in short a good communicator.

Since his death many have commented that had ill-health not taken its toll, his career would have continued to develop. His family and his many friends and colleagues agree that Terry's mental world of historical and archaeological inquiry was a huge support and consolation in his final years when the cancer against which he fought so bravely began to restrict his activities. The series of illustrated short articles he wrote for *Carmarthenshire Life* in those last few years bear testimony to that. Carmarthen and west Wales's past, the questions and queries, the source material itself – sites, finds, photographs, documents – writing, reading and communicating with friends and colleagues through the medium of emails and the internet were all of absorbing interest when so many other activities were denied.

*

In conclusion, I wish to thank the Carmarthenshire Antiquarian Society for entrusting me with this publication. Family and friends have encouraged and sustained me and especial thanks go to my co-editor, Patricia Moore of the RCAHMW whose help has been invaluable. Staff at Dinefwr Press have done a splendid job, and have suggested many improvements in layout. Most of all I wish to thank the contributors who have given freely and generously of their time in producing what I think is a remarkable range of papers reflecting very many of Terry's varied interests.

NOTES

1. C. S. Briggs, 'Terry James FSA', in CBA Wales/Cymru Newletter 33, Spring 2007, pp. 13-15.

2. K. Aitchison and R. Edwards, *Discovering the Archaeologists of Europe: United Kingdom, Profiling the Profession 2007/08*, Institute of Field Archaeologists, 2008.

3. P. A. Rahtz, *Rescue Archaeology*, Penguin Books, 1974.

4. Terry James, 'The Story of Bishop Rudd's Almshouses', *Carmarthenshire Life*, Autumn, 2006.

5. Her address was printed in the *Carmarthen Journal*, 31st Jan. 2007, as 'Fond farewell to a man of many talents'.

6. T. A. James, 'A Carmarthen printing apprenticeship', in E. Rees (ed.), *Carmarthenshire Memories of the Twentieth Century* (Carmarthenshire Antiquarian Society, 2002), pp. 202-207

7. Joseph Moxon, *Mechanick Exercises on the Whole Art of Printing*, H. Davies & H. Carter (eds.), New York, Dover Publications, 1978.

8. M. L. Faull, 'Terry James', *Society for Landscape Studies Newsletter*, Spring/Summer 2007, p. 9.

9. T. A. James, *Carmarthen: An Archaeological and Topographical Survey*, Dyfed Archaeological Trust & Carmarthenshire Antiquarian Society, 1980.

10. T. James, 'Photo-planning: the use of vertical photography as an aid to on-site recording, *Archaeolog*, Royal Photographic Society, Archaeology Section, Vol. 11, 1979.

11. G. Williams, 'Survey and Excavation on Pembrey Mountain', *Carms. Antiq.*, Vol. XVII, 1981, pp. 3-33.

12. 'Delilah', successor to an earlier version named 'Samson' was a flat-file Dos-based database package designed by Jo Jefferies for the Central Excavation Unit. Its potential for SMRs was first realised by Dyfed Archaeological Trust.

13. Med. Arch.

14. D. Benson, 'Obituary: Terrence Alan James', *Carms. Antiq.*, Vol. XLIV, p. 174.

15. M. Page, 'News from the Regional Historic Environment Record', *Carms. Antiq.*, Vol. XLIV, p. 5.

16. D. Browne & S. Hughes (eds.), *The Archaeology of the Welsh Uplands*, RCAHMW, Aberystwyth, 2003; K. Roberts, (ed.), *Lost Farmsteads: deserted rural settlements in Wales*, CBA Research Report 148, 2006.

17. D. K. Leighton, *Mynydd Du and Fforest Fawr: The Evolution of an Upland landscape in South Wales.*

18. H. James (ed.), *Sir Gâr: Studies in Carmarthenshire History*, Carmarthenshire Antiquarian Society, Carmarthen, Monograph 4, 1991.

19. A. Davidson (ed.), *The Coastal Archaeology of Wales*, CBA Research Report 131, 2002.

List of Publications

1976

'Carmarthen Tinplate Works, 1800-1821', *Carms. Antiq.*, Vol. XII, pp. 31-54.

1977

(with Heather James) 'Hedges and Landscape History: a study of land use in the Kidwelly area', *Carms. Antiq.*, Vol. XIII, pp. 42-51.

1978

'A Survey of Fishponds, Watercourses and other Earthworks at the Site of Whitland Abbey and Iron Forge', *Carms. Antiq.*, Vol. XIV, pp. 71-78.

'Cardigan', *Archaeology in Wales*, CBA Group 2, 18, p. 54.

1979

(with D. Simpson) *Ancient West Wales from the Air*, Carmarthenshire Antiquarian Society Monograph No. 1.

1980

Carmarthen: An Archaeological and Topographical Survey, Dyfed Archaeological Trust and Carmarthenshire Antiquarian Society, Monograph No. 2.

'The Bishop's Palace and Collegiate Church, Abergwili', *Carms. Antiq.*, Vol. XVI, pp. 19-43.

1982

'Wings over West Wales: Coastal Sites', *Popular Archaeology*, July 1982, pp. 6-9.

1983

'The Logbook of the Brig *Priscilla* of Carmarthen, April to October,1820', *Carms. Antiq.*, Vol. XIX, pp. 43-51.

'The Angel Vaults, Carmarthen: a hitherto unrecorded medieval building', *Carms. Antiq.*, Vol. XIX, pp. 63-65.

Review of I. Soulsby, *The Towns of Medieval Wales*, 1983, in *Carms. Antiq.*, Vol. XIX, pp. 70-74.

'Excavations at Woolworths, Cardigan, 1978', *Ceredigion*, Vol. XV, pp. 335-42.

1984

'Aerial Photography in Dyfed 1984', *Archaeology in Wales*, No. 24, pp. 12-24.

1985

'Excavations at the Augustinian Priory of St John and St Teulyddog, Carmarthen, 1979', *Archaeologia Cambrensis*, Vol. CXXXIV, pp. 120-161.

(with C. Marshall) 'Llangawse, Llanddewi Velfrey', *Archaeology in Wales*, CBA Group 2, 25, pp. 48-9.

1986

'Shipping and the River Towy: Problems of Navigation', *Carms. Antiq.*, Vol. XXII, pp. 27-37.

'Discovering and Monitoring Sites by Aerial Survey', in D. Austin & D. Moore (eds.), *Welsh Archaeological Heritage Conference Proceedings*, Cambrian Archaeological Association & St Davids University College, Lampeter.

1987

(with Heather James) 'Ceramic and Documentary Evidence for Iberian Trade with West Wales', in B. Vyner & S. Wrathmell (eds.), *Studies in Medieval and Later Pottery in Wales presented to J. M. Lewis*, pp. 225-234.

1988

'Cwrt Malle – an Ancient Manor House Rediscovered', *Carms. Antiq.*, Vol. XXIV, pp. 107-110.

'Air Photography in Dyfed, 1988', *Archaeology in Wales*, No. 28, pp. 39-40.

1989

'Medieval Carmarthen & its Burgesses: a study of town growth and burgess families in the later 13th century', *Carms. Antiq.*, Vol. XXV, pp. 9-26.

(with Muriel Bowen-Evans) 'An Interlude in Carmarthenshire (*Cyfoeth y Thylody*: autobiography of Twm o'r Nant), *Carms. Antiq.*, Vol. XXV, pp. 83-87.

'Air Photography by the Dyfed Archaeological Trust 1989', *Archaeology in Wales*, No. 20, pp. 31-34.

'The early origins of churchyard enclosures in south-west wales – a continuing study of siting and morphology', *Bulletin of the CBA Churches Committee*, No. 26, 1989, pp. 9-16.

1990

'The Carmarthenshire Place-Name Survey', *Carms. Antiq.*, Vol. XXVI, pp. 91-94

'Concentric Antenna Enclosures: a new defended enclosure type in West Wales', *Proc. of the Prehistoric Soc.*, Vol. 56, pp. 295-298.

1991

'Where Sea Meets land: the Changing Carmarthenshire Coastline', in H. James (ed.), *Sir Gâr: Studies in Carmarthenshire History*, Carmarthenshire Antiquarian Society Monograph No. 4, pp. 143-166.

'Carmarthen's Civil War Defences: discoveries at Carmarthen Greyfriars excavations 1983-1990', *Carms. Antiq.*, Vol. XXVII, pp. 21-30.

1992

'Air photography of ecclesiastical sites in south Wales', in N. Edwards & A. Lane (eds.), *The Early Church in Wales and the West*, Oxbow Monograph 16, pp. 62-76.

'The Origins and Topography of Medieval Haverford', *The Pembrokeshire Historian*, Vol. 4, pp. 51-73.

1993

'Carmarthen Priory Gatehouse', *Carms. Antiq.*, Vol. XXIX, pp. 23-26.

'A Carmarthen Bay Shipwreck', *Carms. Antiq.*, Vol. XXIX, pp. 93-102.

1995

'The loss of the Brigantine *Amiable Martha* off Laugharne, September 1786', *Carms. Antiq.*, Vol. XXXI, pp. 67-74.

1997

'Excavations at Carmarthen Greyfriars, 1983-1990', *Medieval Archaeology*, Vol. XLI, pp. 100-194.

'Bleddri ap Cadifor ap Collwyn, Lord of Blaencuch and Cil-sant: Fabulator of Arthurian Romance?', *Carms. Antiq.*, Vol. XXXIII, pp. 27-42.

1998

'Place-name Distributions and Field Archaeology in South-west Wales', in S. Taylor (ed.), *The Uses of Place-Names,* St. John's House Papers No. 7, St Andrews, pp. 101-119.

1999

'The Origins and Topography of Haverford', in D. Miles (ed.), *A History of the Town and County of Haverfordwest*, Gomer Press, pp. 11-33.

2000

'Air Photography and the Archaeology of Carmarthenshire', *Carms. Antiq.*, Vol. XXXVI (Millennium volume), pp. 9-22.

2002

'Haverford', in R. F. Walker (ed.), *Pembrokeshire County History, Vol. II Medieval Pembrokeshire*, Haverfordwest, pp. 431-460.

2003

(with Heather James) 'Fishweirs on the Taf, Towy and Gwendraeth estuaries, Carmarthenshire', *Carms. Antiq.*, Vol. XXXIX, pp. 22-48.

2005

'*Hanes Byr*/A Brief History', *Carms. Antiq.*, Vol. XLI (Centennial Year), pp. 7-12.

'Robert Ferrar: Protestant Martyr', *Carms. Antiq.*, Vol. XLI (Centennial Year), pp. 123-136.

'The Coracle and the Car: an historical view of Carmarthen traffic management through time', *Carmarthenshire Life*, November 2005, pp. 11-13.

'Forgotten Views: J. F. Jones – A Carmarthenshire Photographer', *Carmarthenshire Life*, December 2005, pp. 14-17.

'March to the Music of Time: Carmarthen parades recalled', *Carmarthenshire Life*.

2006

'Carmarthen Bay Subscribers to the Lewis Morris Charts of 1748', *Carms. Antiq.*, Vol. XLI, pp. 44-49.

'Saving the photographic slides of J. F. Jones – an exercise in archaeological detection', *Carms. Antiq.*, Vol. XLI, pp. 104-110.

'Bishop Rudd and his Charity: A Footnote', *Carmarthenshire Life*, Autumn 2006, pp. 24-26.

2007

'A Carmarthen Ironmaster Remembered', *Carmarthenshire Life*, Winter 2007, pp. 11-15.

TECHNICAL PAPERS

1979

'Photo-planning: the use of vertical photography as an aid to on-site recording', *Archaeology*, Royal Photographic Society, Archaeology Section, Vol XI.

1988

An Outline Guide to the Cataloguing of Air Photographs by Computer at the SMR, Dyfed Archaeological Trust Occasional Papers No. 1, ISSN 0955-3878.

A Guide to Micro-computer manipulation of SMR data using Delilah and Foxbase software, Dyfed Archaeological Trust Occasional Papers No. 2, ISSN 0955-3878.

1990

'Computers and Place-name Studies' – paper given at a meeting of the Welsh Place-name County Surveys, Gregynog, June 1990.

'Specifications for a computerised Melville Richards Place-Name Archive': proposals submitted to the Board of Celtic Studies Place-name Survey of Wales.

'A Welsh Place-names Database – Software and Hardware Considerations' – paper submitted to the Place-Names Survey of Wales, Cardiff, November 1990.

2000

'The sea and industry: approaches to an integrated computerised database', in *Maritime Technologies: Transactions of the 10th International TICCIH Conference*, Athens, pp. 31-36.

Website:
www.terra-demetarum.org.uk

Erasmus and the Scholar-Printers

Gwyn Walters

INTRODUCTION

In 1983 I was asked by Terry to write an introduction to his planned printing, at the Rampart Press, of the Welsh chapters from the 1722 edition of Camden's *Britannia*. I was both honoured and ready to oblige, for in 1977 I had written about the manuscript of Edward Lhuyd's printer's copy for the 1695 edition. With that behind me, I had in hand a head of steam, shall we say, for Terry's programme on the 1722 edition.

When, in due course, Terry brought out early page-proofs, the quality of the letter-press printing was immediately evident. It was obvious to me that the whole design and execution was in the hands of a master printer. Terry reminded me, further, that this was the first separate printing of the Welsh material in the *Britannia*, and that consequently its presentation in elegant garb mattered a great deal.

Those were happy days. In between spurts of intensive proof-reading, we bantered light-heartedly about early printers and their splendid devices. I remember the Aldine Press at Venice and the Plantin-Moretus Press at Antwerp being on our menu. Taking a lead from those heady days, I would like now to reflect on aspects of the work of scholar-printers of the early sixteenth century. The printers are too big a subject to be dealt with collectively and so in order to get a little authentic flavour, I propose to follow some of the dealings of one author with three of the major printers. The author is Erasmus, arch-humanist and classical scholar of the Renaissance; the printers are Jodocus Badius Ascensius, Aldus Manutius and Johann Froben.

PARIS, ENGLAND AND THE PRESS OF
JODOCUS BADIUS

Erasmus, after six unhappy years at the Augustinian College of Steyn, near Gouda, and having taken priest's orders, studied and taught at the University of Paris. His pupils included the young Lord Mountjoy, who became a firm friend, possibly prompting his visit to England. He arrived there in 1499, already known for his classical erudition and with something of a poetic reputation. He was later described by William Salesbury as 'the most learned, eloquent and recognised teacher in all Christendom of our age and many ages before'. At Oxford, John Colet steered him into a theological mode of enquiry. Their often vigorous debates resulted in Erasmus's early pamphlet on 'Christ's agony in the Garden of Gethsemane'.

But it was the mastery of the Greek language which became a major issue at Oxford. Erasmus criticised Colet's expounding of Paul's epistles without knowledge of the original language. Invoking the manner of Plautus, Erasmus accused Colet of 'trying to obtain water from a pumice-stone'. Greek to Erasmus was essential for the unravelling of purity in the sacred texts, and ultimately advancing theology.

In January 1500 Erasmus left England, but at Dover he suffered the forfeiture of his savings to Custom-house officers. Apparently, he had misunderstood the law relating to foreign currencies. Returning to Paris a virtual pauper, he hastily produced, by intense reading schedules, a collection of adages from the classical literatures, the future expansion of which in enlarged editions would bring him fame. The *Adagiorum Collectanea*, published by Badius, was dedicated to Mountjoy in England. In some 800 proverbial sayings, it sought to foster elegant Latin style in contemporary writings.

It was Badius's first major publication for Erasmus. His name was often styled Jodocus Badius Ascensius, surnamed from his birthplace Asche, near Brussels. He had only established his Paris press in 1499. Before 1499 he was corrector and proof-reader at Lyons under

EPISTOLAE
Gulielmi Budæi Regii Secretarii.

Prelum Afcenfianu.

V̧enundantur in officina Iodoci Badii cũ
gratia & priuilegio in triennium.

Fig. 1: *Device of the Badius Press featuring an advertisement for the Letters of Budaeus.*

Jean Treschel, but at Paris he set up as printer and teacher of the classics, a fundamental scholar-printer combination. His books frequently contain a learned preface written by himself, a virtue he shared with Aldus Manutius of Venice. By 1535 he had printed almost all the Latin classics and important contemporary works. The latter included works of the scholar Budaeus, together with his letters. The title, interestingly, is featured in a modern sale catalogue alongside and virtually incorporated in Badius's printer's device.

This admirable device, amongst the first known representations of a printing press in action, appeared originally in Badius's edition of Priscian's *Institutiones Grammaticae* (1507). Many members and historians of

the book-trade believe the device to be the work of Albrecht Dürer, one conjecture being that Badius met Dürer during a professional visit to the Netherlands.

In 1502 Erasmus visited Louvain, where he refused a professorship, for he was never happy with the nearness of Dutch theologians. Towards the end of 1504, back in Paris, he wrote to Colet in his usual bright imagery, exclaiming, 'how I hurry on, with all sails set, to holy literature!' He was almost certainly referring to his momentous discovery of a manuscript at the monastery of Parc, near Louvain, earlier that summer. It was of Valla's *Annotationes* on the New Testament. Valla's critical textual notes were precisely what Erasmus needed to spur him on to producing a 'purified' text. The first step was to get Badius, in March 1505, to print Valla's manuscript. It stood as a powerful beacon of Erasmus's future plans.

In England again, late 1505, his spirits rose, to see Colet and to stay with Mountjoy. Increasingly delightful was the opportunity to converse with a large circle of competent Greek scholars, not only Thomas More, but also Linacre, Grocyn, Latimer and Tunstall. There was, almost ludicrously, the usual embarrassment of his lack of money, mentioned regularly in his letters. But suddenly a journey to Italy, often expressed in his early years at the university in Paris as the great adventure, became possible. He was to escort two young men to Italy and its universities and to oversee their studies. They were the sons of the court-physician of Henry VII, Giovanni Battista Boerio of Genoa.

In June 1506 the travellers decided to stay in Paris for two months. It enabled Erasmus to use Badius for printing not only a new (but still unaltered) edition of the *Adagia*, but also translations from Greek to Latin of the two tragedies *Hecuba* and *Iphegina* by Euripides. Two letters from Erasmus to friends throw a searching light on his estimate of the importance of Greek and on the difficulties of styling the translation.

The first letter, written earlier in 1501 from Paris, to Antony of Bergen, Abbot of St. Bertin at St. Omer, just possibly refers to Erasmus's discovery of the two tragedies:

> I have accidentally happened upon some Greek books, and am busy day and night secretly copying them out . . . I have already tasted of Greek literature in the past, but merely (as the saying goes) sipped at it . . . I perceive that Latin learning, rich as it is, is defective and incomplete without the Greek; for we

have but a few small streams, while they have pure springs and rivers rolling gold.

He concludes by revealing his intention of 'restoring' the works of Jerome, and to intensify his study of Greek under a Greek teacher. Huizinga suggests it may have been George Hermonymus of Sparta.

The second letter, written in January 1506 in London, is to William Warham, Archbishop of Canterbury, and in fact forms the preface to Badius's edition of the tragedies in September 1506. The choice of translating Greek verse to Latin verse, Erasmus maintained, was an essential literary testing ground, precluding as yet the ultimate task of unfolding early sacred literature in Greek, but a preparation for it. A poor performance with Euripides would only compromise his talent and reputation, leaving the Holy Scriptures undamaged. He would try to convey to Latin ears the force of the original Greek, without resorting to the 'retreat' of the paraphraser or the 'grandiloquence' of Latin tragedy. The task was always to reproduce in Latin the simplicity, tautness and elegance of the original Greek. Humility was Erasmus's forte, and so it was typical of the editor of the *Adagia* to express his graduated approach to Greek expertise in terms of the Greek adage of not attempting to learn the potter's art on a wine jar.

THE JOURNEY TO ITALY AND THE PRESS OF ALDUS MANUTIUS

By August 1506 the party was braving the Alpine roads, and in September arrived in Turin, where Erasmus received the degree of Doctor of Theology, about which he later wrote rather scurrilously. In Bologna, Erasmus worked on an enlarged edition of his *Adagia*, now to acquire a remarkable increase in Greek entries. It was at Bologna on 28 October 1507 that he judged the time was ripe for a vital letter to Aldus Manutius.

The letter was an enthralling concoction of praise, probing and information. A sense of expectation hung in the air. Erasmus began full of admiration for 'the light you have cast upon Greek and Latin literature . . . your splendid types . . . your uncommon learning'. He appreciates Aldus's 'truly Herculean labours'. One can almost feel Erasmus's emotion as he continues: 'I hear that you are printing Plato in Greek types'. (It was printed in 1513 as a small folio. Brunet valued the edition highly.) Erasmus goes on to ask, provocatively, 'I wonder what has prevented you from publishing the "New Testament" long since?' (In fact the text of

Erasmus's *New Testament*, published in Basle in 1516, was incorporated in Aldus's *Biblia Graeca* in 1518, the first published Greek Bible.) With its spectacular large woodcut ornament and initials in red at the beginning of each book up to the fourth Gospel, a copy of the *Biblia Graeca*, the gift of the Earl of Cawdor, sits proudly on the shelves of Lampeter's Founders' Library, together with a copy of the 1522 Froben edition of Erasmus's *New Testament*. The latter has the equally impressive woodcut border decoration of Urs Graf.

Another aspect of the letter is at first confusing, for Aldus is asked to consider printing the two tragedies by Euripides already printed in September 1506 by Badius. That translation, moreover, was praised by his English friends, claimed Erasmus, and Badius had reported the sale of the whole edition. 'But my reputation has not been enhanced thereby,' continued Erasmus, 'so full is it all of mistakes'. Rejecting Badius's offer of a corrected second edition, he admits the fear of Badius 'mending ill with ill'. Ending the letter on a cautious note, he asks Aldus to return the copy of the 'Tragedies' to the bearer in the event of deciding not to print. But it was printed by Aldus in December 1507 in the classic italic letter small octavo series. The future of the relationship with Badius began to look doubtful.

Aldus had set up his press at the Campo St. Paternian (now Campo Manin) in 1490. For some eight months Erasmus found it to be his true element. The *Adagia* was the focus of attention through 1508. The Greek additions made at Bologna were now further augmented by members of Aldus's 'New Academy': Johannes Lascaris, Baptista Ignatius, Marcus Musurus and Jerome Alexander. Notable new author sources included Plato, Plutarch, Pindar and Pausonius. Erasmus's new friend from Alsace, Beatus Rhenanus, who was to have a career in printing establishments in Paris, Strasbourg and Basle, records Erasmus working in a frenzy, writing out and inserting new material, as, simultaneously, Aldus worked at printing. The absorbed manner of Erasmus in the noise and bustle of the press room amazed Aldus. Huizinga encapsulated the scene, with Erasmus depicted as 'lord and master of the printing-office', where a special corrector was assigned to him.

By September 1508 the *Adagia* was ready, in its enlarged form, with a dedicatory preface to William Mountjoy. Its second book begins with the proverb '*festina lente*', and from this Erasmus derives the 'Dolphin and Anchor' symbol, as employed by Aldus in

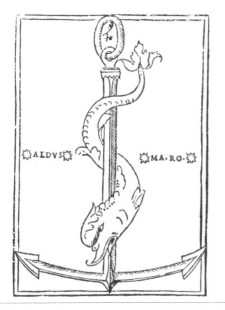

RHETORES IN HOC VOLVMINE
HABENTVR HI.

A phthonii Sophiſtæ Progymnaſmata.   Semipagina.
H ermogenis ars Rhetorica.
A riſtotelis Rhetoricorum ad Theodecten libri tres.
E iuſdem Rhetorice ad Alexandrum.
E iuſdem ars Poetica.
S opatri Rhetoris quæſtiones de componédis declamationibus
       in cauſis præcipuæ iudicialibus.
C yri Sophiſtæ differentiæ ſtatuum.
D ionyſii Alicarnaſẽi ars Rhetorica.
D emetrii Phalerẽi de interpretatione.
A lexandri Sophiſtæ de figuris ſenſus & dictionis.
A dnotationes innominati de figuris Rhetoricis.
M enandri Rhetoris diuiſio cauſarum in genere demonſtratiuo.
A riſteidis de ciuili oratione.
E iuſdem de ſimplici oratione.
A pſini de arte Rhetorica præcepta.

Fig. 2: *Device of the Aldine Press.*

his device. Vincent Cronin signifies the device as being borrowed from medals of the Emperors Titus and Domitian. Alongside the printed device Aldus occasionally added the motto '*festina lente*', a favourite adage of Augustus.

Not having had the opportunity of examining a copy of the 1508 Aldine *Adagia*, I was delighted to find, in leafing through Goldschmidt's scholarly 'Catalogue VII', that it carried an interesting note on the edition. The title of the Catalogue is *Incunabula, Humanists and Reformation Tracts*, and it includes works from the library of Willibald Pirckheimer and other sources. Pirckheimer was born in Nuremberg in 1470 and studied at

universities in Padua and Pavia. He was a friend of Marcus Musurus, and must have been, through him, known to Aldus. He was also a friend of Erasmus, Dürer and Reuchlin. He edited books on Ptolemy and translations of Lucian.

The Catalogue entry, item 135, for the *Adagia* reminds us that here (fol. 113-4) Erasmus extols Aldus 'beyond the Ptolemies as the begetter of a library extending over the entire world'. Even more interesting from a purely bibliographical point of view is a note indicating that 'still preserved on the flyleaf' is a woodcut portrait-bookplate of Pirckheimer by Dürer, with his mark.

The next Catalogue entry, item 136, is Pirckheimer's copy of Erasmus's *Opus Epistolarum*, published in Basle in 1529, a year before Pirckheimer's death. It is similarly adorned. 'It has,' notes the Catalogue, 'a fragment of his woodcut bookplate by Dürer, preserved underneath the recent flyleaf.' It seems that Pirckheimer chose to position these generous gifts from Dürer in the style of an

Fig. 3: *Dürer's portrait-bookplate of Pirckheimer with the artist's mark.*

Fig. 4: *The Pirckheimer bookplate inserted in an Aldine Cicero of 1545.*

illustrated frontispiece, in lieu of an autograph of owner-ship. The subject of the bookplate is the magnificent head of Pirckheimer. Created by Dürer, these plates are an extravagant form of extra-illustration, appearing as they do in Aldine books normally devoid of any illus-tration.

A census of books still carrying this bookplate would be diverting. Shortly after noting the examples in the Goldschmidt sale catalogue, I chanced to find a more complicated case in my own files of printers' ornaments. It is a xeroxed illustration featuring a frontispiece and title-page spread of an undated Aldine, which appears to be a small Aldine octavo of 1545. The frontispiece is, once more, Dürer's woodcut bookplate-portrait of Pirckheimer, presumably glued to the flyleaf. The work is one of those 'anthologised' collections which the

Aldine Press favoured, in this case commencing with Cicero's essays *De Senectute* and *De Amicitia*. The Dürer bookplate is applied in this case by a successor of Pirckheimer, for the work post-dates Pirckheimer's death by fifteen years. This presents no problem when we realise that Pirckheimer's library remained in the family until 1636, when the Earl of Arundel purchased it while on a mission to Vienna.

The nature of early flyleaf illustration is given a further dimension when we read the description of another copy of the Aldine *Cicero* of 1545 in Quaritch's *Catalogue of Aldine Press Publications* (1929), which is based on the library of the Earl of Powis. The annota-tion reads: 'an engraving of *Cicero* inserted as frontispiece'. In view of the contents it appears a logical 'insertion' and not, as in the case of Dürer-Prickheimer plates, signifying ownership – rather, a pleasant example of co-ordinated extra-illustration.

With the *Adagia* published by 1508, Aldus did not want to lose Erasmus's fluent Latinity and competence in Greek, no less his great powers of concentration. He sought to extend his service to December in preparing editions of Plautus, Terence and Seneca's tragedies. Huizinga is eloquent in describing how the ecstatic vision of publishing hidden literatures of the past obsessed both men. Erasmus, as ever, was ready for fresh experiences. The Venetian stay made him realise that England, despite the scholarship and friendship of Colet and More and company, lacked the rich aura accruing to the European scholar-printer.

Yet one more travelling tutorship gave him the opportunity to prolong the Italian venture. He became tutor in Rhetoric to a natural son of James IV of Scotland, then a student at Padua. The usual military uncertainty drove them to Siena and ultimately to Rome, where he was honoured by cardinals and prelates before returning to England.

ENGLAND 1509-1514 AND THE DISCARDING OF BADIUS

The Italian visit was a rewarding experience for Erasmus and was followed by a period in England which for some years seemed to have little documentation. He was probably a house guest of More's for much of the time. What is certain is that by 1511 he ventured to Paris with the manuscript of the remarkable *Praise of Folly*, which was printed by Gilles de Gourmont as *Moriae Encomium* (1511). The title was a delicate play on the name of his London host, and the subject matter a biting satire on folly in all walks of life. This was dangerous territory in that age, despite the work being an immediate and indeed lasting success. The ultimate reaction came when all of Erasmus's publications were condemned in the *Index Expurgatorium* of 1559. It is good to think that Milton found the *Moria* in every hand at Cambridge in 1628. In a world of ill-defined publishing regulation, the work was almost immediately reprinted at Strasbourg as *Stultitiae Laus*.

Badius had been urging Erasmus to complete a further revised *Adagia*, fearing a possible reprint of the 1508 Aldine edition by a German press. But at this period Erasmus began to show unease with the copy-fees offered by Badius. In response, the latter concluded his letter of May 1512 in the grand manner, tinged with sentiment:

I own that by no renumeration could your genius, industry, knowledge, and labour be requited, but the gods will requite you, and your own virtue will be the finest reward . . . You have already deserved exceedingly well of Greek and Roman literature; you will in this way deserve well of sacred and divine, and you will help your little Badius, who has a numerous family and no earnings beside his daily trade.

Responding to Badius's further request for urgent delivery of the revised *Adagia*, Erasmus completed the preface by the turn of the year, and entrusted delivery of Badius's copy to the agent Francis Berckman of Cologne. Berckman's next move changed the whole course of events. He took the copy to Johann Froben at Basle. The role of Erasmus in all this is very much in doubt. What is certain is that in six months he left England 'bag and baggage' for Basle. Beatus Rhenanus, who then worked alongside Amerbach and Froben as editor in Basle, maintained that the connection with Froben always appealed to Erasmus.

Badius reacted with dignity. 'If, however, it is agreeable to your interests and honour,' he wrote to Erasmus, 'I shall suffer it, and that with equanimity.'

BASLE AND THE PRESS OF JOHANN FROBEN

Crossing the Channel from England in 1514 was not accompanied by problems until Erasmus arrived at Calais. There a letter awaited him from the Prior of Steyn requesting his return to the monastery. The Prior, Servetius Roger, criticised his excessive journeying, only to receive from Erasmus a devastating rebuke. Erasmus reminded him that St. Jerome was a much-travelled monk, 'now in Rome, now in Syria, now in Antioch', and that recently the Roman cardinals had paid tribute to Erasmus's learning, 'which our countrymen ridicule'.

Erasmus reached Basle in August 1514, and his reception by German humanists was emphatic. The large printing-office, surrounded by scholars, was virtually a recreation of his experience at Venice. 'I move in a most agreeable Museon,' he commented, 'so many men of learning.' And he could not have been displeased with Froben's device of twin serpents entwining a rod alongside a dove. Although alluding specifically to Matthew X.16 ['be wary as serpents, innocent as doves'], it nevertheless had an affinity to the caduceus of the god Mercury as a symbol of classical learning.

The printing-house dealt not only with the *Adagia*, but also with translations of minor Plutarch texts and a work on Latin construction. Always in the background lurked the presence of Jerome and the *New Testament*. Jerome's letters were Erasmus's passion from youthful days, and now at Basle his work on Jerome was integrated with the labours of Amerbach and Reuchlin and others in the nine-volume edition published by Froben in 1516, the first four volumes containing Erasmus's edition of the letters. Writing to the Hebrew scholar Wolfgang Fabricius Capito on 26 February 1516 he accused professors of theology of almost always having been 'men with an ingrained loathing for good learning'. He recalled that he was blamed for changing the text of Jerome instead of praised for restoring it.

If Jerome was a passion, the *New Testament* was equally demanding. Printed by Froben in 1516, it was Erasmus's greatest scholarly work, and the words of Rudolf Pfeiffer label it the culmination of the journey towards the *'veritas evangelica'*, which was given its first great momentum with the discovery of Valla's manuscript of the *Adnotationes* and its printing, with Erasmus's fine preface, by Badius in 1505. Neither must the role of Colet as instigator of Erasmus's first translation from the Greek be forgotten.

Froben printed the second edition of the *New Testament* in 1518, and a year later Erasmus wrote to Martin Luther's patron, the Elector Frederick of Saxony, complaining of Luther's distrust of scholarly editions of early sacred literature, *'bonae literae'*. As if aggravated by Luther to superhuman effort, Erasmus devoted the whole of the next decade to collaborating with Froben to print a staggering array of texts, thus opening up, in Huizinga's phrase, 'the pure sources of Christianity'. *Cyprian* (1520) was followed by the third edition of the *New Testament* (1522), *Hilary* (1523) and a new edition of *Jerome* (1524). The second half of the decade was of equal force, with *Irenaeus* (1526), *Ambrose* (1527), *Augustine* (1528/9) and finally the Latin translation of *Chrysostom* (1530). All this was speed of work which modern scholarly printing would find extraordinary.

When Erasmus first arrived in England, it was possible to describe him as a young European poet studying in Paris, the *'homo poeticus'* or *'homo rhetoricus'* as he once described himself. The dye of the poet, the humourist, the satirist, the literary man, never left him. We have seen how the *Adagia* and *The Praise of Folly* had a special place in his life. Now *Colloquia* joins that duo. Originally written in Paris for the benefit of his pupils, these simple dialogues illustrating the art of polite conversation were later expanded to include the

Fig. 5: *The 'New Testament' of Erasmus printed by Froben in 1522: the opening of Matthew's Gospel, with woodcut decoration by Urs Graf.*

complex topics of the day, ensuring continued popularity. A Paris manuscript of the early form of *Colloquia* reached Froben in 1518 and was printed with the collaboration of Beatus Rhenanus, but without the consent or knowledge of Erasmus. Offended by such aggressive manipulation of his literary property, no less by textual errors, Erasmus arranged for a new edition at the printing establishment of his friend Maertensz in Louvain. By 1522 the popularity of the work saw editions (largely pirated reprints) appear in London, Antwerp and Paris, across Europe to Leipzig, Vienna and Cracow. Erasmus's close liaison and friendship with Froben prompted him, in March 1522, to bring out a special edition, dedicated to Froben's six-year-old son, Erasmus's godchild, Johannes Erasmius Froben.

In June 1535 Erasmus was at Basle to supervise the publication of the large and somewhat fatigued monument to the art of Christian preaching called *Ecclesiastes*. As early as 1523 it seemed as if he had decided the work was to be dedicated to John Fisher, Bishop of

Rochester. But on 22 June 1535 Fisher was beheaded, as was Thomas More two weeks later. One year on, in July 1536, Erasmus died.

The poet in Erasmus would have responded to what was published at the Aldine Press in 1536. Paulus, Aldus's youngest son, had taken charge of the press in 1533. A prodigious worker, and an even finer scholar than his father, he considerably increased the reputation of the firm during the forty-one years of his period of office. In 1536 he brought about the first separate printing of Aristotle's treatise on poetry, a Latin translation followed by the Greek text and presented in the classic Aldine format of small octavo with italic and Greek letter.

NOTE ON SOURCES

Not having been able, in preparing this study, to visit libraries, I was nevertheless the beneficiary of the delectable habit of collecting important catalogues issued by many London, New York and European antiquarian booksellers. The end-product of this habit is an admirable and unique resource for the history of printing and illustration.

An early admiration of Erasmus was formed when, as a sixth-form schoolboy in Gowerton in 1940, I was pressed by my History teacher, Dr E. D. Lewis, to read Froude's *Life and Letters of Erasmus* (1894) in the summer vacation. The school copy had been mislaid, but amazingly Gorseinon Miners' Welfare Institute Library boasted a copy, and one abiding memory is my enchantment with the prose style of that historian.

Two other books in my possession have provided stimulating assistance. Johan Huizinga's *Erasmus of Rotterdam*; translated by F. Hopman (1952) contains a fine selection of Erasmus's letters, newly translated from the Latin by Barbara Flower.

Fig. 6: Aristotle's 'Poetica' printed at the Aldine Press in the year of Erasmus's death.

Rudolf Pfeiffer's *History of Classical Scholarship 1300-1850* (Oxford, 1978) has chapters of great clarity on Lorenzo Valla and Erasmus, while another, nicely entitled 'Autour d'Érasme', deals with Beatus Rhenanus and Reuchlin.

An appreciated trait of the John Rylands Library, Manchester, was to reprint articles of value from their *Bulletin* as separate publications. Stephen Briggs generously loaned me two of these: Edward Robertson's study of *Aldus Manutius* (1950) and Henry Guppy's *Erasmus* (1936).

Papermaking in West Wales

Terry Wells

In 105 AD, Ts'ai Lun reported the invention of paper to the Chinese Emperor. Ts'ai Lun was an official to the Chinese Imperial court, and I consider his early form of paper to be humanity's most important invention and progenitor of the Internet. Although recent archaeological evidence places the actual invention of papermaking 200 years earlier, Ts'ai Lun played an important role in developing a material that revolutionized his country. From China, papermaking moved to Korea and Japan. Chinese papermakers also spread their handiwork into Central Asia and Persia, from which traders introduced paper to India. This is why Ts'ai Lun is one of the most influential people in history.[1]

That was the suggestion given by Clifford Pickover[2] in response to a survey taken in 1998 amongst leading scientists and mathematicians as to what they believed were the most significant developments of the last two millennia. Certainly, regardless of the true origins, paper, in one form or another, influences all of our lives, either directly or indirectly, it could even be said that it is fundamental to our existence. Even those few in this world that have never seen a sheet of paper will probably be affected in one way or another by government decisions outlined on paper, publicised on paper, distributed on paper and that will ultimately be recorded for posterity on paper.

ORIGINS OF PAPERMAKING

As stated in the opening quote the invention of paper is attributed to China and for approximately 500 years the art of papermaking was confined to that country, but by 610, via Korea, it had been introduced into Japan. Incidentally, the Chinese may have invented paper but the Japanese are credited with the first block printing on paper in about 770. Papermaking had moved into Persia and central Asia by about 750, probably following the

caravan route attempting to connect the Mediterranean with the Pacific. Tradition has it that Chinese papermakers were captured by the Arabs in a battle near Samarkand in 751, thus spreading the art westwards. In 793, there was a factory working in Baghdad, with Chinese workmen introduced by Haroun-el-Raschid. The next known place of production was Damascus, which was to supply Europe for several centuries (particularly with the paper known as Charta Damascena).[3] Paper made its appearance in Egypt about 800 but was not manufactured there until 900, and from there the knowledge was taken to Morocco, and from Morocco to Europe by the Moors. There was possibly a paper mill established at Xativa in Spain in about 1056, but certainly there was a well-established industry there by 1151. The first confirmed papermaking in Italy is at Genoa in 1255 although there is a possibility of an earlier manufactory on the Ligurian coast in 1235. From Italy and Spain papermaking spread to the rest of Europe – France (Troyes) 1338; Germany (Nuremburg) 1390; Belgium 1407; Switzerland (Friebourg) 1411; Great Britain (Hertfordshire) 1494; Sweden (Motala) 1532; Hungary 1546; Netherlands (Altmaar & Dortrecht) 1586; Denmark 1635; Norway 1690. These are the earliest known dates, it is most likely that papermaking occurred before these at these locations. Certainly paper would have been in use in these countries well before these dates, although there was degree of distrust in its use by Europeans simply because paper had been introduced by Moslems; some things in this world never seem to change.[4]

COMMERCIAL PAPERMAKING IN THE UK

The first reference to a paper mill in the United Kingdom was in a book printed by Wynken de Worde in about 1495, this mill belonging to John Tate and was

Fig. 1: Oldest known illustration of a paper mill, engraving by Jost Amman, 1568.

near Hertford. The book was *De Proprietatibus Rerum* by Bartholemaeus Anglicus and had the following verse printed in the colophon:

> And also of your charyte call to remembrance
> The soul of William Caxton, first prynter of this boke
> In laten tonge at Coleyn hymself to auaunce
> That every well disposyd man may theron loke
> And John Tate the yonger, Joye mote he broke
> Whiche late hathe in England doo make this paper thynne
> That now in our Englysth this boke is prynted inne.

Paper was made at the mill for a few years but for how long has not been determined. John Tate died in

1507 and directed in his will that the paper mill be sold. It does not seem to have been a commercial success, possibly subject, even at this early date, to foreign competition, both in paper prices and for the rags to make the paper. Up to the end of the seventeenth century the bulk of the paper used in Britain was imported from the continent, particularly France. By the first part of the eighteenth century papermaking in the UK was well established but high quality papers continued to be imported from Europe. The method of making paper at this time is summarised in figure 1, the earliest known printed illustration of papermaking in the western world, published in 1568. In the background are the water wheel driven stampers for pounding the rags to make the pulp and the press for removing excess water from the 'post'[5] of finished sheets. The vatman can be seen forming a sheet on the mould by dipping it into the vat of pulp. There is a degree of artistic licence in the illustration, the boy carrying the pile of sheets so effortlessly is entirely fanciful. The only stage of the process missing is the couching (transferring) of the sheet from the mould to felt prior to pressing.

Little changed in this method of production until the middle of the eighteenth century when there were two major developments in the paper industry in the UK. The first was the introduction of the rag-engine or hollander, invented in Holland sometime before 1670, which gradually replaced the stamping mills previously used for the disintegration of the rags and beating of the pulp. Using rotating knives against a bedplate, it revolutionised the production of pulp, one Hollander producing in one day as much as eight stampers could do in eight days. This undoubtedly contributed to the fourfold increase in paper production in the eighteenth century. The second development was in the design and construction of the mould used for forming the sheet. Early moulds had straight wires sewn down on to the wooden foundation, this produced an irregular surface showing the characteristic laid marks, and, when printed on, the ink did not give clear, sharp lines. Baskerville, a Birmingham printer, wanted a smoother paper. James Whatman the Elder developed a woven wire fabric, thus leading to his production of the first wove paper in 1757, although it was not in widespread use until the late eighteenth century. Many of the 'laid' papers bought today are wove papers with an impressed laid pattern.

Increasing demands for more paper during the late eighteenth and early nineteenth centuries led to

Fig. 2: *Encyclopédie, ou dictionnaire raisonné des sciences, des arts et des métiers, Diderot, D. 1761.*

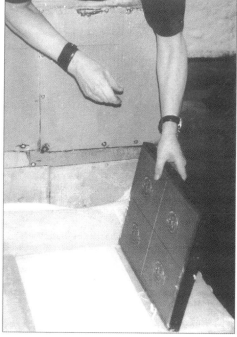

Fig. 3: *Left – papermaker dipping the mould into the vat to form the sheet.*
Right – the formed sheet couched off the mould onto the felt.
(Courtesy of Brian Luker).

Fig. 4: *Fourdrinier paper machine. Wet end on left where pulp is poured onto the web to form the paper, drying cylinders in the centre, take up reel for finished paper on far right.*
(Davis, Charles T., *The Manufacture of Paper*. Philadelphia, 1886).

Fig. 5: *Cylinder mould machine. On left is stone vat with top of cylinder just visible, above that is the take off felt and roller. To the right of that is the press and partially visible on the right is the take off roller.*
(Courtesy of Richard Hills).

shortages of the rags needed to produce the paper. Part of the problem was that no satisfactory method of bleaching pulp had yet been devised, and so only white rags could be used to produce white paper. Chlorine bleaching was being used by the end of the eighteenth century, but excessive use produced papers that were of poor quality and deteriorated quickly. By 1800 up to 24 million lb. of rags were being used annually, to produce 10,000 tons of paper in England and Wales and 1,000 tons in Scotland, the home market being supplemented by imports, mainly from the continent. Experiments in using other materials, such as sawdust, rye straw, cabbage stumps and spruce wood had been conducted in 1765 by Jacob Christian Schäffer. Similarly, Matthias Koops carried out many experiments on straw and other materials at the Neckinger Mill, Bermondsey around 1800, but it was not until the middle of the nineteenth century that pulp produced using straw or wood was utilised in the production of paper.

By 1800 there were 430 (564 in 1821) paper mills in England and Wales (mostly single vat mills), under 50 (74 in 1823) in Scotland and 60 in Ireland, but all the production was by hand and the output per mill was low.[6] The Hollander beater had increased the rate of pulp production, and there were now pressures to increase the rate of papermaking to utilise this. The first attempt at a paper machine to mechanise the process was patented in 1799 by Frenchman Nicholas Louis Robert, but it was not a success. However, the drawings were brought to England by John Gamble in 1801 and passed on to the brothers Henry and Sealy Fourdrinier, who financed the engineer Bryan Donkin to build the machine. The first successful machine was installed at Frogmore, Hertfordshire, in 1803, measuring 8.2m long by 1.2m wide, producing about six metres per minute. The pulp was poured onto an endless wire cloth, pressed between felt covered rollers, transferred to a continuous felt blanket and pressed again, and then wound up on a reel. The reel would have been unwound and the paper cut into sheets and loft dried in the same way as hand made paper. By 1808, Donkin had refined and arranged the forming end of the Fourdrinier machine into a layout which changed little for 150 years.[7] In 1809 John Dickinson patented a machine that that used a wire cloth covered cylinder revolving in a pulp suspension, the water being removed through the centre of the cylinder and the layer of pulp removed from the surface by a felt covered roller (later replaced by a continuous felt passing round a roller) and

pressed and reeled as the Fourdrinier. This machine was the forerunner of the present day cylinder mould or vat machine, used mainly for the production of boards. Both these machines produced paper as a wet sheet which require drying after removal from the machine, but in 1821 T. B. Crompton patented a method of drying the paper continuously, using a woven fabric to hold the sheet against steam heated drying cylinders. After it had been pressed, the paper was cut into sheets by a cutter fixed at the end of the last cylinder. These improvements in the development of the paper machine were reflected in paper production:[8]

Year	No. of machines	Machine production in tons	Hand production in tons
1804	3	10	14950
1810	17	4793	14278
1820	32	8873	12675
1830	72	21313	9377
1840	191	33463	9937
1850	267	57535	5426
1860	340	95971	3839

By the middle of the nineteenth century the pattern for the mechanised production of paper had been set. Subsequent developments concentrated on increasing the size and production of the machines, often adapting existing machines where necessary There are paper machines in use now where the core of the machine is over one hundred years old. Similarly, developments in alternative pulps to rags, mainly wood and esparto grass, enabled production increases. Conversely, despite the increase in paper production, there was a decrease, by 1884, in the number of paper mills in England and Wales to 250 and in Ireland to 14 (Scotland increased to 60), production being concentrated into fewer, larger units. Geographical changes also took place as many of the early mills were small and had been situated in rural areas. The change was to larger mills in, or near, urban areas closer to suppliers of the raw materials (esparto mills were generally situated near a port as the raw material was brought in by ship) and the paper markets.[9] Despite the urbanisation one still gets glimpses of the 'rural roots' of the industry, at the end of the nineteenth century, Home Park Mill, Hemel Hempstead:[10]

> . . . remained a cosy old-fashioned mill that shut down
> to let the workers help with the harvest. At eleven every

morning the Manager and his foremen used to adjourn to the Mill Cottage for bread, cheese and beer.[11]

The change to fewer, larger, mills continued into the twentieth century and, from the 1950s on, papermaking become more and more sophisticated and technical. With the advent of computer controlled machines larger mills could be controlled more efficiently by fewer workers. We are supposed to be heading towards a 'paperless society' yet worldwide production of paper doubled in the last twenty years of the twentieth century to almost three hundred million tons annually. Modern paper machines are up to ten metres wide, up to one hundred and fifty metres long, run at a production rate of up to two thousand metres per minute and will produce 300,000 tonnes a year. Or, put another way:

> It is half as wide as the distance between the wickets on a cricket pitch, and it makes one and a quarter miles of paper in a minute. That means that a champion distance runner would take around five minutes to run along the length of one minute's production.[12]

WHAT IS PAPER?

But what is paper? The dictionary definition usually goes along the lines of: 'A material made of cellulose pulp derived mainly from wood or rags or certain grasses'.[13] Not strictly true as paper can also be made from materials other than cellulose, such as asbestos and leather, unfortunately, the same dictionary also describes papyrus[14] as a form of paper, a popular misconception. So to say that there is some confusion as to what is paper is probably an understatement; it is a little like electricity, we take it for granted and use it without really knowing how it is made. Dard Hunter provides us with a better definition:

> To be classed as a true paper the thin sheets must be made from fibre that has been macerated until each individual filament is a separate unit; the fibres intermixed with water, and by the use of a sieve-like screen, the fibres lifted from the water in the form of a thin stratum, the water draining through the small openings of the screen, leaving a sheet of matted fibre upon the screen's surface. This thin layer of intertwined fibre is paper.[15]

This basic process has not changed in the last two thousand years although the methods of achieving it

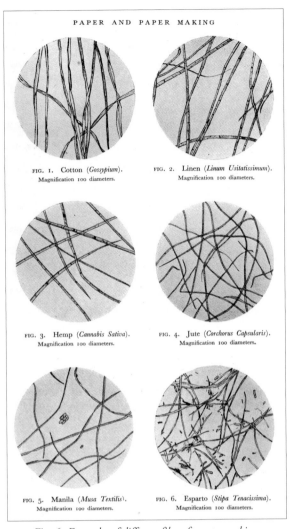

PAPER AND PAPER MAKING

FIG. 1. Cotton (*Gossypium*).
Magnification 100 diameters.

FIG. 2. Linen (*Linum Usitatissimum*).
Magnification 100 diameters.

FIG. 3. Hemp (*Cannabis Sativa*).
Magnification 100 diameters.

FIG. 4. Jute (*Corchorus Capsularis*).
Magnification 100 diameters.

FIG. 5. Manila (*Musa Textilis*).
Magnification 100 diameters.

FIG. 6. Esparto (*Stipa Tenacissima*).
Magnification 100 diameters.

Fig. 6: *Examples of different fibres for papermaking.*

have. The fibres are usually cellulose, a long polymer made of repeating units of glucose that produces a remarkable material. Cellulose has structural rigidity, does not decompose easily, and, important for papermaking, has a multitude of hydroxyl groups for hydrogen bonds. Paper exists because of hydrogen bonds.

Paper can be found in over 14,000 different forms, the choice of source materials and the papermaking process being tailored to produce the desired end product. The process can be split into several stages: fibre selection/pulp production; beating; forming; and drying/finishing.

Commercially, the choice of fibre is effectively limited to wood (mainly birch, eucalyptus, spruce and southern hardwood), bagasse, cotton, esparto, flax, hemp and straw.[16] However, on a smaller scale virtually any plant can be used to provide fibre and is probably only limited by imagination and determination. The first stage of fibre extraction usually either involves a mechanical process such as grinding wood chips or a retting process as is used on flax or hemp, the end result is the same, the cellulose fibres are exposed. The fibres are then either further treated in water mechanically to produce a mechanical pulp or cooked in alkali or acid solutions to produce a chemical pulp. Needless to say, there is some degree of cross over between the two processes resulting in thermo-mechanical and semi-chemical pulps. Some pulps are also bleached as part of the process. The pulp is then subjected to beating or refining in water to further separate and fibrillate the fibres, now generally between a rotating grinder and bedplate, historically, stamper beaters had been used which had a vertical pounding action. The choice of fibre, the degree of grinding or cooking of the pulp, bleached or not and the amount of beating or refining all combine to produce a stock (i.e. pulp that has been beaten and refined) of the desired quality for making the chosen paper. For example, a high quality drawing paper would be made from a well-cooked, bleached cotton pulp whereas sack paper would be made from a medium cooked unbleached softwood pulp. Linen and hemp fibres have the strength for office papers, whereas esparto produces softer bulkier paper. Some beating/refining is done just to reduce fibre length, some to produce more fibrillation, it is dependant on the fibre and the machine involved. The possible combinations are enormous.

Formation of the sheet, whether by hand or machine, is essentially the same. The fibres in a 0.1-1.0% solution with water are strained through a mesh leaving a sheet of matted fibre, this is then dewatered, by press or rollers using felt on one or both sides, and is then ready for the final drying process.

Drying can take days or seconds. Hand-made paper is hung in drying lofts, a particularly thick paper can take several days to dry. Paper machines have a series of heated cylinders, the web of paper is pressed against them and is dried in seconds. After drying the paper can be sized to prevent ink absorption, calendered to compress and polish the sheet, coated or laminated, dependant on the final product and use.[17]

Paper is a remarkable substance with a multitude of uses, some obvious, some not, it is also re-useable, re-cyclable and bio-degradable!

PAPERMAKING IN WEST WALES

Papermaking in Wales has never been a large industry, the majority of the mills recorded being in the north and east of the Principality. However, there is evidence of five paper mills in west Wales (the old Dyfed area), two in Carmarthenshire and three in Pembrokeshire, no evidence for papermaking has been found in Ceredigion. The two in Carmarthenshire were located in Glannant Road, Carmarthen and at the Iron Forge on the river Gwendraeth (adjacent to Mynyddygarreg) above Kidwelly. Two of the Pembrokeshire mills were in Haverfordwest, one in the parish of St Martin, the other in the parish of St Thomas. The other was in the parish of Prendergast, just outside the town of Haverfordwest.

CARMARTHENSHIRE

Carmarthen Paper Mill
The earliest recorded date for the mill in Carmarthen, as a paper mill, is 1792. It is mentioned as one of the properties in a lease to vest possession of 28 September 1825:

> . . . a paper mill formerly a water corn grist mill called Velinganol in the town of Carmarthen let to Revd David Charles on a 99 years lease from Michaelmas 1792 at £18 p.a.[18]

It is assumed that the mill was converted from a corn mill to a paper mill at or around this time. The area where the mill is situated has a long history of milling still reflected in the names found in the area: Millbank Cottages; Millbrook Crescent; Glannant Road (by the side of the stream) and Water Street. There were at least three mills in the area at the same time. The mill water supply must have been a robust one as it supplies two mills in the area of the paper mill, travelling on the supply a third mill in Catherine Street. From there it goes on, as an over-ground stream, to supply the tannery and slaughter house before eventually being diverted underground to empty into the river near the quay. One assumes it must have been a pretty noxious fluid by the time it reached the river!

The owner of the lease, the Rev. David Charles (1762-1834) is perhaps better known for his activities as a Calvinistic Methodist minister, hymn-writer and rope-maker. He was born 11 October 1762 at Llanfihangel-Abercowin, a small village about eight miles from Carmarthen, with his grandfather an ardent Methodist and his brother, Thomas, an Anglican priest it is per-

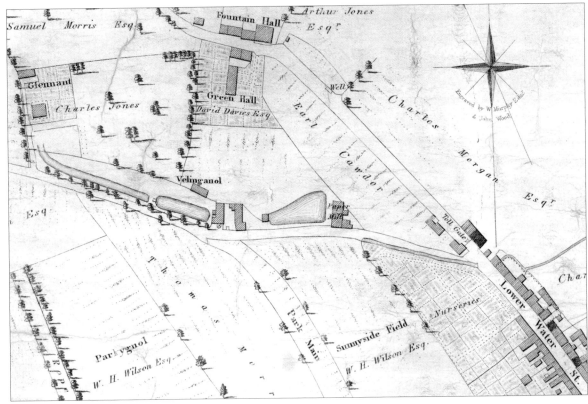

Fig. 7: *Carmarthen paper mill, 1834.*
(Carmarthenshire Archive Service).

haps not surprising that he ended up most noted for his religious connections. However, this was not to be till later in life as his time in education was cut short by the death of his father, following which he was apprenticed to a flax-dresser and rope-maker in Carmarthen, with a further term of apprenticeship in Bristol, unfortunately there are no details of whom he was apprenticed to.[19] He was certainly back in Wales by 1791 as he was married on 1 November to Sarah Phillips at St. Mary's Church, Haverfordwest, Pembrokeshire. Sarah was the daughter of Samuel Levi Phillips, a Christianised Jew and wealthy banker of Haverfordwest.

How David Charles came to be acquainted with papermaking is not known, it is possible that the mill was established in order to make use of the waste from his and other local rope making businesses, old ropes and hemp waste being prime sources of raw material for papermaking. His father-in-law, Samuel Phillips, certainly had connections with the papermakers in Haverfordwest,[20] so it is possible he had seen the works there and realised the potential.

The next reference to the mill is in 1797 in which David Charles is rated for 'a mill', the first reference to it being rated specifically as a paper mill is in the same volume for 1799.[21] In common with many other paper mills, the mill suffered a fire, the *Carmarthen Journal* reporting on 16 February 1821 that:

We are concerned to state, that a fire broke out on Saturday morning last, in the Paper Manufactory of Mr Charles, near this town, which, aided by a high wind, destroyed a considerable quantity of paper &c, together with the whole of the internal machinery, notwithstanding that every possible effort was made to check the progress of the devouring element. It appears that this unfortunate occurrence was occasioned by a quantity of paper, placed over a standing grate to dry taking fire and communicating the flames, which spread with awful rapidity, to the roof of the building. The extent of the loss sustained, cannot as yet be precisely estimated. Unfortunately, neither the premises, nor what they contained, were insured. Two Fire engines were at work for some hours, and the unremitting exertions of a number of persons assembled on this distressing occasion, even at the imminent peril of their lives, bore ample testimony to the friendly and anxious solicitude they felt for the interests of their worthy and suffering neighbour, and for which signal instances of kindness, he requests, through the medium of this paper, to express his grateful thanks.

The Cambrian of 17 February 1821 also reported the incident:

> We regret to state, that the paper-mill and carding-manufactory of Mr D. Charles, near Carmarthen, were totally destroyed by fire on Saturday morning last . . .

This is the only known mention of the carding-manufactory. It also raises the question of the rebuilding of the mill, if indeed it was rebuilt. In the 1792 deed, the paper mill is referred to as Velinganol, yet on the 1834 map of Carmarthen,[22] Velinganol and the paper mill are discreet buildings. Checking the rate books has not helped as they do not name the mills or, apart from the paper mill, distinguish uses, the only help is that the number of mills rated does not change. Whatever the answer, David Charles seems to be back in business by 1822 as he is supplying a local bookbinder, David Morris. The mill seemed to have produced a range of papers, but evidence is not plentiful, and as yet no watermark attributable to the mill has been found. The ledger of David Morris,[23] gives some information on paper types produced:

Mr Charles, papermaker, King Street

1822		
2 December	1 ream Crown printing	0-16-0
1826		
10 March	1 ream broken demy	0-10-0
3 July	1 ream demy	0-15-0
23 July	1 ream crown	0-13-0
7 August	1 ream crown	0-12-0
26 August	1 ream crown	0-12-0
2 October	1 ream crown	0-12-0
1827		
11 April	Coard (*sic*) to send boxes to Lampeter	0-1-0
28 April	1 ream crown	0-12-0
28 April	1lb twine	0-1-4
23 August	2 balls twine	0-0-10
6 September	1 ream crown	0-12-0
27 September	1lb twine	0-1-4
22 October	1/2lb twine	0-1-13
6 December	twine	0-1-0

1828		
1 March	twine	0-3-8
28 April	1 ream crown	0-12-0
14 July	1lb twine	0-1-8
1829		
28 December	1lb twine	0-1-8

Two surviving bills for 1801[24] give some further information:

Mr David Charles – Bill for Kitchen paper	
– 2 Reams	£1-0-0
Bought of David Charles 2 Reams	
Royal Hand @ 10/-	£1-0-0

Despite being in existence at the time of the founding of the *Carmarthen Journal* in 1810, the mill seemingly did not produce paper suitable for printing it. The printers, Wm Evans & Co, purchased several types of paper from Joseph Lloyd & Sons, Gun's Mills, Gloucester. There are several invoices from Lloyds, many of which take the form of letters, one of 21 October 1836 for 50 reams of fine demy being of interest for the inclusion of:

> I am happy to inform you they are well bought as we are now selling at better prices and everything connected with the manufactory of paper is still looking up.[25]

David Charles had a stroke in 1828 and died six years later, his obituary makes no mention of either his rope or paper businesses, however, under the terms of his Will drawn up on 13 July 1826[26] his wish is that:

> . . . if my son David should be inclined to continue and carry on the Business that he may have the Ropeyard and Paper Mill and Stock in Trade at a fair valuation . . .

It appears that his son did carry on the paper trade up until the 1850s but it does not appear to have ever been a major part of his business, perhaps competition from bigger, better and mechanised mills was making his concern unprofitable. The evidence from the census returns suggests that it was never a large business, probably employing no more than one or two papermakers at any one time.

The summary statistics for the 1831 census list two papermakers for the county of Carmarthen. In the 1841 returns there is only one listed, John Davies, aged 50, shown as not being born in the county of Carmarthen.

By 1851 he has died, the only other papermaker listed for the whole county is Thomas Biggin aged 76, born in Scotland, lodging in St Clears.[27]

Evidence for papermakers prior to the census returns has been found in baptism registers. In the register of Heol Awst Independent chapel,[28] between 7 February 1799 and 23 July 1805, three children are recorded to Samuel Davies, Paper Mill & Mary. Similarly, between 16 November 1805 and 10 November 1810 three children are recorded to Evan Davies, Paper Mill & Anna. In the graveyard of the chapel there is a burial of Evan Davies, Papermaker, who died on 1 August 1815, aged 37. Two of David Charles's four daughters are also recorded in the baptism register of Heol Awst, Sarah on 28 October 1792 and Jane on 1 December 1793, both are recorded as being the children of David Charles, Ropemaker. His only son, also David, was born in 1803, but by this date David Charles had moved allegiance to Water Street Calvinistic Methodist Chapel, where he began to preach in 1808, unfortunately no baptism records survive for this chapel pre 1806. However, the earliest surviving baptism register for Water Street chapel (1806-1837)[29] does record three baptisms to papermakers: 15 April 1813 – John son of Evan & Hannah Davies (formerly Davies, spinster) papermaker of Llangain; 12 January 1817 – Elizabeth daughter of Evan & Anne Davies (formerly Watkins, widow) papermaker of St. Peters; and 9 February 1835 – Hannah daughter of Evan & Mary Davies (formerly Evans, spinster) papermaker of St. Peters. Similarly, for Penuel Chapel, Priory Street, Carmarthen[30] on 1 January 1810, David, the son of William and Mary Lewis, papermaker, of Waindew is baptised. Another son, Seth, is baptised on 26 July 1815, this time they are recorded as living in Water Street, just round the corner from the paper mill. There are also baptisms recorded to another papermaker and his wife, Jonah and Mary Richard. Mary on 12 April 1813; David on 10 September 1817; Thomas on 11 December 1822; Esther on 6 April 1826 and William on 30 August 1828. Their residence is listed as Water Street for the baptism of David but thereafter as Priory Street. It is interesting to note that the only baptisms that have been found are nonconformist, reflecting the religious leaning of the mill owner.

From the report in Eurig Davies' article[31] taken from the House of Commons Papers of 1852 it appears that the mill in Carmarthen is no longer working, however, the mill is still being rated as a paper mill in January

Fig. 8: *Woollen mill, Glannant Road, Carmarthen, 1948.* (Carmarthenshire Archive Service).

1853,[32] but whether or not it was working cannot be determined. Certainly by October 1858[33] it had ceased operation as it was now rated as a woollen mill, occupied by Evan Jones but still owned by David Charles. By 1860 it had been sold with sitting tenant to Thomas Lewis.[34] It remained as a textile mill up until the mid 1930s when it became a motor body works,[35] by the 1970s it had become a motor factors warehouse. The building was demolished and the site redeveloped by Bro Myrddin Housing Association in 1992/3, however, some hint of the milling history does at least live on in the name of the development – Y Felin (The Mill).

Kidwelly paper mill

The earliest substantiated date for the paper mill at Kidwelly is 2 November 1724. The mill and adjoining forge are leased by Owen Brigstocke to Peter Chetle for a term of 99 years at an annual rent of £50/15/- with two pounds of brown paper and twelve bushels of charcoal. The lease is determinable on the three lives of Peter Chetle, his wife Alice and Lewis the fifteenth the then King of France. It is mentioned in the document as:

> And also the paper mill lately erected and adjoining to the said forge . . .[36]

Bernice Cardy gives an earlier date of existence of 1719 but it has not been possible to confirm this.[37] However, the date of 1724 makes it one of the earliest paper mills established in Wales, probably only beaten by Halghton in Flint which was founded about 1706. The only clue to the type of paper made at the mill is

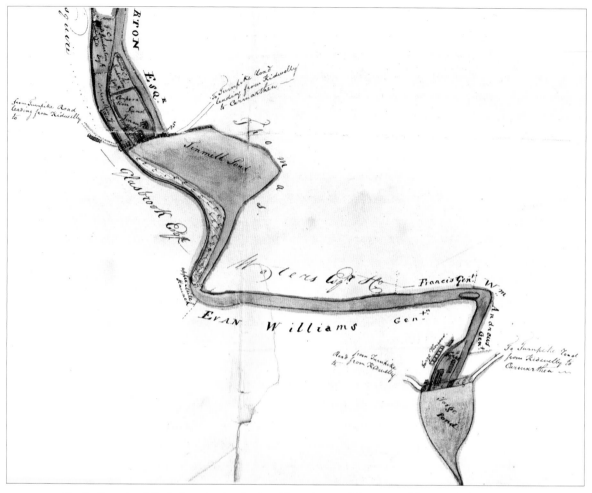

Fig. 9: *Gwendraeth Fach river, showing the tin mills, at the top of the map, and forge, at the bottom, 1808.*
(Carmarthenshire Archive Service).

the brown paper mentioned in the lease above, no paper positively identifiable to the mill has been found. As Kidwelly was a busy port at the time it is quite likely that rope and sail waste from shipping was a major source of raw materials.

Peter Chetle's involvement with the paper mill was short lived. Two exchequer lawsuits resulted in the disposal of some of his properties to settle debts.[38] As part of this the paper mill, together with the forges of Kidwelly, Ponthenry and Whitland, were transferred to Lewis Hughes, attorney and Town Clerk of Carmarthen, on 25 October 1729.[39] Lewis was buried in St Peter's churchyard on 29 January 1730/1. The remainder of the term of the lease was granted to his widow, Frances, on 1 May 1731, this was then transferred to Robert Morgan on 10 April 1733.[40] She married Robert

Morgan in Llangyndeyrn parish church on 29 November 1736, having provided a firm footing for Morgan to build his iron businesses on.

The next recorded tenant at the paper mill is Francis Selman, he is there by 1730 as he is recorded buying cordwood from Arthur Price in an account dated 1 June 1730.[41] The family had been in the area for a few years, he is first found recorded when his son, also Francis, was baptised in Kidwelly church on 15 January 1719/20. Several more children were baptised in the church and his brother, Thomas, married Anna Phillips there on 8 January 1722/3. Thomas Selman was also involved in papermaking, moving to Swansea by 1723 and establishing paper mills at Melin Mynach.[42] Francis Selman was elected onto Kidwelly Borough Council in 1722, holding the office of Bailiff in the same year, eventually being elected an Alderman and becoming Mayor in 1733. He died shortly afterwards and was buried in Kidwelly churchyard on 29 January 1734/5, recorded as 'Alderman'. Interestingly, in his Will drawn up on 27 January[43] shortly before his death he describes himself as 'Papermaker', obviously attaching some importance to the title.

The forge and paper mill now seem to enter a period of decline as in 1740 an action is brought by the owner Owen Brigstocke against Robert and Frances Morgan for failure to keep the buildings in a state of good repair. Even allowing for some exaggeration on the part of Brigstocke's solicitor the buildings must have been in a fairly dire state:

> . . . did permit and suffer the said Forge and Paper Mill and the two outhouses parcells of the said demised premises to be uncovered for want of slating tiling or thatching thereof by reason whereof the rafters beams underpinnings & timbers of the said forge & paper mill & two outhouses became rotten ruinous and in very great decay and also did permit and suffer all the floors and walls of the said forge and paper mill and outhouses to be in great decay for want of necessary repairing thereof . . .[44]

The deed goes on in similar manner concerning the doors, hammer beams, bellows, water wheels and other machinery. Repairs necessary to the forge amounted to £76-10-0, those for the paper mill to:[45]

For timber to mend the press & putting up	0:15:0
For the scrue and making	0:18:0
For the capsill & making being carried away	0:15:0
	£2: 8:0

It may have been that the decay had already started before the property was demised to Frances, but whatever the case they were held responsible, apparently making no effort to make repairs up until proceedings were started on 29 September 1740. The last found mention of the paper mill as a working mill is when it and the forge are properties in a disentailing action in 1746.[46] Papermaking had apparently ceased by 1766 when the forge was sold with freehold to Robert Morgan as it is cited as:

> . . . being minded to sell and dispose of the iron forge called Kidwelly Forge and the paper mill or scite of a paper mill therein wherein a paper mill formerly was . . .[47]

PEMBROKESHIRE

The available secondary literature carries some confusion over the naming, and the history, of the mills in the Haverfordwest area.[48] Haverfordwest Mill, or Mills, seems to be a generic term for any of them, also, the names of Cleddau, Harford, Hartsore, Millbank, Pren-

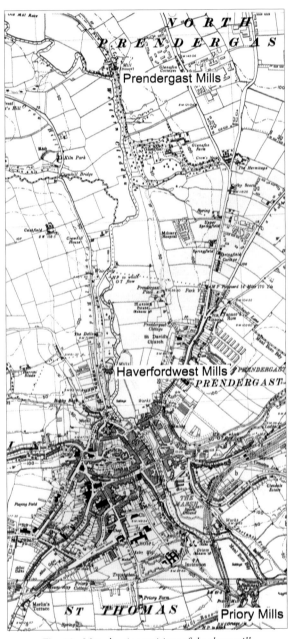

Fig. 10: *Map showing positions of the three mills at Haverfordwest.*
(Ordnance Survey 1948).

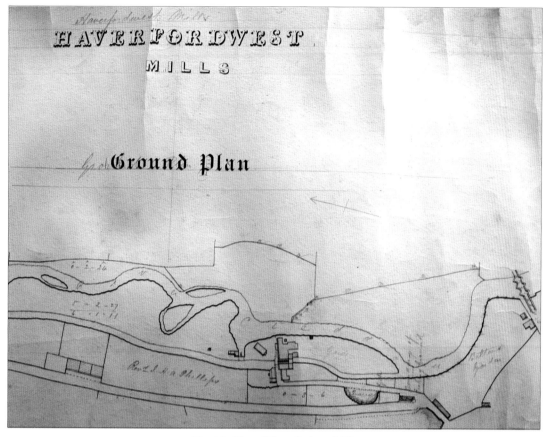

Fig. 11: *Plan of Haverfordwest Mills.*
(Pembrokeshire Record Office. DB/13/2).

dergast and Priory have all been used. The use of 'Mills' rather than 'Mill', does not necessarily mean more than mill, it also refers to more than one waterwheel operating at one site. When writing about the mills I have used the predominant name with the name of the parish of location for additional clarity.

Haverfordwest Mills, St Martin
The first reference to a paper mill at the site is in a mortgage deed of 30 August 1766:

> . . . formerly three water corn grist mills, since two water corn grist mills and two tucking or fulling mills, now or lately two paper mills and a snuff mill . . .[49]

An earlier lease and release of 13/14 February 1764 refers to the same mill as:

> . . . now two water corn grist mills and two tucking or fulling mills . . .[50]

indicating that the paper mills were established sometime between 1764 and 1766. The owner of the mills at these dates was Robert Ferrier of Haverfordwest, Gent. In 1771 a moiety of a corn mill, snuff mill and paper mill in the parish of St Martin was for sale (as Hartsore Mills).[51] Several transactions take place on 14 March 1772 involving John Howells and John Phillips of Haverfordwest and Walter Rice Howells of Maesgwyne, Carmarthen, referring to Harford Mills,[52] it is also at this point that the merchant William Gough of Prendergast becomes involved with the property. Later, in 1778, Gough's son in law, Morgan Meylett of Lawrenny, Esq[53] also becomes involved, but only for a short while as he dies in 1779, his wife Anne being the sole executrix of his will. Morgan's will makes no mention of the paper mill, William Gough dies in 1790 but his will has not survived. However, the mills, and other properties, had already been conveyed to his daughter Anne by lease and release on 24/25 November 1789.

There is £700 secured against the mills borrowed from various people, Anne discharges the debts with monies inherited from her husband and thus gains ownership. Her brother Thomas Gough agrees to relinquish claim to the mills in exchange for the settlement of the debts.[54] She remarried to the Revd John Evans on 15 April 1790 in St Martin, Haverfordwest,[55] but retained control of her interest in the paper mill in her own right –

> . . . sole and separate use of the said Anne Evans for life without the control and not liable to the debts or engagements of the said John Evans . . .[56]

This explains the appearance of Ann Evans as a papermaker in the Universal British Directory of 1791. Richard Lloyd of Haverfordwest, Gent, leased the mill for three lives in 1805.[57] By 1815 it in the possession of Thomas Lloyd, he forms a partnership with John Phillips, draper, to grind corn and make paper in this mill and Priory Mill.[58] Possession of the mills is confirmed by the 1816 Excise List where two mills in Haverfordwest, Nos. 446 & 447, are held by Thomas Lloyd & Co.[59] According to notes made by H. E. S. Simmons,[60] No. 447 was reallocated to a mill in Birmingham in 1839, this means that the Haverfordwest Mills must have been No. 446 as the 1841 and 1851 census returns record the mill as occupied by Benjamin Harvey. Pigot's Directories for 1830 and 1835 only record one paper maker for Haverfordwest, Benjamin Harvey, St Martin. Harvey and his family arrived in Haverfordwest sometime around 1824, prior to this he had been establishing paper mills in Peterhof, Russia, and must have taken over the mill shortly after arriving. *The Cambrian* newspaper reports on 31 March 1832 that:

> On Friday se'nnight, about ten o'clock at night, an alarming fire broke out in the extensive paper mills occupied by Mr Benjamin Harvey, at Haverfordwest, but by the very active and judicious exertions of the persons assembled immediately on the ringing of the alarm bell, it was got under in the course on an hour, with comparatively trifling injury.

The Cambrian describing it as extensive paper mills is not an exaggeration as there had been as many as four water-wheels working at one time.[61] By 1861 it is occupied by two of Benjamin's sons, Jesse and Job, the third son, Joshua, occupied Prendergast Mills. Benjamin Harvey died at Haverfordwest Mills on 2 February 1861. Under the terms of their father's will, proved 12 March 1861, the three sons inherited equal shares as tenants in common during the residue of the several terms of lives created by the several leases under which the properties were held.[62] In the 1871 census the mill appears to be not recorded, it presumably is vacant as Jesse and Job have moved to Talbenny although Job is still listed as a paper maker.[63] The mill is leased to Samuel Rees in August 1871 for 21 years,[64] he also holds Priory Mill, St Thomas parish, which is where he lives with his brother, John, both listed as corn millers. The inventory of papermaking equipment transferred with the lease indicates that it was still a hand-making mill. Samuel Rees did not carry on the papermaking as shown when the mill is advertised for lease again in 1875, described in the particulars as:

> The corn grist mill is alone in working order at present; but only a few years ago a paper manufactory was carried on at these premises on an extensive scale, and where a large fortune was realised.[65]

Prendergast Mills, Prendergast

There have been claims of papermaking at Prendergast in the early part of the nineteenth century, however, I believe the first evidence for papermaking at the Prendergast site is the listing of Millbank Mill as a new mill in 1842, Excise No. 216,[66] established by Benjamin Harvey. However, we already know he was not occupying it as he is listed at Haverfordwest Mills in both the 1841 and 1851 census returns. In support of the start date of 1842, in a sale notice for the paper mills in 1890, it is advertised as having been:

> . . . used as a going concern for upwards of half a century.[67]

Prior to being converted to a paper mill, Prendergast had been a cotton mill, occupied by Matthew Topham. The premises were advertised for sale, along with the residence, grist mill and numerous other buildings in 1804.[68] Eleven years later, Thomas Lloyd agrees not to convert his mills in Prendergast into either paper or corn mills. At this time they are used in manufacturing cotton and as a water corn grist mill.[69] We already know from the Excise list that there were only two paper mills in Haverfordwest in 1816. No. 446 was Haverfordwest Mills, and I believe No. 447 to be Priory Mill, St Thomas, for reasons to be discussed later. If this is correct, as No. 447 was not reallocated until 1839, there could not

Fig. 12: *Advertisement for Prendergast Mills in Worrall's Directory, 1875.*

have been papermaking at Prendergast until after this date. The mills were leased to Benjamin Harvey on 29 September 1840 for the three lives of his sons, together with the residence of Millbank Cottage,[70] this I think is where the confusion over the naming of the mills has crept in. It is my belief that Millbank Mill and Prendergast Mill are one and the same. Prendergast Mill appears twice in the 1851 census return, under separate numbers next to each other, occupied by James Phillips and Thomas James, both papermakers. Millbank appears in the census returns for 1861, occupied by Benjamin's son, Joshua and recorded next to Prendergast Mill, still occupied by James Phillips. The idea that the two mills are one entity is reinforced by the 1871 census return where there are again two entries for Prendergast Mill, with the same occupants as were in the 1861 census for Millbank and Prendergast. In the 1881 census it is listed only as Millbank, now occupied by Samuel Read, a papermaker from Airdrie, Lanarkshire, leased for twenty years from Fanny Letitia Lloyd and others in 1874.[71] At some point, maybe when the mill was set up in 1842, a paper machine was installed, utilising the water power

already in place which had powered over 1500 spindles when it was a cotton mill.[72] The Lloyd and Harvey families evidently retained interests in the mills as Read also leases premises in Prendergast from Jesse and Job Harvey of Prendergast Mills in 1874.[73] Interestingly, in Craig's Paper Mills Directory, 1876, mill No. 216 is listed as Cleddau Mill, Samuel Read & Co, Haverfordwest, adding yet another name to the site. In Slater's Directory for 1880 it is listed as Prendergast Mills, the choice of name seems almost arbitary. Samuel Read never seems to make a success of it, in 1875 he went to Liverpool to sell paper and only managed to secure a small trial order and, in a letter to his cousin, Joseph John Read, states that orders are slack and he is thinking of stopping for a day or two. Samuel had borrowed £1,300 from Joseph John Read to secure the lease, under the terms of which he had absolute title to the water-wheel and other machinery, he assigns these on 17 April 1875, under a Bill of Sale, to Joseph as extra security. This Bill of Sale was re-registered on three further occasions in 1880, 1885 and 1890 showing the debt was never paid off. Samuel Read died insolvent on 27 September 1890, owing Joseph £3515/17/3.[74]

In the 1891 census the mill is listed as Millbank but unoccupied. The next occupier is David Oliver Evans, a Cardiff paper merchant, who leases the mill sometime in 1891. In a letter from John Harvey & Son to Messrs Davies, George & Co., dated 20 December 1890, they state that the owners have no objection to a new lease with the option to purchase for £1650, the equivalent of twenty years rent.[75] An acknowledgement from the Breconshire Millboard Company, dated 15 May 1891, details their acceptance of £146/12/- of Messrs D. O.

Fig. 13: *Ruins of Prendergast Mill in 2007.*
(© ceridwen http://www.geograph.org.uk/photo/410543).

Evans & Co., Cardiff, for stock in trade and machinery belonging to Prendergast Mill sold to them by the administratrix of Samuel Read.[76] However, he apparently only lives there a short while as by the 1901 census he is back in Cardiff. The return shows that his two older children, born in 1892 and 1893 were born in Cardiff and his four youngest children, born between 1895 and 1900 were born in Haverfordwest. This appears to be the last papermaking at Prendergast.

Priory Mill, St Thomas
A paper and corn mill near Haverfordwest was advertised to let in 1798, the advertisement stating that the trade had been long established and the workmen settled at the place about twenty years.[77] It is my opinion that this is Priory Mill as Haverfordwest Mills had by now been making paper for over thirty years and would surely been advertised as such. James Ablart, a Gloucestershire papermaker, is shown as being in Haverfordwest in 1781.[78] Ablart had been in partnership with Thomas Reeve at Wotton-under-Edge but this was dissolved in 1773[79] and he was made bankrupt the following year.[80] How long he was in Haverfordwest is not known but he was back in Gloucestershire by 1784, showing in the Poll Book for St Philip Out Parish.[81] The previous year a corn and paper mill in the parish of St Thomas was for sale by order of the assignees of Anne Rhode, widow, a bankrupt, the mill was let to David Morris.[82] Anne was the wife of John Rhode who died in 1780 and by the terms of his will dated 12 December

1778 inherited all his property. It may be that James Ablart came to Haverfordwest to set up the paper mill but had left before Anne's bankruptcy, the circumstances of which are not known.

In 1815 John Phillips and Thomas Lloyd formed a partnership in the business of papermaking and corn grinding at the paper and corn mills for a term of fourteen years, after seven years it could be terminated by either party if so desired. This partnership was to operate at the mills:

> . . . commonly called and known by the several names of Priory Mills and Haverfordwest Mills with certain cottages and lands thereto belonging situate in the several parishes of St Thomas in the town and county of Haverfordwest and the hamlet of the parish of St Martin in the county of Pembroke.[83]

Lloyd had possession of the mill by lease for his life and that of Morgan Lloyd or the survivor of them. We already know that in the 1816 Excise List there are two paper mills in Haverfordwest, both shown as belonging to Thomas Lloyd & Co. I have demonstrated the case for the Haverfordwest Mills being No. 446 and Prendergast Mill still being a cotton mill, therefore, Priory Mill must be mill No. 447. On 31 May 1825, Thomas Lloyd leased the mill to John Rees, miller, for his natural life, or twenty-one years, from 25 March 1825, should he die before twenty-one years are passed and has bequeathed the lease. The premises are detailed as the:

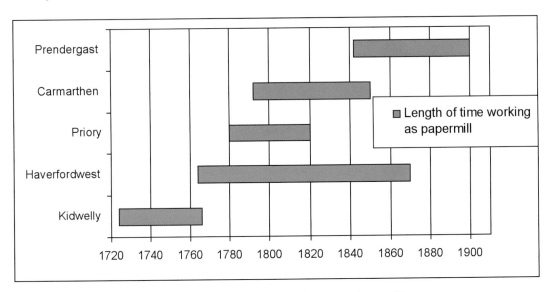

Fig. 14: *Bar chart showing length of operation of papermills.*

. . . water corn grist and paper mills called Priory Mills . . . in the occupation of John Rees . . . situate and lying in the parish of St Thomas and headweir of the said mill in the parishes of St Thomas and Saint Issels Harold-stone.[84]

There is a short inventory of equipment at the mill but no papermaking equipment is listed, Rees is to leave the mill in good and sufficient repair at the end of the lease, except for the lofts over the paper mill. This suggests that they are already in disrepair and it can perhaps be presumed that papermaking had ceased at the mill by 1825. Lloyd was still making paper at Haverfordwest Mills and one of the clauses of the lease is that Rees is:

. . . not to make paper without leave and licence of the said Thomas Lloyd.[85]

John Rees surrenders his interest in the mill on 2 October 1865, as far as I have been able to determine paper was not made there again, certainly not after 1839 with the reallocation of the mill Excise number.[86]

CONCLUSION

Papermaking in west Wales, whilst never a large industry, nevertheless existed for around 175 years, from *c*.1724 in Kidwelly to *c*.1900 in Haverfordwest. The chart above (*Fig. 14*) gives an idea of the length of time of papermaking in the mills. While the two Carmarthenshire mills appear to be completely separate enterprises, the three mills in Pembrokeshire link at one point or another through two families, the Harveys and the Lloyds, owning, and/or operating, more than one mill at any one time.

ACKNOWLEDGEMENTS

Thanks are due to Edna Dale-Jones and Heather James for general encouragement and information; Peter Bower of the British Association of Paper Historians for technical advice; the staff of Pembrokeshire Record Office.

NOTES

1. 'What is the most important invention in the last two thousand years?' In *Edge 48*, 4 January 1999.
2. Clifford Pickover is a research staff member at the IBM T. J. Watson Research Center. He is the author of over 20 books translated in 10 languages on a broad range of topics in science and art.
3. A cotton paper characterised by its glossy and silken appearance.
4. Compiled with information mainly from: Dard Hunter, *Papermaking: The History and Technique of an Ancient Craft*. 2nd edition 1947, and Richard Hills, *Papermaking in Britain 1488-1988: A Short History*. 1988.
5. Pile of sheets of paper interleaved with sheets of felt.
6. A rough estimate for production by hand is twenty-three tons of paper per vat per year. Production is restricted by two factors, the speed of the vatman and the maximum size of the mould that can be handled.
7. Richard Hills, *Papermaking in Britain 1488-1988: A Short History*. 1988.
8. Tillmans, M., *Bridge Hall Mills: Three Centuries of Paper & Cellulose Film Manufacture*. 1978.
9. British Association of Paper Historians www.baph.org.uk. December 2007.
10. Home Park Mill was built by John Dickinson in 1825, converted to a colouring mill in 1890, later pro-duced gummed tape and eventually closed in 1989. www.hemeltoday.co.uk. December 2007.
11. Joan Evans, *The Endless Web: John Dickinson & Co. Ltd. 1804-1954*. 1955.
12. Bolton, Tom, 'The International Paper Trade', *The Quarterly, The Journal of the British Association of Paper Historians*, No. 54, April 2005.
13. Webster's Dictionary 2007.
14. Papyrus is made by pasting thin layers of reed stalk together and, therefore, by the definition that follows in the text, is not a true paper.
15. Dard Hunter, *Papermaking: The History and Technique of an Ancient Craft*. 2nd edition 1947.
16. Bagasse is sugar cane waste, esparto is a perennial grass from Spain and north Africa.
17. Much of the information in this section has been taken from Ian Hendry, 'The Miracle of Paper: Some Thoughts after 50 Years in Paper', *The Quarterly, The Journal of the British Association of Paper Historians*, No. 59, July 2006.
18. CRO Plas Llanstephan 406.
19. *The Dictionary of Welsh Biography down to 1940: under the auspices of The Honourable Society of Cymmrodorion*, Blackwell, Oxford, 1959 & J. E. Lloyd, *A History of Carmarthenshire*, London Carmarthenshire Society, Cardiff, 1939.

20. Samuel Phillips loaned £130 to William Gough and his two children, Thomas Gough and Anne Meylett, secured against the paper mills, in 1788. Pembrokeshire Record Office (PRO) HAM/SE/21/24.

21. CRO/CPR/65/31.

22. CRO/MUS/786.

23. CRO/MUS/363.

24. CRO/CV/4352.

25. CRO/JF/Unlisted – a volume containing pasted in invoices 1833-42 sent to Wm Evans & Co., Carmarthen, printers and proprietors of the *Carmarthen Journal*.

26. SD/1835/32.

27. David Charles is listed in each census as a ropemaker, employing four in 1861.

28. CRO/CNC/42/1.

29. The National Archives (TNA) RG4/3817.

30. TNA RG4/4437.

31. E. Davies, 'Paper-mills and Paper-makers in Wales 1700-1900'. In *National Library of Wales Journal*, Vol. XV, Summer 1967, pp. 1-30.

32. CRO/S/MB/25.

33. CRO/S/MB/27.

34. CRO/MUS/42.

35. In the 1934 borough rate book, CRO/S/MB/94, there is no evidence of the motor works, by 1938 it is in existence, CRO/S/MB/100.

36. NLW. W Evans George 571.

37. Bernice Cardy, 'Paper-making in Swansea'. In *The Quarterley, The Journal of the British Association of Paper Historians*. No. 48, December 2003.

38. See M. C. S. Evans, 'The Pioneers of the Carmarthenshire Iron Industry'. In *The Carmarthenshire Historian*, Vol. 4, 1967.

39. CRO Trant/Yelverton 110.

40. NLW W Evans George 1288.

41. CRO C/V 13/378. The name is recorded as Francis Solomon but is undoubtedly the same person.

42. See Bernice Cardy, n. 37, for more information.

43. SD/1735/46.

44. NLW W Evans George 1288.

45. NLW W Evans George 1293.

46. NLW W Evans George 658-9 & 662.

47. CRO Trant/Yelverton 459.

48. The information available all seems to derive from the work of A. H. Shorter.

49. PRO HAM/SE/21/16.

50. PRO HAM/SE/21/14-15.

51. *British Chronicle* or Pugh's *Hereford Journal*, 20 June 1771.

52. NLW Maesgwynne 200 14 March 1772 and PRO HAM/SE/21/17-20 13/14 March 1772.

53. Anne Gough and Morgan Meylett were married in St Mary, Haverfordwest on 27 Oct. 1774. PRO HPR/2/9.

54. PRO HAM/SE/21/22-27.

55. PRO HPR/25/8.

56. PRO HAM/SE/21/28-30.

57. PRO HAM/SE/21/31.

58. NLW Eaton Evans & Williams 3689-90.

59. Excise General Letter, 8 October 1816.

60. Simmons, Herbert Edward Sydney, Research notes (survey and historical) compiled over forty years on the wind and water mills of Great Britain. Science Museum Library, London.

61. NLW Eaton Evans & Williams 11394.

62. NLW Eaton Evans & Williams 10030.

63. Both are presumably still involved in papermaking as in NLW Eaton Evans & Williams 8698, a lease dated 24 March 1874, Jesse and Job Harvey are referred to as paper-makers of Prendergast Mills.

64. PRO HAM/SE/21/32-33.

65. NLW Eaton Evans & Williams 11394.

66. TNA CUST 139/10 1837-43.

67. NLW Williams & Williams 17275.

68. *The Times*, 20 December 1804.

69. NLW Eaton Evans & Williams 3689.

70. NLW Eaton Evans & Williams 8223.

71. *ibid*.

72. According to the advertisement in *The Times* in 1804 the mill had been designed to operate to a much larger capacity, this suggests that the water power would have been more than ample to drive the machinery to make paper.

73. NLW Eaton Evans & Williams 8698.

74. NLW Williams & Williams 17275.

75. *ibid*.

76. *ibid*.

77. Felix Farley's *Bristol Journal*, 8 September 1798.

78. A. H. Shorter, *Paper Mills and Paper Makers in England 1495-1800*. Paper Publications Society: Hilversum. 1957.

79. A. H. Shorter, 'Paper Mills in Gloucestershire'. In *Transactions of the Bristol and Gloucestershire Archaeological Society*, Vol. 71, 1952.

80. *London Gazette*, 17 September 1774.

81. A. H. Shorter, op. cit., n. 79

82. *British Chronicle* or Pugh's *Hereford Journal*, 27 March 1783 & *London Gazette*, 1 July 1783–8 June 1784.

83. NLW Eaton Evans & Williams 3690.

84. NLW Eaton Evans & Williams 4253.

85. *ibid*.

86. Simmons, Herbert Edward Sydney, Research notes (survey and historical) compiled over forty years on the wind and water mills of Great Britain. Science Museum Library, London.

Carmarthen Printing and Ancillary Trades, 1720-1820

Eiluned Rees

Carmarthen can boast of an unbroken tradition of printing from *c.*1720 to the end of the 20th century. Its association with books goes back much further, for it was from the Augustinian Priory of St John that Sir John Price rescued one of the country's greatest manuscript treasures, the Black Book of Carmarthen.

Sir John Price was a high-ranking Civil Servant entrusted, amongst other things, with the delicate task of overseeing the Dissolution of the Monasteries, but he was also a Renaissance scholar, an antiquary, an author and book-collector, and an ardent Protestant. His Protestant convictions led in 1546 to the printing by Edward Whitchurch in London of the first book in Welsh, known by its opening words *Yny lhyvyr hwnn* ['In this book']. It is an unprepossessing book, but the sentiments that inspired it are touching. Sir John wanted his fellow-countrymen to have access to the Scriptures in their own tongue, and to that end he had put together a basic compilation: the Creed, the Lord's Prayer and the Ten Commandments, together with the alphabet and numerals. The presence of the latter elements is significant, for it indicated that literacy was not widespread in Wales.

Wales had suffered badly in the 15th century from the depredations of the Wars of the Roses, social changes, poor harvests and outbreaks of plague. Enterprising Welshmen tended to seek fame and fortune in London or further afield on the continent. The Tudor dynasty felt gratitude to its compatriots and offered further opportunities for high office. The brain-drain meant that there was little incentive for the development of printing on home ground. The expatriate Welsh spoke English and/or Latin and could buy any

books they wanted in London. Moreover and this was crucial, the London printers exercised strict control over the printing industry, sharing out amongst themselves monopolies of categories of publications. Some concessions were granted to Oxford and Cambridge, but essentially printing was centralised in London, a system well suited to a government ever fearful of survival.

Language posed a problem. Most people in Wales spoke Welsh, but in a plethora of dialects, some of which were mutually incomprehensible. The early printed editions of Rees Prichard's verses, which became known as *Canwyll y Cymry*, were given glosses for North Walian readers. However, there was a universal form of the language used by poets and prose-writers, which was to prove central to the standardisation of the language and to the development of Welsh printing.

The status and survival of the Welsh language were boosted by two factors in the 16th century: the Renaissance and the Reformation. Welsh scholars like William Salesbury, Gruffydd Robert, Morys Clynnog and John David Rhys, influenced by Renaissance scholarship, brought the ancient Welsh language to the attention of the literary world in print. More and more Welsh books were published, and soon there appeared a landmark publication, the 1588 Welsh Bible, translated by Bishop William Morgan. He used a mellifluous form of the afore-mentioned literary language which, universally acceptable, could be used henceforth as a standard for proof-reading. At this stage, Welsh publications had to be heavily subsidised. London printers were reluctant to print limited editions of books in a 'foreign' language. Initially, the patrons were wealthy individuals, but later patronage devolved to societies like the interdenominational *Welsh Trust* (established in 1674) and the Church of England *Society for Promoting Christian Knowledge* (established in 1698). Since literacy was vital to the Protestant cause, both societies promoted education by setting up schools, publishing edifying books and founding libraries. Literacy was permeating all ranks of society, receiving a boost in the steady rise of Welsh Nonconformity. Stephen Hughes, a Carmarthen boy, was associated with the *Welsh Trust* and was instrumental in publishing a cheap edition of the Welsh Bible, amongst other works.

Thomas Jones was a Welsh tailor working in London when he spotted a business opportunity. He realised that once people learned to read, they would want more variety in the way of reading material. In 1679 he became a bookseller/publisher, specialising in Welsh books. In 1695 the Licensing Act lapsed, thereby loosening the stranglehold of the London printers, and Jones moved to Shrewsbury, setting up as a printer. His many publications included an unpretentious Welsh-English dictionary, an anthology of popular Welsh verse, the first Welsh almanack, ballads, chapbooks, ABCs, trade manuals, and popular religious works (especially translations of John Bunyan's books). He established Shrewsbury as the main centre for popular Welsh printing for half a century. Amongst his contemporaries were John Rhydderch and John Rogers, two men of relevance to Carmarthen printing.

The Shrewsbury printers developed an effective distribution network in Wales, comprising itinerant booksellers, chapmen and local agents, and making good use of fairs and markets. Welsh distributors are sometimes named in imprints. In 1714 the name of Nicholas Thomas appears in the imprint of Morgan Llwyd's *Dirgelwch i rai iw ddeall*, printed by John Rogers. In 1719 he appears in the imprint of *Eglurhaad i Gatechism Byrraf y Gymanfa*, printed by Isaac Carter in Trefhedyn, near Newcastle Emlyn. Isaac Carter was the first commercial printer in Wales. There had been instances of clandestine Roman Catholic presses, but Carter was the person who initiated this new era in Welsh history. Trefhedyn may seem an unlikely place for such an important enterprise, but South Cardiganshire at that time had witnessed one of the localised literary and spiritual revivals that spring up in Wales from time to time.

Like Sir John Price, who published the first Welsh book, Carter was motivated by concern for the souls of his fellow-countrymen. He specialised in religious works, though ironically his first publications, in 1718, were two ballads.[1] Although he did not become a printer in order to make money, he had enough business acumen to move from Trefhedyn to Carmarthen in 1725. There was already a printing-house in Carmarthen, that of Nicholas Thomas, the man who had links with Shrewsbury printers and who had encouraged Carter in his venture. His first known publications are dated 1721, but as books took time to go through press, he must have set up the printing-house *c*.1720.

Carmarthen was far better equipped for a new commercial enterprise than Trefhedyn had been. It was an old established town, a flourishing trade centre, with a port; it was an administrative centre for the county and for the Diocese of St David's; it had a grammar school and a nonconformist academy; it had a fairly affluent middle class as well as 'polite' society; its fairs and markets were well attended. In other words, there were potential customers for the services of a printing-house. Even so, making a living was not easy for these early printers. No wealthy patron helped to pay for the equipment needed, and they had to learn the practicalities of working a press, seek custom and finally distribute their wares.

Isaac Carter and Nicholas Thomas were not apprenticed to the trade. Presumably they learned the rudiments of printing in Shrewsbury, either with John Rogers or John Rhydderch, both of whom had business connections with west Wales. John Rhydderch, for example, had the 1734 issue of his almanack *Newyddion oddiwrth y sêr* printed in Carmarthen by Nicholas Thomas and John Williams. The rudiments did not extend to aesthetics, and it was not until the latter half of the 18th century that books printed in Carmarthen became objects pleasing to the eye. The change occurred in 1762, when John Ross, a Scotsman, came to Carmarthen. He had not only served a formal apprenticeship, but he also had seven years' experience as overseer in a London printing house. His mere arrival is noteworthy because it signifies that the trade was well enough established in Carmarthen to attract a professional. Initially, he came to join Rhys Thomas, who had been printing there since 1760, but within two years Thomas moved to Llandovery and later Cowbridge. Ross stayed in Carmarthen until his death in 1807. His arrival was the death-knell of the amateur printer. From now on, Carmarthen printers would serve an apprenticeship. John Daniel, a farmer's son, was apprenticed to Ross. After serving his term, he worked with the King's

Printers in London, returning to Carmarthen in 1784 to set up his own business. He in turn sought apprentices locally. An advertisement in Benjamin Francis's *Marwnad ar . . . John Thomas . . .* (1797) reads: 'Wanted, as an apprentice to a printer, a smart active youth, from the country. Preference will be given to one who can read the Welsh language.' Not all apprentices proved satisfactory, for in *The Carmarthen Journal*, 30 January 1813, Daniel issued a warning:

> To Master Printers, &c. Whereas David Jones, an Indentured Apprentice of J. Daniel, Carmarthen, having absconded and left his master's employ, without any cause or provocation whatsoever: now this is to caution all Master Printers, and others, from harbouring or employing . . . the said David Jones, after this public notice, as legal proceedings will be had recourse to, for recovery of his salary, &c. against such person or persons who may offend against the Statute in that case made and provided. Description: He is of the middle stature, and looks sallow and ghastly: has black hair, which he wear short: chews tobacco immoderately, which gives him a filthy and offensive appearance.

We do not know how many presses there would have been in Daniel's establishment, but it is likely that Carter and Nicholas Thomas and their successors would have had but one apiece. They would have been hand-operated wooden presses [*fig. 1*], bulky items more likely to have been delivered from London by sea rather than by carrier. In time, a press could be bought nearer home from a retiring printer. When John Ross set up in business, he announced that he had a press made in London by a famous carpenter.[2] By the 19th century, presses other than the familiar letter-press came into vogue: rolling presses for copper-engraving and cylinder presses for newspapers. In *The Cambrian*, 8 December 1810, Jonathan Harris advertised 'Letter-press and Copper-plate printing neatly executed.' There is an earlier reference, in *The Cambrian*, 15 August 1807, to 'Copper-plate copies of Hebrew letters and words' being available for a shilling 'at J. Evans and Jonathan Harris, Booksellers, Carmarthen,' but there is no certainty that they themselves printed them at that date. By 1820, all the major printers were offering both copper-plate and letter-press. In 1810 John Daniel published and printed Carmarthen's first (and still surviving) weekly newspaper, *The Carmarthen Journal*. The first two newspapers published in Wales were *The Cambrian* in Swansea (1804) and *The North Wales Gazette* (1808) in Bangor.

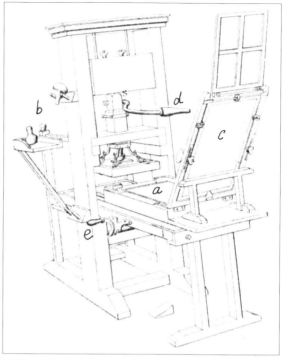

Fig. 1: *An early printing press – 'a': the bed of the press in which the forme of type is fixed; 'b': inkballs for hand-inking the type in the forme; 'c': the platen holding the paper; 'd': when the platen is laid over the forme, the bed is wound into the press, using handle 'e' and the bar 'd' is pulled to 'impress' the type onto the paper.*

Founts of type, like presses, were bought in London, and, again as with the presses, were likely to be passed on in due course. Having set up his business *c.*1720, Nicholas Thomas was announcing in 1721 that new type was shortly to be delivered from London.[3] He acquired a third fount around 1725. Type-founts were not designed to meet the exigencies of the Welsh language, with its preponderance of 'y's, 'd's, 'w's, and accented vowels. Consequently, a publication might contain a mixture of founts, type of all sizes, and indiscriminate use of italic, bold and capital letters. Often two 'v's would be substituted for 'w,' whilst there was no consistency in the use of accents. Shortage of type for a large publication involved distributing a forme after it was printed, thereby slowing the progress of a work through press.

By John Ross's time, such economies did not apply. When advertising his business in 1764, he boasted of having acquired a great many new types from London.[4] Remarkably, he used Hebrew type as early as 1773 and

Fig. 2: *An example of John Evans's Hebrew type in William Higgs Barker, 'A Plain grammar of the Hebrew language . . . Second edition' (Carmarthen, 1814).*
(Reproduced by kind permission of Carmarthen County Museum).

1776, for printing two books by William Higgs Barker, *A Plain grammar of the Hebrew language* and *The Hebrew and English lexicon improved*. John Evans used Hebrew type for a second edition of the former in 1814[5] [*fig. 2*]. He already had it in stock for the benefit of one his good customers, the scholarly Thomas Burgess, Bishop of St. Davids, for whom he printed, amongst other works, the *Rudiments of Hebrew grammar* in 1813. Although no Carmarthen book printed entirely in Greek has come to light, Greek type was used in quotations and on title-pages by John Evans, notably in books by Burgess.

The early printers deserve credit for having made a valiant attempt to embellish their publications with ornament, but that is the kindest observation that can be made. Head-pieces and tail-pieces and decorated initials were used right from the beginning, and

Nicholas Thomas had a primitive frame for one of his earliest publications, *Cyffes ffydd* (1721), and from 1723 onwards he was regularly using a somewhat more ornate frame. It is difficult to tell whether the poor results were due to incompetent presswork or to the state of the ornaments, which could well have been the discarded stock of some English printer. Nicholas Thomas's ornaments were re-used by his successors, Samuel Lewis and Evan Powell, betraying increasing signs of wear and tear as time went by. Isaac Carter's experiment with a two-colour title-page (red and black) for John Goodman's *Maddeuant i'r edifairiol* (1725-6), was one he did not repeat. As with every other aspect of printing, ornamentation improved in quality and execution in the latter half of the 18th century.

Chapbooks and ballads were sometimes crudely illustrated with woodcuts, the illustrations not necessarily having any bearing on the text, but generally, since most Welsh books were religious in content, the need for illustration was minimal. It was only when the habit of reading became more prevalent and led to a demand for a wider range of publications that illustration became a regular feature. Copper-plate printing greatly enhanced the scope for illustration, though it was not widely used in Wales until the 19th century. One of the few examples of ambitious woodcut illustration in Carmarthen is a pictorial alphabet used in a book printed by John Daniel (1801?): Owen Hughes's *Allwedd newydd, i bobl ieuangc i ddysgu darllain Cymraeg* ['A new key for young people to learn to read Welsh']. It had originally been created for English children, and many a Welsh child must have been puzzled as to why the letter A (for Ape) should have a picture labelled 'Eppa'!

Vital materials required for printing included ink and paper. Ink would have been ordered from London, possibly from Beale Blackwell, who was certainly supplying Rees Thomas in Cowbridge in 1783 and the Bala press in 1806.[6] Paper was very expensive, whether it was imported from Holland or France, or manufactured in England. Moreover, the cost rose steadily as the government increased paper taxes. The struggling Welsh printers tended to buy the cheaper variety, which has resulted in the premature demise of many a publication. Paper was transported by sea and subject to the vagaries of the weather. The publication of the third edition of Peter Williams's Bible was held up because 'the ship that carried paper . . . was stop'd by contrary winds at Penarth about three weeks,'[7] and this was by no means a unique occurrence. There were paper mills in Wales by the end of the 18th century and a few manufactured good quality paper, which was on occasion used by Welsh printers for prestigious works. Jonathan Harris of Carmarthen, however, used paper from a Prendergast Mill for a mere broadside: the watermark 'T. Lloyd 1810' appears in *By Command of the King of Kings* in 1810.

As one would expect, there was a marked difference in the quality of press-work between the amateur and the apprenticed printers. The processes of composing type, preparing the bed of the press, inking the formes and pulling the bar require skill – and experience. Help was essential for operating a press, but the early printer's helpers would have been even less experienced than himself. Frequently found at the end of a book was a list of corrections. Nicholas Thomas went a stage further; at the end of Thomas Vincent's *Dydd y Farn Fawr* (1727)

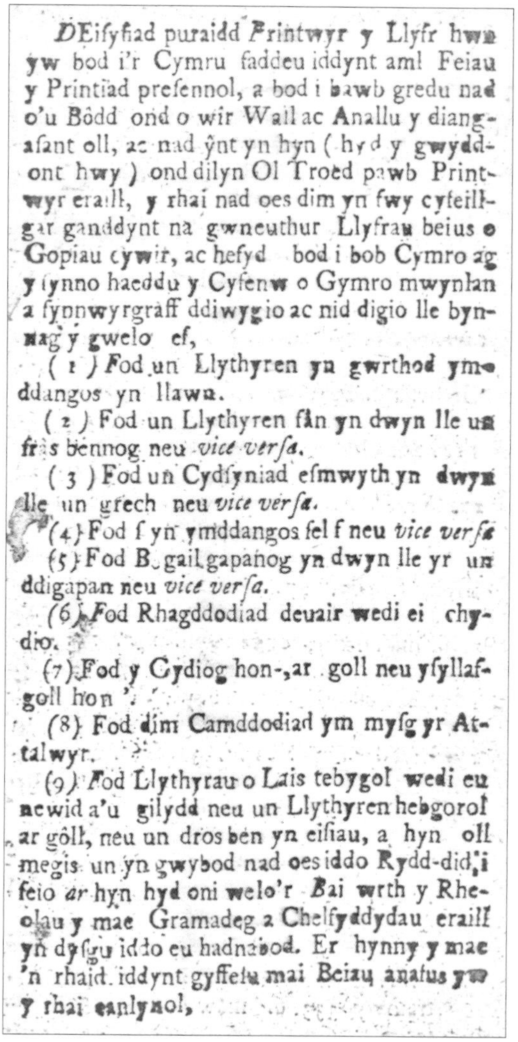

DEisyfiad puraidd *Printwyr* y Llyfr hwn yw bod i'r Cymru faddeu iddynt aml Feiau y Printiad presennol, a bod i bawb gredu nad o'u Bôdd ond o wir Wall ac Anallu y diangasant oll, ac nad ŷnt yn hyn (hyd y gwyddont hwy) ond dilyn Ol Troed pawb Printwyr eraill, y rhai nad oes dim yn fwy cyfeillgar ganddynt na gwneuthur Llyfrau beius o Gopiau cywir, ac hefyd bod i bob Cymro ag y synno haeddu y Cyfenw o Gymro mwynlan a synnwyrgraff ddiwygio ac nid digio lle bynnag y gwelo ef,

(1) Fod un Llythyren yn gwrthod ymddangos yn llawn.

(2) Fod un Llythyren fân yn dwyn lle un fras bennog neu *vice versa*.

(3) Fod un Cydsyniad esmwyth yn dwyn lle un grech neu *vice versa*.

(4) Fod s yn ymddangos fel f neu *vice versa*

(5) Fod B gail gapanog yn dwyn lle yr un ddigapan neu *vice versa*.

(6) Fod Rhagddodiad deuair wedi ei chydio.

(7) Fod y Cydiog hon-,ar goll neu ysyllafgoll hon '.

(8) Fod dim Camddodiad ym mysg yr Attalwyr.

(9) Fod Llythyrau o Lais tebygol wedi eu newid a'u gilydd neu un Llythyren hebgorol ar gôll, neu un dros ben yn eisiau, a hyn oll megis un yn gwybod nad oes iddo Rydd-did i feio *ar* hyn hyd oni welo'r *Bai* wrth y Rheolau y mae Gramadeg a Chelfyddydau eraill yn dysgu iddo eu hadnabod. Er hynny y mae 'n rhaid iddynt gyffesu mai Beiau anafus yw y rhai canlynol,

Fig. 3: *Nicholas Thomas's apology for printing errors in Thomas Vincent, 'Dydd y Farn Fawr' (Carfyrddin [sic], 1727).*
(Reproduced by kind permission of the National Library of Wales).

is a whole page listing common errors [*fig. 3*]. Loosely translated, it reads thus:[8]

> The earnest Entreaty of the Printers of this Book is that the Welsh forgive them the many Faults of the present Edition, and that everyone believe that it was not with their approval but from genuine Error and Inability that they escaped, and that in this they are only (as far as they know) following in the Footsteps of all other Printers, to whom there is nothing more congenial than to make faulty Books of correct copy, and also that every Welshman who wishes to deserve the title of an amiable and sensible Welshman may correct and not be angry wherever he sees,

That one Letter refuses to appear in its entirety.

That one Lower-case Letter takes the place of a capital letter or vice versa.

That a soft consonant takes the place of a harsh one or vice versa.

That ſ appears as f or vice versa.

That a Vowel with a circumflex takes the place of one without a circumflex or vice versa.

That a compound Preposition is joined together.

That this Hyphen - is missing or this apostrophe '.

That there is no Mis-placing of the Punctuation.

That Letters of a similar sound are transposed or one inessential Letter is missing, or an extra one wanting, and all this as one knowing that he has not Liberty to find fault with this until he sees the fault according to the Rules which Grammar and other Arts teach him to recognise. Despite that they must confess that grievous Faults are the following . . .

By the end of the 18th century, more presses needed more hands and those hands now had to be skilled. One of the first employees John Ross took on was an overseer for the Welsh publications, because unlike his pre-decessors he was a 'foreigner' who had not yet learned the language. His overseer was Evan Thomas, a compositor who had worked in printing offices in Shrewsbury and Chester, and who was also a poet and almanacker. Ross, to his credit, lost no time in learning the language himself. There is no evidence to indicate how many presses or how many employees the later printers possessed. The presence of press figures[9] in certain books printed by John Ross and John Evans complicates the picture instead of clarifying it. It is in any case problematic as to whether press-figures were linked to presses or pressmen, but in Carmarthen the mystery deepens. John Ross used figures 0 to 4, with 3 in different sizes or inverted. John Evans used the figures 0, 2, 3, 4, 5, 6, 7 and 9. Evans would not have had nine presses, but even if the figures were linked with pressmen, the use of 0 and an inverted 3 makes little sense. What is certain is that the output of a printing-house, in works printed and in the size of editions, would warrant the use of more than one press.

Despite the size of editions, the actual publishing process changed little in the period under review. Carmarthen printing was more akin to Shrewsbury printing, not only in appearance, but also in that the printers had to rely on their own initiative rather than on patronage to make a living. The primary need was for customers and it must be stressed at the outset that very rarely indeed did a local printer undertake the cost of a publication. The cost was borne by whoever was publishing the work, be it the author, translator, compiler or editor. Since these people were rarely wealthy, by far the most popular system of publication was by subscription. Although the onus for gathering subscriptions lay with the publisher, the printer would help by placing at his disposal whatever facilities he had. The first step was to issue proposals describing the projected book, stating the price and requesting that half be paid beforehand and the remainder on receipt. When the work were a large one, as was the case with editions of the Peter Williams annotated Bible, it would be issued in 1/- parts. The proposals were distributed separately or printed at the end of another publication. Work would not commence until there were enough orders to justify a print-run, which in the early days could be as low as two or three hundred copies. The advance subscriptions would go towards the high cost of paper. Spreading the cost suited the subscribers, few of whom had much ready money. They usually, though not always, had the pleasure of seeing their names in subscription lists at the beginning or end of a publi-cation [*fig. 4*]. The publisher would canvass family, friends and, if he were a preacher, congregations, but vital to the system was the trade network already set up by the printer. The network comprised local agents such as booksellers, shopkeepers, etc. and, most important, itinerant booksellers. The agents collected the names of subscribers and in due course delivered the books, and in return they were given free copies or copies at trade discounts to sell on their own account. Itinerant book-sellers travelled extensively, from market to market, from fair to fair, and without their services, the system would have collapsed. Their names appear and reappear as agents in imprints; fifteen itinerant booksellers are present among the distributors of John Evans's *Cofrestr o lyfrau Cymraeg* (1822).

Books and pamphlets, unless otherwise stated, were issued in blue wrappers or boards [*figs. 5 & 6*]. Some printers offered a bookbinding service, in which case two prices would be quoted in the proposals, for unbound and bound copies respectively. Bookbinders were occasionally part of the establishment, but more often they were freelance binders who had an arrange-ment with the printer. Such an arrangement operated between Crispianus Jones and Nicholas Thomas. Thomas placed advertisements for Jones's bookselling and bookbinding business in his publications, and knowing he could call on the binder's services, he could

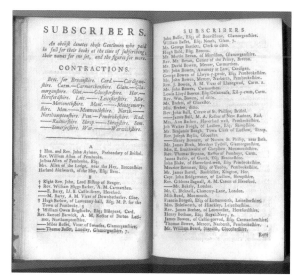

Fig. 4: *The opening pages of the 19-page subscription list to Morgan Williams, 'A Treasury of theological knowledge . . . Vol. 1' (Carmarthen: John Ross and John Daniel, 1791).*

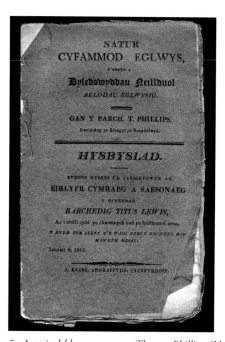

Fig. 5: *A typical blue wrapper on Thomas Phillips, 'Natur cyfammod eglwys' (Caerfyrddin: John Evans, 1815). The wrapper has been used to advertise a forthcoming publication.*
(Reproduced by kind permission of Carmarthen County Museum).

state in the imprint of Andrew Jones's *Llyfr du y gydwybod*: '*Preintiedig gan Nicholas Thomas, lle gallwch gael Printio pob math ar gopiau ai beindio am bris gweddaidd*' ['Printed by Nicholas Thomas, where you may have all sorts of copies and have them bound at a reasonable price']. A bilingual notice by Crispianus Jones in 1731 is more specific about his binding: '*That all sorts of old and decay'd books are neatly bound gilt or plain in calf, sheep or morocco very cheap.*'[10] He also offered to repair books.[11]

It was not unusual for cobblers to take up bookbinding, as did Benjamin Simon of Abergwili, who achieved renown as a manuscript copyist and poet. His bindings are identifiable from the tooling, and like most Welsh bindings of the period, they are functional rather than beautiful. There is a possibility that there was in 1770 a bookbinder in Carmarthen capable of high-class work. In the National Library of Wales are two 1770 books. One is the Alltyrodin Commonplace Book, which belonged to David Lloyd. Handsomely bound in morocco, rather than in the prevalent sheep or calf skin, it is beautifully gold-tooled. What links it with the locality is a copy of the Peter Williams Bible, which has the same gold-tooling. The latter was presented to Peter William's son John and it remained in the family until purchased by Principal J. H. Davies in the early 20th century. The evidence is circumstantial rather than conclusive, but it would be nice to think that they were

Fig. 6: *An example of marbled boards on William Higgs Barker, 'A Plain grammar of the Hebrew language . . . Second edition' (Carmarthen: John Evans, 1814).*
(Reproduced by kind permission of Carmarthen County Museum).

executed in the town. The demand for quality work was limited and much of a bookbinder's work would be fairly routine, as is evident in the surviving register for 1818-28 of David Morris.[12] The most interesting part of the register is his list of clients, which includes contemporary printers, booksellers and stationers in the town.

Printers could never have survived on the proceeds of book-printing. What kept them solvent was jobbing printing. By its very nature, jobbing printing is ephemeral and so very few of the thousands of items that oiled the wheels of society have survived. One cannot overestimate the value of this aspect of the printing trade. The convenience of being able to drop into a printing-house and order whatever was needed, assured of prompt delivery, instead of waiting for supplies to arrive from London or Bristol, was a revolution in local economy.

Jobbing printing falls into two main categories: items commissioned on a regular basis and ad hoc material. Amongst the former are legal and administrative forms, for Courts and Solicitors, etc; the plethora of forms connected with local government and the administration of the Poor Law, highways, etc; documents associated with estate management; bill-heads, adver-

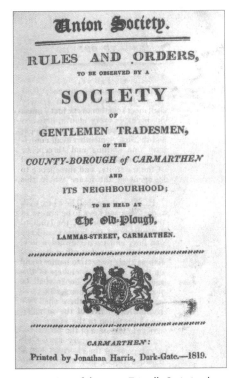

Fig. 7: *One of the many Friendly Societies that appreciated the services of local printers.*
(Reproduced by kind permission of Carmarthen County Museum).

tisements, notepaper, labels and other paraphernalia used by shopkeepers, tradesmen, craftsmen, hoteliers, etc; accounts, notices, annual reports and membership lists for societies, organisations and institutions. By 1820, there was a proliferation of Agricultural Societies, Auxiliary Bible Societies, Savings Banks, Friendly Societies [*fig. 7*] and Literary Societies, including the famous Cambrian Society. Chapels were being founded throughout the county and they, like the churches, needed material that provided the printer with a regular source of income. All kinds of schools were customers, as were book clubs and libraries.

Ad hoc material included notices of sales and auctions of property and stock; posters for theatres, concerts and balls; documents concerned with shipping; notices concerning specific projects, for example, building projects. National and local elections, especially if hotly contested, were a printer's bonanza, and he had no scruples about printing propaganda for all contestants. The Welsh custom of issuing bidding letters on the occasion of a marriage was a useful source of income, as increasingly by 1800 they were being printed instead of handwritten [*fig. 8*]. Another lucrative source were recantations, public retractions of statements made with more haste than discretion. For ephemera, a printer might resort to 'Printing in Gold, Silver, and Flock.' Election addresses and theatre bills were often printed on silk, sadly not a durable medium [*fig. 9*].

In connection with jobbing printing, there were ancillary services on offer. Amongst the Cardiganshire Quarter Sessions Records is an account of the disbursements of Herbert Lloyd, Clerk of the Peace, in connection with a '*special order concerning Robberies and Burglaries*' in 1786. In addition to paying John Ross £2 for printing two hundred in English and £2 for printing two hundred in Welsh, he gave Ross £1 '*for having such translated into Welsh*'.[13] Printers charged for delivery and for 'posting up,' that is, displaying posters on hoardings, doors and shop windows. Jonathan Harris was paid £54.2.5 '*for paper, printing, packing, and carriage of Deanery parcels, &c*' in 1808.[14] Booksellers had flourished in Carmarthen long before the advent of printing. Dawkin Gove, a 17th century mayor of Carmarthen, sold books on a considerable scale; an inventory of his stock taken at his death in 1692 lists multiple copies of books, amounting to £30.10.1 in value.[15] Bookselling escalated in the 18th century, predictably. Printers acted as booksellers too, selling their own publications and those of other printers. Their names would appear in

CARMARTHEN, *July* 22, 1806.

AS we intend to enter the matrimonial ſtate on Tueſday the 5th day of Auguſt next, we purpoſe to make a *Bidding* on the occaſion the ſame day at the ſign of the *Six-Bells*, near the Church, when and where the favor of your good company is moſt humbly ſolicited; and whatever donation you may then be pleaſed to confer on us, will be gratefully received, and cheerfully repaid, whenever demanded on a ſimilar occaſion, by

Your much obliged humble ſervants,

JOHN REES,
MARY DAVIES.

☞ The young man's father and mother (Thomas Rees, Cryer, and wife) his brother (David Rees) and aunt (Anne Morgans) deſire that all gifts of the above nature, due to them, may be returned to the young man on the above day, and will be thankful for all additional favors conferred on him.

Alſo, The young woman's father and mother, (Thomas Davies, Taylor, and wife) her brother and ſiſters, and aunt, (Elizabeth Smith) requeſt that all gifts of the ſaid nature, due to them, may be returned to the young woman on the above day, and will be thankful for all other favors beſtowed on her.

J. Daniel, Printer, Carmarthen.

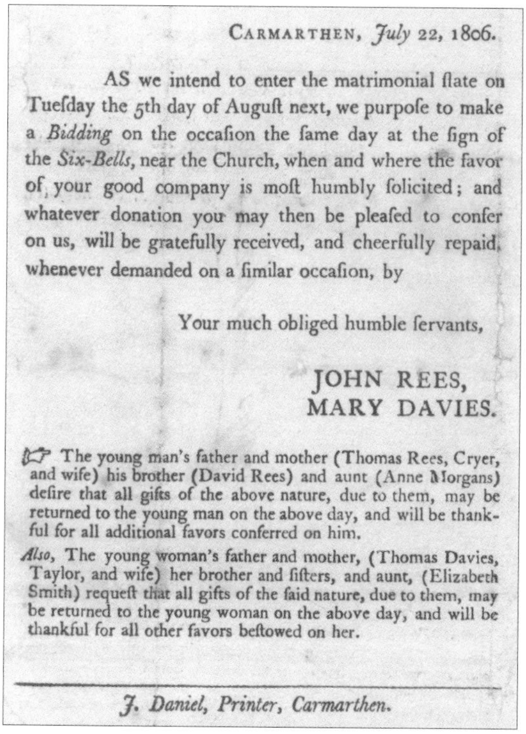

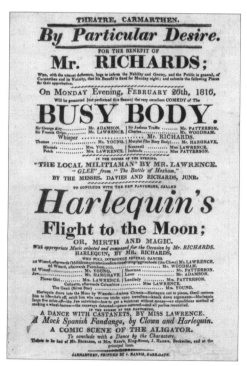

Fig. 8: *A bidding letter.*
(Reproduced by kind permission of Carmarthen County Archives).

one another's subscription lists. Subscribers to Thomas Heywood's *The Life of Merlin*, printed by John Evans in 1812, had amongst its subscribers booksellers and printers from Holywell, Newport, Haverfordwest, Aberystwyth, Swansea, Dolgellau, Cardigan, Bala, Merthyr Tydfil and London. They also dealt in second-hand books. From the outset printers had advertised a forthcoming publication of the author's or of their own [*fig. 10*], but as their output increased, the advertisement was replaced by a full-page list of publications. In turn, the lists evolved into catalogues. John Daniel appended eight-page catalogues to the almanacks of John Harris from 1797 to 1800, and they included stock neither associated with him nor the almanacker. After 1800, separately-issued catalogues became common. *A Catalogue of books at reduced prices, by Ann Scott (successor to the late John Ross)* (1808), has an extra dimension, as it contains *Fruit and forest trees*. Her husband, Walter Scott, was a market gardener. John Evans published several catalogues, the ones dated 1822 and 1825 being so comprehensive that they can be used as check-lists for contemporary Welsh publications. In 1812, he produced a 24-page catalogue of books published by subscription: *Cofrestr o lyfrau gwerthfawr, yn cael eu cyhoeddi*

THEATRE, CARMARTHEN.

By Particular Desire.

FOR THE BENEFIT OF

Mr. RICHARDS;

Who, with the utmost deference, begs to inform the Nobility and Gentry, and the Public in general, of Carmarthen and its Vicinity, that his Benefit is fixed for Monday night; and submits the following Pieces for their approbation.

On MONDAY Evening, FEBRUARY 26th, 1816,

Will be presented (not performed this Season) the very excellent COMEDY of The

BUSY BODY.

Sir George Airy............ Mr. ADAMSON. | Sir Jealous Traffic .... Mr. PATTERSON.
Sir Francis Gripe.......... Mr. LAWRENCE. | Charles.................. Mr. WOODHAM.
Whisper .... Mr. RICHARDS.
Thomas .... Mr. YOUNG. | Marplot (the Busy Body).... Mr. HARGRAVE.
Miranda .... Mrs. YOUNG. | Scentwell .... Miss LAWRENCE.
Patch .... Mrs. LAWRENCE. | Isabinda .... Miss PATTERSON.

IN THE COURSE OF THE EVENING,

"THE LOCAL MILITIAMAN" BY MR. LAWRENCE.
"GLEE" from "The Battle of Hexham,"
BY THE MESSRS. DAVIES AND RICHARDS, JUNR.

TO CONCLUDE WITH THE NEW PANTOMIME, CALLED

Harlequin's
Flight to the Moon;
OR, MIRTH AND MAGIC.

With appropriate Music selected and composed for the Occasion by Mr. RICHARDS.

HARLEQUIN, BY MR. RICHARDS,
WHO WILL INTRODUCE SEVERAL DANCES.

1st Wizard, afterwards Odditibumquirumcioosfumcioosfrizlegriggrinoboski (the Clown) Mr. LAWRENCE.
2d Wizard, afterwards Pantaloon........................ Mr. WOODHAM.
3d Wizard .... Mr. YOUNG. | Showman .... Mr. PATTERSON.
Jew...................... Mr. HARGRAVE. | Lover .... Mr. ADAMSON.
Flower Girl .... Mrs. LAWRENCE. | Landlady .... Mrs. PATTERSON.
Colinette, afterwards Columbine .... Miss LAWRENCE.
The Genii (Silver Star) .... Mrs. YOUNG.

Harlequin drove into the Moon by Wizards—Ambres Chinois—Harlequin cut to pieces, Genii restores him to life—he's off, catch him who can—no tricks upon travellers—knock down arguments—Harlequin leaps five miles off—the Jew outwitted—how to get a waistcoat without money—an expeditious method of making a wheel-barrow—the runaways detected—peace restored—and all parties reconciled.

IN THE COURSE OF THE PANTOMIME,

A DANCE WITH CASTANETS, BY MISS LAWRENCE.
A Mock Spanish Fandango, by Clown and Harlequin.
A COMIC SCENE OF THE ALIGATOR.
To conclude with a Dance by the Characters.

Tickets to be had of Mr. RICHARDS, at Mrs. REES's, King-Street, J. HARRIS, Bookseller, and at the principal Inns.

CARMARTHEN, PRINTED BY J. HARRIS, DARK-GATE.

Fig. 9: *A theatre poster printed on silk.*
(Reproduced by kind permission of Carmarthen County Archives).

WATKINS A LLOYD,
ARGRAFFWYR, LLYFRWERTHWYR, LLYFRRWYMWYR, &c. &c.,

Yn cymmeryd y Cyfleustra hwn i hyspysu i'w Hewyllyswyr da, ac i bawb yn gyffredin, eu bod yn dwyn y Gelfyddyd o argraffu yn mlaen, ger llaw y *Dderwen, Heol-y-prior, Caerfyrddin*. Yn diolch i bawb ag sydd wedi eu ffafrio hwy â'u Gwaith, ac yn dymuno Parhad o'u hewyllys da tu ag atynt, gan sicrhau y bydd i'w Gwaith gael ei wneud mor ddiwall, mor hardd, ac am Bris mor rhesymol ag y gwna rhyw rai ereill ef yn Nghaerfyrddin.

**** Llyfrau, &c. o Lundain, ar y Rhybudd byraf.*

Mae yn barod i'r Wasc, ac a gyhoeddir yn fuan,

GAMUT,
NEU,
GLORIAN PERORIAETH:
AT BA UN Y 'CHWANEGIR
CASGLIAD O HYMNAU,
O WAITH YR AWDWYR HYNOTAF,
YN NGHYD AG AMRYW O RAI NEWYDDION.

Yr ydys yn bwriadu cyfieithu i'r Cymraeg, Traethawd ffhagorol ar sancteiddrwydd, o waith y Parchedig John Hunt, Gweinidog yr efengyl yn Newport-pagnel, mewn dull o bregeth ar 1 Thes. 5, 23. Mae yr awdwr yn dangos, 1. Natur sancteiddrwydd, a pha mor belled mae yn cyraedd, fel y gellir gwybod pa un a ydym yn feddiannol arno ai peidio. 2. Ei ddymunoldeb, i'r dyben i annog meddianwyr i fod yn ddiolchgar i Dduw am dano, ac i ereill weled eu diffyg o hono. 3. Dangos y ffordd a'r moddion ag mae yn cael ei weithredu mewn 8 o bethau neillduol. 4. Cymhwysiad, neu amryw gasgliadau defnyddiol.

Pris Un Swllt a Chwe' Cheiniog.

Trelech, Hydref 6, 1809.

*** Derbynir enwau, nid ydys yn ymofyn arian yn mlaen, gan y Cyfieithydd yn Nhrelech, a chan Watkins a Lloyd, Heol-y-prior, Caerfyrddin.

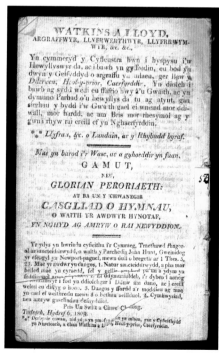

Fig. 10: *An advertisement by Watkins and Lloyd in James Owen, 'Trugaredd a barn' (Caerfyrddin, 1809).*
(Reproduced by kind permission of Carmarthen County Museum).

trwy ragdaliadau, yn rhanau. He guaranteed delivery of part issues to the house of the subscriber, carriage paid. The most attractively printed catalogue is Jonathan Harris's *Catalogue of Welsh books*, 1818, a fine example of functional typographical lay-out.

Carmarthen had links with the book-trade beyond Wales, primarily with Shrewsbury, Chester, Bristol and London. The condition of the roads improved somewhat after the setting up of the Turnpike Trusts in the latter half of the 18th century, and the carrier system worked reasonably well. Carmarthen had the advantage of being a port, which facilitated trade with Bristol. Transport by sea was cheaper than by land. The early printers, as has been shown, were closely linked with their counterparts in Shrewsbury. By 1800, Carmarthen printers had forged closer links with the London book-trade. Both John Ross and John Daniel had worked in London and presumably had personal contacts there. In 1791 they jointly printed *A Treasury of theological knowledge*, compiled by Morgan Williams, and the imprint reads: 'Carmarthen: Printed and sold by John Ross and John Daniel; sold also by Messrs E. and T. Williams, No. 13 Strand; and Stanley Crowder, Pater-noster row, London; and Joseph Lloyd, Wine-street, Bristol, 1791' [*fig. 11*]. In turn they were agents for a London publication: *Y Weinidogaeth lwyddiannus . . .* 'Llundain: Argraphwyd, ac ar werth gan T. N. Longman ac O. Rees, ac yng Nghaenfyrddin [*sic*] gan J. Ross ac J. Daniel [1800?].' *The Carmarthen Journal*, 3 October 1812, contains a list of 'Valuable and useful books now publishing by B. and R. Crosby . . . London . . . and to be had of J. Daniel, J. Evans, J. Harris and J. White, Carmarthen, and by all other booksellers.'

Owen Rees was an influential partner in the firm of Longman, apparently a very popular, sociable man, whose retirement party is mentioned in all his obituaries! His brother, Thomas, was also apprenticed as a book-seller, but he followed in his father's footsteps by becoming a Unitarian minister. Being based in London for much of his career, he retained links with the trade and was commissioned to write volumes, including one on *South Wales*, for the series of *The Beauties of England and Wales* (1815). In the introduction to that volume, he acknowledges the help of his

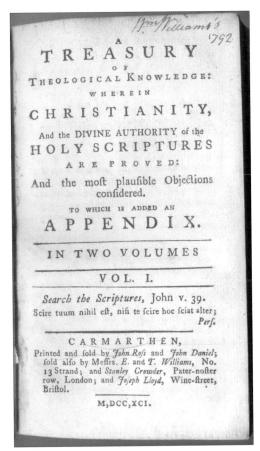

Fig. 11: *Note the London and Bristol agents in the imprint.*

self of the medium of his Paper to procure contributions from other quarters'.[16]

intelligent friend, Richard Philipps, Esq. the able Editor of the Caermarthen Journal; who, besides collecting for me such information as was to be found in the circle of his acquaintance, kindly availed him-

Early notices in *The Carmarthen Journal* highlight the London links: 'Advertisements and orders received by Messrs Taylor & Newton . . . London,' 'Regularly filed at Peele's and Chapter Coffee Houses, and may be seen at the Auction Mart, London.'[17] Several Welshmen were active in the London trade at this period. Vaughan Griffiths was another who named Ross as an agent in an imprint.[18] William Davies of Cadell and Davies came from Welshpool; Evan and Thomas Williams were brothers from Cardiganshire whose London bookshop specialised in books of Welsh interest. The old-established links with Bristol are evident yet again in *The Carmarthen Journal*, 7 January 1820: 'Filed also at the New Commercial Rooms, Bristol, and various other places of public resort.'

Mention has been made of second-hand books. Crispianus Jones was selling books, including second-hand school-books, every market and fair day in Market Street near the Exchange and every other day from his home in 1723.[19] Printers and booksellers supplemented their second-hand stock by placing advertisements for libraries and 'parcels of books' in newspapers and by attending auction sales. An annotated sale catalogue of the Peterwell estate, 1791, shows that John Ross bought £25 worth of books.[20]

Booksellers and printers included stationery in their stock – a vast array of items, as may be seen in an advertisement in *The Rules, orders and premiums, of the Society for the encouragement of agriculture . . . in the county of Cardigan*, printed by Ross in 1787:

> Writing paper, plain, gilt, or black-edged, vellum, parchment, cyphering and copy books, shop-books, Champante's best sealing-wax, wafers, ink-pots, slates, &c. A neat assortment of Ladies and Gentlemen's pocket books from the Maker, in Turky and other bindings, with or without instruments. Maps and prints, plain and coloured, drawing-books, watch-papers, copies and black lines for writing, Gilbert's pencils, &c. Also sells, liquid Japan ink, Walkden's fine British ink powder for records, Bailey's Patent Blacking Cakes, fine scented Pomatum, Durham Flour of Mustard, patent smelling bottles, pasteboards for binders, fine mill'd boards for clothiers, camel hair pencils and water colours in shells, &c &c. And all the patent medicines.

The link between selling books and patent medicines was one of long-standing, though few stocked patent medicines on the scale of John Daniel. In fact, even after he ceased being a printer in 1812, he continued in business in his 'Patent Medicine Warehouse' near the Town Hall, selling patent medicines, books, stationery and music, until he announced in *The Carmarthen Journal*, 26 February 1819, that he had 'disposed of his stock' to John Evans. The range of activities undertaken by members of the book-trade grew to be quite formidable. In common with their English counterparts, they ran Stamp Offices or became insurance agents.

By the end of the 18th century, literacy had made great strides; the Circulating Schools of Griffith Jones had made a potent contribution to existing missions to educate the masses. The trickle of books that came off the Carmarthen presses in the first two decades of their existence became an avalanche by 1820. The improve-ment in the quality of presswork encouraged people who had hitherto gone to England to have their works printed to have them printed locally. Increased demand in turn led to an increase in the number of printers who could co-exist in the town successfully and amicably.

From the outset, there was a preponderance of pamphlets and modestly-sized books in the Welsh language. There were, of course, exceptions, even at the outset, one being a volume of 393 pages, *Choice Collections, collected out of large and valuable volumes . . .* printed by Carter in 1726. The Methodist Revival and a corresponding surge in the strength of other Nonconformist bodies boosted trade by way of hymns, sermons, elegies and doctrinal disputations. The contribution of the Church of England was enhanced by the founding of the *Society for Promoting Christian Knowledge and Church Union in the Diocese of St. David's*. The Unitarians too were good customers. Printers did not allow any personal religious conviction to interfere with work; they would print anything for anybody as long as they were paid. The size of editions increased dramatically. A few hundred copies per edition became thousands; a formidable 8,600 copies were produced of the colossal Welsh Bible with a commentary by the Reverend Peter Williams, printed by Ross in 1770.

A variety of books were now coming off the Carmarthen presses. With what pride would the *Charter of the Borough of Carmarthen*, printed by Ross in 1765 have been received, or the subsequent *Charters of confirmation* by John Daniel and John Evans in 1796 and 1812. Ballads and chapbooks continued to be published, and it became possible to have locally-printed almanacks. Mathew Williams had the issues for 1777 to 1797 of *Britannus Merlinus Liberatus* printed by Ross, and John Harris had *Vox Stellarum et Planetarum* for 1790-1806 printed by John Daniel. On a more elevated plane, Ross printed two Welsh periodicals, the fortnightly *Trysorfa Gwybodaeth* (1770) and the quarterly *Miscellaneous Repository* (1795-96).

Books were not cheap and so amassing libraries was still the prerogative of the affluent. Incidentally, producing book-plates for gentlemen's libraries was one of the printer's ad hoc jobbing printing tasks; David Powell was producing plates as early as 1762. For avid readers who lacked the means to become collectors, access to Circulating Libraries was welcomed. Both John Ross and John Daniel had set up Circulating Libraries by the

1780s. John Ross's terms were 4 shillings per quarter. Hannah White established a Circulating Library *c.*1816, a Reading Room in 1815 and a Book Club *c.*1818.

By 1820, the printer was a figure of substance in the town. This elevation of status owed much to Ross. He was a deacon in Heol Awst chapel and a sheriff of the town. John Daniel built the houses in John Street, named after him. Edward Williams, 'Iolo Morganwg', notes in his diary in 1796 that 'the printing office, and bookselling shop of Mr. Daniel would appear respectable even in London.'[21] John Evans commissioned a family portrait from the artist, Hugh Hughes. Printers played an important role in Carmarthen until the end of the 20th century – one has only to think of the name of Spurrell. Life would have been impoverished without them, because their services were required by all ranks of society, by all trades and professions. John Ross is rightly commemorated in a plaque in Lammas Street, but the contribution of Nicholas Thomas and Isaac Carter should be commemorated too, for their vision and courage in establishing a trade that had more repercussions than they ever dreamt of.

PRINCIPAL PRINTERS, BOOKSELLERS AND BOOKBINDERS IN CARMARTHEN, 1720-1820

The list is by no means definitive and dates are often approximate. Printers in bold type.
They were also booksellers and stationers.

Lewis Barnikel/Barnakel. *Bookbinder,* 1776-82. Near Church, Priory St.

John Breden. 1730?

Isaac Carter (*d.1741*).1725-33. In Trefhedyn 1718-25.

John Daniel (*1755-1823*). Apprenticed to John Ross and worked in London. Printer 1784-1812. King St. 1784-92; Lower Market St. 1792-1818; 'Guild-hall Square, near the Hall' 1808. Ceased being a printer 1812, but continued as bookseller, stationer, music seller and patent medicine vendor. 'Patent Medicine Warehouse, near the Town Hall,' 1819. Printed and published *The Carmarthen Journal*, 1810-September 1812.

John Powell Davies. 1819-45. Printed *The Carmarthen Journal* February 1819-January 1820.

Sarah Davies. *Bookbinder,* 1790.

Lewis Edward. *Bookbinder,* 1762-73.

David Evans. 1820-23. Son of John Evans. Spilman St. Printer and publisher of *The Carmarthen Journal* March 1820-23.

John Evans (*1774-1830*). 1795-1830. Son of Titus Evans, printer in Machynlleth. Priory St. 1795-1813; Lammas St./Heol Awst 1808; Lower Market St. 1813-30; Guildhall Square 1813-1830.

William Griffiths. *Bookbinder,* 1766.

Jonathan Harris (*1784-1838*). 1807-32. Apprenticed to William Collister Jones, Chester. King St. 1807-8; Dark Gate/Porth Tywyll 1808-32.

Crispianus Jones. *Bookseller and bookbinder,* 1723-31.

David Jones. *Bookbinder,* 1795.

James Jones. In partnership with Joshua Watkins. 1811. 44 Priory St.

Lewis. 1799. In partnership with John Ross.

John Lewis (*d.1755*). *Bookbinder, bookseller, stationer.* 1719-55. King St. Mayor 1750. Shot dead by rioters.

John Lewis. *Bookseller,* 1766-86.

Samuel Lewis. 1743-49. King St.

Thomas Lewis. *Bookbinder,* 1704.

Richard (?) Lloyd. In partnership with Joshua Watkins. 1809-10. 'Ger llaw y Dderwen,' Priory St.

John Morgan. *Bookseller and bookbinder,* c.1742-45. Water St.

David Morris. *Bookbinder,* 1791-1839.

H. Morris. *Bookseller.* 1766-76.

Zecharias Bevan Morris. 1801-18. Lower Market St. Previously in Swansea.

Richard Philipps. 1820. Printed and published *The Carmarthen Journal* January-March 1820. Edited the newspaper from 1810 onwards, published it from September 1812-March 1820.

David Powell. In partnership with Evan Powell. 1762. Priory St.

Evan Powell. 1752-65. In partnership with David Powell 1762. Priory St.

David Rees. 1810-1819. Spilman St. Printed *The Carmarthen Journal* September 1812-February 1819.

M. Rhydero. *Bookseller,* 1782-85.

Richard Rhydero. *Bookseller and publisher,* 1768-76. In partnership with John Ross 1771, 1773. Market Place, near the Town Hall; 'Opposite the Hall.'

W. Rhydero. *Bookseller,* 1812.

David Richards. 1815.

John Ross (*1729-1807*). 1762-1807. In partnership with Rhys Thomas 1762-63; with Richard Rhydero 1771, 1773; with John Daniel occasionally 1791-94, 1800?; with Lewis 1799. Lammas St./Heol Awst 1762-72, 1781-1807; Priory St. 1772-81.

Ann Scott (*d.1842 aged 107*). Sister and successor of John Ross. 1807-08. Lammas St./Heol Awst.

Benjamin Simon (*1703-93*). *Bookbinder and manuscript copyist*, c.1740 onwards. Abergwili.

Martha Taylor. *Bookseller*, 1765-71.

David Thomas. '*Vendor of books*', 1726. Convicted of counterfeiting stamps, but spared execution.

Evan Thomas (*1733-1814*). 1767. Journeyman printer with Ross.

Nicholas Thomas (*d.1741*). c.1720-33, 1736-41. In partnership with John Williams 1731-33. In Hereford 1734-35?

Rhys Thomas (*1720?-90*). 1760-64. In partnership with John Ross 1762-63. Lammas St./Heol Awst. Moved to Llandovery and later Cowbridge.

Joshua Watkins (*1769?-1841*). 1809-11. In partnership with Hannah White 1809; with Richard (?) Lloyd 1809-10; with James Jones 1811. King St. 1809; 'Ger llaw y Dderwen,' 44 Priory St. 1809-11.

Hannah White (*d.1860*). 1809-60. In partnership with Joshua Watkins 1809; with sons George White White and Isaac White White 1818-60.

Isaac White White. 1818-60.

John White (*1762-1818*). 1809-18.

John Williams. 1731-33. In partnership with Nicholas Thomas.

John Williams. *Bookseller, stationer*, 1763-77. Heol y Groes.

Walter Williams. *Bookseller*, 1715?-16.

NOTES

NLW = National Library of Wales.

CRO = Carmarthen County Record Office.

For details of books printed in Carmarthen before 1820 and for illustrations of ornaments used by printers, see: Eiluned Rees, *Libri Walliae . . .* (Aberystwyth, 1987), and Charles Parry, *Libri Walliae . . . Supplement* (Aberystwyth, 2001).

1. *Cân o senn iw hên feistr Tobacco* [by Alban Thomas] and *Cân ar fesur triban*.
2. H. Evans, *Ymddiddan rhwng hen wr dall, a'r Angeu* (Caerfyrddin: J. Ross, 1764), Sig. A1v.
3. *Cyffes Ffydd . . . Wedi ei gyfieithu gan R D [i.e. Rees David]. Printiedig yng Nghaerfyrddin gan N. Thomas i'r Cyfieithydd, 1721*. Advertisement on last page.
4. See footnote 2.
5. William Higgs Barker, *A Plain grammar of the Hebrew language . . .* Second edition (Carmarthen: Printed and sold by John Evans . . . Sold also, by Messrs. Crosby & Co . . . London, 1814).
6. Eiluned Rees, 'The Welsh printing-house from 1718 to 1818', in Peter Isaac, ed. *Six centuries of the provincial book-trade* (London, 1990), p. 111.
7. NLW, Cwrtmawr 181A, f.53.
8. I am deeply indebted to Mrs Mary Burdett-Jones, Aberystwyth, for this translation.

9. Pressmen sometimes added press figures, Arabic numerals or symbols, to a forme before going to press, on a page that did not have a signature.
10. Quoted in Ifano Jones, *A history of printing in Wales* (Cardiff, 1925), p. 36.
11. '*Fod pob mâth ar lyfrau i gael eu cyweirio gan Grispianus Jones . . .*' Advertisement in *Dull priodas ysprydol* (Caerfyrddin: N. Thomas, 1723-4).
12. CRO, MUS 363.
13. NLW, Cards/QS/08/4/1788-1800.
14. *Society for Promoting Christian Knowledge and Church Union in the Diocese of St. David's* (Carmarthen: Jonathan Harris, 1810).
15. NLW, St. David's Probate Records.
16. p. viii.
17. *The Carmarthen Journal*, 4 January 1812, and other issues.
18. *The Will of God that the children of religious parents should be church members . . .* (London: Printed & sold by V. Griffiths . . . and sold also by J. Mathews, Strand; and J. Ross, Carmarthen, 1798).
19. *Dull priodas ysprydol* (Caerfyrddin: N. Thomas, 1723-4).
20. *Acct. of silver plate, books, china, pewter . . . late the property of Jno Adams of Peterwell Esqr. Sold by auction at Carmarthen . . . 1781*, NLW, Gogerddan papers.
21. NLW, Add. Ms. 13115B, p. 363.

Early Travellers and their Printed Images of the Tywi Valley

Jill & Conrad Davies

Engraving is no more an art of copying than the English language is an art of copying Greek or Latin.[1]

The period between 1730 and 1850 was the great age of the topographical print. These prints enabled those who journeyed into and explored Wales's countryside to provide illustrated accounts of their travels. Sometimes the prints were copied from paintings or sketches by great artists of the time such as J. M. W. Turner and David Cox. Others were produced from drawings by the travellers themselves, for many were artists. The prints represent a wide range of techniques: wood engravings, line engravings on copper and later steel, etchings, soft-ground etchings, lithographs and aquatints. This article provides a selection of prints of the Tywi valley. It is by no means comprehensive but aims to represent the work of a range of artists and engravers and the techniques they employed in a broadly chronological order.

Attitudes to the landscape have altered since the days of the early travellers. 'The transition from fear and loathing to veneration of unspoiled countryside is largely the result of the journals of the early tourists'.[2] Poor land was associated with poverty and starvation, therefore it appeared melancholy and its beauty could not be appreciated. By the closing decades of the 18th century tourism was becoming established and by the turn of the century a spate of travel books extolling the beauties of Wales were persuading ever growing numbers to visit. George Borrow, ascending Snowdon from Llanberis with his daughter in 1854, described how 'Groups of people, or single individuals, might be seen going up or descending the path as far as the eye could reach'. A little later, at an inn in Bangor, he reported that on a Saturday night 'the house was thronged with people who had arrived by train from Manchester and Liverpool, with the intention of passing the Sunday in the Welsh town. I took tea in an immense dining or ball-room, which was, however, so crowded with guests that its walls literally sweated'.[3]

The short-lived periodical *The Cambrian Magazine*, published in 1773, had copper engravings of Newton House and Golden Grove by Mathew Williams.[4] In 1775 H. P. Wyndham's *A Gentleman's Tour through Monmouthshire and South Wales* appeared, to be followed by his *A Tour through Monmouthshire and Wales* in 1781 and *A Tour to Milford Haven* by 'Mrs Morgan' in 1795. B. H. Malkin's publication of 1804 described his tours of south Wales in 1803 with illustrations by Laporte. Writing about the Tywi valley in the vicinity of Golden Grove, Aberglasney and Llandeilo he states 'The whole of this newly opened track is rich and beautiful; but it still partakes the general character of the views that are not adapted to the pencil.'[5]

These were all travel books; the first attempt at a guide book was probably George Nicholson's *Cambrian Traveller's Guide Augmented by Extracts from the Best Writers,* published in 1808 with further editions in 1813 and 1840. The book, which has a number of errors (Llanelli is 'in Caernarvonshire'), carried a map engraved by S. J. Neele. Despite being complimentary about Carmarthen ('Caermarthen is one of the most wealthy and polite towns in Wales', a remark copied directly from Barber's *Tour throughout South Wales and Monmouthshire* published in 1803), there are criticisms of many places of interest. 'St Peter's wants the venerable

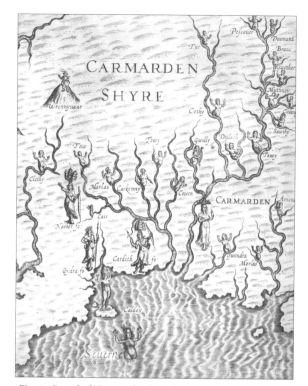

Fig. 1: *Detail of 'Carmardenshyre' from Drayton's Poly-Olbion. 1612. Copper engraving, 250 x 180 mm. William Hole sculpt.*
(Authors' collection).

Ere she Carmarthen get: where Gwilly making haste
Bright Towy entertains at that most famous town
Which her great Prophet bred which Wales doth
    so renown:
And taking her a harp, and tuning all the strings
To Princely Towy there she of the Prophet sings.

The map was engraved by William Hole who, together with William Kip, had engraved the maps for the sixth edition of Camden's Britannia in 1607. It provides a typical example of line engraving executed on copper. Copper, being a very soft metal, would produce only some 300 copies before showing wear. The plate could then be reworked and further copies produced.

Before the middle of the 17th century landscapes only existed in the backgrounds of portraits, replacing the family coat of arms which earlier had been used to identify the sitter and the family. From 1660 to 1700 Welsh landscapes invariably showed the topography surrounding the houses, usually as a bird's eye view, again a mark of identity.[7] By the end of the 17th century figures began to be included.

Some of the earliest engravings on copper plates of the Tywi valley are those of the Buck brothers. Samuel, the leading partner, (1696-1779) and his younger brother Nathaniel (*fl.*1724-1759) were Yorkshire men who combined drawing and engraving skills with publishing. Samuel's first publishing project, in 1720, was a series of views of northern towns. In 1726 he announced his intention of systematically recording ruins throughout England because he wanted to 'rescue the mangled remains' of 'these aged & venerable edifices from the inexorable jaws of time' by visiting and recording them.[8] The project was later expanded to include Wales.

The engravings were stylistically quite different from earlier landscapes in that, although the architectural details were accurately transferred from the drawing to the copper plate, details could be redrawn or added for effect. The early engravings made little attempt to show the texture of foliage or crumbling walls but as the brothers became more experienced the plates improved, becoming more realistic with figures appearing.

The illustration (*Fig. 2*) is of the original drawing for the Carmarthen townscape which was published in 1748 and is now in the Carmarthenshire County Museum. The foreground figures were drawn by H. F. B. Gravelot,[9] who was a French artist active in London from 1732 to 1755. Among his pupils at the St. Martin's Lane Academy was Gainsborough. Gravelot was a lead-

characteristic of storied windows . . . *shedding a dim religious light*, of these it has been stripped, to introduce sashes and other decorations equally inconsistent'. Golden Grove 'does not answer by any means to its name' while Middleton Hall suffers because 'the style of its architecture but ill comports with the imposing, tho' simple, majesty of the surrounding countryside'.

In 1612 the poet Michael Drayton (1563-1631) published a series of songs describing the landscape of England and Wales under the title *Poly-Olbion*, the first part consisting of eighteen songs. Each song is illustrated by a curious map (*Fig. 1*). The maps are without title, county boundaries or scale. Rivers and hilltops are decorated with allegorical figures of hunters, shepherds, herdsmen and water nymphs.[6]

Five of the songs relate to Wales. The fifth song is illustrated by a map of *Penbrokshyre and Carmardenshyre*. It is of no geographic significance but Fig. 1 shows the river Tywi with its tributaries and the strange figures. As the river approaches Carmarthen, Drayton sings:

Fig. 2: *The South-East View of Caermarthen. 1748. Drawing for a copper engraving, 315 x 820 mm. S. and N. Buck.*
(Courtesy of Carmarthenshire County Museum).

ing book illustrator of the day and introduced French style figures, so unmistakable in the Carmarthen prospect.

Friar's Park, the Castle, St. Peter's Church, the Free School and the Priory are among the places of interest listed below the image. Also below the drawing, obviously added later, appears 'The Original Drawing – executed by Saml. and Nathl. Buck in 1748. Certified by Mr. Reid, Keeper of Prints in the British Museum'. There are minor differences between this drawing and the print. Shipping at the quay and boats and coracles on the river were added, as well as the narrative text on Carmarthen, as appears on all Buck prints. Prints published after 1735 have the words 'published according to Act of Parliament' or 'published as the Act directs'. The Copyright Act was passed as a result of a campaign led by Hogarth; copying a print without permission was forbidden for fourteen years from the date of the original publication. As a result the production of engravings now became more profitable and prolific.

The Revd William Gilpin (1724-1804) encouraged the fashion for Welsh landscape that resulted in mountain scenery becoming the centre of English ideas about Wales. From 1768 to 1776 he recorded impressions from his tours in notebooks, later publishing them as picturesque tours 'in which writing and illustrations complement one another to sing the praises of nature'.[10]

> We travel for various purposes; . . . The following little work proposes a new object of pursuit; that of not barely examining the face of a country; but of examining it by the rules of picturesque beauty; that of not merely describing; but of adapting the description of natural scenery to the principles of artificial landscape.[11]

With these words Gilpin started a cult which involved tourists searching out the best views and analysing them in terms of perspective and other elements of pictorial composition, which he termed the 'picturesque'.

The leading proponent of the picturesque was Sir Uvedale Price (1747-1829),[12] who laid out his Herefordshire estate on these principles, aiming for variety and irregularity. Whereas Gilpin looked for a classical or Gothic ruin in his landscape,[13] Price preferred a dilapidated cottage. The picturesque landscape had to show form, texture and variety of colour. The other movement which greatly influenced landscape art was the 'sublime' which was associated with ideas of awe and vastness. The painting it influenced tended to look for nature as perfection; figures were either almost absent or, in Wales, represented as 'Ancient Britons', very often as blind harpists. These two theories induced an addiction to Welsh tourism among English travellers and artists.[14] Inevitably most were drawn to north Wales and the comparative few who ventured into the south tended not to linger in the Tywi valley. Few made much attempt to understand the culture, let alone the language, of the Welsh, who consequently tended to be regarded as quaint, foreign peasants or wildly romantic figures. The major exception was George Borrow, fluent in Welsh and so interested in the people that he insisted on walking everywhere.

Interest in Wales was growing; the hugely influential Richard Wilson (1713-82) returned from Rome in 1756 and over the next decade painted a large group of Welsh landscapes. His paintings were finding a ready market among Welsh intellectual leaders and the appreciation of romantic scenery was commonplace among

Welsh gentry and their extended English families.[15] Thomas Jones (1742-1803) became one of his students in 1763. Traditionally known as Thomas Jones Pencerrig, he was a Welsh landscape artist of considerable talent and inventiveness, now regarded as far ahead of his time. He is best known as an artist of the ordinary landscape, such as those in and around his family home, or the brilliantly painted, blank whitewashed walls seen opposite his studio at Naples. [16] In 1775 his only published project, *Six Views in South Wales*, was supported by an impressive list of subscribers, made possible by his gentry connections. There is a huge difference in style between the work of Jones and that of the Buck brothers; composition and shading are now important and line engraving on copper was developing to meet this need.

Although greatly influenced by Wilson, who, following continental masters of the 17th century, was concerned with the ideal landscape rather than an exact record of a particular place, Jones has here (*Fig. 3*) shown an actual view of riverside Carmarthen.[17] The watercourse in the foreground, where the hulk is beached, is a pill running parallel to the Tywi with its busy shipping.

The upper end of the pill can clearly be seen in the Buck drawing (*Fig. 2*).

Jones added short historical essays to each print. These suggest that he was an artist interested in the place as well as the landscape. In this sense these are the earliest examples of a Welsh artist promoting his home country in image and text, although the Buck brothers had always included a brief dedication, usually to the particular patron, below each engraving. Jones was only a minor figure in his own lifetime because he showed nature as it was while the critics wanted the picturesque.[18]

By 1750 Welsh intellectual life was changing.[19] Thomas Pennant (1726-1798) was born just a few years before the Buck engravings began to appear. The Cymmrodorion Society was formed in 1751 and Pennant was one of its 'corresponding members', highly regarded as a naturalist, traveller and writer. Welsh speaking, from Flintshire, he corresponded with European scholars, most notably Linnaeus. In the early 1770s he travelled widely in Wales and published *Tours in Wales* in three volumes from 1778 to 1783. His *A Tour in Scotland and*

Fig. 3: *Caermarthen. 1775. Copper engraving, 229 x 300 mm. T. Jones pt.*
(Courtesy of A. Scott).

43

Fig. 4: *Denefawr Castle. 1777. Sepia aquatint, 230 x 300 mm. P. Sandy fecit.*
(Authors' collection).

a Voyage to the Hebrides was dedicated to Joseph Banks, who had returned from the *Endeavour* voyage in 1771 and had become a figure of international scientific significance.[20] Banks had a very strong connection with Edwinsford, for his uncle, Robert Banks-Hodgkinson,[21] had married Bridget, elder daughter of Thomas Williams of Edwinsford in 1757. Banks spent considerable periods of time there both before and after his return from the *Endeavour* voyage, in 1767 staying for three months.[22] As one of the leading intellectuals in London he had a wide circle of friends, many of whom were invited to join him at Edwinsford. Among them was Paul Sandby (1731-1809) who, with other distinguished guests, joined Banks's party in 1773.[23]

Sandby was described in his obituaries as 'the father of modern landscape painting in watercolours'. As a founding member of the Royal Academy he played a pivotal role in the promotion of watercolour as a medium for professional artists. In his depiction of the Welsh landscape in the mid-1770s he was breaking new ground from the point of view of technique and also of subject matter. The delicate landscape of Dinefwr (*Fig. 4*) is typical of the detail in his work and his prints were well ahead of fashion.[24] It was not until the end of the 1770s and the following decades that Wales became a

popular area among travellers and artists in search of the picturesque and the romantic and to a considerable extent this was due to the publication in 1775 of *XII Views in Aquatinta from Drawings Taken on the Spot in South-Wales Dedicated to the Honourable Charles Greville and Joseph Banks Esquire by Their Ever Grateful and Much Obliged Servant Paul Sandby, R.A.*[25] Sandby assembled the material for these aquatints during the seven weeks he was based at Edwinsford in the summer of 1773.[26] His son, Thomas Paul, wrote in a memoir that 'this journey he ever after remembered with the fondest delight, having experienced from Sir Joseph Banks an attention and kindness, which called forth in him the highest feeling of respect and affection for his liberal patron and wealthy friend'.[27] The tour resulted in two views of Edwinsford; one of these was produced as an engraving by William Watts (1752-1851) titled *Edwinsford, the Seat of R. Banks-Hodgkinson, Esq.*[28] Sandby's watercolours were used as the basis for engravings by others so the number of Welsh subjects deriving from him 'must be immense'.[29]

The fine sepia aquatint *Denefawr Castle* (*Fig. 4*) was Plate XI of the *XII Views of Wales*. The original of all Sandby's aquatints were printed in sepia or dark brown and not issued hand-coloured as were later aquatints.

The park landscape with the white cattle and a herd of deer contrasts well with the castle in the background. Sandby had toured in north Wales with Sir Watkin Williams Wynn before his stay in Edwinsford and the two tours provided material for four sets of prints as well as reprints in 1812; in all some thirty-five aquatints over a period of thirteen years. *XII Views in South Wales* (1775) did not include either Edwinsford or Dinefwr. *XII Views in North Wales* followed in 1776 and *XII Views of Wales* in 1777. The fourth set, *XII Views in North and South Wales* was not published until 1786; it included *View near Edwinsford*. Another aquatint, *Near Edwinsford*, appears to have been produced separately.

The early *XII Views in South Wales* (1775) have affinities to the topographical engravings of the Buck brothers, which were always of ancient buildings or whole towns and in which the landscape was of negligible importance in comparison to the buildings. Here the landscapes are important, but in *Views in North Wales* of the following year Sandby was to make an ancient building or a town the centrepiece of only four out of twelve prints. By 1780 Sandby was often relegating the main subject to the background with the foreground occupied by picturesque scenery, as in Fig. 4. A recent Royal Academy exhibition contrasted an earlier print of Windsor Castle with *Roslin Castle*, where he included the figure of Lady Frances Scott, an amateur artist, sketching using her camera obscura.[30] It is thought that the figures in the aquatints are connected with incidents on the actual tour, such as the bull attacking the artist in his tent which appears in one of the prints of Carew Castle.

Aquatint engraving is a form of etching but no engraving tool is involved. It is a complicated tonal engraving method which is particularly suitable for reproducing watercolours. Until recently it was thought that Sandby pioneered the use of the technique in England; but the first aquatint was published in 1771 by Peter Perez Burdett,[31] a Liverpool artist who died in 1793.[32]

By 1800 romanticism was supplanting the picturesque.[33] Artists were choosing subjects that were wild, exotic or mysterious. J. M. W. Turner (1775-1851), one of the greatest figures in landscape painting, painted pictures that were increasingly personal and free, with detail subordinate to the effects of colour and light. In 1795 he toured South Wales, resulting in two outstanding views of the Tywi valley. The watercolour *Llandilo Bridge and Dynevor Castle* was exhibited in the Royal Academy in 1796. The regard for the reality of the objects is still present although the castle has been brought forward towards the picture plane. But the picture as a whole has another interest, for the carefully delineated bridge is set in an effect of light that made its own poetic appeal to the artist and is set off by the women washing clothes below it. *Llanstephan Castle by Moonlight, with a Kiln in the Foreground* (1795-6) with the castle magically outlined against the flaring lime kilns, is in the Tate collection. Despite his prolific output, nearly nine hundred prints, neither picture was reproduced as an engraving. Engraving was Turner's primary means of communication.[34]

A colleague of his, John Landseer, father of the famous animal painter, led a campaign for the full recognition of engravers by the Royal Academy. One of his arguments was that engraving, far from being merely a copying process, was rather one of translation. Over the years Turner employed over eighty engravers, often selected when young and rigorously trained. They had to be responsive to his requirements but were still expected to use their artistic judgement. Turner had an extraordinary sense of the balance of light and shade; Ruskin commented that Turner 'paints in colour, but he thinks in light and shade'.[35]

Letters describing a tour through part of South Wales by a pedestrian traveller; with views, designed and etched by the author was published in 1797. The author was the Breton antiquarian Count Armand Louis Bon Maudet de Penhouët (1764-1839). His view of *Llandilo war Bridge* (*Fig. 5*) is very misleading since the greater part of the seven arch stone bridge was still standing at the time. As mentioned earlier, Turner had visited Llandeilo in 1795, the same year as Penhouët, and his 1796 watercolour shows that only two of the arches had been destroyed. Penhouët's over-emphasised near-complete dereliction of the bridge is indicative of the growing romantic movement. The etching is crudely executed but is interesting partly because of its lack of finish. Etching is a method of producing printing plates by allowing acid to bite through a design prepared with an etching needle on the wax ground of a metal plate.

Cymro, in an article in the *Cambrian Register* for 1796, published in 1799, 'reviews' the work of several authors. His article is titled *Cursory Remarks on Welsh Tours or Travels*. In it, more than cursorily, he demolishes the opinions of tourists who, despite travelling quickly, feel entitled to make derogatory remarks on the character of the Welsh and their lifestyles. Not content

Fig. 5: *Llandilo war Bridge. 1797. Etching, 90 x 154 mm. Comte de Penhouët.*
(Courtesy of Carmarthenshire County Museum).

with pointing out gross errors picked up from casual anecdotes he goes into detail on 'the mania which usually affects travellers of attempting to explain Welsh words and names'. While allowing that 'a French emigrant' (Penhouët) is probably entitled to a certain amount of compassion, he states that:

> His descriptions are of towns and castles – and woods – and rivers, etc., etc., most miserably spelt; and they are *adorned* with plates, most of which want something more than an asterisk to remind us of the places they are intended . . . 'to present or disfigure'. All of them, indeed, except two of Caerffyli Castle, and one or two about Pont ar Pridd, might have had their delin. or sculp. . . . in London; and then, shaken in a bag, might have been called Llandilo *war*, or Morgam, or Castle cogh, or any other miscalled place, indiscriminately, as they happen to come out.[36]

John Thomas Barber (1774-1841) unusually combined the careers of artist and founder of insurance offices. He became a student at the Royal Academy in 1791 and exhibited there regularly from 1794 to 1806. His *A tour through south Wales and Monmouthshire* was published in 1803, when the fashion for such works was approaching its peak, and is much more interesting to read than the majority of its contemporaries. It was

dedicated to Sheridan and its intention was to enable the tourist to travel using only a single guide book, for he 'selected from the best authorities an account of those few parts which he had not had the opportunity of visiting'.

After an horrendous voyage from Bristol to Swansea, vividly described, Barber travelled along the coast, visiting Llansteffan on his way to Pembrokeshire and Aberystwyth. He then made his way down the Tywi valley to Swansea. Altogether there are twenty aquatints in the book, including *Llanstephan Castle, Dinevawr Castle* and *Careg-cannon Castle*, all made from Barber's drawings. How many more might there have been if 'several drawings' had not been 'utterly spoilt' while crossing the flooded Loughor after visiting Glynhir waterfall?[37]

The beautiful sepia tones of the Llansteffan print (*Fig. 6*), the work of Joseph Jeakes, an important London aquatint engraver, are not only interesting as a work of art but also in the situation depicted, best described by quoting from the text.

> A farming party . . . proceeding with goods for Carmarthen market . . . a robust young fellow driving a couple of cows; he wore the general dress of all the country, a short blue coarse cloth coat, and breeches of the same open at the knees; but he also possessed the luxury of shoes and stockings. A sledge[38] laden

Fig. 6: *Llanstephan Castle. 1803. Sepia aquatint, 120 x 180 mm. J. T. Barber delin. J. Jeakes sculpt.*
(Courtesy of A. Scott).

Fig. 7: *Tŷ Gwyn the Farm of Sir Richard Steele in the Vale of Towey. 1804. Coloured aquatint, 95 x 120 mm. E. Donovan.*
(Courtesy of A. Scott).

with sacks of grain followed, drawn by a horse on which a lusty wench sat astride, as the peasant girls generally do . . . clothed in a brown jirkin and petticoat, but with her lower extremities uncovered . . . her hands were busied in knitting. Two other . . . girls followed on foot, with their fingers similarly employed, and with large baskets of eggs and poultry on their heads. . . . A comely dame . . . with a sort of side-saddle . . . was probably the mistress, and her superior condition was evident in her dark blue worsted stockings, ponderous shoes and small brass buckles.

In about 1812 Barber added Beaumont to his name and from then on was usually known as Barber Beaumont. His interests had changed; he became one of the largest fire insurers in Britain. He wrote on a range of topical issues and was appointed magistrate for Middlesex and Westminster. He founded the Philosophical Institution which later became part of London University. He died, a very wealthy man, at the County Fire Office in Regent Street and was buried in his private cemetery at Stepney.[39]

Edward Donovan (1768-1837) was an artist and a noted natural historian. Originally a man of considerable wealth, a lifetime of collecting natural history specimens led to his financial ruin. He published many works, including *British Insects* and ten volumes on *British Birds*, and was a Fellow of the Linnaean Society. In the five summers 1800 to 1804 he toured south Wales, resulting in the *Descriptive excursions through South Wales and Monmouthshire*, which was published in 1805. The work was in two volumes with thirty-one coloured plates.

'The vale unfolds a prospect of unrivalled beauty, placid, open, lovely and luxuriant'; this was Donovan's description of the Tywi valley in the second volume. He spent some time in Carmarthen, describing the bridge, quayside and town. An evident admirer of Sir Richard Steele, he describes his life at Carmarthen and gives a full account of his nocturnal funeral:

> It is traditionally well known to the inhabitants of this city, that his remains were conveyed with great pomp from the house in which he died (on 21st September 1729) to the church for interment. To increase the solemn grandeur of the ceremony, it was performed at night, and no less than four and twenty attendants, each carrying a branch of lighted torches, formed part of the retinue in the funeral parade.[40]

It is no surprise that of the two illustrations of the Tywi valley one is of the home of Richard Steele. This small image (*Fig. 7*) is a very fine coloured aquatint.

Following tours between 1811 and 1813 John George Wood, F.S.A. (1768-1838) published his seminal work under the title *The Principal Rivers of Wales illustrated*. The work consisted of a series of views from the source of each river along its course to the sea. The views were accompanied by 'descriptions, historical, topographical and picturesque'. Both text and illustrations were the work of Wood himself. He was an accomplished artist and from 1807 to 1809 was lecturer in perspective at the Royal Institution.

The illustrations were in the form of soft-ground etchings 'accurately done from Nature by the Author himself; he therefore ventures to answer for their accuracy'.[41] Soft-ground etching involves the use of a special high-tallow ground to cover the printing plate. The drawing is made on paper with a soft pencil, the paper is placed over the wax and redrawn. When the paper is removed some of the wax comes away from the plate. It is then bitten and printed as with a normal etching. The resulting print has the appearance of a soft pencil drawing and has a plate-mark.

No more than two hundred and fifty copies of *Principal Rivers* were to be printed after which the plates were to be destroyed. One hundred and fifty-three subscribers are listed. Subscribers from the Tywi valley included Lord Dynevor, Bishop Thomas Burgess, Admiral Foley of Abermarlais and Sir William Paxton of Middleton Hall.

The account of the Tywi valley is illustrated by thirteen plates.[42] The upper reaches of the Tywi particularly attracted Wood's attention; 'indeed the scenery about Ystrad Ffin partakes more of the sublime than that of any other part of this incomparable river'. He mentions a property of Lord Cawdor's called 'Nant y Miwn' (*sic*), residence of the manager of the extensive lead mines nearby employing about two hundred workmen. Unfortunately, no illustration of the lead mines was included although Wood made striking etchings of industrial sites in other areas. *The Towy Bridge at Llandovery* is better known as Dolauhirion Bridge, 'an elegant bridge of one arch, eight-two feet six inches in span, built by Edwards'.[43] The panoramic view of *Llandilovawr* and the Tywi valley looking southwest is a double page. It shows the meander of the Tywi above and below the arched stone bridge. Newton House and the tower of Dynevor Castle are seen together with the church of St.

Fig. 8: *Dryslin Castle. 1812. Soft-ground etching, 170 x 238 mm. Drawn & etched by J. G. Wood.*
(Authors' collection).

Teilo. On the horizon in the centre of the plate Nelson's Tower is featured. This is the earliest print to show the tower built by Sir William Paxton to commemorate the victories of Lord Viscount Nelson. Construction of the tower was completed *c.*1807.

Wood shows Dryslwyn Castle (*Fig. 8*) as much less ruinous than it is today. There was no bridge crossing the Tywi but a coracle is shown on the river just below the point at which the river could be forded when conditions were favourable. There was a ferry at Dryslwyn until *c.*1890; the ferryman lived in a cottage nearby. A stone bridge was opened at Dryslwyn in November 1901. Wood's panoramic view of *Caermarthen* depicts the width of the Tywi valley in its lower reaches with its wide meanders. The seven-arch stone bridge dominates the centre mid-distance and the large number of ships alongside the quay reflects the town's importance as a port. One or two ships are seen downstream below Green Castle. The tower of St. Peter's church dominates the townscape. In the text Wood

mentions the 'extensive tin mills belonging to Messrs Harris, Morgan and Jones which when in full work are capable of making five hundred boxes of tinplate per week' but made no illustration of the mills working. The final etching is that of *Llanstephan Castle* taken from across the estuary at Ferryside and emphasising the castle's strategic location. The number of boats suggests a busy estuary carrying the shipping traffic to and from Carmarthen, fishing vessels and a ferry connecting Llansteffan to Ferryside. In his introduction Wood refers to the 'difficulty of the Welsh orthography' and claims to have gone to considerable trouble to ensure the correct spelling of Welsh names. Despite his efforts the work is riddled with spelling errors.

Between 1794 and 1796 John and Josiah Boydell published *A History of the River Thames* in two volumes containing seventy-six plates aquatinted by J. C. Stadler. The two volumes were intended as the start of a major series on *An History of the Principal Rivers of Great Britain* which never materialised but the full title appeared as a general title to volume one.[44] Wales is fortunate that J. G. Wood completed such a comprehensive study of all its major rivers.

Hugh Hughes (1790-1863) has been claimed as the first truly national artist of Wales.[45] He travelled in Wales for three summers from 1812, not as a landscape artist searching for the sublime but as a portrait painter who took commissions from his own people. He lived in the period when the publication of books of engravings was at its height, almost all involving the skills of an author, an artist and an engraver. In 1818 Hughes decided to produce a work, *The Beauties of Cambria*, which would be entirely his own, an enormous undertaking, particularly for one who had only limited training as an engraver. Born in Pwll-y-gwichiaid farm on the marshy area below the old village of Llandudno, his family migrated to Liverpool in 1802 because of the depression caused by the Napoleonic Wars. There the family lived among many other Welsh emigrants, including sculptor John Gibson, who had been born near Llandudno at the same time as Hughes. The two boys probably attended Sunday school together.

Hughes was apprenticed to a wood engraver in 1804 and his interest in painting grew in the artistic environment of Liverpool.[46] The development of wood engraving in Britain owes much to the achievements of one man, Thomas Bewick (1753-1828), who perfected the art using box wood cut across the grain and the tools of the metal engraver. Line engravings and etchings are made by the intaglio process where the incised lines hold the ink; wood engraving is a relief process where the raised areas print black. There are no plate-marks. This technique enabled both illustrations and text to be printed on the same machine.

Hughes painted the portraits of many of the Methodist leaders and thousands of copies of the engravings were sold. He moved to London in 1814; by 1818 he had set himself up as a wood engraver in Wilderness Row, Clerkenwell, and was ready to embark on his great work. From 1819 to 1821 he travelled the length of Wales making drawings, using his grandfather's house in the Conwy valley as a base where he engraved the blocks.[47] *The Beauties of Cambria* was a great success and his standing with the cultural leaders was greatly enhanced. However he remained loyal to the Nonconformist middle class, dividing his time between London and Carmarthen, where he was very friendly with the printer John Evans, who owned the *Carmarthen Journal*

and published *Seren Gomer*. One of his best and most well known paintings is the group portrait *The family of John Evans, Carmarthen, at breakfast*.

Hughes was radical in his beliefs and this led to his being excommunicated from Jewin Crescent chapel, London, which by 1828 was his place of worship. This was as a result of a petition he raised, as a firm believer in the individual conscience, in favour of the Emancipation Bill. In 1832 he moved to Caernarfon and again started travelling through Wales painting portraits. Although he visited Betws-y-Coed frequently he made no professional contact with the artists' colony there.[48] By the middle of the century photography had undermined his market but Hughes struggled on, holding small travelling exhibitions in a tent.[49] His last journey was to Malvern; he never returned. Although a devout Calvinistic Methodist all his life, tragically he was buried there in an unconsecrated pauper's grave.

This small wood engraving of the falls on the Llwchwr (*Fig. 9*) is a particularly attractive example of the views in *The Beauties of Cambria*. The attention to detail and the very fine incised lines depicting delicate ferns and foliage is remarkable in such a small image. Hughes acknowledged that the historical accounts were taken from Pennant's *Tours in Wales* and Thomas Rees's *Description of South Wales*. His topographical accounts were from his own observations as shown by his description of the waterfall 'A most striking contrast is effected by the blackness of the rock over which it falls, with the almost unequalled clearness of the stream.'

The Beauties of Cambria consisted of sixty views, each with an accompanying page of text. Six views are from Carmarthenshire, three being from the Tywi valley – *Dinevor Castle*, *Nelson's Tower* and *Llanstephan Castle*. *Kidwelly Castle* and *Carreg Cennen Castle* are also featured, together with *Glynhir Water Fall*, included here partly because it was very rarely used as a subject. The work was originally published in six parts and printed in London between 1819 and 1823. There were about four hundred and fifty subscribers, headed by Sir Watkin Williams Wynn. Many London Welsh names appear on the list. There were twenty-two subscribers from Carmarthenshire, including W. du Buisson of Glynhir, Lord Dynevor, H. L. E. Gwynne of Rhyd y Gors, David Morley and John Jones, M.P.

John Henry Robinson (1796-1871) is not one of the most well known landscape artists, probably because his biography concentrates entirely on his work as an engraver, a field in which he had huge talents. Born in

Fig. 9: *Glynhir Falls. 1824. Wood engraving, 125 x 165 mm. H. Hughes.*
(Courtesy of National Library of Wales).

Fig. 10: *A Distant View of Cerig-Cenning Castle from Golden Grove, in the Vale of Towy, Carmarthenshire, Sunset, Milking. 1831. Lithograph, 220 x 285 mm. J. H. Robinson del*[t]. *On stone by G. Childs.*
(Courtesy of Carmarthenshire Record Office).

Bolton, he was apprenticed as an engraver at the age of eighteen but was able to set up on his own as a book illustrator only two years later. By 1823, living in London, he was so well established that he received 800 guineas for a plate, from which a thousand impressions were sold.[50] Between 1826 and 1855 Robinson fought a long battle to win respect from the Royal Academy as a professional engraver. He was one of the nine eminent engravers who, with Landseer, petitioned the House of Commons in 1836 for an investigation into the state of engraving in Britain, and with many other artists in 1837 he petitioned the king for the admission of engravers to the highest rank in the Royal Academy. In 1856 he was elected 'an associate engraver of the new class', by which time his profession was almost obsolete. He did not become a Royal Academician until 1867.[51]

Robinson travelled widely in south Wales, as evidenced by the number of lithographs after him held in the National Library of Wales as well as one watercolour, *Oystermouth Castle and Bay*, painted *c*.1850. The image of Carreg Cennen Castle (*Fig. 10*) is very much a product of the romantic movement; with the distant castle seen through a gap in the trees as if lit by the setting sun. Its position is further emphasised by the contrast with the milkmaid and the cattle in the twilit foreground.

Like most of Robinson's landscapes it was lithographed by George Childs, about whom little is known. He was very active as a lithographer between 1826 and 1873, coinciding very closely with Robinson's career. He lithographed *Kidwelli town and castle,* and *Llacharn Castle* in Carmarthenshire and ten further views in south Wales for Robinson. Robinson occasionally did his own lithography.[52] The process of lithography is discussed with Fig. 13. Childs worked for Hugh Hughes for the lithographs of *The Interior of Carnarvon Castle* and *Vale of Festiniog*.

An artist particularly associated with Wales is Henry Gastineau (1791-1876). He was a drawing master and a prolific landscape painter in the picturesque genre. During his lifetime he exhibited some one thousand, three hundred and forty-one works, nearly all at the Old Watercolour Society.

The most comprehensive work of topographical prints of Wales was published by Jones & Co. in 1830. The book was titled *Wales Illustrated. A series of Views comprising the Picturesque Scenery, Towns, Castles, Seats of the Nobility and Gentry, Antiquities, etc. Engraved on Steel from Original Drawings by Henry Gastineau*. The complete work consisted of two hundred and twenty-four prints, eighty-eight of north Wales and one hundred and thirty-six of south Wales with two vignettes, utilising thirty-one different engravers. A number of editions appeared and the two sections were either bound as one or as two separate volumes. The pages were not numbered and some copies do not include a list of plates. This makes collating difficult, the more so because some copies do not contain all the prints. The work was first published in parts, each containing four views only. These specimen copies were used in advertising and to interest prospective subscribers. Many of the prints were used in Woodward's *History of Wales* (1853) and also Tillotson's *Picturesque Scenery in Wales* (1860).

The view of Llandovery Castle (*Fig. 11*) is from upstream on the river Brân. 'Llandovery . . . is nearly surrounded by rivulets'.[53] Also prominently featured, with some artistic licence, is the tower of Llandingat church.

Wales Illustrated contains eight illustrations with accompanying text relating to the Tywi valley: *Llanstephan, Llanstephan Castle, Sands at Llanstephan, Caermarthen, Vale of the Towy near Caermarthen, Grongar Hill, Caercennin Castle* and *Llandovery Castle*. It would appear that Gastineau was much impressed by Llansteffan and its environs since it accounts for three of the eight illustrations. Gastineau engravings are so well known that the expertise used to produce them is often overlooked.

David Cox (1753-1859) was a leading watercolourist during an age of particular excellence in watercolour art. The first decade of the 19th century saw the emergence of many of the classic artists of the English School of watercolourists and the foundation of the 'Old' Watercolour Society, of which Cox was president.[54] He first visited Wales in 1805 and became the centre of the artists' colony at Betws-y-Coed, holding court at the Royal Oak and offering generous advice and encouragement to the numerous young artists of the next generation who, unlike those before them, came to stay in Wales. By 1852 he had been 'given the status of the old man in the early Victorian art world, second only to Turner' (who had died the previous year).[55]

In 1836 Thomas Roscoe published *Wanderings and Excursions in North Wales*. It became the most influential guidebook to Wales in the mid-19th century.[56] It has been described as 'the pinnacle of design and repro-

Fig. 11: *Llandovery Castle. 1830. Steel engraving, 108 x 150 mm. H. Gastineau.*
(Authors' collection).

Fig. 12: *Vale of the Towey, Nelson's Tower, and Dryslyn Castle in the centre;*
Grongar Hill on the right – from Dynevor Park. 1836. Steel engraving, 118 x 146 mm. D. Cox. W. Radclyffe.
(Authors' collection).

ductive engraving in England, alongside the work of Turner and his engravers'.[57] However, the text is extremely turgid.

The two prints from the Tywi valley depicted in his *Wanderings and Excursions in South Wales* are *Vale of the Towey* (*Fig. 12*) and *Carmarthen*, both steel engravings after Cox. The *Vale of the Towey* demonstrates the engraver's remarkable ability to depict so much in such a small compass. The engraver was William Radclyffe (1783-1855), of Birmingham. Some of these prints were used in Gweirydd ap Rhys's Welsh publication '*Hanes y Brytaniaid a'r Cymry*' of 1872, albeit as rather poor reproductions involving a photographic technique.

Cox, although he painted in oils in the latter stages of his career, largely drew directly from nature and through his scenes the wind is usually blowing; foliage, sea and sky are in motion. This is obvious in another of his paintings in the Tywi valley, that of Dryslwyn Castle, where the leaves blowing in a stiff breeze hint that the weather is deteriorating and therefore the haymakers must hurry to get the crop harvested. His style was broad and vigorous on a rough wrapping paper which was later made commercially and marketed as 'Cox paper'. He devoted much of his time to teaching and wrote several instructional books on watercolour. By the time of Cox and his contemporaries the attitude of painters to the Welsh had changed considerably from that of late 18th century travellers who had largely regarded them as primitive or pagan as part of their search for the sublime landscape.

> Against a background of great social unrest, reassuring images of loyal and pious peasants, such as those which had made George Moreland famous, now sold best on the English art market. Such subjects with a Welsh or Irish context held the additional attraction of 'national character' for an audience increasingly interested in the idea of ethnicity . . . however the depth of David Cox's sympathy with the common people was unusual. Cox was a provincial rather than a metropolitan Englishman, from a middle-class tradesman's background and unpretentious by nature. Furthermore he was a devout Nonconformist.[58]

The lithographic stone (*Fig. 13*) bears two images dated 1853, one of Nelson's Tower and the other of Clearbrook Cottage. Both were, at the time, the properties of Edward Abadam of Middleton Hall, Llanarthne. Another similar stone depicts two views of Middleton Hall mansion. The stones were donated to

Fig. 13: *Lithographic stone depicting Nelson's Tower and Clearbrook Cottage. 1854. Stone, 430 x 280 x 60 mm.*
(Courtesy of Carmarthenshire County Museum).

the Carmarthenshire County Museum by the last of the family to reside at Middleton Hall, Major W. J. Hughes, great-grandson of Edward Abadam. The four images first appeared in *A visitation of the Seats and Arms of the Noblemen* by J. B. Burke, in 1854. The tower image is titled *Tower to the memory of Lord Viscount Nelson in Middleton Hall Park, Carmarthen 1853. Lithograph by Augustus Butler.*

The Tower has unrivalled views of the Tywi valley to the east and west including Dryslwyn, Golden Grove, Dinefwr and Carreg Cennen castles. Travellers during the late 18th century and beginning of the 19th century, such as Skrine[59] (1798), Lipscomb[60] (1801) and Carlisle[61] (1802), were almost unanimous in their praise of the mansion and park. Barber[62] (1803) described it in kind terms but added, while admitting that he had not visited the estate, 'unfortunately it is already neglected'.

Lithography was invented in Germany in 1798 by Aloys Senefelder and was soon widely used for music printing. It was the first fundamentally new printing technology since the invention of relief printing in the 15th century. It is a planographic process in which the printing and non-printing areas of the plate are all at the same level, as opposed to intaglio and relief processes in which the design is cut into the printing block. Lithography is based on the physical repellence of oil and water. Designs are drawn or painted with greasy ink or crayons on specially prepared limestone which is then moistened with water, which the stone accepts in areas

Fig. 14: *The Warren, Taliaris Park, Llandilo. 1847. Chromolithograph, 215 x 358 mm. Aaron Penley.*
(Authors' collection).

Fig. 15: *Opening of the South Wales Railway – The Carmarthen Station. 1852. Wood engraving, 118 x 118 mm.*
Illustrated London News, *25th September 1852.*

not covered by ink. An oily ink, applied with a roller, adheres only to the drawing and the print is made by pressing paper against the inked drawing. The size and weight of the stone are obvious from the image. An almost unlimited number of prints could be produced providing the stone was kept wet and a regular supply of ink maintained. One great disadvantage of the method was the handling and storage of the heavy blocks of limestone.[63] Normally, after use, the drawing would be erased and a new image substituted. It is unusual for lithographic stones such as these to survive; they were probably bought by Abadam from the publisher and were subsequently used to produce letterheads for use at the mansion.

This period coincided with a growth in interest in watercolour painting by amateurs and books of instruction, often with chromolithographs to study and copy, were published, following in the footsteps of Wood, Cox and others. One such is *Sketching from Nature in Water Colours*, written and illustrated by Aaron Edwin Penley (1806-70) and published in 1869.[64] Penley was a painter and drawing-master who exhibited sporadically in the Royal Academy from 1834 to 1869 and showed over three hundred works at the New Society of Painters in Watercolours. He was appointed painter in watercolour to Queen Adelaide, painted a miniature of Queen Victoria from an actual sitting, and taught her son Prince Arthur. He also enjoyed success as a drawing-master in the West Country before taking up appointments with the East India Company and the Royal Military Academy.

Penley is best known today for his technically competent, attractive landscapes with conventional composition. He travelled widely in Britain and is known to have visited Wales, making sketches to be transformed into chromolithographs for his books, of which the scene at Taliaris (*Fig. 14*) is typical. The original was probably painted in 1847. It shows a misty view over the trees and the hidden tributary Dulais to the Tywi valley. *Sketching from Nature in Water Colours*, referred to above, contains a print titled *Study of Stones on the North Side of Taliaris, near Llandilo, South Wales*. In the Taliaris Collection in the Carmarthenshire Archives there is a watercolour called *Black Mountain and Vale of Towey from The Warren* with an almost identical viewpoint to Fig. 14. It is in a sketchbook with many other paintings by 'M P', Mary Peel, sister of William Peel of Taliaris Park. She died in 1879; few of the sketches are dated but dates of 1846, 1849 and 1850 appear occa-

sionally, so it may be reasonable to suppose that she had contact with Penley during his visit.[65]

On 17th September 1852 Carmarthen witnessed the colourful celebration of the opening of the South Wales railway between Carmarthen and Llanelli. A full report of the event appeared in the *Illustrated London News* on September 25th. It was the reporting of such events which led to the rapid growth in the use of wood engravings in the mid-nineteenth century. Before photography was widely established these engravings were extensively used in periodicals of the time such as the *Illustrated London News*, *Punch* and *Graphic*. In this way illustrated records of important historical and social events have survived. Sketches of the events were sent to London where specialist wood engravers prepared the blocks for printing so that the opening of the railway at Carmarthen could appear in the *Illustrated London News* only eight days later. A disadvantage of wood engravings from periodicals is that the text on the verso shows through the paper and detracts from the illustration.

Full page and even double page illustrations often appeared. Such large pictures were composed of several blocks clamped together. The overall sketch was drawn; the blocks were then separated and passed to a number of engravers. Finally the blocks were clamped together again and finished off by the master engraver. Occasionally careful study of the printed picture will show small lines where some of the individual blocks were joined.

Fig. 15 shows the scene of celebration at Carmarthen station, then at Myrtle Hill, while another, on the same page, showed the surrounding countryside with a train approaching the station. The account reports that:

> The celebration of the opening was designed by William Morris, Esq., the worthy Mayor of Carmarthen, who has most generously borne the whole of the extra expenses from his private resources. The weather was delightful. The streets through which the procession was to pass were decorated with triumphal arches. At twelve o'clock the procession was formed. It consisted of the Carmarthen town council and the Mayor; Valentine Davis, Esq., T. C. Morris, Esq., H. E. Stacey, Esq., G. Davis, Esq., wore robes as ex-Mayors. The mayors of other towns, together with a large number of gentlemen followed; after which there was the Bronwdd (*sic*) band. The procession was headed by about thirty sailors, bearing union-jacks, etc., a band of musicians, a portrait of General Picton, and a very prettily designed banner by Mr. John Davis, cabinet-maker. The procession walked all the way to Myrtle Hill through a dense crowd of people.

Arrived at the station an imposing spectacle presented itself, the banks for half a mile being densely crowded.

It might be argued that the reporter should not be included among the travellers who visited south Wales. Although a correspondent often reported on a specific item of news some would spend considerable time on a story and get to know the people and background well. One of the best known is Thomas Campbell Forster, correspondent for *The Times*, who reported on the Rebecca Riots in 1843.

John Piper (1903-1992) does not qualify as an early traveller but as an artist who visited Carmarthenshire frequently and made many watercolours and prints of the area he deserves inclusion, particularly for his illustration of Dyer's *Grongar Hill*. The work was published as an edition of 175 by the Stourton Press in 1982 with four pages of lithographs, all in a lovely black and cream. Two pages, each a triptych, depict Grongar Hill and Dryslwyn Castle. The centre page spread, illustrated below, shows an unusual view of Grongar Hill with Cwmagol farmhouse as the focal point. All were drawn by Piper directly on to plastic.

In his foreword Piper explained his fascination with Dyer's poem:

(it) struck me as one of the best purely topographical poems in existence, because it is so visual. I did some drawings of the hill and the neighbourhood. Dyer, born in 1700, was trained as a painter. He is rather patronizingly referred to by Dr. Johnson and positively criticized by silly old Gilpin for getting his foregrounds mixed up with his middle distances (or something) but was generally much praised . . . I have loved the poem ever since I first read it, and I return to it whenever I feel depressed about the countryside getting spoilt – they are almost as sylvan and undisturbed as they were when I was young, and the single-line railway track has not been made into a double one; it has been taken up, which, I suppose, would have pleased Ruskin, too.[66]

Piper collected old topographical guide books, especially those from the 18th century. 'He was inspired by their . . . illustrations and as a result took lessons at the engraving department of the Royal College of Art'.[67] He looked at fragments of buildings not with the eyes of a

Fig. 16: *Grongar Hill. 1982. Lithograph, 220 x 410 mm. John Piper.*
(Courtesy of the estate of John Piper).

57

historian but as an artist, seeing them partly as abstract shapes but always as things of beauty.[68] He used Dryslwyn Castle as the subject for a lithograph in 1953 and Grongar Hill in *English, Scottish and Welsh Landscapes* published by the Curwen Press in 1944. Piper was a master of lithography:

> one of the most innovative 20th century printmakers. I see him as an artist who had the best possible understanding of the Modern Movement, its aims, techniques and freedoms, and at the same time created works of moving beauty. Piper absorbed the principles of cubism, surrealism, abstraction and Pop Art and combined them with his personal knowledge of stained glass and Romanesque carving.[69]

In the foreword to *Grongar Hill* Piper revealed his delight in the Tywi valley:

> On a first camping expedition in Pembrokeshire more than 60 years ago a friend and I were astonished by the Vale of Towy, between Llandeilo and Carmarthen.

It was quite clearly the Promised Land – a wide, verdant, smiling, fertile, welcoming vale that Blake might have thought up, lying between ranges of highish hills that never become mountains; the perfect setting for classical landscapes with figures by Poussin and Claude, not to mention classical landscapes without figures by Alexander and J. R. Cozens and J. M. W. Turner. Here in a few miles between these pleasant towns the illustrations in the English aquatint books published between 1790 and 1825 or so blossom into life at every bend, as if not only some but *all* of them had been done here. The green, partly wooded hills rise and fall happily on each flank, with a tower here or a hill and a whitewalled farm there in a shallow combe . . . with the Towy winding around the perimeter of its tree-girt ground.

Has there ever been a greater accolade for our incomparable valley?

> *Is nef nid oes un afon*
> *Lased a hardded â hon.*

ACKNOWLEDGEMENTS

Grateful thanks to Dara Jasumani of Carmarthenshire County Museum for the bulk of the photography. A. Scott for access to his fine library, and staff at Carmarthen Record Office.

NOTES

Very many prints were bound in books where the pages have been trimmed inside the plate marks. All measurements given here include image, title and any inscription.

1. John Landseer, quoted in J. Gage, *Colour in Turner: Poetry and Truth,* (1969), p. 10.
2. Tony Newbury, *Travelling for Pleasure* (Gwasg Gomer, 1994), p. 12.
3. George Borrow, *Wild Wales*, 1862.
4. *The Cambrian Magazine* was published in Llandovery and ran for two issues only. It was the first periodical to feature Welsh opinion.
5. B. H. Malkin, *The Scenery, Antiquities and Biography of South Wales* (London, 1804).
6. The map showing the Severn has choirs and harpists in the estuary. The work was re-issued in 1613 with a new title page and again in 1622 with twelve additional songs and ten extra maps.
7. Peter Lord, *Imaging the Nation* (UWP, 2000), p. 81.
8. S. Buck, 'Proposals for the publication of . . . twenty-four views of castles . . . in the counties of Lincoln and Nottingham', 1726, quoted Ralph Hyde, *Buck, Samuel (1696-1779)*, Oxford Dictionary of National Biography, 2004.
9. Lord, op.cit., n. 7, p. 104.
10. William Gilpin, *Hints to form the Taste and Regulate ye Judgment in Sketching Landscape*, mss., *c.*1790. Yale University British Art Centre, exhibited at *An American Passion for British Art*, Royal Academy, 2007-08.
11. William Gilpin, *Observations on the River Wye, and several parts of South Wales relative chiefly to picturesque beauty made in the summer of the year 1770* (London, 1782).
12. Price was a cousin of Thomas Johnes of Hafod.
13. Gilpin suggested that Tintern Abbey would be much improved if large parts of it were demolished.

14. Lord, op.cit., n. 7, p. 160.

15. Lord, op.cit., n. 7, p. 130. The letters of Elizabeth Presland, written when she was staying at Peniarth and quoted by Lord, show that an enjoyment of scenery was by no means unusual.

16. Judy Egerton, *Jones, Thomas (1742-1803)*, Oxford Dictionary of National Biography, 2004.

17. Wilson also produced detailed realistic drawings such as *The Arbra Sacra on the Banks of Lake Nemi, c.1755*, a beautiful chalk impression of a large tree. Jones's sketchbooks from Hafod have many delicate drawings of trees. They were only acceptable to Gilpin because of the faithful reproduction of the scenery which Johnes had already improved along accepted lines.

18. Lord, op.cit., n. 7, p. 151.

19. Lord, op.cit., n. 7, p. 106.

20. The dedication was more than justified; Banks had supplied Pennant with a great deal of information which was rarely acknowledged.

21. A former merchant venturer at Bristol, Banks-Hodgkinson became a country gentleman and took over the running of the estate when his father-in-law died. He was High Sheriff in 1784.

22. H. B. Carter, *Sir Joseph Banks 1743-1820* (Winchester, 1988), p. 49. On 25 September, Banks and his uncle set out on one of their journeys. From Edwinsford to Llandeilo was an easy first stage to Carmarthen. They noted Dynevor Park as they passed as 'one of the Prettyest things in South Wales'.

23. Carter, op.cit., n. 22, p. 121.

24. Pennant's famous *Tour in Wales* was only published in 1778, and Gilpin's Wye Tour pictures, though carried out in 1770, were not published until 1782; neither artist used aquatint.

25. Lord, op.cit., n. 7, p. 132.

26. Peter Hughes, *Paul Sandby's Tour of Wales with Joseph Banks*, The Burlington Magazine, Vol. 117, No. 868 (July 1975), pp. 452-457.

27. Hughes, op.cit., n. 26.

28. Watts, a pupil of Sandby, lived for most of his life in Wales and Bath and was well known for the high standard of his etchings, engravings and aquatints. It is generally accepted that the best work in English line engraving on copper was done in Watt's lifetime.

29. Peter Hughes, op.cit., n. 26.

30. Paul Sandby, *Roslin Castle*, aquatint, 1780. Yale Centre for British Art, exhibited at *An American Passion for English Art*, Royal Academy, 2007-08.

31. Ian Mackenzie, *British Prints*, Antique Collectors' Club, 1988, p. 68. It is generally accepted that Burdett had learnt the aquatint technique from J. B. Le Prince in Paris. Only three aquatints by Burdett are known.

32. Luke Herrmann, *Paul and Thomas Sandby*, Batsford, 1986, p. 43. 'The Russian Princess Dashkoff and Charles Greville were pupils of Sandby and are both cited as being involved in this important innovation. Until recently Sandby was thought to have introduced this effective new technique, which was first developed by the French artist Jean Baptiste Le Prince in the late 1760s, into England. It is now commonly accepted that Greville purchased the formula of the aquatint process from Burdett and presented it to his master. However, Dr. Ball has pointed out that the Russian Princess was almost certainly a pupil of Le Prince, either when the French artist was in Russia from 1758 to 1764 or while she herself was in Paris before coming to England and that it may have been through her that Sandby gained his knowledge of Le Prince's aquatint method'.

33. Lord, op.cit., n. 7, p. 160.

34. A. Lyles and D. Perkins, *Colour into Line, Turner and the Art of Engraving,* Tate Gallery, 1989, p. 9. Turner used etching, soft-ground etching, aquatint and mezzotint but not lithography. 'By means of the illustrated topographical tour or the souvenir Annual he could demonstrate his powers to everyone with access to a library. He was aware of the possibilities of engraving as publicity from the earliest moments of his career . . . Most of his watercolours were painted specifically to be translated into an engraved form . . . Although he never attempted line engraving, a technique traditionally tackled only by professionals, he tried his hand at most other printmaking processes'.

35. Lyles and Perkins, op.cit., n. 34, p. 11.

36. Cymro, 'Cursory Remarks on Welsh Tours or Travels', *Cambrian Register*, vol. 2, 1799, p. 449.

37. J. T. Barber, *A tour throughout South Wales and Monmouthshire* (London, 1803).

38. A *car llusg*, literally a 'drag cart'.

39. Robin Pearson, *Beaumont, John Thomas Barber*, Oxford Dictionary of National Biography, 2004.

40. Edward Donovan, *Descriptive excursions through South Wales and Monmouthshire*, 1805.

41. J. G. Wood, *Principal Rivers of Wales* (London, 1813), advertisement.

42. Thirteen Tywi valley views were printed in elephant quarto; three (Llandovery, Llandilovawr and Caermarthen) are double page panoramic views. They are: 'Source of the Towy Vechan', 'Pont y Cledach', 'Towy at Ystrad Ffin,' 'Ystrad Ffin', 'Fall of the Towy at Ystrad Ffin', 'Towy Bridge at Llandovery', 'Llandovery', 'Llandovery Castle', 'Llandilovawr', 'Dynevor Castle, etc. in the Towy Valley', 'Dynevor Castle', 'Caraig Cennin Castle', 'Dryslin Castle', 'Talley Abbey', 'Llandilo Rhonllys Bridge', 'Caermarthen', 'Llanstephan Castle'. All are dated 1812 with the exception of Llandovery Castle (1811).

43. Wood, op.cit., n. 41, p. 107. William Edwards, who built Pontypridd bridge in 1755.

44. R. V. Tooley, *English Books with Coloured Plates* (London, 1987), p. 108.

45. Brynley Roberts, foreword to the exhibition catalogue *Hugh Hughes:1790-1863, Artisan Painter* (NLW, 1990).

46. Peter Lord, *Hugh Hughes:1790-1863, Artisan Painter*, Exhibition catalogue (NLW, 1990), p. 2.

47. Lord, op.cit., n. 46, p. 4.

48. Lord, op.cit., n. 7, p. 197.

49. One of the foremost Welsh photographers was John Thomas, another emigrant to Liverpool. Some of Hugh Hughes's early portraits, now lost, are known only from Thomas's photographs.

50. Julia Nurse, *Robinson, John Henry (1796-1871)*, Oxford Dictionary of National Biography, 2004.

51. Julia Nurse, ibid.

52. As an example, Neath Abbey, 1830.

53. H. Gastineau, *Wales Illustrated* (1830).

54. G. Reynolds, *Watercolours A Concise History* (Thames and Hudson, 1992), p. 102.

55. P. Lord, *Clarence Whaite and the Welsh Art World, The Betws-y-Coed Artists' Colony 1844-1914* (NLW, 1998), p. 15.

56. Lord, op.cit., n. 55, p. 34.

57. S. Wildman, *David Cox* (Birmingham, 1983), p. 64. Quoted by Lord, op.cit., n. 55, p. 34.

58. Lord, op.cit., n. 7, p. 285.

59. Henry Skrine, *Two successive tours throughout Wales* (London, 1798).

60. George Lipscombe, *Journey in South Wales* (London 1802).

61. Nicholas Carlisle, *A topographical Dictionary of the Dominion of Wales* (London, 1811).

62. Barber, op.cit., n. 37.

63. Stones were eventually replaced by plates made of zinc or plastic.

64. *The English School of Painting in Water-Colour* is the most highly rated of a series of Penley's works. It was published by the firm of Day and Son, one of the largest and most prominent lithographic firms of the second third of the nineteenth century. Day and Son occupied an exceptional position amongst both lithographers and publishers in Britain. The firm attracted many talented draughtsmen and grew quite large, lithographing a great volume of high quality work. They also began to publish many books which contained their own plates – a very unusual activity for lithographers in England at that time; indeed, the art of lithography in colours was raised to new heights by some of the magnificent books they published. Day and Son held this unique position as both printers and publishers of fine quality books with colour plates for more than twenty years, and their decline during the mid 1860s is perhaps indicative of the increased mechanisation and other changes that were occurring in the trade during that time.

65. CRO, Taliaris Muniments, 73-80.

66. Earlier in the foreword Piper refers to Ruskin being 'startled' by a railway in the Derbyshire dales.

67. R. Ingrams and J. Piper, *Piper's Places* (Chatto and Windus, 1983), p. 54.

68. Ibid., p. 36.

69. Orde Levinson, *Quality and Experiment; Catalogue Raisonné*, 1996.

Artists' Depiction of Carmarthen Quay

Ann Dorsett

Carmarthen's Quay did not become a subject in its own right for the professional artist until the nineteenth century. Even in the nineteenth century, depictions of the Quay were topographical rather than artistic studies. As the Quay's fortunes rapidly declined in the twentieth century, so it attracted the attention of some of the town's most notable artists.

The earliest known depiction or visual reference to the Quay is found in the town plan of Carmarthen within John Speed's Carmarthen map of 1610. The town plan shows a bird's-eye view of the quay with three ships moored in the Tywi. A more pictorial view of the Quay is seen in *The South View of Carmarthen – Castle & Town* (see p. 42 for an illustration) published in 1740 by the brothers Samuel and Nathaniel Buck (1696-1779 and *fl.*1727-1753 respectively). The brothers travelled Britain making drawings on the spot during the summer months and subsequently engraving or etching the scenes in the autumn of that year, for publication for their subscribers in the following year.[1] Carmarthenshire County Museum is fortunate in having in its collections the original drawing for the more panoramic South East View of the town. *The South View of Carmarthen* clearly shows ships moored in the river and along the Tywi's northern bank. The busiest part of the quay at this time is not shown in the Buck print, as it was further downstream, at Island Wharf.[2] Later, eighteenth century views of Carmarthen as a town seen from the southern bank of the river and dominated by its castle were largely derived from the Buck engravings of the southern view.

A number of English artists travelled to Carmarthenshire during the 1830s. David Cox's engraving of Carmarthen from about 1830, is possibly the most dramatic view produced of the town.

Cox (1783-1859) shows the river front as a hive of

Fig. 1: *Carmarthen Quay, engraved in about 1830 by David Cox.*
(Collection: Carmarthenshire County Museum).

61

Fig. 2: *An engraving of a view of Carmarthen of about 1830-1831, from an original study by Henry Gastineau.*
(Collection: Carmarthenshire County Museum).

industry, with shipbuilders at work on the river bank and large ships moored together next to the quay, which is merely glimpsed in the distance. A decidedly more romantic and tranquil view was engraved by Thomas Barber for *Wales Illustrated* and published between 1830 and 1831. The Barber engraving is almost certainly taken from a drawing by the topographer and landscape painter Henry Gastineau (1791-1876). The engraving clearly shows the stone quay, which had been extended towards the bridge in 1808 and the warehouses and houses that had been built along the Quay.

We have a far more detailed view of the quayside huddle of buildings and warehouses in a watercolour drawing of the 1840s or 1850s by the west country artist, Alfred Keene (1821-1893).[3]

Little is known about the artist, who was art master at the Hermitage, Bath but he certainly painted another busy port, Bideford in Devon. Nothing is known about his visit or visits to Carmarthenshire but three other drawings by him of the Llansteffan area have survived: *The Ferryhouse*, *The Cliff, Llanstephan* and *The Beach*. Keene's Carmarthen quayside is somewhat down at heel. There is a typical small trading vessel moored at

the quay and small boats are pulled up out of the Tywi onto the quayside. We can see two men fishing from a raft or pontoon floating on the river. The buildings appear shabby in this drawing and speak of a town where poverty was rife. One quayside house has bed linen or washing slung out of an upstairs window and a garment or maybe a brown sail has also been thrown over a garden gate. A little horse and cart are shown turning into the quay. They are approaching the strange, brown, wedge shape which covers the site of present day Towy Works. At first glance this appears to be a shadow but it does not correspond with any building or feature in the landscape. This could be a huge pile of manure, as there was indeed a dealer in manure located on the quay. Other fascinating details shown by Keene are the thatched roofs still to be found on Carmarthen houses in the 1840s. The bridge glimpsed on the right is the mediaeval town bridge, which was lit by two gaslights and another single gaslight is shown fixed high on a wall to light the quayside.

The quay became one of the favourite subjects for Carmarthen's most distinguished amateur artist, Benjamin Archibald Lewis (1857-1946). As manager of

Fig. 3: *'Carmarthen Quay and Castle', a watercolour painting painted in the 1840s by Alfred Keene.*
(Collection: Carmarthenshire County Museum).

Fig. 4: *A large watercolour of Carmarthen Quay; painted in 1899 by Benjamin Archibald Lewis.*
(Collection: Carmarthenshire County Museum. Copyright: the artist's estate).

Fig. 5: *A small, detailed etching of the buildings of the west end of the Quay.*
The etching by William Jones was probably made in about 1910.
(Collection: Carmarthenshire County Museum).

Fig. 6: *A view of Island Wharf, painted in 1928 by Benjamin Archibald Lewis.*
(Collection: Carmarthenshire County Museum. Copyright: the artist's estate).

Carmarthen's gasworks, B. A. Lewis lived close by in the manager's house, which was at the foot of Morfa Lane. Family members have described his daily routine of waking early in the morning and walking out along the riverbanks or quayside to draw, before starting work for the day in the gasworks. The river and the quay with their proximity to home, were therefore some of his constant subjects. One of B. A. Lewis's most lyrical paintings is *Carmarthen Quay* painted in 1899.

This accomplished watercolour is one of two painted by him of a familiar sight, the Tywi at high tide. It depicts a large sailing vessel moored in the river, almost certainly about to leave with the tide. It was of course the high tide that allowed large ships to sail into Carmarthen's port. The two men in the rowing boat may be sailors leaving the ship or possibly one of the port's pilots. The town and quay are seen in the distance; the white building glimpsed to the left of the ship's stern is the Pothouse. B. A. Lewis studied for a time at Carmarthen School of Art and also produced a number of small but dramatic etchings of the quay and river. He may have been influenced by the Art School's long-serving

principal, William Jones, who also produced an etching of the river area *West End of the Quay, Carmarthen.* Jones's etching is very detailed and shows a small part of the stone quay and the foot of Quay Street.

B. A. Lewis's watercolour paintings are very much those of the talented amateur and he certainly gave a rather glamorous gloss to a somewhat down at heel area, as seen in his watercolour of 1928, *Island Wharf.*

The dilapidated buildings and equipment are here lit by wonderfully warm sunshine. Some of his more interesting later paintings of the quay were directly influenced by his professional artist son, Edward Morland Lewis (1903-1943). The Lewis family remember that artistic competition between father and son could be rather fierce. The National Museum of Wales has a fine oil painting by B. A. Lewis of Carmarthen's quayside warehouses, which clearly shows the influence of Morland's sombre, Camden Town palette, as does Carmarthenshire County Museum's small oil study.

Another fine painting of the quay painted in this period also exists in the collections of Carmarthenshire County Museum, painted by J. C. Midgley in 1926,

Fig. 7: *An undated study in oils of the Quay by Benjamin Archibald Lewis. It was probably painted during the 1930s.*
(Collection: Carmarthenshire County Museum. Copyright: the artist's estate).

Fig. 8: *'The Quay, Carmarthen', one of Edward Morland Lewis's most significant paintings of Carmarthen, probably painted between 1930 and 1935.*
(Collection: Carmarthenshire County Museum. Copyright: the artist's estate).

who was then Principal of Carmarthen School of Art. However, possibly the finest depiction of this scene is *Carmarthen Quay* by Edward Morland Lewis.

It was probably painted during the early 1930s, when the artist was living in London. Carmarthenshire and west Wales remained some of Morland Lewis' favourite subjects until his tragically early death on active war service in 1943. *Carmarthen Quay*, which is a large oil painting, is suffused with a silvery light, while the distant quay and buildings are reduced to slabs of muted colour.

NOTES

1. For a re-evaluation of the importance and accuracy of the Bucks' topography, see A. Wilkes, 'Pioneers of Topographical Printmaking: Some Comparisons', *Landscape History*, vol. 2, 1980, pp. 59-69.
2. For more detailed information about the development for the town and quay, see T. A. James, *Carmarthen: An Archaeological and Topographical Survey* (Carmarthenshire Antiquarian Society, 1980).
3. Terry James's advice and enthusiasm were invaluable to Carmarthenshire Museum Service's staff when Alfred Keene's *Carmarthen Quay and Castle* was first for offered for sale.

Christopher Williams and Carmarthenshire

Dylan Rees

It could be reasonably argued that the reputation of the artist Christopher Williams has diminished somewhat since his death in 1934.[1] In the years immediately following his death, the Art Establishment in Wales adopted what might charitably be described as a dismissive response to his work or less charitably as positively vituperative. Sir Cyril Fox, in a footnote to a letter written by Williams' wife Emily, noted 'pictures quite impossible . . . cannot be considered of sufficient artistic importance to warrant the occupation of space in the exhibition gallery of this institution.'[2] This attitude prevailed well into the post-war period when, in response to a request for space in the National Museum to display a proposed exhibition of the artist's work in 1951, the Keeper of Art wrote to his Director: 'This artist is deplorably bad, but on the other hand he is greatly admired by the uncritical in S. Wales . . . I cannot imagine why his turgid and empty painting should be held up for the admiration of schoolchildren and teachers.'[3] The only serious academic study to date of aspects of his career largely continued the trend describing him as a 'mediocre artist'. 'With historical hindsight Christopher Williams emerges as an almost comically unsuccessful figure.'[4]

There have been a number of attempts to restore his standing in more recent years, the most important of which was a major exhibition to mark the centenary of his birth in 1973.[5] If, however, market forces in the art world are an effective barometer of an artist's worth, then these attempts have yet to see any success in auction house prices. In his day Christopher Williams was one of Wales's most celebrated and lauded artists, whose talent as a skilled, perceptive and sensitive portrait painter was very much in demand. Many celebrated politicians, educationalists and literary figures sat for him and these works remain in many instances accessible to the public.[6] Yet the range of his work sets him apart from many of his Welsh contemporaries such as Augustus John or Margaret Lindsey Williams who were also very highly regarded at the time. To his skill as a portrait painter must be added a passion for landscapes executed quickly from a palette rich in vibrant colours, and also allegorical works on a grand scale, revelling in the symbolism of the myths and legends of his beloved Wales and also frequently suffused with the artist's essential humanity.

Christopher Williams was an extremely gifted and complex character who deserves to be appreciated by a much wider audience. While such an aim is beyond the scope of this article, it is hoped that bringing his artistic contribution to a wider audience will stimulate further interest in, and appreciation of, his life and work. The central purpose of this study is to explore Christopher Williams' connection with Carmarthenshire and to cover briefly some of the main features of his career.

The Williams family roots lay deep in the soil of Carmarthenshire. Christopher Williams' grandfather, David Williams (1809-1896) was a farmer in Llangain who later took over the tenancy of the Mill at Llanllwch. Despite the fact that the Mill only had four acres of land it clearly presented a better commercial proposition than the farm. In 1851 he was already employing a general labourer as well as relying on support from his expanding family.[7] He and his wife Rachel had eight children – Margaret, Mary, Esther, David, Evan, Henry, Thomas and John. Evan Williams (1845-1915), Christopher Williams' father, was born in the parish of St. Peter's, Carmarthen. Of David Williams' immediate family, his elder brother Evan (1814-1899) set up a successful cabinet-making business at Tanners Hall, Llandovery, which was continued by his three sons David, Henry and William. David's sister Anna,

Fig. 1: *Portrait in oil of 'David, The Cabinet Maker'.*
(Collection: Mr Duncan Rabagliati.
Copyright: the artist's estate).

Fig. 2: *Portrait in oil of William Williams, cabinet maker,*
Tanners Hall, Llandovery.
(Private Collection. Copyright: the artist's estate).

married John Jones of Hendre Farm in the parish of Llanstephan.

Economic circumstances in the 1860s presented lots of opportunities for those living in the countryside where jobs were difficult to find. The growth of the railways offered for the first time cheap and easily available transport from most rural areas. This new-found mobility allied to the rapid expansion of the South Wales coal industry resulted in an influx of workers, builders and traders into the valleys of Glamorganshire.[8] Among these new migrants, many of whom came from rural Carmarthenshire, was Evan Williams, a young man of enormous energy and drive who was determined to take advantage of the boom conditions on the coalfield. He sought his fortune in the rapidly expanding coal and iron producing communities of the Llyfni valley. As his son would later recall:

> My father . . . left school when he was eleven years of age to go into a flour-mill, and ultimately opened a shop of his own in Commercial Street Maesteg. He specialized in tea, and made this known to the general public by hanging an enormous tea-pot above his shop

window. That shop quickly became known as 'Shop Williams Tebot'.[9]

His hard work secured for him a comfortable lower middle class lifestyle. By Victorian standards he was moving up the social ladder as suggested by his marriage in 1869 to Mary, the daughter of Margaret and Christopher Williams, an accountant with the Llyfni Ironworks Company. In later life, Evan established himself as a pillar of the local community, assuming a prominent position in local government, becoming chairman of the local council and serving as a deacon in his local Congregational chapel. A daughter, Louisa Mary, was born to the young couple in 1871, followed shortly afterwards on 7th January 1873 by a son, Christopher. Evan's happy family life however was shattered by a double tragedy. His wife died on 27th January 1873, shortly after giving birth to their son Christopher and this was followed two weeks later by the death of his infant daughter.

These difficult early circumstances were partly dealt with when Evan was able to gain the services of a local midwife whose daughter Diana became a wet-nurse for his infant son. According to Christopher Williams his childhood, despite the lack of a mother, was a very happy one.[10] As a small boy he roamed around the sides of the mountains and played happily in the streets. The language of the hearth was Welsh and both he and his father regularly attended the local Congregational chapel every Sunday. The bond between the motherless only child and his father was very strong and Evan came to adopt, in Christopher's view, all family roles – mother, sister and brother. Although Evan had moved away from his family in Carmarthenshire, he retained close links with them. These links were if anything strengthened and became increasingly more important to him during his long years of widowhood. His young son spent many a summer holiday with various aunts and uncles dotted across the county. Christopher remembered with particular fondness the many holidays he spent with Evan's sister Margaret and her family.

Margaret Evans, who was Evan's eldest sister, ran a grocery shop at 95 Lammas Street in Carmarthen.[11] By all accounts Evan and Margaret were very close. As a

widow herself Margaret was very well placed to empathise with her brother's plight, and appears to have been willing to support him in every way possible. Margaret's own daughter Mary was staying with her uncle in 1881 and may well have been helping with looking after her young cousin, in addition to plying her own trade as a milliner.[12] During his visits to Carmarthenshire the young Christopher was taken around the large number of relations in his extended family and struck up close bonds with many of them. A place he appeared to have visited often was his grandfather's mill at Llanllwch, where some of his earliest sketches were made.[13] In later life when he became an artist, his family and the locations he knew from his youth would provide the subjects and inspiration for many of his works.

By the 1880s Evan's business was sufficiently successful for him to be able to afford a private education for Christopher. It had been his wife's desire that if she had a son he would become a doctor, and Evan was determined to honour this wish. Aged thirteen the young Christopher was sent away to a minor public school in

Fig. 3: *The Orchard, Hendre Farm. Oil on canvass.*
(Private Collection. Copyright: the artist's estate).

69

Cardiff. Although he appears to have excelled at art and frequently visited the museum to view the paintings, this was by all accounts an unhappy time for him.[14] He remained in Cardiff for three years before moving on to Oswestry High School. The choice of this school on the Welsh border was primarily dictated by the fact that it catered for the education of boys from Nonconformist backgrounds. For Christopher Williams the contrast between the two schools could not have been greater. He enjoyed his time at Oswestry and appears to have flourished as a student. As far as his father was concerned a career in medicine beckoned. But Christopher was increasingly drawn to an alternative vocation – becoming an artist. The turning point for him came on a visit to Liverpool in 1892, with a school friend. Left to his own devices for a few hours he visited the city's Walker Art Gallery. While wondering around he chanced on a painting – *Perseus and Andromeda*, by Lord Leighton, one of the most celebrated artists in Victorian Britain. Later he wrote of this encounter which had brought him enormous joy: 'In a few minutes I had made up my mind and said emphatically – I am going to be an Artist.'[15] All that now remained was persuading his father to agree to this change of educational direction. On returning to Oswestry, with his mind clearly made up on what he wanted to study, he was unable and unwilling to concentrate on his Matriculation Examinations, which he failed. Evan was uncomfortable with the new direction his son proposed taking and took some persuading to agree to this change in career. Such was the closeness of the relationship between father and son that Evan was reluctantly won around, following which he agreed wholeheartedly to support his son in every way possible.

Christopher Williams' first formal tuition took place in 1892 under the guidance of F. J. Kerr, an artist who specialised in watercolours and who taught at the Neath Technical Institute. Fred Kerr successfully prepared him to sit the entrance examination for the Royal College of Art in London. He was awarded a scholarship that entitled him to three years of free tuition and he set off for London in 1893. At the end of the course he was successful in gaining a qualification and then continued his studies. Between 1896 and 1901 he was a student at the Royal Academy Schools and was taught by two of the most distinguished painters of the day: John Singer Sargent and George Clauseen. The influence of Leighton, who had initially inspired Williams towards art, can clearly be detected in the teaching and subject content

adopted at the Royal Academy Schools. These included application of rigorous academic method and subject content drawn heavily from classical themes.[16] Leighton died in 1896 and the memorial exhibition of his work which was held shortly afterwards provided Williams with an excellent opportunity to closely study his work. His progress was such that he was awarded the Landseer prize for a portrait. The classical influence was very much evident in two early works which he completed – *Ladas the Marathon Runner* and *Paolo and Francesca*.[17]

While at the Academy Schools another major influence on Williams was emerging: that of G. F. Watts who had a studio in Kensington. He met and got to know the elderly Watts whom he visited several times before his death in 1904.[18] Part of the affinity Williams had for Watts was that he had Welsh roots and his art was infused with moral content. He was heavily influenced by the symbolism and morality displayed in Watts' work and sought to emulate this in his own paintings. Of Leighton and Watts, Williams wrote in a private note:

> . . . admired the classicism of one and the Celtic nature of the other (not an advocate of art for art's sake . . . the highest form of art is that which portrays the deep problems and aspirations of human life and sets people thinking).[19]

Despite having lived away from Wales for a number of years, the absence certainly did nor appear to have diminished his fondness for his homeland; quite the contrary, his ties with the land of his father grew and strengthened. Early on in his professional career he became committed to the ideals of the eisteddfod and was a dedicated supporter of the annual arts and crafts exhibition which became such an essential feature of the National Eisteddfod and the cultural fabric of Wales. He may well have been drawn to the National Eisteddfod as a result of his association with Fred Kerr who was deeply committed to its artistic ideals and was a regular exhibitor. Williams decided to submit a work for the 1897 Newport Eisteddfod. His entry reflects in many ways his sense of place and identity, and is redolent of happy summers spent among his father's family as a young boy. The entry was a depiction of a farm belonging to one of Evan's relatives in Carmarthenshire – *Hendre Farm by Moonlight*. The work which is quite different from the academic studies he was producing as a student in London at the time was commended by the celebrated artist Hubert Herkomer.[20]

Hendre Farm by Moonlight is sombre in tone and Williams clearly used a very restricted palette to convey an atmospheric portrayal of two old and for him, very dear, farm buildings.[21] It is in very marked contrast to the landscapes he painted in the latter part of his career where he relished the use of colour. Over the following years Williams would become a fairly regular exhibitor at the National Eisteddfod's Arts and Crafts exhibitions and would in turn help judge the competition. One of the first eisteddfodau which he helped to judge was at Llanelli in 1903. As the nineteenth century drew to a close he became increasingly interested in Celtic culture, particularly in the myths and legends of his native language. He was introduced to, and was inspired by, some of the greatest treasures of Welsh literature among them the Black Book of Carmarthen.[22] It may have been at this time that he came into '. . . contact with the intellectual circle of the National Eisteddfod and the Pan-Celtic movement . . . which activated him'.[23] Drawing his inspiration from the Mabinogion, he would in the following years produce three works based on female figures central to the tales – *Ceridwen* (1910), *Branwen* (1915) and *Blodeuwedd* (c.1930).

The great emphasis placed on figurative art in the teaching at the Royal Academy Schools and the undoubted talent he displayed as a figure painter, offered him an avenue to support himself through portraiture. His earliest commissioned portrait, completed in 1899, was of a friend of his in London – *Mrs. Sackville Evans.*[24]

The following year while still at the Academy Schools, he and a friend – Fred Appleyard – took a studio at 18 Kensington Court Place. Over the next few years he painted a number of portraits, but probably the one that gave him the greatest satisfaction was the one he made of his father *Evan Williams* (1903), which he exhibited at the Royal Academy.[25] In 1904 he asked if Rowland Williams, who had been elected Archdruid in 1894, would be willing to sit for him. The finished portrait, *Hwfa Môn* (the archdruid's bardic name) in his full ceremonial regalia is a powerful and striking work which was well received when it was exhibited at the Royal Cambrian Academy in Conway in 1905.[26]

After leaving the Academy Schools in 1901, his career slowly progressed and he obtained a number of portrait commissions. In 1904 he married Emily Appleyard, the sister of his friend Fred. There followed a year-long honeymoon through Italy visiting many classical sites and providing much inspiration for his landscapes. On their return they set up home at 71 Eardley Crescent in London and resided there for the remainder of their married life. Although removed from Wales, he sought to visit his homeland whenever he could. His increasing interest in the eisteddfod, and Welsh culture brought him into contact with Thomas Matthews. Matthews, who was slightly younger than Christopher Williams, was emerging as a vocal champion of Welsh art and culture during the Edwardian period. He became a very influential figure in the Welsh-language press where he championed the cause of many Welsh artists among them Christopher Williams. Matthews also had very close links with Carmarthenshire having been born in Llandybie and although a schoolmaster at Lewis School, Pengam, Monmouthshire, he frequently returned to the village to stay with his family.[27] The two became firm friends, sharing not only a love of Welsh culture, particularly visual culture, but also a concern about the lack of art education and promotion of art in Wales.

The many visits which he made to Carmarthenshire provided not only opportunities for him to indulge his love of painting out of doors directly from nature, but also to pursue his developing career as portrait painter. Possibly the most celebrated portrait he painted linked to Carmarthenshire was of Sir John Williams, a former doctor to Queen Victoria, and the greatest benefactor of the National Library of Wales.[28] Sir John lived in Plas Llanstephan, in an area which Christopher Williams knew very well through his family ties.

Fig. 5: *Portrait in oil of 'Sir John Williams, Bart.'.*
First President of the National Library of Wales.
(Collection: National Library of Wales Aberystwyth.
Copyright: the artist's estate).

In a memoir of his youth, he recalls when staying with his aunt in Carmarthen the regular weekly visit of Mari John Cocks, an elderly cockle gatherer from Llanstephan, who came to the town with her donkey cart:

> I was passionately fond of ponies and donkeys but could never get a chance of driving them: then my chance came as the old woman had tea at my aunt's on the way back to Llanstephan after having sold the cockles. I became a great chum of the old woman, so I arranged to meet her at the mile stone on the Llanstephan road coming in. I knew exactly what time she came and jumped into the cart, taking the reins at the same time . . . At the top of the hill where Carmarthen begins, business also began. I would stand up, still holding the reins and shout: 'Fresh cockles all alive oh!' till we had done the round and back to tea and then to the mile-stone where the sweet natured old woman always gave me a penny.[29]

Many years later while working on the portrait of Sir John, Christopher Williams accompanied him one day

to the local ferry crossing from Llanstephan to Ferryside and the railway station as he was setting out for London. They chanced upon the same old woman, who was known to Sir John as a much loved local character. In the conversation which followed she eventually recognised her old friend much to the amazement of Sir John Williams.[30]

During one visit to Carmarthen, Christopher Williams was himself the subject of a portrait by the photographer J. F. Lloyd.[31] The photograph, which is dated *c.*1900, shows the young artist at an unnamed location painting out of doors. Many years after his father's death, Ifor Williams, who was also an artist, offered an insight into his father's working practices and how he delighted in painting directly from nature. Although his livelihood was increasingly dependant on portrait commissions, he enjoyed the freedom which landscape painting gave him. West Wales, including Carmarthenshire, were among his favorite sketching grounds. 'Colour intoxicated him', and this along with the quality of the light led to a number of visits over the years to Spain, Italy and North Africa.[32] During summer visits to either

Fig. 6: *Photograph of Christopher Williams painting*
out of doors c.1900 by J. F. Lloyd.
(Collection: Carmarthenshire County Museum).

Wales or abroad he would take about thirty 16 x 12 inch canvasses with him. According to Ifor, his father was:

> A fast worker, he would finish a 16 x 12 inch (oil) sketch in one sitting of two or two and a half hours, doing sometimes three sketches a day. Rarely did he go back to a sketch. The first impression of a scene was everything to him, and he felt this was lost by going back a second time.[33]

Of the surviving landscapes from Carmarthenshire, almost all are related to views of castles. It appears that a view of Laugharne Castle was painted in his studio based on a preparatory sketch completed while visiting West Wales (*Fig. 7*). Both works are in public collections.[34] The finished oil follows very closely the preparatory sketch, but incorporates a range of darker colours. By far the largest of the depictions of the county's castles is *Dryslwyn Castle*. With its rocky foreground and overcast sky it captures the splendour of a prominent local landmark dominating the valley of the Towy.[35] The scale of the painting may be gauged in the photograph (*Fig. 10*) by an unknown photographer, of Christopher Williams holding the completed work prior to framing.[36]

Christopher Williams's friendship with Thomas Matthews developed and deepened in the years leading up to the Great War. Besides sharing a passionate interest in the Eisteddfod and pan-Celtic nationalism and culture, they were also deeply interested in promoting and publicising Welsh art. Matthews' admiration for Williams' work grew to such an extent that he vested in his friend the hope and desire that he would be the catalyst for the emergence of a new era where painting would challenge the cultural hegemony of music in Welsh life. According to Matthews, an artist must possess the imagination of a bard and through his works depict the highest aims of the life of his nation. Where the medium of the bard is the word, argued Matthews, that of the artist is colour. Both artist and bard, according to Matthews have the power to give people a '. . . glimpse of the promised land. Christopher Williams is a bard of this type. To me there is something uplifting to my spirit in all his pictures'.[37] Matthews' chosen vehicle for promoting Welsh art were the pages of Owen M. Edwards' journal *Cymru*. He wrote at length drawing his audiences attention to the virtues of a range of Welsh artists, among them Margaret Lindsey Williams, Edgar Thomas and Penry Williams to name but a few.[38] He reserved a special place however in his pantheon of Welsh

Fig. 7: *Preparatory drawing of Laugharne Castle, 1906.*
Pencil and crayon.
(Collection: Carmarthenshire County Museum.
Copyright: the artist's estate).

Fig. 8: *An oil painting of 'Laugharne Castle'.*
(Collection: Newport City Art Gallery, gift of
Mrs Emily Williams, 1940. Copyright: the artist's estate).

artists for Christopher Williams. Given the spirit of the time, Matthews believed that Christopher Williams' message was alive and relevant for Wales.[39] He was also in no doubt than that his friend was continuing along the path marked out by Watts, and cited his painting *Why?* as clear evidence of this.[40]

Regular summer visits to the National Eisteddfod and summer holidays spent in west and north Wales provided many opportunities for Williams and Matthews to meet and socialise, and inevitably ponder the condition of the visual arts in Wales. Both were profoundly concerned about how art in Wales was perceived by the general public and the lack of opportunities provided for young artists in Wales. Whereas Matthews used the

Fig. 9: *Preparatory oil sketch for Dryslwyn Castle.*
(Collection: (Collection: Mrs Mair Rabagliati).. Copyright: the artist's estate).

Fig. 10: *Photograph of the artist Christopher Williams holding his oil painting of Dryslwyn Castle.*
(Collection: Mrs Mair Rabagliati).

columns of *Cymru*, and other publications[41] to champion the cause of visual art and art education, Williams adopted a different approach. At the National Eisteddfod held in Llangollen in 1908, Christopher Williams delivered a lecture to the Honourable Society of Cymmrodorion. His theme was an overview of Welsh art, its current position in the nation's cultural life with emphasis on what was lacking, before suggesting ways in which the position could be improved. Williams argued that as far as he could tell the present situation was 'distinctly depressing', as everything favoured music to the neglect of art. He expressed concern that any nascent artistic talent, which might exist among the young was not allowed to emerge because of the poverty of Welsh art schools when compared with those in England. Williams believed that the majority of his fellow countrymen had no real conception of what art really was, and the few that did believed that it merely involved painting pretty pictures. Local authorities in Wales, he considered, were very slow to involve themselves in art education. But where they did – and he cited favourably the Art School in Llanelli as an exemplar, 'things had gone well, and I hope we shall soon hear of a flourishing school there'. As to why this dire situation existed, Williams was both forthright and candid in his analysis:

> In the local Eisteddfodau, where the competitions are generally musical and literary, no encouragement is given to students of Art . . . Our universities and Colleges also pass Art by as a thing unworthy of their energies . . . Chances of training then are lacking in Wales, and the artistic environment is also lacking. In our towns and villages there is no enthusiasm for having things beautiful.[42]

His ambitious blueprint for elevating the status of art in his homeland could be neatly summed up as the four 'P's'. He called on the wealthy to provide Patronage to young artists who might be struggling during the early years of their careers; the Politicians to fight for more galleries and art education; Preachers to speak of the glories and beauty of this world; and lastly the Press, to publicise art in Wales and promote Welsh artists. Christopher Williams' mantra was 'art for the masses, not for the classes only'. His passionate hope was that Wales would become a 'country full of beauty in the cottage home as in the Plas'.[43] Towards the end of his life he made a provision for a number of his paintings to be given to his home town of Maesteg in the anticipation

Fig. 11: *Drawing of Sir Rhys ap Thomas, based upon contemporary data, by Christopher Williams, 1913.*
(Copyright: the artist's estate).

that they would be exhibited possibly in a gallery so that the public, particularly the young, could enjoy and be inspired by them.[44]

Whenever he could, finances and family commitments permitting, Christopher Williams would travel abroad to southern Europe. On two of these journeys, in 1913 to Holland, and 1914 to Italy, Spain and North Africa, Thomas Matthews accompanied his friend.[45] There is some evidence that the two worked together on a number of projects where Williams supplied an illustration for one of Matthews' books, one of which was closely linked to Carmarthenshire. In this work, which is dated 1913, Williams provided an artist's impression, in the form of a black and white drawing, of Sir Rhys ap Thomas, one of the most celebrated figures from the county's history.[46] Matthews was, among his many other activities, a prolific writer. In 1913 he published a biography of the Welsh-born sculptor John Gibson, R.A. At what point he decided to write a biography of Christopher Williams is unclear but it may well have been discussed and started before the outbreak of the First World War.

The biography of Christopher Williams never saw the light of day. Matthews died in 1916 with the work at a fairly advanced if still rather incomplete form. The surviving draft probably reveals more about Matthews' interests and passions than his subject's life and work. In an idiosyncratic text full of literary and cultural references there is precious little of a biographical nature – personal and professional details are as thin as the literary references are numerous. The final chapter is titled *Y Gweledydd* – the Visionary – which neatly encapsulates his view of Williams. It was undoubtedly Matthews' intention to raise the profile of contemporary Welsh art by publishing a biography of a living artist very much at the height of his powers.[47] The choice of the medium of Welsh for publication is interesting; while it would deny access to a significant proportion of the population of Wales, he may well have been targeting the Welsh-speaking middle classes and their new-found industrial wealth. While in one way he considered Christopher Williams as very much the inheritor of a tradition running from the classical Greeks through to John Gibson, Leighton and Tadema, on the other hand he singled him out as a visionary who, in embracing Celtic themes, was heralding a new age in Welsh art. In prose verging on the hagiographic, Matthews, curiously for such a staunch nationalist, singles out Williams' large-scale depiction of the Investiture of the Prince of Wales in 1911 for particular praise. The painting is:

> . . . accurate in every aspect; but more than this he conveys the sprit of the event, not only to those who were present, but also to those who were not there and in such a way that words cannot express, it is second to none among any similar historic work.[48]

There is little doubt that the ties between the two men, artist and critic were close, possibly too close for the one, to form an objective evaluation of the other. Matthews' style, when writing about Christopher Williams, has been described as being suffused with 'florid and sanguine rhetoric'.[49] Whether this is fair and accurate or not is ultimately a matter of literary taste. Both were determined, and contributed in a variety of ways, to elevating the status of visual art in Wales. After Matthews' death, Christopher Williams wrote that: 'We have lost one of the best, and genuine nationalists. I feel the loss of Tom Matthews keenly. Perhaps I knew him as few did.'[50]

In addition to the close links that Christopher Williams had with Thomas Matthews, visits to Carmarthenshire also entailed spending time with his relatives or working on portrait commissions. Christopher Williams was particularly fond of visiting his father's cousins who lived in Tanners Hall, Llandovery.[51] The three brothers David, Henry and William Williams were all cabinet-makers. Two of them agreed at various times to sit for Christopher Williams, who produced honest, un-pretentious portrayals of ordinary artisans. These small domestic-sized portraits (*Figs. 1 and 2*) capture the determination and resourcefulness of these men and contrast sharply with the other portrait he produced in the town. This was a large and quite austere commission he undertook for Llandovery College of Canon Worthington Poole Hughes, MA, one of its Wardens. Williams intended submitting the work to the Royal Academy Summer exhibition in 1927. In the event it was not accepted and the Canon rather wittily observed: 'I am afraid you were disappointed about the portrait. I should have liked to be in the Academy because I have a vain glorious vein in me!'[52] These portraits are good examples of the range of Williams's abilities and sensitivities as a painter spanning works produced purely for private pleasure to those designed to hold their own in a pantheon of the worthy and good of an illustrious local institution. One of the last commissions he accepted from the county was to paint a portrait of John Hinds who had been the Liberal MP for West Carmarthenshire from 1910-23. The portrait was paid for by a subscription list to a testimonial fund, and was unveiled in 1925.[53] An account of the occasion captures the warmth with which the portrait was received:

> . . . the *piece de resistance* was the Portrait in Oils by the eminent Welsh Artist, Mr. Christopher Williams, whose letter was read amidst loud cheers which emphasized the ungrudging appreciation of the Portrait itself by a crowd of 600 discriminating enthusiasts from all parts of *Shir Gar* . . . your Portrait was declared on all hands to be a decided success and worthy of our friend. It is really wonderful and I heartily congratulate you upon it and thank you warmly on behalf of the Committee of Subscribers for the real good work as well as the 'art' you have put into it.[54]

There are very few people alive today in Carmarthenshire who are able to recall directly Christopher Williams' visits to the county. One who is able to do so is Mr Harry Jones (b.1914) of Llanstephan whose mother Maggie was the artist's cousin. He vividly remembers as a small boy meeting the artist:

Fig. 12: *A drawing of Llanstephan Castle.*
(Collection: National Library of Wales Aberystwyth. Copyright: the artist's estate).

I met Christopher Williams for the first time when I was about six years old. We were at the time living at Park Glas Farm in Llanstephan. He would come and visit, and tell my mother – 'Maggie, I am taking Harry down to the Green'. He liked to walk along the path down to the front and sit and look across at Ferryside. He was particularly interested in the castle. I clearly remember him taking out paper and a lead pencil from his pocket, and in what seemed an instant he had made a perfect image of the Castle. I do wish I had kept that paper.[55]

Someone else who remembers Christopher Williams well is Miss May Francis from Carmarthen. She clearly remembers how Christopher Williams came to paint the portrait of her uncle, Henry Jones, of Hendre Farm (*Fig. 13*). Williams was a regular visitor to the farm whenever he was down in Llanstephan and was keen to paint the portrait of his relative. The farmer, however, was unwilling as he considered himself an unworthy subject. Undeterred by his subject's reluctance he decided to paint him without his knowledge. At the end of each working day Henry was in the habit of unwinding by sitting outside the farmhouse and smoking a pipe of tobacco. Williams set himself up in an adjoining out-building with a clear view of his subject and rapidly

Fig. 13: *Portrait of Henry Jones, Hendre Farm. Oil on board.*
(Private Collection. Copyright: the artist's estate).

Fig. 14: *An oil painting of Llanstephan Castle.*
(Private Collection. Copyright: the artist's estate).

captured his image. The resulting work is more an oil sketch than a formal portrait but nevertheless presents the essence of a farmer at the end of his day's labour.[56]

There is little doubt that Williams produced many other works linked to the county which are currently unrecorded. It is known that he painted an *Interior of St. Peter's*, Carmarthen, but its present location is unknown. As interest in this important artist grows and his career is reappraised then more of his works, including some from Carmarthenshire, will, it is hoped, emerge into public view. As this article was going to press, a painting of Llanstephan Castle, but not *Llanstephan Castle by Moonlight* has come to my attention (*Fig. 14*).[57] Shortly after his death, his widow wrote a letter to William Grant Murray, the curator of the Glynn Vivian Art Gallery in Swansea, regarding works that remained in the family's possession: 'Christopher valued them highly himself and felt he would like them to be where they could be seen.'[58] The renewed interest in Welsh Art in recent years and greater appreciation of the benefits of cultural tourism may well help rehabilitate the reputation of Christopher Williams as his works are sought out and a more balanced approach to evaluating his *oeuvre* is undertaken.

ACKNOWLEDGEMENTS

I am deeply indebted to Christopher Williams' great-grandson Mr. Alistair Rabagliati for providing me with an enormous wealth of information relating to his great-grandfather drawn from the family's private papers. The staff of the Glynn Vivian Art Gallery, Swansea, have also been very helpful in allowing me to consult their file on Christopher Williams. Julie Kim and Andrew Gardiner for technical support regarding some of the images.

NOTES

1. David Bell, *The Artist in Wales* (London, 1957), p. 165. According to Bell, Williams' work could be summed up as '. . . flogging a horse which was already dead and squandering his very real talent, instead of conserving it for the smaller, humbler pictures which were really more within his range.'

2. NMW Archive file on Christopher Williams.

3. NMW Archive file on Christopher Williams.

4. NLW, ex 1148, Ruth Richards, 'The Reawakening of Wales: Painting, Ideology and National Culture in Early Twentieth Century Wales' (History of Art MA, University of Sussex, 1989), p. 4.

5. Catalogue of *Christopher Williams Centenary 1873-1973* (Cardiff, 1973), produced by the National Museum of Wales with an introductory essay by A. D. Fraser-Jenkins. See also P. Lord, *Imagining the Nation* (Cardiff, 2000), pp. 330-6.

6. Among the portraits he painted were those of Lloyd George and his first wife Margaret, Sir John Williams, Prof. Sir Henry Jones, Sir John Rhys, Sir Alfred Lyall.

7. Census Returns for the Parish of St Peter's, Carmarthen, 1851.

8. For the growth of the coal industry in the Maesteg area see John Williams, 'The Coal Industry 1750-1914', *Glamorgan County History, Volume V, Industrial Glamorgan* (Cardiff, 1980), pp. 184-5.

9. Jeremiah Williams, ed., *Christopher Williams, RBA, An Account of his life and appreciation of his work* (Caernarfon, 1954), p. 20. To date this is the only significant account of Christopher Williams' life. The author was a close personal friend who drew heavily on the artist's unpublished papers and a now lost memoir of his life.

10. Williams, op. cit., n. 9.

11. Margaret Williams married David Evans from Newchurch parish in 1854. He was a furnaceman at Carmarthen Tinworks. I am greatly indebted to Edna Dale-Jones for providing me with this information.

12. Census Returns, Maesteg, 1881.

13. Williams, op. cit., n. 9, p. 23.

14. In his own words he notes 'Cardiff school life was hell to me'. Of his time there '. . . I had such a miserable life; it was a terrible nightmare'. Williams, op. cit., n. 9, pp. 25-6.

15. Williams, op. cit., n. 9, p. 30.

16. For an account of the approaches and methods which Christopher Williams would have encountered at Royal Academy Schools, see Helen Valentine (ed.), *Art in the Age of Queen Victoria* (London, 1999), pp. 40-47.

17. Both these paintings are now located in Maesteg.

18. For an overview of Watt's life and work, see V. F. Gould, *The Vision of G. F. Watts OM RA* (2004). The evidence for Watts' Welsh roots are somewhat thin: see the Revd. T. Mardy Rees in *Welsh Painters, Engravers and Sculptors 1527-1911* (Carnarvon, 1911), p. 136: 'Watts confessed

19. that he was of Welsh extraction.' This appears to be the main basis for this claim.

19. Fraser-Jenkins, op. cit., n. 5, p. 5.

20. P. Lord, *Y Chwaer-Dduwies Celf, Crefft a'r Eisteddfod* (Llandysul, 1992) pp. 62-3.

21. I am very grateful to Mr. Harry Jones for allowing me permission to view and reproduce this work.

22. Fraser Jenkins, op. cit., n. 5, p. 7.

23. Lord, op. cit., n.5, p. 331; see idem. p. 333, for a reproduction of *Ceridwen*; p. 335 for *Blodeuwedd*.

24. Located in Maesteg Town Hall.

25. Located in Maesteg Town Hall.

26. Reproduced in Lord, op. cit., n. 5, p. 331.

27. See Dylan Rees, 'Thomas Matthews, MA (1874-1916), Llandybie: Historian, Writer and Art Critic', *The Carmarthenshire Antiquary*, Vol. xl, 2004, pp. 129-138.

28. W. Ll. Davies, *The National Library of Wales* (Aberystwyth, 1937) and *The Dictionary of Welsh Biography Down to 1940* (London, 1959), pp. 1055-6.

29. Williams op. cit., n. 9, pp. 23-24.

30. Williams, op. cit., n. 9, p. 24.

31. J. F. Lloyd (1860-1937) who was employed as Chief Clerk to Carmarthen Probate Registry was a talented amateur photographer. Most of his photographs date from around the early 1890s until the outbreak of the First World War in 1914. He mainly photographed his family, friends, Carmarthen town and local events. I am indebted to Ann Dorsett at Carmarthen Museum for this background information. See C. Delaney's article in this volume.

32. Wil Ifan, 'Memories of Christopher Williams', *Western Mail*, 25 July 1934, p. 11.

33. Ifor Williams, 'Aims and Methods', in Williams, op. cit., n. 9, pp. 137-141.

34. *Laugharne Castle*, oil on canvas (290 x 400) 1940, is in Newport City Art Gallery, the gift of Mrs. C. Williams, while the preparatory sketch is located in Carmarthenshire County Museum, Abergwili.

35. The painting is located in the Magistrates Court in the Guildhall, Carmarthen, and was presented by his widow to Carmarthenshire County Council in 1941.

36. I am greatly indebted to Mr. Alastair Rabagliati and the family of Christopher Williams for allowing me permission to reproduce this photograph.

37. *A Souvenir of the Christopher Williams Exhibition* (Maesteg, 1949); T. Matthews, *An Appreciation of Christopher Williams, R.B.A.* This was first published in Welsh in *Cymru*, January 1911.

38. See for example *Cymru*, January 1912–May 1913, January, April, December 1914, February 1916.

39. T. Matthews, *Celf Yng Nghymru* (Caernarfon, 1914), p. 6. This work was originally published in *Cymru* over a number of editions.

40. The painting *Why?* (1913) depicted a scene of utter desperation and destitution on the London embankment and resonates with Williams' concern for the marginalised and socially excluded in British society. In later life he was drawn to left wing politics and became a member of the Fabian Society.

41. See T. Matthews, *Perthynas Y Cain a'r Ysgol (Cyhoeddwyd gan Undeb y Cymdeithasau Cymraeg,* 1916). This book was intended by Matthews to be a guide for teachers and educators on how best to elevate and promote visual art in Welsh Schools.

42. Notes on Wednesday 2nd September 1908, *Transactions of the Honourable Society of Cymmrodorion*, Session 1907-1908, published in 1909, p. vi; T. H. Thomas and Christopher Williams read papers (which were followed by a discussion) on 'The Past and the Future of Art in Wales'. The papers are not reproduced in the volume. Jeremiah Williams must have consulted Williams' own notes, see Williams, op. cit., n. 9, pp. 127-133. For the Art School in Llanelli which was established in 1907 under the patronage of Charles William Mansel Lewis of Stradey Castle, see S. Jones, *Charles William Mansel Lewis* (Aberystwyth, 1998), pp. 49-50.

43. In the years before the First World War there were several developments in Wales to create national collections. In 1907 the proposed National Museum was granted a Royal Charter. An exhibition was held in 1913 which showed works from the collection of the Davies sisters of Gregynog. See J. Ingamells, *Things of Beauty. What Two Sisters did* (Cardiff, 1967).Their collecting which started in 1908 is now very much synonymous with French impressionism although they bought many other works. In the same year an exhibition was held called 'Modern Artists of Welsh Birth or Extraction'. The first attempt to try and collate the work of Welsh artists was by the Revd. T. Mardy Rees, *Welsh Painters, Engravers and Sculptors (1527-1911)*, published in 1912. An important patron who supported Welsh artists in the first half of the twentieth century was Winifred Coombe Tennant (*Mam o Nedd*). See Peter Lord, *Winifred Coombe Tennant – a life through art* (Aberystwyth, 2007).

44. Two of his works which are on public display in Carmarthenshire may be seen in Parc Howard Museum in Llanelli.

45. Mathews refers to this tour in his 'Appreciation of Christopher Williams, R.B.A.' while Williams mentions another visit they made to Holland and Morocco. Jeremiah Williams, op. cit., n. 9, makes no reference to any of Christopher Williams' traveling companions.

46. They worked on at least two projects. The first was a drawing Williams did for a pageant Matthews was overseeing relating to *The Pengam Episode. Investiture of Sir Rhys Ap Thomas as a Knight of the Garter in 1507* (1913). Secondly, he provided a north African illustration for *Dail Y Gwanwyn* (Pengam, 1916) a collection of poems and stories by pupils at the Lewis School where Matthews taught.

47. NLW MS 16331D. Four chapters had clearly been set up and corrected by Matthews in his own hand, with the fifth in mss form. The work was presumably deposited by the printer Hugh Evans a'i Fab, Liverpool, 16 September 1946.

48. op. cit., n. 47, Chapter 4: 'Art, Literature and History', p. 3 of the galley proof.

49. Richards, op. cit., n. 4, p. 14.

50. *Cymru*, 1916, p. 247, letter dated 16 September 1916.

51. For Tanners Hall see A. T. Arber-Cooke, *Pages from the History of Llandovery* (Llandovery, 1976), vol. II, p. 313.

52. The location of the two portraits is known. *David, the Cabinet Maker* – oil on canvas (30 x 26 inches) was exhibited in the Christopher Williams Centenary 1873-1973 Exhibition – Catalogue No. 9. *Rev. Canon William Worthington Poole-Hughes MA*, oil on canvas (50 x 40 inches) is located in the Library of Llandovery College. The sitter was Warden of the College from 1900-1927. I am indebted to Mr. Dai Gealy for drawing my attention to this work and for all his other help and support. For the letter see Worthington Poole Hughes to Christopher Williams, 21 June 1927, Williams Family Papers.

53. I am indebted to Mr. Alastair Rabagliati for providing me with a copy of this list.

54. W. J. Wallis-Jones to Christopher Williams, 28 September 1925. Williams Family Papers.

55. Part of an interview recorded with Mr. Harry Jones on 13 August 2007 transcribed and translated from Welsh. I am very grateful for the help and support provided by Ms Eiluned Rees in helping to arrange this interview. Parc Glas was also known as *Tafarn Llaeth* (Milk Inn) on account of its popularity with holidaying colliers who would visit and drink buttermilk laced with spirits.

56. Interview with Miss May Francis, Carmarthen, 19 June 2008. I am very grateful for the information and insight provided by Miss Francis.

57. Carmarthen Museum, List and catalogue of Paintings sent to Parc Howard, Llanelli. July 1939, *Llanstephan Castle by Moonlight* was exhibited at the 1935 National Eisteddfod at Caernarfon and was offered for sale at 10 guineas. Fig. 14 was painted for Lady Williams probably at the same time as he was working on the portrait of Sir John. There is also a reference to another view of the castle in a letter dated 1902 which he made for Ms Irene Smith.

58. Letter from Emily Williams to W. Grant Murray, 14 May 1935, Glynn Vivian Art Gallery File on Christopher Williams.

John Francis Lloyd . . .
A Carmarthen Photographer

Chris Delaney

Terry James was a highly competent and gifted photographer, who also had a keen interest in historic photographs, particularly those that recorded the social history of his home town, Carmarthen. In my various roles with Dyfed and Carmarthenshire Museum services, we often discussed and exchanged information of new discoveries of historic photographs or of new sites he had identified through aerial photography. I recall in the early 1980s an exhibition we developed for Carmarthen Museum of aerial photographs of Dyfed taken by Terry, showing well-known and newly-identified archaeological sites across the region. He was even more excited than I was, when I showed him the huge pile of glass negatives that became known as the J. F. Lloyd collection.

In 1989, a fortuitous conversation with my neighbour in Picton Terrace, Mrs Jones, led to a donation of glass negatives to Carmarthenshire County Museum. Mrs Jones had in her possession a large number of glass negatives, which had been found behind a wallpapered door in a partition of her attic, by builders carrying out repairs. The house at 19 Picton Terrace, Carmarthen, had been the home of John Francis Lloyd from about 1902 until his death in 1937 at the age of seventy-six. When he retired in 1931 he was Chief Clerk at the Carmarthen Probate Registry and a well-known and respected figure in the town. He was a keen artist, who expressed his talents and enthusiasm through membership of the Arts and Crafts Committee of the 1911 Carmarthen National Eisteddfod, as well as his interest in photography and calligraphy. The latter was demonstrated through illuminated addresses for which he received enormous praise and numerous commissions. There are negatives of his illuminated addresses among the collection, but sadly they are only in black and white.

The J. F. Lloyd Collection in the museum consists of over seven hundred and fifty glass plate negatives, with some ephemeral material, such as negative boxes and several prints. A collection of papers and receipts related to his social and community activities, not the photographic collection, were deposited in the Carmarthenshire Record Office. The negatives were produced by the dry collodion process and are of three sizes. The majority are half plate, 6½ x 4¾ inch (16.5 x 12cms) with several hundred at quarter plate size 4¼ x 3¼ inch (10.7 x 8cms). In addition there are a few 3¼ inch square plates (8.3 x 8.3cms). Unfortunately, there is no record of the plate camera he used, but we do know that he developed the plates in a small darkroom and studio at the bottom of his garden. The majority of the collection is portraits of family members and friends, but there are nearly one hundred and fifty topographical, event, group and social photographs, which are of particular interest for the social and local historian. They were taken during the period 1895 to 1905.

For this article, I have selected a small group of photographs from the collection to illustrate the quality, inventiveness and significance of his work. There are a number of portraits of Lloyd amongst the negatives, which are assumed to be self-portraits, or at least composed by him, even if a member of his family actually took the image. The image of the photographer with an enormous beaming grin [*Fig. 1*] is a favourite and one that I believe reflects the man and his talent. Like many of his pictures it displays a relaxed informality, uncommon in the stiff portraits of his day. He was apparently a popular figure, in demand as an elocutionist and teller of humorous stories. His keen sense of humour shines out from the photograph and we instantly like him.

Fig. 1: *J. F. Lloyd, late self-portrait.*

Fig. 2: *J. F. Lloyd, self-portrait, c.1905.*

Lloyd and his family lived at 10 Morley Street, Carmarthen, where he is recorded as an insurance agent. The move to Picton Terrace was clearly a move up the social ladder, implying an increase in income, possibly from a new post in the probate service. Although he took photographs while living in Morley Street, the majority of the collection was taken after the move to Picton Terrace. Photography was an expensive pastime and the sudden increase in output and the construction of a studio and darkroom, also imply an increase in income. The second self portrait [*Fig. 2*] was taken in his new studio and he is clearly younger than in the 'laughing portrait'. It is a portrait of a confident and affluent man, taking a pride in his new social position. The family having a formal tea in the garden of number 19 Picton Terrace [*Fig. 3*] was taken at about the same time and is another favourite. The picture is balanced and well composed, with the rose arch acting as a beautiful frame for the group. The garden steps lead the eye to the family group, positioned at the centre of the

Fig. 3: *The photographer's family, c.1905.*

Fig. 4: *Funeral at Moriah Chapel, Llansteffan, 1910.*

Fig. 5: *Pallbearers, Moriah Chapel, Llansteffan, 1910.*

image. The photographer's artistic eye is apparent. While the group is actually posed and the picture structured, the sitters are relaxed, pouring tea and serving food. The composition has a modern feel, as the photographer has not just recorded the situation, but also observed it. Again, like the self portrait, the group, wearing their best clothes, is confident and the new affluence is apparent.

As well as portraits, Lloyd was keen to record events of the day and street scenes around the town. He seems to have been able to move around at events taking candid photographs with the ease of a present-day photo-journalist, despite his cumbersome equipment. There is an intriguing group of photographs taken at a funeral, an event rarely recorded by photographers. Llansteffan Castle [*Fig. 4*] is clearly visible, silhouetted against the skyline in one of the two photographs selected for this article. The remainder of the group show the cortège leaving the house, which could be Pilroath near Llansteffan and various shots taken from different angles in the cemetery. The funeral took place at Moriah Chapel, Llansteffan, in the early years of the 20th century and certainly before 1911, when the chapel was refurbished and the large window inserted. Mourners are packed in around the monuments and, remarkably, are all ignoring the photographer. Both sexes are represented at the funeral, although there does seem to be a

degree of separation. Gentlemen wearing their top hats would imply that the deceased was a person of note in the community. Access to the cemetery from the road was like today, via a long set of steep steps and would have presented a challenge for the pall bearers. The coffin is clearly being carried on a wooden bier [*Fig. 5*] by ten of them. The impressive array of floral tributes is again testimony to the status of the deceased. It is feasible that the funeral recorded is that of Esther Harries of Pilroath, who died in August 1910. This group of images is indicative of Lloyd's innovative approach to photography and his understanding of its role in creating records. These are rare and important images.

The photographer was keen to record sporting events and his action shot of a rugby match [*Fig. 6*] is im-

Fig. 6: *Rugby match, Carmarthen, c.1905.*

83

Fig. 7: *The start of a motorcycle race, Carmarthen Park, 1905.*

Fig. 8: *Motorcyclist, Carmarthen Park, 1905.*

pressive. He appears to have set the camera very near to the scrum, presumably hoping that the ball came out on the right side! Again, as with the funeral, he has a knack of positioning himself unobtrusively and close to the action. The cumbersome boots and baggy shorts held up by heavy leather belts are clear to see and are certainly not performance enhancing. Carmarthen Park was opened to the public in 1900 and with its cycle track was soon to become the focus of sporting and other events in the town. Lloyd recorded cycle racing, motorcycle racing, athletics and aerial stunts that were taking place in the park. The two photographs that I have chosen show a motorcycling event that took place in the park at Whitsun 1905. In this instance, the start line up [*Fig. 7*] is posed for the photographer or at least has been delayed for a few seconds to allow the picture to be taken. Everyone is clearly aware of his presence in this picture. The grandstand is full, indicating the popularity of this relatively new sport. The rider in the foreground is thought to be Bert Yates, a works rider for Humber, who had ridden at Pendine the previous day and won. Bert and his bike are the focus of the next photograph [*Fig. 8*], which is of particular interest because of the other rider on the right of the picture.

This is Mansel Davies, who in August 1905 won a race at Pendine on a Humber Motorcycle, possibly the one in the photograph. His brother Walter was employed at Humber's Coventry Works and borrowed the bike for the event. Mansel Davies was from Pembrokeshire and the founder of the family haulage firm, which is still in business today.

Before the days of municipal swimming pools, river swimming was a common and popular practice. Carmarthen's local press regularly recorded accidents and fatalities in the Twyi. Lloyd's photograph shows the *Forth*, a paddle-steamer [*Fig. 9*], coming up river with the main line railway bridge, the White Bridge, in the background. The bridge was demolished in 1911 and replaced by a bascule bridge. The six swimmers in the foreground are not only risking the perils of a high tide on a fast flowing river, but are dangerously close to the paddles and drag of the vessel. The *Forth* is heavily laden with passengers. A regular visitor to Carmarthen, she would occasionally stop at Llansteffan and Ferryside to collect day trippers and return them to Carmarthen.

Carmarthen Quay from the Bulwarks side of the river was a popular view for engravers, artists and later photographers. If a couple of coracle men could be persuaded

Fig. 9: *The 'Forth' paddle-steamer on the Tywi, c.1905.*

Fig. 10: *Carmarthen Quay from the Bulwarks, c.1905.*

to pose in the foreground, then the image was complete. J. F. Lloyd continued this tradition and his photograph [*Fig. 10*] became a popular postcard. The image is well constructed to show the quay and river at high tide within the landscape of the Tywi Valley, with both Llangunnor and Merlin's Hill visible on the right. The photograph can be dated to around 1905, as the five gables of the J. B. Arthurs Corn and Flour warehouses are visible at the bridge end of the quay. Towy Works, which dominates the view today, was not built until 1911.

The photograph of Nott Square [*Fig. 11*] is another excellent example of Lloyd's work in recording the streets and sights of Carmarthen. It is as always well-composed and a pleasing image. There is an element of humour in the composition with the larger than life statue dominating and apparently pointing at the deliberately posed portly gentleman in the scene. The monument to Bishop Ferrar, erected in 1902, is visible inside the cast-iron railings of Nott's monument. Ferrar was burnt at the stake in 1555, during the reign of Queen Mary, in what was then the market square. 1905 marked the three hundred and fiftieth anniversary of his death and it is likely that the photograph was taken either in 1902 or 1905.

The closer we examine and research this collection, the more apparent it becomes that the collection covers a very short time span of probably less than a decade, while the majority of the images actually fall into a five year period 1900-1905. Lloyd was clearly a very talented photographer and it would be interesting to

know why he stopped or indeed if he stopped taking photographs. Are we just looking at a small part of his output that fortunately survived?

Fig. 11: *Nott Square, Carmarthen, c.1905.*

ACKNOWLEDGEMENTS

I am grateful to Dara Jasumani, Ann Dorsett and Anne Wright of Carmarthenshire County Museum for their assistance in researching this collection of photographs, and also to Lynn Hughes who identified individuals in the motorcycle photographs.

J. F. Jones's Slides and Photographs of Carmarthenshire Country Houses

Thomas Lloyd

J. F. Jones and I shared a compulsive common interest: that of recording through photography what was vanishing from the fabric of a rapidly changing world. That world for both of us was primarily restricted to south west Wales. J.F. was doing it thirty years ahead of me and it was only thanks to Terry James's rescue of J.F.'s photograph and slide collection that I realised that I had been following so very much in his footsteps without knowing it. Terry wrote about the challenge of salvaging, cleaning, copying and cataloguing as much of it as he could in the *Carmarthenshire Antiquary*, 2006, and his selfless labour there needs to be saluted again in this Memorial Volume. His dedication and technical expertise has put safely on permanent record a collection that is a prime resource for society and buildings in 1960s and early 1970s Carmarthenshire.

J.F. was better at his hobby than me, because his range was wider: he covered not just threatened and decaying historic buildings but towns, scenery, trains and cars, local events, people – the whole world around him. I just stuck to buildings. J.F. was a museum curator with a professional breadth of vision, perhaps one ahead of his time in realising the transience of so much. What he disastrously failed to realise was that 1960s photographs and slide transparencies were also pretty transient: colours fade, damp distorts, mould grows with enthusiasm and the plastic wallets then used for storing photographs rotted them in damp conditions. Sadly, the great majority had gone beyond restoring but plenty of unique records have happily survived thanks to Terry's invaluable work.

I met J.F. only once or twice in my early teens but already with a most un-childlike interest in the past. My mother would come shopping in Carmarthen and I was

allowed off to go to Quay Street to discover and explore the musty old museum where J.F. reigned. It was a perfect time capsule in itself of an age well before my day, with blobs of broken Roman pottery found in Carmarthen in glass-topped cases with illegible pen and ink labels faded out and curled up in the sun. Strangely enough all this fascinated me. Of course being quite early on weekday mornings, I was the only person there and I remember on the first occasion J.F. emerging from his office in the shadows at the back to interrogate me (as a good inquisitive curator should) as to why I was intruding on his almost private territory. Fortunately, I had already spotted that my grandfather had donated the old (and to me alarming) Mari Lwyd sealed in a tall glass case, so with reference to this I established my youthful credentials and survived my examination (unlike the Mari Lwyd, which had completely dessicated over the years in its sealed glass case and crumbled to dust when the museum was moved to Abergwili). I do not recall much conversation on any visit but I was too young and then much away from Wales at school and he had gone before I could ever know him better.

Curating a county museum in the 1960s was not a glamorous job and J.F. did not write enough in national journals to be much remembered beyond Carmarthenshire. But he was a knowledgeable local antiquary who did his best with the miniscule resources at his disposal and he was for a number of years secretary of the Antiquarian Society. But now, thanks to the recovery of his photograph and slide collections, he takes an esteemed place among the recorders of our county's past.

When Terry first showed me these a few years ago, I was astonished, even peering through their films of mould. Here were many images of buildings that greatly

Fig. 1: *Tregib, outside Llandeilo, 1968.*

interested me, either demolished before I got to them or much diminished in the interval. Others had been violently modernised in the days before conservation building practices had arrived: few of course in those days were listed. Those were times of casual destruction, though at least partly based on the honest belief that the new age could do better. A week may be along time in politics but twenty years utterly transforms a building in decay. The decorative bits that tell so much are the first to go.

Antiquaries are always drawn to ruins and the faded grandeur of past ages. It is in their blood. My dim memory of J.F. was of someone rather formal but his eye for a good photograph was definitely romantic. No squared-up elevational shots here in the correct manner of the Royal Commission's National Monument Record, but rather forty five degree angles from a proper distance (sometimes with a telephoto lens) to show the all-important setting and the genius of the place. Terry also paid full tribute to this in his 2006 article. J.F.'s slide of now demolished Tregib outside Llandeilo taken in 1968 (*Fig. 1*) would have made a classic picture

postcard shot with its reflecting water and pink rhododendron part obscuring the building but blending with the colours of the lime wash and brick chimney. Here is an artist at work rather than curator. It makes me wish to have known him better.

Likewise his shot of isolated Cennen Tower (*Fig. 2*) is a model of careful composition. One can sense that J.F. walked all round it looking for the perfect angle and he chose not to show its front, even though more imposing and complete, but rather the broken side, to emphasise the ruination and empty landscape. It is a photograph of prize-winning quality, with the eye being led from the low stump of building on the left in the deep shade, diagonally up to the entrance tower catching the late afternoon sun. Little is known about this mysterious place, though dark rumours abound as to why Dr Pridham chose to build his lonely castle here in the early 1840s. Very few pictures of it survive and soon after J.F. visited in 1960 or 1961 it was demolished.

Two much more conventional houses that he photographed just in time were Pibwr Wen in Llangunnor and Abermarlais in Llansadwrn, both elegant, square

Fig. 2: *Cennen Tower.*

Regency designs near the banks of the Tywi. The first (*Figs. 3 & 4*) disappeared soon after J.F. visited in 1963 and perhaps he went with that impending knowledge, though the house looks in good enough order in his pictures. I had never been able to find any image of it at all when researching for my book *The Lost Houses of Wales* in the mid 1980s and it was not until a fine 1820s oil painting of the house by the then Carmarthen-based artist Hugh Hughes turned up at auction and was pur-chased by the National Library of Wales that we knew what an attractive and neat house it was. Hughes painted it as new built in 1822; J.F. captured it dying and it had not changed an iota in between.

A house like Pibwr Wen today would be high on many people's idea of the perfect home, carefully planned and easy to run, with all the fireplaces against the back wall of each room, allowing for a central, almost hidden square chimney stack – a great advance

Fig. 3: *Pibwr Wen, Llangunnor.*

Fig. 4: *Pibwr Wen, Llangunnor.*

89

Fig. 5: *Abermarlais.*

in design which came soon before 1800, allowing for the pleasing hipped roof to be quite uncluttered. The side elevation facing the Tywi had its lower windows set in blind arches, a sophisticated Regency feature, which would have showed well to the many people who still travelled up and down the river in the nineteenth century.

Abermarlais (*Fig. 5*) was an altogether more important place, though designed on exactly the same principles with a big central chimney stack and a hipped roof. It was built earlier than Pibwr Wen in 1805 for Admiral Sir Thomas Foley whose health had not allowed him to join his old friend Nelson for the Battle of Trafalgar. In the 1970s when I had wanted to see it, the house was off-limits, being the very private home of the reclusive Miss Campbell Davys and her thirty cats, none of whom welcomed visitors. Rather like Miss Haversham of Dickens' *Great Expectations* and indeed just like the late Miss Woods of Cardigan Castle, the place was falling down around her while she lived there.

Soon after she died in 1980, the house was set on fire. I clambered about in the ruined shell but it was impossible to take meaningful photographs, as huge laurels had been allowed to grow right up against the entrance front, which had not burned away, whereas the inside was quite destroyed and open to the sky, leaving only the planning of the small circular entrance vestibule to be admired. This would have greeted visitors, for Aber-

marlais had been a finely-designed house by the London architect Thomas Bedford, who chose to settle in Llandeilo on the back of this commission and remained in the area as a practicing architect until retiring to Laugharne in the 1820s. (He could therefore have designed Pibwr Wen too, though the Carmarthen architect David Morgan is more likely).

There are therefore not many pictures of Abermarlais. The shell was demolished in 1982 and I had to put up with a miserable snapshot of my own of the burnt-out back elevation for *The Lost Houses of Wales* in 1986. For some reason, it had also escaped attention earlier in the century: there do not for example seem to be any Edwardian picture postcards. J.F. photographed it from across the field on higher ground with a telephoto lens. The slide has now faded but it provides a unique view of the still complete house, showing it in its snug setting with its unkempt garden trees and shrubs and the southern hillsides of the Tywi valley beyond.

No-one alive today ever saw Ffrwd at Llangyndeyrn with a roof on. It has been a shell for the best part of two hundred years, having been abandoned in 1804. Francis Jones wrote up its history in the *Carmarthenshire Antiquary*, 1980, and on a visit had noticed that even after all that time, a little ornamental plasterwork still survived in a sheltered corner. The house had only been built 1747, so lasted as a home for scarcely fifty years but it had been constructed with great strength,

Fig. 6: *Ffrwd, Llangyndeyrn.*

standing as a virtually complete shell even when I got there in the 1980s. What had changed in the twenty years or so since J.F. photographed it (*Fig. 6*) was that the ivy shown here had completely overwhelmed the standing structure, so that I could not see the well-laid masonry and well-squared corners that had gone into this compact double pile building. In fact, just as Abermarlais and Pibwr Wen were fine local examples of Regency house design, so Ffrwd is a very good instance of the previous and ubiquitous local plan form with parallel front and back ranges, each separately roofed with deep roof valley between and chimneys on each of the four gable ends. Ffrwd in fact is an early example, perhaps even one of the very earliest in the area to be built from scratch to this plan, as several others of this mid eighteeenth century date are in fact earlier single ranges with an added front or back one constructed in parallel. The gaunt but rather striking composition captured by J.F. is therefore important and certainly the best view of this historically interesting house.

J.F. had no time to write up a commentary to his photography: at least none survives. It would have been fascinating to know therefore what he thought of the decaying house at Pontbren Arath (between Llandeilo and Bethlehem) with it slipping limestone tiled roof and big protruding gable chimneys (*Fig. 7*). The house is Glanareth, a small mansion in its eighteenth century heyday and what a heyday that was. From here the

Fig. 7: *Pontbren Arath, between Llandeilo and Bethlehem.*

notorious William Powell caused mayhem in the area with upper-class thuggery – bullying men, seducing women, beating up the locals and no doubt stealing from them all. One winter's evening in 1770 his enemies sent a gang of ruffians round to murder him and his repeatedly-stabbed body was left lying on the parlour floor. Many accounts of this grisly story and its aftermath have been written, recounting how the murderers were traced through the prints of their hobnail boots in the snow. A hundred years later when the details were blurred and exaggerated, it was assumed that Powell's house must have been a grander mansion (like that of his equally bad Ceredigion contemporary, Sir Herbert Lloyd of Peterwell) and had therefore been demolished. Francis Jones followed this account in his *Historic Carmarthenshire Homes* in 1987, writing that only a few stones remain to mark the site near the present farmstead. But this farmstead was the mansion and it was in its front room that Powell met his end. It had been built by Powell in the 1760s and still has a date-stone with his name above the front door: it is easy to forget how modest the houses of the lesser gentry were in remoter areas. What one wonders is whether J.F. knew he was recording the murder house or whether his artistic temperament was simply drawn to photographing an old building in decay. Either way, it is as well he did, as the place had slid a great deal further into dereliction by the time I 'discovered' it and realised that I was then able to stand (not without trepidation) in the very place the deed was done. The house has been done

up again now with a newer look, which has probably exorcised the past, but whether by luck or judgement, J.F. has preserved for us a real piece of local history.

Even more deserving of praise was J.F.'s appreciation that change is also loss. If a house is altered, even much for the better, it is not the house it was before. Often the changes are easy to see and are quickly understood when trying to work out the history of a house, but sometimes it is so well done that photographic evidence is the only key. Two examples are illustrated here. The first is Gardde in St Clears, clearly an old house, and helpfully with a datestone of 1697. But it is hard to appreciate what parts of it are of that date when passing by it now, as it is of irregular outline and clearly added to, with all the windows changed. J.F. however stopped by, camera in hand in 1963, when the house was being entirely re-rendered, a once in a lifetime opportunity. What his slide reveals (*Fig. 8*) is that the protruding right hand front is an Edwardian brick addition. Now the house makes sense. The gabled central bay was the 1697 tall storeyed porch with equal wings set back each side – a classic seventeenth century arrangement in fact, of which few examples survive now in the county. (Terry illustrated another in his 2006 article: Coalbrook near Pontyberem in the act of being demolished, yet again an important moment that J.F. had captured.) What will not however show up here, as it is too faint without a magnifying glass, is the outline of blocked 1697 windows on the left-hand side. The single one shown here (somewhat enlarged) once had a pair beside it and there

Fig. 8: *Gardde, St Clears.*

Fig. 9: *Church House, Llangadog.*

was a smaller one above it. Not even the eye of faith can detect the line of a matching upstairs one but the branches partly block the area. What J.F. recorded will probably never be seen again in our lifetimes. And he surely knew it. He must often have moved fast to beat the unforgiving minute – and roads and transport were nothing like they are today.

Finally, Church House, Llangadog (*Fig. 9*). Dr Walters will still be remembered with great affection by many in the area, an old-fashioned practitioner who knew all his patients and called on them regularly when they were ill. When not helping his patients to stand up, he enjoyed travelling to demolition sales of houses that were being pulled down. No doubt he saw salvage as an act of life-saving. He certainly gave new life to the fine four columned classical porch which he purchased from a demolition sale somewhere not too far over the Welsh border in England. Alas his widow could not remember where that was when I inquired. J.F. photographed it being erected in the early 1970s, which gave me great pleasure to study, as I had seen Edwardian postcard views down the street which showed it was not there then and close inspection shows that, great asset to the streetscape that it is, the proportions are not quite right

for the house it sits against. A drum or two has been missed out from each of the columns to keep the height down below the first floor windows. Without this knowledge, architectural historians of the future would have been stumped. It is a fine thing and J.F. shows once again the happy knack of being in the right place at the vital moment, in this instance to perpetuate an act of creativity rather than loss.

This brief article considers only nine out of the 1,600 images that Terry managed to save from J.F.'s amazing collection. The tragedy is that the whole collection of slides and photographs was once a staggering 11,000 in number. Only a little over ten per cent survived. What does remain only saddens us as to what does not. But the past only ever survives fragmentarily (and frankly, we would be quite overwhelmed by it if it all did: think how big the Record Office would need to be if every old deed survived). It is a magnificent collection nonetheless with its coverage of every walk of local life, including many fine houses still in good order. But the vital thing to remember and appreciate is that Terry saved everything that we have of it, in his own unpaid time and for the good of others. He already knew his own time was running out as he brought life back to it.

Nantymwyn, A Carmarthenshire Klondike

Tina Carr & Annemarie Schöne

This photo essay charts the industrial remains now stranded in a remote upland landscape. Nantymwyn, a lead and zinc mine six miles north of Llandovery (NGR SN787447), is presently surrounded by encroaching afforestation. Like many sites of industrial archaeology, it has been abandoned to the elements, left to decay and its rich past largely forgotten.

It was the most important metal mine in South Wales owned and worked by the landowner, the Earl of Cawdor.[1] While profitable; during the years 1775-1797 and 1824-1900, the recorded sales of lead ore were 80,000 tons with the most profitable year being 1779 when the mine made £12,526 13s 11d profit on 2,500 tons of ore raised. Later the mine was leased to Adventurers and small mining companies when the lodes were exhausted and new veins needed to be discovered.

Fig.1: *Nantymwyn and White Hall farmstead, 19th January 1989.*
(Photograph reproduced by permission of Dyfed Archaeological Trust).

This aerial photograph was taken by Terence James as part of a programme of recording the condition of scheduled sites. The shot shows the southern-most reaches of the mine excavations with the Sulphide Mill in the top right hand corner and the foundations of a post mediaeval farmstead (White Hall) situated on the south side of the Nant y Bai valley, a minor tributary of the River Tywi.

Fig. 2: *Nantymwyn, Sulphide Corporation Mill and New Shaft from Angred Shaft Dump, c.1930.*
(Photograph from the National Museum of Wales' collections).

In 1925 the Sulphide Corporation, then one of the world's foremost Lead–Zinc companies and since absorbed by the Rio Tinto Zinc Corporation, was sourcing concentrate for their zinc smelter at Seaton Carew, Hartlepool. They built a power plant and floatation mill at Nantymwyn capable of treating 125 Tonnes of blende (lead ore) a day. The mill went into production in June 1930 but operated for only 4 months due to the collapse in the ore price brought about by the great depression of 1931/32. The company abandoned the property altogether in 1932.

Fig. 3: *The Carmarthenshire Antiquarians visit Nantymwyn on the 15 April 1978. The group is lined up on the site of the Sulphide Mill prominent to the right of centre of the photograph in Fig. 2 above.*
(Photograph from the Terrence James archive).

Fig. 4: *Sulphide Mill, 15th April 1978.*
(Photograph from the Terrence James archive).

Fig. 5: *Sulphide Mill Detail, 15th April 1978.*
(Photograph from the Terrence James archive).

Fig. 6: *Nantymwyn Mine Site 1989.*
(Photograph from the Tina Carr and Annemarie Schöne Archive, Tregroes).

The Nantymwyn Mine Site photograph (Fig. 6) was made concurrently with 'Pigs & Ingots, the Lead Silver Mines of Cardiganshire' a photographic survey of the industrial archaeology of that county begun in 1987, funded by the Arts Council of Wales and the Photographers Gallery, London.[2]

Nantymwyn, was surveyed but was not included in the exhibition or book of the same name simply because its location was outside the remit of the project. It remains an enthralling if enigmatic site, very difficult to interpret due to the many different phases of work and mining techniques employed, from gravity to the later floatation methods designed to extract ever-diminishing percentages of ore from the tailings.

Fig. 7: *Nantymwyn, Angred Shaft Engine House 1989.*
(Photograph from the Tina Carr and Annemarie Schöne Archive, Tregroes.)

This eighteenth century shaft was sunk to a depth of 10 fathoms initially but later sunk deeper to the 35 fathom level. It is one of only four surviving examples of engine houses with chimney stacks in Wales. Parys Mountain, Anglesey and Frongoch, Ceredigion are of the Cornish variety where the stack is incorporated in to the construction. Nantymwyn and Cwmsymlog, also in Ceredigion, differ in that the stacks are completely separate constructions, probably later additions, after the use of the water power from a wheel had ceased. The function of the stack was initially that of a flue for a steam boiler and later modified to ventilate the mine workings.

NOTES

1. G. W. Hall, *Metal Mines of Southern Wales* (Griffin Publications, 1993).

2. T. Carr & Annemarie Schöne, *Pigs and Ingots: the Lead/Silver Mines of Cardiganshire* (Y Lolfa Cyf., Talybont, 1993).

The Present and Future
of Aerial Archaeology in Carmarthenshire

Toby Driver

Despite trying hard to get airborne in the drought year of 1976 it proved too difficult with a lot of very bad visibility throughout the summer. I did try to get into the air with a local flyer who kept his C150 [Cessna 150] in a shed next to his quarry business on Mynydd Crwbin. He used a field with a decidedly hairy cross slope with numerous dips. The chosen day was windy and murky and I urgently wanted to get some shots of the adjacent Mynydd Llangyndeyrn because the heather had been burnt off. He decided to have a go on his own first. He got up but was soon back with sweat running off his brow and shaking his head. That was the end of that.

Terry James, recollecting the early days
of aerial archaeology in west Wales,
unpublished note, January 2006.

INTRODUCTION

The aerial archaeology of Carmarthenshire was discussed as recently as 2000 by Terry James in the Millennium Volume of *The Carmarthenshire Antiquary*[1] in a paper which reviewed many years of discovery and steady progress. Over the years this quiet countryside has revealed many substantial, hitherto lost, monuments. The present contribution firstly reflects upon Terry (and Heather) James' contribution to the aerial archaeology of Carmarthenshire. It then moves on to consider how the geography of the county influences reconnaissance patterns before dealing, in the main part of the paper, with recent progress in the field of the Carmarthenshire Iron Age.

AERIAL ARCHAEOLOGY IN WEST WALES:
ONE MAN'S PROGRESS

Terry James' pioneering tenacity in the early days of aerial archaeology in west Wales was an essential ingredient in pushing the plough-levelled archaeology of this region further up the national agenda. Other aerial archaeologists had overflown the region and published their results, notably Professor J. K. S. St Joseph[2] for the Cambridge University Committee for Aerial Photography (CUCAP), who first overflew west Wales to record its geology and archaeology in 1948. Archaeological sites were also included within the work of general aerial photographers who flew to record the landscapes of west Wales and whose work illustrated regional guides of the 1960s and 1970s.[3] Terry's vision for the application of aerial photography for archaeology in west Wales was given prominence in 1980 by his publication (with Doug Simpson) of *Ancient West Wales from the Air*,[4] a booklet produced from the results of a handful of flights over Dyfed, which served nonetheless to show the considerable promise this method of prospection held for Welsh archaeology. More than three decades later it remains something of a milestone. Later, his many archaeological discoveries during the drought summer of 1984[5] sent shockwaves through the archaeological fraternity.[6]

Published archaeological literature pertaining to aerial discoveries very often overlooks the considerable role of the individual, their personality and perseverance, in the discovery of lost monuments at the extremes of light and season. The summer of 1984 saw an unusual combination of early summer silage cropping, then rain on extremely dry ground, yielding late regrowth of crop-

Fig. 1: *Close to optimum conditions for aerial photography. Low light and exceptional visibility on an autumn afternoon in 2007 near Talley (centre), looking south-east.*
(Crown Copyright: RCAHMW, AP_2007_3391).

marks in weeds and grass in stubble fields[5] repeated with remarkable effect in mid Wales in 2006.[7] Funding for Terry's flights was clawed together to provide a handful of hours in the air. The results were dramatic, and some of Terry's buried concentric antenna enclosures[8] and Romano-British farms have still refused to show so well – or at all – in two decades of reconnaissance since the remarkable summer of 1984. Terry recorded some of his thoughts and experiences of this time in early 2006 (opening quotation) but what we cannot see in his famous pictures of Llangan Church,[9] among others, are the breathless drives to the airfield on summer afternoons, the struggle to keep composed and focused in the cockpit when such archaeological wonders are being revealed in the landscape below, and the late returns home after dark to process film and document the day's discoveries. Without this persistent and insightful individual in the aircraft's passenger seat at crucial times during the 1970s and 1980s the archaeological record of west Wales would still have major omissions; this must not be forgotten when we casually review Terry's more famous discoveries, now so deeply ingrained in the archaeological story of west Wales.

CARMARTHENSHIRE: EXPERIENCING THE COUNTY FROM THE AIR

Carmarthenshire is one of the most varied of Welsh counties in terms of its geographical reach and variation, together with its archaeology, containing within its boundaries an astonishing array of landscapes. Conceptually there are numerous agenda to consider in planning an archaeological flight on a given day. In the south of the county one already has a full list of targets for a reconnaissance flight; the Taf and Tywi estuaries with their great castles and mediaeval towns overlooking areas of intertidal fishtraps and wrecks, giving way eastwards to the military archaeology of Pendine and the industrial and urban landscapes of the great ports centred on Llanelli. Moving north, between the coast and the Twyi valley, the landscape of undulating plateaux and numerous villages and towns is difficult country, slow to reveal any substantial traces of Roman roads or plough-levelled defended enclosures to augment the sparse pattern of already-known monuments. Yet further to the east, inland of Ammanford, one climbs into the wonderful hill country of Mynydd Du/the Black Mountain, crowded with mediaeval castles, deserted settlements, prehistoric sites and industrial remnants of the limestone industry, splendidly recorded by Terry in the past under winter conditions.[10]

The great Tywi corridor, running east from Carmarthen towards Llandovery, is a natural draw for the aerial archaeologist. Terry and Heather James charted the Roman road along this natural thoroughfare and there is still plenty of first-class archaeology to record during the changing seasons. However, more recent aerial discoveries on the peripheries of the Tywi valley starkly illustrate the bias which can affect the task of exploratory reconnaissance, the aerial archaeologist naturally being drawn on most occasions to the riches of a 'honeypot' landscape in the centre of the valley. Thus it is that the undulating foothills of Mynydd Du around Myddfai to the east, as well as the hilly country to the north of a line

linking Carmarthen to Llandovery, are still yielding significant earthwork discoveries. Save for a concentration of archaeological aerial photographs of the Pumsaint/Dolaucothi landscape, Talley Abbey and its environs, and work along the archaeologically productive fringes of the Teifi valley in the northern part of Carmarthenshire, aerial archaeology has only recently made inroads into the hills and uplands of northern Carmarthenshire – with impressive results. What is briefly reviewed in this paper is the recent progress in aerial archaeology over Carmarthenshire from the end of the 1990s to the present day. It draws only on results from Royal Commission reconnaissance, although the Dyfed Archaeological Trust made numerous grant-aided and independent flights over the county in the same period.

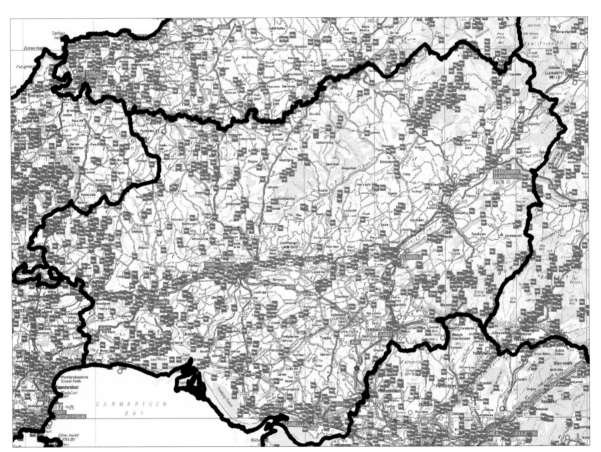

Fig. 2: *Royal Commission oblique aerial photographs, taken for archaeological purposes since 1986, shown in the context of the county of Carmarthenshire. The Roman road along the Tywi valley, and west into Pembrokeshire, is marked by a line of intensive reconnaissance, as is the Dolaucothi landscape (top right), the Mynydd Du/Black Mountain uplands (far right) and the south coast industrial docklands and mediaeval towns around Kidwelly. Great swathes of southern and northern Carmarthenshire have few, if any, specialist oblique aerial photographs. Future flights should aim to redress this imbalance.*

Fig. 3: *The Allt Aber-mangoed defended enclosure near Pumsaint at the moment of discovery in 2002.*
It remains the only later prehistoric settlement recorded near the Roman mines at Dolaucothi.
(Crown Copyright: RCAHMW, DI2007_0184).

REVEALING THE CARMARTHENSHIRE IRON AGE

Carmarthenshire has many substantial Iron Age hill-forts, not least giants like Carn Goch and Gron Gaer, or Merlin's Hill, yet there are great swathes of the county where such remains are largely or entirely absent.[11] It is the job of the aerial archaeologist to continually revisit these archaeologically 'blank' tracts in different seasons and lighting conditions – both low, raking winter light to reveal surface topography and high summer days when the hilltops are parched, revealing buried ditches – in order to test whether the lack of visible monuments represents a genuine pattern of past settlement.

In recent years there have been several important, and quite unexpected, discoveries from the Iron Age which have shown that the complete map of Iron Age Carmarthenshire cannot yet be drawn. Chief amongst these was the first evidence for pre-Roman enclosed settlement in the long-studied Roman mining landscape surrounding Dolaucothi and Pumsaint. As if to reinforce the need for continued aerial reconnaissance in Wales,

and demonstrating how easily aerial archaeologists' eyes can be drawn in a single direction when flying near a 'honeypot' site, a fine Iron Age fort was discovered on a hill overlooking the Cothi valley and Roman mining landscape (NPRN 307331).[12,13] Dolaucothi and its upland environs have been quite intensively flown by generations of aerial archaeologists, both to survey the scheduled Roman leats which link the mines to the hinterland to the north-east and to prospect for un-recorded fragments of the Roman mining landscape. A winter flight by the author on 5th December 2002, from Haverfordwest Airport, was replanned en-route to accommodate worsening patches of weather and shift-ing blocks of cloud. Clearing conditions in late after-noon saw extreme December sunlight strike out over the hills around Dolaucothi, illuminating the land below with a rare quality and direction of light. Thus it was that the Allt Aber-mangoed enclosure was revealed beneath the aircraft. Its significance was clear at the moment of discovery, so there was a chance to share some of the excitement with the pilot. Aside from the

Fig. 4: *The Sugar Loaf hillfort, at the moment of discovery in 2001. The rampart enclosing the northern (near) side of the knife-edge summit is particularly clear.*
(Crown Copyright: RCAHMW, DI2005_0426).

'lost' hillfort quarried away from the summit of Pen y Ddinas, near Llansawel Talley (NPRN 406812), no other Iron Age settlements were known for miles around. Subsequent flights over the site, in good winter light and even under melting snow, have failed to show it again with similar clarity. By good fortune, the site lies within the boundaries of the National Trust estate, albeit by only a few tens of metres, assuring its long-term future.

A further surprising discovery (NPRN 307331)[14] was seen during reconnaissance in 2001 at the Sugar Loaf, a prominent knife-like ridge which dominates a pass on the Carmarthenshire/Powys border. This mountain pass, used both by the modern Llandovery-Llanwrtyd Wells road and the Heart of Wales railway line, also provides a useful passageway for aircraft returning to Haverfordwest Airport from central Wales. Passing by the Sugar Loaf hill on this particular flight, a chance angle of the light revealed a curving rampart around the narrow summit, together with additional cross-banks protecting an entrance at the east. A subsequent field visit confirmed the existence of a denuded gateway, a broad summit terrace and house platforms dug into the north side of the ridge. The previous lack of recognition of this monument, the most easterly hillfort in Carmarthenshire, is all the more remarkable given its position alongside a popular picnic spot and busy road, from where the ridge is climbed by thousands of visitors each year to enjoy the exceptional views.

Further discoveries of Iron Age hillforts and defended enclosures in recent years show that there is still more prospection to do. Quite substantial forts, their ramparts denuded by erosion and cultivation, almost certainly still remain to be found, as shown by the discovery of the bivallate hillfort at Penrhiwyruchain above Cilycwm (NPRN 403827). Occasionally, summer droughts penetrate far enough into the green Carmarthenshire hills to bring the promise of cropmark discoveries there.

Fig. 5: *The Penrhiwyruchain hillfort, a 2.8 hectare hillfort discovered near Cilycwm, only some 2.5km north of the Roman fort at Llandovery. It was initially discovered in the winter of 2005 but this view from autumn 2007 confirmed the presence of denuded bivallate defences on the eastern (near-side) slopes below the summit.*
(Crown Copyright: RCAHMW, AP_2007_3470).

Fig. 6: *Hafod Farm defended enclosure, originally discovered from the air.*
(Crown copyright: RCAHMW, AP_2007_0760).

Conditions were dry enough in July 2006 for crop-marks in grass to be recorded in the hills approaching Llandovery. A particularly rewarding discovery was made at Bronygaer, Llansadwrn (NPRN 404677) in the form of the cropmarks of a polygonal univallate hillfort with bivallate outworks to the north-east, perfectly confirm-ing the previously unexplained 'gaer' place-name evidence.

The further study and investigation of these discoveries is more problematic. While there have been recent pro-jects by the Dyfed Archaeological Trust to investigate Iron Age and Romano-British settlements, as part of the Cadw-funded pan-Wales Defended Enclosures Project,[11] resources for intensive field survey and excavation can-not keep pace with all the research questions that are raised by the landscapes of later prehistoric Wales. A case in point is the slight upland enclosure at Hafod Farm (NPRN 308799), just under 2km north of Carreg Cennen Castle. This probable defended enclosure, originally discovered from the air, has been spared any destructive cultivation in the past. It is quite unmonu-mental compared to an average hillfort. Whether or not it represents the footings for a palisaded enclosure or perhaps an unfinished settlement abandoned during construction, the site remains unusual in the Iron Age of west Wales and is the type of lightly-enclosed site normally only seen as a cropmark. This rare site (and others like it) survives as an earthwork in the modern, intensively farmed landscape, through pure good for-tune.

CONTINUING PROMISE

Carmarthenshire has always been an immensely rich county, archaeologically and historically. Steadily, over the last three decades or so, eyes of aerial archaeologists have had the opportunity to survey nearly all its parts in different lights and seasons. The Romans have long dominated the aerial agenda,[15,16] and the continued promise of further discoveries of Roman forts to add to that at Dinefwr Park,[17] together with the lengths of Roman road yet to be firmly established, means that much aerial exploration still remains to be done. In the case of Roman roads in particular the aerial archae-ologist remains heavily reliant on new information from trusted researchers on the ground, such as Hugh Toller whose indefatigable fieldwork has verified and extended many discoveries originally made from the air.[18] Similarly, the archaeology of the early mediaeval Church yielded extraordinary results for Terry James during many years of exploratory reconnaissance, informed by parallel place-name and map-based research.[19,20]

This paper has demonstrated that the prehistoric period still has much to offer for the flying archae-ologist. With hillforts and defended enclosures being steadily rediscovered over the years, one wonders where the major lowland Bronze Age barrow cemeteries may lie, to rival those known in other parts of Wales. Historic parklands and gardens are found in great numbers in the county, and there is little doubt that there are still new discoveries to be made. The Tywi valley in Carmar-thenshire is of considerable interest to garden historians, being home to the gardens at Aberglasney and Middle-ton Hall, as well as at Dinefwr Park. Royal Commission aerial photography west of Nantgaredig identified the low earthworks of a formal garden extending onto the floodplain fronting Allt-y-gog (NPRN 266166).[21] These are of particular interest as they do not align on the present house and were bisected by the construction of a railway embankment. The earthworks require further research to establish their credentials as belonging to a now-vanished garden. However, their discovery suggests that for any given region there are still lost gardens of some significance to be revealed, both through the tech-niques of archaeological air survey and by other means of fieldwork and documentary research.

Changing approaches to 'The Historic Environment' since the 1980s have seen a widening of research priori-ties to include wider elements of the deserted rural land-scape, from mediaeval and more recent times. The aerial perspective is ideally suited to the recording of wide-spreading and poorly mapped features such as cultiva-tion ridges, quarry complexes and braided trackways.[22] All of these less 'monument-oriented' features attest to the presence of a densely peopled landscape, and of transient activities such as transport, trade and the expressions of the agricultural calendar, which enliven and inform a preoccupation with otherwise 'site-centred' monuments. Coupled with continued aerial recording of present-day Carmarthenshire – where recent work has included the photography of dairies and creameries prior to closure, the Liquified Natural Gas pipeline under construction, or the town centre of Llanelli prior to redevelopment – aerial images in the National Monu-ments Record of Wales can record the changing face of contemporary Wales. Together with historic aerial photography from Cambridge University, images from the Dyfed Archaeological Trust and Terry James's own private flights, these will continue in time to come to enrich the study of Carmarthenshire's hidden past.

Fig. 7: *Research on the ground by Medwyn Parry (RCAHMW) and Roger Thomas (English Heritage) has steadily pieced together the line of the Rhos-Llangeler Stop Line, a Second World War defensive line linking Pendine in Carmarthenshire to Llangrannog in Ceredigion. It was designed to protect mainland Wales from a feared German invasion from the Irish Sea. Aerial reconnaissance in winter 2001, with Medwyn Parry guiding the author's observations, recorded many 'new' sections of the stop line, long thought to have been ploughed away. Without prior, expert, knowledge, this part of the stop line at Pistyllgwion (NPRN 270588), 3km north of Carmarthen, could have been dismissed as a ploughed-out field boundary.*
(Crown Copyright: RCAHMW, CD2003_601_046).

ACKNOWLEDGEMENTS

I am grateful to Heather James for an invitation to contribute this paper and for her patience while I have completed it, and to Chris Musson for helpful suggestions and additions to an earlier draft. My final thanks are posthumously to Terry with whom I last flew over a wintry west Wales in February 2005 out of Haverfordwest Airport, and who continued to provide me with help and advice throughout the long course of the writing and publication of the Pembrokeshire book.

NOTES

1. T. James, 'Air Photography and the Archaeology of Carmarthenshire', *Carms. Antiq.*, Vol. XXXVI, 2000, pp. 9-22.

2. J. K. S. St Joseph, 'Aerial Reconnaissance in Wales', *Antiquity*, Vol. 35, 1961, pp. 263-75 and pls. XV-XLVIII.

3. V. Rees, *South-West Wales. A Shell Guide* (London, Faber and Faber, 1976), pp. 82-83, 88, 128, air photographs by Roger Worsley.

4. T. James and D. Simpson, *Ancient West Wales from the Air* (Carmarthen: Carmarthenshire Antiquarian Society, 1980).

5. T. James, 'Aerial Reconnaissance in Dyfed, 1984', *Archaeology in Wales,* Vol. 24, 1984, pp. 12-22.

6. T. Driver, *Pembrokeshire: Historic Landscapes from the Air* (Aberystwyth: RCAHMW, 2007), pp. 6-7.

7. T. Driver, 'RCAHMW Aerial Reconnaissance 2006', *Archaeology in Wales*, 2006, pp. 143-152.

8. T. James, 'Concentric antenna enclosures – a new defended enclosure type in west Wales', *Proceedings of the Prehistoric Society*, Vol. 56, 1990, pp. 295-8.

9. T. James, 'Air Photography and the Archaeology of Carmarthenshire', *Carms. Antiq.,* Vol. XXXVI, 2000, Fig.11.

10. idem. Fig 14.

11. F. Murphy, R. Ramsey, M. Page and K. Murphy, *A Survey of Defended Enclosures in Carmarthenshire, 2007-08* (Llandeilo: Dyfed Archaeological Trust, Report No. 2007/27, 2008). Unpublished report for Cadw-Welsh Historic Monuments.

12. T. Driver, 'Cynwyl Gaeo, Allt Aber-Mangoed (near Pumsaint)', *Archaeology in Wales*, Vol. 42, 2002, pp. 96-97.

13. B. Burnham and H. Burnham, *Dolaucothi-Pumsaint, Survey and excavation at a Roman Gold-Mining complex 1987-1999* (Oxford: Oxbow Books, 2004), pp. 325-6.

14. T. Driver, 'Sugar Loaf, Llanfair-ar-y-bryn (SN 8348 4278)', *Archaeology in Wales*, Vol. 41, 2001, pp. 118-119.

15. H. James, 'Roman Carmarthenshire', *Carms. Antiq.,* Vol. XXXVI, 2000, pp. 23-46.

16. C. Musson, *Wales from the Air, Patterns of Past and Present* (Aberystwyth: RCAHMW), pp. 58-9.

17. G. Hughes, 'A Roman fort at Dinefwr Park, Llandeilo: an interim statement on a geophysical survey by Stratascan', *Carms. Antiq.*, Vol. XXXIX, 2003, pp.144-7.

18. H. James, 'The Roman road from Llandovery to Pumsaint, Carmarthenshire', in: B. Burnham and H. Burnham, *Dolaucothi-Pumsaint: Survey and excavation at a Roman Gold-Mining complex 1987-1999* (Oxford: Oxbow Books, 2004), pp. 305-312.

19. T. James, 'Air photography of ecclesiastical sites in South Wales', in: N. Edwards, and A. Lane (eds), *The Early Church in Wales and the West* (Oxford: Oxbow, 1992), pp. 62-76.

20. T. James, 'Place-name Distributions and Field Archaeology in South-west Wales', in: S. Taylor (ed.), *The Uses of Place-Names,* (St John's House Papers No. 7, St Andrews, Scottish Cultural Press, Edinburgh, 1998), pp. 101-119.

21. T. Driver, 'The Historic Gardens of Wales from the Air', *Bulletin of the Welsh Historic Gardens Trust,* No. 47, Summer 2007, pp. 1-3.

22. T. James, 'Air Photography and the Archaeology of Carmarthenshire', *The Carms. Antiq.*, Vol. XXXVI, 2000, pp. 18-19.

The initials 'NPRN' used in the paper relate to the Royal Commission's database of National Primary Record Numbers which can be searched for and browsed, with accompanying images, at www.coflein.gov.uk.

The Joys of Enclosures: Aspects of Aerial Reconnaissance in Devon and Somerset

Frances Griffith[1]

There is great sadness in contributing to a book for someone who should have lived much longer, but it is a pleasure to have the opportunity to offer something in Terry's memory. In many ways we followed parallel paths in our aerial reconnaissance endeavours, though Terry and Heather got going a little earlier than I did. We worked in unfashionable areas of the country where the national survey bodies flew but infrequently, but where their pioneering results, if critically examined by the partisan observer, made clear that there was considerably more potential in the application of reconnaissance than the conventional wisdom of the time suggested.[2] For all of us at the end of the 1970s and early 1980s it was a time when the reconnaissance work of regional flyers was not part of their 'proper jobs', when flying was done at first opportunistically (and perhaps irregularly, in both senses of the word), with limited funding – none from public bodies – and we all learned on the job. The initially imperfect results rapidly improved just because those working at this time were highly motivated toward the work, and during the 1980s the bulk of the great wave of important results came from the work of regional flyers.[3] It is a pleasure to recall how the emerging skills of this generation were generously encouraged by the more established practitioners – people like Professor St Joseph and David Wilson from Cambridge, John Hampton of the Royal Commission on the Historical Monuments of England, Derrick Riley and (albeit with some grumbling about archaeologists in general) Jim Pickering. Perhaps most importantly, we also supported one another and shared our learning. We had good networks of friends across the UK and beyond, linked by our enthusiasm for what we were discovering, and those of us working in the south-west and in Wales always saw the challenges and opportunities we had in common. As time went by, the regional flyers contributed significantly to the development of policy and practice in aerial archaeology, and Terry played an important role in both the Aerial Archaeology Committee of the Council for British Archaeology (CBA) and in the earliest years of the fledgling Aerial Archaeology Research Group (AARG).

In retrospect, we can see this as a high water mark in reconnaissance. Since then, two factors have contributed to a significant decline in the amount of locally based reconnaissance that is carried out. One is the significant reduction in (and at times cessation of) support from the national survey bodies for this highly cost-effective exercise, in favour of their own 'core survey programmes'. The other is even more fundamental. In the late 1980s, Gordon Maxwell of the Royal Commission on the Historical Monuments of Scotland, on behalf of the sector, had brilliantly negotiated with the Civil Aviation Authority an exemption which permitted reconnaissance to be carried out even in areas where no Public Transport certificated aircraft were available. However, when this was due for renewal, it was subsequently allowed to lapse by the national survey bodies rather than being renegotiated and maintained. In my own case, in Devon, we managed to surmount the first hurdle, with Devon County Council (DCC) supporting the reconnaissance programme for much of the later 1980s and 1990s, but, when Exeter Flying Club gave up its Public Transport certification, we were unable to overcome the second. On such small matters can significant archaeological progress depend.

Fig. 1: *Roman fort at Clayhanger, 20 June 1989.*
(F. M. Griffith, Devon County Council).

Fig. 2: *Roman fort at Clayhanger, 25 June 1989.*
(F. M. Griffith).

For all of us who were carrying out the first intensive reconnaissance, whether for cropmarks or earthworks, in our own areas, this was a very special time. The sheer scale of what we were discovering was a real source of delight and a stimulus to further work. I think we all felt we had the edge on the better resourced and equipped 'national' flyers and got a lot more from our flights. In those days one's work was less segmented than now, and so one was flying with a head that contained the sites of key planning applications and new road lines, the areas where chance finds had recently come up, the fields currently being walked by volunteer fieldwalkers and so on. I am sure only a prodigy could do this effectively for anything much larger than one or two counties. I am amused at a slide I took many years ago, on which I had simply written 'Mrs Pearce's field' – the hilltop where one of Devon's most indefatigable fieldwalkers had identified a major concentration of neolithic flints, later to be excavated.[4] Of course it later got its National Grid Reference and Sites and Monuments Record number and so on, but this illustrates how the photographs we were taking were of things that had real archaeological context for us and I well remember the pleasure of being able to go out with my late husband to follow up on the ground the sites of particularly interesting new discoveries, often very soon after the flight. Sometimes the results were quite surprising – as for example Figs. 1 and 2. Where I had seen the cropmarks of a Roman fort, the rampart stood clear and upstanding in the field – which subsequently turned out to have a 'Berry' field name on the Tithe Map into the bargain![5] It is true to say that the results of those years of reconnaissance have transformed our understanding of our own areas in ways that surpass our original hopes, and I am sure this is as true of the situation in south-west Wales as it has been in south-west England.

Aerial reconnaissance is different now, and the technology available is changing things very fast. One example is the question of navigation. For the embryonic aerial surveyor, navigation and site location were possibly the hardest skills to develop. They were also about the most important, as a brilliant picture of a staggering new site is of no value at all if it cannot be located. However, the need to work out and record one's track and the location of one's sites has now been superseded by the arrival of GPS (Global Positioning System), while the adoption of digital media has meant that all the juggling with film backs, labelling of films, etc. has also dropped out of the cockpit workload. (Those tasks have joined other obsolete archaeological skills such as the ability to take spot height readings through the level upside down, or to slam on the brakes of the [non-hydraulic] dumper truck at just the right moment to make it tip up and empty itself.) Inevitably, this makes some practitioners of these redundant lost arts feel very old indeed! I was delighted to find, quite recently, that Terry had used exactly the same term[6] as I had to describe the 1970s and 1980s – it was indeed the last of the 'heroic age' of aerial reconnaissance. The friendships made among the regional reconnaissance community were those that commonly characterise heroic ages, and this is just one of the many reasons why Terry has been so sadly missed. Others will expatiate elsewhere on the breadth of his knowledge and competences, but here I would comment that so many of the qualities that made him such a good scholar and archaeologist also made him an exceptional air photographer.

As mentioned above, the good things that have come from aerial reconnaissance have made a tremendous difference to our understanding of many different areas of our archaeology. For example, it has been a pleasure to record Devon's first henge and cursus, not to mention a whole host of Roman forts. But the most significant impact has probably been the change in our appreciation of the level and distribution of activity in what one might broadly term later prehistory, in particular in considering the lowlands. The county's principal area of high ground, Dartmoor, has always had at least its fair share of study, but until quite recently it was suggested that much of the lowlands had been covered with primordial forest until perhaps the Saxon period. A plan published by Ian Simmons as late as 1969[7] shows archaeological sites on Dartmoor, but the area around the high Moor is covered with fuzzy stipple described as 'forest'. One has the feeling he might just as well have written 'here be dragons', for what he was really doing was postulating an explanation for the apparent absence of prehistoric sites here. We can now see that Dartmoor enclosures have benefited from their durable construction (granite) and the limited impact of post-prehistoric disturbance, but that, entirely unsurprisingly, the distribution of settlement enclosures does *not* end at the boundary of the rough ground of Dartmoor, and this has been borne out by recent palaeoenvironmental work.[8] This is made abundantly clear in Fig. 3, where the filled symbols show enclosure sites and hillforts that are known in upstanding form, while the open symbols show the enclosures recorded in aerial reconnaissance by

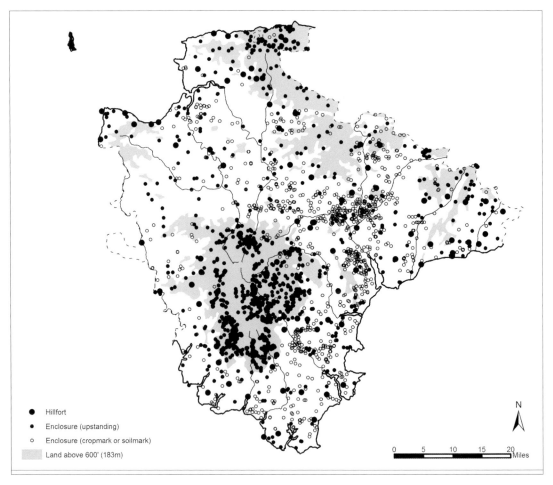

Fig. 3: *Devon enclosures as known 2008. Plan prepared by E. M. Wilkes from information provided by Devon HER.*

the Cambridge University Centre for Aerial Photography, the National Monuments Record and the Devon Aerial Reconnaissance Project.

The picture in Somerset, where reconnaissance has also been carried out by myself and my colleague Bill Horner, is at least as striking (*Fig. 4*). Here a quite large-scale follow-up project has been carried out by the Department of Archaeology at King Alfred's College (KAC), Winchester (now University of Winchester), in conjunction with Somerset County Council. We had recorded 100 enclosure sites, in reconnaissance by Devon County Council on behalf of Somerset County Council, in the 14 x 5km study area they chose, Of these, five enclosures were sampled by KAC (*Fig. 5*), and these have produced dates ranging from the Bronze Age to the post-Roman period, including a full-blown Roman villa.[9]

In general, it is not possible to distinguish between enclosures of different dates, and the distribution maps shown here cannot yet be divided to show settlement enclosures of different periods. In two dimensions, all one has to go on is their (generally very simple) form. For this reason, until recently we might have supposed that the comparison between Dartmoor and lowland Devon might not be very sound, Dartmoor enclosed settlement being conventionally assigned to the 2nd millennium BC, and believed to decline by the end of the Bronze Age.[10] However, although there have been very few recent excavations on Dartmoor, we now know that even on the higher parts of the Moor, enclosed settlement certainly either continues after the Bronze Age or is re-established later. Excavations at Gold Park, near Grimspound, suggest that a stone round house, with evidence of a timber predecessor, on a terrace

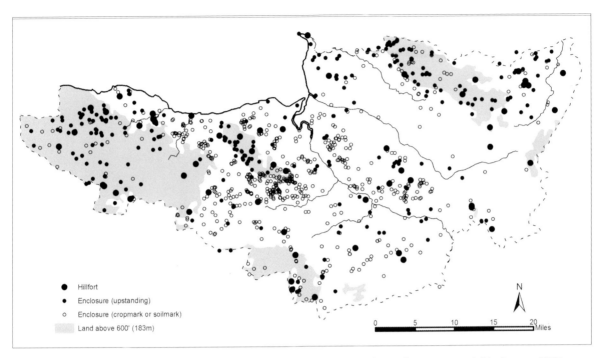

Fig. 4: *Somerset enclosures as known 2008. Plan prepared by E. M. Wilkes from information provided by Somerset HER.*

within an enclosure, was occupied in the Late Iron Age.[11] In terms of its external form this site does not stand out in any way from many others on the Moor. Similarly, ongoing excavations by Sandy Gerrard of a Bronze Age hut circle at Teigncombe, on the northern flanks of Dartmoor near Kestor, have demonstrated that the site was used again in the early Iron Age.[12] On the other hand, the excavations that have so far been carried out on the lowland enclosures have produced rather more sites with 2nd millennium dates than might have been supposed a few years ago (for example, Hayne Lane, Gittisham, below).

Although one can seldom propose dates for sites without excavation, the survey and rescue excavation work that is put in train by their discovery expands our understanding over time. In many ways the problems we face in south-west England are closely paralleled by those in south-west Wales: the Prehistoric Defended Enclosures Project carried out by Dyfed Archaeological Trust and York University under Ken Murphy's direction, which builds so much on the discoveries from Terry's reconnaissance, struggles equally with questions of dating.[13] However, comparison with the work of Welsh colleagues (Driver, this volume), suggests that in south-west England we are *relatively* blessed with dating

evidence, even though colleagues from further east in England might not see it that way!

Since very early in our project, reconnaissance has been followed up by the Devon Post-Reconnaissance Fieldwork Project, a programme of visits to all the 'new' sites discovered, with the objects of understanding their siting on the ground, and, more importantly, finding out who owns or farms them and telling them about the existence and the importance of the sites. This programme of work, which appears to be unusual among regional flying projects (and inconceivable for national ones), has paid huge dividends. Almost none of the newly-discovered sites, save for the odd obvious ones such as a henge, cursus or a Roman fort, has been the subject of any statutory protection. Only the understanding and goodwill of the farmer will protect these sites for the future. One's own comprehension of the enclosures is much enhanced by seeing their exact topographical setting, and very often, when one goes with the farmer into the field where the enclosure has been recorded, both together can immediately spot the place where the site will be – a slight platform, an end of spur, or just the nicest part of the field. The farmer will often be delighted to understand where his predecessors had sited their farmstead, and may then identify all the

Fig. 5: *Complex enclosures at Yarford, Kingston St. Mary, Somerset, 19 June 1990.*
One of the sites investigated by the Winchester South Quantocks Archaeological Survey project.
(F. M. Griffith, Devon County Council).

other factors such as the site's aspect or water sources that would have informed their choice of site. Our project has made friends with many farmers in this way, and in Devon we have in general found responses to the new sites on their land vary from bemused tolerance to great enthusiasm. In addition, when it later comes to discussions with farmers about the inclusion of these sites in Environmental Stewardship Schemes, we are starting negotiations about land management from a good basis. It is certainly very encouraging that the sites we have discovered can now be seen by the farmer as an asset not a source of difficulty.

In expanding our comprehension of the enclosures, three developments of the last twenty-five years have been of great importance: the expansion in rescue archaeological work, the availability of geophysical survey equipment that can cover substantial hectarages in detail, and an expansion in the amount of palaeo-environmental work undertaken, particularly on pollen. This last is lending very considerable strength to our

reading of the chronology of the opening up of the landscape, and strengthening the conclusion that much of Devon was cleared of forest in the later prehistoric period and that by the time of Domesday Book the landscape was at least as open as it is now – a conclusion now also supported by the results of DCC's Historic Landscape Characterisation of the county.[14]

On Devon soils, it is exceptional if anything beyond the coarse outline of a substantial enclosure ditch can be seen from the air (*e.g. Fig. 6*). This however can set in hand serious work. An interesting example is provided by two sites which lay on the line of the proposed improvements to the A30 trunk road east of Exeter. Both of these were only ever recorded, in very faint and fugitive cropmark form, in 1984. This was particularly surprising for the rectilinear enclosure site at Black Horse, Clyst Honiton (*Fig. 6*), which lay less than two miles from the western end of the main runway of Exeter Airport, our base for reconnaissance. We flew over it hundreds of times, knowing it was there, but we

Fig. 6: *Black Horse enclosure DAP/AG 02, 27 June 1984. Compare Fig. 8.*
(F. M. Griffith, Devon County Council).

Fig. 7: *Hayne Lane enclosure DAP/BX 01, 12 July 1984.*
(F. M. Griffith, Devon County Council).

Fig. 8: *Black Horse enclosure, excavated plan, from Fitzpatrick et al. 1999.*[15] (Reproduced by courtesy of Wessex Archaeology).

only ever saw it in that one year of all our flying. The same is true of another site, also recorded only in 1984, this time a single ditched curvilinear enclosure which lay near Honiton, and on which the road scheme likewise made a direct hit (*Fig. 7*). Those single episodes of recognition made it possible for a proper programme of evaluation and excavation to be put in place for these sites before the start of road construction. (In passing one may observe that this is a nice example of not selecting one's most spectacular air photographs for a volume, but rather those with the most material message about the archaeology of one's area.)

The site at Black Horse provided dates from the 8th to the 1st centuries BC, and excavation demonstrated why its cropmarks were so elusive: though very substantial, the ditch of the rectangular enclosure was cut into very light sands, and, despite evidence of cleaning slots in the bottom, had clearly re-filled with the removed soil very shortly after being dug. There was very little difference between the ditch fill and the *in situ* surrounding sand, and this explains why the signature of the ditch was so weak in the aerial photographs – a difference in fill is of course essential to cause a difference in growth of the crop. The photographs in 1984 must have recorded a fleeting moment when the difference was enough to affect the crop. But those few photographs were enough to engender the excavation of the enclosure, and, delightfully, to show that very much more than the enclosure ditch alone survived. Within the enclosure a substantial round house was found, with others outside, and a number of four-post structures (very rare in south-west England) were found both within and outside (*Fig. 8*). By contrast, the site at Hayne Lane, near Honiton, proved to enclose two or possibly three post-built round houses, and the site yielded dates between 1500-800 cal BC.[15]

These two examples are included to demonstrate the point that the results of aerial reconnaissance are valuable not only to identify single sites, but to suggest areas for detailed archaeological examination in advance of large-scale infrastructure works or other landuse changes. Despite all the caveats that any sensible aerial surveyor will apply to the patterns of distribution of sites recorded from aerial reconnaissance, it was clear from the A30 work, for which at minimum a watching brief was carried out for the 21km length of the road, that the aerial 'blanks' on the whole did reflect the gaps of distribution of prehistoric sites in general.[16] Where large-scale evaluation work has been carried out in other areas

– for example the proposed site of Sherford new town in south Devon, or the works around the new power station at Langage on the edge of Plymouth, with its associated gas pipelines, the same general picture has held true, so that it appears that we can use the very partial glimpses of the landscape that the cropmark evidence affords as a more general indicator of the archaeological potential of an area – while remembering all our caveats.

As with the defended enclosures of South West Wales, so in South West England have our enclosures benefited greatly from the application of quite large-scale geophysical survey. Dr Eileen Wilkes (of Bournemouth University, formerly of University of Wales, Lampeter) has been carrying out geophysical survey on a number of the newly-discovered enclosures in South Devon, in collaboration with the writer. This work began with two enclosures at Mount Folly, overlooking Bigbury Bay, where two rectilinear enclosures were found to lie within a complex and apparently contemporary field system (and where a third enclosure never seen from the air has recently been identified by magnetometry). The excavation of parts of this complex has revealed that it is of Iron Age to Romano-British date, and ongoing excavations here are demonstrating once again the presence of major internal features, including at least one terrace-cut round house where archaeological survival is excellent beneath a later seal of hillwash. From the initial trial trenches, a large-scale community excavation project has developed, which is now in its fifth year, yet another of the outcomes of the aerial reconnaissance project.[17]

The existence of more than the surviving bases of the enclosure ditches has been for the writer one of the most encouraging discoveries to emerge from this project in Devon. When the reconnaissance programme started, it was easy for a pessimist to assume (and I did) that all that I was recording were the bases of formerly substantial enclosure ditches, sites which had been so reduced by cultivation that no internal features would survive. The examples above all demonstrate that this is not so, and the programme of geophysical work arising from the reconnaissance offers further comfort in this matter. An excellent example is the site at Thornberry, Chivelstone, in South Devon. Here, aerial reconnaissance in 1984 showed an interesting enclosure whose form was partially reflected in the present day field pattern, although the remains of a number of removed field boundaries can also be seen (*Fig. 9*). The magnetometer survey by Eileen Wilkes (*Fig. 10*) shows however that

Fig. 9: *Thornberry, Chivelstone, from the east. DAP/CR 08, 19 July 1984.*
(F. M. Griffith, Devon County Council).

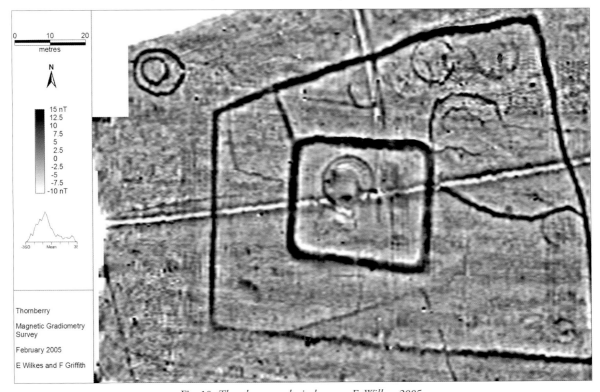

Fig. 10: *Thornberry geophysical survey, E. Wilkes, 2005.*

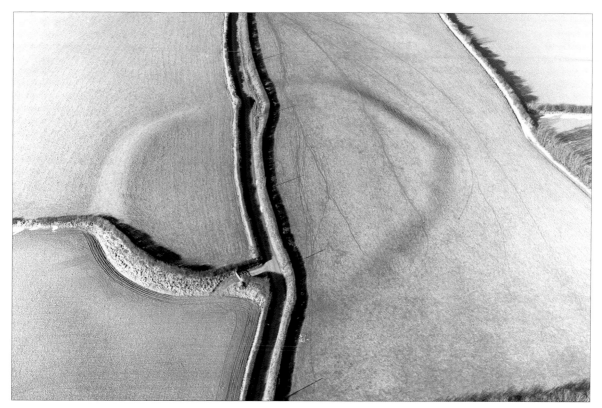

Fig. 11: *Stoke Rivers Hillfort, north Devon. The bank of the hillfort survives within the present-day hedge bank in one quadrant, and as an earthwork reduced by ploughing elsewhere. The ditch can still be seen. Where the modern lane crosses the banks, the nature of the hedge changes as it incorporates part of the bank, and the road itself can be seen to rise up as it crosses the bank. DAP/HZ08, 30 January 1987.*
(F. M. Griffith, Devon County Council).

a whole host of other features survive. Within the enclosure is either a very large round house or possibly a barrow, which itself seems to be partially masked by another rectilinear feature. A whole series of other round houses and linear features can also be seen, all apparently contained within the enclosure, while at the north-west corner of the field something quite different, barely visible on the air photograph as a simple ring ditch, turns out to be a much more complex, probably prehistoric ceremonial feature. All this is immensely encouraging in showing that that which is visible to the aerial observer on Devon soils and in Devon crops is indeed simply the tip of the iceberg.[18]

Mention was briefly made above of the relationship of sites observed in cropmark form to the present day or mapped landscape. This can often help us to elucidate the sequence of development of the landscape. Archaeologists have long understood that a sudden kink in or change of character of a field boundary may demonstrate

the survival of an element of an earlier feature (*e.g. Fig. 11*). Very often the recognition of an archaeological site in cropmark form can elucidate an otherwise inexplicable landscape feature, as seen for example in Fig. 12. In this case, we can say that the enclosure was in existence as an earthwork when the present field system came into being, the latter curving to accommodate the extant site. One cannot say whether the two operated contemporaneously or whether the enclosure was simply an upstanding landscape element that the field system had to accommodate. In much the same way it is possible to relate place-name evidence to archaeological features, and in particular to enclosures (*see below*). Map evidence can help us determine sequence and survival in the same way: in Alphington, near Exeter, the Alphington–Exminster parish boundary (now itself only visible as the cropmark of a hedge line) swings round to respect an enclosure that is now only visible as a cropmark (*Fig. 13*) but whose discovery may explain the strange behaviour

Fig. 12: *Bulland enclosure, Staverton. DAP/CX 04, 20 June 1984.*
(F. M. Griffith, Devon County Council).

of the parish boundary here. We can also recognise sequence in landscape development from cropmarks: the disappearance of the cropmark of a boundary feature as it meets a ring ditch tells us that this was still an upstanding barrow at the time the field boundary was established (*Fig. 14*).

In Devon, far more 'berry' or 'borough' place-names survive in the landscape, at manor, farm, or field level, than we can explain from the presence of upstanding archaeological sites. These derive either from the place-name element *burh* (an enclosure of various sorts, used both for the enclosure around a farm or manor house and for earlier but recognisable enclosures in the landscape such as hillforts) or from *beorg* (a hill or a barrow in the archaeological sense). In late forms it is often hard to distinguish which of these Saxon elements may be the origin of a modern 'berry', 'borough', 'bury' or 'barrow' place-name. However, as Dr Gelling has made clear,

archaeology can often help in this, and the recognition of such sites in cropmark form has done much to elucidate the origins of these previously unexplained names in the Devon landscape – as in the case of Thornberry above.[19] This is a name for which the earliest record we have is the fieldname on the Chivelstone Tithe Map of 1842. However, the presence of the archaeological site here suggests strongly that the enclosure, which we only know as a cropmark, was still obvious as an extant earthwork feature, worthy of naming as a *burh* or 'berry', to the Saxons coming into the Devon landscape. Despite the late date of the record of the field name, it is most likely that it has been innocently preserved, remaining continuously in use for the field long after the enclosure from which it was named was levelled.

Unravelling even the cropmark evidence of an enclosure site can sometimes be complex. Fig. 15 shows an enclosure complex at Horwood in north Devon, lying on

Fig. 13: *Enclosure on Alphington/Exminster parish boundary. DAP/LV 08, 16 June 1989.*
(F. M. Griffith, Devon County Council).

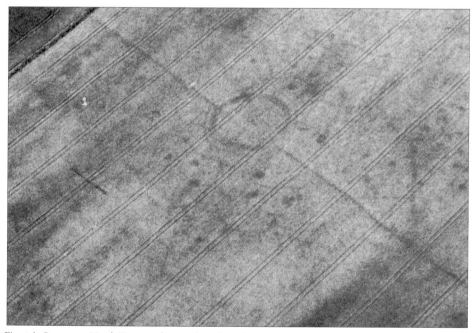

Fig. 14: *Barrow at North Tawton, showing later boundary crossing the top of the barrow (now a ring ditch).*
DAP/YB 03. 5 July 1995.
(F. M. Griffith).

119

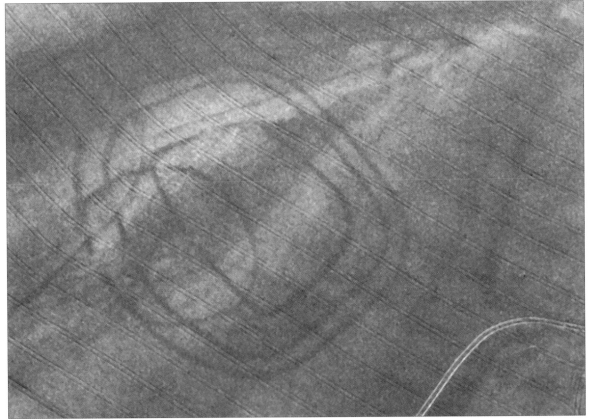

Fig. 15: *Complex enclosure at Horwood, DAP/BK 12, 7 July 1984.*
(F. M. Griffith, Devon County Council).

the end of a spur between two streams. At minimum, we can see a single-ditched curvilinear enclosure, and either a triple-ditched one or a series of enclosures separate from the former, but possibly successors to one another. The single curvilinear enclosure and the triple-ditched complex cannot however have co-existed as their ditches intercut. But they all share the same entrance, and thus, whether the single-ditched enclosure or the triple complex is the earlier, one must have been laid out in reference to the other, to continue the same entrance. Here, equally, we can say with confidence that the whole complex had however been levelled before the present day field system had been laid out, as the existing or recently removed field boundaries (visible on the figure) pay no attention to the layout of the enclosure.

In this brief paper I have outlined only a few of the ways in which the results of the Devon Aerial Reconnaissance programme have fed through into many other parts of the study of the archaeology of our area. The enclosures that have been found in Devon both by our illustrious predecessors J. K. St Joseph, David Wilson and John Hampton, and more recently by myself and Bill Horner (since 1992), are a delight in helping us to re-people the Devon lowland in prehistory. We see things through a glass darkly, and only the crudest of outlines of these sites are generally vouchsafed to the aerial observer. But the discovery of these sites, and the much more detailed work that their identification has engendered in both rescue and research contexts, has greatly helped our still inchoate understanding of the prehistory of lowland Devon and its connections with the wider world, while, viewed in a landscape context, in conjunction with the emerging evidence from palaeo-environmental studies, we can perhaps see a higher level of continuity in the development of the landscape than has sometimes been suggested.

ACKNOWLEDGEMENTS

The work reported here has over time been supported by a number of bodies and individuals. Bill Horner and I are employed by Devon County Council, which has also funded a large proportion of the reconnaissance and post-reconnaissance work, together with RCHME and their successor English Heritage. Reconnaissance in the first two years was supported by several private donors, the Devonshire Association, and by the writer, and of particular importance was a substantial grant from the Department of the Environment, courtesy of Dr Geoff Wainwright, at a critical point in 1984 when it was obvious that the wealth of cropmarks far outran the limited resources available. The flying programme would probably never have got under way without the commitment and support of my first pilot, the late Dickie Dougan, to whom I owe a great debt. Post-reconnaissance fieldwork was funded by DCC and mainly carried out by Rosemary Robinson, with members of the DCC Archaeology Service. Dr Eileen Wilkes' survey of Thornberry was funded by DCC as part of the joint DCC/Bournemouth University South Devon Coastal and Landscape Archaeological Survey project. In the last two years, my work on the results has been supported by a Research Fellowship from the Leverhulme Trust, whose support has been of great importance. In the preparation of this paper I have benefited from discussions with John Draisey, Bill Horner, Heather James, Henrietta Quinnell and Eileen Wilkes. I am also very grateful to Eileen Wilkes for Fig. 10 and for preparing the distribution maps, for which information was kindly provided by the Devon and Somerset Historic Environment Records. I am grateful to Wessex Archaeology for providing Fig. 8 and allowing its reproduction.

NOTES

1. Devon County Council Historic Environment Service.

2. For accounts of this at the time, see for example T. James & D. Simpson, *Ancient West Wales from the Air* (Carms. Antiq. Soc. Monograph, no. 1) 1980; T. James, 'Aerial Reconnaissance in Dyfed, 1984', *Archaeology in Wales*, Vol. 24, 1984, pp. 12-24; F. M. Griffith, 'Aerial Reconnaissance in Devon in 1984: a preliminary report', *Proc. Devon Archaeol. Soc.*, Vol. 42, 1984, pp. 7-10; eadem, *Devon's Past, An Aerial View* (Exeter, Devon Books, 1988), pp. 7-8.

3. For summaries of activity see for example R. Whimster, *The Emerging Past* (London: RCHME, 1989); F. M. Griffith, 'Aerial Reconnaissance in Mainland Britain in 1989', *Antiquity*, Vol. 64, 1990, pp. 14-33.

4. M. Tingle, 'Excavations of a possible causewayed enclosure and Roman site at Membury, 1986 and 1994-2000', *Proc. Devon Archaeol. Soc.*, Vol. 64, 2006, pp. 1-52.

5. S. S. Frere (ed.), 'Roman Britain in 1990', *Britannia*, Vol. 22, 1991, p. 281.

6. T. James, 'Air Photography and the Archaeology of Carmarthenshire', *Carms. Antiq.*, Vol. 36, 2000, pp. 9-22.

7. I. G. Simmons, 'Environment and Early Man on Dartmoor, England', *Proc. Prehist. Soc.*, Vol. 35, 1969, pp. 203-19, Fig. 3.

8. For the Dartmoor/non Dartmoor picture see F. M. Griffith, 'Changing Perceptions of Dartmoor's Prehistoric Context', in 'The Archaeology of Dartmoor: Perspectives from the 1990s', *Proc. Devon Archaeol. Soc.*, Vol. 52, 1994, pp. 85-100, and eadem & Quinnell, H. 'Settlement, *c.*2500BC to AD600', in R. Kain, & W. Ravenhill (eds.), *Historical Atlas of South West England* (Exeter: University of Exeter, 1999). pp. 51-68. For the implications of recent palaeoenvironmental studies of prehistoric lowland Devon see R. Fyfe, A. G. Brown & B. J. Coles, 'Mesolithic to Bronze Age Vegetation Change and Human Activity in the Exe Valley, Devon', *Proc. Prehist. Soc.*, Vol. 69, 2003, pp. 161-82; R. Fyfe, A. G. Brown & S. J. Rippon, 'Characterising the late prehistoric, "Romano-British", and medieval landscape, and dating the emergence of a regionally distinct agricultural system in South West Britain', *J. Archaeol. Science,* Vol. 31, 2004, pp. 1699-1714; and S. J. Rippon, R. M. Fyfe, & A. G. Brown, 'Beyond Villages and Open Fields: The origins and Development of a Historic Landscape Characterised by Dispersed Settlement in South-West England', *Med. Archaeol.*, Vol. 50, 2006, pp. 31-70.

9. See F. M. Griffith, & W. S. Horner, 'Aerial Reconnaissance in Somerset', in C. J. Webster (ed.), *Somerset Archaeology: Papers to mark 150 years of Somerset Archaeological and Historical Society*, 2000, pp. 7-14. Full publication of the South Quantocks project excavations is still awaited, but see C. J. Webster & R. A. Brunning, 'A Seventh-century AD Cemetery at Stoneage Barton Farm, Bishop's Lydeard, Somerset, and Square-ditched Burials in Post-Roman Britain', *Archaeol. J.*, Vol. 161, 2004, pp. 54-81, and http://www2.winchester.ac.uk/archaeology/SQAS.htm.

10. Dating and morphology are further discussed in F. M. Griffith, op. cit., n. 8, p. 93, and eadem, Review of T. Arbousse-Bastide's *Les Structures de l'habitat rural proto-historique dans le sud-ouest de l'Angleterre et le nord-ouest de la France* (BAR Int. Ser. 847, 2000), in *Rep. Trans. Devonshire Assoc.*, Vol. 134, 2002, pp. 261-6.

11. A. Gibson, 'The Excavation of an Iron Age Settlement at Gold Park, Dartmoor', *Proc. Devon Archaeol. Soc.*, Vol. 50, 1992, pp. 19-46.

12. Sundry interim reports by S. Gerrard in Devon HER, and information on the dating of the ceramics from Henrietta Quinnell (*pers. comm.*).

13. The Dyfed Archaeological Trust website (www.acadat.com) contains an excellent series of reports of survey and field-work on a range of enclosure sites studied as part of the Defended Enclosures project.

14. For the palaeoenvironmental picture see R. Fyfe, 'Palaeo-environmental Perspectives on Medieval Landscape Development', in S. Turner (ed.), *Medieval Devon and Cornwall: Shaping an Ancient Countryside* (Macclesfield: Windgather Press, 2006), pp. 10-23 and Rippon *et al.* 2006, op. cit., n. 8; for the DCC Historic Landscape Characterisation project and its account of the development of the Devon countryside, see S. Turner, 'The Changing Ancient Landscape: South-West England *c.*1700-1900', *Landscapes*, Vol. 1, 2004, pp. 18-34, esp. pp. 19-20, and idem, *Ancient Country: the Historic Character of Rural Devon*, Devon Archaeol. Soc. Occ. Paper, No. 20, 2007.

15. The A30 excavations are published in A. P. Fitzpatrick, C. A. Butterworth & J. Grove, *Prehistoric and Roman Sites in East Devon: the A30 Honiton to Exeter Improvement DBFO Scheme, 1996-9* (Salisbury: Wessex Archaeology, 1999), 2 Vols. The dating of Black Horse is discussed on pp. 191-3, and that of Hayne Lane on pp. 122-4.

16. General issues of base geology, cropping patterns, weather, the nature of the sites themselves, genuine site distribution in Devon, etc. are discussed in Griffith op. cit., n. 8, p. 87, while in specific relation to the A30 results see Griffith in Fitzpatrick *et al.*, op. cit., n. 15, pp. 6-8.

17. The project has been reported in a number of interim reports and notes. See most recently E. M. Wilkes, 'Return to Mount Folly: Fieldwork in 2007', *Devon Archaeol. Soc. Newsletter*, No. 99, 2008, pp. 1, 16.

18. Thornberry and other enclosures will be published in F. M. Griffith, & E. M. Wilkes, in prep. 'Hillforts and Enclosures in the South Hams', *Proc. Devon Archaeol. Soc.*

19. 'Berry' placenames are reviewed in M. Gelling, *Signposts to the Past* (Chichester: Phillimore, 1988, 2nd ed.), chapter 6. For the light that aerial archaeology can shed on elucidating these place-names in Devon, see F. M. Griffith, '*Burh* and *Beorg* in Devon', *Nomina*, Vol. 10, 1986, pp. 93-103, and for some more Devon *bury*s and *borough*s see F. M. Griffith, & E. M. Wilkes, 'The Land Named from the Sea? Coastal Archaeology and Place-names of Bigbury Bay, Devon', *Archaeol. J.*, Vol. 163, 2006, pp. 67-91.

A Romano-British Cremation at Allt-y-Cnap Road, Carmarthen

John Purdue, Dee Williams & Ros Coard

(edited and with contributions by Heather James)

CIRCUMSTANCES OF DISCOVERY

On the 19th November 2001, work started on the extension of the Carmarthenshire County Council yard at Allt-y-Cnap Road, Cillefwr Industrial Estate. The extension (centred SN 396190) lies south of the existing yard and covers an area 0.5 hectares adjacent to the northern edge of Ystrad Woods, 2.5 kilometres south west of the Roman town of *Moridunum*. Late in the afternoon of 26th November 2001, the machine excavator driver, Richard Norman, was machining the hillside to create a bank with a 1:1 slope, to define the southern perimeter of the site, when he uncovered a pot containing a cremated bone and associated ceramic material. It is to his credit that the find was reported to the construction site manager Mr Ray Hugget who immediately informed staff at Carmarthen Museum.

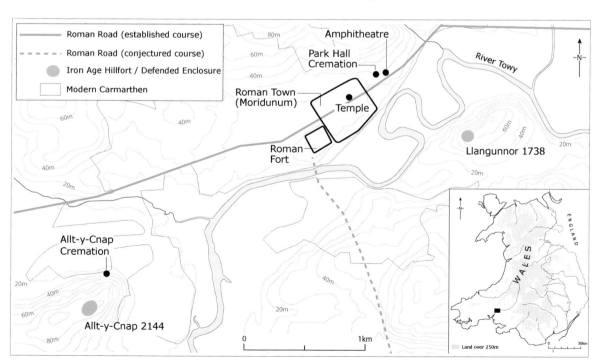

Fig. 1: *Map showing the location of the cremation burial at Allt-y-Cnap in relation to the Roman fort and town of Carmarthen (Moridunum) and Roman roads.*

ARCHAEOLOGICAL RESPONSE

The discovery was verified by Museum Staff Gavin Evans and John Purdue as a Roman cremation, an unusual find in itself and especially in this location at some distance from the Roman town. They in turn informed the Heritage Management section of Cambria Archaeology, advisors to the County Council on archaeology and planning. Lucy Rowly-Williams, Development Control Officer, and Richard Jones, Heritage Management Assistant visited the site on 27th November and recommended archaeological conditions on the progress of the extension work, which were accepted by the County Council, to ensure that no other archaeological remains would be damaged or destroyed without record. Work was resumed away from the area of the discovery allowing sufficient time for John Purdue to clean and further expose the cremation. A further site visit by a member of staff from the County Coroner's Office with Cambria Archaeology Staff in attendance resulted in permission to lift the cremation and remove the material to Carmarthen Museum.

Fig 2: *The cremation burial exposed by archaeological excavation shortly after discovery.*
(Photograph: Carmarthenshire County Museum).

SALVAGE RECORDING AND WATCHING BRIEF

On the arrival at the construction site, it was noted that the cremation was largely intact apart from the damage caused to the urn when uncovered by the machine bucket. A tooth of the bucket had smashed the top of the cremation urn spilling some cremated bones out. The majority of the contents however were contained within the cremation urn, which though shattered, was still *in situ*. The spoil, which had been machined off the burial, had been placed separately from the main spoil in order to allow the recovery of any artefacts from the disturbed burial, and to limit further contamination of the find. The toothed bucket on the machine was replaced with a grading bucket to minimise damage to any surviving archaeology.

Unfortunately, due to the conditions in which the cremation had been found, there was no evidence of the cremation pyre debris being scattered over the urn as had been demonstrated by another Roman cremation recently found at Park Hall, Carmarthen.[1] The cremation was not planned in detail but a full digital photographic record was kept throughout the salvage excavation and watching brief by Museum archaeologist, Gavin Evans and County Council staff. The cremated bone scattered around the cremation vessel by the machine when the burial was uncovered, was bagged separately to prevent contamination of the upper fill within the cremation urn, which still remained *in situ*. These bagged soils were later sorted by hand in post excavation.

The upper fill within the urn was carefully removed and bagged separately from the remaining contents of the cremation vessel. This would limit any contamination, which may have arisen when the vessel was uncovered by the machine. The base of the vessel and the bones within were bagged as one in order to prevent contamination of any surviving residues and environmental evidence. The soil which came from the burial's disturbance was sorted by hand on site over a three day period and fragments of both the cremation vessel and cremated bone, as well as other artefacts were recovered. Although, as noted above, damage to the cremation urn occurred at the time of discovery, it was evident that the cremation urn had also been broken at some time in the past since the worn and dirty edges compared with the clean modern breaks were very apparent.

The stratigraphic sequence (*see Fig. 3b*) was fairly straightforward and it is apparent that soil creep down

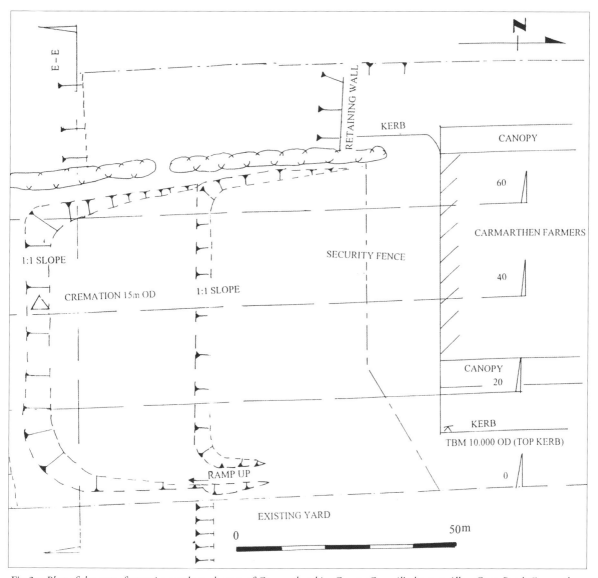

Fig 3a: *Plan of the area of extension works to the rear of Carmarthenshire County Council's depot at Allt-y-Cnap Road, Carmarthen, showing the location of the cremation burial. Plan, scale 1:500.*
(Carmarthenshire County Museum).

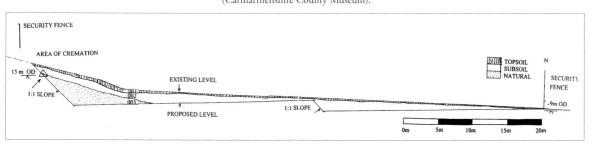

Fig. 3b: *East-facing section across the CCC yard extension showing the location of the cremation burial and its stratigraphy. Plan, scale 1:200.*
(Carmarthenshire County Museum).

the hillslope has moved and distorted the cremation burial to the point that no evidence for a cut or fill for the insertion of the cremation burial was identified albeit that the ground was already disturbed. These processes will have caused the cremation urn to split and might also have displaced evidence of a possible cist containing the cremation. No trace however of this was visible in the vicinity of the find itself.

The bedrock (*003 in Fig. 3b*) on the hill slope is an Ordovician shale of the Arenig system[2] which at the base of the subsoil comprised 80% shale and 20% clay and was of a loose consistency. Above this was a subsoil of homogenous silty clay, some 0.6m in depth and of loose consistency. The topsoil was clearly distinguishable as a dark brown humic soil of 0.3m average depth through the recorded section.

A watching brief was maintained on the remainder of the construction but since only the upper (southern) area of the site involved cutting down into the existing hillslope and the remainder was of spreading and levelling of the surface not all the area of the development involved topsoil disturbance. Nevertheless, sufficient time and opportunity was provided for archaeological observation to be certain that the cremation burial was isolated and no other features were apparent. Sufficient time was also allowed for a thorough examination of the spoil heap from the original machine excavation which revealed the cremation. This allowed more fragments of the cremation urn to be recovered. Further work was carried out in sorting through the cremated bone at Carmarthen Museum following examination by Dr Ros Coard.

CREMATION REPORT
BY DR ROS COARD,
UNIVERSITY COLLEGE OF WALES, LAMPETER

Two contexts – 'central fill' and 'Potbase and contents' were given on the finds bags received for analysis; they have been treated as two contexts for this report but as one for analytical and interpretative purposes. The bone was wet sieved using 4mm and 2mm sieves and air-dried. All of the bone was examined by eye and any showing interesting features were examined under a high-powered light microscope. The bones and artefacts were not numbered but some bones have been bagged separately according to body part.

There is no duplication of bone suggesting that only a single individual is represented. Equally bone fusion is consistent with a single individual. The individual is represented by a wide range of bones, including fragments of skull, vertebrae, rib, scapula, pelvis, limb bones and bones from the hand and feet. However, there are very few bones that are representative of the various body parts and they are highly fragmented. The fragmentation and distortion is partly due to the cremation process but the degree of fragmentation may also be indicative of the treatment the bones received during or after the burning process.

The bones do not give an indication of the sex of the individual. Diagnosis of the sex can be difficult enough with inhumations, but cremations present their own set of difficulties. Metrical analysis has not been undertaken here, apart from some small cranial vault fragments to get a measurement of thickness. Very few bones survive in a measurable form. The bones appear to be gracile and the muscle markings are not pronounced. This could indicate a female. However, this may be complicated by the age of the skeleton. It cannot be ruled out that the individual is a young male.

The eruption and wear rates in teeth are probably the best indicators for ageing an individual at death. Teeth rarely survive the cremation process but this is not the case for the Allt-y-Cnap individual. Several teeth have survived, including molars, premolars and a canine, but they have not survived in such a condition to have retained the occlusal surface and hence be good indicators of the age of the individual. Fragments of the mandible showing the tooth sockets have survived and they do show an adult configuration. The surviving bone epiphyses are fused and suggest an age of at least eighteen years. The auricular surface of the iliac crest (pelvis) shows no obvious age related changes suggesting an individual under the age of twenty four years.[3] Thus the ageing of the skeleton indicates an individual early in the third decade of life (under 24) and by this stage many of the more robust features of the male skeleton may not have fully developed.

The bones show varying degrees of burning but overall most suggest a high firing temperature. The vast majority of the bones are pale in colour falling mostly in the light grey, pale blue and white to pale yellow hues. This is generally indicative of higher temperature burning. Very few bones show the black/blue hues associated wih lower burning. Estimates do vary slightly, but generally the light grey bone indicates a minimum temperature of 600°C (or more precisely 645°C)[4] and the white bone around 700°C or above.[5] The bone surface is extensively cracked, again suggesting temperatures in excess of 600°C.[6]

The total weight of the burned bone is around 674.4g and as such is comparatively light when compared to published sources of known ash weights for adults.[7] However, this figure is an underestimate since a small amount of additional bone was recovered during post-excavation sorting of samples at Carmarthen Museum. The Allt-y-Cnap skeleton falls well within Trotter and Hixon's 'young' category, defined by them as being up to twenty years of age. The ash weight can also be compared with other published Romano-British cremations in Wales, such as the Caerleon Abbeyfield site where only three cremations show a greater survivorship of bone.[8]

Clearly several factors could contribute to the total ash or bone weight being recovered, such as the actual body weight, sex, height and size of the individual. Burial practices may also influence how much or little burned bone is collected depending on the care taken to collect the ash after the firing process. Despite the ash weight, the evidence (i.e the degree of fragmentation and the poor representation of each body part) suggests that the attendants took not a great deal of care over collecting this skeleton from the funeral pyre. Very few of the vertebrae have survived, less than ten recognisable fragments and this picture is repeated for many of the major body parts. The bones are generally highly fragmented with few articular ends surviving and none are sufficiently complete to undertake metrical analysis. Even the most robust small bones survive as fragments. Perhaps however the task was undertaken by inexperienced family or other groups or individuals.

It is noticeable how very little charcoal is present with the cremation; only two tiny fragments have been found with the cremated bone. This may indicate that the bone was picked through fairly carefully and the charcoal was deliberately excluded. Reporting on cremations generally, Mays suggests that a more haphazard collection might have resulted in more charcoal ending up in the urn.[9] It is possible that some process was undertaken to winnow out the charcoal. There are classical references that describe bones being washed with wine before being buried.

Overall and taking the pyre and grave goods into consideration, the following interpretation of the cremation event may be offered. The burial was that of but one individual, most probably a female, with some accompanying exotic goods, including carved bone items and personal adornments. Sufficient bone judged to be enough to represent a body was then collected, not very carefully, along with the remains of the personal adornments and worked bone items. It is not possible to say what happened to the pyre debris that was cleared out, as the context in which the cremation was found was so disturbed. We cannot know whether the pyre debris was scattered over the urn or not as part of the cremation ritual – this may well have been the case with the Park Hall, Carmarthen cremation.[10] Certainly after the body had been burned great care was shown to the dead individual, presumably by close family, with the addition of grave goods to the cremation burial.

THE FINDS
BY DEE WILLIAMS

Introduction

Finds from the cremation can be divided into two categories: pyre goods and grave goods. Pyre goods comprise clothing, ornaments and other objects burnt in the funeral pyre with the body, some of which may be later included with the ashes deposited in the funerary urn. Grave goods comprise objects placed within the urn after the cremation as part of the burial rites. All give clues on the cremation and burial events of the funerary ritual and the care taken for the deceased. Three burnt stones and a lump of fired clay (daub) were also found within the urn although these were probably accidentally incorporated during the gathering of the remains.

The assemblage is a very rare discovery for west Wales and raises a number of interesting questions on the role and treatment of pyre and grave goods. With a dearth of comparable material within the region, it has been necessary to look elsewhere, particularly to cremations excavated in south-east Wales, for parallels.

Pottery and Fired Clay

1. The cremation urn is an almost complete wheel-thrown jar, reconstructed from many fragments, in a grey sandy fabric, hard fired and fully reduced. The jar has a rolled, everted rim with an incipient neck cordon. It has a worn dark grey slip on the exterior surface and is decorated, very simply, with grooves and single rouletted bands. The rim diameter is between 130 and 140mm, the base diameter some 100mm and the height of the vessel some 350mm. The sooty deposit inside the base

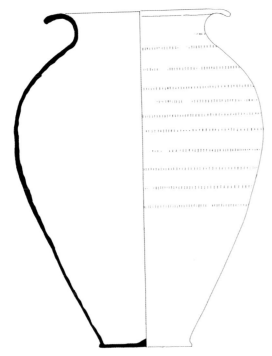

Fig. 4: *Cremation urn, reproduced at ⅛ actual size.*
(Drawing: Heather James).

of the urn is probably a residue from the cremation which it contained.

The urn is not a local product. Although there were local wares both in continuation of Iron Age forms and copying imported pottery from south east Wales, historically west Wales in the late prehistoric and early historic periods was, as far as we can judge, neither a ceramic producing, nor regularly using region. Local wares are generally gritty with frequent gravel inclusions and of poor quality.[11] The cremation urn is a South Wales Greyware product, from kilns in south east Wales, possibly Caerleon and is no later than 150 AD in date. The products of the south east Wales kilns were the most common of the coarse wares in Roman Carmarthen, where any local pottery production was small scale. As with other sites a peak in production and supplies was reached by the early second century.[12] It is uncertain as to whether the Allt-y-Cnap urn had previously been used or whether it was specifically obtained for the burial. The vessel has been damaged during its exposure by earth moving machinery and earlier breaks can be explained by post-deposition soil movement. On balance it would appear that the jar was newly purchased for funerary use.

Such jars are present within other Roman assemblages from the region. The intact cremation urn from Park Hall, Carmarthen is of similar form and fabric though without the rouletted decoration. Surveys of the sparse and often isolated finds of Romano-British cremation urns from west Wales[13] note (where records of earlier finds allow) that the urns are jars of cooking pot form. The two exceptions are a pedestalled urn of 'La Tène III type' from the Roman baths at Pumpsaint[14] and an urn of uncertain context at Cwmbrwyn, Carmarthenshire, a romanised farmstead, which at the time of discovery was compared to examples from Kent.[15] Looking south-eastwards to arguably more 'romanised' areas of south Wales, similar jar forms were used as cremation urns. Compare, for example, possible greyware burial urns of late first-early second century date from the fort at Loughor.[16] Not surprisingly, urn finds from the Lodge Hill Cemetery site at Caerleon were all of either greyware or black-burnished jars.[17]

2. Other finds from within the urn are detailed below but within this sub section dealing with pottery there was only one other ceramic vessel clearly placed with the cremated bone within the cremation urn. Two body sherds from near the base of a jar with the characteristic Severn Valley fabric of an exterior buff-orange and grey core, tempered with fine sands and occasional small red grog pellets and a little surface mica can be associated with a joining base sherd and three more body sherds recovered from the spoil heap.[18] This dispersal is probably due to machine action at the time of discovery since the breaks are all recent. None of the sherds were burnt but too little of the vessel survives to determine the type of jar. A second century AD date is likely. Pottery from the Severn Valley region occurs in significant quantities from sites in Roman Carmarthen from the second through to the fourth centuries AD.

Lamps

The larger of the lamps with the stamp of 'FORTIS' can be dated between 90–150 AD. This has been tentatively identified as being a *Firmalampe* of Loeschcke type X from the Modena workshop in the Po Valley of northern Italy or from one of its branch workshops.[19] The Modena workshop exported far and wide, mainly to the north and northwest provinces and Modena examples are usually in bright brick-red clay and normally without a slip, as here. The lamp factories of Italy usually use the cognomen in full on their lamps such as 'FORTIS', which is inscribed in relief. Few other lamps

Fig. 5: *Lamps from the Allt-y-Cnap cremation burial,
photographed at Carmarthen Museum soon after discovery.*
(Photograph: Carmarthenshire County Museum).

have the makers name in raised letters. However, there is a possibility that the lamp is a provincial product as a number of these types of lamps were copied using the 'Fortis' stamp. The lamp was retrieved intact but not burnt. The nozzle was fire blackened from use in antiquity.

The smaller lamp is possibly a *Firmalampe* of Loeschcke type IX. Production of these began around AD 70, earlier than type X, but both types continued to be manufactured into the second century. This was also retrieved intact but not burnt, and again showed evidence of a fire-blackened nozzle from use in antiquity.

The sherds of a miniature oil lamp were recovered from the spoil heap, which unfortunately had been broken by the contractor's machine bucket. This lamp shows no evidence of previous use in antiquity. The inclusion of these miniature lamps and vessels within children's burials is an aspect of Roman burial practice also noted at Colchester, Essex.[20]

Tile

Five small fragments of tile were recovered from the spoil heap. They were curved and thus were from an *imbrex* or *imbrices*, that is to say the curved tiles which covered the two adjoining edges of the side ridges of the flat *tegula*. Although their primary purpose was as roofing tiles these were used for other purposes. They may here indicate the presence of a tile cist in the burial pit or the provision of a simple cover for the cremation urn.[21]

Glass

1. Four small rim and neck fragments of a flask or unguent bottle of pale blue glass; the rim is out-turned and rolled-in but insufficient remains for the diameter

of the vessel to be established. This rim form is typical of unguent bottles of the first to second centuries AD.[22]

2. One neck fragment from a vessel of indeterminate form, possibly a flask or phial, of colourless glass, very bubbly with several black impurities.

3. Another ten associated fragments (one pale blue, nine colourless) all very small, were retrieved from sieved material.

One, possibly two, unguent containers therefore can be identified but not enough survives to determine their exact form. From the late first century onwards glass vessels were very often added to the grave goods deposit and the majority of glass vessels found with second century cremations are phials or *unguentaria*.[23] These small containers are thought to have contained oils and other costly preparations which were used as unctions in a funerary context.

It is not clear how and when the vessels came to be broken. One possibility is that they were placed on the pyre and shattered in the heat. Another possibility is that, once emptied of contents, they were broken and later scraped up and placed in the urn. The evidence is inconclusive as the fragments are too small to detect signs of heat damage although when examined under the microscope at Carmarthen Museum, the edges of the broken glass showed no sign of melting. It is of note that the urn from the Park Hall Estate, Carmarthen, contained fragments of pale blue bottle glass which were clearly heat-affected and yet were still identifiable.[24] These two Carmarthen cremations add to the still sparse evidence indicating that the Romano-British funerary practice of adding glass vessels to cremation burials had spread across Wales beyond military cemetaries like those at Caerleon.[25]

IRON OBJECTS
BY HEATHER JAMES & JOHN PURDUE

Some iron objects were recovered from within the cremation urn and one from the spoil heap of material from the top of the urn disturbed by the machine bucket. They were corroded and some certainly fire-damaged. However it has not been possible to clean and conserve these objects nor X-ray them so some identifications must remain provisional.

1. Two small but clearly identifiable fragments from sandals, boots or shoes came from within the cremation urn. Carbonised leather still survived around the dis-

tinctive hobnails, one fragment (310mm long, 257mm wide) having five nails, the other (210mm long, 200mm wide) having three. These must be classed as pyre goods, perhaps worn by the deceased at the time of cremation. Only a small, perhaps token, deposit was then retrieved from the ashes and placed within the cremation urn.

2. Two complete nails were found in the upper cremation fill; they are of Manning's Type 1, the most common, with tapering square-sectioned stems which were bent but not clenched.[26] They had round, flat heads, perhaps simply the consequence of having been hammered into wood. They were 55 and 60mm long.

3. A further heavily corroded nail head or tack was recovered from the machine disturbed upper cremation fill.

4. A small corroded fragment, perhaps part of a strap hinge, 26mm long, 3.7mm wide and 2.5mm deep was recovered by dry sieving from the central fill of the cremation. It was perforated by two small tacks, one complete, the other with only a head, 5.2mm apart. At a further distance of 5.2mm was a hole through which another tack would have passed. The small size of this possible hinge possibly indicates the presence of a small wooden box or casket deposited within the cremation urn.

5. A heavily corroded iron object, or two objects fused together was recovered from the spoil from the initial machine bucket disturbance of the cremation. This may be another strap hinge of about 65mm, and has traces of mineralised wood in the join between two parts of the hinge. Fused to this is a twisted square sectioned length of iron of uncertain purpose.

WORKED BONE
BY HEATHER JAMES AND JOHN PURDUE

All of these worked bone objects were recovered from the cremation urn and represent pyre goods later gathered up and placed within the urn.

1. A fine bone hairpin, broken towards the tip, 35mm long showed signs of burning and may have been warped into its present shape by the heat of the pyre. It has minute traces of a residue of green copper salts staining it visible only under the microscope. The pin has a conical head above a collar. This is the earlier of the two types known, identified by Greep as Type A with straight tapering stems in use between the mid first

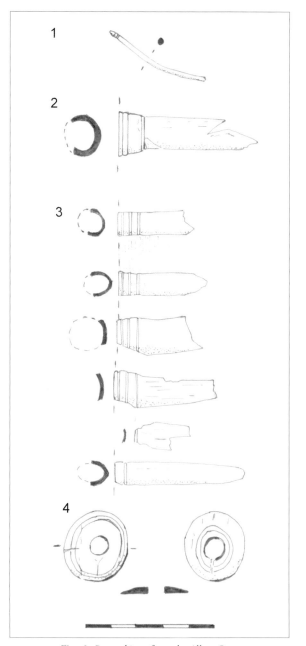

Fig. 6: *Bone objects from the Allt-y-Cnap cremation burial, actual size.*
(Drawn by Heather James).

to the mid third century AD. This example fits his category Type A2.2 well defined as having conical or rounded heads and grooves below making one or more collars.[27] This is the one gender-specific find from the cremation, since hairpins have only ever been recovered from female cremation burials.[28]

2. Four joining fragments form part of a lathe-turned bone tube or cylinder decorated at the presumed opening end. The fragment is 55mm long with an internal diameter of 11mm. The cylinder is slightly tapering with an incised band at its end and a second deeper band below forming a collar. Two further bands below from another collar demarcating the top of the object from its shaft or body. This may have held a toiletry item.

3. Nine fragments, of which five are illustrated, belong to at least six small lathe-turned and incised bone tubes of slightly different diameters. Four have identical, matching incised double bands in three groups at the cut end of the bones. One has but a single decorated zone, again of two bands. It is possible that these are part of the top and bottom of bone 'pipes' joined by bronze binding and forming a musical instrument, a *syrinx* or pan pipes. Greep notes, when citing a single bone cylinder as a possible element from such a musical instrument, that such finds are rare from Roman Britain and often unrecognised.[29]

4. Four fragments of burnt bone from within the urn join to form a complete round disc measuring 25mm in diameter and 3.5mm in depth. It is slightly distorted by heat with clear dark marks from burning on its upper and underside surfaces. There is a perforation 7mm in diameter finally and symmetrically drilled through the disc, though not absolutely centrally located. The disk is domed in profile and two finely-incised bands encircle its outer circumference, quite deeply but sharply cut. On the underside there are also two similar circular cuts but these encircle the perforation.

This object can be identified as the surviving bone button of a 'button and loop' fastener and compared to a similarly sized example from the Legionary Fortress Baths at Caerleon.[30] The button was attached to the loop by a bronze rivet within the central perforation. Complete examples are rare and the type has been studied by Wild who suggests that these are of early Roman date and if used for clothing (and this is far from certain) may have been used on a cloak or cape.[31]

SITE LOCATION, ARCHAEOLOGICAL BACKGROUND & HISTORIC LANDUSE

The discovery of the cremation burial at Allt-y-Cnap was completely unexpected. It is necessary to consider the location of the burial as well as the burial rite itself. Bearing in mind a likely date of late first or early second century for the cremation, the Allt-y-Cnap burial should first be compared with the location of burials in relation to auxiliary forts and *vicus* settlements. At Llandovery, the closest auxiliary fort to Carmarthen to have revealed such evidence, a cremation cemetery was located some 400 m. south of the fort and about 200m west of the Roman road approaching the fort from the south east.[32] At Pumpsaint, poorly recorded finds of a 'cinerary urn containing burnt bones' came from the bathhouse, south of the fort, now known to to be close to the Roman road. Other roadside burials may be in the same general location.[33] Other cemeteries at auxiliary fort sites listed by Pollock, such as Abergavenny, were some 800m from the fort although there is an antiquarian record of a possible cremation burial some 4 km to the north-west. Other cemeteries, cremation and inhumation, at forts like Segontium (Cernarfon) and Brecon Gaer were closer to both forts and roads and this would seem to be the norm for auxiliary forts in Britain.

The Allt-y-Cnap cremation is some 2km distant from the Roman fort site and associated settlement at Carmarthen. Nor is it close to the recently recognised and recorded Roman Road proceeding westwards from Carmarthen to as yet undiscovered destination(s) in Pembrokeshire. This lies 500m to the north (*see Fig. 7*). The Park Hall cremation, discovered in 2001, is in a much more explicable location flanking the road leading from the fort at Carmarthen up the Tywi Valley to forts at Llandeilo and Llandovery. It too is likely to be of early second century date and thus earlier than the defended, formally constituted Roman town to the west and possibly the Roman amphitheatre which lies close to the east of the Park Hall site. There was evidence for other burials at this cemetery site which might have continued in use as burial rites changed to inhumation in the later Roman period. There is possibly some significance to be attached to the Park Hall cemetery being located to the east of a Roman temple, discovered at the Priory Street excavations of late first to early second century date. This temple preceded the formal layout of streets and buildings taken to indicate the establishment of a civitas capital at Carmarthen, at some date between AD 120 and AD 150 and is likely to be of Trajanic date (early second century).[34] The Allt-y-Cnap cremation was an accidental discovery but in so far as could be ascertained from the subsequent watching brief, it was a single burial.

Cremation was not an unknown rite in late Iron Age Britain and there are examples from west Wales of such burials in the defences, or ditches of hillforts and defended

Fig. 7: *Vertical air photograph, Meridian Air Surveys, 1954, reproduced from the air photographic collection in the HER, Dyfed Archaeological Trust, with annotations showing possible hillfort banks on Ystrad Hill and a small enclosure on Allt-y-Cnap Road.*

enclosures. Pollock notes that five out of the six Iron Age sites to produce cremations are located in west Wales. There is some suggestion also that Romano-British burials, both cremation and, in some few instances, in-humation, may have continued an earlier native Iron Age practice of burials on boundaries or at least the periphery of settlements. At present, the only possible settlement context for the All-y-Cnap cremation is a hillfort on Ystrad Hill, Johnstown which lies less than 200m to the south – the burial is in fact on the lower slopes of Ystrad Hill. However, the existence of the hillfort is far from certain.

It was first listed by Savory in his gazetteer of hillforts in Wales.[35] He had identified the site from a vertical air

photograph taken by the RAF in 1946, but subsequent visits by the Archaeology Division of the Ordnance Survey in 1966 and 1967 failed to reveal to them evidence to substantiate Savory's site. They thought that surviving earthworks were either natural or part of an old field bank. An air photograph by Terry James in 1984 seemed also to show at least part of an enclosure, listed as record 2144 on the Dyfed Archaeological Trust's Historic Environment Record. A recent field visit by K. Murphy and R. Ramsay of Dyfed Archaeological Trust as part of a Cadw-funded, pan-Wales survey of pre-historic enclosures concluded that some of the undoubted earthworks on the plateau like summit of Ystrad Hill were natural but others could be part of a defensive bank surviving up to 0.3m in height in parts.[36] The size and shape of the enclosure however could not be recognised on the ground.

It is however important to recognise that the hilltop may well have been subject to some degree of levelling as part of John Jones' landscaping and emparking of his Ystrad estate in the early nineteenth century. Tom Lloyd has drawn my (HJ) attention to the illustration on the sale catalogue of Ystrad in 1843 after John Jones death which shows a prominent and fashionable encircling of the hilltop above the house by a plantation of fir trees.

On balance therefore there remains at least the possibility of there being a hillfort or defended enclosure on the summit of Ystrad Hill which might, conceivably provide a possible context for the cremation burial sited on the northern flanks of the site, just possibly in a liminal position. Several hillforts and defended enclosures surround the site of Carmarthen's Roman fort and town. Most are known only from Ordnance Survey plans, air photographs, antiquarian records or place-name evidence.[37] Only on the largest and most complex site, Merlin's Hill has had some excavation (and that very limited) been carried out and there was no evidence of Romano-British occupation.[38]

Further south, between Llangynog and Llansteffan there are numerous defended enclosures and hillforts of varying size and undoubtedly different dates of origin and occupation. It is interesting to note that the one extensive excavation on such a site, that at Pen-y-Coed demonstrated occupation and use as a farmstead in the Romano-British period but with very little evidence of life styles altered in any way by even the most basic Romano-British 'consumer goods'.[39] Other small defended enclosures in west Wales have however shown plenty of evidence for occupation in the first and second centuries AD.[40] It is thus interesting to note that in addition to possible hillfort earthworks on Ystrad Hill the 1954 air photograph (*Fig. 7*) shows a possible small, sub-circular defended enclosure on Allt-y-Cnap Road adjacent to the former Cill Efwr farm. The air photograph clearly shows the field bank lying over the earthwork, part of a set of field boundaries either side of Allt-y-Cnap Road that seems to perpetuate alignments of former mediaeval strip fields. All this area now lies below an industrial estate, all early traces being lost. Nevertheless, if there was a defended enclosure adjacent to the farm which from its form could be of late Iron Age/Romano-British date, here is another context for the cremation burial.

The most striking feature of the Allt-y-Cnap cremation however is how strongly classical it is in its burial rites. This was also a feature of the Park Hall cremation, also of a young woman. Here though was evidence of possible feasting at the time and site of burial with cremated fragments animal bones, possibly from a sheep, with the human remains. There were also carbonised grape pips within the funerary urn. Care had been taken to remove the fragments of a glass vessel or vessels, together with bone, pottery and iron nails from the pyre there to be placed in the funerary urn. This is similar to the practice at Allt-y-Cnap. Dr Ros Coard has noted in her bone report above a certain lack of expertise in recovering material from the pyre for burial at Allt-y-Cnap which might denote unfamiliarity with the actual practice of such Roman burial rites by local practitioners. Yet the desire of the deceased, or those burying the deceased, for Roman burial rites is manifest. Nevertheless, she points out, bone was collected along with pyre and grave goods, some fairly exotic, placed in the urn. Further, the addition of lamps is intriguing and may suggest that they were part of the cremation ritual. The possibility of pan-pipes being burnt and buried with the deceased female also raises interesting questions. Only the 'monumentality', that is to say marking the grave by a mausoleum or tombstone which is more common in the cemeteries of the legionary fortresses seems lacking. Pollock notes that native influence may account for the rejection of such monuments in favour of barrows or wooden mortuary enclosures. Since, however, it is likely that there has been soil creep down Ystrad Hill (see above) we cannot be sure what, if any, above-ground structures may have marked the Allt-y-Cnap burial.

This completely unexpected discovery cannot be exactly paralleled by any other Romano-British cremations analysed by Pollock and is a rare, important and – at present – mysterious addition to our knowledge of life in and around *Moridunum* in the first and second centuries AD.

ACKNOWLEDGEMENTS

Thanks are due to Gavin Evans, Curator of Carmarthenshire County Museum, Abergwili, whose help and support has made this project's limited budget extend through to post-excavation work and now, publication.

NOTES

1. P. Crane, unpublished Report on the Park Hall excavations, Dyfed Archaeological Trust Report 2001/42, prn 42599.

2. Geological Survey Maps, Sheet 229, Carmarthen, Solid & Drift; A. Strahan *et al. Memoirs of the Geological Survey: The Geology of the South Wales Coalfield, Part X, The Country around Carmarthen* (HMSO, 1909), p. 31.

3. C. O. Lovejoy, R. S. Meindl, T. R. Pryzbeck & R. Mensforth, 'Chronological metamorphosis of the auricular surface of the ilium: a new method for the determination of adult skeletal age at death', *American Journal of Physical Anthropology*, Vol. 68, 1985, pp. 15-28.

4. P. Shipman, G. Foster & M. Schoeninger, 'Burnt bones and teeth: an experimental study of colour, morphology, crystal structure and shrinkage', *Jnl. of Archaeological Science*, Vol. 11, 1984, pp. 307-325.

5. R. A. Nicholson, 'A morphological investigation of burnt animal bone and an evaluation of its utility in Archaeology', *Jnl. of Archaeological Science,* Vol. 20, 1993, pp. 411-428.

6. Idem.

7. M. Trotter & B. B. Hixon, 'Sequential changes in weight, density and percentage ash weight of human skeletons from an early fetal period through old age', *The Anatomical Record,* Vol. 179, pp. 1-18.

8. E. Evans & J. D. Maynard, 'Caerleon Lodge Hill Cemetery. The Abbeyfield Site 1992', *Brittania*, Vol. 28, pp. 205-207.

9. S. Mays, *The Archaeology of Human Bones* (London, Routledge, 1998), p. 223.

10. P. Crane, op. cit., n. 1.

11. D. Brennan, 'The Coarse Pottery' in H. James, *Roman Carmarthen: Excavations 1978-1993* (Britannia Monograph Ser. No. 20, 2003), pp. 255-282, esp. p. 259 for 'local gritty ware'.

12. Idem, Fig. 7.15, p. 257.

13. R. Philpott, *Burial Practices in Roman Britain: A survey of grave treatment and furnishing AD 43-410* (Oxford, BAR 219, 1991); K. Pollock, *The Evolution and Role of Burial Practice in Roman Wales* (Oxford, BAR Brit. Ser. 426, 2006).

14. Royal Commission on Ancient & Historical Monuments in Wales, *Carmarthenshire Inventory* (HMSO, 1908), pp. 58-9.

15. For the excavation at Cwmbrwyn, see J. Ward, 'Roman remains at Cwmbrwyn, Carmarthenshire', *Arch. Camb.*, Vol. 62, pp. 175-208, and for the urn found in the nearby farmyard, J. F. Jones, 'Roman Carmarthenshire', *Carms. Antiq.*, Vol III, 1961, p. 126.

16. R. & L. Ling, 'Excavations at Loughor, Glamorgan: the north-east and south-east angles of the Roman Fort', *Arch. Camb.*, Vol. 122, p. 99-146.

17. Evans & Maynard, op. cit., n. 8, p. 194.

18. P. V. Webster, 'Severn Valley ware: a preliminary study', *Trans. Bristol & Gloucs. Arch. Soc.*, Vol. 94, 1976, pp. 18-46.

19. S. Loeschcke, *Lampen aus Vindonissa* (Zurich, 1919).

20. N. Crummy, *Colchester Archaeological Report 2: The Roman Small Finds from Excavations in Colchester, 1971-9* (1983), pp. 270-3.

21. R. Philpott, op. cit. n. 13, pp. 9-12, for a discussion of stone & tile cists.

22. J. Price and S. Cottam, *Romano-British Glass Vessels: A Handbook* (CBA Practical Handbook in Archaeology, No. 14, 1998), p. 22.

23. Philpott 1991, pp. 115 & 117, K. Murphy, 'Excavations at Penycoed, Llangynog, Dyfed, 1983', *Carms. Antiq.*, Vol. XXI, 1985, pp. 75-112.

24. Ros Coard, pers. comm.

25. D. Zienkiewicz, 'The Glass' in E. Evans & D. J. Maynard, 'Caerleon Lodge Hill Cemetery: the Abbeyfield Site 1992', *Britannia*, Vol. 28, pp. 240-242.

26. W. H. Manning, *Catalogue of the Romano-British Iron Tools, Fittings and Weapons in the British Museum* (British Museum, 1985), see Section R, 'Structural Fittings'.

27. S. J. Greep, 'The Worked Bone' in D. Zienkiewicz, *The Legionary Fortress Baths at Caerleon* (National Museum of Wales & Cadw, Cardiff, 1986), Vol II, The Finds, p. 197.

28. N. Crummy, 'A Chronology of Romano-British Bone Pins', *Britannia*, Vol. 10, 1979, pp. 157-163.

29. S. J.Greep, 'Objects of bone and antler' in A. G. Marvell & H. S. Owen-John, *Leucarum: Excavations at the Roman Legionary Fort at Loughor, West Glamorgan* (London, Soc. For the Promotion of Roman Studies, 1997), Britannia Monograph Series, No. 12, p. 410, No. 6.

30. Greep, op. cit., n. 27, pp. 209-210, No. 22.

31. J. P. Wild, 'Button-and-Loop Fasteners in the Roman Provinces', *Britannia*, Vol. 1, 1970, pp. 137-155.

32. Although records are sparse, J. F. Jones, then Curator of Carmarthen Museum, was alerted to the discovery of urns and pottery, although very little now survives in the collections of Carmarthen Museum; for full details, see records 4084 & 4087, in the Historic Environment Record maintained by Dyfed Archaeological Trust at Llandeilo.

33. Pollock, op. cit., n. 13, p. 232.

34. H. James, *Roman Carmarthen: Excavations 1978-1993* (Britannia Monograph No. 20, 2003), for temple, see pp. 145-150.

35. H. N. Savory, 'List of Hill Forts and Other Earthworks in Wales, V: Carmarthenshire', *Bull. Bd.Celtic Studies*, Vol. 16, 1954, pp. 54-69.

36. Unpublished reports by K. Murphy *et al.* to Cadw, in the Historic Environment Record (HER), Dyfed Archaeological Trust, Llandeilo, site record 2144.

37. For a recent, exhaustive condition survey of all upstanding and cropmark sites of this type, see the reports, n. 39.

38. G. Williams *et al.* 'Recent Archaeological Work on Merlin's Hill, Abergwili', *Carms. Antiq.*, Vol. XXIV, 1988, pp. 5-13.

39. K. Murphy, 'Excavations at Penycoed, Llangynog, Dyfed, 1983', *Carms. Antiq.*, Vol. XXI, 1985, pp. 75-112.

40. G. Williams & H. Mytum, *Llawhaden, Dyfed: Excavations on a group of small defended enclosures, 1980-4* (BAR Brit. Ser. 275, 1998).

Some Preliminary Observations on Sir John Gardner Wilkinson's Survey of the Ogofau Gold Mines, Dolaucothi, of 1868

C. Stephen Briggs

In 'retirement' the pioneer British Egyptologist, Sir John Gardner Wilkinson (1797-1875), researched in South Wales and Southwest England, c.1855-1870. He produced the earliest known detailed topographical survey of the Ogofau, Dolaucothi, Carmarthenshire (SN 665 404). This is described and discussed in the contexts of archaeological discovery and survey, and of historic mining. It brings much new information to bear on the state of the nineteenth-century landscape prior to its industrialisation for gold extraction after 1870. Both circumstantial and direct evidence for the function and dating of the described features are discussed. These suggest heavy dependence upon extensive hydraulic processing to mine unknown metals before gold was recognised in 1844. It seems likely that metals other than gold were being sought before that date. Such a large-scale low-yielding mineral extractive undertaking probably had mediaeval or post-mediaeval origins, although many prefer a Roman dating. Current interpretations rely strongly on antiquarian tradition and limited archaeological evidence, some unpublished. Rigorous archaeometric dating and sedimentological studies should be applied to many of the outstanding investigational problems.

INTRODUCTION

Sir John Gardner Wilkinson (1797-1875) was arguably the Father of British Egyptology.[1] After a successful career abroad, he returned to live permanently in Britain during the 1850s. In 1855 he married Caroline Lucas, who belonged to a well-established Glamorgan family. They moved from London to begin married life in rented property at Tenby and in 1866 they bought a house at Reynoldston on Gower. Thereafter, with Caroline's help, he researched sites, landscapes and some buildings in Derbyshire, Devon and Cornwall, in Pembrokeshire and on Gower.[2] Their travel notebooks are illustrated with accomplished sketches and watercolours which survive in Wilkinson's extensive archive, now owned by the National Trust. Since 1999 this has been the subject of a useful online catalogue at the Bodleian Library, Oxford, where the archive is on deposit. The listing is insufficiently detailed to identify all individual documents.[3]

In 2007, while examining Wilkinson's investigations at some British prehistoric sites, I stumbled upon drawings of Dolaucothi. They include sketches of Roman artifacts from Pumsaint and landscapes showing the Ogofau opencasts and adits, all apparently from Sir John's hand. The present discussion focuses on his remarkable ground survey of these mine-workings, completed by 1868. The other drawings will be published in due course.

Having been acquainted with Terry James for some thirty years, and having worked alongside him during his time at the Royal Commission on the Ancient and Historical Monuments of Wales, I believe his interest would have been fired by this discovery. Terry would have appreciated Wilkinson's skills as a surveyor; his qualities as a cartographer and illustrator of artifacts, his deductive insights as a researching antiquary, and his industry in completing the project. It is therefore a great privilege to publish this component of Wilkinson's work in a collection dedicated to Terry's scholarship.

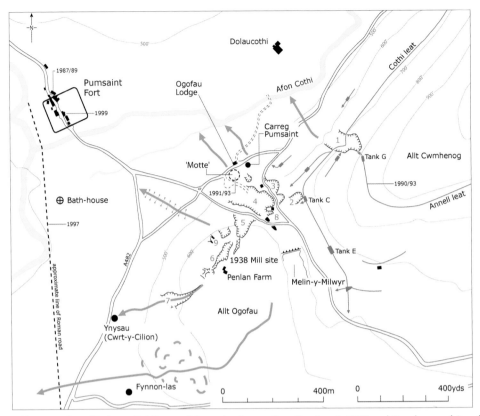

Fig. 1: *General location plan of Dolaucothi Mines and Pumsaint Roman fort after Annels 1995 and Burnham and Burnham, 2004, with additions. The orange arrows added to the plan indicate probable outwash channels. The numbers relate to the following features:*
1- Allt Cwmhenog opencast, 2 – Mitchell Pit, 3 – 'Roman' Pit, 4 – Ogofau Pit, 5 – Niagara Pit, 6 – Penlanwen workings,
7 – Cwrt-y-Cilion trenches, 8 – Davies Cutting, 9 – Upper and Lower Roman adits.

A BRIEF ANTIQUARIAN HISTORY
OF DOLAUCOTHI MINES

The Ogofau was the name adopted to describe caves or adits incised into the eastern bluffs of the Cothi valley just outside and to the east of the village of Pumsaint in Carmarthenshire and towards the southern margin of the Cambrian Mountains. This unusual topography formed part of the Dolaucothi estate, a property belonging to ancestors of the Johnes family from the time of Henry VII until gifted to the National Trust in 1943.[4] With a modest country house of 1792-6 by John Nash, demolished in 1956,[5] the management of its landscape features was typical of the larger farming units of Tywi Valley gentry until the mid-twentieth century.

Today the remaining buildings and farmland are leased out and in the summer months the mines are opened as a visitor and educational attraction. It is widely believed that this was the only gold mine in Roman Britain. The site is felt to be of supreme technological importance in the British Isles with features unique in this country. These beliefs were well-established in the antiquarian literature when the Wilkinsons first came to Dolaucothi during the 1850s.

The object of this article is two-fold: first, to explain the topographical features delineated on the plans and briefly set them in the context of industrial history and archaeological investigation; and secondly, to reflect upon those features and discuss how they and certain other factors may affect the most recent interpretations of the site.

GARDNER WILKINSON AND THE OGOFAU
The Wilkinsons and the Johnes families
It is unclear whether or not the Johnes's knew Gardner Wilkinson before *c*.1855, when he probably accompanied the Cambrian Archaeological Association in its visit to the area. Betha Johnes was already well-acquainted with Wilkinson's wife-to-be, Caroline Lucas, prior to their

marriage in 1856.[6] Distinguished antiquaries and geologists regularly visited Dolaucothi, so the Wilkinsons were among several who enjoyed the well-planted historic estate and its unusual industrial features. Sir John would have soon familiarised himself with the Ogofau during these visits. The Egyptologist no doubt shared the family's enthusiasm for their small but celebrated private museum of local antiquities, as well as for the Cambrian Archaeological Association, of which he became a Vice-President in 1869.

The 1854 edition of Wilkinson's *The Ancient Egyptians: their Life and Customs* included an account of goldmining on the Nile[7] which he had recently obtained from the French Egyptologist, Bonomi, so his counsel on ancient mines was no doubt respected. He undertook this Ogofau survey in 1868, shortly before his health began to decline significantly. The Johneses may have invited him to undertake the task, one for which

he seems to have been eminently well-qualified and which must have been time-consuming and enervating.

Plans of the industrial site: a brief history
Dolaucothi estate plans of the eighteenth century aside (and these provide no information on mining), there are only three significant surveys of the area offering useful background to Gardner Wilkinson's. The earliest is the Tithe Award of 1840.[8] This conveys little to help decipher the landscape around Dolaucothi: the industrial area is shown featureless; it betrays no idea of contemporary agricultural practice, and it gives only the names of landlords (John Johnes of Dolaucothi, George Lloyd of Brunant and Sir James Williams) and their tenants. It is helpful in providing farm names, though less so in not naming individual fields, a practice which is found on many other contemporary Tithe Award Maps.

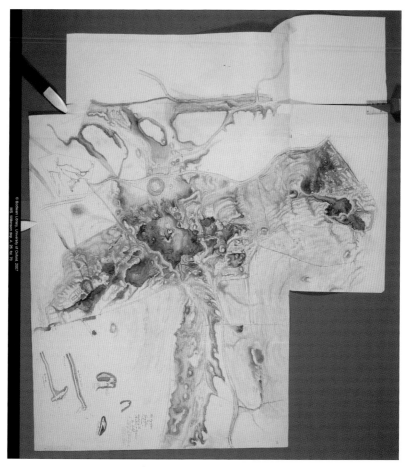

Fig. 2: *Gardner Wilkinson's main plan, 1868, fo. 70.*
(Reproduced by courtesy of the Bodleian Library and with the permission of the National Trust).

137

The earliest detailed accurate survey of the area is therefore the Ordnance Survey First Edition 25-inch (Plans Carms. XVI: 4; XVII: 1, 2 and 5, and IX: 13, 14) of 1888. Curiously, although depicting a number of quarried features, in common with industrial features depicted elsewhere, the Ogofau mines are not so clearly or so extensively engraved in 1888 as upon the Second Edition of 1906. Both editions were made at a time of serious industrial interest, if not also of activity. Thus, Gardner Wilkinson's is the earliest-known detailed survey of the area: it depicts the greater proportion of those features today considered important to an understanding of the landscape on the eve of the first real burst of known industrial activity in the early 1870s.

A numbered plan by Alwyn Annels, from the 1995 site guide,[9] is used here as the basis of Fig. 1 for locational purposes.

Gardner Wilkinson's Plans of the Ogofau

Five plans have survived. They are archived but not indexed among loose papers in an oversize elephant-sized folio (Bodleian MS Gardner Wilkinson A 26; fols. 67, 68, 69, 70 and 71). Two are more-or-less finished pieces (fols. 70 and 71); two are pencil sketches including all original measurements, one of underground and the other of surface features (fols. 67 and 68); and fol. 69 is a preliminary draft for fol. 71.

The most accomplished and complete (fol. 70; here Fig. 2) may be described as Wilkinson's master plan. Finished in a brown colour-wash hachure technique and annotated by a tiny hand in red and black inks, it encompasses the area of opencasting stretching from Allt Cwmhenog in the north through the Ogofau Opencast, to the south end of the opencast trench alongside Penlanwen Farm and the north end of the Cwrt-y-cilion trench. It is entitled: 'The Ogofau or gogofau 'caves' worked by the Britons and Romans for gold, by Gardner Wilkinson, scale of 110 feet [30.35 m] to 1 inch [0.0025 m].' On the reverse he wrote: 'To be sent to the Editorial Sub-Committee Archaeologia Cambrensis – In the case of my death, with the condition of them publishing . . . of this size within three years of my death. Gardner Wilkinson October 1868. If the above condition is not complied with or fulfilled, it is to be returned to my Executors. J. Gardner Wilkinson, Sept. 26th 1870.'

Extracts from this plan are presented at a larger scale to illustrate some of its more interesting features. It is worth observing that a small number of underground tunnels or adits are marked up in red on this plan. Several are marked only 'Cave' while others have more specific names. As is noted in individual cases, some have since disappeared and it has not been found possible to discuss all the sites. A small sketch-map relating this main site survey to Pumsaint and the road system overlies the mapped area close to the road junction triangle centred on SN 6605 4025.

With Fig. 3 we begin closer description in the north, on the Allt Cwmhenog opencasting (numbered '1' in Fig. 1). It is noteworthy that there is no up-to-date archaeological plan, largely due to its inaccessibility post-World War II under heavy undergrowth and forestry plantation. Only outline plans have so far figured in the archaeological literature (e.g. Fig. 1), though the OS 25-inch plan SN 6640 of 1978 offers useful comparison with Wilkinson's and shows his to be slightly askew in some places. His is nonetheless the most detailed plan available and was the first to depict the Cothi leat crossing the opencast. He seems also to have depicted the water tanks ('G' on Fig. 1) which the 1960[10] and 1969[11] plans show at the terminus of the Annell leat. To the south of the opencast area is marked 'Wood of Cwm', 'Henog dell of the old cave . . . or the oldish dell'.

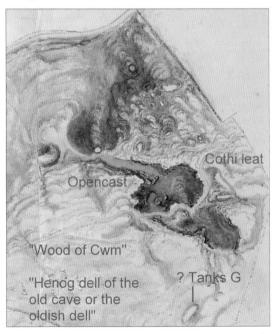

Fig. 3: *Annotated extract from Gardner Wilkinson's main plan showing the Allt Cwmhenog opencast; his map legends are in inverted commas, other text is for cross reference to Fig. 1.*
(Reproduced by courtesy of the Bodleian Library and with the permission of the National Trust).

Fig. 4: *Annotated extract from Gardner Wilkinson's main plan showing the Ogofau opencast.*
(Reproduced by courtesy of the Bodleian Library and with the permission of the National Trust).

Fig 5: *Plan of Gwenno's Cave or Well, fo. 70.*
(Reproduced by courtesy of the Bodleian Library and with the permission of the National Trust).

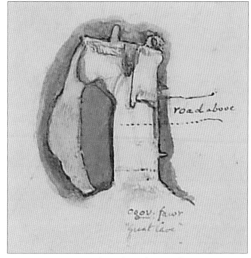

Fig. 6a: *Plan of Ogof Fawr, fo. 70.*
(Reproduced by courtesy of the Bodleian Library and with the permission of the National Trust).

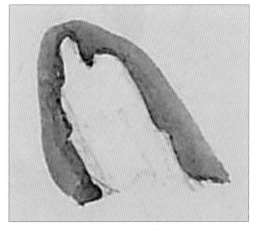

Fig. 6b: *Section of Ogof Fawr, fo. 70.*
(Reproduced by courtesy of the Bodleian Library and with the permission of the National Trust).

Fig. 4 shows the central area of the main plan, focused on the 'Great Opencast' or 'Ogofau Opencast' (numbered '4' on Fig. 1) which is the area now most familiar to investigation and probably where the greatest changes have taken place since 1868. Its most immediately recognisable features within the opencast are 'Ffynnon Gwenno – Gwenno's Well' above which is marked 'rushes', and beyond that 'spring' alongside the track passing through this opencast area. 'Rushes' and 'marsh' are similarly marked above what at that time was the natural stone pillar 'Clochdy Gwenno' or 'bellhouse steeple' where the stream enters the opencast pit. Among several individual site plans provided in the empty margin is 'Ogof Ffynnon Gwenno' (Fig. 5). This lay within the opencast, part of which is marked 'Marshy Ground'. Another marginal plan shows the tunnel that existed beneath the central track passing through the site (Fig. 6a; Fig. 6b may be the section to this or of some other). Upon the floor of the main opencast is a west-facing minor site over which is written 'quartz hammer', and below it, apparently on the floor of the extraction area 'quartz'. This has the first mapped depictions of the site of the Carreg Pumsaint 'stone' and of the so-called 'motte', here titled a 'mound with larches'. A short distance southwest is inscribed 'site of tent', which is presumably where the Australian miners pitched camp *c.*1855 (a fact not previously ascertained, see p. 143). The Dolaucothi estate lodge (built in 1840) is shown as a simple square building, its (presumably productive) rectangular garden beds being

ghosted in. Further to the southwest is marked a 'Spot where nothing will grow well' (centred on SN 6615 4040). This may be coincident with the area where broken quartz waste was observed by Sir Joseph Banks in 1763,[12] and later by Lewis and Jones.[13]

The third extract (Fig. 7) shows 'Pen lan Wen House and Farm', with a mineral extraction trench running below and alongside the farm, and the features now known as the *Roman Adits* below, where, since 1989 when they were opened up for access, they have formed part of the National Trust's 'Miners Walk' (these features are numbered '6' and '9' on Fig. 1). These adits are also among the surveyed sections provided marginally. One (the more northerly) reads 'upper Ogo Hwch, Sow's Cave 5'6" by 5'11" ' [1.65 m by 1.8 m] and the adjoining adit is entitled: 'Ogo Cauge 6'1" by 5'10" [1.55 m by 1.77 m] cave of the bowl' (Fig. 8). These later became respectively OLD LEVEL (ROMAN) and OGOF CAWGIAU (ROMAN LEVELS) on the 1907 OS 25-inch map, before the present titles of *Upper* and *Lower Roman Adit* were adopted. The pencilled drafts preparatory to these sections (fol. 68) are not illustrated here. It seems strange that Gardner Wilkinson should have re-surveyed them when comprehensive plans and sections were already in print, made twenty-four years earlier by the geologist Warington Smyth (Fig. 9).[14]

At first sight, some of the elongated earthworks depicted on the ground adjacent to and west of Penlanwen are a mystery, but archaeological survey in the 1980s recognized them as pillow mounds.[15] Interestingly, several had appeared on the OS 25-inch plan (SN 6640) by 1978.

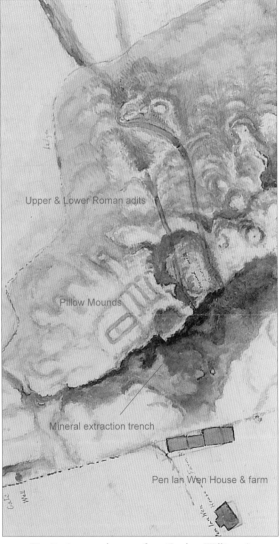

Fig. 7: *Annotated extract from Gardner Wilkinson's Main plan, fo. 70 of the Penlanwen area.*
(Reproduced by courtesy of the Bodleian Library and with the permission of the National Trust).

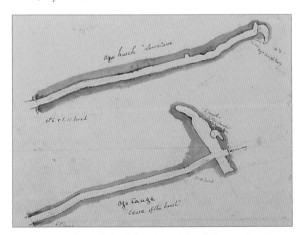

Fig. 8: *Plans of Ogof Huwch and Ogof Cauge, fo. 70.*
(Reproduced by courtesy of the Bodleian Library and with the permission of the National Trust).

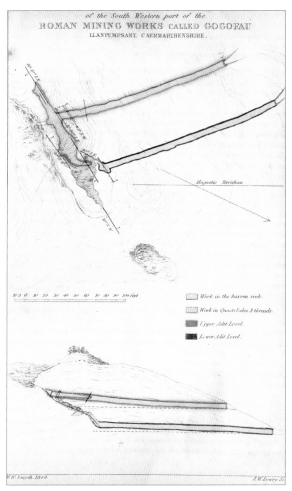

Fig. 9: *Ogof Hwch and Ogof Cauge (Upper and Lower Roman adits), plans by Warington Smyth, 1844.*

One of the most interesting aspects of Wilkinson's plan is his depiction of 'Melin-y-Milwyr' (soldiers' mill) which is in a different location to the water tank now known by that name today (Fig. 10). Wilkinson's Melin-y-Milwyr seems to be in the same position as the water tank named as 'Tank E' by Jones and Lewis in the 1960s (see Fig. 1). Wilkinson here depicts the earth-work bank. To the south he marks 'Melin-y-Milwyr' and, significantly, the plan records 'channel cut in rock' 'varying' . . . '6 ft (c.1.8 m) wide' just beyond the point where the leat leaves the tank at the southeast corner (at OS SN 6070 4004). Its course continues, well-marked as far as the next hedge (at OS SN 6691 3999), before Wilkinson demonstrates its westward descent with a streak of darker watercolour. The 'modern sand pit' immediately north-west of the 'Melin' is also shown.

Wilkinson's plan is of great value for the west side of the valley between Allt Cwmhenog and Allt Ogofau through which runs the minor road between Pumsaint and Caio villages. He records features before the area was heavily used and altered by twentieth-century mine-workings. Along the eastern slopes of Allt Ogofau he marks what appears to be a watercourse with the legend 'Rhyd y Saison site of battle between Britons and Saxons' with 'marsh' added both above and towards the west. There is little trace of the tank now known as Melin-y-Milwyr on this plan unless the hedge bank between the road and the watercourse is the dam wall. Jones and Lewis make it clear that this, their Melin-y-Milwyr, was used as a washing facility by the twentieth century mine,

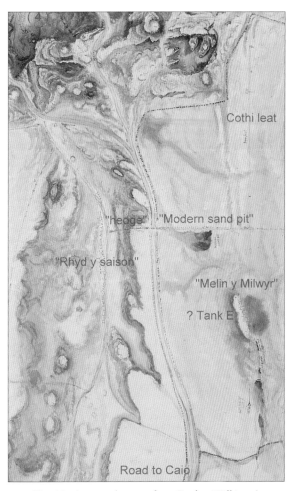

Fig. 10: *Annotated extract from Gardner Wilkinson's main plan, fo. 70, of the Melin-y-Milwyr area, with his map legends in inverted commas.*
(Reproduced by courtesy of the Bodleian Library and with the permission of the National Trust).

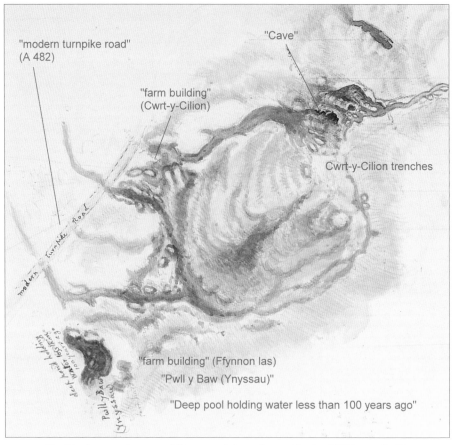

Fig. 11: *Annotated extract of Ynysau and the pool area, Gardner Wilkinson, fo. 69.*
(Reproduced by courtesy of the Bodleian Library and with the permission of the National Trust).

but considered the Roman pottery found in the dam wall make-up indicated a Roman origin to the feature. A period of subsequent re-use in the seventeenth century was also suggested from pottery found in the same location. The possibility that the pottery was residual must now be given serious consideration.

The *Cwrt-y-cilion Trenches*[16] south of Penlanwen appear to have been surveyed separately. Entitled simply Ogofau, fol. 69 is a comprehensive colour-wash plan which depicts but does not name the farm long known as Ynysau (at SN 6583 3968). Known as Cwrt-y-cilion from the late nineteenth century until the later twentieth, it lies close to and east of the main road, the A482, going south from Pumsaint which is here clearly marked 'modern turnpike road'. Alongside Ffynnon-Las Farm, the next holding to its south (at SN OS 6588 3937), is inscribed 'Pwll-y-Baw (Ynyssau)'. Adjacent to and west of the farm is a vine-leaf-shaped feature

appearing to define a former pond (centred on OS SN 6585 3933). A bend in the road today accommodates its original shape. A much smaller pond lying slightly to the north-north-west of this was still marked on the OS 25-inch plan in 1978. Wilkinson's simple legend reads 'with water in it 100 yrs ago or less'. This seems to have been the preliminary version of fol. 71 (Fig. 11), which preserves a smaller image and repeats the same condition of publication on its exterior as appears on the reverse of fol. 70. It otherwise differs little from fol. 69, replicating: 'Pwll y Baw Deep pond holding water less than 100 years ago' and 'Ynysau', adjacent to which is additionally written but faintly, 'farm buildings' to which is also added – 'the Islands – is a name given to all these farms'. Although Lewis and Jones perceptively described this feature as 'a small opencast that is gradually being filled by silted material',[17] at present there appears to be no greater evidence to favour that interpretation over its use as a pool or reservoir. Further investigation is clearly needed.

This particular draft is important in that its heavy watercolour technique conveys a strong visual impression of hydraulicing activity covering the entire hillside behind and to the east of Ynysau (Cwrt-y-cilion) and as far south as, if not to beyond, Ffynnon-Las Farm. This impression is borne out to a greater degree by the broken-up nature of the ground as seen on vertical aerial photographs of 1975, particularly between the two farms.[18] This minor landform (centred on OS SN 658 393) seems to result from the deposition of outwash detritus brought from the area immediately to its northeast, and, given the detail of Wilkinson's record and the very different nature of the surrounding land in 1975, it appears more likely to have been man-made and related to mining or hydraulicing, than natural in origin.

Gardner Wilkinson's surveys in context

Though the masterplan is a more-or-less finished drawing, sight-lines and some measurements are still visible on it. In contrast, the preparatory drawings are covered in figures and calculations. Mr Robert Protheroe-Jones's examination of them suggests the use of chains and tapes, rather than theodolite or plane table. These are likely to have been used to achieve a geometrically-based technique known as trilateration.

Taken together, fols. 70 and 71 are such truly remarkable pieces of survey achievement and graphic illustration that it seems useful to consider their place in the history of archaeological survey, a field closely related to military topographical mapping. Although accurate plans of relatively small sites have survived from the later seventeenth century, General Roy was essentially the first to apply large-scale survey techniques to the accurate mapping of archaeological monuments at the end of the eighteenth century.[19] He was responsible for the first detailed recording of Roman roads and forts on Scottish O.S. maps. Although his example was followed in Ireland by the short-lived topographical survey of the 1830s, and by others who mapped ancient sites for the Ordnance Survey in England during the 1840s and '50s, the introduction of competent large-scale archaeological survey is usually attributed to Augustus Lane-Fox, later General Pitt-Rivers, whose mensuration of sites on Cranborne Chase appeared in print only in the 1880s.[20] Competent in his depictions at both small- and large-scales, Gardner Wilkinson seems to have anticipated him by at least a decade. So in common with his other work, particularly in the uplands,[21] Wilkinson's

unpublished view of the Ogofau in 1868 sets him among the foremost archaeological surveyors of his day.

A HISTORY OF MINE EXPLOITATION AND INVESTIGATION

The seventeenth-eighteenth centuries

Interestingly, although Edward Lhuyd supposed the Ogofau 'to have been Copper-mines of the Romans',[22] the hillside appears to have suggested no real potential for profit to Chauncey Townsend[23] who undertook several remunerative ventures recovering copper and lead nearby in Cardiganshire.[24] And when in 1767 Sir Joseph Banks described the site, its leats, the Carreg Pumsaint, the opencasting and spoil heaps, he twice stated that he had no idea what metal had been found there.[25] Uncertainty as to what metal might be won then beset the activities of the Johnes family, who, having begun a new extractive venture in 1797, described it simply as 'A Lead and Copper Mine'.[26]

The Hoard of Roman Gold Jewellery 1796 and 1815

Although the Johneses venture vainly promised lead and copper, belief in the Ogofau's potential to yield gold had been strengthened when a hoard of Roman jewellery was found in a field not far from the mine the previous year.[27] In this and in a later discovery several pieces of goldwork came to light: two chains, a necklace, the fragment of a serpent armlet, a rod and two wheel-shaped ornaments. An onyx seal was found separately. Today these objects are divided between the British Museum and Carmarthenshire County Museum. Though not at present demonstrable that they were made of local gold, this was a spectacular treasure which captured the antiquarian imagination and became an important catalyst in associating the mine-workings with both the Romans and the alchemists' dream.

The Ogofau in the nineteenth century

The Johnes family reacted positively to the Picturesque landscaping movement by beautifying their estate and making the Ogofau accessible with new paths in the earlier nineteenth century.[28] Visitors included the geologist Roderick Murchison who, in 1839, described the area and agreed its workings should be attributed to the Romans.[29] By this time, the colonists had assumed a serious place as founders of the mine, even if there was still uncertainty about what metal they took from it.

A breakthrough came in 1844, when Warington Smyth, a colleague of Murchison's from the Geological

Survey, described a particle of gold in quartz from the site.[30] Equally convinced of its Roman origins, he was probably the first to draw attention to comparative mining sites in Roman Europe. Then, soon after the gold-obsessed John Calvert had attached great importance to this single 'specimen of gold in the Museum of Economic Geology from 'Oogofau' near Caio, a Roman mine' in 1853,[31] a group of Australian miners is said to have lived in a 'little tented camp' at the site, in a venture of which little is currently understood.[32]

John Gardner Wilkinson, who probably first visited the Ogofau around this time, would have been *au fait* not only with these industrial developments, but also with all the contemporary antiquarian lore. As already noted, he had probably attended the Llandeilo meeting of the Cambrian Archaeological Association which visited the place in 1855.[33] Soon after his survey, the *Mining Journal* reported that further activity had brought a strange engine named *Gnion Eur Glawdd*, or Fairy of the Goldmine.[34] This development heralded several phases of intermittent reconnaissance and extraction which only really came to an end in 1940.

But whatever the mine's industrial fortunes, speculation upon its antiquity certainly prospered. Writing in 1909, Prof. Francis Haverfield estimated that 4 million tons of rock had been extracted from the site, mostly in ancient times. Reckoning for the value of Roman tailings and blocks which they had extracted and intended to crush, he believed the contemporary miners' surmise of a production figure of *c*.1 million ounces of gold.[35] This amount was more recently reduced to 24,000 Troy Ounces;[36] still a respectable figure given the geological milieu believed to have produced it. These earlier speculations, together with an important description of all the ancient artefacts and features then known from the site, soon formed the basis of Bosanquet and Haverfield's account in the Royal Commission on Ancient Monuments' volume on Carmarthenshire which, in summarising what had gone before, unpopularly speculated upon a Norman, rather than a Roman date for the mine's exploitation.[37]

Oliver Davies and the Roman Mines of Europe

As promotion of the mine's promise ebbed and flowed, in 1935, one of its re-openings offered the opportunity for scholars to examine the archaeological potential of some ancient debris encountered underground. Oliver Davies, who was already well advanced in researching Roman mines throughout Europe,[38] seized the oppor-tunity. Unhappy with the Royal Commission's conclusions after investigating for himself, he reported his own findings on a defensive note. It was not 'justifiable to throw doubts on [a] Roman date' due to the convincing testimony of 'settlement-evidence in the valley, the use of cross-cuts and of an aqueduct, the graffiti on the gallery walls, the heavy iron hammer, and the numerous mill-stones . . . which could be paralleled in Roman times'.[39] Several wooden artifacts were found, one of which was later reconstructed into the pattern of a Vitruvian waterwheel.[40] Dated by radiocarbon to 50 B.C.,[41] this artifact still assumes a critical role in interpreting the mine.

A complex mining site defined 1960-1993

The mining site and the Roman Fort have both benefited from a series of investigations since 1960 which are summarised and discussed in a recent monograph by Drs Barry and Helen Burnham, University College of Wales, Lampeter.[42] This monograph reviews all work undertaken around the mines since 1960 and shows how they were first surveyed in detail 1960-70 by the late Prof. G. B. D. Jones and Dr P. R. Lewis. They comprehensively interrogated many visible and accessible earthwork features, dealing variously with the leats and undertaking excavations on the fort site in Pumsaint itself.

A new team began work in 1983. This was a partnership between mining engineers from University College of Wales, Cardiff and archaeologists from the then St David's University College, Lampeter. Investigations included survey, fieldwork and excavation and considerable re-interpretation. They surveyed the environs of a possible mill site behind the Pumsaint stone and interpreted it as a mediaeval or post-mediaeval stamp-mill, an interpretation at first strongly upheld in print but eventually to be withdrawn in the light of later investigations.[43] Geophysics, excavation and ground survey were also brought to bear on the fort, the vicus, the early road through the village of Pumsaint, and the 'bathhouse' site. Complementary investigation focusing on the mining complex included transects of the Annell leat and the exposure and detailed investigation of an ore-processing floor near the proposed mill complex adjacent to the 'motte' feature. Two radiocarbon dates taken from its stratigraphy are now felt to assume an important place in dating the entire mining complex.[44]

As might have been expected, the cultural deposits encountered at Pumsaint fort were well-stratified and contained diagnostic, even if not always closely datable cultural debris. This indicated military occupation between AD75 and AD120, a later Roman phase being associated with an unusual cellared timber building. Little evidence for metal-working other than the sort normally expected on Roman forts was encountered.[45] Diagnostic cultural debris continued to prove fugitive within the mining area. Reviewing the ceramic dating evidence Peter Webster has suggested that the admittedly poorly stratified later second and third century material from Melin-y-Milwyr seems to indicate that the main period of mining activity might not co-incide with the main period of the fort and fortlet's occupation. Post mediaeval pottery comes from Melin-y-Milwyr and from one at least of the leats. Nonetheless, in reaching conclusions which re-emphasise the site's potential for Roman mining, *Dolaucothi 2004* emphasises 'a significant Roman interest in the mines' whilst allowing that most if not all of the surviving surface features cannot be proven to be of Roman date.[46]

In 2000 a Franco-British team commissioned by the National Trust undertook a survey looking at both topographical and underground features.[47] Its useful survey data remain unpublished, but its text presented a number of speculative conclusions largely unsupported by direct evidence. In 2002 this was followed by a complementary non-interpretational NT-commissioned EDM ground survey from the Dyfed Archaeological Trust. Findings from these unpublished investigations were subsumed into the *Dolaucothi 2004* monograph.

Both these recent studies – the Franco-British study of 2000 and *Dolaucothi 2004* – are in broad agreement that most of the irregular topographical features like opencasts are exclusively man-made, and that many, if not most earthwork features on the site result from hydraulicing activities – either for hushing or ore-processing. And in this regard, an outcome of the Franco-British work was the suggestion that mining hydrology had at some time sent water from the Great Opencast to continue its descent in a nor-westerly direction across the road towards the Afon Cothi.[48] This idea was not a new departure, but echoed the important questions originally posed by Lewis and Jones, when in 1970 they published an aerial photograph indicating the sites of four places where silt-laden outwash had indubitably left the working mine.[49] Gardner Wilkinson's drawings, and brief discussion of his interpretative technique relating to Fig. 11 in particular, emphasise the need to map and examine these outwash channels and their deposits

besides underlining the potential for southward extension of the processing activities that produced them.

DISCUSSION
Some mineral processing problems
Current speculations about the nature and chronology of mining at the Ogofau present problems about processing which require further explanation. The first practical question concerns the viability of the lithologies apparently exploited from Roman times until the mid-nineteenth century.

Gold occurs both in quartz veins and finely dispersed in the pyritic component of Silurian siltstones at the Ogofau. Successful recovery of gold from this siltstone requires ore pulverisation on a scale that was poorly developed before the scale of mechanisation that became available in the nineteenth century. It is therefore improbable that mines earlier than this could have been aimed at recovering that metal and it must be emphasised that the idea of mining gold there began only after 1846. It is worth recalling Haverfield's acceptance of four million tons as the estimated quantity missing, removed from the opencast before nineteenth-century mining began, a figure reduced to half a million tons by Annels in 1995. Extraction of such a large volume of such apparently poor ore and intervening rock would be remarkable for any period and has serious implications for the quantity and type of rock waste to be anticipated in dumps on or near the site.

Space does not permit of detailed discussion here, but the claim that analysis of the processed sediments from the excavations actually demonstrate that gold was the metal being extracted is not beyond debate.[50] And although there is a tacit belief that vein gold in quartz was the Romans' main quarry, that such a limited amount of crushed quartz spoil has so far been mapped in the mining area must bring that belief into question. So the recovery of gold from adits and galleries before *c.*1850 is still very much in question.

The Ogofau and the quest for gold in Ancient Britain
It might usefully be pointed out that during the nineteenth century Dolaucothi's promotional mining potential was continuously served by opinion of dubious objectivity. So it is hardly surprising that successive historic mining speculations yielded relatively small amounts of gold due to the poor quality of the recoverable ore. Interestingly, some 800 tons of quartz and ancient tailings were crushed for a yield of 92 ounces of

gold in 1905,[51] which might suggest that whoever had originally deposited those tailings had been trying to recover a metal other than gold.

It must seem odd that in an area of intermittent mineralisation where copper and lead-silver mines were often exploited productively during post-mediaeval times,[52] such great effort had to be expended on recovering any mineral at all from deposits as apparently barren as those of the Ogofau. The question as to why the Romans may have sought gold so assiduously from such unyielding lithologies is routinely explained with reference to the belief that indigenous peoples must have established the enterprise. This explanation, in its turn, is popularly underpinned by the claim that free gold and placer deposits could be readily recognized and exploited at this spot. Questions about the geological sustainability or reality of this explanation are rarely asked.

Yet free gold is found in small quantities at many locations throughout Britain and Ireland. It can be panned from many Northern Irish rivers,[53] has been recovered by panning and in nugget form from parts of Scotland and is not uncommon in streams throughout the northwest and west of England, and Wales.[54] In North Wales it has been noted in Anglesey and Clwyd, and it occurs alluvially along the Mawddach and its tributaries in Merioneth. There, 'by diligent and selective panning it is . . . possible to obtain pea-size nuggets from stream banks cut into the finer river gravels, and more particularly from the stretch of the Afon Wen lying immediately south of Capel Hermon'.[55]

Archaeologists have regularly rehearsed how the Romans probably took stream-borne or placer deposits from the Cothi, even though its presence has never been demonstrated there. They have gone on to argue that the Romans removed virtually all the free gold from both the workable Ogofau lithologies as well as from any secondary deposits.[56] But these claims seem hardly credible given that the geological literature is bereft of supporting evidence of free gold even after centuries of investigation.[57] With so much alluvial gold available in so many rivers elsewhere in Wales, it has to be asked how far it would ever have been necessary for the ancients to mine for it anywhere in Britain before the Industrial Period. Expensive mining along the Cothi makes even less sense when stream-borne samples have been collected with relative ease from the River Sannau above Llanfynydd (around OS SN 55 28) no more than 15kms to the southwest.[58]

Given these geological facts, it is hardly surprising that one anonymous authority on gold worldwide remarked of the Ogofau adits in 1850 that 'such openings, to judge from the vast amounts of sterile quartz rubbish at their mouths must have been more for the purpose of employing the idle hours of their soldiery than for profit'.[59]

Dating, chronology and human activity

There is at present no conclusive dating for the Ogofau mines. Five radiocarbon dates have been obtained from the entire mining area. Two come from the Cothi leat excavations[60] and two were more recently taken from the ore-processing floor.[61] All derive from contexts lacking other datable materials. As already noted, a date was earlier taken from the wooden fragment generally considered to have been part of a 'Vitruvian de-watering wheel' found unstratified underground.[62] However, it has never been explained where a wheel 11 ft 8 ins [3.55] in diameter was actually used underground for de-watering.

Charcoal sampling for radiocarbon dating without complementary culturally diagnostic artefactual evidence is notoriously unreliable because peat and bog timber were major sources of fuel before coal. Derivative charcoal often yields dates anachronous to the activity being dated.[63] A dating technique like optically-stimulated luminescence now needs to be applied in ancient mining studies generally. Unaffected by the same sampling difficulties, this should at least provide confirmatory or complementary dates from future excavations. Though expensive, it has been applied in many different circumstances worldwide and ought to prove of value for such an unusual site as the Ogofau.

As noted above, Roman pottery from the mine site and its environs is poorly stratified and in the case of Melin-y-Milwyr and the Annell leat it was found in association with some sixteenth- or seventeenth-century potsherds. These latter may equally be indicators of a construction date and now demand full description in print.[64]

At least one aerial photograph of the area below the mines betrays features probably indicative of Roman agricultural settlement.[65] Had that settlement extended further into the Ogofau hillside, it might be expected that it would have left evidence such as potsherds in the ploughsoil. So in this regard, potsherds could be anticipated in the leats and tanks lying within close compass of the Roman fort. None of the artefactual material so far used to support a Roman date for the mine actually derives from reliable stratigraphies offering evidence of Roman activity independent of the fort.

Although some parts of the leats have been investigated by pollen and sedimentation analysts, there is strong reason for believing that much more information may be had from systematic laboratory investigation on the mine's outflow channels. Particulate studies of river gravels and sediments would obviously be necessary both for the outflow channels and for the Cothi itself. Such investigations might follow the approach employed during the 1980s in the Ystwyth Valley[66] and which have since been undertaken and enhanced elsewhere more recently.[67]

A serious line of investigation which has so far escaped discussion here is the question of how far the open-casting and its overburden has been subjected to erosion by natural, as well as human agency. River sedimentation studies may also help provide some of the answers to this question.

Conclusions

Preliminary examination of Sir John Gardner Wilkinson's plans of the Ogofau confirms a great deal that is already known about the mine. However, this archive material is particularly valuable because it also locates topographical features now lost or altered. It is demonstrable that Wilkinson believed mineral hydraulicising activity extended south to include silt-laden outflows around Cwrt-y-cilion Farm (now Ynysau) and Ynysau (now Ffynnon Las) which clearly require detailed survey and scientific investigation.

Interpretations of both the function and dating of the Ogofau currently depend more on indirect than direct evidence. A greater degree of caution would therefore seem to be due in promoting either the notion of gold mining before *c.*1850, or of an exclusively Roman origin for the site, until more confirmatory evidence can be assembled. And as, in spite of two centuries' observation and investigation, there is at present equally poor geological evidence for river-borne gold or placer deposits as there is archaeological evidence for pre-Roman mining, both need to be proven before the public is further tantalized by the press into believing them.[68] Just as Gardner Wilkinson undertook exhaustive topographical surveys to the highest standards of his day, all future work seeking to date and ascertain the nature of the Ogofau workings ought to be based upon the most up-to-date investigative technologies available.

ACKNOWLEDGEMENTS

This paper could not have been written without grants from the Cambrian Archaeological Association and the Carmarthenshire Antiquarian Society which enabled me to undertake research and defrayed photographic reproduction costs. My interest in Dolaucothi was for long nurtured by the late George Boon, who encouraged critical scholarship. I am indebted to Richard Suggett and others for bibliographical assistance and to John Wiles, particularly for sharing his knowledge of Roman settlement around Pumsaint. Dr E. Plunkett Dillon and Mr Paul Faulkner dealt with formal applications to undertake fieldwork on the National Trust's Dolaucothi Estate. At a late stage in this writing, Robert Protheroe-Jones gave generously of his expertise and it is to be regretted that all his useful suggestions could not be absorbed into the study. I owe a debt of gratitude to Heather James for her editorial forbearance. The essay's presentation and accuracy of its factual content owe much to her dedication and punctiliousness as an editor. All opinions and any outstanding errors are entirely the author's responsibility.

Last, but not least, thanks are due to the National Trust for permission to reproduce material from the Gardner Wilkinson deposit at the Bodleian Library, and to the staff of the Library's Manuscript reading room for their amicable assistance.

NOTES

1. The Oxford Dictionary of National Biography online (*ODNB*).

2. C. S. Briggs, 'A monumental contribution? Sir John Gardner Wilkinson's neglected surveys of 'British' sites in perspective', in P. Rainbird (ed.), *Monuments in the Land-scape* (Oxford, Oxbow, 2008), pp. 239-248; C. S. Briggs, 'An Egyptologist abroad: Sir John Gardner Wilkinson and some *British* monuments in Gower', *Gower*, Vol. 59 (2008), pp. 13-29; G. Gabb, *Swansea and its History*, Vol. 1 (Llan-dybïe: Dinefwr Press, 2007).

3. J. A. Flynn, *Catalogue of the papers of Sir John Gardner Wilkinson 1797-1875* (online from Bodleian Library website, 1997).

4. J. Martin (née Methuen-Campbell), *Guide to the Gold Mines at Dolaucothi* (National Trust, u.d.).

5. R. F. Suggett, *John Nash Architect – Pensaer* (Aberystwyth NLW/RCAHMW, 1995), p. 121.

6. NLW Dolaucothi correspondence, *passim*.

7. J. Gardner Wilkinson, *The Ancient Egyptians: their Life and Customs* (London: John Murray, 1854), pp. 140-45.

8. NLW Conwil Caeo/Cynwyl Gaeo Tithe Award.

9. A. E. Annels & B. C. Burnham, *The Dolaucothi Gold Mines: Geology and Mining History*, 2nd and 3rd eds. (Cardiff: Univ. Wales, 1986; 1995), fig. 2.

10. G. B. D. Jones, I. J. Blakey & E. C. F. Macpherson, 'Dolaucothi; the Roman Aqueduct', *Bull. Board Celt. Studs.*, Vol. 19 (1960), pp. 71-84.

11. P. R. Lewis & G. B. D. Jones, 'The Dolaucothi Gold Mines I: The Surface Evidence', *Antiqs. Jnl.*, Vol. 49 (1969), pp. 244-272, *passim*.

12. G. E. Evans (ed.), 'Journal of a tour in Carmarthenshire A.D. 1767 [by Sir Joseph Banks]', *TCASFC*, Vol. 15, 1921-2, pp. 14-18 & 23-4; For Banks see *ODNB*.

13. Lewis & Jones loc. cit n. 11, p. 255 (Tank G); Banks's account of quartz is mentioned in G. E. Evans, op. cit., n. 12.

14. W. W. Smyth, 'Note on the Gogofau or Ogofau Mine, near Pumsaint, Carmarthenshire', *Mems. of the Geological Survey*, Vol. 1, 1846, pp. 480-484 and pl 1

15. G. A. M. Gerrard, 'Pillow Mounds in the Dolaucothi mining complex' in D. Austin, 'Excavations and Survey at Bryn Cysegrfan, Llanfair Clydogau, Dyfed, 1979', *Med. Archaeol.*, Vol. 32, 1988, pp. 161-3.

16. The feature was first named Cwrt-y-cilion by Jones and Lewis, op. cit., n. 11, p. 252.

17. Jones & Lewis 1969, op. cit., n. 6, p. 252.

18. RAF AP 75 384 1410, copy in National Monuments Record, Aberystwyth.

19. For Roy see *ODNB* and P. Ashbee, 'Field Archaeology: its origins and development', in P. J. Fowler (ed.), *Archaeology and the Landscape: Essays for L. V. Grinsell* (London: John Baker, 1972), pp. 38-74, espec. 51-4; for the O.S., in Ireland see idem p. 57 and C. S. Briggs, 'Prehistory in the

Nineteenth Century', in S. M. Pearce (ed.), *Visions of Antiquity: The Society of Antiquaries 1707-2007*, *Archae-ologia* III (The Society of Antiquaries of London, 2007), pp. 226-265; at 231 and 234. For the O.S. in England see idem.

20. M. Bowden, *Pitt Rivers: The life and archaeological work of Lieutenant-General Augustus Henry Lane Fox Pitt Rivers, DCL, FRS, FSA* (Cambridge: University Press 1991) and Briggs, op. cit., n. 19, p. 236.

21. Briggs in Gower 2008, op. cit., n. 2.

22. W. Camden, *Britannia*, revised by E. Gibson, 1695 & 1722, see 1984 edition *Camden's Wales*, set & printed by T. James (Carmarthen, Rampart Press, 1984), p. 48b.

23. NLW Powys MSS corresp. 3128.

24. W. Rees, *Industry Before the Industrial Revolution* (Cardiff: Univ. of Wales Press, 1968), Vol. ii, pp. 571, 576.

25. Evans, op. cit., n. 12.

26. *The Times*, 26th May 1797, p. 3, col. c.

27. The discovery is best explained in R.C.A.M, *An Inventory of the Ancient Monuments in Carmarthenshire* (London, H.M.S.O., 1917), pp. 25-7; see also J. Johnes, 'Com-munication . . . relating to some gold ornaments found in Carmarthenshire', *Arch. Jnl.*, Vol. 7 (1850), pp. 173-4, and V. E. Nash-Williams, 'The Roman Gold Mines of Dolaucothi (Carms.)', *Bull. Board Celt. Studs.*, Vol. 14, 1950, pp. 79-84.

28. I am indebted to Caroline Kerkham for this information.

29. R. Murchison, *The Silurian System* (London: John Murray, 1839), pp. 367-9.

30. Smyth, op. cit., n. 14, p. 481.

31. J. Calvert, *The Gold Rocks of Great Britain and Ireland* (London, Chapman & Hall, 1853), p. 127.

32. A. E. Annels and B. C. Burnham, op.cit., n. 9, 3rd edn., p. 42.

33. *The Times*, Cambrian Archaeological Association, Sept. 7th, 1855, p. 8, col. c.

34. *The Mining Journal*, 11th Nov., 1871, p. 995. This refer-ence is kindly provided by George Hall.

35. F. Haverfield, 'Roman Dolaucothi', *TCASFC*, Vol. 5, 1909-10, pp. 14-15.

36. R. Protheroe-Jones in C. J. Arnold & J. L. Davies, *Roman and Early Medieval Wales* (Stroud: Sutton Publishing, 2000), p. 97.

37. R.C.A.M., loc. cit., n. 27, pp. 25-32.

38. O. Davies, *Roman Mines in Europe* (Oxford Univ. Press, 1935).

39. O. Davies, 'Finds at Dolaucothy', *Arch. Camb.*, Vol. 91, 1936, pp. 51-7.

40. G. C. Boon & C. Williams, 'The Dolaucothi Drainage Wheel', *Jnl Rom. Studies*, Vol. 56, 1966, pp. 122-7.

41. The radiocarbon date (90, + or – 70 B.C.) was first mentioned by G. C. Boon while reviewing the *OS Map of Roman Britain* (1979) in *Archaeol. Cambrensis*, Vol. 128,

1979, pp. 165-6; detail was later provided by G. B. D. Jones and K. Maude: 'Dating and Dolaucothi', in B. C. Burnham & J. L. Davies (eds.), *Conquest, Coexistence and Change: Recent Work in Roman Wales, Trivium*, Vol. 25 (Lampeter: SDUC. 1990), pp. 169-171 and in *Britannia*, Vol. 22, 210-212 (same title).

42. B. Burnham & H. Burnham, *Dolaucothi-Pumsaint: Survey and excavations at a Roman gold-mining complex 1987-1999* (Oxbow: Oxford, 2004).

43. D. Austin & B. C. Burnham, 'A New Milling and Processing Complex at Dolaucothi: Some Recent Fieldwork Results', *BBCS*, Vol. 31, 1984, pp. 304-313; B. C. Burnham, 'Dolaucothi: Roman mining; revisited', in B. C. Burnham & J. L. Davies (eds.), op. cit., n. 41, pp. 161-168; B. C. Burnham, 'Dolaucothi revisited', in T. D. Ford & L. Willies (eds.), *Mining before Powder, Peak District Mines Hist. Soc. Bull.*, Vol. 12, 3, 1995, pp. 41-7; B. C. Burnham, 'Roman Mining at Dolaucothi: the Implications of the 1991-3 Excavations near Carreg Pumsaint', *Britannia*, Vol. 28, 1997, pp. 325-336; B. C. & H. Burnham, op. cit., n. 42, pp. 225-286.

44. P. Q. Dresser, 'Radiocarbon determinations', in Burnham and Burnham, op. cit., n. 42, pp. 269-70. The two dates are SWAN-38 2630±70BP (Cal 925BC-427BC) and SWAN-37 1890±60BP (Cal 43 BC-AD331). Although neither sample sits easily with what is known of the dated Roman occupation locally, the possibility that they may represent recycled charcoal was not considered by the excavators.

45. Burnham and Burnham, op. cit., n. 42, pp. 62-66, in Peter Crew, idem, 'Iron slags and other metal-working debris', pp. 140-142.

46. Burnham and Burnham, op. cit., n. 42, p. 317.

47. B. Ancel, B. Cauuet & I. Cowburn, *The Dolaucothi Gold Mines, Carmarthenshire, Wales, U.K. Archaeological Appraisal, Franco-British Team* (Unpublished Report for the National Trust, Wales, April 2000).

48. Ancel *et al.* op. cit., n. 47, master plan.

49. P. R. Lewis & G. B. D. Jones, 'The Roman Gold-Mines at Dolaucothi', *Carms. Antiq.*, Vol. VI, 1970, pp. 90-100, esp. p. 99. Neither this reference nor the topic is noticed in Burnham & Burnham, 2004.

50. A. E. Annels, 'The analysis of the processing residues' and 'The results of the gold analyses', in Burnham and Burnham, op. cit., n. 42, pp. 270-280.

51. J. M. Maclaren, *Gold, its Geological Occurrence and Geographical Distribution* (The Mining Journal, London, 1908).

52. G. Hall, *Metal Mines of Southern Wales* (Griffin Publications: Kington, Herefords., 1983), pp. 39-49.

53. C. S. Briggs, J. Brennan and G. F. Freeburn, 'Irish Prehistoric gold-working; some geological and metallurgical considerations', *Bull. Hist. Metallurgy Gp.*, No. 2, pp. 18-26.

54. D. Cooper, Gold in Britain: New prospecting methods and new discoveries', *Earthwise: British Geological Survey*, No. 12 (June 1998), pp. 34-5; Anon, *Recent Exploration for Gold in Britain*, u.d. pamphlet (*c.*1990), with distribution map; Anon, *Minerals in Britain: past production; future potential, Gold* (British Geological Survey, DTI, u.d., probably post-2000); Anon, *Recent Exploration for Gold in Britain*, u.d. pamphlet (*c.*1990). with distribution map.

55. T. M. Thomas, 'The Mineral Industry in Wales – A Review of production trends, resources and exploitation problems', *Proc. Geol. Assoc.*, Vol. 83, 1972, pp. 365-384.

56. P. R. Lewis, 'The Ogofau Roman Gold Mines at Dolaucothi', *Nat. Trust Yrbk 1976-7*, pp. 20-35, p. 29, fn. 44.

57. Burnham & Burnham, op. cit., n. 42, *passim*.

58. W. L. Harris, 'Gold in the Rivers', *Carmarthenshire History*, 7, 1970, pp. 78-9.

59. Anon, Untitled [A review of eighteen books on gold mining worldwide], *The Quarterly Review*, June-Sept. 1850, pp. 395-434; at p. 408.

60. G. D. B. Jones and K. Maude, op. cit., n. 41, pp. 169-171.

61. Dresser, op. cit., n. 44.

62. See n. 40 & 41.

63. C. S. Briggs, 'Peat Charcoal and Archaeological Dating in Post-Medieval Wales', *Archaeol. in Wales*, Vol. 45, 2005, pp. 85-90; C. S. Briggs, 'Burnt evidence and Mined ground: peat and poverty in early mineral extraction practice', in C. Burgess, P. Topping & F. M. Lynch (eds.), *Beyond Stonehenge: Essays on the Bronze Age in Honour of Colin Burgess* (Oxford, Oxbow) pp. 78-89.

64. Burnham & Burnham, op. cit., n. 42, p. 313.

65. Cambridge UAP CBG 82 (Copy in NMR Wales).

66. J. Lewin, S. B. Bradley and M. G. Macklin, 'Historical Valley Alluviation in mid-Wales', *Geol. Jnl.*, Vol. 18, 1983, pp. 331-350.

67. M. G. Macklin, P. A. Brewer, K. A. Hudson-Edwards, G. Bird, T. J. Coulthard, I. A. Dennis, P. J. Lechler, J. R. Miller, J. N. Turner, 'A geomorphological approach to the management of rivers contaminated by metal mining', *Geomorphology*, Vol. 79, 2006, pp. 423-447; cf the useful research recommendations of Burnham & Burnham, op. cit., n. 42, pp. 330-31.

68. 'Gold mines May be as much as 3,000 years old', *Cambrian News*, 20th April 2000; 'Wales's golden age', by Darren Devin, which states: 'It is thought mining began there in the Bronze Age (up to about 1,000BC)', *Western Mail*, Sept 12, 2008. Interestingly, Gardner Wilkinson himself explained how the 'unscientific Britons' had excavated opencasts before the Romans showed they could do better by tunnelling in 'Cromlechs and other remains in Pembrokeshire', *Collectanea Archaeologica*, Vol. 2 (1871), 219-40; at pp. 219-220.

St Peter's and the Men of Old Carmarthen

William Strange

Few people have done more to deepen our understanding of mediaeval Carmarthen than Terry James. This paper aims to explore part of that field and to build a little further on some of the foundations he laid, particularly his concern to explore the history of Old and New Carmarthen and to elucidate the relationship between the Priory and the old town.[1]

The site of the Roman town of *Moridunum* remained inhabited in the early Middle Ages. It was this old town of Carmarthen which Gerald of Wales noted in his *Itinerarium Cambriae*, and whose brick walls were still partially standing when he visited in 1188 (*Itinerarium Cambriae* 1.10). Gerald did not mention the small settlement which had begun to grow alongside the Norman

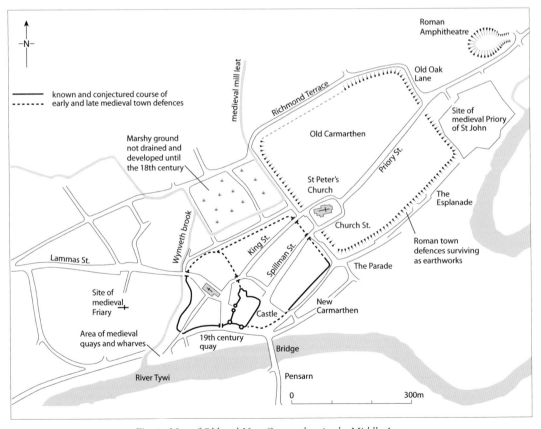

Fig. 1: *Map of Old and New Carmarthen in the Middle Ages.*

castle, commanding the river crossing quarter of a mile south-west of the old town. This more recent settlement grew through the thirteenth century to become a full borough by 1256/7, with a charter modelled on that of Hereford.[2] If Gerald had visited a century later, he could scarcely have avoided noticing the existence of two very different communities, both claiming the name of Carmarthen.

The borough of New Carmarthen was a settler community, its population drawn largely from outside Wales. It was a royal protectorate, sheltered by the castle and by its own walls, and given privileges by its charter. R. A. Griffiths' description is appropriate: New Carmarthen was 'an alien community in a hostile environment'.[3]

New Carmarthen and its growth was part of the local and regional history of South-West Wales. It reflected and influenced the conflict of royal and native power in the region. Seen from a wider perspective, New Carmarthen's development from the twelfth to the fourteenth centuries was also part of a Europe-wide growth of population and stands as an example of the urban expansion of the period. Population increase and urbanisation impacted here on the fringe of Europe as much as in any other region. Disputes over markets, for instance, were frequent causes of litigation wherever lords attempted to take advantage of growing trade. Market disputes happened in the Tywi valley as they did elsewhere, and New Carmarthen's conflicts with its neighbours were a local expression of a much wider struggle for the profits of trade which was going on simultaneously in many places.

The crown had ambitions for the commercial development of its borough of New Carmarthen. In 1305/6 it acceded to a request from the burgesses of New Carmarthen and issued letters patent forbidding the sale of goods in gross anywhere within five leagues (fifteen miles) of their borough.[4]

Other lords, however, had ambitions for their proto-urban centres, too. At some point between 1313 and 1318 the Bishop of St. Davids attempted to promote his manor of Abergwili as a weekly market, an attempt which the burgesses of New Carmarthen strenuously opposed.[5] Carmarthen Priory likewise wanted to promote Old Carmarthen as a trading centre. It was so close to New Carmarthen that conflict between the two was inevitable, and Old Carmarthen suffered several handicaps in the conflict. It lacked New Carmarthen's borough status. Old Carmarthen appears to have been organised as a *vill* or township, and organisationally it

was no match for a fully-fledged royal borough. It did have the one argument on its side, however, which weighed heavily in mediaeval thinking: ancient custom. Old Carmarthen had existed before the new borough, and therefore had a prior claim to be a trading centre; so, at least, the men of Old Carmarthen and their lord, the Prior, argued. This was the defence Prior Robert Daviston attempted, when the burgesses of New Carmarthen complained in 1315 that he was holding markets in Old Carmarthen contrary to royal command. The Prior was unsuccessful because he could not produce documentary evidence for a right he could only claim as based on custom 'time out of mind'.[6]

The existence of two communities, Old and New Carmarthen, therefore caused a number of anomalies and difficulties related to trade and urban development. The administration of justice also created difficulties however, and these difficulties have received less attention. The problems which the existence of Old and New Carmarthen posed for judicial administration are illustrated by a case which arose in 1340 and whose consequences ran on into the following year.

The problems began in either 1340 or 1339. Three felons, David Taverner, John Tredgolde, and Thomas Yonge, had fled to the Friary at the west side of Carmarthen. A fourth criminal, a thief (*ladro*) named Thomas Sathanas, had fled in the opposite direction to the church of St Peter to the east of the borough of New Carmarthen.[7]

The three who had made their way to the Friary all have recognisably English names and may have originated from the borough of New Carmarthen. Young is a common enough name, but it may be significant that, as Terry James pointed out, there was a long-established burgess family by the name of Young in New Carmarthen during the early fourteenth century.[8]

George Eyre Evans transcribed the name of the fourth man as 'Sathavas', but 'Sathanas' ('Satan') seems a more likely reading, and perhaps more of a *nom de guerre* than a given name. The fact that he took a different direction and that his crime is described in a different way suggests that he may have been separate from the group in the Friary.

All four must have been claiming sanctuary in their chosen churches. Under the law of sanctuary a convicted felon could escape justice for a time (typically thirty to forty days) by taking refuge in a church, after which he had to leave (abjure) the king's realm. In Wales this right of sanctuary formalised and put into legal form the

Fig. 2: *St Peter's Church as it may have looked in c.1510, shortly after the south aisle was added but before the vestries were built. The main entrance was through the south door, via a porch that has now been converted into a chapel. The rood screen is based on surviving examples in Wales and like them does not extend into the south aisle. The north transept is shown as a chantry dedicated to Our Lady, as suggested in a document of 1541; its arch was removed in the 19th century. A further guild chapel is conjectured between the piers of the south aisle arcade. The east bays of the south aisle are also interpreted as a chapel. Wall paintings are based on surviving late mediaeval British examples, including the 'Doom' over the chancel arch. St Peter the Apostle iconography is suggested in a number of paintings, including the one facing the south door. Externally the walls are rendered. The roof structures are based on timber roofs from late mediaeval West Wales and the chancel has a typical Carmarthenshire wagon roof. All roofs are shown with steeper pitches than at present, and with local phyllite slate coverings. Floor tiles are restricted to the easternmost bays of the chancel and aisle, while seating is confined to the choir stalls and stone benching in the nave. A lamp burns in the sanctuary.* (Neil Ludlow).

protection (*nawdd*) anciently ascribed to churches and their environs.[9] However, none of the four remained in the churches to the end of their term of sanctuary, and all escaped. The problem this posed for the royal administration was to determine who was responsible for guarding them and therefore who should be punished for allowing them to escape.

There was nothing unprecedented in dealing with escape from prison: in 1339 John Kyng requested and was granted pardon for breaking out of prison at Carmarthen.[10] In view of the fact that, as we shall shortly see, the borough of New Carmarthen had been fined for the escape of Taverner, Tredgolde and Yonge from the Friary, had petitioned the king and had received redress, all by early April 1340, it is possible that the three fugitives in the Friary had made their escape from prison at the same time as John Kyng, in 1339.

Nor was there anything new in dealing with matters of sanctuary. In 1312/13 a man named John le Crouchor (again a non-Welsh name) had fled to St Peter's for sanctuary. We only know about this because of a problem in apprehending him: there may have been many other instances not recorded in our surviving sources.[11]

One new element in 1339/40, though, was the lack of a responsible arresting officer in the Welsh county of Carmarthen. The commotes of Elfed and Widigada, with those parts of Derllys not incorporated into the royal demesne of Carmarthen, together formed the Welsh county of Carmarthen. Each of the commotes had traditionally an officer known as a *cais* (pl. *ceisiaid*) whose function was that of a sergeant or keeper of the peace. They undertook the pursuit and apprehension of criminals on orders from the beadle of the commote. In the case of John le Crouchor who sought sanctuary at St Peter's in 1312/13, the groom to the beadle of Widigada, Ieuan ap Hywel, had failed to tell the *cais*, Rhys ap Aron, about le Crouchor's flight, so that he could not be held. But there were no *ceisiaid* in 1340. No appointment of a *cais* was made in Elfed after 1332 and in Widigada after 1333.[12] With no *cais* to apprehend the four sanctuary seekers of 1339/40, the king's justiciar may have been faced with a novel situation, and may have had to try a variety of different options in order to discover who should now be responsible in such cases.

The king's justiciar in South Wales, Gilbert Talbot, turned first to the burgesses of New Carmarthen and attempted to fine them £20 for permitting the escapes. The burgesses were not willing to accept this responsibility. They claimed they were not liable to provide custody for prisoners beyond the walls of the borough itself, and both the Friary and St Peter's lay beyond their walls. In response to their petition for a remedy the king ordered (April 4th 1340) that an enquiry be made as to whether the burgesses were accustomed to guard felons outside their walls. The consequent inquisition was held on August 7th 1340 before Rhys ap Griffith, deputy of Gilbert Talbot.[13] The inquisition empanelled a jury which found that the burgesses of New Carmarthen had never been liable to provide custody for robbers and felons fleeing to the churches outside their walls. The jury placed the responsibility on the men of the commotes of Widigada (presumably in the case of St. Peter's) and of Elfed (in the case of the Friary).

The crown accepted the jury's findings and on December 2nd 1340 ordered Gilbert Talbot to release the burgesses from their fine, and to make the commotes of Widigada and Elfed answerable for the escapes instead.[14]

The findings of the jury shed some interesting light on the relationship between St Peter's and the borough of New Carmarthen. It has been suggested that St Peter's was a Norman creation, deliberately placed between the two settlements of Old and New Carmarthen in order to serve as a church for both. The Battle Abbey Chronicle recording its grant of St Peter's is however ambiguous and the church could equally well have pre-Conquest origins (see discussion on p. 155). In this important respect, though, the burgesses of New Carmarthen did not see St Peter's as their responsibility. For nearly a century and possibly longer they had had a chapel in their market place, dedicated to St Mary and containing by this time a chantry of the Blessed Virgin Mary.[15] By the mid-fourteenth century parishes had developed recognised boundaries, and St. Peter's parish included New Carmarthen. But though St Peter's may have been a place of burial for the inhabitants of the borough, their relationship with the church appears to have been at best ambiguous. If St Peter's had been a Norman foundation intended to serve New Carmarthen, the experiment had not been a complete success. The attitude of the burgesses in 1340 suggests that St Peter's was not intimately linked to the new borough and makes it seem more likely that St Peter's pre-dated the establishment of New Carmarthen.

Following its order to Gilbert Talbot in December 1340 the crown seems to have failed in its attempt to make the commote of Widigada responsible for the escape of Thomas Sathanas, and turned its attention next to the community of Old Carmarthen.

An order dated 11th September 1341 directed Gilbert Talbot to fine the men of Old Carmarthen the sum of 100s, in other words one quarter of the original fine of £20 levied for the escape of the four fugitives, unless they could show that they were not accustomed to guard escaped felons in this way. The fine was specifically related to the escape of Thomas Sathanas from the church of St. Peter's.[16] It also equals the fee-farm of 100s apparently paid by Prior John Edridge (1281-*c*.1307) to Edward I for the revenues of Old Carmarthen. Terry James estimated that it represented payment from one hundred tenants at 12d per holding.[17]

The order of September 1341 is interesting and perhaps revealing. Talbot was ordered to investigate whether the men of Old Carmarthen were accustomed to provide this kind of guard. Perhaps this was a test case to ascertain who was responsible to apprehend felons and to guard those seeking sanctuary, now that there were no *ceisiaid*. Talbot had failed to get the men of the commote of Widigada to take responsibility and it may have been the men of Widigada who perceived the link between Old Carmarthen and St Peter's which led to the avenue Talbot was told to explore in September 1341.

It is not known how the case of Thomas Sathanas and his escape from St Peter's was finally resolved. The lack of resolution in this case reflects the lack of clarity about the status of Old Carmarthen itself, as the case reveals it. The men of Old Carmarthen evidently regarded the new borough as an upstart and a thing of yesterday. They were conscious of their town's antiquity, but their rivals were armed, as they themselves were not, with written evidence of their privileges. Old Carmarthen was distinguishable from the commote in which it lay, and could be made legally responsible in a way which suggests some measure of communal, if not civic, organisation. But it was the Prior, and not the men of Old Carmarthen themselves, who spoke up for their status, and that fact emphasised the limits of their organisation: like villagers and unlike true burgesses, their lord spoke for them, they did not speak for themselves.

NOTES

1. Terrence James, 'Medieval Carmarthen and its Burgesses: a study of town growth and burgess families in the later thirteenth century', *Carms. Antiq.,* Vol. XXV, 1989, pp. 9-26.
2. Ralph A. Griffiths, 'Medieval Carmarthen', in R. A. Griffiths, *Conquerors and Conquered in Medieval Wales* (Stroud, Alan Sutton, 1994), p. 177.
3. Griffiths, 'Medieval Carmarthen', *Conquerors & Conquered*, p. 187.
4. The burgesses took their stand on these letters patent in subsequent disputes: National Archive SC8/119/5909 (1313).
5. National Archive SC8/311/15527. See also G. E. Evans (ed.), 'Documents relating to the town from the earliest times to the close of the reign of Henry VIII', *Transactions of the Carmarthenshire Antiquarian Society*, Vol. 18, 1924-5, p. 3.
6. Ralph A. Griffiths, *The Principality of Wales in the Later Middle Ages: The Structure and Personnel of Government. I: South Wales 1277-1536* (Board of Celtic Studies History and Law Series. No. 26), (Cardiff, University of Wales, 1972), p. 168 (citing National Archive SC8/119/5908-

11; *Calendar of Close Rolls 1313-18*, p. 370; *Calendar of Charter Rolls* III, p. 397).
7. Evans (ed.), 'Documents relating to the town', pp. 4-5.
8. James, 'Medieval Carmarthen', p. 24.
9. H. Pryce, *Native Law and the Church in Medieval Wales* (Oxford, Oxford University, 1993), pp. 165-203.
10. The request is in National Archive, SC8/256/12790. The grant of pardon in *Patent Roll 13 Edward III*: see E. A. Lewis, 'Carmarthen Castle', *West Wales Historical Records*, Vol. 3, 1912-13, p. 60.
11. Griffiths, *Principality of Wales . . .*, pp. 70-1 & 412.
12. Griffiths, *Principality of Wales . . .*, p. 71.
13. Evans, 'Documents', p. 5.
14. Evans, 'Documents', p. 5, citing Close Roll 14 Henry III, 2 m.12 (*Calendar of Close Rolls 14 Henry III*, p. 588).
15. Griffiths, 'Medieval Carmarthen', *Conquerors & Conquered . . .*, p.189-90 (n.40), on the date of foundation of the chapel: National Archive, SC6/1158/3, Minister's Accounts, Carmarthen 1352/3, on the chantry.
16. National Archive, C47/10/33/6.
17. James, 'Medieval Carmarthen', p. 12.

Pentowyn, Llanstephan – a Pre-conquest Possession of Llanteulyddog (Carmarthen Priory)

Heather James

GRANT TO BATTLE ABBEY

Around 1110 AD Henry I gave the native Welsh religious community of Llanteulyddog in Old Carmarthen, together with St Peter's, later the parish church for Old and New Carmarthen, to Battle Abbey in Sussex. This appears to signal uncompromising change. The Normans had little regard for the native Welsh church, its organisation or its saints, and zealously promoted the reformed Benedictine monasticism of their leading English houses – the 'spiritual arm of a military conquest' according to R. R. Davies.[1] Only a year before the royal grant, the bridgehead castle of Rhydygors lower down the River Tywi had been replaced by a new royal fortress with a small attached borough, known as New Carmarthen (*see Fig. 1, p. 150*). There was in fact a Welsh settlement close to the site, belonging to the religious community of Llanteulyddog sited within the decayed but still visible defences of the Roman town of *Moridunum*. Strategic considerations in controlling the lowest bridging point of the Tywi no doubt lay behind the choice of site for the new castle west of Old Carmarthen and the inhabitants of the new royal borough were incomers, mainly English from the west country and Flemings.[2] Yet leaving Old Carmarthen under the rule of Llanteulyddog clearly indicates some kind of racial – as well as spatial – accomodation between native Welsh and Norman conquerors.[3] Henry I's royal power was sustained in Wales as much by control of his own Marcher lords as subjugation of the native Welsh princes. It is also clear that Battle Abbey's tenure of Llanteulyddog was brief and unsuccessful. It was Bernard, a

former royal clerk and member of the King's Household, whom the King appointed as the first Norman Bishop of St David's in 1115 who lost no time in persuading the King to reverse this decision. *The Chronicle of Battle Abbey* provides much information on these events and includes the first mention of Pentowyn, a possession of what was to become Carmarthen Priory, successor both in location and probably possessions to Llanteulyddog. This detached part of the Priory's estates was situated on the east bank of the mouth of the Taf estuary opposite Laugharne and within the Lordship of Llanstephan (SN 321106). It straddled the mediaeval *via regia* (the royal road), an important routeway from south to west Wales involving a ferry crossing of the River Tywi at Llanstephan and the River Taf between Pentowyn and Laugharne.

The *Chronicle of Battle Abbey* records that King Henry 'gave as his own gift a church founded in honour of the holy apostle Peter in Wales in a town called Carmarthen (*Chermerdi*) with all its appurtenances to be held for ever free and quit. He also gave the church of Battle another church founded there in very ancient times in honour of St Theodore the martyr. To it he added a separate land not far off called Pentywyn, a necessity since it abounded in wheat'.[4]

'Attracted by the pleasantness of the place' as the *Chronicle of Battle Abbey* puts it, (Bernard) 'urgently desired to secure that church to his own right by every means'. Finally, with the election of Abbot Warner at Battle Abbey in 1125, the King gave Llanteulyddog to Bishop Bernard and compensated Battle Abbey with

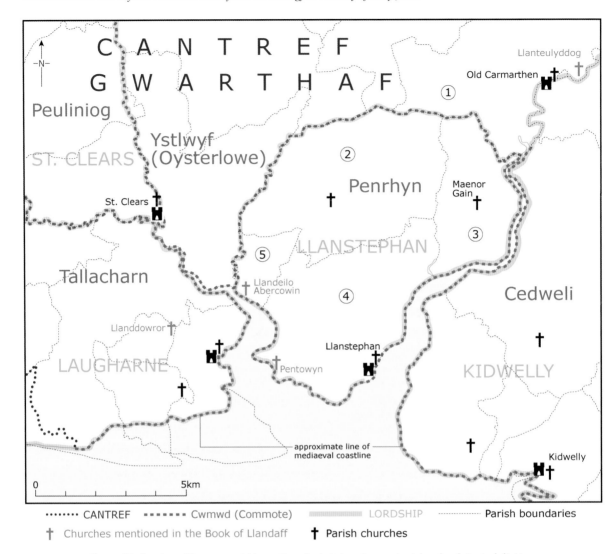

Fig. 1: *The location of Pentowyn within mediaeval administrative, territorial and ecclesiastical divisions.*
Only mediaeval parish churches are marked with black crosses. Numbered parishes are: (1) Carmarthen, St Peter's;
(2) Llangynog; (3) Llangain; (4) Llanstephan; (5) Llandeilo Abercowin.

land from royal lands in Sussex. The brethren in Carmarthen 'quickly returned to England'.[5] Bernard reconstituted Llanteulyddog as a house of Augustinian canons. A new primary dedication to not just a Latin saint but one of the apostles, St John the Evangelist, was given and St Teulyddog attached in a subsidiary role like many other reconstituted native welsh religious houses.[6] It has been suggested that the Augustinian rule was more congenial to and compatible with the native Welsh *clas*.[7] It must also be recognised that Bernard's patron Queen Mathilda particularly favoured the Augustinians, as did many of the leading Norman aristocratic families and

clergy. Another more mundane reason favouring Augustinian houses was that they were cheaper to found, endow and sustain than the older monastic houses.[8] Finally, the king's change of direction may be more firmly in the realm of *real politik*. Searle refers to the dating for the documents from the royal administration for confirmation of this exchange of lands. In the Pipe Rolls for the 31st year of the reign of King Henry I (1130/1) Bernard is recorded as holding the Honour of Carmarthen and thus Henry might have seen the benefits to his valued official securing direct control of an old and important monastic centre in Old Carmarthen.[9]

LLANTEULYDDOG – AN EARLY ECCLESIASTICAL SITE

Who then was Teulyddog, the dedicatee of this refounded native Welsh ecclesiastical house? We can discard the English chronicler's identification of St Theodore the Martyr. Noted fleetingly as one of the companions of Teilo in the *Life* of the saint in *The Book of Llandaf*, Teulyddog is a shadowy figure with no substantial hagiographic reference. Indeed, Baring-Gould and Fisher note that he might be one and the same as Teilo.[10] Evans has given this suggestion much more substance and convincingly argues that *Teulyddog* is a hypocoristic form of *Eliud*, Teilo's alternative and perhaps original name. He further suggests that Teilo might have been given the former Roman town by the early mediaeval Irish ruling dynasty of Dyfed and that his monastery and cult centre was sited there before a later shift to Llandeilo Fawr.[11]

Terry James's 1979 excavations on the site of Carmarthen Priory located enclosure or boundary ditches whose fills produced radio-carbon dates for the eighth or ninth centuries.[12] Documentary evidence complements the location and nature of this early site. A list of 'bishop houses in Dyfed' of probable ninth-century date is included as an archaic survival in later recensions of the Welsh Laws. *Llan Teulydawc* is one of seven named and in a seminal study Charles Edwards suggested that one of these sites was located in each of the seven *cantrefi* making up the early mediaeval kingdom of Dyfed. Llanteulyddog would thus be the bishop house for the large *Cantref Gwarthaf*.[13] Another early mediaeval reference to an abbot at Carmarthen comes from the witness list of a now lost 'celtic' charter at St Davids copied by the Tudor antiquary John Leland.[14]

These scraps of evidence are still as substantial as many others for pre-Norman ecclesiastical sites in Wales. We can therefore suggest that there was a post-Roman, pre-Norman ecclesiastical site at Carmarthen conceivably of fifth- or sixth-century origins but certainly in existence in the eighth to ninth centuries. Its location just outside the eastern defences of a Roman town south of the Roman road leading up the Tywi valley, where a Roman cemetery might be expected, suggests early origins.[15]

A dearth of documentary sources means that we can only guess at the extent of lands and subordinate churches that such an early monastic house might have possessed. Geraint Dyfnallt Owen, who made a detailed study of the Priory estates, points out that although in comparison with other monastic houses in west Wales, Carmarthen Priory was quite wealthy, most of its revenues were derived from 'spiritualities' rather than 'temporalities' – that is to say advowsons and tithes of subordinate churches, rather than landed estates.[16] The mediaeval Priory never had a rich and powerful patron, English or Welsh, but built up its estates by means of exchanges, purchases and gifts. Apart from much land within Old Carmarthen and properties acquired in New Carmarthen, there were lands around the town and some outlying granges and manors. The focus of this article is on Pentowyn, one of these outlying possessions since it was, as we have seen, a part of Llanteulyddog's lands in the early twelfth century at the time of conquest and quite possibly much earlier. Whilst information on its mediaeval history is sparse, so little is known of the kind of estates pre-conquest native Welsh ecclesiastical houses owned that it is worth looking at Pentowyn in more detail, both as an estate and also its possible place within lands and churches belonging to St Teilo, a major early Welsh saint with cult centres at Llandeilo, Penally and possibly Carmarthen. It also throws some light on pre-Norman field systems in west Wales.

PENTOWYN IN *THE BOOK OF LLANDAF*, WELSH TERRITORIAL UNITS AND ST YSTYFFAN'S CHURCH, LLANSTEFFAN

It is well known that Bishop Bernard spent much of his episcopate locked in a bitter struggle with Urban, Bishop of Llandaff, over the boundaries of their respective dioceses. Bernard proved himself to be a champion of St David in his mission to establish what was, finally, the biggest diocese in Wales and to claim metropolitan status for it. Llandaff's claims were justified on the basis that it was the spiritual and temporal inheritor of the patrimony of St Teilo. *The Book of Llandaf*, a collection of saints' lives and charters, was produced and deployed in support of these claims. Wendy Davies's study of these charters has provided compelling evidence that amongst the outright forgeries and edited documents there is a core of very early land charters of sixth- and seventh-century date relating to estates in south-east Wales. Much of the material supposedly relating to gifts of estates to Teilo in west Wales is, however, corrupt or late.[17] Yet it was in west Wales, not south-east Wales, that the cult of Teilo originated. Reuben Davies has recently studied *The Book of Llandaf* from a different perspective characterising it as a 'monument to the learning and literary culture of early twelfth-century Wales'.[18] Bishop Urban and and his officials had knowledge (and perhaps written lists) of churches associated with Teilo and his cult. There is, moreover, independent archaeological and documentary evidence for early origins for some at least of the Teilo sites in west Wales.[19] A spurious charter purporting to date to the eighth century but most probably derived from a list and notes of Teilo churches drawn up in the eleventh century (Llandaff *253 (143 J[20]) is ordered by the cantrefs of Dyfed, Ystrad Tywi and Brecon and Elmael. For Cantref Gwarthaf we find:

VI.	*Lannteliau lanndibrguir mainaur*	Llanddowror
VII.	*Lannteliau trefcerniu*	Crinow, or poss. Trelech ar Bettws
VIII.	*Lanntoulidauc icair*	Llanteulyddog in Carmarthen
IX.	*Lann teliau aper coguin*	Llandeilo Abercywyn
X.	*Lannteliau penntiuinn*	Pentowyn, Llanstephan.

All but the last identification are given by Gwenog-fryn Evans, the editor of the facsimile edition of the Llandaf charters,[21] who in many cases used information from Egerton Phillimore, author of the voluminous footnotes on place-names and other subjects in the scholarly three-volume edition of Owen's *Pembrokeshire* of 1906. However, for the last entry in the list, Phillimore suggested Pendine, an identification adopted by Baring-Gould and Fisher, although they admit that no confirmatory dedication has survived.[22] Pentowyn is a more likely identification, particularly since in this list Teilo churches in the well-established territorial unit of Tallacharn (here termed a cantref) are separately identified and this is where Pendine should be.

The best evidence for firmly locating Pentowyn in the parish of Llanstephan on the east bank of the River Taf comes from a fourteenth-century entry in the Cartulary, described in detail below, where the Prior was in dispute with the Lord of Llanstephan. Places named as bounds can be identified today (*see Fig. 2*). William Rees, in his *Map of South Wales and the Border in the XIV Century* marks two chapels, 'St Teilo' at Pentowyn and 'Eglwys Trewyn or Trefwenyn' at Pentrewyn. Unfortunately, Rees's sources for his map locations have not survived and cannot always be traced – these two chapels being a case in point. The name 'sinshill' (saint's hill), discussed below under open-field farming, attached to the hill above Pentowyn, gives some support to the

likelihood of a former chapel at Pentowyn – a normal feature on a monastic grange. No surface traces survive today but the field name Parc y Spitt (from ysbytty, meaning hospice) may indicate its location (*see Fig. 2*). In view of a pre-conquest association with Llanteulyddog and the suggested identification in the *Book of Llandaf* lists, the lost dedication might well be to Teilo. Eiluned Rees strongly supports William Rees's location of Eglwys Trewyn at Pentre-wyn (SN 325130) and further draws attention to the descriptor 'eglwys', not 'capel' as potentially significant.[23] There is moreover a reference to 'Eglwys Tref Wenyn' in an early fourteenth-century *Inquisition Post Mortem* for Amabillia de Laundry – a knightly family holding lands in and around Llandeilo Abercywin.[24]

We have already seen that there is ninth century evidence, in the list of Bishop Houses for the existence of *cantrefi* as ancient administrative and territorial divisions. Smaller divisions of *cwmydau* (commotes) were features of the larger *cantrefi*. It is widely accepted that many of these units were adopted by the mediaeval Welsh church to form their new units of archdeaconries and deaneries. Parish organisation itself came late to Wales and again earlier ecclesiastical organisation such as mother churches with dependant chapelries often survived in later parish boundaries. The southern half of the Lordship became the parish of Llanstephan. Further up the Taf on its eastern banks, at the confluence of the Afon Cywin with the Taf, was the church of Llandeilo Abercywin, listed, as we have seen as a Teilo church in *The Book of Llandaf*'s list. The dedication is further evidence for a concentration of Teilo churches and estates in south-west Carmarthenshire. It is likely that the estate unit became the small parish of Llandeilo Abercywin, held as a knight's fee of Llanstephan by the Laundry family. Carmarthen Priory, however, had the spiritualities of the church as revenue – the remains perhaps of a more extensive pre-conquest Llanteulyddog estate? Most of the northern half of Penrhyn became the parish of Llangynog, with a detached unit to the east, Maenor Gain, becoming the parish of Llangain.

These older units also dictated many of the territorial boundaries of the new Norman lordships and their feudal – and racial – subdivisions. Pentowyn lay within the commote of Penrhyn Deuddwr which was simply appropriated as the Norman Lordship of Llanstephan. This lordship was, like Laugharne (Tallacharn) and St Clears, a 'barony' held directly of the King's Principality of Wales and owed suit to the County Court at Carmarthen. It was further divided into two: Llanstephan being the 'Englishry' and Penrhyn the 'Welshry' which were separate lordships and, later, manors. It is beyond the scope of this short article to look at the wider perpetuation – or dismemberment – of native Welsh territorial units following the Norman conquest.[25] Not least amongst the contributions that a full publication of the Carmarthen Cartulary could make is to further document these for Carmarthen and its hinterland. Certainly the new royal castle and county of Carmarthen virtually obliterated the older Welsh unit of Derllys. Penrhyn Deuddwr though was a 'natural' territorial unit in that it comprised most of the peninsula of land between the lower reaches and estuaries of the Tywi (to the east) and the Cywin, tributary to the Taf, to the west with a northern boundary also defined by eastward and westward flowing streams (Nant y Coedcae and Nant y Pwntan). This became the lordship of Llanstephan divided between the 'englishry' of the southern half focussed on its castle and small borough at the strategically important mouth of the Tywi estuary and the Welshry of Penrhyn to the north. The Priory's estate at Pentowyn predated this Anglo-Norman legal and racial division and it seems likely that its lands fell within both administrative divisions.

There is no firm evidence historically, architecturally or archaeologically to prove that Llanstephan Church itself occupies a pre-Norman site but the rapid construction of a castle within the ramparts of an Iron Age hillfort and the location there of the caput of the new lordship suggest seizure of an existing centre of Welsh lordly power. In terms of location therefore Llanstephan is the prime candidate as a 'mother-church' of the commote. Then there is the dedication to 'Ystyffan' – anglicised as Stephen the first martyr. In admittedly late hagiographic traditions, he is termed 'Confessor' to St Teilo.[26] This role of 'confessor' is a device often found in late hagiography to associate an obscure, and perhaps early saint, with a later, more powerful one.

However, no such continuation of native Welsh pieties could survive unaltered in the new world of the Norman lordship of Llanstephan, bitterly contested as it was in the twelfth and early thirteenth centuries when the resurgent Welsh sought to revive the kingdom of Deheubarth under Rhys ap Gruffydd and regain their lost lands. The castle changed hands no less than four times during this period. In addition to the reformed monastic orders such as the Benedictines, favoured as we have seen by the incoming Normans, the first generation of

conquerers, as befitted a warrior aristocracy, were early patrons of the newly-founded Crusading Order of the Knights Hospitaller. The Order may even have gained a foothold during the bishopric of Wilfred, Bishop Bernard's predecessor (d.1115), associated with Flemings like Letard Litelking or Wizo of Wiston. Slebech Commandery was established in the first half of the twelfth century. Some time between 1160-1170, and certainly before 1198, Geoffrey de Marmion, Lord of Llanstephan, granted the church to the Knights together with a carucate of land, a fishery in the River Taf and a boat at The Ferry for transport across the Towy.[27] Details of this grant can be gained from later confirmations. The carucate, a large area of land of some 100, or perhaps 120 acres, was between 'Goer' (Gower) and 'Longam Forestam'. These lands are difficult to locate today. Phillimore, in his copious notes to Henry Owen's magisterial edition of George Owen's *Pembrokeshire* locates the land in Penrhyn, west and northwest of Llangynog.[28] A carucate[29] implies ploughlands and although the relict traces in the modern field boundaries of former open-field cultivation around Llangynog are not as pronounced as at Llanybri and Llanstephan, it is likely that there were common fields around this early nucleated settlement in Penrhyn where the Commandery held its landshares.

Valuable though these lands were for the Knights, it was the spiritualities – the tithes and oblations from Llanstephan Church – which were even more substantial. The Knights had the 'predial' or 'great' or 'rectorial' tithes, based on a tenth of crops produced. At an early date these were 'commuted' to cash payments. Out of their revenues they had to pay for a vicar to perform services and provide pastoral care but the figures given in a surviving account from the Slebech Commandery for 1336 show the difference between this income and expenditure: £40 was received from a potential total of £60 (£20 from the fishery not received in that year) and £8 was paid out for the vicar who also had the small tithes.[30] The Priory's grange of Pentowyn was not exempt from payment of tithes to the Knights.

The Knights' wealth and their exemptions incurred the hostility of both the regular Church and laymen and by the later Middle Ages it is clear that they had to pay out for protection and often to lend money, disadvantageously, to the Crown. They often leased out their scattered possessions to 'farmers' or tenants who could profit thereby. So in 1338 we find that the Slebech Commandery thought it prudent to retain two local knights to look after their interests: Stephen Perot for Pembrokeshire and Richard Penres of Llanstephan, at a fee of £2 p.a. The Penrees family lost their Lordship in 1377, not to be restored until the 1390s; during part of that period Richard II's favourite Simon de Burley held Llanstephan. He was in fact 'fermor' or lessee of the 'frary' or regional unit of the Knights' estates in Carmarthenshire and Gower. So when he fell from grace in 1388 and the Lordship reverted to the Crown, the surviving accounts give a rare picture of the extent and value of the Knights' tithe revenues for Llanstephan.

Thirty shillings were received as sheaf tithes from 'Pentewi', £5 11s 8d from 'Don and Rowisdon' and £4 19s 2d from 'Rowisley and Alenysdon'.[31] This gives a good idea of the relative areas of the Pentowyn landshares and the open fields of the Down. The formula to calculate this predial tithe was 1d per day for the harvester or a sheaf of corn.

PENTOWYN – A GRANGE OF CARMARTHEN PRIORY

There are few twelfth-century charters in the Carmarthen Cartulary relating to Bishop Bernard's re-establishment of Llanteulyddog as a House of Augustinian Canons after the brief Benedictine interlude. At some time after 1125, but before 1148, Bishop Bernard issued a charter granting the Priory two carucates of land at Cwmau with their tithes and offerings. This land may have been part of Llanteulyddog's estate.[32] Also in the Carmarthen Cartulary is another contemporary document which relates to Pentowyn, which we have seen was certainly part of the estate of Llanteulyddog in the eleventh century if not earlier.[33] In this document he orders Maurice Fitzgerald not to intrude onto the holding which he, Bernard, has given back to Carmarthen Priory. This is an interesting example of the loss of control over ecclesiastical lands which afflicted St Davids and other Welsh churches in the early years of the Norman conquest. Maurice was one of the sons of Gerald of Windsor and Nest, daughter of Rhys ap Tewdwr, the last Welsh king of south Wales. One of their sons, David, succeeded Bernard as Bishop of St Davids in 1134 and he made his brother Maurice steward of the lands of the bishopric. Maurice later took a leading role in the Norman Conquest of Ireland, securing the office of Justiciar. In the early years of the conquest, Gerald, Constable of Pembroke Castle, had ravaged St David's lands in Pebidiog in 1096 and the family's stewardship of church lands was often close to

complete appropriation of their revenues. Curbing the encroachments of the Fitzgeralds was a high priority for Bernard and he appointed Henry, Earl of Northumberland, son of David I, King of Scotland, as steward of the lands of the Bishopric.[34] Julia Barrow notes the obscurities in this text, not fully understood by the seventeenth century copyist of Peniarth Ms 401D, the sole copy of the mediaeval cartulary. It is possible that there are phrases within this document reminiscent of the 'sanction' clauses identified by Professor Wendy Davies as one of the key components of the 'celtic' Latin charters which could further suggest the antiquity of the Pentowyn estate.[35]

No accounts survive for Carmarthen Priory and so use has to be made of a few documents in the Cartulary and accounts which survive for the Lordship of Llanstephan in the later Middle Ages, for the years when it had escheated to the Crown during the minority of an heir or had been forfeit to the crown. Details of Carmarthen Priory's lands and income are given in the *Valor Ecclesiasticus* of 1535, an assessment of clerical incomes organised to allow Henry VIII's appropriations by his able minister Thomas Cromwell. Pentowyn was described as a 'grange' and valued at 66 sh. 8d. Whilst principally associated with Cistercian Houses, such as, in west Wales, Whitland Abbey, other monastic houses organised their outlying lands in similar ways. Typically, a grange would contain a cluster of buildings – a granary, byres, accommodation for the lay brothers and peasant workers, and a chapel. Many granges were leased out by the later Middle Ages to tenants, the mother house receiving only a rent rather than produce. Many such sites became profitable farms after the Dissolution and Pentowyn was no exception.

The Priory was leased by several people in the sixteenth century as the records of the Court of Augmentations show, but it seems that Pentowyn was soon detached from the Carmarthen Priory lands and advowsons and became part of the estate being built up by the Lloyds of Plas, Llanstephan and their successors, the Meares. There is nothing in the present-day former working farmhouse and buildings at Pentowyn of possible mediaeval build.

We therefore have little information on how the Priory's grange at Pentowyn was organised, especially on the crucial question as to how early it ceased to be farmed 'in demesne', i.e. directly by the Priory, and became let out to tenant farmers for rent. Generally this process accelerated in the later Middle Ages after the highpoints in terms of population and seigneurial demesne-farming in the thirteenth century. A group of documents in the Priory Cartulary, however, regarding a dispute in the later fourteenth century give valuable evidence on the agrarian regime and diversity of resources.

The Revd William Strange's article on the 'Men of Old Carmarthen' in this volume highlights one case amongst many of disputes over jurisdiction, and thus revenues, between Old and New Carmarthen. The late Professor R. R. Davies has drawn attention to the large revenues which the King and the great English Lords were extracting from their Welsh possessions in the 1360s and 1370s, notwithstanding the ravages caused by the Black Death just over a decade earlier. 'None,' he wrote, 'were more determined or more grasping than the Black Prince'.[36] As eldest son of Edward III and Prince of Wales, Edward's officials pursued every avenue in his Honour of Carmarthen to raise money and this involved a challenge to the Prior, Lord of Old Carmarthen, on many counts. Of interest in our context is the charge made against the Prior that he had unjustly appropriated forty acres of marshland at 'Penrhyn' within the lordship of Richard de Penrice (or Penres/Penrees) Lord of Llanstephan and tenant-in-chief of the Black Prince. The case was heard in Carmarthen Castle before Thomas de Bradestone, Constable of Carmarthen Castle and Justiciar of South Wales. Despite arguments by the Prince's agent William le Younge, Prior John Martin's case that he had held the lands from time immemorial was upheld by the twelve jurors.[37]

That was not however the end of the matter; indeed one wonders whether this was simply a device by the Prince's agents to get money from the Priory. Lawyers in the thirteenth century had expressed concern about the large amounts of land held 'in frankalmoign' – lit. free alms – by the Church and religious houses which were undying corporations. The King therefore never received his feudal revenues owed when estates were inherited or granted. These concerns culminated in Edward I's Statutes of Mortmain of 1279 and 1290 which forbade the gift or alienation of lands in 'mortmain' – lit. dead hand – to the Church. In practice however licences for a fee were quite readily available. So we find within the Cartulary another document from Prince Edward dated 1369 where he confirms, for a fine of 40 shillings, from Prior William, the right to purchase land from Robert de Penrice for the Priory's exclusive use as Common of Pasture for all their animals on their land of 'Pentewy' (Pentowyn). Usefully this land's boundaries are listed and

although not all the places can be identified the general location is quite clear. The description is as follows:

> Edward . . . Prince of Acquitaine and Wales . . . concede and give licence . . . to William, Prior of the Church of St John the Evangelist of Carmarthen and the Convent of that place . . . in pure and perpetual alms from Robert de Penrice, Lord of Llanstephan, common of pasture for their animals of all kinds on the land of the said Prior and Convent at Pentowy now and for all future time ? to wit: to pasture such animals there yearly on all the lands of the said Robert in the Lordship of Llanstephan, within the following boundaries:

> . . . from the land of the said Prior and Convent until Stone Bridge adjoining Mondegu Mill (Pendeggy), close to that place where Mondegu river runs into the Taf. From the stone bridge eastward unto the burgage of Morabri, and from the said house until Richard's lake, thence eastwards to Somer's Way hafod, so unto Alexander's dike, so unto Norris's dike, thence unto Thonel's Cross, and so downwards to Stony Ford, thence unto the foss (bank or ditch) of the Park there, thence from that side towards the South, and so unto Taf River, and so unto the Prior's land at Pentowyn, in the following manner:

> . . . in all the uncultivated fallow and marsh lands within the said limits, during the whole year, and on his arable and meadow lands, and his Montagu meadows from the time when the corn shall be gathered in until the same lands be resown, and from the hour in which the hay shall be mown and ricked until the feast of the Purification of Our Lady (2nd Feb.). And no other person than the said Prior and Convent and their successors shall have common of pasture within the above named boundaries . . .[38]

The starting point can be firmly located as there still is a stone bridge crossing the 'Mundegy' brook on the minor road leading down from Llanybri and close to the entrance to Pendeggy Mill, one and the same with the mediaeval Mondegy. The boundary then extended up the steep hill and hollow way to the boundary of one of the burgage plots of Llanybri. The name 'Richard' must be linked to demesne lands listed in the 1409-1410 accounts of 'Castel Ricward' which could not be let in that year.[39] Eiluned Rees has drawn my attention to the 'moor' called 'Castilrichard' in the later account for 1479-1480 which produced no income 'because submerged by the sea'.[40] The 'Lake' is from *lak,* a Middle English term for stream in common use in the anglicised areas of south-west Wales.[41] Castle Richard as an

Fig. 2: *Annotated extract from OS Sheet SN31, 1:25,00 Provisional edition, 1950 showing locations, and general locations of boundary features listed in the 1369 Award in Carmarthen Cartulary.*

entity may therefore have extended both to the east and west of Nant Crymlyn, but since the order given for the bounds means that Richard's lake lies somewhere between the Llanybri burgage and 'Somersway hafod' (i.e. on the eastern side of the Nant Crymlin), I tentatively suggest that it may be the spring at SN337131 and the small rivulet emerging from it. 'Somersway hafod' suggests that in the fourteenth century the high hill north of Llanybri was then unenclosed hill pasture with a hafod or summer dwelling on its fringes. However, there was an Anglo-Norman estate of Martinsgrove in this area (the names 'Lan-Martin' and 'Coed Lan Martin' perpetuate the location of this holding) so it is

probable that the boundaries of the Prior's lands then extended northwards along the lower slopes of the Nant Crymlyn. Alexander's dyke, and Norris's dyke cannot be exactly located but were probably enclosed drained meadows on the valley floor. Thonel's (later Welshman's) Cross is probably the cross roads of Pont felin-y-cwm. A ford may have preceded the present-day Pont yr Hendre and the Priory lands will thus have extended across to the western bank of Nant Crymlyn. The 'foss' (bank or ditch) of the park may refer to enclosed land belonging to Hendre. The present enclosed marshland is of two phases of eighteenth and nineteenth century work and the mediaeval confluence of the Nant Crymlyn and the Afon Taf would have been much further inland than today. The suggested location of these bounds are marked on Fig. 2.

This agreement shows the importance for the mediaeval farmer of upland and saltmarsh pastures, so that the stock could be kept off the meadows and away from the arable lands until the hay was mown and the corn harvested. Hay was an extremely valuable resource to the mediaeval lords for their horses and to all farmers for winter fodder. There is no mention of 'stinting' – that is limiting the numbers of beasts to be pastured – so there was clearly sufficient land for this. After harvesting, the arable fields were thrown open as pasture until spring sowing. There is little doubt that all around Llanybri and Llanstephan down to the coastal edges there were extensive arable lands organised as open fields – that is to say in unfenced strips of land, whose ownership and tenanting was intermingled requiring a complex system of regulation and co-operation detailed from much more extensive mediaeval English sources in accounts and court rolls and subject of an extensive literature.[42]

Returning to Mondegu marsh it is difficult to see how various, potentially conflicting, rights could be exercised without encroachment unless by this time the meadows, if not the saltmarshes, were enclosed in separate fields – perhaps that is what the references to Alexander's and Norris's dike imply. The latest (1479-80) Ministers Account states that the Mondegy meadow of the Lord's was six acres in extent. The valuable 'Mondegu' (Pendeggy) Mill was owned by the Lords of Llanstephan and tenants were obliged to use it; probably Pentowyn grain was milled there. However, returns could vary – for example, in 1388-9 rents normally £6 16s 8d from his two mills was down, because the mill at Mondegu stood idle from Michaelmas to the feast of St Andrew (29th September to 30th November). Rents were also received from tenants at 'Moghire', today's Mwche Farm. The Lord's income was also supplemented by dues payable on transporting animals to Llanstephan's fairs and markets – for example the Lord, or the royal steward Thomas Smith, failed to collect a customary 1½d for each capon 'having a certain way over the Marsh of Mundegy' in 1388. Four shillings were collected from the sale of rushes from Mondegy marsh. Rents were low in the early-fifteenth-century accounts due to the depradations wrought by Glyndŵr and his local supporters, although we learn from the 1411 account that people as well as geese were supposed

to pay a toll for crossing 'a certain way in the lord's marsh of Mondegy'.

Another resource exploited by both the church and secular lords were the 'fisheries' in the Towy and Taf. Fish weirs were built in the estuaries of the three rivers of the Gwendraeth, Towy and Taf.[43] Both the Prior of Carmarthen and the Knights had a fishery in the Taf but the exact site of their weirs is not known. However, a feature showing on the 1946 vertical RAF photograph might show the site of the Pentowyn weir (*see Fig. 3*). The extensive inquiry ordered by Prince Edward into the Prior's rights held before Thomas de Bradestone also included his rights to erect fish weirs in the River Towy, although it unclear whether this includes fish weirs in the river as well as in the inter-tidal estuary.[44]

MEDIAEVAL OPEN FIELD CULTIVATION

We rerurn in this section to where the article began – namely the productive arable lands of Pentowyn singled out for notice in *The Battle Abbey Chronicle*. It is evident from field and documentary evidence that these were organised as large open fields where the Prior and the Lord's 'demesne' lands were scattered as strips within communally cultivated fields. The evidence is partly in the present form and shape of field boundaries, often with the curving reversed 's' shape of the former furlongs. Comparison between recent OS Landranger maps and the 1841 Tithe Map for Llanstephan and the William Couling Enclosure Map of 1810 shows many now lost strip fields within surviving larger fields. There is in addition a large number of deeds and other documentary evidence for the steady process of exchange and consolidation of strips and enclosures within the former open fields to create separate farms. Thus new farms at Laques, Laques fawr, Down Farm, Ffynnon Down, Lord's Park and Park-y-Vicar for example were created in the sixteenth and seventeenth centuries. In some instances the former name of the open field is assumed by its successor farms and this seems to have been the case with Down Farm from the area known as The Down. The later mediaeval Ministers Accounts noted above make it clear that by the fourteenth and fifteenth centuries the demesne lands had been rented out to tenants, many of whom were enterprising peasant farmers slowly building up consolidated holdings whose names have been perpetuated in some instances by modern farms.

There is, however, one probable open field that survives only in field names which is relevant to Pentowyn and that is 'sinshill' or saints hill, a name evidently given to the field east of Pentowyn and south-west of Llanybri. It is interesting to find that during this period in the later fourteenth century, when the Priory was defending its possessions, it was also receiving fresh gifts of land from local people. Llanybri was a nucleated settlement which might have had 'bond' status at an earlier period but by the later Middle Ages had commuted its 'boon-works', or services, for a fixed rent. It also possessed free peasant farmers who were well on the way to building up a nucleus of lands and, by the later fifteenth and early sixteenth century farms, in their own right. Alice Barrett and her son Richard Symond (presumably Alice had remarried) granted by their own charter, witnessed at

Llanstephan in 1367, twenty-three acres of land and 8d of rents to the Priory.[45] A family connection is inescapable when we see that the Prior by this date was Brother William Symond. No need here it seems to seek licence to alienate the land. Where was this land? Six years earlier a charter witnessed amongst others by the bailiff of the Lord of Llanstephan, Walter Wynter, records a grant (perhaps in fact a purchase) by John Frances and his wife Alice, daughter of Philip Randolf, of sixty acres of arable land on Saints Hill in the lordship of Llanstephan. The donor's title came through Alice's ancestor Walter Randolph, who had been granted the land by William de Camville, Lord of Llanstephan in the early fourteenth century. It seems likely that the twenty-three

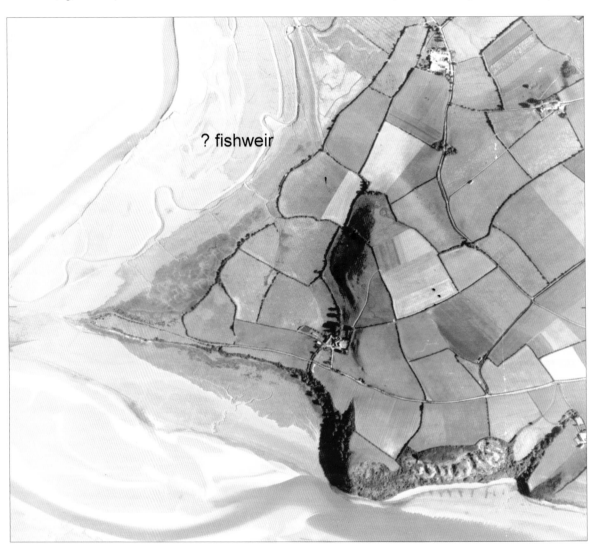

Fig. 3a: *Vertical air photograph, RAF 1946, 106 G./UK/1625. July 46, photograph 1182 showing Pentowyn.*

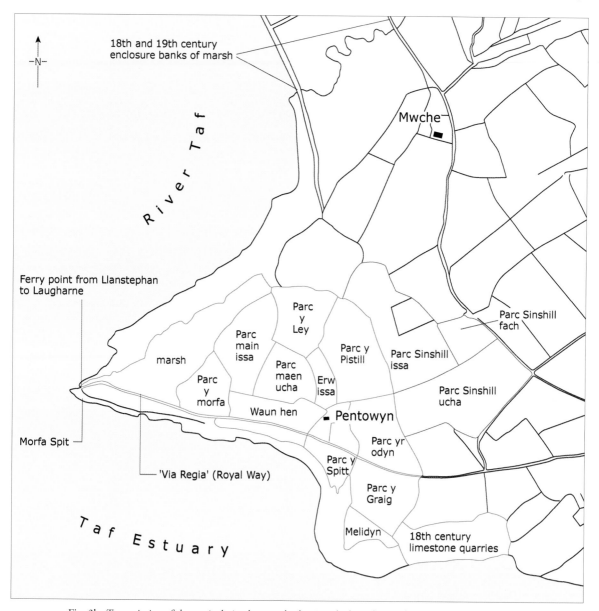

Fig. 3b: *Transcription of the vertical air photograph, showing the boundaries of Pentowyn's lands taken from Llanstephan Tithe Map with field names from the Tithe Schedule.*

acres later given to the Priory was part of these lands on Saints Hill adjacent to Pentowyn. The implication is that these lands were intermingled in one large open field.

It is not the purpose of this article to describe the high mediaeval open field systems of Pentowyn, Llanybri and Llanstephan although they deserve a more extensive treatment. The question is to what extent were they pre-Norman in origin. It was recognised by an earlier generation of agricultural historians, on whose shoulders much modern work still stands, that communal tenure and cultivation were a feature of the more densely settled lowland areas of pre-Norman Wales.[46] To a certain extent the layout of such open fields was a reflection of the undulating topography dissected by numerous small steep sited cwms or valleys such as we find over the southern part of the Llanstephan lordship – a more pastoral and woodland dependent economy may have characterised the Welshry of Penrhyn.

Communally-organised arable cultivation systems took different forms and it has been suggested that the extensive co-axial strip system of Manorbier for example is of pre-Norman date.[47] Such systems can be of great antiquity. Other models have been put forward by the late Glanville Jones for Welshries.[48] It has also been argued for Pembrokeshire in particular that the newly-founded planned Flemish settlements of the early twelfth century were associated with a whole 'landscape package' of newly organised field systems.[49] Certainly the strip fields still fossilised in the present day landscape in Llanstephan village bear a close relationship to the settlement plan with its burgage plots arguably of post-conquest foundation. But Llanybri, a nucleated settlement, has a much more native-Welsh radial plan and still has an extensive relict open-field system radiating out from its core.

The above can only be a brief introduction to what is a very complex subject. However, given the early reference to Pentowyn ploughlands and the known turbulence of the area throughout the twelfth and early thirteenth centuries, it seems unlikely that conditions allowed the kind of wholesale landscape reorganisation suggested for parts of Pembrokeshire. So extensive open-field arable production may well have characterised the pre- as well as the post- conquest landscape of Llanstephan. Sparse though the evidence is, I also suggest that there were early and probably extensive ecclesiastical estates associated with the cult of Teilo. It is unlikely that these could have been created anew in the troubled conditions of the ninth and tenth centuries. Pentowyn, and possibly other of the mediaeval Priory's possessions, may thus already have been part of Llanteulyddog's estate in the eighth to early ninth centuries.[50]

Finally, to return to *The Battle Abbey Chronicle's* encomium for Pentowyn – its abundance of wheat. It is common in discussion of mediaeval Welsh settlement and agriculture to quote Gerald of Wales' celebrated descriptions of the Welsh:

. . . the whole population lives almost entirely on oats and the produce of their herds, milk, cheese and butter. They eat plenty of meat but little bread.

. . . they content themselves with wattled huts on the edges of the forest . . . Most of their land is used for pasture.[51]

Historians and archaeologists then generally observe that there were in fact considerable areas of lowland arable production in Wales and indeed nucleated settlements. In fact Gerald was well aware of this and in other parts of his *Journey Through Wales* and his *Description of Wales* he notes areas rich in corn and other cereals. Coming as he did from Manorbier, where the de Barri family had expropriated what was clearly a very rich native Welsh *maenor*, he must have known that his pastoral, nomadic characterisation of the Welsh was but a partial picture. However, as Robert Bartlett has observed, such characterisations in the twelfth and thirteenth centuries of peoples – Celts (Welsh, Bretons and Irish), Slavs, Scandinavians, those on the fringes of what were regarded as the European heartlands as pastoral and nomadic, and thus essentially uncivilised, was a common aspersion. It justified their conquest and the seizure of their lands. 'In some ways pastoralism became a cultural yardstick' and 'the arable-pastoral polarity was given a moral colouring'.[52] When much of the early mediaeval landscape of south and west Wales is examined in detail, it becomes apparent that much of it, as I suggest at Pentowyn, was already organised and exploited in ways which the Normans simply appropriated and expanded rather than created anew.

ACKNOWLEDGEMENT

I am most grateful to Eiluned Rees for reading and commenting on this paper; I have benefited from her extensive knowledge of Llanstephan and Llanybri but any remaining errors or misinterpretations are mine.

NOTES

1. R. R. Davies, *The Age of Conquest Wales 1063-1415* (Oxford University Press, 1991), p. 181.

2. For the origins of the mediaeval castle and town see T. A. James, *Carmarthen: An Archaeological and Topographical Survey'* (Carmarthen: Dyfed Archaeological Trust & Carmarthenshire Antiquarian Society, 1980).

3. I have explored this further in 'Carmarthen', in P. Denison (ed.), *Conservation and Change in Historic Towns,* CBA Research Report 122, 1999, p. 261.

4. E. Searle (ed. & trans.), *The Chronicle of Battle Abbey* (Oxford Mediaeval Texts, 1980), p.124.

5. Searle, op. cit., n. 4, pp. 134-5.

6. The primary example of this was the addition of St Andrew to the Cathedral Church dedication of St Davids; Pill Priory, a dependency of St Dogmaels Abbey, the reformed *Llandudoch* was dedicated to St Mary and St Budoc.

7. Defined as an 'ecclesiastical or quasi ecclesisatical community, referred to in the Welsh laws headed by an abad (abbot), and thus, perhaps, of monastic origin, which was associated with the major or mother churches of the pre-Conquest Welsh church'. J. Wyn Evans, 'The Survival of the *Clas* as an Institution in Medieval Wales: Some Observations on Llanbadarn Fawr', in N. Edwards and A. Lane (eds.), *The Early Church in Wales and the West,* Oxbow Monograph 16, 1992, p. 33.

8. F. G. Cowley, *The Monastic Order in South Wales 1066-1349* (Cardiff: UWP, 1977), p. 29.

9. C. Johnson & H. A. Cronne (eds.), *Regesta Regum Anglo-Normannorum Henrici Primi 1100-1135* (Oxford, 1956), p. 368.

10. S. Baring-Gould & J. Fisher, *Lives of the British Saints,* (Cymmrodorion Society, 1907-1913), Vol. 8, pp. 251-2.

11. J. Wyn Evans, 'Aspects of the Early Church in Carmarthenshire', in H. James (ed.), *Sir Gâr: Studies in Carmarthenshire History* (Carmarthen: Carms. Antiq. Soc., 1991), pp. 249-351.

12. T. A. James, 'Excavations at the Augustinian priory of St. John and St. Teulyddog, Carmarthen, 1979', *Arch. Camb.,* Vol. CXXXIV, 1985, 120-161; see p. 128 for radiocarbon dates.

13. T. M. Charles-Edwards, 'The seven bishop-houses of Dyfed', *BBCS*, Vol. 24 (1970-2), 247-262.

14. Terry cited E. Phillimore, 'On a 9th century Dyfed Charter', in H. Owen (ed.), *Owen's Pembrokeshire,* Cymmrodorion Record Series, 1897-1906, Vol. 4, pp. 428-429; G. Thomas, 'A lost manuscript of Thomas Saint, Archdeacon of St. Davids, 1500-1513', *Nat. Lib. Wales Jnl.,* Vol. XXIV, 1986, pp. 309-338.

15. Burial was forbidden within the walls of Roman towns.

16. G. Dyfnallt-Owen, 'Agrarian Conditions and Changes in West Wales during the 16th century with special reference to Monastic and Chantry Lands', Ph.D. Thesis, Univ. of Wales, NLW 1935/50; idem, 'The Extent and Distribution of the Lands of the Priory of St John at Carmarthen', *Carms. Antiq.,* Vol. 1, Part 1, 1941, pp. 21-29.

17. W. Davies, *The Llandaff Charters* (Aberystwyth: NLW, 1979); W. Davies, *An Early Welsh Microcosm* (London: Royal Historical Society, 1978).

18. J. R. Davies, *The Book of Llandaf and the Norman Church in Wales* (Boydell Press, 2003), p. 148.

19. See the unpublished Reports to Cadw for the 'Early Medieval Ecclesiastical Sites Project' for Carmarthenshire and Pembrokeshire by Neil Ludlow, Historic Environment Record, Dyfed Archaeological Trust, Llandeilo.

20. Ref. No. in W. Davies, 1979, op. cit., n. 17, p. 126.

21. J. Gwenogvryn Evans, *The Text of the Book of Llan Dâv* (Oxford, 1893, NLW facsimile edition 1979).

22. S. Baring-Gould & J. Fisher, *Lives of the British Saints,* Cymmrodorion Society, 1907-1913, Vol. 7, *S. Teilo,* pp. 226-242.

23. E. Rees, in litt.

24. Phillimore, E., op cit., n. 14, Part II, p. 389, n. 31.

25. One notes however the perceptive comments by the late R. R. Davies in *The Age of Conquest: Wales 1063-1415* (Oxford Univ. Press, 1987, p'back 1991), pp. 12-13, 20-217, 264-5, on the fragmentation of Wales, the antiquity of some units but the changing fortunes of others and the efforts of later antiquarians to reconstruct a single fixed system which can never have existed contemporaneously.

26. S. Baring-Gould and J. Fisher, op. cit., n. 19, Part 8, pp. 367-368. His other dedication is at Llanstephan in Radnorshire, again in proximity to a Teilo site.

27. W. Rees, *A History of the Order of St John of Jerusalem* (Cardiff, 1947), p. 114

28. H. Owen (ed.), *The Description of Penbrokeshire by George Owen of Henllys* (London, Cymmrodorion Record Series, 4 Parts). Part II, 1897, p. 389, n. 29 by Egerton Phillimore.

29. See 'Notes on Weights and Measures', pp. 280-282, in W. Rees, *South Wales and the March, 1284-1415* (Oxford Univ. Press, 1924).

30. The 1338 account is printed in J. R Rees, 'Slebech Commandery and the Knights of St John, *Arch. Camb.*, Vol. XIII, 1896, p. 37.

31. F. Green (ed.), 'The Lordship of Llanstephan', in *West Wales Historical Records* (Carmarthen, 1927), Vol. 12, pp. 122-123.

32. Carm Cartulary 8 – also 7, p. 38, in J. Barrow (ed.), *St David's Episcopal Acta 1085-1280* (Cardiff: South Wales Record Society, 1998), No. 7, p. 38.

33. As above, No. 6, p. 36.

34. Bernard's close links with the Scottish court are described in J. Barrow, op cit., n. 32, p. 33.

35. W. Davies, 'The Latin charter tradition in western Britain, Brittany and Ireland in the early medieval period', in

D. Whitelock *et al.* (eds.) *Ireland in Early Medieval Europe*, pp. 258-280. I refer to the phrase 'Quod si quis contra hoc venire temptavit et donationem nostram infirmare vel diminuere, precipimus ut ilico ipse et omnis terra eius interdicatur et nisi se emendavit tertio vocatus excommunicetur'.

36. Davies, op. cit., n. 1, p. 403.
37. Thomas Phillips (ed.), *Cartularium S. Johannis Bapt. De Caermarthen* (Cheltenham, 1868), pp. 31-32, Nos. 82 & 83 (hence Carm. Cartulary).
38. Translation by Alcwyn Evans.
39. F. Green, op. cit., n. 31, Vol XIII, 1928, p. 47.
40. Idem, p. 77.
41. B. G. Charles, *The Place-Names of Pembrokeshire* (NLW, Aberystwyth, 1992), Vol. II, p. 789.
42. The best starting point is A. R. H. Baker & R. A. Butlin, *Studies of the Field Systems in the British Isles* (Camb. U.P., 1973), esp. M. Davies, 'Field Systems of South Wales', Ch. 11, pp. 480-529.
43. Llanstephan Lordship's weirs are discussed with others in H. & T. James, 'Fish weirs on the Taf, Towy and Gwendraeth estuaries, Carmarthenshire', *Carms. Antiq.*, Vol. XXXIX, 2003, pp. 22-48.
44. Carm. Cartulary 62/120 1355.
45. Carm. Cartulary No. 81/88.
46. M. Davies, 'Field Systems of South Wales', in A. R. H. Baker & R. A. Butlin (eds.), *Studies of Field Systems in the British Isles* (Camb. Univ. Press, 1973), p. 482.
47. J. A. Kissock, 'Some examples of co-axial field systems in Pembrokeshire', *Bull. Board Celtic Studies,* Vol. 40, 1993, pp. 190-197.
48. Amongst his extensive publications; G. R. J. Jones, 'Forms and Patterns of Medieval Settlements in Welsh Wales', in Della Hooke (ed.), *Medieval Villages: A Review of Current Work* (Oxford Univ. Committee for Archaeology, Monograph 5, 1985), pp. 155-162.
49. J. Kissock, 'God made Nature and Men Made Towns': Post-Conquest and Pre-Conquest Villages in Pembrokeshire', in Nancy Edwards (ed.), *Landscape and Settlement in Medieval Wales* (Oxbow Monograph, 81, 1997), pp. 123-137.
50. See the comments on federated ecclesiastical communities of, for example, Teilo in W. Davies, *Wales in the Early Middle Ages* (Leicester Univ. Press, 1982), pp. 162-164.
51. L. Thorpe (ed. and trans.), *Gerald of Wales: The Description of Wales* (Penguin Books, 1978), pp. 233 & 252.
52. R. Bartlett, *Gerald of Wales: A Voice of the Middle Ages* (1982 & Tempus, 2006), pp. 133-134.

The Advowson of Abernant Church

J. Beverley Smith

(with additional notes by Heather James)

Terry worked on the Cartulary of Carmarthen Priory[1] right up to his final weeks, in particular trying to get the entries in date order and to locate all the places and persons mentioned. Some detailed maps were prepared. Terry worked mainly from the remarkable manuscript translations and notes on the Cartulary put together by Alcwyn Evans, a Carmarthen Antiquary of the nineteenth century. It was Terry's aim to publish a new edition of this important historical source but he realised that he needed, as co-editors, a mediaeval Welsh historian and a palaeographer familiar with the seventeenth-century hand of the sole surviving copy in order to check Phillipps's transcript. The Carmarthenshire Antiquarian Society has resolved to seek to publish the Cartulary in its Monograph series. Terry sought information and advice from friends and colleagues, none more so than Professor J. Beverley Smith, who was Chairman of the Royal Commission on the Ancient and Historical Monuments of Wales during the period that Terry worked for the Commission. With characteristic generosity and scholarship, he responded at some length to Terry's inquiry relating to the advowson of Abernant Church and his communication is published here. A few further notes on the grant and the church have been added at the end by one of the editors (HJ) of this volume.

Three documents in the *Cartulary* of Carmarthen Priory have a bearing on the circumstances in which the Priory came to hold the patronage of the church of Abernant, namely Nos. 41, 42 and 43.

No. 43 may be taken first. This is Edward I's charter of 15 May 1290, at Westminster, confirming the grant of the advowson of the church of Abernant and the chapel of Cynwyl to the Priory Church of St John the Evangelist, Carmarthen. The charter recites that Richard ap Meredudd ap Richard, in the king's prison for trespasses against the king, by charter granted Abernant to the church of St John and the canons, so that the canons should thereafter, day-by-day, celebrate the memory of Stephen Bauzan, Richard Giffard and others who had died serving the king in the area. The reference is to the disaster at Cymerau in 1257. Robert Tibetot, justiciar of West Wales, is among the witnesses to the charter.

The charter is enrolled on the Charter Roll. The entry in the calendar[2] is brief and omits the names of witnesses, and it reads Maredudd ap Robert rather than Maredudd ap Richard, but it provides a means of access to a full Latin text that could prove to be more accurate

than that which appears in the *Cartulary*. More important, it authenticates the *Cartulary* text, providing a record contemporary with the grant of the charter.

With regard to Maredudd ap Richard, some instructive documents may be cited. Abernant and Cynwyl are located in Elfed, a commote which came under the crown's immediate lordship in 1241 when Henry III created the English and Welsh counties of Carmarthen, Derllys forming the English county and Elfed and Gwidigada the Welsh county. The rule of the princes over Elfed was extinguished at that point, and, though there were subsequent periods when royal control was tenuous, the princes' exercise of power of advowson in Elfed and Gwidigada ceased. Thus there is no need to associate the church of Abernant with any member of the princely lineages after 1241.

Maredudd ap Richard can be identified in the survey made in 1268 of the county of Carmarthen.[3] Under the Welshry of Carmarthen in 'the commote of Elfed and Derllys' the first named tenants are Maredudd ap Richard and Rhys ab Owain and Richard ab Owain, who held their *tenementum* in Elfed and Derllys, render-

169

ing two cows or ten shillings, at the lord's choice. This identification, and the association with Elfed, is helpful in relation to the key document that follows.

In Liber A, a volume compiled by royal clerks in the reign of Edward I, we have, dated 23 January 1289, a document made by Maredudd ap Richard ap Maredudd of Elfed by which, in the presence of John Pdrych (*sic*), prior of Carmarthen, and thirteen named Welshmen at Carmarthen, he declares that he had come before Robert Tibetot and made his submission *de alto et de basso* placing life and limbs, lands and tenements at the King's will. The conditions provided that he and his wife should reside at the home of a burgess, within the walls of Carmarthen, until the king's coming and the declaration of his will, Maredudd offering a thousand marks in security. Robert Tibetot provided a sum of six pence a day to Maredudd and his wife pending the king's coming.[4] Maredudd ap Richard had clearly been involved in the rebellion of Rhys ap Maredudd and the treatment accorded him, in the presence of a number of Welshmen (several of whom can be identified), indicates a wish on the part of the authorities to restore an understanding between lord and community.

A good ten years later, between 1298 and 1301, the account rolls for the principality of West Wales were recording sums received by the crown for lands of Maredudd ap Richard which had come into the king's hands and been leased at rent.[5] They were described as forfeited lands in 1301 in an account roll returned by the prior of Carmarthen in his capacity as treasurer, that is, chamberlain, of West Wales. In that year, in what was effectively the declaration of the king's will that had been foreshadowed in 1289, a financial penalty of £200 was imposed on Maredudd ap Richard in justice's sessions held before John de Havering, justice of West Wales. Maredudd paid £26 13s 4d of the fine in the same year, but he died before 1304-5. For in that financial year his son Maredudd Fychan paid £140 in part payment of the fine. This last entry indicates that Maredudd ap Richard's estate had not been forfeited in its entirety and that his son, being in a position to undertake to meet the obligation imposed on his father, was in possession of part or the whole of the paternal inheritance.

The document of 1289 provides the setting for document No. 41 in the *Cartulary* and does much to establish its authenticity. Maredudd ap Richard ap Maredudd grants the church of Abernant and the chapel of Cynwyl to the priory, defining the lands and

rights associated with the church. The charter is undated, but it bears the names of witnesses that include Robert Tibetot, and the other names are consistent with a transaction *c.*1289-90. The reference to Tibetot as *tunc justiciario West Wallie* reflects the writing of the text into the *Cartulary* at a later date.

It is therefore clear that the advowson of Abernant was held, not by a member of a princely lineage (as we have anticipated already) but by a freeman of the commote of Elfed. This is perfectly feasible, and there are instances of church patronage being vested in non-princely families, notably in the shared patronage of some 'portionary' churches in Gwynedd. Its grant to the priory was part of the process by which Maredudd ap Richard ap Maredudd endeavoured to make his peace with the king, who then confirmed the grant. The prior, John Istrigge (or Edrich) was actively involved in the transactions, and he may already have made an association with the royal administration in south-west Wales that would bring him the responsibilities of treasurer by 1299.[6]

This leaves us with No. 42 in the *Cartulary* and this is a perplexing document. Enacted in the name of William de Braose, it begins with a reference to the burning of the town of Carmarthen and the priory by Maredudd ap Richard and the subsequent forfeiture of Maredudd's lands, circumstances in which Braose, with the consent of Hubert Walter, archbishop of Canterbury and Justiciar, granted the church of Abernant to the priory of Carmarthen. The attack, though not the forfeiture, would be consistent with the indications in the other documents of Maredudd ap Richard's involvement with Rhys ap Maredudd. But the document is placed in an historical setting when William be Braose was bailiff of Carmarthen and Hubert Walter was Justiciar of England, that is *c.*25 December 1193 – 11 July 1198. The names of the numerous witnesses to the transaction could be examined so as to establish whether the document is likely to be authentic or spurious, but this may not be necessary.

The issue of the advowson of Abernant can be resolved by placing Nos. 41 and 43 in the setting created by other records of the late thirteenth century, and especially the document in the name of Maredudd ap Richard himself in Liber A. The prior seized the opportunity created by Maredudd ap Richard's submission following insurrection, and his own association with the royal administration, to secure the advowson of Abernant for the priory. There are several cases in the records

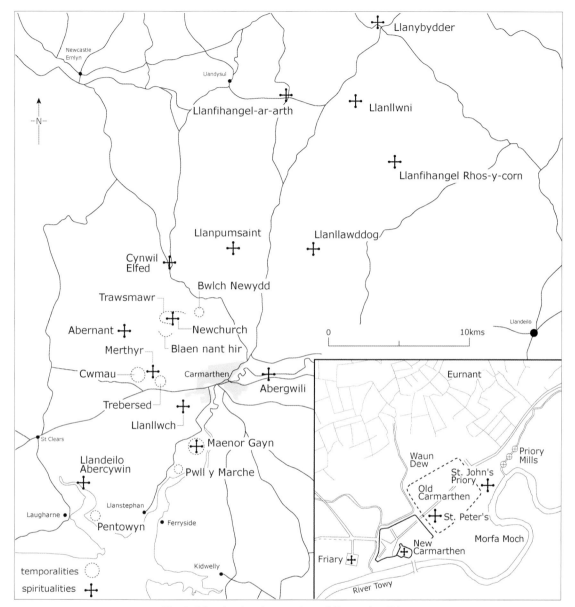

Fig. 1: *Map showing the possessions of Carmarthen Priory.*

of the King's Bench in the post-conquest period in which the crown claimed the advowson of Welsh churches previously held by princes. In this case the transactions concern an advowson, held by a freeman, who was probably a person of some standing in the commote of Elfed, that came into the priory's possession in the situation created by the involvement of some of the men of south-west Wales in insurrection with Rhys ap Maredudd in 1287. Edward I completed the transaction by confirming the grant of advowson of

Abernant to the priory in 1290, the year in which, as *Brut y Tywysogyon* relates, Rhys ap Maredudd 'was seized in the woods of Mallaen through the treachery of his own men'.[7]

As noted in the accompanying article on Pentowyn, a large proportion of Carmarthen Priory's revenues were derived from its 'spiritualities' in comparison with its 'temporalities' or landed estates. Appropriation of a church, that is to say the rights to its tithe and other revenues, was widespread in the Middle Ages. At Aber-

171

nant, following Maredudd ap Richard's grant, the Prior and canons received the greater tithes and dues such as mortuary dues; in return they appointed a vicar at a lesser stipend to provide pastoral care. The majority of the Priory's possessions were in the commotes of Elfed and Widigada and the former Derllys, subsumed into the Honour of Carmarthen.

Although detailed discussion cannot be entered upon in this paper, it is interesting to note that many of the Priory churches display archaeological and tenurial evidence for an early origin. It is indeed possible that some at least were pre-conquest possessions of Llan-teulyddog, the native Welsh ecclesiastical precursor of Carmarthen Priory. Abernant however, as Beverley Smith has established above, was in lay hands in the twelfth and thirteenth centuries. The church seems to have had an early importance belied by its small, two-celled mediaeval building. It had two chapels of ease: Troed y Rhiw, now extinct, and Cynwil Elfed, now a large church in its own parish. Cynwil remained a dependent chapel of Abernant throughout the Middle Ages but the church was much enlarged in the fifteenth

century probably due to the increasing wealth of the area and the growth of Cynwil village. The parish of Cynwil was later carved out of Abernant which was in origin therefore of considerable size. Another indicator of an early importance is the very large churchyard which surrounds the small mediaeval church. This is taken as one of the characteristics of early origin in the recent pan-Wales, Cadw-funded *Early Medieval Ecclesiastical Sites* project.[8]

Together with the advowson, Maredudd ap Richard also granted to the Priory an acre of land next to the cemetery. It may be that this was actually land within the large churchyard which could have been divided into segments as for example at Llandyfaelog, another early site.[9] The portionary rights noted here by Beverley Smith can also be found in some other Carmarthenshire churches and indicate churches controlled by Welsh kin groups. These lay owners may have seized churches formerly belonging to native monastic sites when the latter fell victim to decay and despoliation – this certainly seems to have been the case with Llandeilo, an important early Teilo monastery. Alternatively, churches

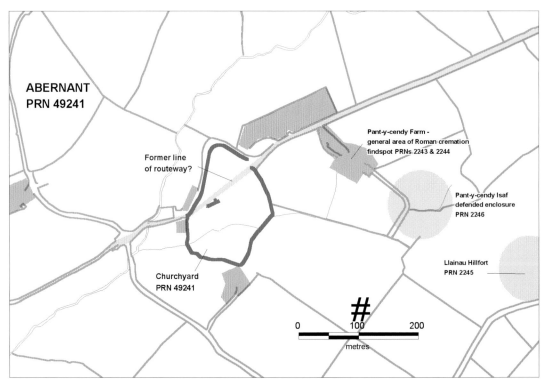

Fig. 2: *Map of Abernant Churchyard showing other early sites in its vicinity – reproduced from N. Ludlow, 'Early Medieval Ecclesiastical Sites project, Stage 2: Assessment and Fieldwork, Carmarthenshire Part 1 Overview', Report 2004/2.*
(By permission of Dyfed Archaeological Trust).

may have been established by lay founders – in some cases the obscure saints to whom they were dedicated may in fact be the lay founder.

Abernant is dedicated to a Latin saint – St Lucia – which might possibly be an anglicisation of the Welsh Lleucu, supposedly one of the many companions of St Ursula, virgin and martyr and be a post-conquest re-dedication. However, there are a few Welsh churches dedicated to St Lucy of Syracuse. A more powerful native Welsh cult, that of Cynwil, is represented in the dedication of Abernant's chapel at Cynwil Elfed. Cynwil is also culted at Conwil Gaeo, an important early church in the commote of that name. Other mediaeval churches within the commote of Elfed were Newchurch where the Priory had both the advowson and lands and which was a chapel of ease to Carmarthen, and Merthyr, also belonging to the Priory whose original dedications are obscure. These were both subsidiary chapels to Carmarthen St Peter's up to modern times.[10] Trelech a'r Betws seems to have been a Teilo church and is very much at the westward extremities of the commote. There are therefore some grounds for suggesting that Abernant might have been in origin a, if not the, mother church for the commote of Elfed. Interestingly, the authors of the recent 'Pevsner' volume for Carmarthenshire and Ceredigion, noting the 'huge' churchyard, draw attention to the fact that 'Abernant was a traditional place of burial for several surrounding parishes'.[11]

NOTES

1. T. Phillipps (ed.), *Cartularium S. Johannis Baptistae de Carmarthen* (Cheltenham, 1865). This is a rare book, privately printed, and is a transcript of the sole surviving MS of the Cartulary, NLW Peniarth MS 401D, a seventeenth century copy of the lost original.
2. *Calendar of Charter Rolls,* ii (1257-1300) p. 345.
3. Marquess of Bath MSS, Longleat MS 624.
4. J. G. Edwards, (ed.), *Littere Wallie* (Cardiff, 1940), p. 183.
5. M. Rees, (ed.), *Ministers' Accounts for West Wales 1277 to 1306* (London, 1936), pp. 68-9, 86-7, 194-5, 206-7, 384-5.
6. R. A. Griffiths, *The Principality of Wales in the Later Middle Ages, Vol. 1: South Wales 1277-1536* (Cardiff, 1972), p. 168.
7. T. Jones, (ed.), *Brut y Tywysogyon or The Chronicle of the Princes* (UWP, Cardiff, 1952), p. 121.
8. Unpublished reports of this project by N. Ludlow are in the Historic Environment Record for Dyfed, maintained by Dyfed Archaeological Trust at Llandeilo; the 'Overview' Report for Carmarthenshire (project record number 44753, report 2004/2) is particularly informative. For churches see N. L. Ludlow, 'Spiritual and Temporal: Church Building in medieval and later Carmarthenshire', *Carms. Antiq.,* Vol. XXXVI, 2000, pp. 71-86.
9. T. A. James, 'Air Photography of Ecclesiastical Sites in South Wales' in N. Edwards and A. Lane, (eds.), *The Early Church in Wales and the West* (Oxbow Monograph 16, 1992), pp. 62-76, esp. p. 73 for Llandyfaelog, Carms.
10. See the lists compiled by A. W. Wade-Evans, 'Parochiale Wallicanum', *Y Cymmrodor,* Vol. XXII (1910), pp. 23-124.
11. T. Lloyd, J. Orbach & R. Scourfield, *The Buildings of Wales: Carmarthenshire and Ceredigion* (Yale UP, New Haven & London, 2006), p. 116.

From Chapel to Cloister

A study in continuity and change over seven centuries

J. Wyn Evans

INTRODUCTION AND SUMMARY

Over the past seven centuries, the area immediately to the north of St Davids Cathedral on the south bank of the river Alun has been marshy riverbank, churchyard in active use, chantry college and chapel complex, picturesque vista and desolate ruin. For three years, at the beginning of the twenty-first century, the picture changed. From November 2004 until May 2007 there was intense building activity on that part of the Cathedral precincts, issuing in the refurbishment and recovery of the Cloisters, which were opened by their Royal Highnesses The Prince of Wales and The Duchess of Cornwall on 23rd June 2008.

The result of the work undertaken over the past three years has been the physical re-connection, for the first time in several hundred years, of the Cathedral and the buildings to the north of it. The convenience and shelter offered by such a link, which covers a relatively short distance, conceal a long and complex process leading back to the 1920s and before.

Successive deans and chapters, in consultation with successive bishops of St Davids, had made known their intentions of recovering that part of the curtilage for the use of the Cathedral and the furtherance of its mission. The delay in realising these intentions, before work actually began on site in November 2004, was a result of factors beyond their control.

The length of time between the conception and the realisation of the final scheme reflects in part the complexity of the consultative and planning processes. There were two such: the one secular and the other ecclesiastical. Given the sensitivity of the site and its religious, cultural, historical and architectural signifi-

cance, it is not surprising that the planning process was both long and intricate. It involved both consultation with voluntary groups and the granting of planning consents by the relevant statutory bodies. Archaeological assessments were undertaken and, where necessary, excavation in advance of construction.[1]

This lengthy sequence has been educative, illuminating the kind of process which must have exercised the Cathedral authorities in the past when they undertook works of this magnitude. The related issues of design, choice and sourcing of materials, and the nature and standard of workmanship have also been instructive. The mediaeval and early modern process, however, must probably have involved less bureaucracy, minimal consultation and no form filling.

It was equally illuminating to observe the physical processes of construction in both timber and wood marrying traditional craft skills and materials. To see Des Harries, the Cathedral's regular banker mason, shaping the stones for the outer doorway of the new North Porch and then constructing a Romanesque outer doorway from them was a revelation and a sight not normally seen in recent decades. Equally, to see Dai Howells, the other mason, finishing the pointing of the outer wall of the West Cloister in such an imaginative and creative manner was also a cause for wonder.

The thread running across the centuries and linking the various works and building phases on the site of the Cathedral has been, as it remains, that of response to need. In particular, there was the necessity, which emerged at different times, to meet the needs of the Cathedral through the construction and reconstruction of buildings. A particular challenge facing St Davids in

Figs. 1a and 1b: *Collecting stone from Caerbwdi beach below the mediaeval stone quarries in 2006; stone cutting by Des Harris, cathedral mason.*
(Photographs: Maggie Hemming).

the twentieth century was that posed by the increasing number of tourists, visitors and pilgrims to which the cathedral authorities had to respond both positively and practically for both their material and spiritual needs. This was the period from the 1920s onwards when St Davids, like other cathedrals in the United Kingdom, came back to life and found itself the object of increasing interest. This led to an exponential rise in numbers – up to three hundred thousand by the 1990s.

There was a further consideration which the Cathedral Chapter had to bear in mind, especially from the late 1950s onwards. The Cathedral fabric required serious attention and the Cathedral Architect was requested to set out a coherent long-term programme for the conservation and repair of the building. This programme itself followed on from both a major campaign initiated in the 1930s to eradicate the death watch beetle which had ravaged the timberwork in the building and the need to catch up on essential repairs delayed for the duration of the Second World War.

The approach adopted in this paper makes implicit assumptions about continuity, and not only the continuity of the existence of the site over time. There is continuity in the way a living historic site like St Davids in daily, even hourly, use over the centuries, demands a coherent strategic approach to its continued management in the present and its survival into the future. There is also continuity in the need for knowledge about previous approaches to the site and an awareness of how decisions that have to be taken in the present are influenced by decisions affecting the site and buildings taken in the past. This is especially true at St Davids, given the quirky nature of the building and the cramped

nature of the site; and the consequent remedial work which has had to be undertaken over the centuries.

This study is offered as a tribute to Terry James and is not only an expression of a valued and fruitful friendship of long standing but will also stand as a recognition of Terry's long-standing interest in St Davids as well as his contribution to the St Davids Cathedral Fabric Advisory Committee of which he was a member, as the 2004-2007 Cloister Scheme was moving through its planning and construction phases.[2]

SECTION I

Adam Houghton and the College of the Blessed Virgin Mary

The story begins in the third quarter of the fourteenth century. At that point in the life of the Cathedral the particular need of the time was met by the foundation, 'with the assent of our chapter' of a 'certain chapel or chantry (*cantariam*), of one master and seven presbyters.' It was collegiate (*per modum collegii*) and the members were bound to reside and to serve the Most Highest in the same chantry, which was dedicated to, and named for, the Blessed Virgin Mary. It was located 'on the soil of our sanctuary and our cathedral church of Menevia, on the North side of the said church of Menevia'.[3]

There can be no doubt, not only from the description of the location, but also from the name and dedication, that this was the site on the bank of the river Alun to the north of the Cathedral occupied today by the vaults beneath Cloister Hall and its garden, together with St Mary's Hall and the Cloister linking the complex with the Cathedral.

The wording of the charter – the references to 'our chapter'; 'our cathedral', 'our sanctuary' – makes it clear that the founder was the contemporary bishop of St Davids. From 1361 to 1389, this was Adam Houghton.[4] His life and career, in both its local and national character, its clerical and secular aspects, its royal and court patronage and its international links made him the ideal person to offer a solution of this nature to the contemporary problems facing his Cathedral and its mission.

Houghton was a Doctor of Civil Law of the University of Oxford and in 1376 he was named as a commissioner appointed to settle a dispute between the University and the Faculty of Laws. His diplomatic and administrative skills were however employed on a stage wider than the university. He had, as a king's clerk, been involved in business for the king in France in 1360 and 1361; he headed a commission to negotiate peace with France in 1377; and in the same year was appointed Lord Chancellor of England, a post he held until 1378. In 1380, he was involved in the marriage negotiations of Richard II and Anne of Bohemia.

Adam Houghton was clearly, therefore, a person possessing initiative, drive, influence and ability. His involvement in the business of government had given him access to patronage at a very high level. He made use of those links in order to bring about the foundation of the Collegiate Chantry of the Blessed Virgin Mary. The need to access and the ability to command and persuade those with power and money to support what was clearly an expensive enterprise in terms both of capital and revenue was especially necessary in St Davids, given its isolation and the poverty of resources and the scarcity of personnel.[5]

Similar considerations were to influence the Cathedral authorities from 1999 to 2007 as they put together a campaign both to raise funds and to gain the necessary permissions to realise the recovery of the Cloisters. There is a curious symmetry between the fourteenth and twentieth-century situations in that it was the state in its various guises which provided both permissions and substantial amounts of funding in the modern period, while Houghton was dependent on an equivalent royal and court patronage. The main difference

Figs. 2: *Near vertical air photograph of St Davids Cathedral from the north-east; Porth-y-Tŵr is on the lower left and part of the mediaeval Bishops' Palace on the top right. The new Clositers and St Mary's Hall are on the centre right of the photograph.*
(Air photograph 2006: T. Driver. Crown copyright, RCAHMW).

lies in the disendowment of the Church in Wales which meant that neither the episcopal revenues available to Houghton nor the resources which the Cathedral Chapter could draw on in the late fourteenth century were available in the late twentieth century. Instead it was a public appeal to which a very large number of private donors, grant-making bodies such as the Heritage Lottery Fund, the European Regional Development Fund and the Friends of the Cathedral and the Representative Body of the Church in Wales responded which made them the patrons of the works undertaken.

Fig. 3: *Common Seal of the Masters and Fellows of St. Mary's College, St Davids from a deed of 1529, John Luntley Master. The shield to the left probably has the arms of John of Gaunt, the central image is of the Virgin Mary supporting her child and below, the Master at prayer; the arms to the right are probably those of Bishop Houghton, on a fess between six crosses crosslet, three leopards' faces. Donated by Mr Thomas Lloyd to the Cathedral Library.*
(Ex inf. D. Williams).

Houghton was well aware of the isolation and slender resources available to the Cathedral, since he had been born within Dewisland, the episcopal lordship which lay around the Cathedral in an area running up to Fishguard to the north and Newgale to the south. His birthplace is traditionally pointed out as Caerforiog in Whitchurch, which is marked today as the site of a mediaeval moated site and lies just yards outside the border of the parish of St. Davids (SM811268).[6] His origins, as his name implies do not appear to be Welsh. Some light may be thrown on his immediate antecedents by the Black Book of St Davids which mentions a Master Adam Houghton. This may well be a reference to Houghton. Given, however, that the Black Book was compiled in 1326 and Bishop Houghton died in 1389, and although it is possible that he was a very young Master of Arts in 1326 it is more likely that this was a relative, possibly an uncle, of the same name.[7]

Houghton was well acquainted with the Cathedral; it may be that he had received his early education at St Davids, perhaps as a chorister in the cathedral school. It was, however, his experiences in government as a king's clerk, in effect a combination of royal civil servant and minister of the crown, together with the patronage of the court and in particular that of a powerful and wealthy personage, which enabled him to carry out his intentions at St Davids. The influence and patronage to which he had access are revealed in the names of the co-founders of the chantry college: John of Gaunt, fourth son of Edward III and Duke of Lancaster; and Blanche his wife. Moreover, when it came to endowing the new chantry college with churches for the support of the master and seven presbyters, he not only drew on the episcopal income to purchase the patronage of five churches within the diocese of St Davids, but he was also able to influence the patrons who ranged from John of Gaunt and Blanche to Guy de Brian, John of Haroldston and Nicholas Audley.[8]

That is not to say however, that the bishop did not overreach himself. The appropriation of the hospital at Whitwell, a few hundred yards outside the Close to the south of the Cathedral had occurred with the assent of the Chapter but without royal licence. So, in 1390, tactfully, perhaps after Houghton's death in 1389, Richard II issued the licence for £20.[9] Houghton's omission to gain a licence sounds entirely in character for he is said not only to have excommunicated a pope, probably the anti-pope Clement VII (r.1378-94), but also to have commemorated the fact in the stained-glass windows of the chapel of his foundation.[10]

The ostensible purpose of the foundation was, as with any chantry, to make constant intercession, through the saying or singing of masses, for the souls of the departed, especially the patrons of the chantry. In the case of St Davids, the first person to be so commemorated was, according to the statutes, the Lady Blanche, wife of John of Gaunt who although alive at the time of the initial foundation in 1365 had died in 1368, before the compilation of the statutes of the College in 1372. Alongside her are named Henry of Lancaster, her father who had died in 1361, and also John of Gaunt and Bishop Adam who were to be interceded for as long as they remained in this life; and such intercession was to continue after their deaths. It is also worthy of note that linked with them is William de Courtenay, 'special friend and benefactor of this chantry'. Courtenay was Archbishop of Canterbury from 1381 to 1396.[11] The statutes make a point of emphasising his input into securing the foundation of the chantry and then go on to say that he too would be prayed for after departing this life. In addition Houghton mentions the bishops and canons of Menevia, his parents and the benefactors of the said chantry and the souls of other faithful departed. Mass commemorating Blanche was to be celebrated daily; mass for the others on Wednesdays and Fridays at the Cathedral's high altar.

Mention of the Cathedral's High Altar may seem strange. The chantry was equipped with a large and splendid early Perpendicular chapel which is the most prominent part of Houghton's complex to survive. It is a substantial building, and from the surviving detail must have been expensive both to construct and to furnish and adorn. The mediaeval shell which, after its re-roofing in the 1960s, forms St Mary's Hall, is set over a substantial vault. Prior to the most recent scheme, which placed a refectory on an inserted mezzanine within the former chapel, the building seemed extremely large and spacious; too large indeed for a master and seven presbyters.

Although neither description nor traces remain of the liturgical arrangements within the chapel, it is clear from the very full and detailed statutes that accommodation had to be found for the daily singing of the Office of the Blessed Virgin Mary antiphonally under the direction of the Precentor of the chantry.[12] Consequently, there must have been stalls of some sort or another in the chapel, probably to the west of the substantial main altar. The difference between the floor levels of the sacristy and the main chapel is such as to suggest that there were the usual three footpaces leading up to the altar, which was flanked on its north side by the very large and elaborate tomb of Adam Houghton himself. The height off the ground of the alabaster ledger stone on which his effigy probably lay makes the same point. Put together, this evidence would suggest

that a substantial area of the east end of the building was taken up with the altar and stalls.

Two-thirds of the way down the chapel there is a door on the north side. It is possible that this was once covered by a transverse screen running north and south in the body of the chapel, dividing the area reserved for the college to perform the office and the liturgy from that reserved for those who wished to attend and hear the same.[13] The door communicates with a corridor in the thickness of the wall which leads both upwards to rooms in the tower and downwards, via a spiral staircase, to basement level and out by another door into the courtyard, now the 'peace garden', to the north of the chapel and lying between it and the domestic range of the college. That range, which housed the master and seven fellows and their servants, was itself set on a first-floor vault which substantially survives beneath the modern house set asymmetrically upon it.

In any case the chapel, whatever its putative internal fittings, seems overlarge for those who sang services there, however elaborate the liturgies which they were called upon by the 1372 statutes to perform within it. A more basic question, however, is why Houghton founded the College in the first place, since even a cursory glance shows that in many respects it duplicated the prime functions of the Cathedral, which lay only a few yards to the south of it.

The prime function of the cathedral body, the corporate collegiate body known as the Chapter was, as it still is, to perform the *Opus Dei*; that is: to say, or in particular to sing, the services, the offices and the Eucharist in choir every day, ferial or festal.[14] The Precentor was the member of Chapter charged with the responsibility for overseeing the performance of the liturgy.[15] There were however problems affecting the Cathedral in the 1360s, both generic to secular cathedrals of the old foundation such as St Davids and specific to St Davids itself because of its location.

Specifically, the foundation charter states that Bishop Houghton, John of Gaunt and his wife Blanche were moved to found the College because of the slender resources of the Cathedral, which meant that the liturgical standards of the Cathedral were poor because of a shortage of priests who could sing well, a deficiency which could only be rectified by bringing in priests from England.[16] It is ironic that Houghton makes that point, since he was a prime example of an able priest who had travelled in the opposite direction to England and who had only returned on his elevation to the episcopal

Plan

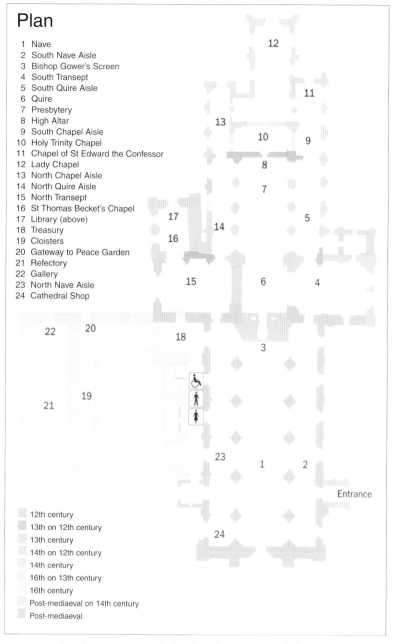

1 Nave
2 South Nave Aisle
3 Bishop Gower's Screen
4 South Transept
5 South Quire Aisle
6 Quire
7 Presbytery
8 High Altar
9 South Chapel Aisle
10 Holy Trinity Chapel
11 Chapel of St Edward the Confessor
12 Lady Chapel
13 North Chapel Aisle
14 North Quire Aisle
15 North Transept
16 St Thomas Becket's Chapel
17 Library (above)
18 Treasury
19 Cloisters
20 Gateway to Peace Garden
21 Refectory
22 Gallery
23 North Nave Aisle
24 Cathedral Shop

12th century
13th on 12th century
13th century
14th on 12th century
14th century
16th on 13th century
16th century
Post-mediaeval on 14th century
Post-mediaeval

Fig. 4: *Plan of the Cathedral from the 2008 Cathedral Guide.*
(Reproduced by permission of St Davids Cathedral and Jarrold Publishing, copyright reserved).

intervening period to the extent that drastic countervailing measures were called for.

It is the more likely however that the low musical standards at St Davids were due to a fundamental issue facing secular cathedrals of the old foundation like St Davids. It was a problem which had faced them from the very beginning when the Normans had introduced them into Britain. In secular, as opposed to monastic cathedrals, the canons, the individual members of chapter, were supported not only by a common fund drawn from churches and lands held in common ownership by the community as a whole, but also by individual prebends bearing the names of a specific manor or group of estates or churches, assigned to each canon in his own right.[17] This led to large-scale clerical absenteeism and was appreciated not only by those who were able to enjoy such lucrative canonries, without cure of souls, *in absentia*, but also by kings and popes who could see that advantages of getting salaries for their protégés or servants without any outlay on their own part. It has been pointed out that the secular cathedrals were the single most important instrument for the diversion of surplus wealth from the grass roots of English and Welsh parishes, to support not only the most sophisticated features of the mediaeval church but also the careers of the men who actually ran 'the ramshackle twin engines of church and state'.[18]

A classic example of such a career is, of course, that of Adam Houghton

bench. The irony becomes sharper when we consider that he was Precentor of the Cathedral between 1339 and 1352 and presumably suitably qualified in liturgy and music. It may be the case that when Houghton returned to St Davids as Bishop in 1361, he found that both musical and liturgical standards and, more probably, the Cathedral's revenues had also declined in the

himself. His royal service was supported by the income from a number of benefices, including prebends of St Davids Cathedral, but it is noteworthy that, although his service to the crown and the court continued after he became bishop, he resigned such preferments.[19] Further he turned the access and contacts he had made to good use to the benefit of the Cathedral through the foundation and endowment of St Mary's College. The setting up of the College still begs the question of whether it was the correct solution to the problem of non-residence by placing it adjacent to the Cathedral which was itself, as it still is, a collegiate church, housing and served by a corporate body whose prime function is the regular performance of the liturgy.

It is clear from both the foundation charter and the statutes of the College that Houghton's perception of the Cathedral's liturgical competence was low when he came into office in 1361.[20] This raises the question as to why he did not attempt to reform the Cathedral foundation itself rather than duplicate resources in this extravagant way, not least because there was already an answer of long standing associated with the Cathedral.

In fact, cathedrals themselves were well aware of the consequences of the non-residence of those enjoined to keep perpetual residence, especially where music and liturgy were concerned; moreover, they had devised a solution to answer the problem. Cathedrals had put in place a set of 'singing deputies', Vicars Choral, *Vicarii Chorales*, who were enjoined to perpetual residence on behalf of their non-resident principals, for each canon had his own deputy.[21] Vicars Choral had to live communally and were not supported by prebends, but by a common fund. In time they developed into a separate corporation with their own estates. Their function was to sing the services, assisted by the choristers.

This was a fairly elaborate and demanding set of tasks, hence the importance of the post of Precentor. He had oversight of the liturgy and had therefore to possess a high degree of expertise. That, in turn, involved detailed acquaintance with the Use of Sarum (Salisbury), which St Davids had adopted by 1224, fairly early in the sequence of those cathedrals to adopt the Sarum Use.[22] The Sarum Use made the Cantor/Precentor responsible for all services. This in turn meant that he had to keep perpetual residence and to have the necessary disciplinary powers to maintain standards, not least where the Vicars Choral were concerned.

The irony of Houghton's approach to the foundation of the College is thus even more compounded when it is recalled that he was the Precentor of the Cathedral between 1339 and 1352, and charged with both perpetual residence and with disciplining and training the Vicars Choral. He did indeed, in the set of statutes which he promulgated to his Chapter in 1368, take steps both to improve the musical performance and the standards of residence and discipline of the Vicars Choral.

This did not however appear to have satisfied his requirements, nor did his endowment of the four boy choristers in 1363.[23] He thus set up the College of St Mary to remedy the situation, complete with both two choristers and a precentor of its own, but to be under the governance of the Precentor of the Cathedral.

It may well be the case that Houghton adopted this solution because this was the fashionable way to express religious intention; the kind of institution to found and endow at the time. Indeed, Blanche's brother Henry, Duke of Lancaster had founded the Newarke College, Leicester, or the College of the Annunciation of Blessed Virgin Mary of the Newarke to give it its full title. It was a chantry college, whose purpose was to pray for the House of Lancaster.[24]

St Mary's College was better endowed than the Cathedral, therefore, attracting the kind of musically and liturgically qualified cleric whom Houghton had in mind. The standards attained would therefore be higher than those manifestly not attained by the Vicars Choral, who may well have attained their position by default, perhaps as superannuated choristers. In any case, their emoluments were far smaller than those intended for the collegians of St Mary's. Furthermore, the College was not prebendal, hence its revenues were to be shared in common and could not be diverted by either the master and seven fellows or the papacy or the crown for the support of careers away from St Davids. This would facilitate perpetual residence, or at least discourage non-residence. Moreover, separate endowments did not encroach on the resources of the Cathedral.

The recognition that the chantry college, as closely linked as it was with the Cathedral – which in any case had its own Lady Chapel – was in some sense duplicating the work and intentions of both the Chapter and the college of Vicars Choral, may be the reason why at the end of the fifteenth century a merger between the College and the College of Vicars Choral actually occurred, probably as part of another reform of the liturgy under Bishop John Morgan.[25] It may equally have been due to the rationalisation and consolidation of resources. However successful this merger may have been, within a few decades circumstances changed again. This time, it was not changes in the musical and liturgical practices of cathedral or college that were being called for, rather a root and branch reformation which would see the college swept away and its buildings reduced to ruin.

SECTION II

Dissolution, Neglect and Decay

Tranquillity and silence rather than the sound of many voices singing masses and psalms characterised this area of the cathedral precincts for some considerable time before 2007. It was the tranquillity and silence of abandonment, neglect, vandalism and decay. The period between the second half of the sixteenth century and the early twentieth century saw the dissolution and abandonment of the College, with the consequent demolition and asset stripping of the buildings. The seventeenth century saw parliamentary soldiers destroying the library housed in the upper range of the West Cloister.[26] The eighteenth century saw the conversion of the remains of the College into pauper housing and at the end of the century, the architect John Nash vandalised the fine early Perpendicular chapel windows, cannibalising their stonework for his distinctive Gothick Perpendicular West Front built in 1793.[27] The nineteenth and twentieth centuries, the period when the major restoration of the Cathedral was undertaken, saw, as part of that process, the conservation, partial reconstruction and recovery of both Chapel and Cloister. It was viewed as the logical conclusion of the wider campaign to secure the survival of the fabric both of the Cathedral and the buildings ancillary to it within the Close.

As a result, for some three and a half centuries between 1550 and 1965, the chapel lay unroofed, stripped of its lead and glass; the College vaults survived (as they still do) to their full height and a house was built on part of the basement of the east range; and the outline of the Cloister gradually became harder to make out, as the garth became filled up with soil to such an extent that walls and walkways disappeared. The garth also became the burial place of infant and stillbirths.[28]

The west range of the Cloister appears, however, to have survived longer than the rest of the enclosure. That may be due to the fact that it seems at one time to have accommodated both library and school: *Over yᵉ west cloister was formerly a free school or library for the use of the college.*[29] Both of these had either been removed or destroyed by 1776, when a print by Hooper and Sparrow shows the outer west wall of the cloister as still standing at that date.[30] The Cloister, thus, appears to have survived whatever damage was done to this area of the Cathedral in 1648, though it has clearly been shorn of the roof of its upper storey. Not only does the wall clearly link the Cathedral and the west front of St Mary's

Chapel but traces of the bottom doorway of the (missing but now restored) vice are clearly shown.

The school was moved, probably in the mid sixteenth century, to the edge of the churchyard to the north of the South Gate and the schoolroom was constructed over the basement containing the former cathedral workshops. As for the library, the visit of Parliamentary soldiers in 1648 led to the destruction of the surviving contents. The location of the library is unknown but there is strong evidence to suggest that may well have been in the cloister area in the mid to late sixteenth century. There is an entry in the Chapter register for 1568 which speaks of Chantor (Precentor) Thomas Huett sending to Bishop Richard Davies 'certain extracts from the grants and Statutes of the Church of St David'. Archdeacon Payne in his gloss on this entry states *inter alia* that Bishop Davies' second son had obtained a few leaves of Cicero, 'written on parchment, that came out of the library adjoining to the cathedral of St Davids . . .'[31] This would accord well with a location in the west range of the Cloister after the school had been removed.

It is reasonable to suppose that the wall fell victim to the same forces that removed the tracery of the chapel windows. According to Jones and Freeman all the 'windows were shorn of their tracery, and apparently of a large portion of their ashlar jambs to furnish materials for the present west front of the cathedral'. The west front, into which these genuine windows were set (to Jones and Freeman, 'clearly of very best Early Perpendicular' and 'beautifully proportioned') was that built in 1793 by John Nash in a mock Perpendicular eighteenth century Gothic Revival style.[32]

It was not, however, the visitation of Parliamentary soldiers in August 1648 that began the process of ruin and abandonment of College, Chapel and Cloister. Over a century before, Bishop William Barlow, as a proponent of the reformation of the Anglican Church, had attempted to move both the Cathedral and the episcopal residence to Carmarthen. In this Bishop Barlow partly failed. He and his successors up to the present day moved to live in the former College of Abergwili outside Carmarthen. The Cathedral remained at St. Davids on its ancient site, as it still does.[33]

The Cathedral itself did, however, suffer in that Bishop Barlow on 1 March 1538 slighted the shrine of St David. He managed to gain possession of the relics and forward them to Thomas Cromwell, who, although this is speculative, probably had them destroyed. If

Fig. 5: *Print by Hooper & Sparrow, 1776.*

Barlow's correspondence with Cromwell is to be believed, his programme of reform entailed the improvement of the condition of the College and its *'poor collegians'*, who appeared to be in difficulty because of the expenditure of the Chapter on the major rebuilding work of the cathedral.[34] In the event it was one of those poor collegians, a Cambridge graduate by the name of Stephen Green who was responsible for seizing the relics in the shrine and handing them over to Barlow.[35] As matters turned out later, however, the College itself and the poor collegians attached to it became as much victims of the Reformation as the shrine.

The last phase in the life of St Mary's College, Chapel and Cloister begins with two Acts of Parliament, dating from the end of the reign of Henry VIII and the beginning of that of Edward VI. A depleted Treasury, following wars with France in 1544 led to the passing of an Act of Parliament intended to dissolve chantries, colleges, guilds and hospitals and transfer their property to the Crown. To that end, Commissioners were appointed on 14 February 1546 to visit all establishments in such categories. Among those appointed for South Wales, as might have been expected, was Bishop Barlow.[36]

The articles sought to discover the name and numbers of chantries and similar institutions; the nature of

the charitable foundation under which they operated; whether they were parish churches – and if not, how far distant they were from such churches; the yearly value of the lands and property that were associated with them; the value of the ornaments, plate and chattels which belonged to them; and sixthly and lastly, and perhaps most interestingly, how many chantries and such institutions had been dissolved since 1535-36 and been obtained by people without the King's licence, and hence how much they were worth. In the case of St Mary's College, which heads the answers for Pembrokeshire, the answer to the second Interrogatory, informs us that the College had been founded to 'fynd' (support) a Master, whose salary was £20 per annum; seven fellows and two choristers at an annual cost of £26.15s.6d; and supported *'other dedes of charitie'*, though these are unspecified. The return unfortunately names neither the Master, nor the fellows and choristers.

It does, however, note at the end of the answer to this second interrogatory that:

The said Colledge hath byn altered from y^t foundacion &Adyoinyd & annexid to the Cathedral Churche ther to the maynteynance of the Maister and xxii vicars Chorall & viiith qeresters with other seruauntes for the mayn-

*teynance of god seruyce within the said Cathedrall
Churche as apperith by a writing called the Reformacion.*

The answer to the third question, which asked
whether the chantry was or had been a parish church,
received the reply:

> [The College] *ys no Paryshe Churche but is within the
> Churcheyarde of the Cathedrall Churche of Saynt Davys.
> The nomber of houselyng people belonging to the said
> Churche of Saynt Davyd ar by common estimation
> abowt xiiii*[th] *or xv hundred . . .*

The land and possessions of the college appeared at
least in 1546 to have produced a yearly income of £84
and 17 shillings, which was used up completely in supporting the Master (£20), twenty Vicars Choral, eight
choristers and other servants (£26.10s.8d), the stipend
of one priest to singing in the chapel of St Ishmael's, in
Carmarthenshire (5s.) a substantial sum of £28.0.2d in
paying tenths, 24s.2d for synodals and proxies for four
churches, eight pence for a fine, one hundred and fourteen shillings for fees and wages. There was in addition
a sum of twenty-five pounds and twenty-two pence
spent on 'reparacions'.

What precisely these 'reparacions' were, is unclear
from the entry. Was it that the fabric of the College, the
Chapel or the Cloister were under repair? Was it the
erection of buttresses in the Cloister garth? It may also
have been the construction of the upper stage of the
West Cloister to house the school and library. It may
equally well have been repairs the College had had to
carry out in the churches whose patronage was vested in
it.

In any case, the sum total of expenditure was eighty-
four pounds and seventeen shillings, which exactly
matched the income. In addition, the answer to the fifth
interrogatory reveals that the value of the plate and
chattels owned by the college was thirty-two pounds
and three shillings.

It is instructive to compare this valuation with that
made for the *Valor Ecclesiasticus* in 1535 – hence the
significance of the last Interrogatory.[37] The return for
the *Valor* was made by John Luntley, described as
*clericus et socius eujusdem Collegii Beatae Mariae Virginis
prope Eccl' 'Cathedral' Meneven'.* This designation is
slightly disingenuous, since Luntley was in fact the
Master of St Mary's College from 1524 to 1542, while
also being Archdeacon of Cardigan and Precentor of the
Collegiate Church of Llanddewi Brefi.[38]

The value of the said College and manor of Whitwell
(value £6.6.8), 'of the foundation of Adam recent
Bishop of St Davids' was £6.6.8d. It then proceeds to
list the parish churches held by the College, together
with their values, namely Nevern (£27), St Ishmael's
(£16) Haroldston West (£6.13.4d), Cilycwm (£16),
Marloes (£11.13.4), Llansanffraed (£10.0.0), Llanreith
(£5.0.0), Manorowen (£2.10.0s), Llanstinan (£4.13.4).
The income thus derived from these churches and the
manor came to £111.16.4d, giving a total, after
synodals and procuration fees of £5.12.0 were deducted,
of £106.3.6d. This compares with £84.17s in 1545.
Whether like is being compared with like is difficult to
tell: for the 1546 Survey does not itemise the
components of the income; nor does it mention any
churches owned by the College. Instead the fourth
question asked about income derived from 'lands and
possessions' rather than churches.

In any case, the death of Henry VIII on 28 January
1547 caused the 1545 Act to lapse. The College's reprieve
was however only temporary. The new reign of Edward
VI saw a new Act passed in December, and a new body
of Commissioners appointed. More detail about the
College survives than in the 1546 Survey as can be seen
from the Certificate of Dissolution (Certificate 74, No.
20), published by Francis Green in 1921.[39]
It refers to the:

> *Colledge, called our Lady Colledge, founded by one
> Adam Hutton and one John, duke of Lancaster and
> Dame Blanche his wif, for a Master, seven Fellows and
> two Queristers, and about sixty years past the same as is
> reported was united to the cathedral church of Saynt
> Davis, to the intent to have a master of the same colledge
> founde and 27 vicars corall, 8 queristers and other ser-
> vants.*

It is interesting that it informs us that the revised
foundation funded twenty-seven rather than twenty-two
Vicars Choral. The latter figure, as set out in the earlier
document corresponds to the number of prebends and
canonries occupied by the members of the Cathedral
Chapter. Given that the Vicars Choral, as the name
suggests, were the (choral) deputies of the Canons,
twenty-two is the number that might be expected.
When the names of those listed in the certificate are
counted, the number of Vicars Choral is twenty-one not
twenty-seven. When, however, it is realised that Stephen
Green, the Master of the College was also the Sub-
Chanter of the Cathedral, which was technically a post

held by the senior Vicar Choral, then it is clear that the tally is correct and that the number twenty-seven is an error, perhaps a misreading of xxvii for xxii. Certainly the sum of £71.00, which included £20 as Green's stipend together with £51 for those of the Vicars Choral corresponds with a number of twenty-one rather than twenty-seven. It is worth at this point, therefore, looking in more detail at the personnel who made up the College foundation in the years immediately prior to its suppression; as well as noting what happened to some of the survivors.

The change to the Foundation is specified in the Chantry Certificate, as happening about sixty years past, which should place it around 1488/89. The actual date is not given. Nor is there any reason given as to why it happened. One suggestion may be that the change may have occurred a few years later than 1488; that sixty was an approximate number. This would square more with an entry in the Statute Book where the change is associated with John Morgan who became Bishop in 1496, though, to complicate matters the relevant statute is dated 1501. On the other hand 1488 was the year in which John Morgan became Archdeacon of Carmarthen; he was also Dean of Windsor, so he may have had an influence on the college prior to his elevation to the episcopal bench.[40]

By 1504, the year of Archbishop Warham's metropolitical visitation, we are presented with a snapshot of the whole corporate and clerical establishment of the Cathedral. The names of the members of Chapter, Vicars Choral, Choristers and Chantry priests are given. The Master of the College was Richard Raydr LLD, the Fellows were Sir Thomas Bacon, Sir William Stevyns, Sir Johnes . . . Sir Philip Lewis, Sir Thomas Cortner and Sir William Laurence, seven in all.[41]

The 1548 Certificate gives the location of the College as being in the parish of St Davids and on the north side of the Cathedral church. Significantly, or ominously, in the light of what followed the certificate makes the point that the College is covered with lead. It then proceeds to give the dimensions of the church (chapel) as being twenty-four yards long; and nine yards broad, the vestry (which was on the south side and housed in a three-storey structure) as being seven yards long and five yards broad; and a stair, presumably the stairway under the tower leading up from the Cloister was six and a half yards long and three and a half yards broad.[42]

The ecclesiastical possessions of the College are not given in detail, the aggregated total being given at

£89.6.8, and the non-ecclesiastical lands and tenements are given a value of £6.10.4, which accords well with that given for the manor of Whitwell in the *Valor* in 1535, namely £6.6.8d. The value of £95.9.8, given as that of the ecclesiastical benefices in 1535 (less £5.12.10 in synodals and procuration fees, making £89.16.10), is of the same order as the £89.6.8. noted in 1548.

As for the master and presbyters of the dissolved college, a document of 1553, shows that they, along with the other surviving chantry priests of the Cathedral were still being paid their promised pensions, even though some of them were Vicars Choral – whose College had not been suppressed.[43]

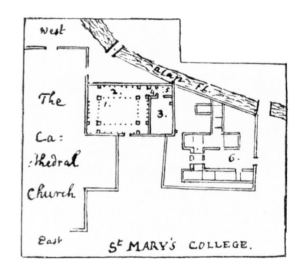

Fig. 6: *Lord's plan from E. Yardley, 'Menevia Sacra'.*

A plan of the ruins which now characterised the area to the north of the cathedral was made by Joseph Lord in 1720 and included by Edward Yardley in his *Menevia Sacra*, written probably between 1739 and 1760. Lord described the site thus:[44]

The Quadrangle & Cloyster (1) which are contiguous to ye north side of ye Cathedral Church, are now almost in ruins; there being now only round ye walls some remains of pillars, which give us a notion of what it hath been. The west Cloyster (2) was formerly a Free School, or a library for ye use of ye College (during which time, that which is now ye School, in ye churchyard, was a store-house, & work house for ye use of ye Church). The other three sides of ye Cloyster were covered with lead, & served only for shelter, & were supported by pillars neatly wrought, as appears by ye remains of those round ye walls. The Chapel, dedicated to St Mary (though some say to St Peter) stood on ye north side of the Quadrangle (3), joining to ye Cloysters. It was a curious building; on ye south & north sides it hath three windows of about 24 feet high & 9 feet broad, & at ye east end a window something larger. In ye south west corner stands ye Tower (4), under or through which is ye entrance from ye Cloysters to ye Chapel. This Tower is 70 feet high, & all well built, being ornamented with true Free-stone, as are also ye windows of ye Chapel. Over ye south-east corner was a small room (5) with a door from ye Chapel into it; which I take to 'have been a vestry. The length of this Chapel,' in ye clear within, is 69 feet 9 inches from east to west, agreeable to the height of ye Tower: ye breadth 22 feet 9 inches: ye height of ye side walls 45 feet. Underneath the whole extent of this Chapel is a vault (with launcets to let in light) said to have been a charnel house.

Yardley made his own additional comments:[45]

The College (6) on ye north side of the Chapel, was a large pile of building, vaulted all under it. In this College ye seven Fellows (& Master) had their appartments, according to the appointment of ye founder Bishop Adam Houghton, who endowed it with £100 per annum. Most of – ye walls are still standing, though all uncovered except two small parts inhabited by two cottagers. From the College there was a way that led directly into ye Chapel through ye gardens, which lay between ye Chapel & College. It was surrendered to ye Crown in King Edward VI's reign, with lands belonging to it, on part of which stands ye ruins of a Chapel called Whitewell, about 500 yards south of ye Close of St Davids. The College and lands are set by lease upon paying some small acknowledgment to the Crown.

This was the condition, ruinous and abandoned, of this part of the cathedral curtilage for several decades after Lord and Yardley's descriptions. The depredations made by Nash were, as we have seen above, noted by Jones and Freeman and it seems that the domestic buildings were still being leased from the Crown in 1811.[46] It was only in the first half of the twentieth century that serious plans for the recovery and reuse of the Chapel and Cloister were drawn up.[47]

SECTION III

Recovery and Reconstruction:
The 2007 Cloister Scheme in Context
In July 1994, in my report to Chapter, I, newly appointed as Dean of St Davids, drew my capitular colleagues'

attention to the possibility of 'putting the cloisters back into commission'. It was not until September 2007, however, that the new Cloister complex became accessible to the public in its entirety. The opening up of the new facilities marked the climax of a strategy of recovery, restoration and enhancement undertaken over the previous several decades. Such had been the growth in numbers of pilgrims, tourists and visitors that not only the physical facilities but the mission and liturgy of the Cathedral had been affected. The previous thirty years had seen an exponential rise in the number of people visiting the Cathedral, peaking in the early 1990s at nearly three hundred thousand per annum. Thus, as far as the Cathedral was concerned, the significance of the Cloister scheme lay in two areas: that of strategic planning for the long-term future needs of the Dean and Chapter and, secondly, that of the need to continue the programme of repair and conservation of the fabric of the Cathedral and its ancillary buildings, such as St Mary's Hall.

Therefore, in order to realise both the strategic programme and the urgently needed conservation work, suitable stone had to be found, preferably locally. This led to a campaign for the reopening of the mediaeval quarries at Caerbwdi from which had come the Cambrian sandstone used in both the building of the Cathedral in the twelfth, and the Palace of the bishops, in the fourteenth centuries.

In March 1999, therefore, the Dean and Chapter launched its Millennium Appeal to fund the five elements identified as part of a strategic programme, embracing both conservation and recovery. The first element was the re-facing of the badly laminated West Front. The second was the rebuilding of the organ; the third, the recovery and re-roofing of the only surviving mediaeval gateway leading into the Close, Porth y Tŵr; and the fourth was the provision of another two bells to create the long planned Royal Ring in the adjacent bell tower.

It was only after the first four elements had been completed in 2002 that the way was open to carry out the fifth and last: the rehabilitation of the Cloister area. The first four elements had been completed at a cost of £1.9 million. The total cost of the whole project was estimated at £4.2 million but came in at around £4.5 million, of which the final cost of the Cloister was about £2.55 million. The Cloister project, given its significance and cost, was made the subject of a separate Cloister Appeal. This fifth and last element of the Millennium programme had several aims.

First of all, there was the intention of upgrading the facilities of St Mary's Hall, the former Chapel of the Chantry College of the Blessed Virgin Mary. This was not the first time that the Cathedral Chapter had given consideration to recovering the Chapel and the Cloister.

In 1929, an appeal was launched to raise £20,000 'to complete the work of restoring the ruins'.[48] The force behind the appeal was William Williams (Dean 1919-1930), whose vision, drive and energy matched those of Houghton centuries before. Williams was well acquainted with the Cathedral and its problems and with the campaign which had been waged by his Victorian pre-decessors in restoring the cathedral at a cost of £50,000. Interestingly he saw, rightly, the beginning of the Victorian campaign as 1849, rather than 1863. He had served as Canon Residentiary under four of them, James Allen (Dean 1878 to 1895), Evan Owen Phillips (1895-97), David Howell (1897-1903) and James Allan Smith (1903-1918).

Williams had not been idle since his appointment in 1919. He had spent £10,000 in furnishing the eastern chapels, installing new heating and electrical lighting machinery and overhauling the organ. Since work was complete on the Cathedral, it was now the time 'go forward' and turn to the ancillary buildings which were in a state of ruin. His intentions were threefold: to re-incorporate the Octagonal Tower as a Belfry (an anonymous benefactor had given money for a peal of bells); to take steps to preserve 'the spacious Palace' at a cost of £8,000; and to repair the Chapel of St Mary's College at a cost of at least £6,000. Dean Williams thought that the right use of the former chapel, 'as it was consecrated' would be for a retreat and clergy study house.

He had another piece of work in mind too, were the funds to allow it: the remodelling and resetting of the buttresses on the north side of the nave wall, which at present are a serious disfigurement to the Cathedral; to bring the lovely Cloisters to light and shape; and to strengthen the walls of the old sacristy and piscina.

It was not just the lack of funds, however, which prevented the whole programme as outlined in the appeal pamphlet from being accomplished. The Bishops' Palace went into the guardianship of the state in 1932, which meant that responsibility for its upkeep rested elsewhere. Williams' death in 1930, which occurred after the repair and the recommissioning of the Bell Tower, did not prevent the conservation and consolidation of the Chapel ruins, following a grant of £3,000 from the Pilgrim Trust in 1931, or the placing of a hut within the ruins for gatherings of clergy.[49] The major obstacle, however, to the completion of the programme was the discovery of severe death watch beetle infestation in the cathedral roof timbers. The Second World War also supervened and in the immediate aftermath the Cathedral authorities were concerned to catch up with necessary maintenance and repair.

It was not until 1961 that the committee of the Friends of the Cathedral, which had been formed to meet the challenge of the cost of fighting the death watch beetle, discussed the possible restoration of '*St Mary's College in a simple form, e.g. putting in windows and providing a room which could be used for meetings and possibly as a refectory*'.[50] Perhaps the Friends had been stimulated to consider the possibility of restoration by the very full and informative talk on St Mary' College at St Davids, given by R. J. Tree at the annual Friends Festival the year before. The address began by saying that '*it is easy to imagine then being rebuilt, and serving some useful purpose*'.[51]

In 1966, the roofless ruin of the Chapel was opened as a multi-purpose hall, for the use both of the Cathedral and the parochial congregation. By the mid 1990s it had become a victim of its own success, in that there were several activities, including the parochial Sunday School, youth activities, parish teas and a series of successful craft exhibitions, all making demands on a single space. Plans had, at least since 1990, been afoot to improve and enhance the facilities of the hall; with a view above all to increase accommodation within the great height of the main floor.

The insertion of a mezzanine floor almost doubled the usable space in the hall. It enabled the provision of a hundred seat Refectory, on two floors, with the removal of the stage, display and exhibition space – the Cloister Gallery – was created at the East end of the main floor. The undercroft, which at one time housed boilers and an electricity-generating set, and from 1994-2002, a Lapidarium, now houses a pair of smaller energy-efficient boilers and storage and staff spaces in connection with the Refectory above. The space at the east end of the Undercroft became a music rehearsal and resources centre available for the wider community, other choirs and musicians who use the Cathedral, as well as for the Cathedral Choristers and Lay Vicars Choral, who for the first time in a generation, were housed under the same roof as their robes and the Music Library.

Fig. 7: *The new refectory in St Mary's Hall showing the mezzanine floor.*
(Photograph: Maggie Hemming).

When the Cathedral Choir took up their new accommodation in the Undercroft of St Mary's Hall, they were returning to a site with which they been associated in the Middle Ages. In the meantime, they had moved from a practice room, now demolished, in the grounds of the Treasury, to the North Transept and then to the South Transept. By then the Choir, or rather the three choirs had outgrown the space available to them in which to rehearse and robe.

In 1991, the Chapter resolved to create a new Song School by roofing over (with a glass roof) the space formed by the angle of the two easternmost buttresses supporting the North Transept and the Nave. Unblocking the Romanesque doorway in the East face

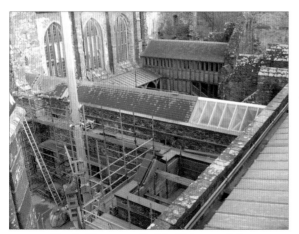

Fig. 8: *The west wall of the Cloisters and the new North Porch under construction.*
(Photograph: Maggie Hemming).

of the Transept provided access from the Cathedral. It soon became clear that the space was too small to house choir, choir robes and music library which had to remain in the parvise over the South Porch. There was also a general lack of ventilation. The choirs thus welcomed their new accommodation, which left the problem of what to do with what were both a new construction and a substantial space.

The answer lay in the creation of a Treasury in which the Cathedral's treasures of Restoration and later silver; mediaeval Episcopal crosiers, the surviving woodwork of the eighteenth-century organ case, nineteenth century textiles (including the cope worn by Bishop Jenkinson at Queen Victoria's coronation in 1838) can, for the first time, be properly conserved and displayed. Books from the Cathedral Library, which is located above the Chapel of St Thomas Becket off the North Transept, are also regularly displayed in the Treasury.

The Treasury lies in the north east angle of the area that would once have been the south corner of a cloister connecting St Mary's College and the Cathedral, utilising the Romanesque doorway in the west face of the transept as an access point. The space was both defined and constricted following the construction of the easternmost pair of buttresses erected against both the north aisle of the nave and the east wall of the north transept. Indeed, the whole of the area immediately against the north wall of the nave had been similarly affected by the construction of the other buttresses running from east to west. Their continued presence has posed a challenge to successive Cathedral architects and certainly during the present campaign their removal was seriously suggested. They are, however, by now part of the historic fabric of the Cathedral and have thus been retained. They furnish not only two walls of the Treasury but also serve to define the newly constructed walk along the south side of the new Cloister. This feature has been covered with a glass roof to let in the maximum amount of light and is also designed not to transgress the sills of the north nave windows. Before the roof was constructed, necessary conservation work was carried out on the reveals and mullions of the windows; indeed the regular conservation programme of the Cathedral was modified to allow this to happen.

The buttresses further served as a division between the lavatories, including facilities for the disabled, which were newly created in this area, offering a solution to a problem that had long exercised successive Deans and Chapters. From time to time various locations had been

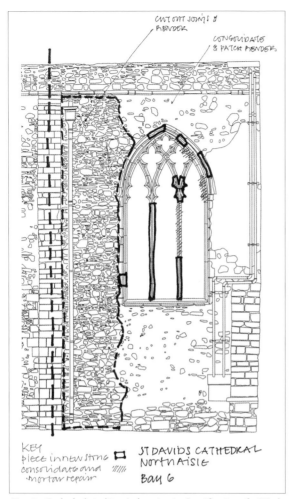

Fig. 9: *Cathedral Architect's drawing in Specifications for Works for the new Cloisters, Bay 6, North Aisle.*
(Reproduced by permission of Peter Bird, Cathedral Architect, Caroe and Partners, Wells, Somerset).

always been doubt as to whether the south side of the garth had ever been completed. The project was not however conceived as an exercise in antiquarianism. On the contrary, it would be for providing the Cathedral with sorely needed facilities, both for its own mission and ministry and also for the 280,000 visitors who come to the Cathedral each year.

It was clear that the west range of the Cloister had had a storey above the walkway and that the east range had been of three storeys above the walkway, since it had accommodated a two-storey sacristy entered from the former Chapel. It was decided to leave the East range at two stories, leaving the view of the top storey as it was. Both the east and west ranges and the arcades of the walkway beneath were realised in timber, as was the south walk against St Mary's Hall.

Fig. 10: *The North Cloister walk and the Two-Storey East Range.*
(Photograph: Maggie Hemming).

suggested including St Mary's Hall, the former Nash Chapter House by the South Gate and the Bishops' Palace. It was indeed in the Palace that they were and are still located. It was, however clear that they were both too small and especially in bad weather too remote from the Cathedral, so it was resolved to place them nearer the main building for the relief of both congregations and tourists. It was possible to utilise a new sewer laid for the Choir room lavatory in 1992.

The main thrust of the Millennium campaign, however, was to recover and recreate the fourteenth century Cloisters, destroyed in the seventeenth and eighteenth centuries. They had originally connected the Cathedral with St Mary's College, though there has

In the east range the enclosing wall survived to a substantial height. The corresponding wall in the west range had entirely disappeared with the exception of one or two courses remaining above ground. This wall therefore had to be reconstructed. The outer walls of both the east and west ranges then served as anchor points for the oak framing and structure of the Cloister. This enabled the upper ranges in the east and west to house meeting rooms suitable for small and medium sized groups linked to the parish and the diocese; and also an education and retreat centre for the use of the many groups, especially from schools and parishes, who visit the Cathedral annually.

Fig. 11: *The North Porch, with a romanesque style doorway, built from the Caerbwdi stone shown in Figs. 1a and 1b.*
(Photograph: Maggie Hemming).

riverbank. Although, as Dean, I had suggested to the architect that Gothic not as a pastiche but as expressed in a twenty-first century idiom would be very acceptable, he produced a Romanesque design expressed in twenty-first century form, as can be seen from the actual round-headed doorway as constructed in purple Caerbwdi ashlar.

Prior to the building of the Porch, there had been no access into the nave of the Cathedral from the College Chapel. The Cloister was not connected to the Nave at that point; and the north door was to the west and outside of the line of the west wall of the Cloister garth. Access from the Cloister into the Cathedral appears to have been through the doorway in the east face of the north transept only.

Following the construction of the porch and the creation of the junction between it and the south cloister walkway, the area at the foot of the stair to the upper west has been formed into a pleasant concourse, since the glass of the walkway roof here rises to the full height of the west range to clear the top of the particular nave window into which fragments of surviving mediaeval glass had been inserted.

As this is – and was – a Cloister, at its heart lies the secret garden of the cloister garth. The grassy oblong along whose edges are planted roses and herbs, retains that sense of tranquillity and calm that the original builders of the fourteenth century no doubt intended. Just as pilgrims and the original denizens of St Mary's College enjoyed a space of rest and refreshment as they made their way to and from the Cathedral, so do contemporary pilgrims and tourists appreciate the breathing space offered by the central space, as they make their way between the Cathedral and the new refectory.

With the Cathedral and St Mary's Hall linked again, circulation between the two buildings has been re-established not least due to the North Porch. This is an entirely new construction, single storey, but resting on both a piled and rafted foundation, because of the soft and wet nature of the ground at this point nearest the

ACKNOWLEDGEMENT

I am grateful to Dr. David Williams for supplying information and a photograph (*Fig. 3*) of the College Seal. For further details see D. H. Williams, *Catalogue of Seals in the National Museum of Wales* (Cardiff 1998), Vol. II, p. 47.

NOTES

1. The archaeology and archaeological discoveries made between 1996 and 2007 are the subject of a separate paper by Jerry Samson, the Cathedral archaeologist, which will appear in Evans and Wooding (eds.), *The Condition of Menevia* (forthcoming), as will a paper by Peter Bird, the Cathedral Architect on the work done on the fabric and fittings of the Cathedral in the twentieth century. Cambria Archaeology (2004) and Cambrian Archaeological Projects (2005, 2006) undertook the work and the report (CAP 364) by Phil Evans and Dr Amelia Pannett has been received by Chapter.

2. An earlier version of this paper was given to the St Davids and Dewisland Historical Society in June 2007 and to the Broadhaven Historical Society in 2008. I am grateful to both societies for their questions and comments.

3. W. Dugdale, *Monasticon Anglicanum,* J. Caley, H. Ellis and B. Bandinel (eds.) (London, 1819, 1830), Vol. VI, p. 1388a. I am grateful to Dr Sally Harper for this reference; and also for giving me permission to use her most informative and useful paper, 'And all in accordance with Sarum Use', in Evans and Wooding, op. cit., n. 1.

4. G. Williams, 'Adam Houghton' in *Oxford Dictionary of National Biography,* online edn. May 2008 [http://www.oxforddnb.com/view/article/13863] accessed 28 July 2008; F. Green, 'Pembrokeshire Parsons: Appendix 1', *Hist. Soc. of West Wales Trans,* Vols. IV, V & VI (1917) p. 273; G. Williams, *The Welsh Church from Conquest to Reformation* (Cardiff 1962), p. 168; G. Williams, 'The Church,1280-1534', in *The Pembrokeshire County History* (Haverfordwest, 2002), p. 315.

5. Williams, op. cit., ODNB, n. 4.

6. B. G. Charles, *The Place-Names of Pembrokeshire*, 2 Vols. (NLW, 1992), Vol. I, p. 339.

7. J. W. Willis-Bund, *The Black Book of St Davids* (London, Hon. Soc. Cymmrodorion, 1902), p. 95, which refers to Master Adam Houghton as a juror in the Upper Bailiwick of Pebydiog; and p. 119 which notes that he holds three acres of land in Priscilly at a yearly rent of 6d.

8. Dugdale, op. cit., n. 3, Vol. 6, p. 1388a.

9. Dugdale, op. cit., n. 3, Vol. 6, p. 1390b.

10. E. Yardley, *Menevia Sacra,* F. Green (ed.), (Cambrian Arch. Assn. London, 1927), pp. 57, 58.

11. M. Powicke and E. B. Fryde, *Handbook of British Chronology* (London, 1961, 2nd edn.), p. 211.

12. Harper (forth.), op. cit., n. 3, p. 10.

13. Jerry Sampson, makes the same suggestion in his report to Chapter on the archaeological implications of the cloister scheme (8th March 2001) (*penes me*) quoting W. B. Jones and E. A. Freeman, *The History and Antiquities of St Davids* (London and Tenby, 1856, facsimile edn., Pembs. Co. Council, Haverfordwest, 1998), p. 186.

14. P. Barrett, *Barchester: English Cathedral Life in the Nineteenth Century* (London, 1993), p. 57.

15. Harper, op. cit., n. 3, pp. 6-7; W. H. Frere, *The Use of Sarum* (Cambridge, 1898, 2 Vols.), Vol. I, p. 3 *et passim*; see also P. Baxter, *The Use of Sarum* (Reading 2008).

16. Dugdale, op. cit., n. 3, p. 1388a.

17. B. Dobson, 'The English Vicars Choral: An Introduction', in R. Hall, R. and D. Stocker, *Vicars Choral at English Cathedrals, Cantate Domino, History, Architecture and Archaeology* (Oxford, 2005), pp. 1-10, but see pp. 3 and 4.

18. Dobson, op. cit., n. 17.

19. Williams, 'Houghton' op. cit., n. 4.

20. Dugdale, op. cit., n. 3, Vol. 6, p.1388a.

21. J. Barrow, 'The Origins of Vicars Choral to 1300', in Hall and Stocker, op. cit., n. 17, pp. 11-12.

22. Harper, op. cit., n. 3, pp. 5-6.

23. Harper, op. cit., n. 3, pp. 8-9.

24. P. Jeffries, *The Collegiate Churches of England and Wales* (London, 2004), p. 205.

25. Harper, op. cit., n. 3, p. 11; F Green, 'St Mary's College at St Davids', *Hist. Soc. of West Wales Trans*. Vol. VIII, 1919-1920, pp. 21-24.

26. J. W. Evans, 'St Davids Cathedral: The Forgotten Centuries', *Jnl. of Welsh Eccles. History*, Vol. 3, 1986, pp. 73-92, but see pp. 82-84; R. Fenton, *A Historical Tour through Pembrokeshire* (Brecknock, 1903 & facsimile reprint, Haverfordwest 1994), p. 33, note n.

27. Jones and Freeman, op. cit., n. 13, p. 186.

28. As recorded by the Revd Nathaniel Davies in his MS family tree. I am grateful to Mrs Sheila Anstead, the great-great grand-daughter of the Revd Nathaniel Davies (1808-1886) one time Minor Canon, Prebendary and Master of the Cathedral Grammar School, for sending me a copy of Davies' family tree. See my paper on Davies in 'The Schoolmaster and the Dean', in Evans and Wooding, op. cit., n. 1.

29. Yardley, op. cit., n. 10, p. 373.

30. It is reproduced as illustration 18 on p. 40 of W. Evans and R. Worsley, *Eglwys Gadeiriol Tyddewi/St Davids Cathedral* (Yr Oriel Fach Press, St Davids, 1981), but wrongly captioned.

31. H. T. Payne, *Collectanea. Menevensis*, NLW MS SDCh/B 27 & 28, Vol I, p. 198.

32. Jones and Freeman, op. cit., n. 27, pp. 186-187; I have always felt personally that Nash's Strawberry Hill Gothick West Front was better suited to the genuine late Perpendicular profile of the sixteenth-century nave than its successor of 1878, which when it was refurbished in 1999 revealed surviving traces of Nash's mouldings.

33. T. Wright (ed.), *Three Chapters of Letters relating to the Suppression of the English Monasteries* (London, 1968), pp. 183-186. 183-6.

34. Wright, idem, p. 186; J. W. Evans, 'The Reformation and St Davids Cathedral', *Jnl. of Welsh Eccles. History*, Vol. 7, 1990, pp. 1-16.

35. For details of Green's career, see A. J. Brown, *Robert Ferrar* (London, 1997) pp. 308 & 324.

36. E. D. Jones, 'Survey of South Wales Chantries', *Arch. Camb.,* Vol. XXXIX, Part 1, June 1934, pp. 135-155, esp. pp. 136 and 142 -143.

37. J. Caley (ed.) *Valor Eclesiasticus temp. Henry VIII* (London, Record Commissioners, 1810-1834, 6 Vols.) Vol. IV, p. 382.

38. Green, op. cit., n. 4, App. I, p. 145.

39. Green, op. cit., n. 25, pp. 21-24.

40. Green, op. cit., n. 4, pp. 275-6.

41. Yardley, op. cit, n. 10, p. 383.

42. Green, op. cit., n. 25, p. 21.

43. Yardley, op. cit., n. 10, p. 377.

44. Idem, p. 373.

45. Ibid.

46. Fenton, op. cit., n. 26, p. 40.

47. W. D. Caröe, 'Recent Excavations at St Davids, Bishop Houghton's (1361-1389) Cloister', *Arch. Camb.,* Vol. LXXXIX, Part II, December 1934, pp. 279-290; W. D. Caröe, *Some notes upon Architecture with a digression upon Church Bells* (privately printed, Abergavenny, 1932); W. Williams (et al.), *An Appeal for £20,000 to complete the work of restoring the ruins* (St Davids, 1929), gives an idea of what was intended and what was actually achieved in the 1920s.

48. Idem, p. 1. and *passim* for what follows in the next paragraphs.

49. M. Wight, *St David's The Pilgrim's Guide* (Gloucester, 1959, 4th edn.), p. 53.

50. The relevant minute book of the Friends is at present in my possession.

51. R. J. Tree, 'St Mary's College at St Davids', in *The Annual Report of the Friends of St Davids Cathedral* (Llandysul, 1961), p. 7, and *passim*; this paper is a valuable contribution to the discussion.

'A Plot within the Close of the College Church': Abergwili Bishop's Palace and College Revisited

Neil Ludlow

The Bishop's Palace, Abergwili (NGR SN 44052096), now the home of Carmarthenshire County Museum was, until 1972, a palace of the Bishops of St Davids. It occupies a gently sloping terrace flanking the Tywi floodplain, within a parkland landscape typical of the Tywi valley (*Fig. 1*). Acquired by the bishops by the 13th century, Abergwili became the site of a collegiate church, whose precise form and location are unknown.

The college was moved to Brecon in 1541, after which the present Palace was established. The Palace was variously altered and rebuilt during the post-mediaeval period, and the park appears to have been first formally landscaped in 1801-1803. With its adjoining agricultural land, it now comprises over 10ha under multiple owners, mainly Carmarthenshire County Council and the Church in Wales.

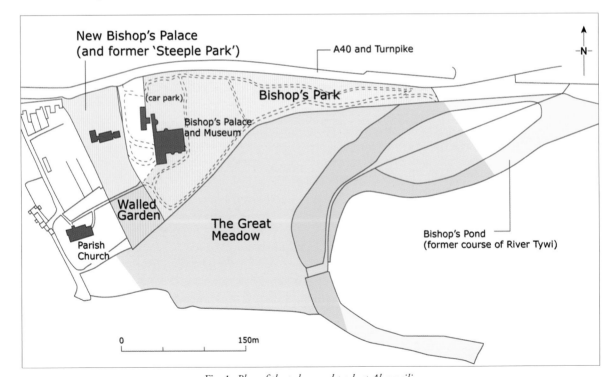

Fig. 1: *Plan of the palace and park at Abergwili.*

In a typically comprehensive yet concise account of the Palace, Terry James argued that the present Palace buildings were adapted from the mediaeval collegiate church and cloister soon after 1541.[1] The present paper expands on Terry's arguments in the light of recent work suggesting two separate building complexes within the Abergwili demesne. Thus the Palace may instead have been adapted from a pre-existing episcopal lodging and the college may have been located elsewhere within the episcopal demesne – or vice-versa. Evidence for the layout of the mediaeval buildings, and the surrounding landscape, is also discussed, and dates for the (re)construction of the post-Reformation palace are suggested. This reappraisal of the site was part of a landscape, environmental and documentary study, augmented by targeted geophysical survey, that was undertaken by Dyfed Archaeological Trust in 2005 at the request of Carmarthenshire Museums Service with a view to developing the Palace grounds for greater public use and enjoyment.[2]

COLLEGE CONSTITUTION, *c.*1290-1541

Abergwili was described as a Manor of at least 600 acres when sold in 1986 and was a possession of the Bishop of St Davids, held as demesne, in the early 14th century.[3] We do not know for how long it had then an episcopal possession, but the neighbouring parish church was in episcopal hands by 1222 at least when it was 'restored' to the cathedral.[4] Later, a distinct, collegiate church was established at Abergwili by Bishop Thomas Bek (1280-93). It appears that it was initially established, in 1283, at Llangadog, but was soon after transferred to Abergwili, possibly in 1284[5] or more likely in 1287.[6] The original founding charter has been lost but the college at Abergwili may have been under construction in 1291 when Bek was granted licence to 'stop the way in Abergwili which leads from Carmarthen to Dryslwyn, provided that he makes a like way in his own ground' suggesting that the road had to be realigned around the college buildings or precinct.[7] Abergwili was definitely the site of the college by 1296,[8] but it was still being referred to as Llangadog College, after its parent, in the confirmation charter of 1329 (Cal. Patent Rolls 1327-1330, 438), while it retained Llangadog's dedication to St Maurice but not, it seems, St Thomas the Martyr.[9] Bek also founded a college at Llanddewi Brefi, Ceredigion, while a further college, St Mary's, was established within St Davids Cathedral Close in 1377.

The foundation of chantry chapels and colleges, within which priests were endowed to perform an intercessionary mass daily for individuals after their death, proliferated in the 13th century and lasted until the close of the mediaeval period.[10] As at Llangadog and Llanddewi Brefi, they were normally established within pre-existing parish churches. Abergwili however appears, unusually, to have been established on a virgin site. Even more unusually, there is no indication in the sources that either of the four St Davids colleges had any kind of commemorative function. Instead of intercessionary masses, we read in the *Valor Ecclesiasticus* of 1535 that Abergwili then supported 'four priests, four choristers and two clerks celebrating Divine Service there every day in the week'.[11] Similarly, Llanddewi Brefi comprised a Precentor and twelve prebendaries,[12] while the later St Mary's College, at St Davids, was founded for the maintenance of a Master and seven priests and two choristers.[13] Moreover, in a confirmation of its foundation charter Abergwili College was under the jurisdiction of the Bishop who, effectively acting as Dean, had a stall in the choir and a voice in the chapter[14] and held the collegiate church as a perpetual vicarage.[15] It may be that the constitution and function of these Welsh colleges owed more to native Welsh models of liturgy, and cure, than to those of their English counterparts. For example, the Precentor was the head of the chapter, as the Bishop was at St Davids, regarded as a continuation of the practice of the native Welsh Church.

In direct continuation of the original endowments of Llangadog, Abergwili College comprised twenty-one prebendary canons, endowed with the revenues from twenty-one parishes, later twenty-two, that mainly lay in Breconshire and Radnorshire, where the Bishop held much property.[16] They were drawn in equal number from the three superior orders of the clergy – seven canons, seven deacons and seven subdeacons each of whom maintained a perpetual vicar of his own degree. There were also five clerks in minor orders ('vicarios'), and choristers ('certain singing men and boys').[17] By the 14th century, youths were under instruction at the college. In the *Valor*, the college itself was 'worth by the year . . . 13s 4d', with 'a portion of the prebend of Llangadog £18, and of the church of the parish of Myddfai £13 6s 8d . . . are worth £22 with the pensions annually received . . . from 22 prebends . . . and so the whole exhibition is worth annually £42'.[18]

The residentiary system common to all mediaeval cathedrals did not fully develop in the colleges; the

Abergwili canons were not, at first, obliged to reside at the college.[19] There are numerous references to absentee prebendaries, who merely collected their revenues, and many canons were pluralists, holding prebends at other colleges by Papal dispensation.[20] However, in 1331, perhaps in attempt to rectify this, Bishop Gower annexed the prebend of Llanfynydd to the Precentorship, and created two new offices of Chancellor and Treasurer who were, upon forfeit of their profits to the canons resident, bound to perpetual residence.[21] This may again reflect a particularly Welsh identity.

Bishop Bek also founded a town at Abergwili.[22] Though occasionally referred to as a borough, it appears to have received neither charter nor constitution. However, the bishop was granted market rights in May 1290, and again in September 1291 (*Cal. Charter Rolls* II, 343 and 405). The grant of a fair followed in April 1313 (*Cal. Charter Rolls* III, 216).

COLLEGE LOCATION AND LAYOUT

Where were the college buildings? Those at Llangadog and Llanddewi Brefi have gone but were clearly associated with pre-existing parish churches, whose rebuilding as large, cruciform structures may have been contemporary. At Abergwili, the pre-19th century parish church featured a four-bayed aisle south of the nave which could feasibly represent the collegiate church.[23] However, part of the church, including its temporalities, had been granted to Carmarthen Priory in 1269[24] although the advowson remained, by courtesy, in the hands of the bishop. Monastic patronage may therefore lie behind the addition of the aisle, while all contemporary sources appear to make the distinction between the collegiate church and the parish church.

Bishop Bek's licence to alter the Carmarthen to Dryslwyn road, mentioned above, suggests that a pre-existing road had to be realigned around his college. The new diversion has continued in use ever since. We can now be fairly certain that the original road was part of the Roman road leading down the Tywi Valley to *Moridunum* (Carmarthen) largely followed by later routes including the turnpike and present A40.[25] Thus an intact section of Roman road remains preserved within the Abergwili demesne and as a firm, dry metalled surface may have been utilised for mediaeval buildings whether collegiate or bishops' lodgings (*Fig. 4*).

We have seen that the college was valued at £42 annually in the *Valor Ecclesiasticus* of 1535. This is a considerable sum. Whilst not in the same league as

the major monasteries of the region, variously worth between £118, and £164,[26] it does compare favourably with some of the smaller houses like St Dogmael's Abbey, valued at £87, Pill Priory, at £67, and – interestingly – the small priory on Caldey Island which was valued at only £5 10s 11d.[27] The college itself was worth 13s 4d annually, the remainder of the valuation relating to income from its prebends. This compares with a valuation of £6 6s 8d (out of a total of £106 3s 6d) at St Mary's College, St Davids.[28] However, as Terry has pointed out with reference to Carmarthen Priory, the revenues recorded in the *Valor* were mainly drawn from spiritualities, 'and we have no way of knowing if these were spent on constructing and maintaining prestigious buildings'.[29]

Nevertheless, the sources for Abergwili suggest that a complex of buildings was present, and that they were probably arranged around a cloister. In addition to the church, a chapter house was singled out in a certificate of induction of 1400.[30] After Gower's statute of 1331, there was presumably accommodation for all the canons. An account of Bishop Barlow's transfer of the College to Brecon in 1541 describes it as housing 'a multitude of prebendaries, canons (and) choristers'.[31]

The present Bishop's Palace is, in essence, a group of chambers arranged around four sides of what was formerly an open court, later roofed over. Terry suggested that it represents the collegiate church, cloister, and chapter house, which were converted for domestic use by the Reformation Bishop William Barlow (1536-48), after his transfer of the college to Brecon.[32] He saw the college as following the normal monastic, conventual layout, suggesting that the canons' lodgings – possibly communal and including a dormitory and refectory – were integral, but allowed that they may have been housed in a separate building or buildings. The Bishops' Registers contain numerous accounts of the duties performed by the Bishop at Abergwili and, as Dean, he would also have had accommodation at the college. I suggest that his apartments, however, may not have been integral with the college buildings.

St Mary's College at St Davids may, although later, and worth more in 1535, be offered for comparison. Here we are fortunate in having a plan and description from the early 18th century by Archdeacon Yardley.[33] It comprised an open quadrangular cloister, measuring 33.7m north-south and 26.8m east-west, occupying 840 square metres (*Fig. 2*). It was not flanked by any buildings except to the north, where stood the collegiate

Fig. 2: *Comparative plan of St Mary's College, St Davids, and Abergwili Palace.*

church. This was a 'curious building' 22m long (east-west) and 10.4m wide (north-south) and 45' high, with a tower, 75' high, attached to the south side of the west wall. The canons accommodation was in a detached, sprawling block of buildings, measuring overall 30m north-south by 36.3m east-west (and occupying 1440 square metres overall), to the north of the chapel. No separate chapter-house has been identified. In comparison, the Palace at Abergwili measures 25.5m north-south and 29m east-west, with a total area of 767.5 square metres (*Fig. 2*).

The Black Book of St Davids – the detailed inventory of the holdings and assets of the Bishopric that was compiled in 1326 – contains one very terse reference to the college, reading 'The Lord (Bishop) has a plot within the close of the college church, and is worth yearly 6d' (*j placea infra clausura ecclesie Collegium*).[34] This is an interesting entry for two reasons. Firstly, it indicates a separate episcopal enclosure within or perhaps below the college close (*infra* can carry either meaning in mediaeval Latin). Secondly, it may thus suggest separate lodgings for the Bishop within or adjacent to the College close. From this entry alone it is of course not possible to say whether the present Museum (former Bishop's Palace) is within the college or the wider Bishops' close. Suggestions locating these two distinct entities within the Abergwili demesne are further developed below.

The evidence, actual and potential, is threefold. Firstly, geophysical survey techniques can locate buried structures within the present Park adjacent to the Museum. Secondly, there is the archaeological record of earlier structures revealed during works within the Park, although it must be emphasised that no modern archaeological excavation has taken place. Thirdly, there is the map and documentary evidence. Resistivity survey was undertaken as part of the 2005 project over a large area to the south and east of the Palace, and a smaller area in the kitchen garden. Unfortunately, the results were inconclusive; despite a 'wide variation in ground resistance across the site' the 'interpretation of the results has been problematic due to the poorly defined and amorphous nature of the anomalies'.[35] Other geophysical techniques, and perhaps survey in different weather conditions, might however produce better results and geophysical survey must remain a potential source of information on the site.

Secondly, stone walls were seen 20 metres east of the present palace, in a pipe trench dug in 1977, at approx. NGR SN 44092095.[36] They may be the same as the 'foundations of buildings . . . traceable in the surrounding lawn', observed by the Royal Commission in 1913.[37] Furthermore, wall-lines were observed as parchmarks, southeast of the palace, in 1927-49 when they were excavated, revealing a 4ft depth of stone walls.[38] No buildings are depicted in either location on a 1796 estate map (*Fig. 3*), so these walls belong to the early post-mediaeval period at the latest, and could therefore represent collegiate buildings or the bishop's residence. Alternatively, they may represent the remains of post-mediaeval palace outbuildings that had gone by 1796.

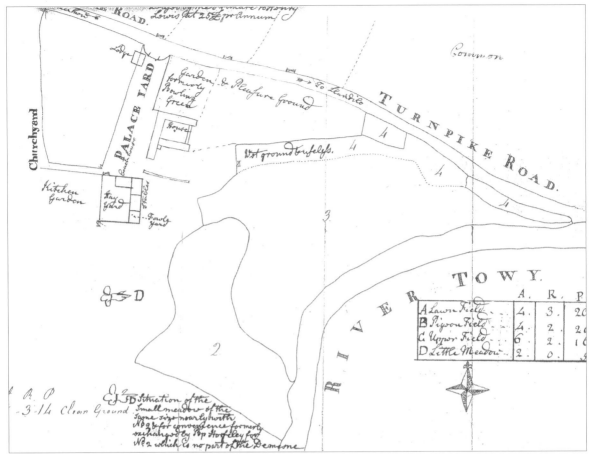

Fig. 3: *The estate map of 1796.*
(National Library of Wales, St Davids Map Book, 1796).

Documentary and map sources provide more information. The estate map of 1796 shows a group of buildings, now entirely gone, 20 metres southwest of the present Palace at SN 4404 2090 (*Figs. 3 and 4*). They formed two sides of a square enclosure, labelled 'Hay Yard'. Might these buildings have had earlier origins, as the site of the college? The *Valor* of 1535 gives a valuable glimpse of the layout of the college precinct, describing 'three closes with the circuits therein, to the said college annexed, whereof one of them is called Ludfield which is worth by the year . . . 13s 4d'.[39] These 'three closes' appear to represent three walled enclosures. It is not possible to identify them with certainty – while the name 'Ludfield' appears to have been lost – but might they refer to the collegiate cloister, a complex (perhaps around a yard) of Bishop's chambers, and a third enclosure? It may then be that the present Palace evolved from a pre-existing Bishop's

lodging, while the 'Hay Yard' was adapted from the collegiate cloister.[40]

The Hay Yard was aligned approximately east-west, and measured approximately 26.4m north-south by 27m east-west, with a total area of 701 square metres, i.e. slightly smaller than the Palace. However, two pictures from the late 18th century[41] show that the east side of the yard was occupied by tall, substantial building, with a loft, used as a stable block (*see Fig. 5*). The post-Reformation decline of former monastic or collegiate buildings into agricultural use was not unusual; I have discussed this with reference to Whitland Abbey.[42]

THE BISHOP'S PALACE – A MEDIAEVAL
BISHOP'S LODGING?

I would like now to discuss the evidence for the Palace having been the site of a bishop's lodging, rather than the College. It has been seen that a lodging for the

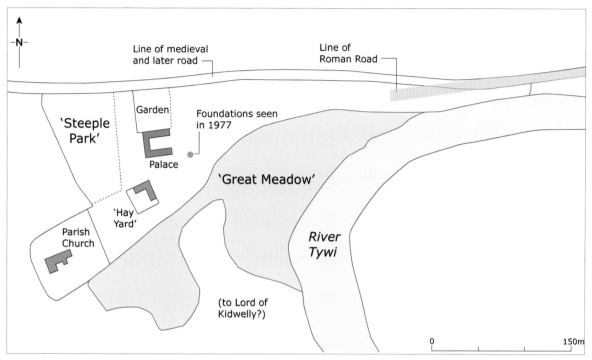

Fig. 4: *Plan showing the present Palace, the former Hay Yard, Steeple Park and Great Meadow, with the parish church, parchmarks/foundations, and line of Roman road.*

Bishop, separate or otherwise, was apparently present at Abergwili College before 1541. This has previously been suggested by, *inter alia*, Glanmor Williams and Michael Thompson.[43] One nineteenth century writer went a stage further by suggesting that 'portions of (it) may be incorporated in the present Palace'.[44] Did the Bishop's 'plot within the close of the college church' mentioned above, that was 'worth yearly 6d' in 1326, represent this lodging? If so, where was it? To what degree could it qualify for the term 'palace'? Was it a favourite episcopal residence before the removal of the College in 1541?

The magnificent Bishop's Palace at St Davids, as we see it today, was the work of Bishop Henry Gower in 1328-47. Its predecessor was of uncertain form, but was described as a *'mansio* fit only for servants and animals where the palace should be' in 1328.[45] Nevertheless, the 'stone buildings' there were valued at 2s in the *Black Book*[46] or four times as much as the 'plot' at Abergwili. However, an *Extent* of the bishop's holdings compiled in 1328, on the death of Bishop Martin values the St Davids site at 6d – the same as Abergwili in 1326[47] and just because no buildings within the plot at Abergwili were specifically mentioned, it doesn't mean there weren't any. For instance, the *Extent* describes the Bishop's

Palace at Lamphey, Pembs. – where a fine hall and ancillary buildings had already been built – as 'a messuage with its gardens worth 3s 4d per annum', the former bishop's lodgings at Trevine (Pembs.) as 'a messuage worth 12s annually', and those at Wolfscastle (also Pembs.) as 'a *mansio* worth 4s per annum'. The valuations make interesting reading, particularly the comparison between Lamphey, with its extensive buildings, and Trevine, a site favoured by Bishop Martin of which nothing is known. Nevertheless, as ever, they cannot be interpreted too literally – the fine Bishop's castle at Llawhaden (Pembs.), which was by now largely complete, was 'worth nothing per annum beyond the outlay'.

No mention is made of Abergwili in the 1328 *Extent*, but this need not be significant – as its editor, Francis Jones, points out, it 'does not include all the lands and revenues by any means. Either the keeper who made the return was responsible only for those manors extended, or the record is incomplete'.[48] Nevertheless, in 1342, the Statute Book recorded an order to bring seven of the bishop's houses into good repair. These were at St Davids, Trevine, Llawhaden, Lamphey, Llanddewi (Gower), Llanddew (Brecs.) and Llandygwydd (Ceredigion).[49] Those that were ruinous were to be demolished and their materials used for repairing the others. This may suggest that either there was no residence worth recording at Abergwili, or that it was ruinous.

The situation may have subsequently changed. Frequent visits to Abergwili were recorded during the tenure of, for example, Bishop Hugh Pavy (1485-95), who performed ordinations there in 1485, 1486 and 1487.[50] He, at least, spent enough time at Abergwili to warrant lodgings suitable to his station. While no mention is made of any Bishop's lodgings at Abergwili by Leland recording in the 1530s, the residences at Llanddewi and Llandygwydd are also omitted from his account.[51]

Where were these lodgings? In 1594, after their transfer to Brecon, the canons claimed that it was 'late custom of some of (them) to reside for part of the year at the College of Abergwili, Co. Carmarthen . . .'[52] This sounds like it refers to a period *after* 1541, meaning either that the conversion to an entirely private palace had yet to take place, or that the palace was separate from the collegiate buildings, which were still standing for some time after 1541. And in 1548-54, Bishop Robert Ferrar described the hall of his palace at Abergwili as being 'ruinous', and he had perforce to use the 'great chamber adjoining' as his hall, suggesting that it was already an old building in 1541.[53]

So perhaps the mediaeval bishop's lodgings occupied the present palace site. Does the present building have any attributes that may have mediaeval, domestic origins? Terry suggested that the present Bishop's Palace was adapted from a series of buildings arranged around three sides of an open courtyard. This plan-form is not confined to ecclesiastical buildings, being widely adopted in British episcopal residences from the 14th century onwards.[54] Whilst Abergwili Palace is very different from the palace at St Davids itself, the latter is exceptional and unique in Welsh domestic architecture of the period. Neither can it be compared with Lamphey Palace, with its dispersed assemblage of buildings, nor Llanddew which is in effect a fortified manor-house

Fig. 5: *A drawing showing the Palace, and stable block (left) in 1784, from the east.*
(Cardiff Public Library MS 3.237).

resembling a castle. However, the nature of Trevine, Llandygwydd and Llanddewi remains unknown.

It may be significant that, at Abergwili, 'a close called *ymaenduy*' is mentioned in a letter of 1541.[55] If the place-name is the modern welsh *maendy*, we can read this as a stone house or building, often carrying the meaning of the house of a religious order.[56] It may represent one of the 'three closes' recorded in the *Valor* of 1535 and is a further suggestion that separate, and substantial domestic lodgings were already present. So it is possible that one of these 'closes' may represent the collegiate cloister (possibly the 'Hay Yard', as discussed above?), while a second may have been represented by the bishop's lodging, by definition seemingly arranged around a yard.[57]

However, in summary, there is no *direct* reference to an episcopal residence at Abergwili before the sixteenth century. And none of Bishop William Barlow's letters, written between 1536 and 1548, directly mentions any pre-existing residence.[58] Yet the evidence presented above does strongly suggest two separate buildings or groups of buildings within the mediaeval college precinct: the college itself and a bishop's residence. So Terry's case is still a strong one, whilst his demonstration that the present palace building, in plan, and even structure, preserves a mediaeval layout – be it college or residence – is of lasting value.[59]

THE REMOVAL OF THE COLLEGE, 1541

Abergwili College was spared dissolution under Edward VI's Chantries and Colleges Act, of 1546, by virtue of having been, for a second time, moved – this time, to Brecon. It was re-established – and rededicated as Christ's College – within the recently-dissolved Dominican Friary at Llanfaes, south of the town, where it still survives as Brecon College. The transfer was undertaken in 1541 by Bishop William Barlow (1536-48). The prebends were conveyed to the new college, and all persons connected with Abergwili College were free to reside at Brecon. Barlow successfully petitioned King Henry VIII that Abergwili was a remote place, and one 'where few spoke English', and it has been suggested his motive was to rescue both the income of Abergwili College, and the property of Brecon Friary, from Dissolution by combining the two.[60] However, Brecon College did not entirely escape the Chantries Act being subject to the accompanying survey, in which it had 'no cure of souls' but had a Reader of Holy Scriptures, a Grammar Master, an usher, 20 scholars and a stipendiary priest.[61] The canons had to repeat the case for their exclusion from the Act as late as 1594.[62] Llanddewi Brefi College survived the Chantries Act, being active into the 17th century,[63] but was subject to Chancery proceedings to confirm whether or not it was collegiate.[64]

The removal of the college may have been the first stage of Barlow's proposed transfer of the See from St Davids to Carmarthen, in order to provide space for an episcopal palace of the appropriate quality. He then petitioned Henry VIII's Chamberlain, Thomas Cromwell, to transfer St David's Cathedral itself to the recently dissolved Franciscan Friary at Carmarthen.[65] This proposal was ultimately unsuccessful, but had seen the gutting of St David's Bishop's Palace and the sale of Lamphey Palace, while the other episcopal residences – Llawhaden Castle, Trevine, Llanddewi in Gower, etc. – were either disposed of or allowed to fall into ruin. By 1554 Abergwili, with Brecon, was the only habitable episcopal residence left to the bishopric.

THE POST-MEDIAEVAL PALACE, 1541-1627

It is not known with certainty when the post-mediaeval Bishop's Palace took shape. Bishop Barlow 'had alienated the most profitable parts of the (episcopal) estate, and impoverished the diocese.'[66] His successor, Robert Ferrar (1548-1554), found parts of the building were 'ruinous' and worked hard to clear debts and improve the management of the episcopal estate. He bought three detached parcels of land totalling 104 acres to increase revenue, for which he was criticised by his enemies and accusers. He does not appear however to have had the revenues or given priority to repairing the bishops' lodgings although he resided at Abergwili, using 'an adjoining chamber' to the ruinous main buildings.[67]

However, an extensive programme of work must have been undertaken at some time during the late sixteenth or early seventeenth century, for an inventory from 1713 refers to the presence of a Long Gallery, an Elizabethan feature *par excellence*.[68] Moreover, a description of the Palace in 1796 suggests that it was then, though altered, still fundamentally 'Elizabethan' in character. In that year, Iolo Morgannwg recorded that it was then 'a mass of low buildings, the additions of one age to those of another, and of that to those of the preceding' and that it seemed 'to have been built about 150, or 200 years ago', while 'most of the chimney-tuns (were) channelled in the taste of the time of Queen Elizabeth'.[69] A near-contemporary account, from 1791, describes the Palace as 'a venerable old mansion . . . although it is irregular and not lofty' and the whole 'was built of rough stone'.[70]

It is possible that Bishop Richard Davies, 1561-81, was responsible for this work. The sources indicate that he was firmly installed at Abergwili, transforming it into 'a powerhouse of intellectual and spiritual energy'[71] but such endeavours did not necessarily need a new palace to sustain them. An account written in 1582 by his successor, Bishop Marmaduke Middleton (1581-90), complained that '. . . all his lands, even to his very doors, were in lease by his predecessor (i.e. Davies). All the Spiritual Livings worth £10 per year were advowsoned. Himself in great debt to the Queen and others. His livings in annual rents not above £150 . . .' Middleton added that 'all his houses, except one, (were) down to the ground, and that one in most extreme ruin' clearly meaning Abergwili. Moreover, Davies' leased properties may have included the Palace (or precinct) itself – his will mentions a 'lease of Abergwili'.[72]

Did Middleton undertake any work on the Palace in the eight years following this complaint? Or is the present palace later still? Middleton's successor, Bishop Anthony Rudd (1594-1614), was an absentee, residing at his estate at Aberglasney, Carms.[73] He was succeeded by Bishop Milbourne (1615-21), who furthered the destruction of the other episcopal properties, procuring for example a licence to demolish Llawhaden Castle, and the hall, chapel, cellar and bakehouse at St David's Palace.[74] Milbourne may then be either a likely candidate, possibly having concentrated his resources on Abergwili, or an unlikely one, generally dismissive of all his Welsh properties.

William Laud (1621-27), later Archbishop of Canterbury under Charles I, built 'a chapel or Oratory' within the Palace 'at (his) own charge'.[75] It was consecrated in 1625, four years into his incumbency, and dedicated to St John Baptist after his Oxford College. It has been suggested by a number of authorities that Laud's chapel was essentially the chapel that remains at the Palace to this day – still referred to as 'Laud's Chapel' – on the first floor of the south range. The present detail and fittings are all 20th century, but the dimensions conform to those given by Laud. As there was presumably a pre-existing chapel, Laud's work may have represented a refit; it was described as 'an old chapel' in 1791 although, according to Archdeacon Yardley, Bishop Ottley 'had fitted up the decent chapel' in 1713-23.[76] Terry suggested that 'if Laud had gone to the expense of building a new chapel, it is possible that

other works were carried out at the palace at this time'.[77] However, during his episcopacy, Laud visited his diocese only twice. The first occasion was in July-August 1622 when he began his visitation at Brecon College, went on to St Davids, 'visited at Carmarthen', then left for England. In August 1625 he 'came safely to (his) own house at Abergwili (and) consecrated the chapel or oratory', staying at Abergwili until November.[78]

In my view, it is most likely that either Bishop Middleton, 1581-90, or Bishop Milbourne, 1615-21, were responsible for the post-mediaeval palace, while stylistically, Laud's episcopacy represents the latest date at which an 'Elizabethan' palace, as described in the sources, could have been built.

THE BISHOP'S PARK

The present Bishop's Park and gardens may also have mediaeval origins, possibly being coterminous with the college precinct. In addition to the 'plot within the close of the college church', the *Black Book* lists the Bishop's other direct possessions at Abergwili as including an 'island in the River Tywi containing a stang of pasture worth yearly 3d'; the Lord of Kidwelly had 'the other half of the island'.[79] Might this pasture be represented by the 'Great Meadow', the water-meadow on the Tywi floodplain, at NGR SN 442 209 to the southwest of the present palace (*Fig. 1*)? A former loop of the Tywi, now dry, crosses the meadow and is followed by the parish boundary; it may represent the boundary with the Lord of Kidwelly's land in 1326.

The *Black Book* mentions gardens at five episcopal manors – Lamphey, Llandygwydd, Llawhaden, Trevine and Wolfscastle.[80] We have seen that Abergwili, during the early 14th century, is unlikely to have been a residence worthy of a garden.[81] But it is possible that the 'three closes' of the *Valor* were large enclosures, rather than the small courtyards discussed above (*see Fig. 4*). They may suggest an early origin for the present park curtilage, and its tripartite division into the area of the Palace itself, with the park proper, the area to the west and southwest of the Palace – including the Hay Yard and suggested college site – and the Great Meadow. Whilst such large areas are not normally termed 'closes' in contemporary sources, the name 'Ludfield' does suggest a large agricultural enclosure. It may also be significant that a tripartite division is again hinted at in Bishop Ottley's Inventory of 1713, where three fields are listed but not individually named.[82] So in area, and general configuration, the park or palace curtilage may have remained unchanged throughout the post-mediaeval period.[83]

But when was the palace curtilage turned into an appropriate setting for the Palace? There is little evidence in the sources for any 'formal' landscaping until the beginning of the 19th century. However, in view of what was happening elsewhere in Wales during the earlier post-mediaeval period, and locally at Coedcenlas, Haroldston and Landshipping, Pembs.[84] it is possible that some form of Renaissance garden or park may

have existed. It might be expected that whoever was responsible for the erection of the present Palace – Bishops Middleton, Milbourne or Laud – would wish for it to be seen against an appropriate landscape for their age and tastes. There remain therefore a number of interesting but unanswered questions about the mediaeval and post-mediaeval college, Palace and Park all worthy of further research – be it through more geophysical survey, archaeological excavation or documentary research.

NOTES

1. T. A. James, 'The Bishop's Palace and Collegiate Church, Abergwili', *Carms. Antiq.*, Vol. 16, 1980, pp. 19-43.

2. N. Ludlow, K. Murphy, R. Pryce, D. Sabin & K. Donaldson, 'Bishop's Park, Abergwili: Historic Landscape Survey', 2005; unpublished Dyfed Archaeological Trust client report, copy held in the Dyfed Archaeological Trust's Historic Environment Record (hence HER) for Carmarthenshire, Ceredigion and Pembrokeshire at DAT offices, Llandeilo.

3. Welsh Church Commission, 'Episcopal and Capitular Manors: proposed transfer to the University of Wales', 1944, unpublished Inland Revenue Valuation. A copy is held in the Historic Environment Record (HER) for Carms, Ceredig. and Pembs. maintained by Dyfed Archaeological Trust, Llandeilo.

4. J. C. Davies (ed.), *Episcopal Acts relating to Welsh Dioceses, 1066-1272,* Historical Society of the Church in Wales, Vol. 1, D.455, p. 353.

5. J. W. Willis-Bund (ed.), *The Black Book of St. David's, 1326* (London, Hon. Soc. of Cymmrodorion, 1902), p. liii.

6. J. Caley, H. Ellis & B. Bandinel (eds.), *Dugdale's Monasticon Anglicanum: a History of the Abbies and other Monasteries, Hospitals, Friaries, and Cathedral and Collegiate Churches, with their Dependencies, in England and Wales* (Record Commission, 1817-1830, 6 vols.), Vol. 6, Part 3, pp. 301 & 1376.

7. G. E. Evans, 'Bishop Beck stops a road at Abergwili', *Trans. Carmarthenshire Antiq. Soc & Field Club (hence TCASFC)*, Vol. 1, 1905-6, p. 65; see also further discussion and references in T. A James, *op. cit.* n. 1.

8. G. E. Evans, 'Abergwili – Notes on its Canons', *TCASFC*, Vol. 1, 1905-6, p. 94.

9. R. A. Roberts, *The Episcopal Registers of the Diocese of St Davids, 1397-1518, Vol. III: A Study of the Published Registers* (London, Hon. Soc. Cymmrodorion, 1920), p. 137.

10. R. Morris, *Churches in the Landscape*, 1989, pp. 362 & 364-5.

11. J. Caley (ed.), *Valor Ecclesiasticus temp. Henr. VIII* (Record Commission, 1810-1834, 6 vols.), Vol. IV, p. 410, 'collegium sancti Mauricii de Ab'guilly'.

12. E. Yardley, *Menevia Sacra* (ed.) F. Green, *Cambrian Archaeological Association,* 1927, pp. 404-5.

13. G. F. Webb, 'St Davids Cathedral and St Mary's College', *Archaeological Jnl.*, 1962, Vol. 119, pp. 330-332.

14. G. E. Evans (ed.), 'Christ Church, Abergwili: 1283-1540', *The Carmarthenshire Antiquary*, Vol. IV, 1962, p. 186.

15. R. F. Isaacson (ed.), *The Episcopal Registers of the Diocese of St David's 1397-1518* (London, Hon. Soc. Cymmrodorion), 2 Vols., Vol. 1, pp. 306-7.

16. W. B. Jones and E. A. Freeman, *The History and Antiquities of St. David's* (London 1856 & facsimile edn. 1998, Pembrokeshire County Council), pp. 299-300.

17. *Menevia Sacra*, op. cit., n. 12; Yardley transcribed Patent Roll, 12 Ed. 1, m. 9, 1284 and Patent Roll 3 Ed. III for these extracts, pp. 419.

18. *Valor Ecclesiasticus*, n. 11, quoted by Roberts, op. cit., n. 9, pp. 137-8.

19. G. E. Evans, op. cit., n. 14, p. 186.

20. T. A. James, op. cit., n. 1, p. 21, citing *Cal. Papal Registers, 1198-1304*.

21. *Menevia Sacra*, op. cit., n. 12, pp. 422-3.

22. I. N. Soulsby, *The Towns of Medieval Wales. A Study in their History, Archaeology and Early Topography* (Chichester, 1983), Abergwili, pp. 68-9.

23. S. Lewis, *A Topographical Dictionary of Wales*, 1833; CRO St Davids Map Book 1811; T. Rees, *The Beauties of England and Wales*, Vol. 18, *South Wales* (London, 1815), p. 338.

24. T. Phillips (ed.), *Cartularium S. Johannis Bapt. De Caermarthen* (Cheltenham, 1869) no. 36, pp. 10-11, noted by Roberts, op. cit., n. 9, p. 73.

25. The late Professor Barri Jones first identified causewayed lengths of Roman Road south of Merlin's Hill and the present A40 between Nantgaredig and Abergwili; see

G. D. B. Jones, 'The Towy Valley Roman Road', *Carms. Antiq.*, Vol. VIII, 1972, p. 4; for detailed mapping see HER, Dyfed Archaeological Trust, Llandeilo.

26. N. Ludlow, 'Whitland Abbey, Carmarthenshire: a Cistercian site re-examined, 1994-99', *Arch. Camb.*, Vol. 151, p. 47.

27. N. Ludlow, 'Pill Priory, 1996-1999: Recent Work at a Tironian House in Pembrokeshire', *Medieval Archaeol.*, Vol. 46, 2002, pp. 41-80.

28. *Menevia Sacra*, op. cit., n. 12, p. 374.

29. T. A. James, 'Excavations at the Augustinian Priory of St John and St Teulyddog, Carmarthen, 1979', *Arch. Camb.*, Vol. 135, 1985, pp. 19-43.

30. *Episcopal Registers*, op. cit., n. 15, Vol. 1, pp. 160-161.

31. More extensive extracts from this Account of Bishop Barlow's closure of Abergwili and transfer of all residents books, organs and vestments to his new Christ Church College at Brecon (BL MS Cleopatra E IV, f. 141) than that quoted by Terry is in G. Dyfnallt Owen, *Elizabethan Wales* (Cardiff, 1964), p. 199.

32. T. A. James, op. cit., n. 1.

33. *Menevia Sacra*, n. 12.

34. *The Black Book*, op. cit., n. 5, p. 241.

35. D. Sabin and K. Donaldson, 'The Geophysical Survey', in Ludlow *et. al.*, op. cit., n. 2, pp. 49-54.

36. T. A. James, op. cit., n. 1, p. 28.

37. Royal Commission on Ancient and Historic Monuments in Wales, *Inventory: Carmarthenshire*, HMSO 1917, p. 4.

38. T. A. James, op. cit., n. 1, footnote 61, p. 34.

39. Roberts, op. cit., n. 9, pp. 137-138.

40. Interestingly Ian Soulsby's plan of Abergwili places the collegiate church in this general location, southwest of the present Palace (Soulsby, op. cit., n. 22, p. 69).

41. NLW D6182, Byng 1784, f. 251.

42. Ludlow, op. cit., n. 26, pp. 64-5.

43. G. Williams, *The Welsh Church from Conquest to Reformation* (Cardiff, 1976), pp. 78-9, 163; M. W. Thompson, in his *Medieval Bishops Palaces in England and Wales* (Aldershot, 1998), pp. 182-3, hedges his bets somewhat. He listed the ten known residences of the mediaeval Bishops of St Davids according to their type and function, following the manorial organization of bishoprics in mediaeval Britain, i.e. each with its See Palace, its London residence, manor castles and other manor houses. He suggested that 'a house was possibly associated with the college' at Abergwili.

44. G. E. Evans, op. cit., n. 14, p. 187.

45. R. Turner, 'St Davids Bishops Palace, Pembrokeshire', *Antiquaries Journal*, Vol. 80, 2000, pp. 87-194.

46. *Black Book*, op. cit., n. 5, p. 13.

47. F. Jones (ed.), 'Medieval Records relating to the Diocese of St Davids', *Jnl Hist. Soc. Church in Wales*, Vol. 14, pp. 9-24, citing NA E. 152, no. 16.

48. Idem, p.14 and pp. 16-20, citing NA E154/1/48 KR Inventories, the latter further evidencing an inventory taken at the death of Bishop Bek in 1293, which is comprehensive in all other respects but entirely omits Abergwili – where the collegiate church, and a market, were flourishing – from its list of manors.

49. Archdeacon Yardley, writing in the mid 18th century, gives some indication of the residences favoured by various bishops. David Martin died at Llandygwydd, which Yardley regarded as his chief residence (*Menevia Sacra*, n. 12, p. 50), though other sources suggest that Trevine was his favourite (R. Turner 2000, n. 45, pp. 165-6), as it was for Bishop Robert Tully, 1460-81 (idem. p. 76).

50. Recorded in the *Episcopal Registers* (op. cit., n. 15, Vol. 2, pp. 468 & 511; also described by Roberts, op. cit., n. 9, p. 101). As all business would have been conducted in the Chapter House, it is unsurprising that no reference to lodgings is recorded in the *Registers*. The *Registers* are not complete – there is a long hiatus between 1410 and 1482, and further long gaps in the 16th and 17th centuries, see J. C. Davies 1945, 'The Records of the Church in Wales', *Nat. Lib. Wales Jnl.*, Vol. 4, p. 6.

51. L. Toulmin Smith (ed.), *The Itinerary in Wales of John Leland in or about the years 1536-1539* (London, 1906, 5 Vols.), Vol. 3, pp. 58 & 114. Trevine, on the other hand, is described as a piece of Llanrhian parish, where the Bishop of St David 'hath a place' (p. 65), while Llanddew was 'sumtime a veri place of the bisshops, now no thing but an onsemeli ruine' (p. 109), and Lamphey was '. . . a place of stoone after castel fascion . . .' (p. 115).

52. E. G. Jones (ed.), *Exchequer proceedings (Equity) concerning Wales, Henry VIII – Elizabeth* (BBCS History & Law Ser., No. IV, Cardiff, 1939), NA E62/17, pp. 305-7.

53. An account from 1581-90 also describes the Palace as 'in most extreme ruin' (*Menevia Sacra*, n. 12, pp. 398-9). See also T. A. James, 'Robert Ferrar: Protestant Martyr', *Carms Antiq.*, Vol. XLI, 2005, pp. 123-136.

54. M. W. Thompson (op. cit., n. 43), notes that earlier episcopal residences, such as East Meon (Hants.), and Mayfield (Sussex) were not courtyard-based (pp. 130-133), but the courtyard plan developed thorough time via, for example, Sonning Manor (Berks.), Southwell (Notts.) and Croydon (pp. 129, 137-8), to the huge complexes at Knole, Hatfield and Hampton Court.

55. T. H. Lewis, 'Carmarthenshire and the Reformation Movement', *TCASFC*, Vol. 14, 1919-21, pp. 33-38.

56. *Geiriadur Prifysgol Cymru: A Dictionary of the Welsh Language*, Cardiff 1990, *maendy*, p. 2309.

57. The 1796 map, like the *Valor*, suggests a tripartite division of the site, which is a recurring theme – three fields were recorded in 1713 (NLW Ottley 1), although whether all sources are refer to the same features is open to question. Three walled enclosures of approximately equal size are shown in 1796 (*Fig. 3*) the Palace, the Hay Yard and a third labelled 'Garden . . . formerly Bowling Green' immediately north of the Palace; all would qualify for the

term 'close' in its mediaeval context. If the latter is one of the 'closes' referred to in 1535, then the surviving stretch of wall along its west side may have mediaeval origins. This raises interesting questions as to other possible sites for both the cloister, and any residential buildings. However, the third enclosure may equally be represented by the Kitchen Garden (NGR SN 44012088), or the field at SN 43982096, called 'Steeple Park' in 1796 (or *Parc Clochty*), possibly in reference to the church steeple or a clock tower on the palace, or to an entrance tower to the college (James 1980, 30). And, of course, its possible that the 'closes' of 1535 may refer to none of these at all.

58. *Menevia Sacra*, n. 12, pp. 388-390; T. H. Lewis, op. cit., n. 55, pp. 36-7.

59. A. Jones, 'The Property of the Welsh Friaries at the Dissolution', *Arch. Camb.*, Vol. 91, 1936, pp. 30-50. An account from 1936 may be mentioned in passing. This suggests that a pre-Reformation Palace is specifically mentioned in the sources, *viz.* 'there was a college or chantry' at Abergwili 'where stood the Palace of the Bishops', and gives a reference to PRO, Minister's Accounts 5598, m.7, *dorse* (pp. 34-5). However, it is not clear whether the 'Palace' is mentioned specifically in the original source or whether it was just the author's assumption.

60. Jones, op. cit., n. 59.

61. E. D. Jones, 'Survey of South Wales Chantries, 1546', *Arch. Camb.*, Vol. 89, 1934, pp. 135-155.

62. E. G. Jones, op. cit., n. 52, pp. 305-7, citing E62/17.

63. *Menevia Sacra*, n. 12, pp. 132 & 404-5.

64. J. C. Davies, op. cit., n. 50, p. 17.

65. *Menevia Sacra*, op. cit., n. 12, pp. 388-90.

66. T.A. James, op. cit., n. 53, p. 125.

67. Idem, p. 134, n. 22, citing Foxe's *Book of Martyrs*, which gives Ferrar's responses to the 56 accusations made against him.

68. NLW Ottley Papers, Ottley 1, 'The View of the Dilapidations of the Palace of Abergwilly, with the Outbuildings, Garden and Court Walls, and other appurtenances to the Palace', 18 Aug. 1713.

69. M. B. E. Evans (ed.), '*Sir Gaeriad:* Some Comments on Carmarthenshire and its people by Iolo Morgannwg', *Carm. Antiq.*, Vol. 24, 1988, pp. 41, 47; from NLW MSS 13115B.

70. G. E. Evans, 'The Episcopal Chapel, Abergwili Palace', *TCASFC*, Vol. 23, 1932, pp. 86-7.

71. G. Williams, 'Bishop Richard Davies', in *Welsh Reformation Essays* (Cardiff 1967), pp. 151-190.

72. *Menevia Sacra*, op. cit., n. 12, pp. 398-9, 'Bishop Middleton's Account of the Diocese'.

73. T. A. James, op. cit., n. 1, p. 24.

74. J. W. Evans, *St Davids Bishops Palace & St Nons Chapel* (Cardiff Cadw Guidebook 1991), p. 20; see also *Menevia Sacra*, op. cit., n. 11, pp. 104-5.

75. D. L. Baker-Jones, 'William Laud, Bishop of St Davids', *Carms. Antiq.*, Vol. III, 1959, pp. 32-33.

76. *Menevia Sacra*, op. cit., n. 12, p. 121.

77. T. A. James, op. cit., n. 1, p. 26.

78. Laud was not kept busy by canonical duties during this second visit – only one man offered himself for ordination but was declined, and no confirmations took place (Baker-Jones, op. cit., n. 75, pp. 32-3).

79. In 1326 the manor also comprised a 'water mill, worth yearly 20s, two (fish) weirs on the Tywi, and one on the Gwili, worth yearly 10s, and wreck of goods, and perquisites, worth yearly 7s', *The Black Book*, op. cit., n. 4, pp. 241-251.

80. Summarised in E. Whittle, *The Historic Parks and Gardens of Carmarthenshire* (Cardiff, Cadw, 1992); but see also her 'The Historic Parks and Gardens of Carmarthenshire', *Carms. Antiq.*, Vol. 36, pp. 87-102.

81. Lamphey Palace, in contrast, was associated with an extensive park by 1326, comprising 68.8ha and including three orchards, 'the fruit of which with the fruit of the curtilage' included apples, cabbages and leeks, four vineyards, 48 acres of woodland, four fishponds and containing 60 head of cattle, as well as deer. R. Turner, *Lamphey Bishop's Palace and Llawhaden Castle* (Cardiff, Cadw Guidebook, 1991), pp. 8-9. No real comparisons can be made with Abergwili Park which can only have occupied 6.03ha at most, including the Great Meadow.

82. NLW Ottley Papers, op. cit., n. 68.

83. Unless the attempts by Bishop Ferrar (1548-54) to 'enclose the highway near Carmarthen' (T. A. James, op. cit., n. 1, p. 24), represented an effort to enlarge it.

84. C. S. Briggs, 'A new field of Welsh cultural heritage: inference and evidence in gardens and landscapes since *c.*1450', in P. Pattison (ed.), *There by Design: Field Archaeology in Parks and Gardens* (Oxford, BAR 267); E. Whittle, 1992, op. cit., n. 80, pp. 13-20.

The Topography of Mediaeval Cardigan

Seamus Cunnane

At the southernmost end of Ceredigion, just above where Afon Mwldan flows into the tidal waters of the Teifi, the river curves round a ridge on its right bank, a kilometre before it broadens into its estuary. Mediaeval Cardigan straddled that ridge.

The motte and bailey of Old Castle stands at the point further west where the estuary begins. It seems likely, though it cannot be proved, that this is where Roger of Montgomery built a fortress when he swept through Ceredigion in 1093. Later the name Din Geraint

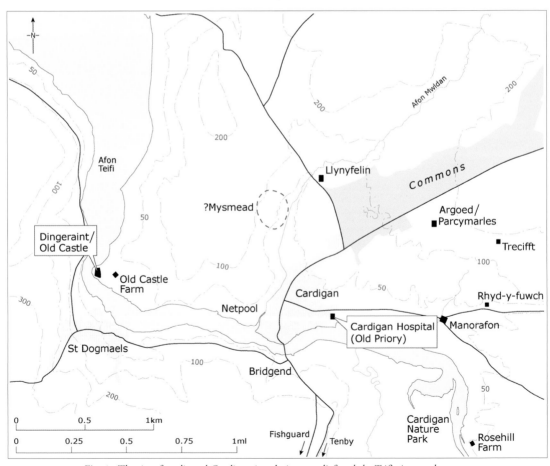

Fig. 1: *The site of mediaeval Cardigan in relation to relief and the Teifi river and estuary.*

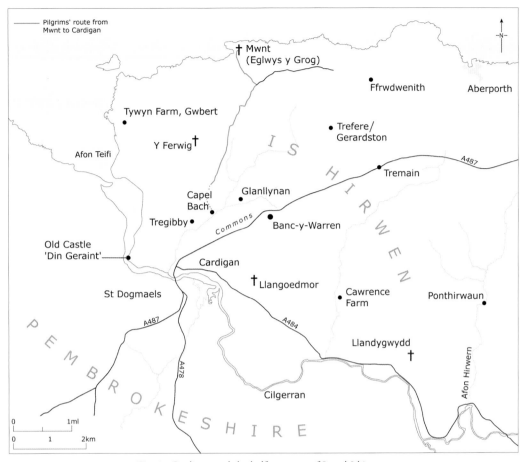

Fig. 2: *Cardigan and the half commote of Iscoed Ishirwern.*

was attached to it, giving rise to the belief that its origin was Welsh.[1] Old Castle was too small to accommodate a defensible settlement and the river was too difficult to bridge at that point. Little wonder it was abandoned.

There is no clear date for the foundation of Cardigan, but it was soon after AD 1109, thus allowing us to settle on 1110.[2] Its purpose was to dominate Ceredigion, of which its name is an anglicised form. Its immediate lordship was the half-commote of Iscoed Ishirwern, which stretched in a rough triangle between the Teifi, the sea and the Hirwern (now Hirwaun as in Ponthirwaun) that flows into the Teifi seven miles upstream. Within that district the part least affected by the colonisers was Llandygwydd, which was associated with the Bishop of St. David's, and Llangoedmor, despite the presence of the Mortimers in their fortress at Coedmor. Llangoedmor was in the Welshry; it held its Petty Sessions at Cauros, now Cawrence Farm.

The colonisers built a strong wooden castle. It withstood the Welsh forces that destroyed Norman French power at the battle of Penparc in 1136 and a raid by Dublin Danes in 1138. Rhys ap Gruffydd destroyed it in 1165, rebuilding it in stone after reaching an accord with Henry II in 1171. To celebrate his new castle he held the great Eisteddfod in 1176, which has been the icon of all *eisteddfodau* since then, thus making Cardigan's Castle nationally significant.[3]

THE TOWN WALL

Cardigan was probably smaller to begin with than its later dimensions as a walled town. Terry James suggested[4] that its northern boundary was the crossing from Black Lion Mews to Ebens Lane, both of them side streets off High Street. It makes sense. If correct, the town would have formed a rough quadrant with the castle occupying one quarter; but because the boundary cut across the ridge it was no use to Robert Waleran when he walled the town in the 1240s, instead he followed the natural contour of the ridge, beginning with the castle at the riverside. Terry pointed out that a dogleg at the end of Ebens Lane had probably marked the limit of the unwalled town, but in order to follow the contour Waleran had to widen the original settlement by some yards on either side. The town wall running west from the Castle incorporated Teifi Gate and passed by the quay, eventually curving north towards New Gate at the end of Quay Street. It then followed the ridge along today's property boundaries between High Street and the Mwldan area until turning eastward towards Bartholomew Gate, near F. W. Woolworth today. A dry ditch once ran outside the walls; a trace may be seen where the road dips slightly to the north of Bartholomew Gate at the top of College Row. The wall continued eastward briefly before turning south to Wolf Gate at the end of St. Mary Street. Its effect was to change the shape of the town from a quadrant into something resembling a pear.

Towers may have guarded the gates or protected the wall where its alignment changed. One such may be the northwest corner south of College Row. Speed's map (*Fig. 4*) shows only one tower east of Bartholomew Gate where the wall turns south. Terry James' 1978 dig (before F. W. Woolworth obliterated about 120 feet of the wall when extending its shop) found its remains. It may have become a prison after the Prison Tower in the castle became dilapidated and before a special lock-up was built along what is now the Woolworth frontage. Terry reported: 'Parts of the (nearby) mediaeval wall survived intact in its lower courses. In section it was about 1.63 metres wide and the interior was faced with ashlar'.[5] Today there are two breaks in the town wall on its western side allowing access to the Mwldan from Eben's Lane and Market Lane. These are post-mediaeval, made when the wall had decayed.

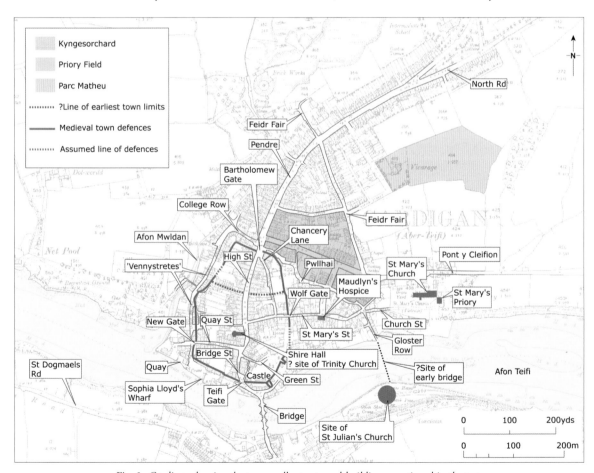

Fig. 3: *Cardigan showing the town walls, streets and buildings mentioned in the text.*

TWO BRIDGES

The defining element in Cardigan's topography is its interaction with the Teifi, whose tidal waters gave it its haven and port.

Sir Samuel Meyrick refers to a tradition that Cardigan Bridge once stood upstream of its present position.[6] If so, the town began with a bypass road, which after the bridge was moved near the castle it was not to regain for 750 years. It was probably wooden and hardly massive, perhaps sufficient for a pack-horse, with heavy traffic such as oxcarts crossing immediately downstream over a weir-like structure. Gloster Row seems the most likely site (*see Fig. 3*). There is no documentary support, yet the topographical evidence is good. To reach the present bridge from Pembrokeshire the Fishguard and Tenby roads need to take a sharp left turn above the town, whereas a bridge at Gloster Row would have given them a gentle curve with an easier slope. Archbishop Baldwin and Giraldus Cambrensis proclaimed the Third Crusade in 1188 precisely opposite Gloster Row. On the mound where Baldwin preached St. Julian's church[7] was built to commemorate the event. Its remains had vanished before July 1802, long before the engine house of Cardigan railway station covered the site in 1885. St. Julian's was probably round like a Templar church, for it was later known as Capel Sidan[8] (meaning a circular knoll, like the Irish *sidhe*). It was however under the control of St Dogmael's Abbey and does not therefore form part of Cardigan's mediaeval churches and chapels.

Heather James has pointed out that on the first edition 25 inch (1890) of the Ordnance Survey, exactly where I postulate the existence of the first bridge, a ferry, with a jetty on the Pembrokeshire side, is marked. The second edition (1906) eliminated both ferry and jetty, of which the only remnant seems to be its foundation. Its disappearance suggests that the ferry had served as the start of a pathway on the south of the Teifi, which the construction of the station in 1885 had blocked, thus rendering it redundant.

In 1970 Alan White made borings for Costain about 250m upstream of Gloster Row, to test the foundations of a bypass bridge eventually opened in 1991. He came across wood. Terry and Heather came[9] to probe his information. Could what he found have been tree trunks *in situ,* perhaps the remnants of ancient woodland? Alan said no; the wood had no knots such as one would expect in tree roots. He had encountered worked wood with clear grain, its vertical posts 8″ wide and about 18″ deep, beginning 20 yards inland and

going 23 yards into the river. He said it was unmistakable, because worked wood was worse than granite; a drill cuts through granite but wood moves with the drill and breaks the bit.

He had come across what looked like an old weir in a place from which the main current had departed and which in consequence had in part become land. Heather suggested that apart from catching fish it could have served as a baffle to protect the bridge from drift-wood that might have piled against it in times of flood. If so, it supports the Gloster Row location. As half of it lies in a field between the Teifi and the Carmarthen road it implies that the river changed course over the centuries. A weir in that position might have accelerated the process whereby, along the length of the town, a large stretch of accrued land built up on the right bank of the Teifi. The grounds of Cardigan Hospital, formerly the Priory, slope perceptibly, suggesting that the river once ran by the present driveway. The Teifi lapped the castle before accrued land separated it. The extent to which the land between the castle and river was created by natural silting or infill remains to be determined. More land was added below the bridge; Sophia Lloyd's Wharf there was only created in 1864.

Upstream of the new bypass bridge and near Cardigan Nature Park, a broad expanse of water and marsh marks an ancient river crossroads. Before the Ice Age a meander by Cilgerran led the Teifi to flow from south to north along the valley below the Tenby road at Troed-yrhiw; it continued north before diverting towards the sea along the present Gwbert Road. During the Ice Age, Irish Sea ice caused a large lake to form. As the ice disappeared, and with it the lake, the Teifi rapidly cut down into the surface to form Cilgerran Gorge, allowing it to flow east-west. The marshy area where the old and new river beds meet facilitates changes in the flow of the main current. Ancient documents describe an island opposite Rose Hill Farm as 'the little island in the river belonging to the Abbot of St. Dogmaels',[10] implying it was part of Pembrokeshire until the Teifi changed course and isolated it (*see Fig. 1*). The 1268 Extent (Longleat 624) states '*In aqua de Teyuy est quedam pastura et extenduntur per annum ad vi d*', implying that the change of course had already occurred by that date.

Nowadays St. Mary's Church seems a quiet enclave, but an earlier bridge by Gloster Row would have placed it near the centre of urban and port activity. It also helps explain why St. Mary Street bends noticeably when it might have been straight. The street originally joined the town with the bridge, not the church. Later, when St. Mary's was built, a by-road linked it with the street at the point where the water from Pwllhai meets the road on its way towards the river (where high tides flood it to this day).[11] When the bridge was moved downstream to its new site the section of the street to its earlier site became disused and the junction to the church became the main thoroughfare, thus leaving St. Mary Street with an otherwise inexplicable bend.

The first bridge was wrecked in the catastrophe of 1136, the battle of Cardigan at Crug Mawr when the Welsh defeated the Norman settlers.[12] Welsh forces destroyed it again in 1231. When the king made Cardigan his own in 1241 and sent Robert Waleran to fortify town and castle it was probably realised that the bridge could only be protected if it was under the castle. They rebuilt it there, of wood, like its predecessor.[13] It was a far more difficult site, for the river runs faster there and instead of a gentle slope to the water there was a direct drop. Worse, on entering Pembrokeshire the road crossed a stream that needed yet another bridge,[14] and this was followed by a sharper gradient than the old bridge would have required.

Cardigan port would once have extended upstream to the first bridge. Maritime activity at that point lends support to the story of Our Lady of Cardigan, a shrine

with Flemish roots which is said to have first appeared where St. Mary's Church now stands. With the building of the new bridge that part of the harbour was lost and shipping moved downstream; but this loss was mitigated by the Mwldan Brook becoming a new focus for quayside activity.

All in all, the theory that the first bridge was at Gloster Row seems highly probable. The new bridge changed the town radically. Its previous polarity had been east-west from Gloster Row along St. Mary Street towards the Cross and (as I believe) Trinity Church with its nearby market, but the new bridge changed this to north-south, with the King's High Road from Pembrokeshire running north across the new bridge, thus relegating St. Mary Street to a lesser role. St. Mary Street is part of the original twelfth-century settlement,[15] though it became extra-mural when the walls were built as it was not feasible to enclose it. Professor Harold Carter[16] incorrectly identifies St. Mary Street as a pre-seventeenth century extension to the walled town. He also seems to rely over-much upon Speed's rather fanciful impression of the number of houses near the church.

SPEED'S MAPS

John Speed published two maps of Cardigan in his *Theatre of the Empire of Great Britain in 1611*. Its

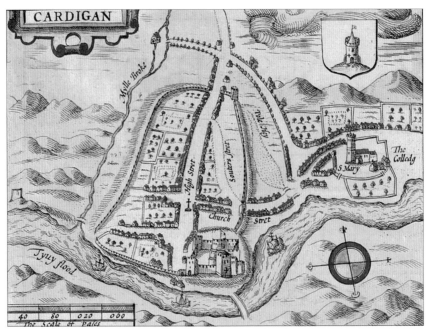

Fig. 4: *John Speed's map of Cardigan, 1610, from his* Theatre of the Empire of Great Britain *reproduced by permission of the National Library of Wales.*

'Second Booke' covered Wales by means of an overall map followed by thirteen county maps. Whilst he openly acknowledged his debt to his predecessors, Llwyd and Saxton, he took pride in his town maps, the first of their kind which he claimed to have surveyed himself. On either side of his map of Wales are six small cartouches with town views. These are rather schematic and for Cardigan the Teifi appears to be flowing in the opposite direction to join the sea on the east. Much more informative is the larger plan accompanying the county map, which combines a bird's eye view of upstanding buildings with a map, but not of course to modern surveyors' accuracy or scale, leading to much distortion; *Feidr Fair* is too close to the walled town. The castle is the wrong shape and its gate and great tower are in the wrong place. I doubt that there were as many burgages as he suggests. He has the gallows in the Netpool instead of on Banc y Warren. Nevertheless this, the earliest map of the town, confirms the general layout of the castle and the town with its wall and tower, streets and burgages, the Cross, St. Mary's Church (and to the south of it the Vicar's orchard, long since incorporated into the churchyard). Speed also shows Afon Mwldan (Mylle Brook) with the Town Mill and its leet stream, the muddy patch at Pwllhai (Pole Hey) with a bridge in St. Mary Street (Church Street) where the Pwll Hai effluent approaches its outlet in the Afon Teifi. New Gate and Bartholomew Gate are not shown, though Teifi Gate and Wolf Gate are included. Two buildings shown on the quayside outside the wall are mentioned in a Coedmor deed of 1507.[17] His caption 'The Colledg' where the former priory stood has led some to infer there was once a school there, whereas the name is used simply in the Latin sense of a community (despite the fact usually it held only one monk, and never more than two). Interestingly, a property in St. Mary Street named the Colledge is mentioned in 1666.[18] We do not know how old it is. It could only have been in the former hospice of the Knights Hospitallers.

THE PILGRIM PATH

Foremost among the pilgrim paths in Wales was that from Ynys Enlli (Bardsey Island, off the western tip of the Lleyn peninsula) to Tyddewi (St. David's) in the south-west. It mostly followed the coast, but at Mwnt Church (Eglwys y Grog) it cut inland to the Teifi crossing at Cardigan. From Mwnt (SN195510) it took the present road until a public path (SN188484) took the pilgrim through Capel Farm towards Afon Mwldan

(SN187475); and then, I believe, followed the stream as far as Cardigan's Town Mill. Not only do parts of that track remain; they have been used by people now alive. Speed then shows a road from Town Mill to St. Mary's Church. This is Feidr Fair (St. Mary's Lane). It is in two unequal sections. West of the A487 road it was called Brick Lane in the nineteenth century when the brickworks, now defunct, existed, but it is once again Feidr Fair. The eastern section from the A487 to St. Mary's Church is a trunk road, while the western part remains an unadopted lane. Cardigan already had a St. Mary's Street, so there must have been a reason for duplicating the name Feidr Fair. I suggest it is that the latter was the final stage of the pilgrim path as it approached the shrine of Our Lady of Cardigan (see Capel-bach below).

STREETS

The most reliable account of Cardigan comes from two detailed Extents made in 1268[19] and 1301.[20] I deal with them briefly for reasons of space. The 1268 Extent does not refer to intra-mural streets, but 1301 names them as follows:

1. St. Mary Street outside the gates: *in vico beate marie extra portas* or, as in 1268, outside the East Gate: *extra portam de Est.* It lay between Wolf Gate and the church. In 1268 it had twenty-one burgesses, ten holding a full burgage each and eleven a half burgage, in total fifteen and a half burgages. In 1301 there were twenty-five burgesses, eight holding one burgage, one holding one and a half, and fifteen with half a burgage each; in total seventeen burgages. They could well have fitted on one side of the street, but the Extents do not tell us whether that was so in this case but see footnote 27.

2. The Knights Hospitallers of St. John are not mentioned in the Extents, for these are statements of revenue, yet in 1160 the Knights were awarded three burgages in St. Mary Street[21] where the Angel Hotel now stands.[22] There they kept a hospice for pilgrims; some came to pray at the shrine of Our Lady of Cardigan in St. Mary's Church,[23] and others were on their way to or from St. Davids or, later, heading for Strata Florida. Named Maudlyns Hospice in the Survey of South Wales Chantries, 1546, it was funded by Territorium Leprosorum/Sickmens Land/Tir y Cleifion,[24] a carucate on the left of the road between the eastern edge of town and Llangoedmor parish. When

Henry VIII abolished pilgrimage in 1536 it still housed 'ympotent and deceassyd' – for which read 'frail and diseased' – men, until it was confiscated.

3. CHANCERY LANE came by its name in a curious fashion. Speed calls it 'Souters Strret'. The Latin *sutor* means cobbler, but at that time the term also described glovers, tailors and craftsmen who banged away at metal, leather or wood. This suggests that it may have been the town's industrial estate. It was suitable if only because houses on the land sloping eastward to the town wall would have been built on piles, thus providing an undercroft where tradesmen could catch the morning light. But that must remain speculation until the site is examined. 'Souter' became 'Suitor', perhaps following the eighteenth century trend to spell words so as to give them a French flavour.[25] It needed only the arrival of a lawyer to complete its transformation into Chancery Lane. The 1301 extent calls it '*In vico de porta lupi usque ad portam bartholomei ex utraque parte*' – 'from Wolf Gate to Bartholomew Gate on both sides' (*Fig. 5*). Wolf Gate was the eastern exit from the walled town, near the castle, and gave on to St. Mary Street. Did it receive its name because of wolves in Coedmor Forest, which it faced, or because its master mason may have carved a wolf over the gate as his personal craft signature? Sixteenth-century documents call it *porta lupini*. At that time St. Mary Street ended at Wolf Gate, while its continuation to High Street was known as Castle Yard. When Wolf Gate decayed the name St. Mary Street superseded Castle Yard.[26] Part of the Wolf Gate archway appears to survive behind 43, St. Mary Street.

4. A particular feature of the Extent escaped Sanders' notice:[27] burgages are named in order, first on one side of Souter Street and then the other. It had twenty-two burgesses, one with four and a half burgages, one with three, one with two, three with one and a half, seven with one and nine with but a half burgage – a total of twenty-five and a half burgages. In this regard Souter Street is more complex than any other part of the town. Philcus had three burgages, a garden and a half burgage separate from those. One of Walter Coyd's three burgages was outside the wall at Bartholomew Gate.

5. BARTHOLOMEW GATE. We can only explain its name by postulating a St. Bartholomew's chapel or oratory outside the town to which it led.[28]

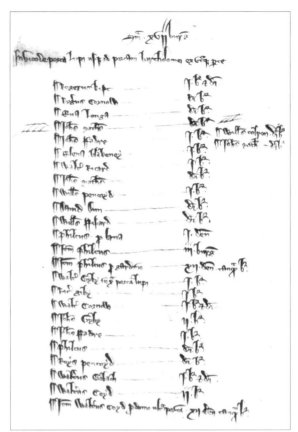

Fig. 5: *Extract from an Extent of Cardigan, 1300-1, listing burgesses 'from Wolf Gate to Bartholomew Gate on both sides' (NA SC 11/771).*
(Reproduced with the permission of the National Archives).

6. HIGH STREET: '*vicus de porta bartholomei usque ad crucem ex utraque parte*' – 'the street from Bartholomew Gate to the Cross on both sides'. High Street now extends to Quay Street but then it ended at Market Lane by the Cross, which has long gone (possibly because of the Puritans, for Speed's map shows that it survived the Reformation). Much of High Street became part of the town only when the walls were built. Its twelve burgesses are fewer than elsewhere. This may account for many of the sixty-eight empty burgage plots mentioned in Walter Pederton, the Justiciar of West Wales' Account for 1298-1300 as 'in decay of the rent'.[29] Twenty-two and three quarter burgages are allocated, of which Walter Blakeney held a block of nine, and moreover paid 8 pence extra '*pro duobus capitibus domus sue*'. What this means is not certain, but perhaps his house had two

turrets, as would have befitted a Constable of Cardigan Castle (1298 to 1301).[30] There is no mention of burgages on Ebens Lane, though it could have accommodated half burgages behind houses on the High Street. The typical burgage had its gable facing the street with a passageway to one side and a cellar beneath. Dimensions were not completely uniform though a frontage of 20 feet was typical. Later on, adjoining burgages were amalgamated and their roofs rebuilt so that the houses now faced the street. There were many stone cellars in High Street, though none remain; often builders destroyed them before word of their existence got out.

7. Between the Cross and the next group of burgages there was a gap. On the left, going south, was open ground between Castle Yard (now upper St. Mary Street) and the bailey wall. On the right (as I intend to argue) Trinity Church stood between Quay Street and the market. Its market monopoly served Cardigan well: no one, under pain of forfeiture, might trade within five leagues of Cardigan except in its market on Saturday.[31]

8. GROSVENOR HILL: '*Vicus castri de cruce usque ad pontem de theyvi ex una parte*' – 'Castle Street from the Cross to the Teifi Bridge, on one side'.[32] This is followed by *in vico a ponte de theyvi usque ad crucem ex parte alia* 'from the Teifi bridge to the Cross on the other side'. These were counted as two streets. Both began at the top of Quay Street. The first, running by the castle ditch, is called *regia strata*: King Street[33] elsewhere, but in the 1301 Extent it is Castle Street. Its burgages (whose demolition in the last century was recorded photographically) formed an island between King Street and the second street, Bridge Street, now known as Grosvenor Hill.

9. CASTLE STREET had sixteen burgesses, five with full burgages and eleven with half a burgage each. BRIDGE STREET took a wider sweep and so had room for more burgages. There were twenty-five burgesses, with twenty-one and a half burgages between them: two with two burgages apiece, twelve with one and eleven with a half burgage, one of whom also paid a sum equivalent to the rent of one eighth of a burgage *pro parvo placio*: a small plot.

10. TEIFI GATE: Sanders[34] misread this name as '*pontem de Cheyni*' instead of '*pontem de Theyvi*' (Teifi).

Unfortunately, Wmffre follows his reading and seeks to explain it by an analogy with Pont-de-chaine at Angers.[35]

11. A few years ago an excavation behind the Green Street cottages by the Castle entrance turned up traces of what looked like a gate. The hope that we had found the great gate to Cardigan Castle seemed unlikely as the remains were so slight that they probably marked the entrance to a bailey, as in Cilgerran and Carmarthen. The remains are aligned with Quay Street and, as the Castle was older than the street, New Gate was probably so placed as to give direct access to the bailey entrance and, behind it, the great gate of the castle with its double portcullis that stood (as I believe) by the Great Tower, thus ensuring that an enemy breaking through New Gate would be in the direct line of fire from the Castle. The excavation was brief, repairs to the cottages being deemed more important than possible discoveries relating to the castle.[36]

12. QUAY STREET: '*In vico*[37] *de cruce usque ad novam portam*' – 'in the street from the Cross to the New Gate'. Its name indicates that New Gate was built after the others, all of which lead to a main road whereas New Gate opens only to the dockside. Presumably the thriving port[38] needed greater access than Teifi Gate provided; its ancillary businesses would have extended to Mwldan Water, thus reinforcing the need for a west gate. The street had thirteen burgesses in ten burgages on one side: seven with single burgages and six with half a burgage. The other had eleven burgesses: eight with single burgages and three with half a burgage – a total of twenty burgages on the one side, twenty and a half on the other.

13. VENNYSTRETES: '*In vicis Luteis vennystretes*'. In 1301 the term is plural, whereas in 1268 it was simply *Fenystrete* and comprised only four waste burgages. Fenny Streets, or muddy streets, is the equivalent of the Latin *vici lutei*. The 1268 Extent implies they were extra-mural, as it distinguishes the borough within the walls, '*burgum infra muros*', from its waste land, '*vasta burgi*', where it locates *Fenystrete*. The 1301 Extent shows that *Vennystretes* was thriving, with fifteen burgesses and fifteen burgages, of whom one had two burgages, another one and a half, ten had a whole burgage each and three had halves. Where was it? Unlike the 1268 Extent, that of 1301 does not distinguish *Vennys-*

tretes from those within the walls, but that may be a rare scribal omission in an otherwise fascinating document. Intra-mural Cardigan is not particularly muddy, but two places outside it are. Pwllhai seems less likely if only because an extra-mural burgage in that district has already been mentioned outside Bartholomew Gate. There remains only Afon Mwldan to the west of Cardigan. Though far from proven, this is rendered more probable because one burgess, *David Pistor*, was a baker, for whose work easy access to water would have been useful. Perhaps the burgages lay near New Gate.

14. CENSARS: the dorse of the 1301 Extent names twenty-one censars who traded in Cardigan Market, each paying twelve pence, the same as for a burgage.[39]

CHURCHES

Cardigan had two churches, St. Mary's and Holy Trinity. St. Mary's belonged to a Benedictine Priory which was not conventual[40] in that it never held more than two monks, and usually only one. The Prior employed a secular vicar for pastoral work. A door apparently leading to a night stair in the south-east corner of the chancel indicates that Priory and church were attached. Though first mentioned in the time of Rhys ap Gruffydd, St. Mary's was a de Clare foundation. Its mother house, Chertsey Abbey, lay in de Clare territory in Surrey. Like the hospice belonging to the Knights of St. John, it probably dates from between 1158 and 1165 when the de Clares appropriated Cardigan for the second and last time. How long it has been a parish church is not known. To deal with it *in extenso* is not possible here.

The great mystery of Cardigan's topography is the location of Holy Trinity, which has long disappeared. It went under various names, many of them variants of Llanddwy.[41] Silas M. Harris' explanation[42] is perhaps most succinct: 'Lando or Landov represents the Welsh Landou, i.e. Llandwyf or Llandwy, church of God; in the twelfth century it was natural to render this, 'church of the Holy Trinity', for that was the time when dedications under that form were becoming general'. He instances Llandow, Glamorgan, Llanddew, Breconshire, and Llanddwy, near Dineley's Ffynnon Drindod.

Most scholars support a countryside location. Professor Ralph A. Griffiths is perhaps most eloquent. Holy Trinity, he states, 'with a refuge and a Welsh name . . .

may well have been an old Celtic chapel somewhere in the countryside around Cardigan'.[43] The relatively fertile land would have been populated before the Normans came and a pre-existing rural chapel would not have been out of place.[44] Yet if Holy Trinity was ever a rural Celtic chapel it did not remain such, for it is never referred to as anything but a church.

One would imagine that Cardigan's church was within the town it served rather than in the countryside, for Mass-going was not an optional extra but a vital element of communal life to the extent that some would have attended daily Mass. A town church would have been preferable during the turbulence of the early twelfth century. Yet Professor Ralph Griffiths[45] points to the example of Aberystwyth, whose parish church was just over a mile away at Llanbadarn. Of course, Llanbadarn was an established monastic site long before Aberystwyth existed, whereas as yet we can only speculate whether Holy Trinity was pre-Norman or rural. Unlike Aberystwyth, which came to have a chapel, *Capel Mair*,[46] within the town, if Cardigan lacked Holy Trinity in its early days then all it had left was St. Peter's Chapel in the Castle, which was minuscule and more an oratory than a place for communal worship. It could not provide for the town as it was just a room over the gate as in Cilgerran Castle and would have held only a handful. It could be used only when the gate was closed, for when it was open the portcullises were drawn up into the chapel.

Of the four attempts to locate Holy Trinity Emily Pritchard made two. An enthusiast who assembled a mass of material, not always reliable, she lacked judgment. She wrongly thought Holy Trinity was a priory staffed by monks, whereas it was an ordinary church whose revenues went to Llanbadarn Priory, itself a dependant of St. Peter's Abbey, Gloucester.[47] R. H. Malden, M.A.,[48] proved the documents she relied upon[49] were late fourteenth century forgeries perpetrated by Gloucester Abbey, in which the reference to Holy Trinity is itself a late interpolation.

First she said that Holy Trinity was one and the same as the later church and priory of St. Mary;[50] the Chertsey Benedictines had simply taken it over and changed its name. But this cannot be, for a crucial element in the legend of Our Lady of Cardigan is a physical distinction between the two churches.

In 1906 she proposed that Holy Trinity was at Glandwr cottage[51] near Rhyd-y-Fuwch on the eastern outskirts of Cardigan by the road that forks left at

Manorafon. She thought Glandwr may once have been *Llandwr*, which in turn could have derived from *Llan* and *d'eau*, i.e. church by the water! Apart from the aberrant etymology, her explanation also fails because it places Cardigan's church in the neighbouring parish of Llangoedmor. She further identified a well near Glandwr as Trinity Well, whose alleged existence has so bedevilled local research that it deserves to be disposed of once and for all.

Cardigan's Trinity Well does not exist and never did.[52] The sole evidence is in Thomas Dineley's *The Account of the Official Progress of His Grace Henry the First Duke of Beaufort through Wales in 1684* (facsimile edition, London, 1888), whose fascinating illustrations seem to have dulled the critical faculties of its readers. On p. 247 the book gives a skimpy account of Cardigan with a drawing of an unrecognisable building, and on p. 248 there is a sketch of Trinity Well with a pierrot-like figure on stilts. But it was the indexer, not Dineley, who assigned Trinity Well to Cardigan, though Dineley added to the confusion by illustrating places such as Cardigan that the Duke did not visit. Nor did the three-week journey follow the sequence of Dineley's illustrations, for they would have had the Duke doubling on his tracks like a snipe. Dineley's Trinity Well is Ffynnon Drindod, in Llanfihangel-y-Creuddyn, north of the Ystwyth near Llanilar, about a mile below Trawscoed[53] and near the church of Holy Trinity or Llanddwy.[54] Pilgrims drawn there by the well's reported curative powers also frequented its fair and the tavern; hence Dineley's illustration of a pierrot.

Another site for Cardigan's Holy Trinity Church emerged when Professor William Rees' 1934 map placed Landou five miles from Cardigan, near Blaenannerch, seemingly confusing it with Llwyn-Ddu. Despite his erudition, his attribution is not accepted.

Iwan Wmffre has recently advanced a novel solution: 'The most likely candidate (for Holy Trinity) must be the farm *Capel* whose dedication or earlier history is otherwise unknown . . . In view of the situation of *Capel* it is likely that (Holy Trinity) fair was a large event held outside the town walls, on the waste ground of *Rhos Tre Aberteifi*'.[55] His argument is attractive: we are looking for Holy Trinity: the name *Capel* is ecclesiastical, and since its dedication or earlier history is otherwise unknown it is the most likely candidate for the missing church. I do not agree. Receipts from the Holy Trinity fairs do not suggest they were of the size or consistency that Dr. Wmffre seems to envisage.[56]

Again, Holy Trinity was a church, not a chapel. May I suggest gently that adequate consideration has not been devoted to the important distinction and consequent difference in status between them. The church was the centre of worship for the parish. A chapel served those some distance from the church; it could also promote devotion in a place regarded as holy. Churches were essential; chapels were optional and sometimes desirable (though just to complicate matters, monastic places of worship were churches).

Regardless of where or by whom it was built, Holy Trinity was the chief place of worship for Cardigan and was thus a church, not a chapel, as the records show. To demote it to *Capel*[57] is to imply that, uniquely in Wales, in Cardigan the name *Llandduw* lost the element *Llan*. This adds a gratuitous complication to a mystery that is already too complex.

Iwan Wmffre does not seem to realise that, far from referring to Holy Trinity, Capel Farm received its name from the pilgrim track already mentioned. His interest seems focused on the Farm, but it was *Capel-bach*, just below it, that gave the farm its name. *Capel-bach* seems to have been a wayside oratory where the pilgrim paused to pray before departing to make his devotions at the Shrine of Our Lady of Cardigan in St. Mary's Church there. He might then lodge at the Knights' Hospice before crossing the Teifi and setting out for the Shrine of St. David.

The fact that *Capel-bach* is an old mile[58] from the Cardigan Shrine evokes the Slipper Chapel near Walsingham. Like *Capel-bach*, it is by a stream, an old mile from the great Marian Shrine. Walsingham pilgrims, including the kings of England – among them Henry VIII – prayed at the Slipper Chapel before removing their shoes (hence its name), fording the stream and walking the final mile barefoot. We have no records of Wales' pilgrim path, but the parallel between *Capel-bach* and the Slipper Chapel is inescapable, and to dismiss the idea that *Capel-bach* served a similar purpose – a respite for prayer before crossing Mwldan Brook barefoot on the final mile to Our Lady of Cardigan – is to be blind to the depth of Catholicism in mediaeval Wales.[59] Walsingham's fame was far greater than Cardigan's – it was known internationally – yet in its own setting Cardigan's shrine was renowned, as Bishop Barlow testified when reporting its destruction to Thomas Cromwell.[60] The suspicion that this iconoclastic ideologue exaggerated its fame to his master so as to acquire greater cachet by getting rid of it is allayed by a rescript from Pope Julius II, dated 3 September 1512, granting pilgrims at Cardigan the spiritual privileges they would have received if they had visited the major basilicas of Rome.[61] Moreover, the shrine had a chantry priest who was funded by lands in Cardigan and Llangoedmor to sing the Lady Mass daily for pilgrims;[62] and Harris, citing Burnet, states that Cardigan was the shrine that received most pilgrims and offerings in those parts.[63] The idea of *Capel-bach* as a wayside oratory for pilgrims thus fits its location better than Dr. Wmffre's rather Procrustean alternative.[64]

As we have seen, the sites proposed for Holy Trinity do not persuade. If any site remains it must be within the parish it served; otherwise it could hardly have been the town church, for Llangoedmor and *Y Ferwig* would be just as convenient. The only remaining places that suggest themselves within the parish, Old Castle (SN 164464), Tregibby (183474) and perhaps Glanllynan (196479), are speculative and lack support.

Holy Trinity's dedication does not settle whether it was Welsh or Norman; it could have been either.[65] Its Welsh form, *Llanddwy*, and the status of its lands as a *refugium ecclesie* might advance its claim to be pre-Norman and therefore non-urban, were there no countervailing argument. But there is: the thirty-two year rule in Cardigan of Rhys ap Gruffydd brought about an enormous advance in Cardigan of Welsh culture even apart from his great Eisteddfod of 1176. Professor Ralph Griffiths has drawn our attention to Rhys' influence.[66] In addition, Rhys re-named the town *Aberteifi*, and without detriment to its heterogeneous inhabitants whom he accepted and welcomed, he presided as legislator over a renaissance of Welsh law by adopting, re-editing, expanding and applying the laws of Hywel Dda. Well after his time, in the early fourteenth century, they were still in use at Coedmor Petty Sessions.[67] It could well have been Rhys who applied Welsh law to Holy Trinity by extending to its lands the status of refuge. The argument remains open: we cannot draw a firm conclusion, but neither can one decide on the basis of Welsh names or Welsh legislation that Holy Trinity was Celtic.

There are other problems. Since Holy Trinity's carucate was nearby[68] we might identify it through its lands if only we could find them. But the Priory lands are complex. It had two carucates in Tremain, and another belonging to the church in *Y Ferwig* in which the Priory had a one third share. The difficulty in finding the Holy Trinity carucate is that the Priory estate passed through

a series of owners after the Reformation, two of whom – the Phillipses of Tregibby (later of Cardigan Priory) and the Pryses of Gogerddan – united their own possessions with it, thereby increasing its size from approximately 500 acres to 1700. I have so far failed to disentangle them, so the lands of Holy Trinity remain undiscovered.

Again, in the 1268 Extent (Longleat 624) 'the lands of Landou/Terra de Christchirche' were rented to fourteen men, all Welsh, for only four shillings (two shillings in 1299).[69] Since the going rate for rented land was four pence an acre,[70] the carucate[71] was plainly let out cheaply. Why did the money go to the king? It is unlikely that it had been exchanged for other land while retaining the name of the church,[72] for it was still acknowledged as church land in 1424 and 1428. The King must have taken it into care, and the only reason that makes sense is that it was in the wardship of the king while awaiting resolution of the long-lasting dispute over its ownership between St. Peter's Abbey, Gloucester, together with its Priory in Llanbadarn, and St. Peter's Abbey, Chertsey and its Priory in Cardigan.

How did the dispute come about? Whoever built Holy Trinity, the first colonists used it. When they were routed in 1136 only Cardigan Castle was left to them until 1158, when the de Clares retook the town and revitalised it, bringing in the Chertsey Benedictines who took over the pastoral care of Cardigan and built their own priory church. This was seen as infringing the rights of Llanbadarn and Gloucester, who instituted legal action to recover what they considered to be theirs, even to the extent that, towards the end of the fourteenth century, they created outrageous forgeries. Meanwhile, the king held the land.

Halfway through the fourteenth century Landou disappeared from his accounts, which would suggest that a settlement had been reached, were it not that the forgeries were devised nearly fifty years later. Were they a last-ditch attempt by Gloucester to revive a claim it had already effectively lost? Other explanations escape me.

No attempt to locate Holy Trinity has so far met with agreement. This is an attempt to state the case and arrive at a conclusion:

Holy Trinity is older than St. Mary's. Whether it was Celtic, and adopted as parish church by the Normans (if it pre-existed Cardigan, could it have been on the very site where they established the town?), or whether the Normans built it, we cannot say. It is not a chapel but a church – the two are in different categories. As it dates from at least 1110 we must find a later date for St. Mary's; by far the most likely is when the De Clares captured Cardigan in 1158.

The shrine legend confirms that Holy Trinity is the older church. It survives in Bishop William Barlow's report to Thomas Cromwell in 1538. Barlow recounts how Thomas Hore, the Prior, related to him that:

> . . . the Image now situate in the church of Cardigane whiche ys used for a greate pilgrimage to this present daye was founde standing apone the Ryver of Tyve beinge an arme of the see and her sonne apon her lappe and the saide taper bernynge in her hande . . . the same ymage was carried thens unto Christes Church of Cardigane and the sayd ymage wold not tarry there but was founde thre or fower tymes in the place where now is buylded the church of our Lady and the taper burnynge in her hande which continued styll burnynge the space of nyne yeres with out wastynge until the tyme that one foreswore hymselfe thereon. And then it extincted and never burned after.[73]

From this, certain facts emerge: St. Mary's was the church of Cardigan in Bishop Barlow's time (Holy Trinity no longer existed; it was not in the *Valor Ecclesiasticus* of 1536); Holy Trinity was earlier, for the legend implies that St. Mary's did not exist until the image in effect declined to be housed in "*Christes Church of Cardigane*", and that St. Mary's was built to accommodate it.[74] This means that Holy Trinity had once been the parish church, and at the very least suggests that it could have been in the town. Prescinding from its historicity, the purpose of the legend was to explain why St. Mary's was built in a place one would not expect to find a church and why this later church, because of its shrine, came to supersede Holy Trinity. The legend must therefore refer to the time before Rhys ap Gruffydd expelled the de Clares from Cardigan (whether the shrine actually dates from then is another question).

Holy Trinity was thus the parish church and had pastoral care of the parish before St. Mary's existed. Despite being awarded to the Priory it continued indefinitely as the parish church. The Priory became responsible for pastoral care not because of St. Mary's – being a monastic church it carried no implications as to its status in parish life – but in virtue of its possession of Holy Trinity. Once it had established the predominance

of its church and Shrine the Priory probably kept Holy Trinity alive until the dispute with St. Peter's, Gloucester had been resolved. One suspects that the Priory was interested in Holy Trinity less as a building than for its legal status as parish church. When the argument was won St. Mary's became parish church and Holy Trinity was allowed to fall into disuse.

Towns held their fairs on their church's feast. Trinity Fair[75] was observed in Cardigan long after Holy Trinity ceased to be the parish church; the final reference to it is, almost incredibly, as late as 1587.[76] On the score of Cardigan's patronal feast alone, and even without other evidence, we must place Holy Trinity at the very beginning of the town's history, antedating St. Mary's.[77]

I think Holy Trinity was within the town walls of Cardigan, where the Shire Hall now is and exactly where one would expect to find a church: by a crossing in the centre of town and next to the High Cross and market. So close is the conjunction between church and market in other places that markets tended to stray into churchyards, if only to ensure the honesty of traders, who would incur the sanction of sacrilege if they cheated on holy ground. When I suggested this to Terry, he said 'Why didn't we think of that before?' Support for the view is mounting.[78]

Cardigan's first Hall was the *aula competens*[79] in the Castle where the Justiciar presided over the Great Sessions every six months. They appear to have been held there in 1343. A grant of 1249 to the men of Cardigan allowed them to form a guild of merchants, as in Bristol, who would have needed a meeting place.[80] We do not know when they transferred from the Castle, though it was well before the present Shire Hall was newly erected in 1764 between the Market and Quay Street. It is a fair assumption that an earlier Shire Hall stood on the same spot as that of 1764. Eight pence was spent to clean the Sherehall in 1487;[81] Sherehall is mentioned in 1489,[82] Guilde haule in 1566[83] and Sheere Hall in 1652.[84] Vital to this theory that the Shire Hall occupied the same site as Holy Trinity is the fact that Holy Trinity and Shire Hall do not overlap; all references to Shire Hall come after Holy Trinity had vanished from the records save for its Fair. Could the guild of merchants (about whom we hear little) have claimed the derelict church and used its nave as their Hall? Speculation, perhaps, but it makes sense of what is otherwise a mystery.

Rhys' charter says Holy Trinity lands were adjacent to it; i.e. the church did not lie within them but was nearby, unlike St. Mary's two carucates, which were not adjacent as they were three miles away in Tremain. Yet Holy Trinity's lands may well have been near Cardigan, for when the Cardigan Commons were surveyed in 1855 almost all the broad swathe of land north-west of Cardigan, from the Teifi to the Commons and including the present Ysgol Gyfun Aberteifi with its extensive playing fields, belonged to the Priory Estate, then in the possession of the Miles family. If Holy Trinity occupied the site of the Shirehall, those lands would qualify as being adjacent to it. It seems probable that they included the Holy Trinity carucate. If so, they were ideally situated for, lying next to the port, they would have enabled an outlaw sheltering within them to escape the kingdom. But we cannot prove it as yet, for post-Reformation enlargement of the Priory Estate has muddied the waters. Nonetheless, on present knowledge a town location for Holy Trinity cannot be ruled out on the basis that its lands are not nearby.

Professor Griffiths argues that in the Ministers' Accounts the Holy Trinity lands are listed not under Cardigan but under the commote of Iscoed.[85] His point is valid but three factors mitigate its force. It can be argued that it is listed separately from the town precisely because the revenue was both temporary and extraordinary. In any event the Accounts are not the model of logic one might desire. Revenue in 1298-1300[86] is listed as follows: the vill of Cardigan, the land of Anian ap Wilym (miles outside), Landyen, the Netpool (just by the town), incoming burgesses at Felindre and Llanerchaeron (both many miles away), the lands of Hugh de Cressingham and of Nest, widow of Roger Mortimer (both in Llangoedmor), two mills in Cardigan, lands at the king's demesne at Gardeston (three miles out), at Warrentreehill (two miles out and assigned to the constable), Cardigan Island, Holy Trinity fair in the town, and petty tolls in Cardigan. Similar disorder can be found elsewhere.[87] Finally, since Holy Trinity is near its lands, placing those lands in the commote would remove it from the parish it was meant to serve and leave the churches of Llangoedmor (2 miles) and Ferwig (2.5 miles) equally convenient for the townspeople.

The debate as to whether Holy Trinity was within the town of Cardigan is still undecided, but I believe there now exists a strong presumption in its favour.

CARDIGAN'S ENVIRONS AND HINTERLAND

I can only give an outline of Cardigan's hinterland. It lay to the north and west, for Pembrokeshire was

immediately to the south and to the east the Knights Hospitallers owned the land as far as Llangoedmor. The Priory was allowed to make burgages on land allocated to it near St. Mary's but does not seem to have done so. Certain properties near the town are identifiable today.

PRIORY FIELD

When Edward I was in Cardigan on 22 Nov. 1284 he allowed Walter Gobach to give the monks a five-acre field 'called 'Croft atte Greteditch' in the suburbs of Cardigan . . . notwithstanding the statute of mortmain'.[88] The boundaries of Priory Field still exist: Pwllhai, Williams Row, William Street and Feidrfair. On the west it abutted the town ditch, as its name 'Greteditch' implies. The Pwllhai boundary is winding because it followed the edge of the muddy area in the triangle between Pwllhai, St. Mary Street and the town ditch. Priory Field met William Street at the point where the latter now bends, just west of Bethania Chapel, which lies within the field. Neither William Street nor Priory Street then existed.

PARC MATHEU

Between Feidrfair, Pontycleifion, the Knights Hospitallers' lands and Heol-y-Sarne (North Road) was a holding named Parc Matheu or Mathew,[89] including the present Penralltddu which backs on to the Hospitallers' land. It seems to have extended west as far as the main road. In the 1301 Extent John Matheu held three half-burgages in Chancery Lane (PRO SC 11/771). John Matheu (his son?) was reeve of Cardigan on 14.8.1344 (PRO E/163/4/34 m.2d).[90]

THE ROAD NORTH

The King's High Road left Bartholomew Gate, crossed the town ditch and headed towards Aberystwyth. Today it has two names: Pendre, and beyond it North Road, but it was then known as Heol y Sarnau.[91] The *sarn* was a stepped crossing over a rivulet in the common lands, about 700 yards north. The water now flows beneath the rugby field and is culverted where the *sarn* once was, just below the grounds of the modern Catholic Church. It joins a similar rivulet (also culverted) to flow through the Hospitallers' lands before joining the Teifi.[92]

KYNGESORCHARD

West of Priory Field was the two-acre enclosure of Kyngesorchard, later known as *Perllan y Barrett*.[93] Its northern boundary was the present William Street, with Williams Row to the east, the town ditch to the south and the main road to the west. In 1700 a substantial house named was built halfway along that road. It was named Pendre, and eventually gave its name to the street, displacing the older name of *Heol-y-Sarnau.*

MYSMEAD

Mysmead[94] is hard to place. Wmffre's suggestion[95] that it overlaps with Parc-y-Reiffl cannot be accepted because that would place Mysmead within the town's common lands, whereas it was a property like any other. My guess is that it lay near Mwldan Water on the right bank below Llyn-y-Felin. One hopes that, in seeking the origin of the name, the possibility of a connection with the Latin *messis*, or harvest, is not overlooked.

AFON MWLDAN AND ITS MILLS

The Mwldan stream rises in the King's Manor of Gerardston (see below) in Tremain parish and flows about four miles to join the Teifi two hundred metres below the town bridge of Cardigan. It played a vital role in Cardigan's mediaeval port and ancillary industries. As the name implies, it also accomodated Cardigan's most thriving mediaeval industry: woollen milling. Its correct title was Mwldan Brook or Mwldan Water, but today it is called The Mwldan from the Latin *molendinum* or mill. Dr Wmffre's suggestion that its older name was *Llynnan* is appealing, for the name *Mwldan* could not have pre-dated its industrial function.[96] In 1298-1300, the King rented out two woollen mills (Felinban and Town Mill) to Flemish colonists. The land near *Felinban* (the fulling mill) on the other side of Mwldan Brook is *Cnwc-y-Deintur,* the hill of the tenterhooks. A third mill is recorded in 1302-3 and 1340-5,[97] but where it was is not known unless it was upstream where we have New Mill today – a name first recorded in 1405. In recent times New Mill was a grist rather than a woollen mill, but (as Dr Gereint Jenkins informs me[98]) some mills had two sets of equipment, one for wool and the other for corn; if the fulling mill encountered lean times, the miller might switch to grist milling. Two new mills are referred to in the early fifteenth century.[99] Coming so soon after the wars of Owain Glyndŵr, one assumes that they may have replaced others that had been damaged or destroyed. By royal edict Welsh wool was not counted among the wools of England as it was too rough, but that made it ideal for tapestries; hence perhaps the heavy Flemish involvement in Cardigan's

mills. Arras, a noted centre for tapestry, was Flemish territory at the time. It may be relevant to the origin of the Taper Shrine in St Mary's, Cardigan, that in Arras there was a devotion connected with a taper, deriving from a story that the Blessed Virgin Mary appeared to a bishop there and gave him a candle.

THE COMMON LANDS

Cardigan's common lands began at a triangle that once contained pools to water the cattle, where the cenotaph and the town gardens are today. They then expanded laterally on both sides of the Aberystwyth road, though mostly to the west, where they stopped short of *Cnwc-y Deintur* (the hill of the tenterhooks) that led to *Felinban* (the fulling mill) on the river Mwldan. They ended a mile and a quarter to the north at a ridge, now four hundred and seventy feet above sea level, formed by debris accumulated along the margin of ice in the Ice Ages. The commons were known in Welsh both as *Rhos-y-Saison*[100] and *Parc y Dre*. Early editions of OS maps record an 'entrenchment', possibly Iron Age, named as Crug Llwyn-Llwyd (DAT HER site 5215) in the west-ward dune, now lost to sand extraction. Its mediaeval name, *Cnwc y Saeson*, indicated that it marked the outer limit of the common lands of an English colony.

CRUG MAWR/BANC Y WARREN

The dune to the north-east of the commons has two names, both of them still in use. The original name, Crug Mawr, is also the name of the nearby farm. The Constable of Cardigan Castle owned Crug Mawr Farm along with its neighbour, the evocatively-named *Cwrt*, which may have been his ordinary residence. Crug Mawr became the gallows hill. Its Anglo-Saxon title, Warren Tree Hill,[101] has become *Banc y Warren*, and is today used more commonly than Crug Mawr. Among those who died there was Hugh David Coch, Vicar of Llanarth, who was hanged, drawn and quartered in 1593 when he fell foul of the Elizabethan religious and political establishment.[102]

The main road once went to the east of Crug Mawr through the Constable's farm (doubtless allowing him to keep an eye on traffic). So Giraldus Cambrensis tells us in describing his journey with Archbishop Baldwin from Cardigan to Lampeter in 1188: they left 'Crug Mawr, that is, the big hill, on our left soon after riding out of Cardigan'.[103] Today's road is a stiff ascent to the west of Crug Mawr that might have proved too much for mediaeval ox-carts. A further indication of the change of route is that north of Crug Mawr the road from the King's Manor in Trefere takes a straight line to the east of the hill (a line now obscured by the modern style of engineering road junctions). Beyond Crug Mawr the original and the newer road rejoin at the junction leading to Trefere.

Crug Mawr must have been a key element in the battle of Penparc when the Welsh destroyed Norman power in 1136. Sometimes, when seen on a late summer evening, in the kind of light that seems to accentuate its outline, I wonder whether the slight imperfection in its symmetry may not indicate concentric defensive rings hastily thrown up for that battle and now almost eroded by the passage of time.

Tremain

North of the commons is Llangoedmor parish, which was once a broad stretch to the coast from Llangoedmor to Mwnt until the Normans carved a rough circle from it to form the parish of Tremain, including the King's Manor and the Benedictine lands, leaving only a narrow strip to connect Llangoedmor with Mwnt. In that strip lies the hamlet of Penparc, so named because of its proximity to *Parc y Dre*.

Gerardston/Trefere

The Lord (later the King) held a demesne of two and a half carucates in Tremain. Nominally three hundred acres, they actually amount to four hundred and fifty (possibly including former waste land). Its name was Gerardston. Trefere is simply its Welsh form (Gerardston >Treferedd >Trefere). It became King's land when he appropriated Cardigan. References to it are innumerable.[104] PRO SC 11/771, under the heading *Particule de Ville de Cardygan*, records 44s 2d as rental for 132.5 acres in 1300-1301 and 29s 4d for pasture which, since it fetched less, may have approximated to the same acreage. Trefere was divided into four in the eighteenth century: Trefere Uchaf (possibly the original house: 221498) was on a rise facing south with Trefere Bella to its east, Trefere Fawr to its south and Trefere Fach (later absorbed into Trefere Fawr) nearby to its southwest. Trefere Fach had a cottage named, evocatively, Pentref, at the lowest point of Gerardston where one might expect workmen to have their abodes. The 1976 Cambridge Aerial Survey disclosed crop marks around Pentref that indicated a long-disappeared hamlet. The names of nearby farms, *Llain* and *Llain y Bettel*, suggest

strips worked by men on the estate. In 1517 a list of parishes from which a tenth was collected does not mention St. Michael's, Tremain but includes Trefereu.[105] Was this a simple error or does it suggest a chapel of ease in the hamlet?

The Priory lands in Tremain

Rhys ap Gruffydd's charter confirmed two carucates of land to the Priory of St. Mary in Cardigan[106] '. . . *que jacent ab aquilonari parte vie que ducit versus Bleynporth a Catlavas usque ad vadum Arturi . . .*'; i.e. to the north of the road leading towards Blaenporth from Canllefaes to Arthur's Ford. Difficulties with place names are endemic, and easily understood in the context of an English or Norman scribe taking down a Welsh name that is probably mispronounced by the speaker. Canllefaes Uchaf begins where a spring of water rising by the main road runs west towards *Afon Mwldan*. The name Arthur's Ford is an instance of the mediaeval tendency to find traces of Arthur everywhere. The correct name is Arberth, a stream that begins behind Trefere Bella and flows south towards the Teifi east of Llechryd. The name *(perth)* probably refers to a boundary hedge between Gerardston and the Priory lands. Between those two rivulets were the monks' two carucates, which today comprises three farms: Canllefaes Uchaf, Treprior and Ffynnonwen. Just before one arrives at the two demesnes there is a farm with the indicative title of Vagwr (*Y Fagwyr*: wall, enclosure).

Parc y Marles

Parc y Marles, now called Argoed (188466), would have fitted so snugly into the south-eastern corner of the town's common lands that its exclusion seems deliberate. It was first recorded as *Le Malros*,[107] explained by Iwan Wmffre on the analogy of Marloes in Pembrokeshire, which B. G. Charles traced to Malros, meaning 'hill-spur'. Wmffre thus sees it as referring to 'the long spur' from Banc y Warren to Cardigan. The transposition of consonants from Malros to Marles would be an instance of a well-known phenomenon (also known in biblical analysis) whereby the more difficult version of a word is seen as earlier than the simpler one on the ground that with the passage of time people would tend to simplify it.

The reason that the hypothesis, which seems to make sense, does not convince, is twofold: the hill-spur does not exist and there is only a gently undulating slope of which Parc y Marles is an indistinguishable element. More importantly, an alternative derivation came to light twenty years ago when two passages in the late 13th century Ministers' Accounts (n. 29, p. 297), brought me up short:

> *From Adam le Mouner holding certain land, called Le Malros, of my Lord the Prince in farm for so much money a year, at my Lord's pleasure; for that farm for the present year: 12d proved.*

> *From Adam Le Muner and David Hickeman holding three mills of my Lord the Prince's near Cardigan in fee farm . . . for that farm for the present year: £6.13s 4d proved.*

Adam le Mouner (Adam Molendinarius) means Adam the Miller. He rented the King's woollen mills on *Afon Mwldan* to the west of the common lands. Why should he also rent land some distance away that lacked either mills or water? Could he have needed marl? If so, for what? Could it by any chance bleach wool? Dr. Geraint Jenkins, author of two books on milling, advised me to consult the Soil Survey at Trawscoed. They said Parc y Marles did indeed contain marl, for it had been the bed of the Teifi before the last Ice Age. They had never heard of marl as a bleaching agent but promised to look into it. They rang in amazement some days later to say they had found that marl would indeed bleach wool.

It seems that my query had brought to light an industrial usage that had been forgotten for ages. Given that, I think that a derivation from the known use of Parc y Marles is preferable to Iwan Wmffre's otherwise attractive hypothesis.

TRECIFFT

This farm is east of Parc y Marles (194465). Dr Wmffre says: 'The surname, which is likely to have been English) is not otherwise known.' It is in fact Flemish, and its modern form is *Kieft*.[108] A man of that name told me it may originally have been *Kievet*, meaning plover. Walter Kyft held half a burgage in 1268 (Longleat 624), Roger Kift[109] had one and a half burgages in Chancery Lane in 1301 (SC 11/771) and John Kyft the Elder is mentioned on 9 September 1394 (CPR). Terry James suggested that the Cardigan Kifts may be related to Kifts in Carmarthen, an important burgess family in the later 13th century.[110]

OTHER LAND HOLDINGS

Among the lands omitted from the above brief sketch are those of the Welsh freeholders. Most notable among them are the three carucates Gwilym ap Gwrwared[111] and his son Eynon ap Wilym held in *Y Ferwig*,[112] including Towyn Farm, Gwbert (164510), where Lewis Glyn Cothi would later stay; and Ffrwdwenith (233514), west of Aberporth. Dafydd ap Gwilym would be born of a branch of this family.

ACKNOWLEDGEMENTS

I hope this brief outline of one aspect of Cardigan's complex history will help clarify issues for future study, if only by provoking disagreement, for thereby lies progress. My thanks are due to those who have helped and advised me, most of all Terry James.

NOTES

1. Professor Ralph Griffiths suggests its Welsh name originated (perhaps when Rhys ap Gruffydd controlled Cardigan [1165-1197]) as the rise of the Arthurian legend led people's fancies to localise the names of certain characters such as Geraint. R. A. Griffiths, 'The Making of Medieval Cardigan', *Ceredigion*, Vol. XI, 1990, pp. 98, 106.

2. W. J. Lewis, *The Gateway to Wales* (Dyfed Cultural Services, 1990), favours 1110. Emily Pritchard's claim that St. Mathaiarn founded a church there in the fifth century is worthless. E. Pritchard, *Cardigan Priory in the Olden Days* (Heinemann, 1904), pp. 1-3. Legend locates Mathaiarn in Ceredigion, not Cardigan. There is no evidence of a pre-Norman settlement or church on the site of the town.

3. D. J. C. King, 'The Castles of Cardiganshire', *Ceredigion*, Vol. III, 1956; see also unpublished reports on recent excavations and recording in Dyfed Archaeological Trust's Historic Environment Record (HER).

4. Orally to the author in 1979.

5. T. James, Excavations at Woolworth's Cardigan 1978', *Ceredigion*, Vol. V, 1983, pp. 337-343.

6. S. Meyrick, *The History and Antiquities of the County of Cardigan* (Brecon, 1907), p. 19.

7. PRO B. 3/4349. Lands of Dissolved Religious Houses: 5287. 27-28 Henry VIII. Its remains had vanished by July 1802 and in 1885 the engine house of Cardigan railway station covered the site, see Griffiths, op. cit., n. 1, p. 132 n. 96.

8. Sir Richard Colt Hoare looked in vain for the chapel, presumably because he searched south of the existing bridge, not up river opposite Gloster Row. M. W. Thompson (ed.), *The Journeys of Sir Richard Colt Hoare through England and Wales, 1793-1810* (Alan Sutton, 1983), p. 227. D. W. Lloyd told the author that when he was young his family employed a workman who once lived on the knoll and was known as Twm Shidan. The field was known as Parc y Capel.

9. On 25 January 1983.

10. PRO SC6/1161/6 M.6, 1432-4: R. A. Griffiths, *The Principality of Wales in the Later Middle Ages* (UWP, 1972), p. 429.

11. Speed's map of 1610 (my Fig. 4) shows a bridge at this point. The flow is now culverted; see E. R. Horsfall-Turner, B.A., *Walks and Wanderings in County Cardigan* (Bingley, Yorks., Thomas Harrison and Sons), p. 173.

12. The mediaeval chronicler, Florence of Worcester, whose narrative is so colourful as to evoke doubt as to its objectivity, relates that: 'When the bridge over the river Tivy was broken down it was a wretched spectacle to see crowds passing to and fro across a bridge formed by the horrible mass of human corpses and horses drowned in the river'.

13. When the footbridge was being built in 1975 a 55' length of wood, 11" square, was found at the bottom of the Teifi. It had three joints placed symmetrically, the central joint being a right angle and the others acute angles, suggesting that they emerged from a common base to support a long beam. Over the years my efforts to have it preserved failed, and it was cut into sections, three of which remain. It plainly precedes the stone bridge. The latter existed in 1638 and may date from 1604. Nigel Nayling, M.A., a dendrochronological specialist at University of Wales, Lampeter, told me (conversation 26 July 2008) that because the wood is elm it is not susceptible to dating.

14. The stream, by Siop Penbont, is now culverted, but in 1996 its arched bridge came to light during road works. It seemed to be an eighteenth-century rebuild.

15. PRO SC 11/771: The Extent of 1268 (Longleat 624) shows St. Mary Street was flourishing by then. Its prominence is due less to its proximity to St. Mary's, which pre-dates, than to its connection with the original bridge by Gloster Row.

16. H. Carter, *The Towns of Wales* (UWP, 1965), p. 190.

17. CRO, Coedmor Collection D/LL. 1/172, 1507.

18. CRO, Colby 69, 1666. One wonders where it could have been. The only building that suggests itself is Maudlyns Hospital, the former property of the Knights Hospitallers.

19. The 1268 Extent (Longleat 624) was made when Prince Edward transferred his lands to Edmund before going on Crusade.

20. The 1301 Extent (PRO SC 11/771) was made when Edward I transferred the same lands, which he had previously recovered, to his son Edward, Prince of Wales. I. J. Sanders' edition in 'The Boroughs of Aberystwyth and Cardigan in the early fourteenth century', *BBCS*, Vol. XV, 1954, pp. 282-293 is useful, despite several errors; e.g. he exaggerates the size of the town to include Pendre and misplaces New Gate; see also n. 27.

21. The Knights' Commandery was at Slebech in Pembrokeshire. The 1268 Extent records that Henricus Slebech owned half a burgage in the street.

22. The NLW Kyle documents establish this. Kyle 11 (1571/2, l.4) has in vico ibidem appellato Our Lady Street et ibidem manifeste agnotum de tenura Sancti Johannis. Kyle 34 (4 Nov. 1652) refers to a Burgage . . . call St. John's Hould in St. Mary's Street. A lease dated 8 April 1823 refers to the Angel Inn . . . formerly . . . known by the name of Saint John's hold.

23. Pending a full treatment of the shrine, 'Our Lady of Cardigan' (*Welsh Saints and Shrines*, No. 2, 1954) by the Reverend Silas M. Harris is recommended. It may be accessed on cardigantaper.org.

24. E. A. Lewis & J. Conway Davies (eds.), *Records of the Court of Augmentations relating to Wales and Mon-*

mouthshire (UWP, 1954), Cardigan 6/9/13, p. 227. The name explains the road name by St. Mary's Church: Pontycleifion (Bridge of the Sick). A rivulet from the Hospitallers' land towards the Teifi, now culverted beneath the road, was presumably once bridged; hence the name.

25. Honour in place of honor; blue instead of blew.

26. There is no record of buildings in Castle Yard until the seventeenth century.

27. Sanders, op. cit., n. 20. Halfway down the manuscript list there is a tiny dot that at first sight seems accidental. Below it are burgages from Wolf Gate to Bartholomew gate (*see Fig. 5*). It is not certain whether the order of burgages on the other side of the street is in the same or the reverse direction, though the latter seems more probable. Something like that apparently accidental dot (or an equivalent such as a gap) is found on other streets elsewhere. The burgesses' names provide fascinating clues as to their origin or occupation, but that has no place in a study of topography.

28. Cfr. n. 64 below.

29. Myvanwy Rhys (ed.), *Ministers' Accounts for West Wales 1277 to 1306, Part I* (Cymmrodorion, 1936), pp. 131, 217.

30. idem, p. 125.

31. CPR 23 May 1280.

32. Sanders, op. cit., n. 20.

33. The King Street sign was removed and until recently lay in the Council yard by the Mwldan in Cardigan. Where it now is I do not know.

34. Sanders, op. cit., n.19.

35. I. Wmmfre, *The Place-Names of Cardiganshire*, 3 vols. BAR British Series 379(I) (Archaeopress, 2004). The encyclopaedic range and depth of this magnum opus is such that one cannot envisage a future history of Ceredigion that does not rely upon it. But see 'Pont Aberteifi', Vol. 1, p. 17.

36. S. Wardle, T. Jameson & M. Locock, 'Excavation at Green Villas 2003', unpublished excavation report in Dyfed Archaeological Trust's Historic Environment Record (HER), prn. 49, 166.

37. Vicus can mean either a street or a quarter/district of a town. In this instance it bears the latter sense, as the Cross was not directly at the top of Quay Street.

38. J. F. Lydon, 'Three Exchequer Documents from the Reign of Henry III', *Proceedings of the Royal Irish Academy*, Vol. 65, Section C, No. 1, 1966, pp. 15-17: 'Cardigan castle occupied a key position . . . in . . . 1257 . . . arrangements seem to have been made for carrying another £440 of Irish treasure to Wales . . . to Cardigan . . . A troop of 400 went (from Ireland) to Cardigan . . . perhaps the most unusual cargo of all was cloth which was seized in Drogheda to be sent to Cardigan for one thousand satellites there'. I believe Cardigan exported wool to Flanders until the Carmarthen staple was set up in 1326. It also had a thriving fishing industry. Crafts such as boat-building and sail-

making would have flourished; in 1414 a keel for the king's barge was laid in Cardigan harbour (for coastal defence).

39. Valuable notes on censers/chensars are to be found in Rhys, op. cit., n. 29, p. 239, distinguishing them from burgesses 'de vento et de vico'.

40. Fulfilment of the monastic offices requires at least six monks.

41. See Rhys, op. cit., n. 29: Landyen (p. 81), Landu (p. 97), Landeu (p. 203), Landou (pp. 303, 369); also Landew PRO Ministers' Accounts [General Series] Bundle 1158, No. 3, de Southwallia); Landw (*Arch. Camb.*, 1877, Vol. 1, p. clxxiii); 'ecclesiam sancteTrinitatis que dicitur Landov cum una carucate terre adjacente que est refugium ecclesie' (CPR, Nov. 22, 1424 and Nov. 19, 1428); Christes Church of Cardigane (Harris, op. cit., n. 23); and terram de Christchirche (1268 Extent, Longleat 624).

42. Op. cit., n. 23.

43. Griffiths, op. cit., n.1, p. 104.

44. Griffiths, by e-mail, 12 Oct. 2007.

45. Griffiths, op. cit., n. 1.

46. G. Morgan, *Ceredigion* (Gwasg Gomer, 2005), p. 224.

47. Even the redoubtable Dom David Knowles relied upon Emily Pritchard without cross-checking her sources. D. Knowles & C. N. L. Brooke, *Heads of Religious Houses England and Wales 940-1216* (Cambridge UP, 1972), p. 86.

48. R. H. Malden, 'The Possession of Cardigan Priory by Chertsey Abbey', *Trans. of the Royal Historical Society*, 3rd ser., Vol. V, 1911, pp. 141-156.

49. Pritchard, op. cit., n. 2, pp. 7-17 and 18-26.

50. Op. cit., p. 17.

51. Her letter (*Archaeologica Cambrensis*, 1906, p. 74) was in answer to a critical review of her book.

52. Even Silas M. Harris (op. cit., n. 23) follows Emily Pritchard's opinion that it existed.

53. *The Welsh Gazette*, 15 May 1924, tells of the well and how the Trawscoed family abolished the fair.

54. Harris, op. cit., n. 23.

55. *Capel*, Vol. 1, p. 3. I. Wmmfre, op. cit., n. 35.

56. Rhys, op. cit., n. 29: 8s. 9d. 1298-1300 (p. 83); 3s. 3d. 1298-1300 (p. 99); 7d. 1304-1305 (p. 367).

57. A graphic indication of the lower status of Capel is implied in R. E. Latham's *Revised Medieval Latin Word-List* (OUP, 1965), p. 68, where an alternative meaning of capella is 'portable equipment of chapel', implying that its furnishing was of a lesser order. The term 'chapel' was also given to oratories whether open to the public or not. In Ireland the meaning of 'chapel' changed after the persecutions following the Reformation. Catholics, dispossessed of their churches by state power, were forced to worship in secret, often in the open air. When persecution slackened and they could begin to build once more, such was the bigotry of the Ascendancy that it proved wise to keep their heads down by referring to their new churches

as chapels. In Carlow the back street where they were eventually allowed to build is still called Chapel Street even though it has long held a cathedral.

58. An old mile is an approximate figure, generally about one third longer than the statute measurement. From Capel-bach the pilgrim could reach Cardigan by different routes. Today we go by New Mill Road towards the Aberystwyth Road and then into town, but then he could follow Afon Mwldan past Felinban almost to Town Mill before branching left on Feidr Fair.

59. In spiritual terms two journeys from Ynys Enlli to Tyddewi were considered equal to a pilgrimage to Rome, and three such journeys were the equivalent of one to Jerusalem. Not that they were, in terms of distance.

60. *Letters and Papers*, 29 Henry VIII, f. 118: 'the image now situate in the church of Cardigane, whiche ys used for a great pilgrimage to this present daye'.

61. *Papal Letters*, Vol. 19, 1503-1513, Julius II, Lateran Registers, Part Two, 12 Sep. 1512 (Dublin, Irish Manuscripts Commission, 1998): 'to all the faithful of either sex . . . for all future time'.

62. There are many post-Reformation references to the chantry lands, in phrases such as 'Tir y Channtry', 'Land lately belonging to chantry John ap Ieuan', or 'Lands granted to maintain priest or cantor to Mass of St. Mary in the parish church'; Also NLW Kyle 1, l.4, 03.(1537), 'Burgagium cantuariae ecclesie Ste Marie'; Kyle 3, (1548,) l.7; Kyle 24, (1583)' a burgage late of Our Ladies lands'; PRO 310/34/206, 25.06.1567 and 26.06.1587; CRO: Coedmor 123, 21. 10.1620 and 145, 25.10.1620. There were 12 statute acres of chantry land in Cardigan parish and nine Welsh acres in Llangoedmor.

63. Harris, op. cit., n. 23.

64. In the 1847 Tithe Map Capel-bach was a house. Today its walls stand about two feet high. As yet we do not know whether it is the mediaeval building or a replacement, though it seems to be orientated. Could Cardigan's north gate have been named Bartholomew Gate because of the dedication of Capel-bach?

65. P. O. Ríain, 'The Saints of Cardiganshire', *Cardiganshire County History* (UWP, 1994) states (p. 392) that such dedications, which are rare in Wales and Ireland, probably mostly post-date the arrival of the Normans.

66. Griffiths, op. cit., n. 1.

67. PRO SC2 217/17: 29 Ed. 1: m.3, section 7. 'Comitatus de Kardigan tentatus die Martis in festo Apostolorum Philippi et Jacobi anno regni regis Edwardi xxx' (2 May 1301); 'XIId de Morithit Du quia iudicatus fuit in camlour. Plegium Kedivor ap Lewelyn'. The 1268 Extent (Longleat 624) refers to the pleas and perquisites of the Welshry of Cardigan, which comprises one third of the commote. As late as 11 Oct. 1484 Richard Mynours is appointed steward of the king's commotes called 'Walshe Courtis' in Cardigan and Cantremawre (CPR). For my information on Rhys and his expansion of the Laws of

Hywel Dda I am indebted to a conversation with Professor Emeritus Dafydd Jenkins of UCW Aberystwyth. Land was still measured in Welsh acres in Llangoedmor in the 17th century; see references to the chantry lands in n. 58 above.

68. Charter of Rhys ap Gruffydd: CPR 22 November 1424 and 19 November 1428 'Sciatis me . . . dedisse . . . ecclesiam Sancte Trinitatis, que dicitur Landov, cum una carucate terre adjacente'.

69. Rhys, op.cit., n. 29, p. 81.

70. PRO SC11/771: rental of Gerardeston etc. (1301).

71. A carucate, or a season's ploughing, can vary from 60, 90, 100 or 120 (the large hundred) acres. In Tremain the two and a half carucates belonging to the king and the two belonging to the Benedictines measure 180 acres per carucate. Whether that is due to subsequent reclamation of waste land or to a different measurement of acre I do not know.

72. Such an exchange may have taken place in another instance: that of the Knights Hospitallers. One cannot be certain, as the relevant document, NLW No. 11477 of the Slebech Collection (1308) is a rewritten compilation of earlier records. It suggests that before the Knights were given their burgages in Cardigan with a carucate they held '"in the land of Kardigan a church que dicitur de villa Gerbaund et Alfwynne" in the time of King Henry'. My guess is that they lost the land they first held after the battle of 1136, and in 1160 were given the Cardigan properties as compensation. I think the original property lay near St. Michael's, Tremain (the church in question), and was probably Ffynnonwen Farm; but this was later awarded to Cardigan Priory. The late Mr. A. D. Lewis, who was born close by, told me that local people always pronounced Ffynnonwen as Ffynnonowen, i.e. St. John's Well. Such evidence as we have is scarcely coercive, but it needs to be recorded in case something transpires in the future.

73. British Library, Cotton Ms., Cleopatra E. IV., Folio 118.

74. British Library Cotton MS., Cleopatra E. iv., ff. 141, 143. It is quoted in Pritchard and Harris, nn. 2 and 23 above.

75. The 1268 Extent (Longleat 624) records two fairs, each of three days, one at the Feast of Holy Trinity and the other at that of Saints Simon and Jude (28 October). The latter is not mentioned in the rentals, implying that only Trinity Fair was observed.

76. NLW. Noyadd Trefawr Collection, No. 419, *Y Llyfr Plygain, 1612* (republished 1931 by Gwasg Prifysgol Cymru) shows that five fairs, all of them on feasts of the Blessed Virgin Mary, had at long last superseded Trinity Fair.

77. This brings up an intriguing speculation. The legend attending Our Lady of Cardigan may perhaps be an attempt to explain why one church in effect usurped the status of another that preceded it.

78. T. Lloyd, J. Orbach and R Scourfield, *The Buildings of Wales: Carmarthenshire and Ceredigion* (Yale University Press, 2006), p. 445.

79. PRO C145/33/31 4 Ed I.

80. CPR 26 Oct. 1249.

81. 'Pro mundacione domus de la Sherehall'. Longleat 594: 1-2 H VII.

82. PRO SC6/H VII/1622: 3-4 H VII.

83. NLW Kyle 8, 14.12.1566. The new Shire Hall continued to be called the Guildhall: on 1 October 1776 the minute book of Cardigan Borough, 1653-1838, refers (p. 269) to ringing the Guildhall bell to summon the Burgesses to a meeting. A later minute (p. 361) indicates that this was the custom.

84. NLW Kyle 34, 4.11.1652, also 'apud Aulam villae de Cardigan', NLW Kyle 51.

85. Griffiths, op. cit., n. 1, p. 126.

86. Rhys, op. cit., n. 29, p. 81.

87. Rhys, op.cit., n. 29, pp. 97, 203 and 297-303.

88. Cal. Welsh Rolls 22 Nov. 1284. Mortmain forbade the transfer of land to an ecclesiastical body without the lord's permission.

89. NLW Gogerddan Old Schedule 1 Nov 1709, Parc Matthew Issa, Tyllwyd p. 45; Tyllwyd 167/168/169/84, all between 1713 and 1714; Ceredigion Muniment room, Packet 364, 11 Apr 1938, and Deeds 1909.

90. Griffiths, op. cit, n. 1, p.419

91. A sarn was a causeway or stepping stones. The earliest reference to Pendre as a street name seems to be the following note: Paid towards making Pendre Street from the gaol to the Turnpike in the year 1788: £13.12.10 (NLW: St. David's Collection: Cardigan, No. 132. For Heol-y-Sarne, cfr. NLW Kyle 16, 7 Feb 1576/7; Heol y Sarn, Kyle 24, 8 Oct. 1583; NLW Noyadd Trefawr 173, 8 Mar. 1574 and 225, 24 Jul. 1581; and many from NLW Tyllwyd: 11, 53, 58, 59, 61 (where it is called King Street), 62, 64, 76, 77, 81, 86 and 183, between 1 May 1625 and 10 Feb. 1783.

92. n. 24 supra.

93. 'Kyngesorchard' PRO SC 6 1159/2 and 1159/3 (1387-88); SC 6 1622 (1487-88); Longleat 594, 1485-86; 'King's Orchard'; NLW Cwrt Mawr 30.11.11619 & 11.10.1633.; 'Pellen y Bared' NLW Kyle 11 27.1. 1571/2; 'Perllan y Barret' NLW Kyle 20 3.3.1581; see also NLW Tyllwyd 614 1(1697); 64, (1700) 183, (1716); also nos. 289, 81, 11 and 86. Some assume the property belonged to a person called Barrett; the name is probably from 'pared' (L. paries), a wall, partition or boundary, as in Trebared farm to the west.

94. NLW Morgan Richardson 1673 (1763); CRO Colby 72, (1715); Colby 71 (1726/7): Ceredigion Deeds, packets

352 and 355. For Washmeade and Middlemeade see CRO Coedmor 120 (1599).

95. Wmffre, op. cit., n. 35, Vol. I, p.15.

96. Wmffre, op. cit., n. 35, Vol. I, p. 6.

97. Rhys, op. cit., n. 29, pp. 83, 297 and 365.

98. Pers. comm. 11 Dec. 2007.

99. PRO, SC/1222/12 H IV, 1410 and 1411.

100. Ceredigion: Cardigan Minute Book 1653.

101. It was doubtless convenient that Gallows Hill was on the Constable's lands where he could observe it. The name appears in many documents in various forms, e.g. 'Watrehul', 'Waryntrehulle', 'Warentrehulle', Rhys, op. cit., n. 29, pp. 83, 299, 365; 'Warantrehulle', PRO SC6/1218/6, m.6, 1307-14; 'Waretrehulle', PRO LR12/43 22 Ed III; 'Waretrehull', PRO SC6 1159/2, 'Wartrehull,' *Arch. Camb. Supplement*, Vol. 1, 1877, p. clxxiii; 'Water Hill', CRO Coedmor 144 (1596); NLW Cwrt Mawr 207 (1633), 'lands called Water Hill', NLW, Cwrt Mawr, p. 125 (1633).

102. S. Cunnane, 'Ceredigion and the Old Faith', *Ceredigion*, Vol. XII, No. 2, 1994.

103. L. Thorpe (ed. & trans.), *Gerald of Wales: The Journey through Wales* (Penguin, 1978), p. 177.

104. As always, spelling varies: 'Gerardston', 'Gerardeston', 'Gerardiston', 'Girardestone', 'Gardestone', Rhys, op. cit., n. 28, pp. 83, 97, 203, 297, 299 and 365: CPR 1328, p. 204. Cal. Welsh Rolls, 1278, p. 166: NLW Bronwydd 2898, p. 377, 13.10.1641, Bron. 2861, p. 420, 15.6.1666, Tyllwyd 302 23-25.5.1633, Tyllwyd 78, 26.2.1702; also Tyllwyd 9, 11, 79, 80, 85, 89, 92, 305. Its Welsh form first appears in the 14th century as Trevereth, then Treveredd and eventually Trefere.

105. R. F. Isaacson (ed. & trans.), *The Episcopal Registers of the Diocese of St. David's 1397-1518*, Vol. II (1407-1518), p. 826.

106. CPR 19.11.1428; also CPR 22.11.1424.

107. Also: Le Malros: Rhys, op. cit., n. 29, p. 365; Terra de malros: PRO SC6/1218/84; Park y Marlys: NLW Bronwydd 7117 (1718), p. 506; Marls Field: Borough Council Minutes 1880: CDM/2/27 and 31.

108. Wmffre, op. cit, n. 35, p. 12. Some 20 years ago a footballer named Kieft played for Holland.

109. Not Kist as in Sanders (n. 20).

110. T. James, 'Medieval Carmarthen and its Burgesses', *Carms. Antiq.*, Vol. XXV, 1989, p. 20.

111. CPR 1252, P.126.

112. 1268 Extent (Longleat 624): Eynon et Gunewaret heredes Willelmi Gunewaret tenent iii carucates terre apud Berewye et reddunt per annum V sol . . .

Place-names in Early Printed Maps
of Carmarthenshire

D. Huw Owen

Terry James's extensive knowledge of place-name studies and cartography was amply displayed in his numerous activities and publications covering a wide chronological span. A most significant contribution to the Carmarthenshire Place-name Survey involved setting up a database for entering and interrogating the information collected for the Survey.[1] Studies, such as those of the changing Carmarthenshire coastline,[2] and, with Heather James, of fish weirs on the Taf, Towy and Gwendraeth estuaries,[3] were based on a number of documentary and cartographic sources. In the latter, local place-names were skilfully used to locate lost local fish weirs. The former was accompanied by the reproduction of extracts of several maps, plans and charts, including Christopher Saxton's depiction of the Carmarthenshire coastline, 1575-6. Terry was very interested in my work as Keeper of Pictures and Maps at the National Library of Wales, and we had frequent discussions concerning acquisitions, especially at the time of the Library's purchase in 1986 at a Sotheby's auction of Christopher Saxton's map of Wales, c.1580.[4] Saxton, and two other major figures in the history of cartography, Humphrey Llwyd and John Speed, were responsible for early printed maps of Carmarthenshire and Wales. An examination of data contained in their maps, especially those relating to the specific places named by them, and the actual form of place-names, together with a consideration of contemporary observations by visitors to the area, Welsh poets, and genealogists, would seem to be a most appropriate subject for this memorial volume.

Sir Edward Don's account of his visit to mid and south Wales from his home in Horsenden, Bucking-hamshire in 1524, recorded in his book of household accounts and related material (1510-1551), represents 'a travel journal [which] provides us indirectly with rare insights into the Wales of the 1520s'.[5] Sir Edward was the owner of property in the lordship of Kidwelly, including the house at Penallt approximately a mile west of the town. A circuitous route for the journey was taken with the party travelling from Horsenden to Pembrokeshire via Newcastle Emlyn, and then to Carmarthen, after calling at Carew Castle to see Sir Edward's kinsman, Sir Rhys ap Thomas, the most powerful figure in south Wales during the reigns of Henry VII and Henry VIII.[6] They stayed for a fortnight at Carmarthen, named as 'Carmardyn', 'Carmarthyn', 'Carmarddyn', 'Carmardeyn', 'Kermerdyn' or 'Kermarddyn', and then, for three weeks, at or near 'Kydwelly', where he received rents from his estates at 'Kydwelly' and 'Pennalte/Penalth' [Penallt]. Whilst at Kidwelly, beer and wine were brought there, possibly by ferry from 'Lanstaffen', and documents were prepared in relation to Sir Edward's dispute with the abbot of 'Whytlande/Whyghtlande'. On the return journey, the party called at 'Newton', the ancestral home of Sir Rhys ap Thomas, and 'Langedoc' [Llangadog], the small market town under the patronage of the Bishop of St. David's.[7]

Whilst Sir Edward's visit to Carmarthenshire in 1524 was of a personal nature, John Leland's travels in the area, forming part of his extensive tour of England and Wales, were in an official capacity following his appointment as 'King's Antiquary' in 1533, with instructions to search monastic libraries for antiquities and records. Notes were compiled during his visit to Carmarthenshire in 1536-9, a crucial period which witnessed the dissolution of the monasteries (1536-40) and the Acts of Union between England and Wales (1536-43). The union legislation established an uniform administrative framework for the thirteen Welsh shires, which were represented on the county maps of Christopher Saxton and John Speed. Leland identified twelve commotes in three cantrefi, two of which were named as 'Cantref Vaur' and 'Cantref Bachan', in 'Estratewy'. One market was identified, at 'Cairmardine', and nine castles: 'Cairmardine', 'New Castel', 'Clare Castel', 'Llanstufan', 'Lacharne', 'Lanamdeueri', 'Dineuer', 'Dryslin/Drisloyn' (corrected to' Drislluen'), and 'Kerikennen'. The latter seems to have caused some confusion as Leland, having referred to Carreg Cennen in the list of castles as being three miles from Dinefwr 'at the roote of Blake Montaine', then states that the commote of Iscennen, in which Carreg Cennen was located, 'hath no notable castel or goodly building or toune'. Kidwelly does not appear on this list, but his observations on the town includes the comment that the old town is 'nere al desolated, but the castel is meately wel kept up'. Variant forms for 'Lananeri' and 'Llanameveri' [Llandovery], 'Landistufan' and Talacharne are also presented, and other places mentioned include 'Llanethle' and 'Penbre', and the commotes of 'Eskenninge' [Iscennen], and 'Carnobthlon' [Carnwyllion]. The list of abbeys and priories comprises 'Carmardin Priori'; 'Teguin ar Tave' [Whitland]; 'Talley Priory'; 'Aberguili, a collegiate church', and Llandilavaar', and the following rivers are mentioned; 'Brane'; 'Cowe'/'Cowen'; 'Cothey'; 'Dules'/ 'Dulesse'; [Dulas]; 'Kennenn'; 'Lochor' [Llwchwr]; 'Marleis'; 'Tava'; 'Tewe/Tewi'; 'Vendwit'/'Vendraith' 'Vendreth'/'Wendreth', 'Wendraith Vaur' [Gwendraeth Fawr]; 'Vendrath' 'Wendreth Vehan' [Gwendraeth Fach].[8]

Leland has been described as 'the first English topographer',[9] and the antiquarian content of his notes was mirrored in the work of Humphrey Llwyd, a leading Renaissance scholar, whose writings and maps reflected the contemporary respect for tradition and vernacular languages. A native of Denbigh, he represented the borough as its Member of Parliament, and was actively involved in the efforts which led to the Act of 1563, authorising the translation of the Bible and Book of Common Prayer into the Welsh language. One of his most important historical works was the *Cronica Walliae*, an English translation of the Welsh and Latin texts of mediaeval Welsh chronicles and related texts.[10] In view of the significance of his map of Wales, it is of interest to note the forms of the local place-names which appear in the *Cronica*. Humphrey Llwyd's background was undoubtedly responsible for his greater familiarity with the topography of north and north-west Wales, and several errors relating to locations in south Wales have been identified.[11] However, his description of the various regions of Wales contains several references to places in Carmarthenshire, which appear in this work. 'Caermerdhynshire' is described as the third part of the 'kingdome of Wales called Dinevwr'. The towns and castles of the shire included 'Caermerdhyn', 'Dynevwr', which was the Prince's seat of the countrey, Newtowne, Llandeilo, Llanymdhyfri, Emlyn . . . Llanystyffan' and others. This list also significantly includes 'Swansey, nowe in Glamorgan called Abertawy upon the sea'. The shire was considered to be 'the strongest part of all Southwales' with 'highe mountains, great woodes and fayre ryvers, specialy Towi'. The course of this river was traced from its source 'not ferre frome Wy runneth south to Llanymdhyfri and thence south west by Lhandeilo and Dinevwr and to Abergeweili and Caermerdhyn and at Llanystaffent to the sea'.[12] Also his account of military campaigns in south-west Wales contains references to 'Llanymdhyfri', 'Dynevwr' and 'Lhandeilaw Vawr' (1214), 'Kydwyli', 'Karnwylhyon', 'Caermardhyn', 'Saynt Clare', 'Thalbocharne' [Laugharne], 'Llanystephant' and 'Newe Castell in Emlyn' (1215) and 'Drosolan' [Dryslwyn].[13,14]

Humphrey Llwyd's map, *Cambriae Typus*, the earliest map of Wales, was published in 1573 by Abraham Ortelius in Antwerp in the *Additamentum* to his *Theatrum Orbis Terrarum* (1570). An important feature of his map of Wales, and one which was in contrast to the works of other sixteenth-century cartographers, was his use of the names for the traditional Welsh kingdoms, presented in Latin, Welsh and English, and the use of the three languages for place-names. Therefore, extending across south Wales, DEHENBARTIA appears in capital letters, and on the top left hand side, 'Deheubart' and 'Sut Wales'. 'Cantremaur' (in bold letters) is located on the west bank of the river Tovius [Tywi], and, on the east bank, in smaller italic print, 'Cantref Bychan' beneath an even smaller wording 'Swt wallie regia' referring to ' Dinefer', the traditional base of the rulers of Deheubarth, 'Tryslwyn', another important Welsh stronghold, is shown further down the Tywi valley. Latin and Welsh names are provided for Carmarthen, the county town: 'Maridunum' and 'Caerdfyrdhyn', with a reference made to its association

Fig. 1: *Part of Humphrey Llwyd's map from*
Cambriae Typus, *1573 [c.1617].*
(Reproduced by permission of Carmarthenshire Record Office).

with Merlin. Welsh names are also provided for the fortified centres of 'Talacharn', L.ymdyfri' and 'Ceydwyly', and the other places names are 'S. Clere', 'L. Ysmael', 'L. Stephan', and 'L. Gadoc'; and the rivers 'Bran', 'Lhychwr', 'Tovius', 'Wandres' [Gwendraeth], and, presented in bilingual form, 'Tivius,/Teifi', and 'Lochar/Llychwr'.[15] (*see Fig. 1*).

The use of the three languages, and the priority given to the Latin, and especially the Welsh language, may be attributed to Humphrey Llwyd's scholarly instincts, wide learning and Welsh background, and errors or inconsistencies in the map may be explained by the practice of employing foreign artists or engravers.[16] A reasonably accurate representation is presented of the course of the River Tywi, as also was the case with the rivers of north Wales, with which Llwyd was probably more familiar, and this is in contrast to the rivers in south-east Wales flowing into the Bristol Channel which were shown in diagrammatic form. Other defects in Llwyd's map included the failure to denote Gower, and the distortions of Anglesey, the Llŷn Peninsula, and St. Bride's Bay and Milford Haven in Pembrokeshire.[17]

The maps which resulted from Christopher Saxton's topographical survey of England and Wales undertaken in the period 1573-8, were far superior in their depiction of the outline of Wales.[18] This survey had been commissioned by Elizabeth I's government motivated by political and military considerations, with the Welsh

coast considered to be a very vulnerable target for an invasion. Whilst these maps were technically superior, there were inconsistencies in the presentation of place-names, and this largely resulted from the use of interpreters to assist Saxton, a Yorkshireman, communicate with a largely monoglot Welsh-speaking population. In 1576 magistrates in Wales had been required to provide Saxton with guides 'such as do best know the cuntrey' and also to 'set forth a horseman that can speke both Welsh and Englishe to safe conduct him to the next market towne'.[19]

The maps published following the survey were the atlas of England and Wales (1579), and the wall-map of England and Wales (1583).[20] The atlas contained seven maps depicting the thirteen shires of Wales, and these seem to have been made available originally as single sheets. Neighbouring Glamorgan and Pembrokeshire were presented as single sheets, but Carmarthenshire was grouped with Cardiganshire, Radnorshire and Brecknockshire on one sheet. The 1580 map purchased by the National Library of Wales in 1986, entitled *Cambriae* (*quae nunc vulgo Wallia nuncupatur*), contained many identical features to the wall-map, but contrasting elements including the lower-case forms, in manuscript, for the names of the shires as in Carmarthenshire, in the 1580 map, and of capital forms in the printed wall-map. Other features, including the sailing vessel in Carmarthen Bay; one of the eight vessels depicted on the entire map, and tree symbols, were also presented in manuscript, whilst the geographical outline, county boundaries, town symbols and town and river names were engraved. The combination of manuscript and engraved forms strongly suggests that the 1580 map was a proof for the 1583 wall-map, and there was a very strong resemblance between the two in terms of the presentation of the place-names of Carmarthenshire.[21]

There was, however, a marked contrast between the relevant information provided by these maps and the 1579 atlas. A general map of England and Wales in the atlas, entitled 'Anglia', located only two places in the area extending westwards from the town of 'CARMARTHEN' to the borders of Pembrokeshire and Cardiganshire, namely 'Lacharne' and 'Newcast'. On the other hand the map of the county in the same atlas located seven places in the area extending westwards from Carmarthen (rendered as 'Carmarden' on the map) as far as St. Clears ('S. Cleare'), and then southwards to Carmarthen Bay. These were 'Capel Llanlloch', 'Llan-

Fig. 2: *Part of Christopher Saxton's map 'Radnor, Breknok, Cardigan et Caermarden' (1578) in his*
Atlas of England and Wales *(1579).*
(Reproduced by permission of Carmarthenshire Record Office).

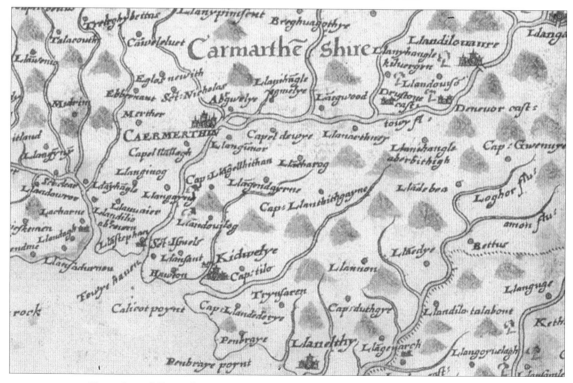

Fig. 3: *Part of Christopher Saxton's map,* Cambriae (quae nunc vulgo Wallia nuncupatur).
(By permission of Llyfrgell Genedlaethol Cymru/The National Library of Wales).

ginog', 'Llangayng' 'Llandilo abercowen', 'Llanvaier', 'Llacharne', 'Llanstephan' and 'Llanyhangle Abercowen'. Another eight places were located in the area south and west of St. Clears extending to the boundary with Pembrokeshire, that is, 'Llacharne', 'Llansadurnen', 'Pendyne', 'Llandowror' 'Marras', 'Egloskemen', 'Llandach', and 'Eglesvaier Keffig'. All these places appeared again in the maps of 1580 and 1583, but with variant forms for 'Pendine', 'Sct Clear', 'Egloiskemen', and 'Llandagh'. Also, a comparison of the area extending along the courses of the rivers Gwendraeth Fawr and Loughor, from source to mouth, reveals that whereas the only place located on the general map was 'Llanelthy', a total of twelve places were identified in this area on the 1579 map. These were, in addition to 'Llanelthye', 'Capel Llandedery', 'Trynsaren', 'Llannon', 'Llanedye', 'Llandebea', 'Capel duthgye', 'Llangenarche', 'Pembray', 'Capel Gunllo', and 'Parkreame' (*see Fig. 2*). Ten of these appeared again on the 1580 and 1583 maps, with 'Parkreame' and 'Capel Gunllo' omitted; and varying forms presented for 'Llanelthy', 'Llanedye', 'Llangenarch', and 'Penbraye'; and identical forms for the other five. Other notable omissions on the 1580 and 1583 maps were the mansions of Glanbrân, Ystrad Wallter, Cwmgwili, Llwynhywel, and Golden Grove.[22]

The maps of Humphrey Llwyd and Christopher Saxton directly influenced the work of John Speed, who published in 1611 his *Theatre of the Empire of Great Britain*, comprising four books. 'The Second Booke: containing the Principality of Wales', including a map of Wales, and maps of the thirteen Welsh shires with town-plans which, in the Carmarthenshire map, featured a plan of the county town, Carmarthen. The title was modelled on Ortelius's atlas, which contained Llwyd's map, and the outline of Wales, together with the place and river names, were based upon Saxton's maps. The most significant original contribution made by John Speed was in the compilation of the town plans which accompanied the county maps. A key to the plan of Carmarthen contained the words 'The Priory', 'S. Peters Church', 'The Key' and ' The Castell', and the following streets: 'Priory', 'S. Peters',

'Water', 'Spilmans', 'Kings', 'High', 'S. Maries' and 'Key'. Whereas 'Carmarden' appeared in bold on the map, the title of the map, and also that of the town plan referred to 'CAERMARDEN'.[23]

The county map and town plan were accompanied by a detailed description of the county, which contained a discussion of the various names for the county town: the Latin 'Maridunum' and 'Muridunum', the Welsh 'Caer fridhin' and the English 'Caermarden', and an intriguing reference to 'the ruines of *Carreg-Castle*' east of the town. This would seem to refer to the castle of Carreg Cennen, which is incorrectly located on the map, with Speed repeating Saxton's error as he also had placed this castle beneath the castle of 'Druslen', the parish of 'Llanyhangle Aberbithigh' and the mansion of 'Golden Grove' (see Fig. 3).[24] There were stated to be ten castles, twenty-eight rivers, five market towns, and eighty-seven parish churches in the county, and their names are listed in the table presented after the map of 'all the Townes, Rivers, and memorable places mentioned in Caermarden-shire'. The nine castles identified by Leland are located here, with the exception of Carreg Cennen, with Leland's apparent confusion concerning this castle shared by Saxton and Speed. The other castles shown by Speed were 'Carmarden', 'Llanstephan', 'Llacharne', 'Druslon', 'Denever', 'S. Claire', 'Newcastle emlyn', 'Llanymthefry' and 'Kidwyly'. The rivers in-

Fig. 4: *Part of John Speed's map, 'Carmarthenshire' in* Theatre of the Empire of Great Britain, *1611.*
(Reproduced by permission of Carmarthenshire Record Office).

cluded 'Brane', 'Cothy', 'Cowen', 'Gwendrath vaure' [the Gwendraeth Fach, although shown on the map, is not named], 'Gwilye', 'Lloughor', 'Tave', 'Towy' and 'Tyvy'. The market towns, in addition to 'CAERMAR-DEN', were inserted in capital letters: 'KIDWELLYE', 'LLANDILO', 'LLANELTHYE', 'LLANGADOKE', and 'LLANYMTHEFRY'.

The descriptive account and list of names do not refer to other significant features shown on the map, and especially the mansions which, again with distinctive symbols, were the homes of the predominant gentry families. Close family ties linked many of the owners of these country houses. Several were associated with the Dinefwr family. 'Newton', a fortified manor-house, had been the home of Gruffudd ap Nicholas, a dominant figure in the political life of south Wales in the first half of the fifteenth century.[25] He was the grandfather of Sir Rhys ap Thomas, whose grandson, Sir Rhys ap Gruffudd, was executed in 1531, and his possessions forfeited to the Crown. Sir Rhys ap Thomas's daughter, Gwenllian was the wife of Hywel ap Rhydderch of Ystrad Wallter, near Llandovery, which was shown on Saxton's county map as 'Istradwalter'. Their son, David Powell, was High Sheriff in 1550 and 1561, and both he and his son, George Powell, were Justices of the Peace. The family in possession of 'Abermarlas', in the parish of Llansadwrn, was descended from Ednyfed Fychan, steward to the princes of Gwynedd in the thirteenth century, and his wife, Gwenllian, daughter of the Lord Rhys of Dinefwr. The name 'Jones' was adopted in the early sixteenth century, and Sir Henry Jones was Sheriff of Carmarthenshire in 1574 and 1584, Cardiganshire in 1553, and Brecknockshire in 1580. His uncle, Richard Jones, had married Elizabeth, the heiress of 'Comgwily' in the parish of Abergwili, and resided at Cwmgwili. 'Golden Grove' had been built by John Vaughan in the period 1560-65, and his son Walter was Sheriff of Carmarthenshire and Cardiganshire, and Mayor of Carmarthen. In the Llandovery area, 'Lloynhowell' was the original home of the Gwynne family, whilst a member of this family, Rhydderch Gwynn, of 'Llanbrayne' (Glanbrân), with its fenced deer-park shown on Saxton's map, was High Sheriff of the county in 1573.[26]

Many members of these gentry families were patrons of poets and were praised by them. At least ten poets were the beneficiaries of the patronage of the Jones family of Llanegwad and Abermarlais.[27] Bardic compositions often referred to gentry homes, as in Lewis Glyn Cothi's eulogies to Philip ap Maredudd ap Philip,

and John ap Philip of Cil-sant, in the parish of Llanwinio [shown by Saxton as 'Kilsant' on his map], and his ode praising Hywel ap Henri ap Gwilym ap Thomas Fychan of Parc y Rhun in the parish of Llandybie ['Parkreame' on the map].[28]

Lewis Glyn Cothi (*c.*1420-89) whose name associated him with the forest of Glyn Cothi, near Llanybydder, referred to 'gaer verdin' in his ode to Lord Herbert, 'aber marleis' in his poems in praise of Morgan ap Tomas and Harri ap Tomas, 'llan ymddfri' also in the latter, and 'dinefwr' and 'kedweli' in his poem in praise of Owain ap Gruffudd ap Nicolas.[29] Carmarthenshire place-names identified by Ieuan Deulwyn (*fl.* 1460) include 'llangadog', 'lannedi', 'Gaerfyrddin', 'llan dailo', 'llan Egwad', 'llan arthne', and 'hidweli'.[30] He was a native of Kidwelly, and Lewys Dwnn, the poet and genealogist who was reared in Montgomeryshire, was also associated with this town as his mother was a descendant of David Dwnn of Kidwelly. He became a deputy herald, and his lists of pedigrees include references to 'Sir/Tref Gaer Vyrddin', 'Llan Edi', 'Llan Dybie', 'Kydweli/Kydwely/Kidweli/Kidwely', 'Llan Ym Ddyfri', 'Abergwily', 'Llangathen', Llanysteffan', 'Talacharn/Lacharn', 'Llansadern', 'Landeilo Vawr', 'Llann Egwad Vawr', 'Y Drenewydd Y Ninevor', 'Abermarlais' and 'Llangadog Vawr'.[31]

Lewis Dwnn belonged to the same family as Sir Edward Don, who stayed in Carmarthenshire in 1524. Whilst Sir Edward Don, John Leland, Christopher Saxton and John Speed were visitors to the area from England, and Lewys Dwnn and Humphrey Llwyd were both scholars primarily associated with localities in north Wales, their works are relevant for the local historian in Carmarthenshire. The information presented on the places which feature in their writings and early printed maps, together with the compositions of local poets, has contributed significantly to our awareness of the relative importance of localities within the shire at this time, and our understanding of the topography and toponomy of Tudor and early Stuart Carmarthenhire.

ACKNOWLEDGEMENTS

I am grateful to Professor J. Gwynfor Jones, Cardiff, who read an early draft of part of this paper; Mr Terry Wells and the staff of the Carmarthen Archives Service, and for the permission granted by the Service reproduce the three maps in Figures 1, 2 and 4; and the staff of the National Library of Wales, and for the permission granted by the Library to reproduce the map in Figure 3.

NOTES

1. Terrence James, 'Carmarthenshire Place-name Survey', *Carms. Antiq.*, Vol. XXXIV, 1998, pp. 128-129.

2. Idem, 'Where Sea meets Land, The changing Carmarthenshire coastline', in Heather James (ed.) *Sir Gâr, Studies in Carmarthenshire History, Essays in memory of W. H. Morris and M. C. S. Evans* (Carmarthen 1991), pp. 143-166.

3. Heather James and Terrence James, 'Fish weirs on the Taf, Towy and Gwendraeth estuaries, Carmarthenshire', *Carmarthenshire Antiquary*, Vol. XXXIX, 2003, pp. 22-48.

4. D. Huw Owen, 'Saxton's Proof Map of Wales', *The Map Collector*, Vol. 38, 1987, pp. 24-5.

5. R. A. Griffiths, 'Travelling between England and Wales: the itinerary of Sir Edward Don in 1524', *Carms. Antiq.*, Vol. XL, 2004, p. 6.

6. Idem, *Sir Rhys ap Thomas and his Family: A study in the Wars of the Roses and Early Tudor Politics* (1993), pp. 44-86.

7. Ralph A. Griffiths (ed.), *The Household Book (1510-1551) of Sir Edward Don, An Anglo-Welsh Knight and his Circle* (Buckinghamshire Record Society, no. 33, 2004), pp. xlviii, 114-20.

8. L. Toulmin Smith (ed.), *The Itinerary in Wales of John Leland in or about the years 1536-1539* (1906), pp. 3-4, 57-61, 113-5.

9. D. Hey (ed.), *The Oxford Companion to Local and Family History* (1996), p. 277.

10. Humphrey Llwyd, *Cronica Walliae* (ed.) Ieuan M. Williams (2002).

11. Ibid., p. 24 for comment that 'Llwyd's special interest in Welsh place-names and topography [was] in its own way a manifestation of the priority still being attached in his age to the authority of antiquity'.

12. Ibid., p. 243.

13. Ibid., pp. 77, 79, 81.

14. Ibid., pp. 193-6, 223.

15. Humphrey Llwyd, *Cambriae Typus*; F. J. North, *The Map of Wales before 1600 A.D.* (1935), pp. 54-9; Olwen Caradoc Evans, 'Maps of Wales and Welsh Cartographers', *The Map Collectors' Circle* (1964); Ann Perkins, 'Some maps of Wales, and in particular of the counties of Pembrokeshire, Cardiganshire and Carmarthenshire', *Carms. Antiq.*, Vol. VI, 1970, pp. 60-1; D. Huw Owen, *Early Printed Maps of Wales* (1996), pp. 1-5, plates 1, 4; Iolo and Menai Roberts, 'Printed Maps of the whole of Wales, 1573-1837', Part 1, *The Map Collector*, Vol. 68 (1994), pp. 35-36.

16. North, op. cit. n. 15, pp. 59-60.

17. Idem, pp. 57-9.

18. Idem, pp. 59-61, Ifor M. Evans and Heather Lawrence, *Christopher Saxton: Elizabethan map-maker* (1979), pp. 41-2, Owen, op. cit., n. 15, pp. 4-6, plates 2, 3, 5, 7, 8.

19. Sarah Tyacke and John Huddy, *Christopher Saxton and Tudor Map-makers* (1980), p. 32; National Archives, *Privy Council Register, 2/11*, pp. 44-5.

20. Christopher Saxton, *An Atlas of England and Wales (1579)*; R. A. Skelton, *Saxton's Survey of England and Wales, with a facsimile of Saxton's wall map of 1583* (1974); Evans & Lawrence, op. cit., n. 18, pp. 20-39; Tyacke & Huddy, op. cit., n. 18, pp. 24-45.

21. Owen, op. cit., n. 4, pp. 24-5; idem, *Early Printed Maps*, op. cit. n. 15, pp. 7-9.

22. Skelton, op. cit., n. 20, p. 5 considered that 80-90% of the names on the county maps in the 1579 atlas were presented on the 1583 wall-map.

23. John Speed, *Theatre of the Empire of Great Britain,* Part II, (1611); Owen, op. cit., n. 15, plate b.

24. Tom Hopkinson, 'Four centuries of Carmarthenshire Cartography', *Carms. Antiq.*, Vol. XLII, 2006, pp. 129-130, drew attention to the location of 'Carreg Castle' in Saxton's map of Carmarthenshire as that of the thirteenth-century Castle Rhingyll, and suggested that this represented either an error by Saxton, if his intention was to refer to the far more significant Carreg Cennen castle, or was an important omission. Speed's adherence to the information contained in Saxton's map, and his comments in his descriptive account suggest that Saxton was mistaken.

25. Griffiths, op. cit., n. 6, p. 165, n. 29 suggested that Gruffudd ap Nicholas had moved to Newton, his new home, soon after 1425.

26. Ibid., pp. 11-25; Francis Jones, *Historic Carmarthenshire Homes and their Families* (Carmarthen, 1987), pp. 3-4, 60-1, 203-4, 48, 83-5, 118-9, 74; *The Francis Jones Treasury of Historic Carmarthenshire,* C. Charles-Jones (ed.), 2002, p. 112; R. K. Turvey, 'Household, Court and Localities: Sir Thomas Jones and the rise of "That great family of Jones of Abermarlais:"', *Welsh History Review,* Vol. 22, 1, 2004, pp. 29-51.

27. Ibid., p. 47; E. R. Ll. Davies, 'Noddwyr y beirdd yn sir Gaerfyrddin' (unpublished MA thesis, University of Wales, 1976, pp. 160-176.

28. Jones, op. cit., n. 26, 1987, pp. 32 & 145.

29. E. D. Jones (gol.), *Gwaith Lewis Glyn Cothi, Y gyfrol gyntaf, Testun llawysgrif Peniarth 109* (1953), pp. 4, 59, 63, 71; idem, *Gwaith Lewys Glyn Cothi (Detholiad)* (1984), pp. 19, 43 & 144 for comment that 'Cedweli' was the form of the place-name used by Lewys Glyn Cothi; Dafydd Johnston (gol.), *Gwaith Lewys Glyn Cothi* (1995) pp. 52, 56, 60, 254.

30. Ifor Williams (gol.), *Casgliad o waith Ieuan Deulwyn* (1909), pp. 46, 49, 51, 60, 67, 91.

31. Samuel R. Meyrick (ed.), *Heraldic Visitations of Wales (by Lewys Dwnn)*, Vol. 1 (1846), pp. 24, 26, 93, 94, 99, 131, 139, 143, 145, 147, 150-1, 195, 198, 207, 210, 213-4, 217, 237.

Sir John Perrot's Deer Park at Cyffig

Ken Murphy

In 1583, Sir John Perrot began construction of a deer park for the 'recreation of gentlemen'[1] in the demesne of the Lordship of Laugharne, in what is now Carmarthenshire, a few kilometres southeast of Whitland (grid reference SN226151). The park was very short-lived: Perrot's death in 1592 signalling the beginning of its end. The is now little trace in the landscape of the former park apart from the place-name element 'pale' used in several farms – Great Pale, Old Pale, Little Pale and Pale Gate. The term pale refers to the stout fence constructed around the park.

Sir John Perrot, who was born at Haroldston, near Haverfordwest in Pembrokeshire, rose to become one of the most powerful individuals in southwest Wales. The lordships of Carew and Laugharne were granted to him, and Elizabeth I appointed him Lord Deputy of Ireland. He was also a member of the Council of the Marches, a member of the Privy Council and responsible for the naval defence of south Wales. However, he made many enemies during his political career, eventually leading to him being accused and tried for treason. He was sentenced to death, but died before the sentence could be enacted. There seems to no truth in the rumour that he was the illegitimate son of Henry VIII,[2] but his temperament and business methods resembled those of the king. Indeed, it is rare not to find references to legal disputes concerning Perrot's land dealings, and other aspects of his business, in the numerous collections of documents held by the National Library of Wales and other archives relating to south Wales. His acquisition of land for Cyffig deer park included deception, and is a typical example of his *modus operandi*.

At Carew Perrot had set about transforming the mediaeval castle into a residence fit for an Elizabethan gentleman. A vast new wing was added to the castle (unfinished at his death), and a deer park for the recreation of Perrot and his friends created nearby. A similar scheme was underway at Laugharne Castle, but on slightly more modest, but nevertheless still grand, scale. Here, though, no suitable land close to the castle was available for a deer park; therefore Perrot chose a tract of demesne 8km to the northwest, on the northern fringes of the lordship in the parish of Cyffig. This comprises some of the highest land in the lordship, rising to over 170m above sea level, although on its northern fringes it falls steeply away to the valley floor of the Tâf at a little over 10m above sea level. It seems likely that much of this high ground was rough, unenclosed land prior to the creation of the deer park.[3]

Not all the land required for the park was under Perrot's control; his acquisition of the additional required land led to a protracted dispute, which was researched by P. C. C. Evans in his 1940 thesis. The following account is taken from his thesis,[4] which is largely based on the proceedings of the Star Chamber.[5] Morgan Phillips of Picton owned three acres of land at a place called Wenallt that Perrot needed to complete his park, plus an acre on the mountain at Cyffig. An agreement to exchange land was agreed on February 23rd 1583, with Perrot giving Phillips three acres at Dolerwydd and receiving three acres, a cottage with one acre and another acre. Although Phillips gave more than he received, he was satisfied as his newly acquired land was 'bottome' and very fertile. At the same time Perrot and Phillips took the opportunity to rationalise their holdings by exchanging other lands. Phillips marked trees with an axe to delimit the proposed deer park and began to erect a fence around his newly acquired lands. Soon after, Perrot began construction of a pale around the park. However, Phillips quickly realised he had been duped. The land he received from Perrot carried an annual rent of £80 payable to the Earl of Northumberland; no such rent was payable on the land he had given. Perrot refused to discuss to matter and pressed on with construction, gathering 30 retainers armed with weapons 'invasyve and defensyve' at Wenallt. Phillips accused Perrot of erecting his paling beyond the agreed boundary and 'settinge the same pale malyciouslly throughout messuage and cottage'. Realising that there was little point in remonstrating with Perrot, Phillips took matters in his own hands and on the night of June 13th 1583 between midnight and 3 o'clock in the morning with 30 men ('desperate and evill disposed persons' according to Perrot, armed with 'halberds, swords, javelins, forrest bills, pikes, hatchets, axes, saws and bows and arrows' 'fytter to raise tumultus rebellyous then to preserve good order') tore down 20 perches of the new pale. Perrot filed a suit against Phillips, and Phillips bought a counter-charge. The case was to be heard by the Court of the Council of the Marches, but as Perrot was a member of the Court it was transferred to the Star Chamber. Before the charge could be heard Phillips sought the assistance of his cousin Eynon Phillips, and he, with 30 of his men on October 30th 1593 cut down the same 20 perches of the pale. Perrot re-erected it and once more it was cut down. The Star Chamber eventually found in Perrot's favour and ordered Phillips to pay £20 for each of his two acts of riot and his servants to pay £5 for each of their offences. In all, it cost Phillips somewhere in the vicinity of £340. Perrot presumably completed his park soon after the Star Chamber's ruling.

A survey carried out in 1595, three years after Perrot's death, contains a detailed delineation of the park:[6]

> We find at Kifficke a Park impaled, containing four myles three quarters compass, every myle 1800 yards, wherein by estimac'on 300 acres, whereof we find of copses and groves 12 acres, which we value to be worth xiii[s] iiii[d] for the wood; also we find one other parcel of timber trees of 100 years growth or thereabouts, which we value every tree, with bark, top and lop to be worth 4s, Silly ground, heathes and ffurzes, the number of c.IIII[XX].II (182) acres, which we do value ye aforesaid grounds to be worth per ann. 6*l* 13*s* 4*d*.
>
> Also we find without the pale belonging to the park of meadow ground 13 acres.[7]

It is unclear whether the park actually functioned as a deer park during Perrot's lifetime, as an inventory of his goods and chattels made on the 27th April 1592 following his death lists in the park only 18 colts, 40 oxen, one bull and six heifers in the custody of William Dod.[8] However, it is likely that even in death Perrot was still evading the law and that his agents were concealing his goods and chattels for in 1613 there certainly were deer in the park as it was reported that one Rees Pythergh was accused of carrying away the palings of the park and that the keeper of the park had destroyed the whole herd of deer ' killing them in and out of season and powdering and barrelling them up for the entertaining of guests'.[9] He was also accused of ploughing up the park. The following year, 1614, it is recorded that £1,600 of cattle and sheep were kept in the park.[10]

Following Perrot's death, the Lordship of Laugharne was granted to the Countess of Northumberland, who had little direct contact with southwest Wales and therefore had no interest in maintaining the deer park. Laugharne Castle, the deer park and other properties where leased out as a package, and then divided and sub-let to other tenants.[11] Apart from the sources cited above, documents of this period refer to the park in a formulaic manner, apparently copying the wording of the 1595 survey, such as in a grant of 1627:[12] 'that park of Kiffick inclosed with pales containing by estimation in circuit four miles and three quarters . . .' It is not until 1633, when much of the former demesne of Laugharne was then the property of Sir Sackville Crow, that new evidence becomes available. In that year an inquiry into his property records that he owned:[13] 'Kiffick Parke, alais the old parke'. Fifty years had now passed between Perrot founding the park and it being referred to as an old park, presumably an acknowledgement that its intended original function had long since ceased. It is not known, however, when the several farms that still exist (ruinous in the case of Old Pale) were carved out of what had been the deer park, but as Crow is known to have been an improving landlord – he drained Laugharne Marsh in 1661[14] transforming it from pasture subject to tidal inundation into rich arable farm containing several farms – it is likely that the conversion of what had been marginal land into enclosed land-holdings probably began, and was, perhaps, completed during his lifetime. The establishment of farms was certainly complete by 1756 when a document records 'All those . . . several ffarms, Lands and Tenements called Pale',[15] and one suspects that by then the landscape resembled that of today. This landscape is shown on the tithe map[16] and on maps included in a sale document of the Westmead Estate.[17]

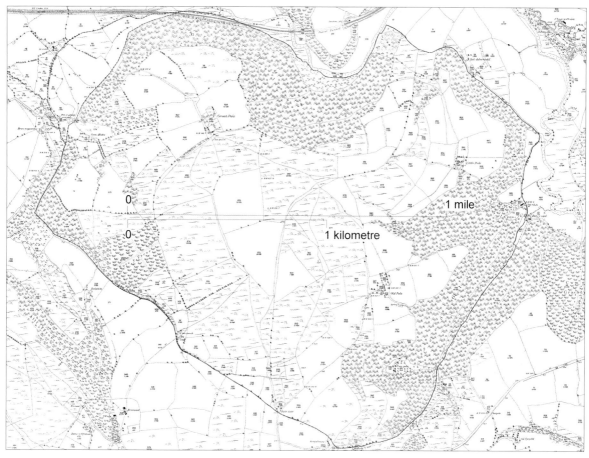

Fig. 1: *The boundary of Cyffig deer park plotted onto the 1888-89 Ordnance 1:2500 1st Edition map.*

Plotting the location of the fields recorded on the tithe map and on the Westmead sale maps belonging to the several farms containing the place-name element pale reveals the extent of the former park. The south side of the park is defined by a hedge-bank of conventional size for the area, but clearly of importance as many other hedge-banks run up to it but do not cross it. An (the only?) entrance into the park was probably at a place now called Willow Glyn (formerly Pale Gate). To the north-west of Pale Gate the hedge-bank/deer park boundary runs on the south side of a stream in a narrow, steep-sided valley. The boundary follows the stream until it approaches Pen-y-Graig farm. For the next 1,000m the course of the former pale is unclear, with one of two routes possible. The area between the two possible routes may be the 13 acres outside the pale, but belonging to the park, mentioned in 1595. The park boundary then follows the junction of a steep slope and the floodplain of the River Tâf. This boundary is now nothing more than an ordinary hedge-bank. At Wenallt the course of the pale diverges from the floodplain to follow a small stream in a deeply incised valley, or rather the boundary is represented by a low bank to immediately to the south a small stream. The parish boundary follows this low bank. The park boundary then emerges onto fairly level ground and runs up to Pale Gate. The boundary of the park is shown plotted onto the Ordnance Survey 1888-1889 1:2500 map (*Fig. 1*). This plotted boundary measures 8,290 yards or 8,550 yards if the slightly longer course on the northwest side is followed (the 1595 survey estimated it at 6,750 yards) and the park area comprises 4,168,000 square yards following the shorter boundary course on the northwest side (3,072,000 estimated in 1595). It is interesting to note that the area between the two alternative boundaries shown on Figure 1 is 152,400 square yards, which roughly corresponds to the area of meadow of 133,120 square yards estimated lying outside the pale in 1595.

NOTES

1. P. C. C. Evans, 'Sir John Perrot', unpublished University of Wales thesis, 1940, National Library of Wales 1940/20, p. 158.

2. R. Turvey, *The Treason and Trial of Sir John Perrot* (Cardiff: University of Wales Press, 2005), p. 4.

3. A map over a century later, dated 1697, shows that much of high ground along the northern edge of the lordship was still then largely unenclosed. NLW Llwyngwair 1123, 'A Rough Draught of Roscough Lands . . . and Mountain Containing about 760 acres'.

4. Op. cit., n.1, pp. 158-163.

5. A catalogue of the Star Chamber proceedings has been published by Ifan ap Owen Edwards, *A Catalogue of Star Chamber Proceedings Relating to Wales* (Cardiff: University Press Board, 1929), see p. 134.

6. The Castle Lordship and Manor of Tallaugharne otherwise Laugharne with the Members. 2nd October 1595. Original document held by Laugharne Corporation.

7. The acre in the 1595 survey consists of 10,240 square yards, which is 2.16 times greater than the statute acre of 4840 square yards.

8. *Archaeologia Cambrensis* 1866, Carmarthen – An inventory of all and singular the Goods and Chattells y^t Sr John Perrot had wthin ye said Countye y^t xxviith of Aprill last past, 1592.

9. T. I. J. Jones, *Exchequer Proceedings Concerning Wales* (Cardiff: University of Wales Press, 1955), p. 125.

10. Ibid., p. 305.

11. Anon 1939, Exchequer Proceedings: James I, *Trans. Carm. Ant. Soc. and Field Club*, 29, 116-121.

12. NLW 10118E Vol. 1 Laugharneshire Documents. Land Revenue and Involvements. South Wales Involvements Vol. 10 folio 108. Grant of the Manor of Tallaugharne, 20 July 3 Charles I, to Francis Bacon.

13. Anon 1938, Crow, of Westmead, Laugharne, *Trans. Carm. Ant. Soc. & Field Club*, 28, p. 82. The following is from an Inquiry held on 4 April 1633 into the property of Sir Sackville Crow: Lease of Lordship of Laugharne from 1616/17, formerly granted to William Lord Knolls, for 21 years after the death of Dorothy, Countess of Northumberland. Sir Sackville Crow also owned Kiffick Parke, alias the old parke and other lands late in occupation of William Smaleman Esq.

14. A document dated 29 March 1660 sets out Sir Sackville Crow's intention to build a sea wall across Laugharne marsh the following year. NLW Llwyngwair 14264.

15. Carms Record Office, Glasbrook 1/2. 'Pre-nuptial settlement of Cornwallis Maude and Lititia Vernon, August 7 1756'.

16. NLW. Kiffig Parish Tithe map (1839) and Apportionment (1840).

17. Westmead was the name of the mansion and estate founded by Sir Sackville Crow. The sale document 'Particulars of the Westmead Estate' is not dated, but probably mid-19th century.

The Trenches at Falkland, Fife:
a Legacy of Royal Deer-management?

Simon Taylor

In 1997 on one of Terry's visits to Scotland when he was working on the prototype of the Scottish Place-Name Database, we went to see the Buzzart Dikes.[1] The Dikes enclose an irregular oblong area on Middleton Muir[2] just under a mile long on the north and south sides, by *c.*650 yards along its western margin (the best preserved section) and 470 yards on the eastern. Although identified by antiquarians as a Caledonian camp and associated with the battle of Mons Graupius, they have more recently been convincingly interpreted as the remains of a mediaeval deer park.[3] They are on the lands of Glasclune, Kinloch, Perthshire, and start *c.*2 kilometres west of the castle of Glasclune, on the gently sloping, south-facing edge of the Grampians.[4] It was a bright, fresh, windy day when Terry and I were there, and we walked the whole perimeter, impressed by the good state of preservation, especially at the western end, both of the upstanding dike or embankment and the interior ditch. It is in fact one of the many mediaeval or early modern deer enclosures to be found throughout the Scottish countryside, which are often associated with castles and high-status houses, and which Christopher Dingwall has termed 'a neglected heritage' (Dingwall 2007).

It was through Terry's interest in such landscape features as The Buzzart Dikes that I myself first became aware of the importance of deer-management in mediaeval Scotland, and its physical legacy in the landscape. In this volume dedicated to his memory I am therefore very pleased to have this opportunity to present to a wider audience the evidence for one such feature, hitherto unrecognised, in Fife in east central Scotland, a region which Terry had visited several times. I must stress at the outset that I am not an archaeologist or a landscape historian, nor am I an expert in animal man-

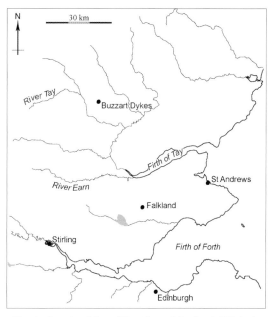

Fig. 1: *Location Map of East Central Scotland. Fife is the peninsula between the Firth of Forth and the Firth of Tay.*
(Drawn by Gilbert Márkus).

agement: the prism through which I view the past is very much that of toponymics.[5] I could not, therefore, have reached the tentative conclusions set out below without much input and advice from a wide range of people with expertise and knowledge very different from my own. In particular I would like to mention Mairi Davies (Historic Scotland), Christopher Dingwall, John Fletcher, Rod McCullagh (Historic Scotland), Paula Martin, Douglas Speirs (Fife Council) and Ninian Stuart of Falkland. This does not mean that they agree with me, and I take full responsibility for what follows.

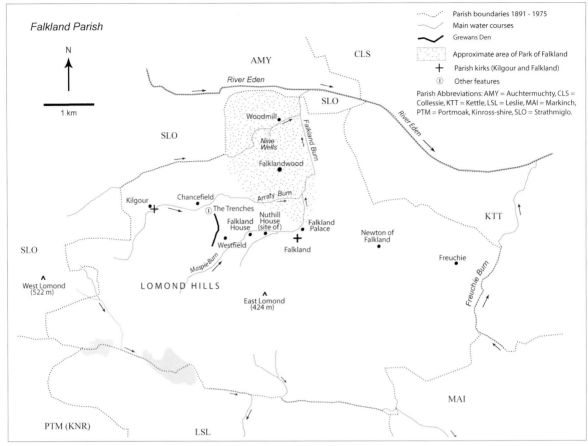

Fig. 2: *Parish of Falkland, Fife.*
(Drawn by Gilbert Márkus).

Hunting at Falkland under the Stewarts

Falkland first appears in the record as the name of a royal thanage, its thane, Macbeth (Mac Bethad), witnessing a document of *c*.1128 (*St A. Lib.* 117-8). About 30 years later, *c*.1160, Falkland was given by King Malcolm IV to Earl Duncan (Donnchad) I of Fife (*RRS* i no. 190). Falkland lay in the mediaeval parish of Kilgour, and it was not until the early seventeenth century that the name of the parish was changed from Kilgour to Falkland, with the removal at that time of the parish kirk to the burgh of Falkland.

The castle and lands of Falkland remained in the hands of the earls of Fife for over two centuries, until they were recovered by the Crown, in the person of James I (1406-37) in 1425, on the forfeiture and execution of Murdoch, earl of Fife and duke of Albany, the king's cousin. Following this royal acquisition, throughout the fifteenth and early sixteenth century, the Stewart

kings went about systematically creating a hunting palace, much of which still stands, and a large hunting park, which can be defined as an enclosed game reserve surrounded by a ditch and bank on the top of which was a palisade (Gilbert 1979, 215). This has left several important traces both in the landscape and in the place-nomenclature. Probably the most important example of the latter is Falklandwood, now the name of a farm, the house and steading of which is at NGR NO248086, and on the west side of which part of the enclosing bank survives. The royal hunting park is very much defined by the lands of the farm of Falklandwood, along with those of Woodmill, the steading of which lies *c*.1 kilometre to the north. In a charter of 1625 to John Murray earl of Annandale, mention is made of the office of forester of Falkland, with profits, (and) 'the office of maintaining the walls, embankments and the paling of the grove and woods of Falkland' (*officium sustentandi* muros, aggeres et lie *peilling* saltus et silvarum de *Falkland*) (*RMS* viii no. 826). Part of the embankment, mentioned above, is still clearly visible,[6] and the paling or fence is referred to in the name *Palingback*, marked on Ainslie's map of Fife (1775), which would have lain beside the north edge of The Park of Falkland at around NO250100.

James II (1437-60), son of James I, grew up a keen huntsman and was frequently at Falkland, where he kept dogs.[7] The chief quarry was deer, and during the reign of his grandson, James IV (1488-1513), another very enthusiastic huntsman, the royal accounts contain frequent references to the management of deer in the royal parks throughout the kingdom, especially at Falkland, which seems to have played a central role in the stocking of other royal deer parks.[8] The first recorded use of a gun in a stalk was in 1508, when James IV stalked in Falkland Park 'with a culverin'.[9]

The Trenches

On the Falkland Estate, a short distance south-east of Chancefield, and to the south of the Arraty Burn, is a feature known as The Trenches (NO234079, NMRS No. NO20NW 8). This consists of at least six deep trenches separated by high embankments, each trench between about 150 and 200 metres long. They run down a west-facing slope, converging on a point near the Arraty Burn. In plan they look like a half-closed fan, with its apical point to the west (*see Fig. 4*). Because they lie so close to the old route from Falkland westwards, the NMRS suggests that they are hollow-ways, that is very old tracks which have left deep grooves or trenches in the landscape. The argument would be that when one became unusable because of mud, another, parallel, route would have been taken, and another hollow-way created. For various reasons this explanation is unsustainable, not least because of the high number of trenches involved, and because there is evidence that some bedrock has been cut away in at least one of the trenches. It is much more likely that they were created as part of a single, concerted and managed construction effort.

Our first certain reference to them is on Thomas Winter's 1757 plan of Nuthill, which shows them much as they are today, and calls them 'The Trenches, an Old Fortification' (*see Fig. 3*). It is even more unlikely that they are fortifications than that they are hollow-ways. The fact that they are so described, however, shows that they were old enough for their original purpose to have been forgotten by the mid 18th century.[10]

I would propose that they were created in the late middle ages as part of the royal deer-management strategy. Within the general context of this strategy, in which royal funds were invested, the primary evidence is provided by two, perhaps three, place-names, two of which

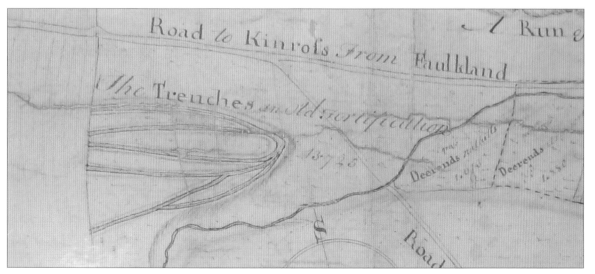

Fig. 3: *Detail from 'A Plan of the Estate of Nuthill, the Property of William Thomson Esq., surveyed by Thomas Winter, Anno 1757', in possession of the Falkland Estate, Falkland, Fife. It the earliest representation of The Trenches, which it terms 'an Old Fortification'. Note also the fields or enclosures called 'Deerends' to the west (right-hand side). The 'Road' lower right is 'Road to Arngosk', i.e. Arngask, a place on the way to Perth. Reproduced by kind permission of Ninian Stuart.*
(Photo: Heather James).

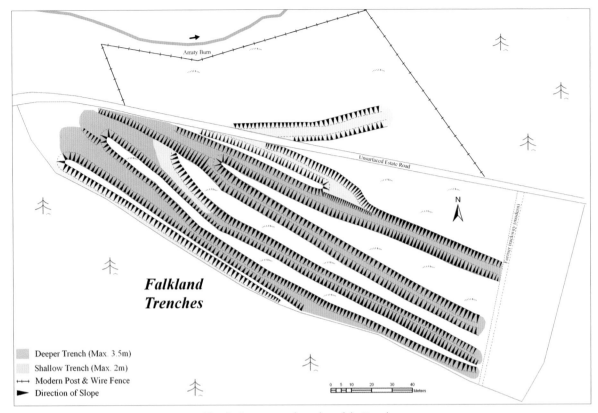

Fig. 4: *Accurate modern plan of the Trenches.*
(Supplied by Douglas Speirs, Fife Council Archaeologist).

appear on the above-mentioned Falkland Plan/1757, and one of which appears on Blaeu (Pont) East Fife. The first of these is the name of two small fields, each called *Deerends*, immediately west of the Trenches, on the other (north) side of the Arraty Burn (called the *Den Burn* on the Plan). They now form the south-east corner of the arable lands of Kilgour, more specifically the south-east corner of the field called the East Haugh (NO232080), now afforested. I would suggest either that the Trenches themselves were known as Deerends (a word which does not occur in *DOST* or *SND*), or that an element has been lost, e.g. *Deer Trench Ends or the like. Whatever the exact meaning of this name, it does strongly indicate that there is a connection with deer in the immediate vicinity of the Trenches. The second place-name on the Falkland Plan/1757 which suggests a connection with hunting is *Greyhound Den*,[11] a small den or valley running down from the Lomonds and heading directly towards the east end of the Trenches, near the west edge of the fields of Westfield. Greyhounds were hunting dogs, and this small, natural valley, now

completely under trees, may explain the location of the Trenches. The Den stops some 150 metres short of the east end of the Trenches, but modern agricultural and forestry activity may well have obscured a physical link between the Den and the Trenches. The third place-name is that applied to the Arraty Burn on Blaeu (Pont) East Fife, which appears as *B. Deir*, presumably for *Burn(e) of Deir*, i.e. *Burn of Deer. This is the burn which flows right beside the west end of the Trenches, and along which, as I suggest below, the deer may have been driven towards Falkland Park.[12]

As we have seen (*Hunting at Falkland under the Stewarts*), the actual hunting of deer at Falkland, at least by members of the Scottish court, took place in Falkland Park, to the north of the Palace, and about 1.5 km east of the Trenches. My working hypothesis is that this elaborate structure was made not for the hunting of deer but for their capture, as well as their sorting, to stock the royal park at Falkland and to supply other royal parks throughout lowland Scotland, especially Stirling (see *TA* references, below). That some kind of deer capture was going on at Falkland is made explicit in a record in 1506, in which one John Balfour is paid to range the countryside (probably the Lomonds) with blood hounds (Sc *raches*) to drive deer to the Park.[13]

The question then arises as to how the deer were directed towards the Park after being concentrated through the Trenches at a point beside the Arraty or Den Burn (*B. Deir*). The answer may well lie in the burn itself, which for most of its course between the Trenches and the Park runs through a deep and distinctive den or valley, which could have acted as a natural funnel, enhanced perhaps by a paling fence along the top of each side.

A final answer to the puzzle of the Trenches must await further archaeological and documentary investigation, not only of the feature itself, but also of its wider

context, and of similar features elsewhere in Scotland and beyond. At Fyvie, Aberdeenshire, for example, there are earthworks, also in woodland, which bear at least a superficial similarity to those at Falkland. Known as 'Montrose's Camp', they are supposedly related to a clash in 1664 between the Marquis of Montrose and the Earl of Argyll (NJ771392, NMRS no. NJ73NE 10).[14] Perhaps the most striking parallel to the Falkland Trenches so far identified is a set of fan-like trenches at Parkmill, Tarbolton, Ayrshire, south-west Scotland, NGR NS442268 (*Fig. 5*).[15] The presence of this feature, combined with nearby place-names containing the element *park* (viz Parkmill and Parkhill), which in older Scottish place-names always refers to emparked land (as opposed to modern Scots, in which *park* usually refers to a field), alone indicates the possible existence of a hunting park.

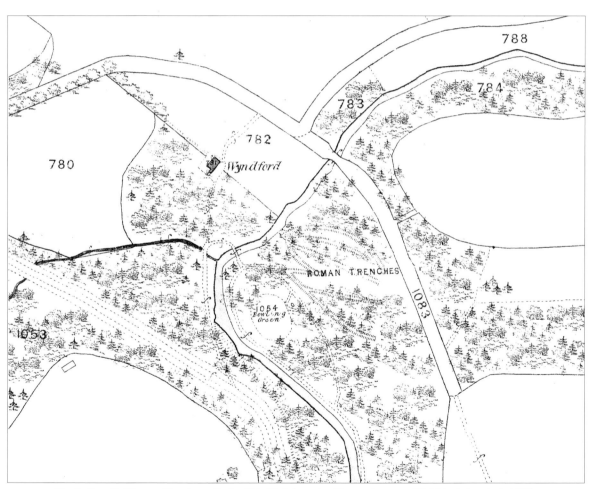

Fig. 5: *So-called Roman Trenches at Parkmill by Tarbolton, Ayrshire, as shown on OS 25 inch 1st edn (c.1858).*
For the possible significance of Wyndford in connection with deer-management, see footnote 39, above.
(Image supplied by Christopher Dingwall, reproduced by kind permission of the Trustees of the National Library of Scotland).

Fig. 6: *Copper alloy mount of a stag's head found in 2007 at the Falkland Trenches. Length 5 cm.*
(Photo Douglas Speirs).

At the end of 2007 a remarkable find was made on one of the embankments of the Falkland Trenches: this was a decorative mould-poured copper alloy mount of a stag's head, viewed from the front (*Fig. 6*). There is still debate amongst archaeologists as to what exactly this object represents; one theory, especially attractive in the context of this chapter, is that it is a badge of office of one of the royal officials occupied with deer management at Falkland. There is another theory, however, which suggests that it is a 19th-century drawer-handle![16] The Trenches of Falkland clearly still have a story to tell, and this chapter is only the beginning.

APPENDIX

'The extant evidence for Falkland park allows a fairly full picture of the running of a park in the late fifteenth and early sixteenth centuries to be drawn' (Gilbert 1979, 220).

This Appendix contains some references from the first decade of the sixteenth century to deer hunting and management at Falkland from the Accounts of the Lord High Treasurer of Scotland in the reign of James IV (1488-1513) (*TA* ii, iii), showing the intensity of deer-hunting activity around Falkland at this time. The original Scots text is given (apart from the Roman numerals, which have been modernised), with modern English translations, where deemed necessary, in end-notes. Place-names have been italicised. Note the mention of the building of a deer fold. While I do not think that this refers to the Trenches themselves, it may well refer to a structure connected with them.

These have been interspersed chronologically with some references taken from the *Exchequer Rolls* (*ER*) xii showing other aspects of the royal hunting estate at Falkland, including the feeding of boars and swans. Note that even for the period covered here (1502-1508), the list of entries relating to Falkland as a hunting estate is not exhaustive.

TA ii, p. 151
21 June 1502
Item, the samyn day, to the man that kepis the park of *Faukland*, 7s.

p. 394
8 Sept. 1503
Item, to him [Andro Aytoun] that he gaif the men that hed the Kingis cursouris and meris fra the *Tor Wod* to *Faukland*,[17] 4s.

p. 407
24 Nov. 1503
Item, to ane man to pas to *Kynneil* for the deir nettis and to haf thaim to *Faukland*,[18] 8s.

p. 408
25 Nov. 1503
Item, to Maister Levisay, Inglis man, that takis deir in *Faukland*, be the Kingis command,[19] 28s.

p. 419
13 Feb. 1504
Item, to ane man brocht the quik deir fra *Faukland* to *Strivelin*, 6s.

p. 424-5
27 March 1504
Item, to the Queenis Yemen brocht ane quyk deir fra *Faukland* to *Strivelin*,[20] 14s.

Item, in *Faukland,* to tua men tursit tua bukkis to *Strivelin,*[21] 14s.

Item, to the man that woke the fald all yeir quhair the deir wes tane,[22] 14s.

p. 425

Item, payit to him [i.e. Andro Matheson] for making of the fald to tak the deir in, 21s. 4d.

Item, payit to the said Andro that he laid doun for carying of xj littaris with deir, sindry tymes, ilk littair 14s., and 4s. mair amang thaim,[23] summa £7 18s.

Item, payit to the said Andro he laid doun for schoing of the Quenis littar hors that bure the deir all Yeir,[24] 18s. 8d.

ER xii, p. 196

1504

Et Thome Duncan ad pastum aprorum in *Faulklande,* i bolla i firlota ordei.[25]

p. 197

Et per solutionem factam ortulano de *Faulklande* percipienti in anno duas celdras avenarum, de anno compoti, ii celdre avenarum. Et eidem ad sustentationem fossarum et palorum parce de *Faulklande* de eodem anno, ii celdre avenarum. Et ad reparationem fovearum prati de *Faulkland* de dicto anno, i celdra avenarum . . .[26]

Et per liberationem factam ad pastum ferarum et cervorum in *Faulkland* pro captione eorundem animalium et postea missorum versus parcam de *Strivelin* de mandato domini regis, vi bolle iii firlote avenarum . . . Et eidem per liberationem factam in una celdra quindecim bollis avenarum ad pastum quinque aprorum et trium cignorum in *Faulklande* a quinto Octobris usque festum Natalis Domini infra hoc compotum, i celdra xv bolle avenarum. Et eidem in/p. 198/pabulo unius equi regis in *Faulkland,* Jacobo Averie cum eodem remanente circa captionem cervorum missorum ad Strivelin tempore hiemali diversis vicibus, v bolle avenarum.[27]

ER xii, p. 205

Stirling 5 July 1504

Et eidem [Johanni Strivelin, rotularor<i>] pro expensis unius le stalcar et duorum servitorum ejusdem

laborantium per duocedim dies circa captionem cervorum et ferarum tempore solemniationis matrimonii domini regis, xl s. . . . Et pro structura et edificio unius le fauld in parca de *Faulklande* pro cervis capiendis de mandato domini regis, xiiii s. Et pro cariagio octo cervorum de *Falkland* versus monasterium de *Edinburgh* tempore maritagii domini regis,/p. 206/xxviii s.[28]

TA ii, pp. 474-5

15 Jan 1505

Item, payit to James Avery for his expens and folkis with him passand to the *Torwood* at thre sindry tymes and to *Faukland,* to draw the Kingis staggis[29] and bring- and thaim to *Edinburgh* and *Faukland,*[30] £3.

Item, to the said James for ane mannis expens kepand/ p. 475/the said staggis in *Faukland* 3 days, ilk day 8d.,[31] summa 22s.

TA iii, pp. 171-2

November 1505

In one month alone, the following expenditure is recorded:

11 Nov.

Item, for deir nettis quhilk Yeid to *Faukland,*[32] £6 18s.

Item, to Maister Levisay, Inglisman, to pas to *Faukland* to tak deir to send to *Strivelin,*[33] 42s.

17 Nov.

Item, payit to Andro Mathesoun that he gaif in *Faukland* for carying of deir to *Strivelin* vj tymes, and iiij men with ilk littar, by the Yeman that passit, ilk tyme 14s.; summa £4 4s.[34]

Item, for schone to the littar hors, 4s.

Item, for schoing of the Kingis thre staggis quhilk wer send to Edinburgh,[35] 6s.

Item, for bigging of the deir fald in *Faukland,*[36] 18s.

Item, for making of ane stalp and the irn graith to the samyn, be the kingis command, to sla foxes in the park of *Faukland,*[37] 6s. 6d.

Item, payit to the vicar of *Kilgour* the teynd silvir of the Kingis staggis in tua Yeris,[38] 16d.

/p. 172/

Item, to him he laid doun to xxxii men divers dayis with Maister Levisay at the deir taking; ilk man on the day, 8 d; summa 21s. 4d.

Item, to him he gaif John Balfour passand with raches in the cuntree to drif the deir to the park, and for wynding of the hay Yard for deir taking,[39] 14s.

p. 180
27 Jan. 1506

Item, to Andro Matheson for the littar passand this winter bipast xvi tymes to *Strivelin* with deir, to foure men passand tharwith ilk tyme by the Yeman, ilk man on the day viii d., bidand furth ilk tyme thre dayis and ane tyme foure dayis for the wateris stoppit thaim;[40] summa £6 10s. 8d.
/p.181/
Item, for making of ii littaris for carying of deir, 4s.
Item, to the werkmen that tuke the deir in the fald, in drinksilvir, 5s.

Item, the thrid day of Februar, to James Avery quhilk he gaif be the Kingis command to the man that caryit the deir fra *Faukland* and kepit the park, 28s.

TA iv, 115
1508

Item, the secund day of Maij, in *Faukland*, to Johne Methuen that Yeid with the King to stalk ane deir with the culveryn,[41] 14s.

p. 134
1508
12 July

Item, payit to Andro Matheson for carying of deir divers tymes, mending of the hay Yard and Yett thairof, and of the deir fald mending divers tymes contenyt in his bill,[42] £5 9s.

GLOSSARY

boll: 'A measure of capacity for grain, malt, salt, etc., or of weight, varying for different commodities and in different localities' (*DOST*). 'It was 12 gallons using the normal Scots measure of ale, or about . . . 218 litres' (Barrow 1981, 173).

chalder: sixteen bolls
firlot: fourth of a boll
yeman: an official next in rank to a gentleman of the household. The grades next below the *yeman* (yeoman) are the groom and the page' (*TA* i, Glossary, p. 447).

BIBLIOGRAPHY

Barrow, G. W. S., 1981, *Kingship and Unity: Scotland 1000-1306* (London).

Dingwall, C. H., 'Deer Parks in Scotland – a neglected heritage', in *The History, Ecology and Archaeology of Medieval Parks and Parklands*, ed. I. D. Rotherham, *Landscape Archaeology and Ecology*, Vol. 6, September 2007 (being papers from a conference held at Sheffield Hallam University in September 2007), 25-8.

DOST: *Dictionary of the Older Scottish Tongue*, ed. W. Craigie and others 1937-2001. Accessible on DSL website.

DSL website: Dictionary of the Scots Language/Dictionar o the Scots Leid, an electronic edition of two earlier works, the *Dictionary of the Older Scottish Tongue* and the *Scottish National Dictionary*, on-line at http://www.dsl.ac.uk/

Dunf. Reg.: Registrum de Dunfermelyn, Bannatyne Club 1842.

ER: *The Exchequer Rolls of Scotland*, ed. J. Stuart and others 1878-1908 (Edinburgh).

Gilbert, John M., 1979, *Hunting and Hunting Reserves in Medieval Scotland* (Edinburgh).

PNF 2: Simon Taylor, with Gilbert Márkus, *Place-Names of Fife*, Vol. 2 (Central Fife between Leven and Eden), (Donington), [volume 2 of a 5 volume series], (forthcoming).

RMS: *Registrum Magni Sigilli Regum Scottorum (Register of the Great Seal)*, ed. J. M. Thomson & others, 11 volumes, Edinburgh 1882-1914 (reprinted 1984).

RRS i: *Regesta Regum Scottorum*, vol. i, (*Acts of Malcolm IV*), ed. G. W. S. Barrow (Edinburgh 1960).

SND: *Scottish National Dictionary*, ed. William Grant et al. (1931-76). Accessible on DSL website.

St A. Lib.: Liber Cartarum Prioratus Sancti Andree in Scotia, Bannatyne Club 1841.

TA: *Accounts of the Lord High Treasurer of Scotland*, ed. T. Dickson and Sir J. Balfour Paul, 1877-1916.

Watson, W. J., 1926, *The History of the Celtic Place-Names of Scotland* (Edinburgh and London; paperback edition, with Introduction, corrigenda and addenda, and a full W. J. Watson bibliography, by Simon Taylor, Edinburgh 2004).

NOTES

1. The name Buzzart is probably a variant of Scots *bizzard*, older *bussard* or *bussart* 'buzzard', while Scots *dyke* always refers to wall or other kind of upstanding enclosure. It was presumably so named because buzzards used the dikes as convenient perches.

2. Middleton is a division of the lands of Glasclune, appearing as Middleton of Glasclune (*Middletown of Glasscloon*) on Stobie's map (1783). For more on the name and place Glasclune, see n. 4, below.

3. Full details and references can be found on the RCAHMS Canmore website, NMRS Number: NO14NW 2.

4. Early forms of Glasclune, Kinloch, are: (Matthew mair of) *Glasclon* c.1250 x c.1340 *Dunf. Reg.* no. 332 [mair (Latin *marus*), a court official]; in tota baronia mea de *Glasclune* 1363 x 1366 *RMS* i no. 221 [Thomas Bisset (*Bysset*) gives to Isabell countess of Fife on their marriage 'all my barony of Glasclune']; (all lands of) *Glasclune* 1370 *RMS* i no. 350 [David II to John Herring (*Herynge*) all the right of all the lands of Glasclune resigned by Bisset].

   The name probably derives from Gaelic *glas chlaon* 'green slope'; for *claon* used as a noun (as opposed to its more common usage as an adjective meaning 'slanting, oblique'), see Watson's discussion of Clyne, Sutherland (1926, 335). The mediaeval castle of Glasclune (NO15 47), now a dilapidated but still impressive ruin, perched on the western edge of the den or deep, narrow valley of the Glasclune Burn, is approached on the south-west up a long, even slope, probably the eponymous *claon*. The Glasclune Burn here forms the parish boundary between Kinloch parish on the west and Blairgowrie parish on the east. Glasclune Castle is on the eastern edge of the extensive lands of Glasclune.

5. Some of this article has been adapted from the Introduction to Falkland parish in *PNF* 2.

6. Along the east side of Cash Wood, between Falkland and Strathmiglo, at around NO237087.

7. See Gilbert 1979, 40 and notes for references.

8. See Appendix for details.

9. *TA* iv, 115 (see Appendix); Gilbert 1979, 57 and note; see also ibid. 56-7 for a definition of stalking.

10. In the mid-19th century there was a local belief that they were of Roman construction. While the OS Name Book (27, 59) endorses their military use, it is sceptical of a Roman connection, as under Trenches is written: 'The remains of extensive military defences, consisting of about six ditches running nearly parallel to each other, but approximating towards the west. They are supposed by Col. Millar to have been constructed by the Roman General previous to occupying the Camp of Pitlour . . . No other traces of any works in connection with these trenches are known to any person in the place. There seems no sufficient evidence to suppose that these works were constructed by the Romans.'

11. This is now Grewans Den.

12. This seventeenth century map is notorious for its transcription errors, and it is possible that *Deir* represents an original Den: we know that this burn was known as Den Burn in 1757 (Falkland Plan/1757). However, B<urn of> Den is a very unlikely construction for this common Fife burn-name.

13. *TA* iii, 172, for details of which, see Appendix.

14. I am grateful to Mairi Davies for drawing this to my attention.

15. I am grateful to Christopher Dingwall for drawing this to my attention.

16. I am grateful to Douglas Speirs and Ninian Stuart for information on this object.

17. 'to him who paid the men that brought the king's coursers and mares from the Tor Wood (by Stirling) to Falkland'; *cursour* is defined by *DOST* as 'a large powerful riding horse or war-horse; a stallion'.

18. 'to a man to go to Kinneil (West Lothian, on the south shore of the Firth of Forth) for deer-nets and to bring them to Falkland'.

19. 'to Master Levisay, Englishman, who captures deer in Falkland, by the king's command'; on 6 Dec. 1503, another payment (of 29s. 6d) was made to Levisay in the same terms (*TA* ii, p. 409).

20. 'to the Queen's yeomen (who) brought a live deer from Falkland to Stirling'.

21. 'to two men (who) carried two bucks to Stirling'.

22. 'to the man that watched the fold all year where the deer were taken'.

23. 'paid to the said Andrew (Matheson) (the money) that he had laid out for carrying eleven litters with deer, at various times, each litter 14s., and 4s. more among them'; at the same time Matheson was also paid for carrying swans and bears to Edinburgh to the comptroller.

24. 'paid to the said Andrew Matheson (the money) he laid out for shoeing the queen's litter horse which carried the deer all year'.

25. 'And to Thomas Duncan for feeding the boars in Falkland, 1 boll and 1 firlot of barley'.

26. 'And for payment made to the gardener of Falkland who was in receipt of 2 chalders of oats a year, from the year of the account, 2 chalders of oats. And to the same man for the maintenance of the ditches and fences of the Park of Falkland from the same year, 2 chalders of oats. And for the repair of the embankments of the meadow of Falkland from the said year, 1 chalder of oats . . .'

27. 'And for the provision made to feed the game and red deer in Falkland, for the capturing of the same animals, which were afterwards sent to the park of Stirling by command of the lord king, 5 bolls, 3 firlots of oats . . . And to the same man for the provision made of 1 chalder 15 bolls of oats to feed 5 boars and 3 swans in Falkland from the 5 October until Christmas, within (the year of) this

account, 1 chalder 15 bolls of oats. And to the same man for the fodder for one horse of the king in Falkland, with James Avery staying with it, for the capturing of red deer sent to Stirling various times during the winter, 5 bolls of oats.'

28. 'And to the same man [to John Stirling, the comptroller] for the expenses of one stalker and his two servants working for 12 days on the capturing of red deer and game at the time of the lord king's wedding, 40s. . . . And for the structure and building of one fold in the park of Falkland for capturing red deer by command of the lord king, 13s. And for the transportation of 8 red deer from Falkland to the monastery of Edinburgh (Holyrood) at the time of the lord king's wedding, 28s.'; the wedding of James IV and Margaret Tudor took place on 8 August 1503.

29. *TA* ii, Glossary under *staggis* 'young horses' (ref. p. 135 [1505: Item, for iiii bos bittis to the Kingis staggis).

30. 'paid to James Avery for his expense and that of others with him going to the Tor Wood (south-east of Stirling) at three different times, and to Falkland, to "draw" the king's *staggis* and to bring them to Edinburgh and Falkland'. Gilbert suggests that 'drawing deer' meant using nets, 'encircling them before driving them into a fold or enclosure' (1979, 220-1). The main meaning of Scots *stag* is 'young horse' (*DOST*). In this and the following entry Gilbert takes it to mean 'stag' (i.e. male deer).

31. 'to the said James (Avery) for one man's expense for keeping the said *staggis* in Falkland, for 33 days, each day 8d.'.

32. 'for deer nets which went to Falkland'.

33. 'to Master Levisay, an English man, to pass to Falkland to take deer to send to Stirling'.

34. 'paid to Andrew Matheson for expenses he incurred in Falkland for carrying deer to Stirling six times, with four men with each litter, by the yeomen who went back and forward, each time 14s., total £4 4s'.

35. 'for the shoeing of the king's three young horses which were sent to Edinburgh'; see comment under *TA* ii, pp. 474-5, above.

36. 'for building the deer fold in Falkland'.

37. 'for making a trap and the iron required for the same, by the king's command, to kill foxes in the Park of Falkland'.

38. 'paid in cash to the vicar of Kilgour (older name for Falkland parish) the teind or tithe of the king's *staggis* over two years'; for the *staggis*, see comment under *TA* ii, pp. 474-5, and ns. 29 & 30 above.

39. 'paid to John Balfour for ranging through the countryside (probably around Falkland; J. M. Gilbert suggests this means the Lomond Hills (1979, 220)) with bloodhounds to drive the deer to the Park, and for the construction of a wattle enclosure to catch them'. For a discussion of the phrase 'wynding of the hay yard for deir taking', see Gilbert 1979, 220. Note also the place-name Wyndford, referring to a ford over the Parkmill Burn by Tarbolton, near the apex of so-called Roman Trenches (see p. 239, and Fig. 5). *TA* iii, Glossary under *wynding* has 'possibly making narrow entrances or alleys'.

40. 'to Andrew Matheson for the litter coming and going this past winter 16 times to Stirling with deer, to 4 men who accompanied it each time with the yeomen, paying each man per day 8d., staying away each time for 3 days, and once for 4 days, because the flood-waters stopped them'. Falkland is almost certainly the source of the deer in this and the following two entries.

41. 'to John Methven who went with the king to stalk a deer with a culverin (an early form of hand-gun)'.

42. 'paid to Andrew Matheson for the transportation of deer several times, for the repair of the enclosure and its gate, and for repairs carried out on the deer fold several times, as contained in his bill'.

At the Margins: the Dynamics of Post-Mediaeval Land-use and Settlement around the Farm of Sarn Faen in the Twrch Valley, Carmarthenshire

Muriel Bowen-Evans and Anthony Ward

Historical and archaeological evidence illustrate the emergence, development and decline of an upland farm, Sarn Faen, on the Black Mountain, Carmarthenshire. It is likely that transhumant exploitation of valued grazing and associated transient settlement led to enclosure of common land and the creation of a hill farm at the limits of viability, perhaps in the late seventeenth and the early eighteenth century. Viability was sustained with the advent of opportunities for complementary industrial and agricultural employment in the nineteenth century. It appears that the farm had ceased to be occupied before the Second World War. We offer this paper in Terry's memory with recollections of many enjoyable and fruitful field trips to the Black Mountain in the 1980s and early 1990s when every visit brought new discoveries.

INTRODUCTION

The Golden Grove Estate archive contains a map dated to 1789 of the farm of Sarn Faen on the south-eastern slopes of the Black Mountain, Carmarthenshire (*Fig. 4*). The farm is located on the west bank of the valley of the Afon Twrch and, surrounded by common land, it marks the maximum altitudinal extent of agricultural enclosure on the Carmarthenshire side of the Twrch (*Figs. 1 and 2*). Intriguingly the map is annotated with the words 'Old Walls' in a position approximate to a rectangular foundation and other features which are visible on the bank of the Twrch, to the north of the farmhouse recorded on the map which presently survives in a ruinous condition. The foundation is an example of numbers of often compartmented rectangular structures on the Black Mountain which show some elements of variability in their essentially simple construction. With the exception of one partially excavated example in the Garw Valley, they are undated but are argued as the remains of settlement structures mostly of the late Mediaeval to early post-Mediaeval centuries, many of which could have been connected with seasonal exploitation of the uplands.[1] There are

examples of other such structures recorded through field work in the Twrch Valley both within and beyond the boundaries of Sarn Faen.[2] Documentation for late mediaeval and early post-mediaeval land-use on the Black Mountain is rare compared to some other upland regions of Wales and therefore the coincidence of historical evidence, possibly from the mid-seventeenth century and certainly from the mid-eighteenth century onwards, early cartographic data and archaeological field remains at and around Sarn Faen provides an important opportunity to explore the dynamics of the exploitation of an area of upland landscape in the region.

THE LOCATION AND TOPOGRAPHICAL SETTING OF SARN FAEN

The enclosed area of Sarn Faen farm (centred SN 7700 1504) is located on ground with a south-easterly aspect rising from the often precipitous west bank of the Afon Twrch at around 250m OD to around 380m OD below Cefn Carn Fadog. The enclosure is carved out from the upland common and is isolated from a wedge of enclosed farmland to the south-west between the

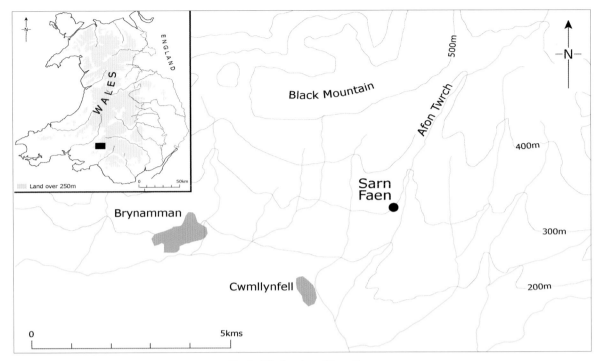

Fig. 1: *The location of Sarn Faen.*

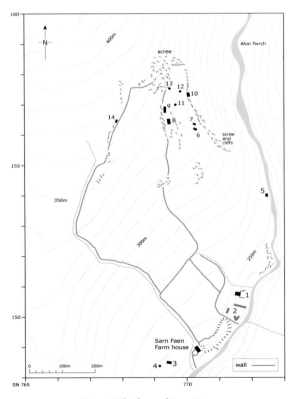

Fig. 2: *The farm of Sarn Faen.*

villages of Cefn bryn-brain and Ystradowen on the A4068 in the extreme south-east corner of Carmarthenshire. Brynaman and Cwmllynfell are locally important centres (*Figs. 1 and 2*). On the Breconshire side of the Afon Twrch, agricultural enclosure extends further to the north to Llwyncwnstabl with the abandoned farm building of Dorwen lying opposite Sarn Faen high on the east bank of the river.

The steep and often rocky Millstone Grit slope to the west of the Twrch is interrupted by a narrow band of Carboniferous Limestone. Today there is little differentiation between the character of the enclosed area of the abandoned farm and the surrounding landscape, with very poorly drained soils and impoverished vegetation comprising grass, bracken and reeds. A few trees provide shelter in the immediate vicinity of the farm building (*Fig. 3*).

THE HISTORICAL EVIDENCE FOR THE FARM
The farm of Sarn Faen[3] (lit. 'stony causeway') was part of the Golden Grove Estate and thanks to this there is a certain amount of documentation in the estate collection at the Carmarthen Record Office. The Vaughans of Golden Grove were also manorial lords and therefore the collection includes documents relating to the Lordship of Perfedd and the manor of Gwynfe and Fabon in

which Sarn Faen lies. The boundaries of the commote of Perfedd were largely stable for tenurial purposes through the Middle Ages,[4] into the post-mediaeval period as illustrated by a mid-eighteenth century perambulation of the bounds.[5]

Unfortunately, the references discovered in the Golden Grove archives (listed as Cawdor/Vaughan in the Carmarthenshire Record Office) are not sufficiently early or comprehensive to provide a key to the use of the site in the Middle Ages but two Rentals of the seventeenth century contain data which may be relevant. One is undated but is of the middle of the century (C/V 8399), the other is for the year 1669 (C/V 8400). The properties are grouped by parish and as is often the case in Rentals, are un-named. The lists include tenants, annual rents and occasional marginal note. The holdings in the parish of Llangadog for both dates include an unoccupied tenement with a value of eighteen shillings. The 1669 Rental describes it as 'A Ten (ement) upon the Mountain neere Llwyn y Cwnstabl.' This landmark is in the neighbouring parish of Ystradgynlais across the Afon Twrch. Of the holdings which can be identified as Vaughan property there was nothing located closer to Llwyn y Cwnstabl than Sarn Faen and for this reason it is tentatively suggested that this was the unoccupied holding.

The first unambiguous reference to Sarn Faen is from 1752 and shows it to have been rented by one John Morgan for 19s. 6d. per year (C/V 8395). He is described on another occasion as a farmer of Rhosmaen, Llandeilo (C/V 7694). He seems to have sublet it, as his under-tenant, Lewis Llewelin, was still there in 1768.[6] John Morgan relinquished his tenancy in 1765 or earlier. In 1767 Richard Vaughan leased the property for three lives, to the Reverend Thomas Lewis, the incumbent of Llangadog, the lease being back-dated to 1765. The annual rent had more than trebled to three pounds, and so it continued to 1829 when the lease was surrendered (C/V 7694). During this period there was also a change of terminology. In 1755, it was described as 'A cott on ye B.M.' (C/V 5959), but in 1767 it was referred to as a messuage, tenement and lands. The extent of Sarn Faen in 1767 is unstated but when the farm was mapped in 1789 it consisted of just over eighty-nine acres. Since the rent was as in 1767 it seems likely that the 1767 acreage was as in 1789. In the later eighteenth century the farm failed to find a buyer when the Golden Grove Estate tried to sell some of its Black Mountain property.

The occupations of the heads of household returned in Censuses were: in 1841 collier, 1851 and 61 farmer, 1871 farmer and shepherd, 1881 (the same person as in 1871) farmer, 1891 a coal miner and in 1901 a colliery stationary-engine driver. The 1891 Census included a query about housing and Sarn Faen was in the category of '5 rooms or more'. On the evidence of Electoral Lists and the Cawdor Rentals, occupation continued through

Fig. 3: *Sarn Faen on the south-west slope of the Twrch Valley looking north; the farmhouse lies in the cluster of trees.*
(Photograph A. Ward).

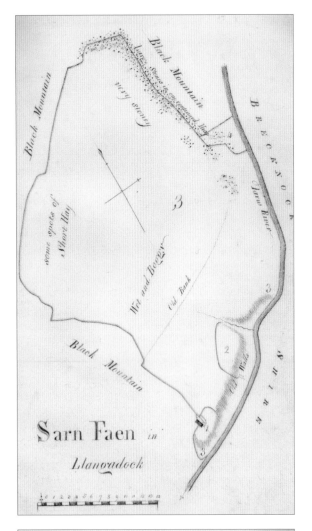

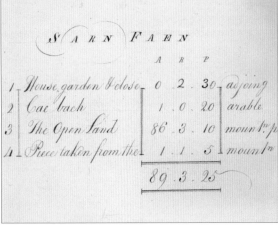

Fig. 4: *1789 Golden Grove Estate Map
of Sarn Faen.*
(Reproduced by permission of Carmarthenshire Record Office).

the early decades of the twentieth century. The last-discovered annual rentals are for the sums of £9 in 1928 and £10 in 1933. No one was in occupation at the outbreak of the Second World War although RAF aerial photography shows the farmhouse still had a roof in 1947.[7] It is not known when the fields north of the farm ceased to be used as formal enclosures. There is no indication that boundaries have been maintained for many decades.

THE CARTOGRAPHIC EVIDENCE
FOR THE FARM

The 1789 map (*Fig. 4*) and the accompanying schedule of the land and its use (C/V 5852) provide a helpful insight into the disposition of the farm bounded by the river to the east, named as the 'Tarw River'[8] and the Black Mountain common on the other three sides. The fields total in extent eighty-nine acres, three rods and twenty-five perches. The farmhouse with enclosures to front and back (annotated '1') described as 'garden' and 'close' are two rods and thirty perches in extent and are at the southern extremity of the area defined as the farm. To the north-east above the steep river bank is 'Cae bach' (annotated '2') which is just over one acre with the schedule indicating arable usage.[9] 'Old Walls' are noted along the slope of the river bank. By far the largest unit on the farm (annotated '3') is described as 'The Open Land' and is over eighty-six acres in extent. It is apparently without subdivisions thought worthy of record other than an 'Old Bank' indicated as an ephemeral feature extending towards a rocky area above the river. To the north of this bank the ground is marked as 'Wet and Boggy', echoing its present day condition. Higher up the slope 'some spots of Short Hay' presumably reflect potential for fodder.

The northern and north-eastern edge of 'The Open Land' coincides with a linear band of stipple, a convention seemingly indicating rock and stone, and described as 'large stones in one continuous line'. Across this band runs a dotted line that can be surmised as indicating a boundary. However, there are only a few short stretches of wall currently visible amongst the outcrop and low cliffs of the area and no boundary is recorded on subsequent mapping (see below) although the craggy rock on the ground certainly forms a natural boundary. Immediately to the west, the ground is described as 'very stoney'. A small enclosure (annotated '4'), noted in the schedule as just over one acre in extent and described as 'Piece taken from the mountn', is recorded adjacent to the river. No trace of the enclosure can currently be seen on the ground and it is not recorded on the next detailed mapping of the farm namely the Tithe Map and Schedule dating to 1839 (*Fig. 5*).

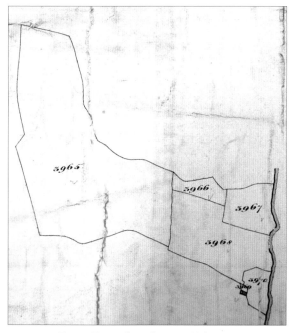

Fig. 5: *Extract from the 1839 Tithe Map of Llangadog, showing Sarn Faen.*
(Reproduced by permission of Carmarthenshire Record Office).

Indeed the Tithe map demonstrates that the extent of the farm had apparently declined by almost half to some forty-seven acres. Comparison with the estate map shows that the particularly steep and craggy north-eastern portion of the farm as defined in 1789 had been excluded by 1839. The necessity of paying tithe may have argued in favour of a realistic statement. Nor is this area mapped by the Ordnance Survey as integral to the farm. The 1812 two inch to a mile draft Ordnance Survey map shows a still more restricted roughly square area of enclosure lacking internal sub-division with the farmhouse at its south-eastern corner, which may reflect the ephemeral character of the physical boundaries higher up the slope in the early nineteenth century. However, the first edition one inch Ordnance Survey map (sheet 41, published in 1831) following revision undertaken in May and June 1826[10] shows the boundaries of the farm enclosing apparently the same area as the 1839 Tithe map. The extent of the enclosed area remains the same on later large scale Ordnance Survey

maps[11] although the Inland Revenue Valuation of 1910 reverts to the 1789 estate map calculation of extent as just over 89 acres of which 40 acres were agricultural land (T/DV/2/87 Quarter Bach).

The position of the farmhouse is constant from the 1789 estate map onwards. The detail of the 1877 surveyed OS 25-inch map (*Fig. 6*) is sufficient to show that by then the house with an immediately adjacent small yard or paddock to the south-west had essentially achieved the plan visible today. The 1789 estate map and the 1839 Tithe map, however, show a small yard to the north-east of the house. The different locations of the yards appear to be real, even making allowance for both the smaller scale and perhaps greater imprecision of the earlier mapping. It indicates an intervening change in the focus of the building from its north-eastern to its south-western frontage which is supported by analysis of the fabric of the remains of the building. The 1877 OS map shows the paddock south-west of the property approached by a track from the south-west which can no longer be seen.

STRUCTURAL EVIDENCE VISIBLE ON THE FARM

Evidence relevant to the development of the farm is described in relation to the ruined farmhouse and its congruent small enclosures; the fields of the farm; a rectangular foundation and adjacent stone piles on the river bank in a position coinciding with the 'Old Walls' marked on the 1789 estate map; and a cluster of dry stone wall buildings at the northern edge of the boundaries of the farm.

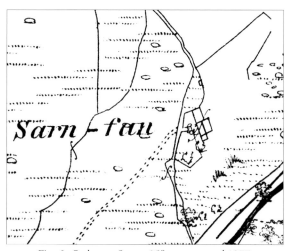

Fig. 6: *Ordnance Survey 25" map surveyed 1877.*

Fig. 7: *Sarn Faen farmhouse 2008 from the south.*
(Photograph A. Ward).

Fig. 8: *Sarn Faen farmhouse 2008 from the north-west.*
(Photograph A. Ward).

The Farmhouse

The farmhouse is located at 240m OD on a promontory between the Afon Twrch and a stream flowing from the north-west into the river (*Figs. 7, 8 and 9*). The 19m long building range aligned NNW-SSE comprises a house with byre attached to the NW. The gabled house comprises a principal two-storied residential unit with a single storey lean-to on its northern side and single storied units attached to north-west and south-east (*Fig. 9*). The unit to the north-west was the byre and either the lean-to or the single storied unit to the south-east served as the dairy 'essential to every farm where the cows were kept for milk, butter or cheese'.[12]

The house is described in detail in Appendix 1. A structural sequence can be suggested: the central, core, residential unit is the primary feature to which, perhaps not very much later, a byre was added to the north-west. Next, a smaller unit was added to the south-east at some later date. The residential unit was remodelled with the addition of a symmetrical southerly façade (*Fig. 7*). Arguably, at that point, a door and window in the north wall of the house were blocked and a new door created on broadly the same axis as the door in the south façade which gave access to a newly added lean-to on the north face of the house. Curiously there appears to be no north-facing external exit from the lean-to.

The rearrangement may have coincided with the appearance suggested by cartographic evidence of a small yard and paddock immediately to the south-west and the disappearance of a yard to the north-east.[13] These features are lesser in extent than the 'garden' and 'close' noted on the 1789 estate map and appear to be within the boundaries of these features. This major modification and reorientation of the residential unit appears to have taken place between 1839, when the yard to the north-east is still recorded on the Tithe map, and the 1877 OS 25-inch map when the current building plan with small paddock to the south-west is illustrated (*Figs. 4, 5 and 6*). The symmetrical front elevation of the house also suggests a remodelling in the third quarter of the nineteenth century (the suggested date of the bricks) in imitation of the industrial housing which is now prevalent in South Wales.[14] As noted above, the 1891 Census records the house as having five rooms or more, suggesting two-up and two-down, with the lean-to at the back.

The Old Walls

Terracing along the brow of the steep river bank north-east of the farmhouse (*Fig. 2*) leads to the enclosure

named on the 1789 estate map as 'Cae bach'. A rectangular foundation (Structure 1) (*Fig. 10*) lies at right angles to the steep slope on an artificial platform at around 240m OD. A boulder wall revets the face of the platform which is approached from the south by a track. The foundation measures 12 metres NW-SE by 5.8 metres NE-SW and is divided into two compartments The north-western compartment, internally 6.8 by 3.4

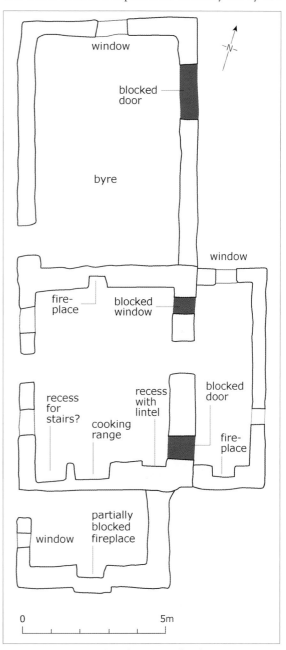

Fig. 9: *Plan of Sarn Faen farmhouse.*

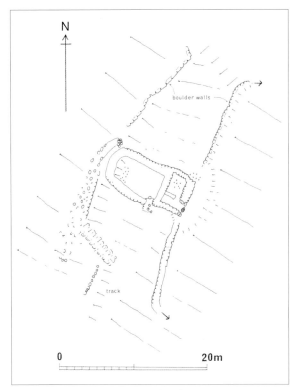

Fig. 10: *Dry stone building foundation – Structure 1.*

metres, comprises dry-stone boulder walls up to 1 metre high with a 0.8 metre wide entrance at the south-eastern corner. The south-eastern compartment measures 2 by 4 metres, the dry-stone walls standing between 0.5 and 1 metre high. It is partially sub-divided and is entered across a sill stone through a 1 metre wide entrance in the end wall. Boulder banks run at right angles from each corner of the eastern end of the building partially enclosing an area on the steep slope leading down to the river bank. South of the building are three stony piles (2) which look likely to be, at least in part, the consequence of field clearance. The general area of these features (*Fig. 2*) corresponds with the position of the 'Old Walls' on the 1789 Estate map (*Fig. 4*).

Structures at the Northern Edge of the Farm
A group of rectangular dry-stone foundations is located on the slope towards the northern limits of the farm enclosure at between 320 and 350 metres OD (*Fig. 2*) on natural terraces in the lee of rock exposure (*Fig. 12*). Structure 6, accessed by a 1 metre wide entrance, measures 12.4 metres NW-SE by 6 metres NE-SW, having coursed stonework standing up to 1 metre high (*Figs. 11 and 12*). It is paired with another structure (7) 15

metres to the north, a foundation 5.2 metres N-S by 8 metres E-W on a slight platform scarped in the slope. Coursed walling survives up to 0.8 metres high and there is a 1.3 metre entrance in the south wall (*Fig. 11*). Around 100 metres further north a compartmented building (10) is located on top of a low cliff. Tumbled dry-stone walls between 0.4 and 0.6 metres high define a northern unit measuring 5.2 metres N-S by 2.5metres E-W entered by a 1 metre break, with a smaller unit to the south around 2.6 metres N-S by 2 metres E-W (*Figs. 2 and 11*). A sub-annular foundation around 4.5 metres across is located 4 metres to the west. There are three other lesser sub-annular stone foundations (*Fig. 2, No. 11, 12 and 13*) further to the west.

Structure 9 is relatively complex (*Figs. 13 and 14*). The principal range measuring 18 metres NW-SE by 5 metres NE-SW comprises two conjoined units of contrasting form. The walls of the northern compartment stand at 1.5 metres high with up to ten courses of stonework in place. Internally it is 7.4 metres NW-SE by 2.8 metres NE-SW with a 1.4 metre-wide entrance at the south-eastern corner where two sill stones are visible. Some laid flat slabs within the interior indicate a paved floor. The compartment abutting to the south is 8.4 metres NW-SE by 5.2 metres NE-SW; the south-eastern down slope end is constructed of larger boulders forming a platform which roughly levels the interior of

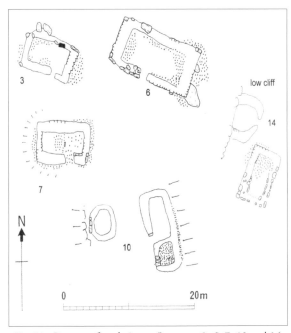

Fig. 11: *Dry stone foundations – Structures 3, 6, 7, 10 and 14.*

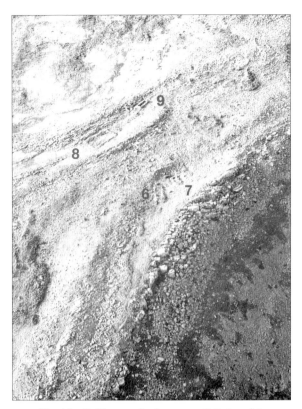

Fig. 12: *Air Photograph of structures 6, 7, 8 and 9.*
(Crown Copyright, RCAHMW).

the structure. It is sub-divided by a wall broken by an entrance. Its surviving walls at 0.3 metres high contrast in scale and style of construction with those of the northern unit which are comprised of parallel facings of boulder and slabs retaining a rubble core. Immediately to the south is another rectangular foundation 8.8 metres NW-SE by 3.8 metres NE-SW with the same style of construction; it is conjoined with a simpler unit built against the low cliff. Twenty-two metres south is a large enclosure (Structure 8), 22 metres NW-SE by 12.5 metres NE-SW, defined by walls at places around 1 metre high which again are made up of parallel facing slabs and boulders retaining rubble. There is a 0.8 metre-wide entrance visible in its northern wall (*Fig. 13*).

Other Features on or Immediately Adjacent to the Farm
Other structures on the farm, all of dry-stone-build, include: to the south-west of the farmhouse, a single-unit rectangular foundation 7.8 metres WNW-SSE by 4.8 metres NNE-SSW (*Figs. 2 and 11, No. 3*) with an oval boulder structure 4 metres across (*Fig. 2, No. 4*) located 34 metres distant; on the west bank of the Afon

Twrch, a small rectangular foundation 4 metres long (*Fig. 2, No. 5*); and, at just under 370 metres OD immediately beyond the bank of the north-western boundary, a rectangular building, 7 metres SW-NE by 4.6 metres NW-SE with coursed walling to a height of 1.2 metres, accompanied by a simple shelter against a cliff face (*Figs. 2 and 5, No. 14*). A leat feeding off the Afon Twrch crosses the south eastern slope of the farm to the north of the farmhouse just above the 250m

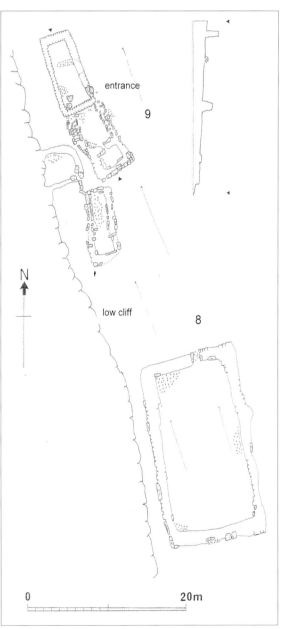

Fig. 13: *Dry stone foundations – Structures 8 and 9.*

Fig. 14: *Dry stone structure 9 from the north.*
(Photograph A. Ward).

contour.[15] The leat was built in the early 1820s to service a colliery at Cwymllynfell.[16]

THE DEVELOPMENT OF SARN FAEN FARM

The dry-stone rectangular foundations described within and close to the farm are typical of others which have been described elsewhere on the Black Mountain[17] and recorded more widely in many parts of upland Wales.[18] Such structures in Wales are usually associated with transhumant exploitation of these uplands with the permanently-settled hendre expanding its activity to exploit seasonally available pasture at the upland hafod or lluest.[19] Although designation of function is not always apparent, some can be seen as human dwellings or shelters of varying degrees of scale, for example: structures 1, 7, 9 and 10 with integral or congruent compartments and also associated ancillary structures serving as animal shelters (e.g. the structure attached to 9); folds or pens (e.g. 4, 6 & 8); and structures with other purposes of storage or protection.

They have also been argued by one of us (AW) as integral to a dynamic whereby marginal landscapes initially used only on a seasonal basis became subject to episodes of permanent settlement and exploitation.[20] Recent study has moved away from the presentation of a universal model for transhumance applicable across Wales to one which recognises regional variability in economic circumstances, the chronological parameters of activity, and the mechanics of practice, in the context of broader consideration of rural settlement.[21]

For the Black Mountain only limited historical evidence has so far been found against which to compare the surviving structural remains such as those on Sarn Faen although such documentary and place name evidence as has been published certainly indicates transhumant activity associated with relict settlement.[22] The only archaeological investigation of an example of such settlement on the Black Mountain at Tro'r Derlwyn in the Garw Valley has done little to provide any element of chronological precision, producing radiocarbon dates spanning the very late mediaeval and modern periods. A clay pipe fragment leads to a tentative preference for a mid-eighteenth to early nineteenth century association.[23] While there may well have been activity at Tro'r Derlwyn during these decades, it would be unwise to conclude that activity was limited to this period or indeed that it was necessarily a principal episode of activity.

Historical and cartographic evidence for Sarn Faen provides an opportunity to further understand the development of the farm, and this particular tract of Black Mountain upland. To start with the seventeenth century rents, nineteen shillings and sixpence (and the possibly earlier eighteen shillings), if accepted as relating to Sarn Faen, indicate some enclosure of the common at this epoch. This rent was not the going rate for a cottage alone which would have been let for two or three shillings a year. One of the marginal notes in the seventeenth century Rental illustrates the range of rents in relation to one David Thomas ap Evan and an unknown property: 'whether he hath taken in the ground he promised for which with his former rent of 2s he is to pay 1£.' (C/V 8399).

There was a tendency for rents to increase on the Vaughan properties in Llangadog during the second half of the eighteenth century, but the percentage rise was not consistent in all holdings, a fact that leads to the suspicion of improvements of one sort or another: either enclosure or building. The rent of Sarn Faen more than trebled between 1752 and 1767 and there was also the change in terminology already noted, from a cottage in 1755 to a messuage, tenement and lands in 1767. It might be suggested, therefore, that Sarn Faen was re-made in the middle years of the eighteenth century. It had been acquired by the Vaughan family in the sixteenth or early seventeenth century as a result of some transaction now unknown. One reason for its survival must have been that it had become part of a great estate with a place in the rent roll. Although remote, it slotted in to the formality of estate management. Moreover, various members of the Vaughan family in successive generations held the position of Lord of the Manor of Perfedd. As such they had authority in the Court Leet which controlled matters to do with the commons such as enclosure. If as seems likely there was enclosure at Sarn Faen in the eighteenth century the landlord's position vis à vis the Court Leet could only have been a help.

Added to this was the continued importance of animal husbandry in the area. For example, the undated inventory attached to the probate will of 'Thomas ap Morgan ap Jevan Lloyd of Llangadogge parish, gentleman', who died in 1604 and was buried at Llangadock Church, makes reference to 'wild beasts breed upon the black mountayne.'[24] That they are described as 'wild' may indicate that the husbandry practice on the commons was distinctive even if not necessarily transhumant.

The seventeenth century Rentals show the value placed by the Vaughans on cattle as a source of wealth and the minutes of the eighteenth century Courts Leet show how this aspect of the economy was maintained. Part of the seventeenth century tenancy agreements were services such as 'the herding of 20 Wild Beastes Winter and Summer' or the 'herding of as many Beastes and Sheep as shall be putt to them.' However, no information about the terms of the tenancy between John Morgan and his landlord – or indeed terms of the sub-let has been seen. Residence in the upland or on the margins of the mountain, or possession of an upland

dwelling, would have been essential for cattle herding and indeed guarding of stock from theft.

The pasturing of cattle was one of the main aspects of farming in Perfedd. As the Jurors of the Lordship had commented in May 1709 in relation to the Black Mountain . . . 'the Tenants and Inhabitants have been used Time out of Mind to have Common of Turbarie and also Common of Pasture for all kind of beast without number and other commodities as furze, heath, coales and lime' (C/V554-5). So prized was a stake in the cattle trade that things went out of control in the next three or four decades with inhabitants of Perfedd pasturing cattle from outside the Lordship, a practice which had been expressly forbidden by the Court Leet (C/V 542). Any person grazing sheep, cattle or horses of persons who had no rights of common was to pay twenty-five shillings and eleven pence to the Lord of the Manor for each offence. It was also suggested that persons with a right of common should graze it with sheep, cattle and horses in 'the number equal to their lands'. The disputes continued and in 1763 and 1775 individuals were presented for herding cattle from outside the lordship and fines were imposed.

Perhaps this was the context in which John Morgan's tenancy must be viewed. An attempt has been made to identify him. In 1756 there certainly was a saddler of this name living in Rhosmaen Street, Llandeilo and the difference in occupation does not necessarily rule out the possibility that he was the tenant of Sarn Faen (C/V 8203). Whoever rented the farm had the opportunity of grazing the enclosed land and using the common. The information on the Revd Thomas Lewis' tenancy is equally scanty. It was certainly not the permanent home of his family. Apart from the possibility of grazing cattle there, Sarn Faen offered rest and shelter at the distant eastern end of the vicar's parish which was bounded here by the rivers Twrch and Aman. Head of household information as recorded in the various Censuses shows a mix of farming and industrial roles, reflecting the increasing industrialisation of the Twrch valley[25] and the area south of the Black Mountain and this was perhaps more generally linked to a requirement for economic diversification to maintain the viability of the holding.

The extent of the enclosed land of the farm varied over time although the phasing of episodes of intake is unclear. Presumably there was some intake of unknown extent from the common by the time of the seventeenth century rentals putatively associated with Sarn Faen. The recording of an 'Old Bank' and the description of a small field on the 1789 Estate map as 'Piece taken from the mountn' suggests more than one phase with the latter episode of enclosure perhaps not all that long before 1789 for it to be described in such terms. Particular regard for using natural features to define the farm is apparent: the Afon Twrch to the east; the stream coinciding with the field bank to the south and south-west; and outcrop and low cliff to the north. The acreage of the farm halves in terms of land which is clearly defined by artificial boundaries between the estate mapping in 1789 and the tithe mapping in 1839 although the 1910 Inland Revenue Valuation indicates continued fiscal recognition of its late eighteenth century extent.

The historical and cartographic information demonstrates that there is a dynamic in the evolution of the farm probably over at least three centuries. The archaeological evidence suggests several phases of settlement in the immediate vicinity of the enclosed intake. The 1789 Estate map's reference to 'old walls' at a location which corresponds with rectangular dry stone house foundation (Structure 1), some adjacent enclosure, and field clearance (*Fig. 2*) indicates settlement with a degree of antiquity prior to the by then apparently established farmhouse represented by the present ruins. The cluster of dry stone buildings at the northern edge of the farm is, on the basis of their form, also likely to be earlier than the ruined farmhouse. The farmhouse itself appears to have undergone an episode of remodelling. A sequence can be argued:

> *Episode 1*: the dry stone buildings and ancillary structures at the northern edge of the farm (*Fig. 2, 6-14*) representing the earliest phase of presently visible settlement, perhaps associated with seasonal exploitation of grazing along the Twrch Valley and prior to any local intake of the common.

> *Episode 2*: the rectangular dry stone structure (*Fig. 2, Structure 1*) above the Afon Twrch also representing an early phase of settlement, perhaps but not necessarily fully coinciding with structures 6-14 of Episode 1. Possibly this building too is initially associated with transhumant exploitation but eventually, with an element of field clearance, adjacent enclosure and arable farming, it becomes a more substantial enterprise and the nucleus for an emerging hill farm.

Dating Episodes 1 and 2 cannot be fixed to any source with precision. Presumably transhumant exploitation of these slopes initially predates the period of the mid to late seventeenth century rentals which may coincide with the use of Structure 1 and associated features.

Episode 3: The construction of the farmhouse before 1789, implying a contemporary or earlier abandonment of Structure 1 as a principal dwelling. Speculatively, can the construction of the farmhouse be linked to the change noted in terminology from cottage to messuage between 1755 and 1767; and the trebling of the rent between these dates associated with a significant increase in the acreage enclosed to something approaching that mapped in 1789 including the later further addition of the 'Piece taken from the mountn'? Alternatively the farmhouse could be an even earlier construction, the change in description reflecting only an enhanced scale of enclosure.

Episode 4: the remodelling of the farmhouse with the addition of a new southerly façade around the third quarter of the nineteenth century and its subsequent abandonment before the middle of the twentieth century.

Whatever the precise relative sequence of activity, the waxing and waning of Sarn Faen farm at the margins of viable agricultural exploitation reflects the changing utility of this tract of landscape to different people at various times. Probably from at least the sixteenth and seventeenth centuries the area provided highly valued seasonal grazing for holders of common rights of the Manor of Perfedd who lived north of the Black Mountain. Some of those graziers maintained their interest in the area through the later seventeenth and into the eighteenth centuries eventually extending to more than a transient satellite presence at a distance from principal holdings and progressing to intake and enclosure associated with permanent settlement and some arable activity. Finally, in the nineteenth and into the early twentieth century, a way of life developed continuing farming practices but now combined with employment in the burgeoning industries in the valleys to the south.

APPENDIX 1

Description of Sarn Faen Farmhouse*

The dangerously dilapidated condition of the roofless building range precludes detailed survey. Figure 9 is a measured sketch plan. The central element, the residential house (*Fig. 7*), is built of 0.6m thick walls of

---

* The description is based on the condition of the building when first described and measured in 1995. By 2008 it had become noticeably more ruinous.

stone retaining a rubble and mortar core. Traces of a yellowish rendering or wash are visible on the relatively carefully dressed and pointed external face. The gable walls approach 6m high excluding the chimneys. The 7.5m long frontage contains a central doorway with the 3.5m high elevation containing four symmetrically positioned windows two up two down (*Fig. 7*). Window and door openings in the frontage and the arch of the fireplace in the north-west wall are retained by bricks. Some bricks are stamped "B D B" or "B D B C". Mr Robert Protheroe-Jones identifies these as siliceous refractory bricks and suggests a post-1860 date, with a post-1870 date being likely. The identity of the brick company is uncertain. The farmhouse had certainly acquired its current footprint before the 1877 OS 25-inch survey, a process which may have included the construction of this symmetrical façade (*c.*1870-1900). The lower windows contain a sash frame. There are suggestions in the stonework at the north-western corner of the frontage where it adjoins the byre to the west that the façade could well have been added to an earlier structure. A slate roof is suggested, at least at the latest stage, although with few remaining in the vicinity it is likely that the roof was stripped.

Internally the ground floor of the house measures 6m NW-SE by 5m NE-SW. Although no trace of internal subdivision into rooms survives, this is likely since there are fire places in both gable walls with the flues contained within the walls. The larger fireplace is in the south east wall and is partially occupied by a cast iron oven indicative of a kitchen range. The fireplace in the west wall is brick arched. Wooden joists ran NE to SW 2m above the ground supporting the first floor. A recess in the south-east gable wall to the right of the fireplace wall may be connected with the positioning of steps giving access to the first floor. Alternatively there could have been a centrally positioned stairs. Little can be said about how space was divided at first floor level. Traces of internal wall plaster survive at both levels. There is no evidence of the building ever having being connected to electricity.

The north-eastern wall contains a centrally positioned door giving access to a single story lean-to room abutting, and an addition to the principal building. Either side of that door are blocked apertures. The aperture to the right extending the full height of the wall with the blocking also visible on the outer face suggest a former door; and perhaps a former window to the left with a stone lintel *c.*1m above the rubble which obscures the lower part of the feature. The lean-to is

constructed of carefully dressed stone blocks and is recessed into a natural boulder bank (*Fig. 8*). It runs the full length of the north side of the house and internally is 2.4m wide. There is a fireplace in the south-east wall with the flue contained within the wall. There are window apertures in both north and west walls but apparently no external entrance.

The single story unit to the south-east of the dwelling is also built of mortared stone with traces of whitewash on the external face. The southern face is more carefully constructed than the gable wall which contains numbers of more roughly dressed boulders. The north side is in fact recessed into a natural boulder bank. Entered via a door in the south wall which also contains a window, internally it measures 3.4m NW-SE by 4.9m NE-SW. A blocked fire place is recessed into the end gable of the unit. A substantial chimney projects on the outside of the wall. The roofline is delineated by plaster on the outer face of the gable wall of the house.

The north-western unit of the range appears to be a byre (*Fig. 8*); an exclusively stone built mortared gabled structure without any evidence for a coating of plaster or wash. The apex of the roof against the house is 6m high. Internally it measures around 8m NW-SE by 6m NE-SW. Nothing can be seen of internal fittings or features at ground level amongst the rubble within the interior. A line of joists 1.6m off the ground indicates the presence of a loft lit by a window high in the north-west gable. While currently it is entered through a 1m wide by 1.6m high doorway in the south-west wall where it adjoins the house, there are indications of another entrance at the ruined north-western end of the north wall of the structure providing direct access to the fields beyond. As noted the byre appears quite likely to predate the southern façade added to the original structure of the house. A butt joint where the byre's north wall adjoins the house indicates that it was built on to the original house although the chronology of that sequence need not have been long.

A path fronts the house to the south-west opening on to a small yard in front of the byre. A gate accesses the yard from the open common to the west across a stone slab which bridges the immediately adjacent stream. A low elevation south of the path and yard is enclosed to form a paddock around 19m N-S by 11 m E-W defined by a flat-topped dry stone bank along which grow ash and oak trees. There is no clear indication of an entrance into this paddock on the line of the track indicated on the 1877 OS 25" map.

ACKNOWLEDGEMENTS

We first walked the Twrch Valley with W. H. (Bill) Morris many years ago, benefiting from his intuitive eye for an interesting landscape. Heather James has been a most patient and constructive editor. The assistance of staff at Carmarthen Record Office, National Library of Wales, RCARM (Wales), and the Central Register of Air Photography of Wales is grate-fully acknowledged. Many thanks to Robert Protheroe-Jones, Curator of Heavy Industry at the National Waterfront Museum, Swansea, for his commentary on the bricks through the good offices of Gerallt Nash, Senior Curator of Social History at St Fagan's National History Museum.

NOTES

1. A. Ward, 'Transhumance and settlement on the Welsh Uplands; a view from the Black Mountain' in N. Edwards (ed.) *Landscape and Settlement in Medieval Wales* (Oxbow Monograph 81, 1997) pp. 97-111.

2. D. K. Leighton, *Mynydd Du and Fforest Fawr. The Evolution of an Upland Landscape in South Wales* (RCAHMW, Aberystwyth, 1997; A. Ward, 'An Archaeological Field Survey of Part of the Black Mountain in South-East Dyfed: A Contribution to the Interpretation of Economy and Settlement in the Region from Prehistory to the Early Modern Period', unpublished Ph.D., University of Nottingham, 1993.

3. Other forms of the name which have been discovered include: Sarne ffane (1752); Sarn fane (1784); Sarn Fan (1877); Sarvân (1891); and Sarn fain (1928).

4. D. Rees, 'The Changing Borders of Iscennen', *Carms. Antiq.*, Vol. 24, 1988, pp. 15-21.

5. W. H. Morris, 'Boundaries of the Lordship of the Commote of Perfedd', *Carms. Antiq.*, Vol. 21, 1985, pp. 60-3.

6. Register of Cwmllynfell Chapel, NPR.

7. CPE/UK/2079. 19 May 1947. F20"//16.400' 2158.

8. It is not understood why the river is named as the Tarw rather than the Twrch. The name currently attached to the slopes of the eastern bank of the river is Tyle-garw which perhaps indicates past variability. It may, however, be a reference to the rough (*garw*) hillside (*tyle*).

9. Evidence of former ploughing is visible running north to south in this field on an aerial photo taken by the RAF in 1947 (CPE/UK/2079. 19 May 1947. F20"//16.400' 2158).

10. Undertaken by Thomas Bugden. One inch sheet 41 Ystradgynlais 4. Revision Hill Sketches two inches to one mile. British Library.

11. (Twenty-five inch Carmarthenshire Sheet XLIII.13 surveyed in 1877 and the First Edition six inch map, Carmarthenshire Sheet XLIII SW, based on survey between 1877 and 85 and second edition revised in 1903).

12. E. Wiliam, *The Historical Farm Buildings of Wales* (John Donald, Edinburgh, 1986) p. 24.

13. A small slightly 'hollowed' terrace immediately north of the house is the likely residual remains of an adjoining yard to the north-east.

14. J. Lowe, *Welsh Country Workers Housing 1775-1875* (National Museum of Wales, Cardiff, 1985), p. 38.

15. Not illustrated on figure 2 to avoid over complication of the map.

16. J. Dyfnallt Owen et al., *Hanes Eglwys Cwmllynfell* (Spurrell, Caerfyrddin, 1955) p. 151; the leat, known as 'Feeder Jams', carried water to the Llynfell; D. Powell, 'Industrial Archaeology of Cwm Twrch' in C. S. Briggs (ed.) *Welsh Industrial Heritage* (CBA Res. Rpt. 79, 1992) pp. 66-69.

17. A. Ward, op. cit., No. 1 & 2.

18. K. Roberts, (ed.), *Lost Farmsteads: deserted rural settlements in Wales* (CBA Research Report, 148, 2006).

19. R. U. Sayce, 'The Old Summer Pastures. A Comparative Study' & 'The Old Summer Pastures Part II: Life at the Hafod', *Monts. Colls.*, Vols. 54 & 55, 1956 & 1957, pp. 117-145 & 37-86.

20. A. Ward, op. cit., n. 1, p. 107.

21. K. Roberts, op. cit., n. 18.

22. M. Bowen Evans, 'Dros y Mynydd Du i Frynaman: documentary sources for some farms near Nant Melyn' in H. James (ed.) *Sir Gâr: Studies in Carmarthenshire History*, (Carms. Antiq. Soc., Carmarthen) 1991, pp. 25-35; A. Ward, 'An Incipient Upland Farmstead at Tro'r Derlwyn', *Carms. Antiq.*, Vol. 31, 1995, pp. 17-33; A. Ward, 'Transhumance and Place-Names: An Aspect of Early Ordnance Survey Mapping on the Black Mountain Commons, Carmarthenshire', *Stud. Celtica*, Vol. 32, 1999, pp. 335-348.

23. G. Smith & D. Thompson, 'Results of Project Excavations' in K. Roberts, op. cit., n. 18, pp. 113-132.

24. Carmarthenshire Record Office, Cynghordy Schedule, p. 23, doc. 43.

25. D. Powell, op. cit., n. 16.

Dinas, Cwm Doethïe: Reflections on a Deserted Upland Farmstead

Richard Suggett

In 1998 a small party of rain-soaked but undaunted Carmarthenshire Antiquarians and friends, led by Terry and Heather James, traversed the old township of Doethïe-Camddwr, making their way south-west from Capel Soar-y-mynydd, the famously remote south Cardiganshire chapel, across the hill to the deserted Doethïe valley. On the mountain above Cwm Doethïe the clouds cleared and the sun shone briefly on the valley; it was rather like a glimpse of Shangri-La. We made our way down the hillside examining the fugitive remains of stream-side huts, probably of 'lluest' type, that Terry and Heather had discovered, eventually encountering on the valley floor the ruins of a substantial farmstead named Dinas or 'fortress'. This farmstead is indeed dominated by a 'fortress', actually a large rocky outcrop, sheltering the house from the north. At the heart of the ruined farmstead there is a vernacular house of unusual interest, and we agreed to return to plan it. It was not to be; eventually, with Heather's encouragement, I returned to Dinas to survey the dwelling for this memorial volume. When writing this article I have had the advantage of Terry's and Heather's research notes on Dinas, and of reading Iwan Wmffre's contribution on Cwm Doethïe to this volume. I hope some points of general interest will emerge from these reflections on a deserted farmstead in upland south-west Wales.[1]

DESCRIPTION OF DINAS

The surviving vernacular architecture of south-west Wales tends to be rather late in date, as Peter Smith has shown.[2] Dinas is a house site of more than usual interest because it promises more historical depth than is typically encountered in Cardiganshire and Carmarthenshire. Dinas was an upland farmstead that became increasingly marginal and was eventually abandoned, escaping the great nineteenth- to early-twentieth-century rebuilding that has erased much of Cardiganshire's historic domestic architecture. One can readily appreciate the contrast between the old and the new domestic architecture by following the Doethïe Fawr from the Victorian box-like farmhouse at Tyncornel to the long and low ruins of Dinas. Tyncornel was the last inhabited farmhouse in the valley; the farm was sufficiently viable for the house to have been rebuilt in the mid-nineteenth century, but it was abandoned a century later, not long after the dreadful winter of 1947 that finally emptied several houses in the district that had survived into the twentieth century.[3]

Fig. 1: *On the hill above Cwm Doethïe on 12 Sept. 1998: Luke Suggett, Heather James, Tony Heath, Richard Suggett and Jackie Coughlan.*
(Photograph: Terry James).

Fig. 2: *Photograph of Dinas (right hand side), January 2009, showing its downslope siting.*
(Photograph: Tina Carr and Annemarie Schöne Archive, Tregtoes).

The rebuilding of upland south-west Wales has been so comprehensive that there are very few standing pre-nineteenth-century farmhouses. There are of course many abandoned dwellings – like Dinas – but they tend to be archaeological sites with walls reduced to their footings.[4] Because of the remoteness of Cwm Doethïe, the site of Dinas has not been substantially robbed and – critically for dating and interpretation – the plan of the dwelling is still intelligible. Dinas provides the opportunity to reconstruct the plan of the unimproved upland dwelling, and to place it within the context of the regional architecture of Wales.

Dinas is now a roofless ruin with picturesque moss-covered wandering walls and several substantial birch trees growing within and on the walls. The lateral walls have been gently collapsing for a century or more, though they generally still stand to the level of the window sills, a height of four feet or so. Collapse shows that the walls are regularly about 2 feet 6 inches thick with substantial footings, and rubble-built with generous quantities of clay mortar; a few water-worn stones are mixed with the rather friable stone collected from the hillside outcrops and scree. Dinas is a long range,

some 60 feet (18.3 metres) from upper to lower gable-ends, aligned NW-SE on a sloping site. The house is platformed with the upper gable-end set into an excavated rocky bank and the lower end rising impressively from a spreading platform elevated several feet above the original ground level. The site was evidently carefully selected by the builders of the dwelling, and the labour involved in preparing it was considerable.

Dinas was a longhouse in the strict sense of the term used by architectural historians, whose discussions of this house-type have sometimes seemed arcane, if not occasionally acrimonious. The points at issue were the distribution of the house-type, and the significance of the frequently encountered structural break between house and cowhouse (now reasonably interpreted as an expression of alternate rebuilding).[5] At Dinas, house and cowhouse formed a single long range with the distinctive peculiarity of planning that the dwelling was entered via the cowhouse, the mark of a 'true' (rather than 'derived') longhouse. A central chimney divided the range into upper and lower ends, the *pen uchaf* and *pen isaf* described by Iorwerth Peate. The cowhouse occupied the downhouse, its downslope siting allowing

260

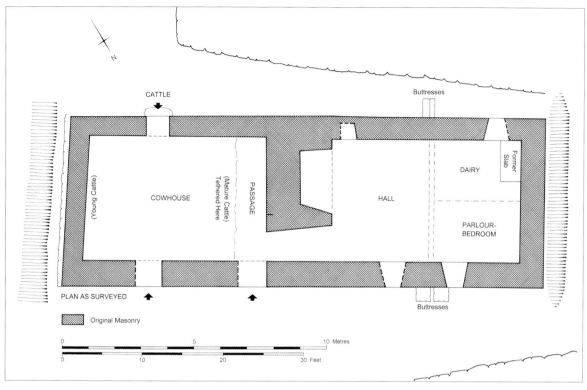

Fig. 3: *Ground plan of Dinas, as surveyed in 2008.*
(Crown Copyright: RCAHMW).

muck to drain away from the range. Cattle entered the downhouse from the doorway on the west side. The dwelling of two bays was sited upslope 'above' the stack and entered from the other side of the range.

The sixteenth- or seventeenth-century visitor to Dinas would have entered from the central doorway in the eastern side of the range. This led into a 'hearth passage' running behind the chimney stack, between house and cowhouse proper. In south Wales certainly (as Iorwerth Peate first described) this passage was called *y penllawr*, i.e. 'the floor's end', conveying that the area was regarded as part of the dwelling, although it often functioned as a feed-passage for cattle tethered in the downhouse.[6] To reach the dwelling proper, the visitor turned right in the passage alongside the jamb of the fireplace and entered the hall or kitchen. The kitchen was heated by a well-made fireplace with good jambs and a shelving back. It lacks an oven; rather surprisingly the wall oven is often a relatively late feature in western Wales.[7] There is a niche (rather than a window), possibly for a lamp, in the north-west wall near the fireplace. An offset window (rather than centrally placed)

lit the partition at the upper (dais) end of the kitchen; it may be safely assumed that the owner's table and bench were placed here. Beyond the partition there were twin inner rooms: a parlour/bedroom with dairy alongside (west). Evidence for lofts has not survived. The plan replicated the hierarchical arrangement of the mediaeval house with outer bay, passage, hall, dais, and inner bay.

Dinas has some of the distinctive features of a mediaeval house but these are overlaid by post-mediaeval elements, which may indeed belong to the original building phase. The hearth-passage (passage behind the fireplace) is present but it was not a full cross-passage with opposing doorways. The fireplace substantially survives though the chimney shaft has collapsed and the fireplace lintel has been removed. So far as one can tell (though there has been wall collapse) the fireplace is fully bonded with the lateral wall, and may therefore be primary, though a slight change of angle at the junction of house and cowhouse was noted.

The roof-trusses have long since disintegrated but the house may have been cruck trussed. This is suggested by

(i). *Dinas: east elevation of the longhouse with the buttresses.*

(ii). *Dinas: west side of the longhouse with detail of the cowhouse doorway.*

(iii). *Buttress detail.*

Fig. 4: *Dinas: masonry details.*
(RCAHMW: Crown Copyright).
(Photographs: Daniel Jones/Richard Suggett).

the way in which the walls on the line of the partition truss have been pushed outwards, needing support externally from large inclined slabs serving as buttresses. The crucks (we may hypothesise) would have been of the western (Gwynedd) type used in mass walling rather than the timber-framed type. These crucks lack the integrated tie-beam characteristic of the timber-framing tradition.[8] The blades of a cruck-truss without the restraint of a tie-beam may spread, as indeed seems to have happened at Dinas.

DOCUMENTARY

Dinas is an unusual survivor in the Cardiganshire context but it belongs to a well-defined house type: the longhouse. These longhouses were the homesteads of pastoral farmers, the most numerous class in the uplands. They are styled yeomen rather than gentry in documents, and they were the freemen or free tenants of manor and lordship. Their farms, judging from the dwellings, were not unprosperous, but they seem to have become less prosperous. These small farms are often documentary blanks – houses and landscapes tend to be the primary sources for the historian of the late-mediaeval to sixteenth-century uplands. These freehold farms were gradually absorbed by their larger neighbours in the seventeenth- and eighteenth-centuries and are often first documented in estate records.

It is therefore not entirely unexpected, but very pleasing, to find that documents relating to Dinas survive from the later seventeenth century in one of the estate collections in the National Library of Wales.[9] The earliest deed records the purchase in 1679 of 'Tir Clyn y Dinas', by Edward Price, gent., from Thomas Nicholas, yeoman, and his heirs. This was the 'killer' deed, witnessed by seven neighbours, that alienated Dinas from a family of owner-occupiers, transferring it to the neighbouring Nantyffin estate on the borders of Carmarthenshire and Cardiganshire. From Nantyffin it passed through marriage to the Glansevin estate, which retained it until the later nineteenth-century break-up of the estate.[10]

Tir Clun y Dinas, or the land of Dinas meadow, became known as Dinas-Foelfraith when part of the Glansevin estate. The deeds show the farm included the lands belonging to *Tir Clun y Dinas* and a contiguous dependant holding called *Foelfraith* or speckled hill, presumably named from the rocky and bracken-covered hill rising behind it. Several fields are named in Clun y Dinas:

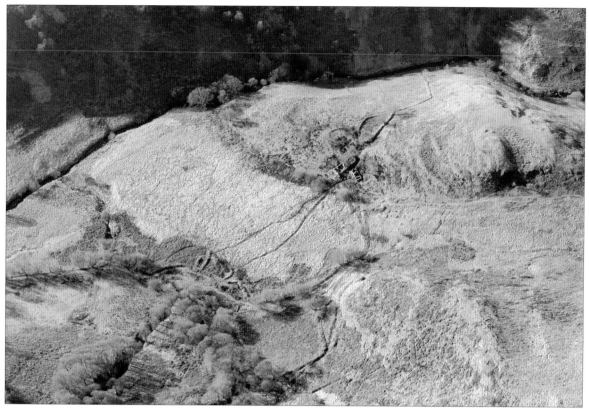

Fig. 5: *Aerial view of Dinas in winter showing the former meadow of Clun y Dinas (centre) between Dinas farmhouse and the probable site of Tir Griffith ap Rees Llewelyn Du (south).*
(Crown Copyright: RCAHMW, AP–2007–5036, photograph: Toby Driver).

Gweirglodd y dinas: the meadow of Dinas;
Pen y bwlch: the head or end of the gap;
Pen yr henglawdd du: the end of the old black bank
  or ditch;
Tir Griffith ap Rees Llewelyn Du: the land of Griffith
  ap Rees Llewelyn Du.

In Foelfraith, separated from Dinas by a stretch of sheepwalk:

Tir cae yn y coed: the land of the field in the wood;
Gwaun bwlch: the meadow of the gap
Pant y bedd: the hollow of the grave.

The 1679 deed acknowledges an existing right of dower, and names a further tenement, *Tyddyn Nant Ieuan*, which may have become detached from the main holding as part of a marriage settlement.

From the information in the deeds a three-generational family tree can be constructed which probably takes the occupation of Dinas back to *c*.1600:

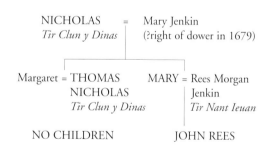

The circumstances prompting the sale seem to have been Thomas Nicholas's lack of immediate heirs, a demonstration of the interconnection between house and lineage.

LAND USE
The lands of Dinas-Foelfraith form a compact group on the east side of the Doethïe. The fields are enclosed by relatively substantial stone walls depicted on the first-edition O.S. six-inch map (1891) and its successors.[11]

Fig. 6: *Dinas from the south showing the house (centre) flanked by outbuildings (right) and barn (left) with garden beyond.*
(Crown Copyright, RCAHMW, AP_2007-5034, photograph: Toby Driver).

They are of uncertain date, and one wonders if they replaced an earlier system of earth banks and hedges, especially as a seventeenth-century field name refers to the 'henglawdd' or old bank. Earth banks were not un-common in the uplands and presumably were originally planted with quickset. The old and denuded banks of former enclosed fields on upland farms were referred to as *corcloddiau* (sing. *corclawdd*) or dwarf mounds by the nineteenth century. They were increasingly regarded as 'ancient' as land use changed, with fields becoming more open as small, banked enclosures were aban-doned.[12]

It is possible to make some suggestions about land use at Dinas. Clun y Dinas, the meadow of Dinas, is the key feature of the site. The meadow spreads out before Dinas (south) rather like an apron. It has not been managed for over a century, and is now very wet through lack of drainage, but it is still full of lush-looking grass in the summer. In winter the ungrazed grass becomes a brown 'feg' (seen in the aerial photo-graph, Fig. 5) contrasting with the surrounding greener pasture.

The pasture to the north and west drops down the steep-sided valley to the Doethïe. To the east there is still some relict woodland on the slope running up to the open ground. A field adjacent to this woodland was probably arable, though no cultivation ridges can be discerned here as they can be on some upland farms. 'Traces of cultivation' were sufficiently noticeable (and remarkable) in these uplands as to be recorded on the later nineteenth-century plan of a neighbouring farm.[13] A small two-bayed barn (barn floor and storage bay) sited west of the house shows that some corn must have been grown at Dinas.

A further range lay on the other (east) side of the meadow facing Dinas and was clearly linked to it. This may have been Tir Griffith ap Rees Llewelyn Du. It is now represented by two bracken-filled walled enclo-sures: a garden and a possible house site with opposed doorways (but probably adapted for agricultural use). It is possible that this house may have functioned as a dower-house, a distinctive feature of some farmsteads of quite modest status in western Wales. An existing right of dower at Dinas was safeguarded in the 1679 deed.[14]

It is now appropriate to turn to some of the issues discussed by Iwan Wmffre in this volume. There was an important distinction between the enclosed fields of a farm and the unenclosed land or mountain ('mynydd') belonging to it.[15] The farms of Doethïe-Camddwr were (as Wmffre puts it) not unlike island oases in a desert of unenclosed rough common. At Dinas, as at other farms, the boundary between enclosed and unenclosed land was marked physically by a substantial stone wall, the product of much determined labour. These boundary walls show some variation in construction. They may stand several feet high; at other places the downslope side is markedly taller than the upslope side, and may appear not unlike a revetment. A nineteenth-century cartographer referred to these 'revetments' in Llanddewi-brefi as 'one-sided mounds indicative of Boundary between Lowland and Upland'.[16]

The unenclosed land was open commonland divided between adjoining farms before enclosure in 1888. Enclosure parcelled up the former open common as fixed sheepwalks, which were then sometimes wire fenced. Yet (as Wmffre explains) before enclosure the common was already divided into sheepwalks attached to individual farms. These sheepwalks, probably of eighteenth-century origin, had in turn displaced an earlier and different system of commons management related to cattle husbandry. Cattle were more inclined to wander than sheep, and those guiding cattle on the summer pastures required shelters (shielings), which were often found grouped together. These 'summer dairies' or *lluestau* are sometimes named in documents and were regarded as a kind of freehold sometimes having walled enclosures for mountain hay. The shieling associated with Dinas has not been identified but a curiously detached portion of sheepwalk (surrounded by the Nant Llwyd sheepwalk) is surely related to the lost *lluest* site, and is indeed adjacent to sites named Lluest Fawr and Lluest Fach (Fig. 7).[17]

The great tracts of unenclosed land associated with the farms of Doethïe-Camddwr are not referred to in surviving deeds. Nevertheless, the full range of enclosed and unenclosed land becomes visible legally in the procedure of levying a fine when the sale of land was formally recorded in the records of the Court of Great Sessions.[18] This procedure required a formal statement of acreage and land use which was recorded in documents known as 'feet of fine', copies of which were retained by the court, the vendor and purchaser. The information was approximate rather than precise, never-

theless some idea of land use, and the relative proportions of different types of land, is given by the feet of fine. The seventeenth-century feet of fines have not survived very unevenly for Cardiganshire, but fortunately the 1679 deed for Dinas had a covenant requiring the seller to levy a fine on the premises in these terms:

> 2 messuages
> 2 barns
> 3 gardens
> 15 acres of land = arable
> 20 acres of meadow
> 30 acres of pasture
> 2 acres of wood
> 200 acres of furze and heath.

The acreage may be approximate but it corresponds quite well with the acreage (257 acres) recorded in the nineteenth century. The proportion of one acre of enclosed ground to three of open ground (67 acres of enclosed land to 200 acres of furs and heath) is reasonable, and the relative proportion of different types of land use is convincing.

The economy of the pastoral farm depended on fully utilising the different qualities of enclosed and unenclosed land.[19] Grazing on the unenclosed ground supported cattle raised for the beef market. In theory, where there was access to commonland, the number of cattle that could be grazed on the common was unlimited. However the cattle summered on the hill had to be overwintered in the cowhouse. The successful pastoral farmer needed to maximise feed production so as to overwinter as many cattle as possible. Cattle were fed during the winter on hay from meadow and mountain. Large hay fields, measured not in acres but in terms of the labour needed to cut them, were required to provide winter feed.[20] Tir Clun y Dinas, the older name for Dinas-Foelfraith farm, conveys the importance attached to the hayground (*clun*) at Dinas.

The Doethïe and neighbouring valley seems to have become progressively less prosperous in the early-modern period as cattle husbandry gave way to sheep. The land was less intensively cultivated and to an increasing extent degraded through mining and tree felling. Freeholders became tenants; woods were felled; the land may have become colder and wetter. Some tenements were abandoned in the eighteenth century and by the early nineteenth century their houses were noted as roofless and ruined. A survey of the neighbouring Fforestresgob (Bishops of St Davids) (1819) by

Henry William Ayres noted that several farmhouses on the Camddwr had 'fallen' or were 'taken down'. Others were collapsing following abandonment, a process that had probably begun in the later eighteenth century since it takes some thirty years for a roof to fall. Troed-rhiwcymer, for example, was in a very ruinous state, 'the roof haveing fallen in some places and the outbuildings are in a worst state.' One Morgan Edwards recollected a great quantity of wood there, 'principally nut trees' of a very large size. So dense was the tree cover then that it was impossible to see a conspicuous animal through the trees, not even a white horse.[21]

Thomas Hoskins, a privileged witness who visited the township of Doethïe-Camddwr to assess the value of the tithes, provided a bleak picture of the valley as he saw it in May 1839. He found that the soil of this mountainous township was 'wretchedly poor', adding 'what little cultivated land there is, is very unproductive and will bear little else but oats or potatoes.' One farm managed 'a light barley' – but only occasionally. The mountain pastures were dominated by sheep with 6,000 sheep vastly outnumbering a stock of 233 cows and bullocks and 38 horses.[22]

Farms were abandoned in the township throughout the nineteenth century. This was not a process without nuances. Some farms expanded to incorporate the land of abandoned neighbouring farmsteads. The small range of outbuildings (outside kitchen, stable, and pig-sty) built near the farmhouse (not depicted on the tithe map) suggests that Dinas remained viable into the nineteenth century. Nevertheless, the house remained unmodernised and when abandoned was still of long-house type without even the addition of a 'polite' entry directly into the dwelling.

CARDIGANSHIRE VERNACULAR ARCHITECTURE IN CONTEXT

Dinas allows us a glimpse of the unimproved pre-Victorian upland farmstead – unmodernised before it became ruined. The platformed siting, the plan form, and the possible cruck-trusses are features that in combination suggest a mediaeval origin. However, Dinas *as it survives* appears to incorporate an integral fireplace and is therefore best considered sub-mediaeval in the sense used by Cyril Fox. A building date in the later part of the sixteenth century is probable. Dinas may well have originated as a late-mediaeval hall-house but it cannot be demonstrated from the surviving structural evidence.

It must be emphasized that unambiguous structural evidence for hall-houses (rather than 'first-floor halls') rarely survives in south-west Wales. In Cardiganshire not one hall-house has been securely identified; in Carmarthenshire conclusive evidence for a hall-house origin has been demonstrated only at a handful of sites. Talhardd (Ffairfach) and King's Court (Talley) have lost their historic roofs, but renovation of Aberdeunant (Llansadwrn) unexpectedly revealed that the principal fireplace had been built against the central cruck-truss of a mediaeval hall. This is a familiar sequence in Powys but an absolute rarity in Dyfed. The problem of the absent hall-house phase in Dyfed is not that there wasn't a phase of durable hall-houses but that the evidence for it has been erased with the demolition of the greater part of the vernacular housing stock.[23]

Dinas was a longhouse in the strict sense of the term. This was a regional house-type, built in either timber or stone, distributed through much of central and southern Wales, and often but not invariably of mediaeval origin. Intensive survey in Radnorshire and Breconshire has conclusively shown that many longhouses still retain evidence of their hall-house origin, despite much rebuilding. In many cases the surviving mediaeval fabric (often a fragmentary cruck-truss embedded in the back of a fireplace) is the merest smile from an otherwise vanished Cheshire cat. Longhouses in Cardiganshire and Carmarthenshire are generally late, often incorporating a central service room, an innovation of the seventeenth century as Peter Smith has shown. Dinas is earlier, with a suggestion of crucks, and bears comparison with the indisputably cruck-framed Llwyn-rhys, Llanbadarn Odwyn, photographed as a curiosity at the turn of the century, and apparently demolished during World War I.[24] These longhouses were the homesteads of a class of pastoral farmers; the plan indeed expresses the interdependence between farmer and cattle. It has to be emphasized that the plan-type was socially as well as geographically restricted to the farmer. The houses of the greater and lesser gentry were of different plan-type from the longhouse and detached from their agricultural buildings. It is these houses that have tended to survive in south-west Wales rather than the dwellings of the farmer.

Why have so few historic farmhouses survived in Cardiganshire? Some basic aspects of construction need to be considered, as well as social factors. An inferior masonry tradition may have reduced the survivability of historic houses in Cardiganshire. One has only to travel to Merioneth to appreciate the importance of substantial masonry for the durability of historic buildings. The building stone in Cardiganshire was often poor and derived from different sources. Houses had low eaves with walls that were not easily altered without local collapse. Moreover, clay was a significant building material, and we may suppose that some substantial houses were built of clay, as in Devon. Undoubtedly a prejudice developed against building in clay, and latterly only cottages were clay-built. Ultimately there was a rejection of vernacular farmhouses in Cardiganshire with their long and low walls and undesirable plans. In some cases these old-fashioned houses were totally abandoned and allowed to become ruined – as at Dinas – or demolished and replaced by storeyed, symmetrical farmhouses detached from their farm buildings. The abundant date inscriptions from the Napoleonic Wars to the First World War tell the story of this late, great rebuilding in Cardiganshire.

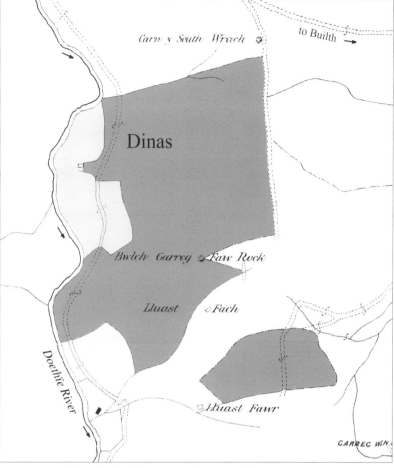

Fig. 7: *Map of the enclosed (lighter tone) and open land (darker tone) at Dinas, Foelfraith, based on a lithographed map of unenclosed land in Llanddewibrefi, c.1864.*
(NLW, WCC, SD Maps/14ii).

POSTSCRIPT

These reflections on Dinas were written sometime after survey. On site, of course, one has different and more immediate responses to a ruined dwelling. One inevitably wonders about the people who have lived in the house, whose labour still marks the landscape. One certainly wonders about that poignant moment when the door was closed for the last time. The census returns tells us that in 1851 Dinas was farmed by Nathaniel Jones (35) and Margaret, his 19-year-old wife, with no family or servants. By 1861 Nathaniel was farming 255 acres; he and his wife had four children and had taken in a lodger, Rees Rowland Pugh, a 40-year-old pauper described as 'blind from birth'. By 1871 the family had increased to seven children aged between 2 and 19, and the blind Rees Pugh still lodged at Dinas. By 1881 many of the children had left, leaving Nathaniel and

Margaret Jones with their youngest sons, David and John, and their daughter, Margaret, now married to a 38-year-old shepherd, Morgan Williams. By 1891 the family at Dinas was reduced to Nathaniel Jones (74) and his unmarried children David (24) and Martha (30). There is no entry for Dinas in the 1901 census, so by this date Dinas had been abandoned.[25] Dinas was then, and still is, farmed from Nant-llwyd on the other side of the hill.

Dinas belongs to an experiment in living that began effectively with the construction of durable hallhouse-longhouses in the uplands in the sixteenth century.[26] They were not the first houses in the uplands of course, but they were resolutely durable and had a mature multi-bayed plan that was refined with the addition of fireplace and central service-rooms. The experiment in living draws to a close in the eighteenth and nineteenth centuries with the progressive abandonment of farmhouses in upland valleys like the Doethïe. Those who remain farming in the hills are often conscious that they are the last representatives of a vanishing way of life, as the title of a recent autobiography by Huw Jones of Cwm Tywi, Tregaron, indeed suggests, *Y Bugail Olaf* or 'The Last Shepherd'.[27]

There are many ruins in the uplands, but unlike Dinas their narratives are not generally recoverable. However, all ruins prompt reflection, and laments on ruined and abandoned homesteads are a familiar theme in poetry from late-mediaeval Wales and Ireland. Dafydd ap Gwilym's meditation on The Ruin (like Dinas characteristically sited between enclosed pasture and open

mountain) comes to mind when contemplating Dinas. In Rachel Bromwich's translation:

> You ruined shack with open gable-end,
> between the mountain and the pasture,
> it would seem grievous to all those
> who saw you once a hospitable home
> and see you now [instead], with ridge-pole broken,
> beneath your roof of laths, a dark and shattered house.

The poet recalls his own characteristically amorous sojourn there, but concludes with sentiments that still retain their resonance:

> Dafydd, the household's span of work is done,
> . . . it was a decent way of life.[28]

NOTES

1. Site surveyed with Daniel Jones of Lampeter, then an IFA student at the Royal Commission. I am grateful to Charles Green for preparing the finished drawings. Grid reference SN 7663 521; NPRN 91330.

2. Peter Smith, 'Historical Domestic Architecture in Dyfed: an Outline', in Tudor Barnes and Nigel Yates, (eds), *Carmarthenshire Studies: Essays Presented to Major Francis Jones* (Carmarthen, 1974), pp. 54-67.

3. Huw Jones, *Bugail Olaf y Cwm*, ed. Lyn Ebenezer (Llyfrau Llafar Gwlad 68, Llanrwst, 2007). See Iwan Wmffre's contribution to this volume.

4. On deserted rural settlements, see generally Kathryn Roberts, (ed.), *Lost Farmsteads: Deserted Rural Setlements in Wales* (CBA Research Report 148, 2006), especially Chapter 5 by Paul Sambrook, 'Deserted rural settlements in south-west Wales', pp. 83-95. On the background, Kenneth Murphy et al., 'Upland Ceredigion: Historic Landscape Characterisation' (Cambria Archaeology Report, 1999). See also the case-study by Andrew Fleming and Louise Barker, 'Monks and Local Communities: the Late-medieval Landscape of Troed y Rhiw, Caron Uwch Clawdd, Ceredigion', *Medieval Archaeology*, Vol. 52 (2008), pp. 1-30.

5. On the longhouse controversy in Wales, see especially the contributions by I. Peate, J. T. Smith, and P. Smith in *Culture and Environment: Essays in Honour of Sir Cyril Fox*, ed., I. Ll. Foster & L. Alcock (London, 1963), pp. 389-444. An overview is provided by Eurwyn Wiliam, *Welsh Long-houses* (Cardiff, 1992).

6. Iorwerth C. Peate, *The Welsh House: a Study in Folk Culture* (3rd edn, Liverpool, 1946), p. 56.

7. Eurwyn Wiliam, '*Yr Aelwyd*: the Architectural Development of the Hearth in Wales', *Folk-Life*, Vol. 16 (1978), pp. 93-199.

8. Ceiling beams are often placed alongside crucks in the stone-walling tradition but are not usually pegged to the blades.

9. NLW, Glansevin 2638 (endorsed 'L') and 2639 (endorsed 'N'). There are related documents are in the Glasbrook Collection, Carmarthenshire Record Office, and in the D. T. M. Jones Collection, National Library of Wales. References are collected in Iwan Wmffre's indispensable *Cardiganshire Place-names* (BAR British Series 379, 3 vols, Oxford, 2004), Vol. 2, p. 503.

10. On the Glansevin estate, see Francis Jones, *Historic Carmarthenshire Homes and their Families* (Carmarthen, 1987). The outlying Cardiganshire parts of the estate had been mortgaged in 1861, NLW, DTM Jones Collection 3396.

11. Sheet Cardiganshire XXXVI N.W., 1st edition published 1891 (surveyed 1885-7), 2nd edition 1905 (survey revised 1904). There is a striking loss of information on the 2nd edition, including the names of uninhabited farmhouses, some field boundaries, and descriptions of prominent features such as 'Rock'.

12. *Corcloddiau* are shown on several annotated maps of farms in Doethïe-Camddwr, based on the tithe map, prepared by D. P. Davies, Aberystwyth, in 1879: NLW, Welsh Church Commission, Maps SD/90, maps of Dreinllwyndu, Rhydtalog, and Tynycornel farms. An 'old bank or clawdd' is shown on NLW, Welsh Church Commission, Maps SD/91.

13. NLW, Welsh Church Commission, Maps SD/90 (Tyn-

cornel) shows traces of cultivation at Nantygwyddel. Terry and Heather James have noted areas of extensive upland ploughing in Doethïe-Camddwr.

14. Richard Suggett, 'The Unit System and the Developmental Cycle of the Family', *Vernacular Architecture*, Vol. 38 (2007), pp. 19-34.

15. David Jenkins, 'Rural Society Inside Out', in David Smith, (ed.), *A People and a Proletariat: Essays in the History of Wales, 1780-1980* (London, 1980), pp. 114-26; idem, *Ar Lafar, Ar Goedd* (Aberystwyth, 2007).

16. NLW, Welsh Church Commission, Maps SD/90 (Rhydtalog).

17. NLW, Welsh Church Commission, Map SD/14ii & Map SD/15.

18. On the procedure, see Glyn Parry, *A Guide to the Records of Great Sessions in Wales* (Aberystwyth, 1995), pp. lv-lix.

19. See further, Richard Suggett, *Houses and History in the March of Wales: Radnorshire 1400-1800* (Aberystwyth, 2005).

20. Cf. the meadow named 'Gwaith Wyth-gŵr', i.e. 'eight-men's work', at Brithdir, NLW, Welsh Church Commission, Maps SD/95.

21. NLW, Welsh Church Commission/ECE/EL/SD 46. Morgan Edwards 'heard others say formerly that this wood was so very thick of large trees that a white horse or other beast could not be seen in any part of it from the opposite steep of Cefn Henfaes'.

22. The National Archives, Kew, Tithe File for Doethïe-Camddwr Township, IR 18/13996.

23. P. Smith, op. cit., n. 2.

24. I. Peate, op. cit., n. 6, pp. 68, 70, figs. 15-16, and esp. fig. 72.

25. Paragraph based on research notes by Terry and Heather James.

26. R. Suggett, op. cit., n. 19, chaps. 11-12.

27. Huw Jones, *Bugail Olaf y Cwm*, ed. Lyn Ebenezer (Llyfrau Llafar Gwlad 68, Llanrwst, 2007).

28. Rachel Bromwich, *Dafydd ap Gwilym: a Selection of Poems* (Gomer Press, Llandysul, 1982), pp. 186-7.

Toponymy and Land-use in the Uplands of the Doethïe Valley (Cardiganshire)

Iwan Wmffre

This short piece attempts to evaluate the particularities of the traditional agricultural economy of the central Welsh uplands, illustrated by the case of the Doethïe valley in Cardiganshire.[1] Use is made of Early Modern documentation relating to the area as well as to oral information collected from the last mountain shepherds.

BACKGROUND

The mountainous spine of central Wales constitutes the widest expanse of open moorland in Britain south of Scotland and is situated on the borders of the counties of Cardiganshire, Carmarthenshire, Breconshire, Radnorshire and Montgomeryshire. Upon being taken to see what had been described to him as 'mountains' in the 1960s, a visiting Italian geographer exclaimed 'Tundra!' – which anecdote is a salutary reminder that not all mountains conform to the schoolbook categories of towering pyramidical peaks. Trees hardly grow above the 300m contour and the coincidence of both these characteristics constitutes a rough-and-ready guide to the traditional Welsh binary distinction between *mynydd* (mountain) and *llawr gwlad* (literally 'floor of the country', that is to say, lowland).

Pumlumon, its highest point at 752m, dominates the northern part of this area, but thence southwards the topography takes the appearance of a dissected plateau whose rounded summits lie at between 400–600m. The only exception is Drygarn-fawr in Breconshire which reaches 645m. North of Drygarn-fawr, the plateau is dissected by waters running into the Elan river whence the derived name of the area Elenydd. West of Drygarnfawr, the plateau is dissected by waters running into the Tywi river and this is where the Doethïe river is situated.

Contrary to the mountains of northern Wales and even to the Brecon Beacons to the south, these central Welsh uplands are characterised by a succession of rounded hills rather than by a profusion of pointed peaks. It is this fact which seems to lie behind the earliest known name of these uplands *Crynfynydd* 'round mountain' (only attested as an earlier alias of *Fforestresgob* 'the bishop's forest' near Ystradffin and in a thirteenth-century reference to the mountains near Garn-gron, Blaen Caron). The later traditional name of these mountains – *Y Mynydd-mawr* 'the great mountain' – was applied partly due to the extensiveness of the upland and partly to distinguish it from the much smaller Mynydd-bach west of it in Cardiganshire. Colloquially, however, the commonest appellation was simply *Y Mynydd* and its inhabitants were distinguished as *Pobl y Mynydd* 'the inhabitants of the mountain'.

The mountain was a vast open stretch of land dominated by moorland grasses on slopes and wetland vegetation on flats and bottoms. Rocky outcrops show themselves in a few areas most especially on steep valley sides. The widespread planting of dense uniform conifer forests (W. *coed gleision* 'evergreen trees') since the 1930s has radically changed the appearance of the land which has a less uniform look than it hitherto possessed.

DEMOGRAPHICS AND CHANGE

In the Doethïe watershed, above its junction with the Pysgotwr, over a period running from the eighteenth to the early nineteenth century, there seems to have been some twenty-eight inhabited houses.[2] By 1841 there were only some sixteen inhabited houses attested with a standing population of sixty-two.[3] The number of inhabited houses declined to five by 1901 with a corresponding decrease in the population to twenty-five.[4] The decline continued throughout the twentieth century and the last inhabited house, Tyncornel, was abandoned in the 1950s.[5] W. J. Lewis, in his otherwise exemplary *Cardiganshire Historical Atlas*, perpetrated a grave error in describing the houses of the Doethïe and neighbouring valleys as *tai-unnos* 'one-night (squatter) houses', typical of the upland fringes of Cardiganshire in the eighteenth and nineteenth centuries.[6] Many, if not most, of the Doethïe houses were long-standing independent agricultural holdings probably mediaeval in origin. The earliest attestations are Cnwchgwyn 1599, Nantgwyddyl 1631, Brobwll, Maesbetws, Tyncornel 1653, Doethïau-fach, Nantiwan 1660, Dinas 1679, Gurnos 1684 (it should be borne in mind that deeds did not exist in Cardiganshire prior to 1536).

The language of the inhabitants throughout this period was exclusively Welsh. Of the 1901 total of twenty-five, fourteen were Welsh monoglots (Maesbetws, Tyncornel, Coli in the upper part of the valley), whilst eleven also had English as well as Welsh (Blaendoethïau, Troedrhiwcymer), with one of the enumerated persons in Troedrhiwcymer being a relation usually resident in Cheltenham. The area was not well served by any ecclesiastical institution. The chapel or oratory that gave its name to Maesbetws was traditionally held to have fallen in ruin around 1716 and having been dedicated to the ancient Welsh saint Celynnin. Whatever credence can be given to these traditions, it is clear that *betws* is a mediaeval term for chapel. In 1821 a nonconformist (Methodist Calvinistic) chapel was erected in the adjoining Camddwr valley and named Soar-y-mynydd. This also acted as the local school until 1947 when the school was discontinued. The circulating schools of Griffith Jones had been active in the Doethïe valley in the late eighteenth century and, despite the reputed primitive lifestyle of *Pobl y Mynydd*, there is no doubt that they were in regular contact with their fellow Welsh of the lowlands, not least the seasonal woolpickers and shearers and the drovers who guided their flocks eastwards from Llanddewi Brefi to the present-day Llanwrtyd Wells (then named Pont Rhyd-y-fere).

PLACE-NAMES

I did not come across many members of the original families of the Doethïe valley, but my enquiries with the shepherds of Llethr, Nantllwyd (of the adjoining Pysgotwr and Camddwr valleys) and of Troedrhiwruddwen supplied me with a respectable collection of names which demonstrated that a great many names were never collected by the Ordnance Survey (OS) mapmakers at the end of the last century. This can be illustrated clearly taking as example the mountainland between the Doethïe and Pysgotwr rivers which belonged to Troedrhiwcymer and the annexed holding of Cnwcheithinog. Maps give us thirteen names (five from pre-OS maps and eight from OS maps),[7] but an interview with Jim Lewis of Troedrhiwruddwen in the 1990s harvested at least twenty-seven further names. These were *Bryndyfran, Carreg Bwlchgwynt, Carreg Llety'resgob, Cnepyngors, Cnepyn Tirda, Craig-yr-olchfa, Craig Troedrhiwcymer, Esgairbedd, Esgairborfa, Esgair Ffosgwellau, Esgair Garregwen, Esgair Rhiwlosg, Gribin-lwyd, Llethrcoed, Llynllwyfen, Pwll-y-foelfraith, Pyllau-mawn, Talcencnwch, Hendre-boeth* (r), *Penrhiwcymer* (r), *Dyfran* (hn), *Ffostegan* (hn), *Nantgelynnen* (hn), *Nant Hendre-boeth* (hn), *Nantnod* (hn), *Pantclunmwynwr, Pomprenwitsh.* The last two were not included in *PNCards* 2004 because of some uncertainties which I had hoped to clear with Jim Lewis in a subsequent interview, but he died not long afterwards and consequently I was unable to verify anything more. The location of *Pantclunmwynwr* at SN 763516 was clear enough, but at the time I was somewhat suspicious concerning its pronunciation (*-moenwr* rather than *-mwynwr*), a suspicion to which I now attach less importance. I was unable to give exact grid co-ordinates for the location of *Pomprenwitsh* from the map, in grid SN 7649, but its position could be easily enough ascertained from an actual inspection of the area as Jim had said it lay directly below Talcencnwch and referred to a single stone which bridged Nantcnwch. There were some other names *Castell* and *Pant-y-gower* somewhere in SN 7649, but I am unable to give any more precise location. Figure 1 contrasts the density of place-names of this area from the maps and those from the oral tradition.

Investigations with my informant established that *Cefn Cnwcheithinog* was an umbrella term for a stretch of upland which covered and included at least three distinct ridges. Investigations also established that the place-name Cors Pwllci had been completely misplaced on OS maps, some 2km from its traditional location. It is evident that the surveying carried out by the OS in the 1880s and 1890s for the 6-inch maps was constrained by factors of time and resources and thus did not always assemble a representative sample of the most important place-names, let alone the majority of names that were then in use. The physical survey could be

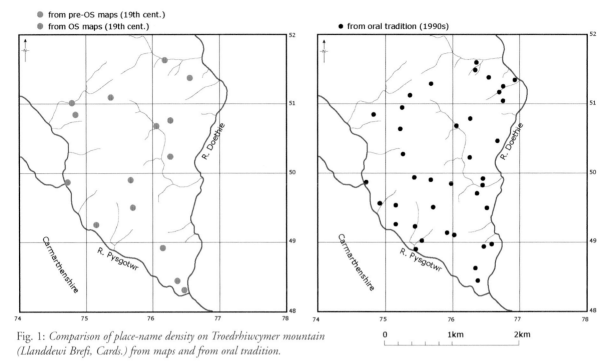

Fig. 1: *Comparison of place-name density on Troedrhiwcymer mountain (Llanddewi Brefi, Cards.) from maps and from oral tradition.*

carried out consistently, whereas the collection of local names depended upon the availability of local informants and there must have been many cases where the shepherds most suited to give toponymic information were at the time of the survey otherwise occupied in driving, selling livestock or helping neighbours in another location.[8] One of the clearest illustrations of the failure of the OS survey in the uplands north of the Doethïe valley is the example of *Esgairwen*, the crowning height of the extensive civil-parish of Caron Uwch-Clawdd at 548m, which was never named on OS maps even though it was still mentioned, albeit no location given, in the 1990s in the local newspaper, the *Cambrian News*, at a period when the status of commonland was being redefined.

The superficially 'featureless' traditional landscape of these uplands (before afforestation) was in fact well known to the men who lived there and who looked after livestock and who had names for each hill, stream and feature of the landscape. These names were developed orally before maps of these districts were ever made and functioned as markers to convey geographical location over a wide expanse of land (to reach a sick or lost creature or person for example). Erwyd Howells[9] relates an amusing illustration given him at the mountain farm Cefnbrwyn (Llangurig, Montgomeryshire) that if one

of the members of the family were to leave their cap on their mountain they could direct any other member to the place and retrieve it simply with reference to the place-names on the open upland. Named places also defined boundaries on the open uplands.

Welsh upland place-names are not so different from those of the lowlands except that they were used to name otherwise unbounded pieces of land. This fact seems to make for a greater awareness of, and interest in, place-names among shepherds than among farmers in the enclosed lowlands and indeed sometimes (credible) reasons were given by upland informants for the names. The impressive repertory of place-names however among male inhabitants of the uplands should not be exaggerated relative to the lowlands. It was not that uncommon among the lowland farmers and farmworkers I interviewed to know not only the names of all the fields on the farm they were attached to, but also those of the neighbouring farms where they had worked co-operatively, which also adds up to a considerable sum of toponymic knowledge.

UPLAND LAND-HOLDING

The Welsh uplands were exploited by the inhabitants and did not constitute wasteland in the strict sense of the term and even though the land was divided into exclusive holdings, the legal landholding status of much of the uplands was different from that of the lowlands. Until 1888 most of the Doethïe valley in the parish and lordship of Llanddewi Brefi had commonland status, excepting those patches of enclosed land surrounding dwellings which were held as freehold and which were like unto island oases surrounded by rough mountain pasture. The Llanddewi Brefi parliamentary enclosure act of 1888 apportioned this common mountain pasture as freehold to particular dwellings and so ended the separate legal status of the upland as commonland, which now became unenclosed freehold (only in some areas of upland, usually nearer the lowland boundary to the west was wire fencing erected to replace formerly open boundaries).[10] However, the paradoxical fact is that the upland commonland was already divided between various dwellings prior to 1888 and so was not 'common' in the generally understood sense of the word. Prior to 1888, most dwellings were surrounded by a small area of enclosed freehold lands (some of which was cultivated) and abutted to an adjoining sheepwalk which was deemed commonland though in practice it belonged just as much to the dwelling as did the freehold lands. The enclosed freehold land and the appertaining sheepwalks of the Doethïe valley in the mid nineteenth century are shown on Figure 2 (based mainly on the tithe map and the later enclosure maps).

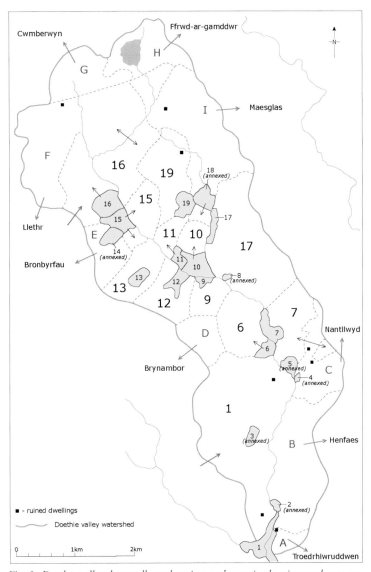

Fig. 2: *Doethïe valley sheepwalks and ancient enclosures in the nineteenth century.*

The legal definition of what constitutes commonland is discussed at length by Gadsden.[11] There is an obvious discrepancy between the 'classic' kind of commonland that prevailed over the lowlands of southern England, which were large stretches of cultivated openfields held in common by a 'manorially' organised village, and the predominant type of commonland in Wales, the uncultivated expanses of rough upland pasture. Villages – on the scale found throughout the English lowlands – were relatively rare in Wales and confined mainly to the anglicised lowland fringes of the country. Nevertheless, even within Welsh Wales a useful distinction can be drawn between lowland common-

land and the upland commonland. The examples of lowland commonland in Cardiganshire tend to be the result of the subdivision of a larger mediaeval unit of landholding, whereby a piece of uncultivated rough ground, usually at one extremity of its bounds, continued to be deemed common for the purposes of thatch, turf and pasture to those farming units which had subdivided from the parent unit. Variously termed *cytir, tir-cyd, cyffredin, cwmins, comins* in Welsh, these types of commonland are technically termed 'appurtenant common' as it is a right confined to a restricted number of landholding units in a lordship as opposed to an 'appendant common' whose rights are open to every landholding unit in a particular lordship.[12] On the other hand, the upland commonland in Cardiganshire, being the uncultivated 'wasteland' of a lordship rather than being the result of the subdivision of mediaeval farming units, can be usefully termed 'seignorial common'.[13] But, as we saw in the case of the Doethïe valley, in the nineteenth century the upland commonland was not shared between every landholding unit in the lordship of Llanddewi Brefi (appendant), or shared between a restricted number of landholding units (appurtenant), but was *separately and exclusively divided* between a restricted number of landholding units exactly as if they were exclusive freeholds.[14] The commonland status of the sheepwalks of the Doethïe valley was probably due both to a historical memory of seignorial rights and to the continuing rights of the lord of Llanddewi Brefi (the Bishop of Saint Davids) to mineral and hunting rights and the appendant rights of turbary, thatch and wool-picking enjoyed by the inhabitants of the lordship.

THE IDIOSYNCRACY OF FFORESTRESGOB'S STATUS

The lands of Cwncheithinog (later Troedrhiwcymer) and Henfaes (later Troedrhiwruddwen) were two of the four constituent parts of the mediaeval *Fforestresgob* 'the bishop's hunting-reserve' and up to the nineteenth century were lands still directly held by the bishop, as opposed to the other mountain landholders who were tenants of the bishop's lordship. Like other mountain farms, these four holdings comprised only a small area of ancient enclosed land, most of their area was open upland. However, when enclosure was considered in the late nineteenth century, in contrast to the rest of the Llanddewi Brefi mountain, the open upland attached to the farms in Fforestresgob were also accounted to constitute freehold land as much as the enclosed land. It is likely that since the Bishop was both freeholder and lord of the land, the common rights to the upland appendant to his freeholds were usually extinguished according to English legal practice. Nevertheless, this had all the appearance of a legal sleight of hand allowing the bishop to avoid payment to secure his part of the mountain commonland which was being enclosed (in contrast to the payments asked of all other owners of sheepwalk rights). Documents preserved in the Cymerau MSS in the National Library of Wales reveal the discontent at this perceived injustice:

> The [Ecclesiastical] Commissioners refuse to allow their sheepwalks to be dealt with under the inclosure of Llan-

ddewi Brefi mountain in a similar way to the sheepwalks of the other owners. (1882 Cymerau MS 177)

> . . . the lands of the Ecclesiastical Commissioners on Llanddewi Brefi mountain and the 2000 acres which they added to the 2000 acres originally owned by them which they were allowed to retain under the inclosure Act while other owners of sheepwalks had to disgorge. (1882 Cymerau MS 174)

When the enclosure of Llanddewi Brefi mountain was first mooted at the beginning of the nineteenth century, the status of the Fforestresgob was clearly problematical as can be seen from the following extract from an article of 1810 penned by 'An independent freeholder' in the *Cambrian* newspaper:

> Question, whether the sheepwalks are to be considered as private property or as waste and common lands, and particularly as to the sheepwalks surrounding Foelallt, and about that part of the lordship called the forest. (*Cambrian* 10/02/1810)[15]

Since the owners of sheepwalk rights already enjoyed exclusive use of their sheepwalks for grazing – their main economic purpose – the Llanddewi Brefi Enclosure Act of 1888 can be seen more as a money-raising scheme that profited the bishop at the expense of these owners, rather than as an emancipatory act that rid the land of an oppressive seignorial monopoly. To emphasise the argument that the enclosure was in fact needless from the point of view of the exploitation of the land, one need only look at the even more extensive neighbouring uplands of Caron parish which, though never enclosed by parliamentary act, today enjoy a practically identical mode of land-use with the enclosed uplands of Llanddewi Brefi.[16]

THE ORIGIN OF THE DIVISION OF THE OPEN UPLANDS

It seems clear that in pre-Conquest Wales most of the mountain wastes were in the jurisdiction of the commotes or administrative divisions of the Welsh kingdoms and that the wastes (*diffaith* in mediaeval Welsh, a substantivised adjective meaning 'desolate' derived from Latin *defectus*) belonged to the Welsh rulers. The southern recensions of the Welsh laws (*Llyfr Blegywryd*) talk of *diffeith brenhin* 'the king's waste' as well as pointing unequivocally to his right to decide the use of that land through his officers: *Maer a chyghellawr bieu kadw diffeith brenhin.* 'It is the steward and seneschal who administer the king's waste.' Charters dating from

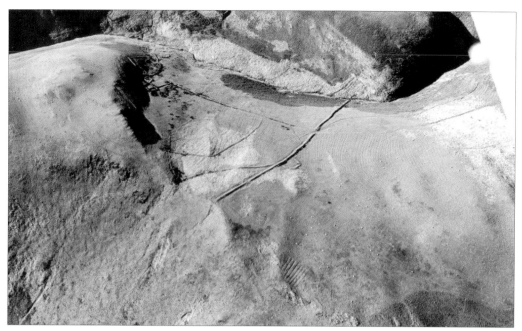

Fig. 3: *Part of Cnwcheithinog (later Troedrhiwcymer) one of the four constituent parts of Fforestresgob, a mediaeval hunting estate of the bishops of St Davids. Air photograph, Jan. 1999, viewed from the north-west, by Terry James, who noted that it was abandoned as a habitation by 1851, replaced by Troedrhiwcymer in the valley to the south. A sheepfold was built over the site of the farmstead, but there are still well-preserved infield and outfield banks, and a palimpsest of cultivation ridges and lazy beds of unknown date. The steep-sided Doethïe valley is at the top left; its tributary Nant y Cnwch is on the top right.*

Fig. 4: *The same area viewed from the north-east; air photograph, Jan. 1999, by Terry James. The former farmstead and sheep fold are here viewed from the north-east, showing traces of cultivation of unknown date, undetectable on the ground.*

the thirteenth century demonstrate that pre-Conquest Welsh rulers were able to bestow the mountain wastes of whole commotes to Cistercian monasteries such as Ystradfflur and Ystradmarchell. The 1202 charter of Rhys Ieuanc ab Gruffudd ab Rhys to Ystradfflur is particularly clear:

> . . . *omnem pasturam de Cantrefmaur et de Cantrefbichan et de quatuor cantredis de Kardegan et nominatim de Penwedic eo molo et eisdem terminis quos carta Mailgonis diffinit data prefatis monachis de pastura Pennwedic* . . .
> '. . . all the pasture of Cantre-mawr and Cantre-bychan and the four cantrefs of Ceredigion, especially that of Penweddig, the mill there and its boundaries which the charter of Maelgwn [Fychan] gave the aforesaid monks because of the pasture of Penweddig' (1336 *Calendar Charter Rolls*: 383–84)

That such upland wastes were considered the prerogative of a ruler (especially by the rulers themselves), did not rule out these same wastes also being considered the assets of the community of the commote as is suggested by the name *Mynydd-y-wlad* 'the country's mountain', the local designation of the *Fforest-fawr* uplands of western Breconshire. A strained polarisation between the rights of the community of the commote on the one hand, and that of the native rulers on the other, need not be implied in these different emphases. If the mountain wastes belonged to the commote, there still remained the practical need for an accepted order for its exploitation, and the native rulers were in the likeliest position to regulate this exploitation, if only as arbitrators.

It seems that both the pre-Conquest Welsh rulers and their successors, the post-Conquest lords, were in a position of being able to dispose of the uplands as seemed fit to them. But whether there was an annual or a rather more permanent allocation of grazing rights to various livestock masters and whether the upland was subdivided in a permanent way is difficult to ascertain as we are simply not well enough informed by the dearth of relevant documentation.

A few things nevertheless do seem clear in relation to land-use in the uplands in places like the Doethïe valley in late mediaeval times. There seems no doubt that the principal economic activity was cattle grazing and indeed the *Black Book of Saint David's* reckoned the stock-carrying capacity of Fforestresgob in 1326 as 240 cows.[17] That there was no mention of sheep in mediaeval times does not preclude their existence on these

mountains at the time, but it does indicate that sheep were not then viewed as the main economic 'cash-crop' that they later became. And whilst there is no doubt that there were periods of economic dominance of either cattle or sheep on the Welsh mountains, the economic dominance of one creature does not necessarily preclude the existence of the other, though their overall numbers would indubitably be affected.[18]

The more abundant documentation for North Wales in late mediaeval times gives us a number of attestations of the Latin term *vaccaria* 'cattle-breeding station' or rather 'cattle ranch' and there is a record of Dafydd ab Llywelyn, Prince of Gwynedd, bestowing the *vaccaria* of Cwmhesgen near Ganllwyd (Merionethshire) to the monastery of Ystradmarchell (1322 *Calendar of Charter Rolls*: 440). The importance of this particular reference is that it shows that a much more extensive stretch of open upland could be subdivided into a network of cattle ranches, a pattern which Winchester has found obtained throughout the uplands of northern England, especially the central Pennines, in the fourteenth and fifteenth centuries.[19] The Welsh equivalent of Latin *vaccaria* may have been *buches* a collective form of *buwch* 'cow', originally meaning 'herd', a term commonly found in the upland toponymy of central and northern Wales, though intriguingly not in southern Wales or the mountains of central Cardiganshire. There is an almost total lack of documentation concerning the Llanddewi Brefi mountain in mediaeval times so that we cannot even begin to guess as to the extent of any 'cattle ranch' in the Doethïe valley. We might interpret Fforestresgob as having constituted one particular cattle ranch, though this is a possibility rather than an established fact. The place-name *Trumda-gwyllton* 'the ridge of the wild cattle' for a particularly remote stretch of upland by Drygarn-fawr in Breconshire implies that *da* 'cattle, livestock' were most usually looked after by herders.[20]

It is known however that cattle are more likely to wander than sheep, a fact which implies that any mediaeval cattle ranch would have been more extensive than the later sheepwalks of the Modern era. The relatively recent sheep-orientated economy of the Welsh uplands is misleading at worst and mostly irrelevant in providing a picture of a mediaeval upland land-use and upland settlement predicated upon the grazing of cattle. As well as deserving a sustained study in itself that has yet to be done, there is no space here to elaborate on features of the cattle-herding economy. I would just like to say in passing that it seems likely that the pattern of wholesale transhumance of herders and flocks with the seasonal occupation of shielings (W. *lluest, hafod*) was more a feature of the cattle-herding economy than that of the later sheep-grazing economy, in the care of full-time shepherds who lived in the mountains the year round. The forage requirement of a cow is roughly equivalent to that of six sheep though this traditional equivalence ratio can vary according to many factors, such as the physiology of the local cattle and sheep, the grazing characteristics of any particular area as well as the pattern of livestock production.

The place-name *Llethrhafodydd* 'slope of the summer-dwellings' in the remotest part of the headwaters of the Doethïe, about two kilometres from the nearest nineteenth-century inhabitation, might imply the existence in the plural of these seasonal constructions in late mediaeval times (since it can be easily demonstrated that the term *hafod* had been replaced by *lluest* by at least the sixteenth century). In the nineteenth century there only existed a ruin, *Magwyr Llethrhafodydd*. However, it is quite feasible that *hafodydd* here means 'summer grazing lands'. The original meaning of *hafod* was indeed 'summer-dwelling' but it evolved to encompass the meaning of 'summer grazing land' which necessitated the coining of new terms to define anew the actual summer construction, namely *hafoty* in northern Wales and *lluest* in central and southern Wales. The term *lluest* is particularly enlightening as its basic meaning was 'camp' and often associated in mediaeval literature with accounts of armies on the move. Both the origin of the word and the examples of the collocation *lle lluest* 'place of encampment' in northern Cardiganshire in the sixteenth and the seventeenth century clearly illustrate the impermanence of such summer dwellings both as regards construction and seasonality. Once again I repeat the particular association of such impermanent summer dwellings with a cattle-herding economy. The term *lluest* has remained part of the living language in northern Cardiganshire, but as the phenomenon it was based upon has evolved, so has its meaning, so that nowadays it means no more than a 'mountain farm', one inhabited all the year round.[21]

THE LATER DIVISION OF UPLANDS INTO SHEEPWALKS

Cattle seem to have been the predominant economic livestock kept on the mid-Wales mountains until the eighteenth century, during which century they were replaced by sheep as the principal economic livestock of the uplands. Indeed the English term *sheepwalk* in itself holds a clue to the origins of the later subdivisions of the uplands found in the mountains of Cardiganshire, an origin that can have no connection with the cattle-herding economy of mediaeval times.

I deliberately emphasised *sheepwalk* as an English term as the Welsh equivalent *libert* has a wholly different origin. Without any particular reference to sheep, the term *libert* is derived from E. *liberty*, which is more familiar in English as the term for a feudal franchise, or area exempt from a certain jurisdiction, a meaning also known in Welsh. I can only speculate that the evolution of the term to refer to sheepwalks was the result of the subtraction of a stretch of upland commonland or waste from the jurisdictional prerogatives of the lord concerning the grazing of livestock. The earliest attestation of the term in this sense is known to be precisely from the Doethïe valley in the early part of the eighteenth century under its English form 'liberty of common'.[22] Lewis Morris in 1747 wrote of 'particular districts or liberties next adjoining to the freeholds or cottages' and 'liberty of grazing belonging to one of the cottages'.[23] The range of use of the term *libert* stretches from the central Cardiganshire mountains to the mountains of central and north-eastern Wales.

The earliest attestation I found for the term *sheepwalk* in Cardiganshire was *sheep walk* in the Ystwyth valley in 1760.[24] A few years later in 1773 Thomas described the Pumlumon area as 'a country of sheepwalks'.[25]

Whilst we must generalise, it is well to remember that developments could take a different turn in other areas. The preponderant development in the Cardiganshire uplands was the division of the upland wastes into separate sheepwalks dependent upon a farm. A contrary case was the upland wastes of the lordship of Ysbyty-Ystradmeurig, locally known as *Comins 'Sbyty* ('the commons of Ysbyty-Ystwyth'), which had a communal shepherd paid for by each of the farmers who sent sheep. Though one might conclude from this that the common was undivided for purposes of ownership, it was made clear to me upon further enquiry that each farm in the parish had its particular sheepwalk or *libert* on the mountain (Iori Davies, Ysbyty-Ystwyth, *pers. comm.*). We shall see below that the term sheepwalk has both agronomic and tenurial connotations, which leads to ambiguity as to what precisely is the legal standing of sheepwalks in the Ysbyty-Ystwyth context (for example, did they denote a customary right only or were they wholly alienable as were sheepwalks in most other lordships?). Nevertheless, it is clear that the arrangements for Ysbyty-Ystwyth mountain constitute a more communal exploitation of the commonland and may well preserve an older system, though this cannot be demonstrated (we may suspect the functional influence of the size and shape of the mountainland concerned, a somewhat smaller and definitely elongated strip of commonland compared to the broad expanses characteristic of the mountain commonland of other lordships).

LEGAL STATUS OF SHEEPWALKS OR LIBERTS

Even if the original subdivision of the commonland uplands into a network of sheepwalks or *liberts* on seignorial commonland or wastes had initially occurred by concession, as Gadsden remarks:

> It is hardly surprising with the passage of time that flock owners often came to look upon the sheepwalk as part of their land in severalty and, if the owner of the waste was an absentee from the area, there was little to counteract this impression. Doubts over ownership seem to have been more prevalent in Wales than elsewhere, probably because some parts of Wales suffered absentee landowners for prolonged periods.[26]

In 1747 Lewis Morris noted concerning the lordship of Perfedd in northern Cardiganshire (and it is worth remembering that he was employed in enforcing crown rights in this crown lordship):

> There hath been time out of mind, a division of the common into particular districts or liberties next adjoining to the freeholds or cottages which all the shepherds thro' boldness or ignorance claim as their own right, and sometimes chase other people's cattle away.[27]

In Llanddewi Brefi too, those freeholders who maintained a right to do as they pleased with their *libert* were quoted as saying 'Why the word *libert* in Latin means free,' to which the Bishop's representatives retorted why should *libert* be applied to sheepwalks 'as distinguished from the freeholds.'[28]

Despite the misgivings of lords it is apparent that a *libert* could be sold (or at least alienated) as can be illustrated in the case of the *libert* of *Llethrllwyd* in the lordship of Pennardd or Caron, which though still retaining commonland status to this day has been attached to different local farms. In 1839, in the tithe map, it was noted as a sheepwalk to Trecefail, but was sold in the 1860s–1870s by the farrier who lived at Blaencroes-fechan to Tŷ-mawr and Alltddu (Llanio) *am damed ogor* 'for a little fodder', and in turn, Tŷ-mawr sold it in the last few years (Sam Jones, Glanrafon-isa, Blaencaron, *pers. comm.*). Another example was given in 1880 by the defendant of Nantmeirch mountain farm near Ponterwyd in northern Cardiganshire: '. . . sheep walks have often been sold and alienated together with the adjoining farm and separately'.[29] A further indication that sheepwalks were treated as freehold are the land prices quoted by George Nicholson in 1813 for Cardiganshire which varied from £3 per acre in Aberystwyth to 15–25 shillings per acre in the hinterland, to 6–9 pennies an acre for sheepwalks.[30] This shows that sheepwalks had a recognised worth and suggests that they could be sold as easily as freehold land.

Gadsden informs us that the right of *common in gross* (i.e. to freely alienate a sheepwalk on its own) is evidenced in northern parts of England and he quotes a legal opinion of 1864:

> There are also lands which in ordinary parlance are called common, although the right of pasture over them is in an individual. Such are the small plots of pasture often in the middle of a waste, called sheepheaves, the soil of which may or may not be in the lord, but the pasture is certainly private property, and is leased and sold as such.[31]

He further argues that the right of *common in gross*, in origin a grant to a person and his heirs, was only perceived by legal opinion as being freely alienable following a case in 1840.[32]

I would like to elaborate on a distinction that may be important when using the term sheepwalk. From its component etymological parts one would be predisposed to understand the term sheepwalk as an agronomic area of land or a pastoral unit wherein sheep remain put without straying far. This is likely to have been the origin of the term, but in its tenurial usage it often meant a 'holding' of commonland which might in some cases correspond to an 'agronomic sheepwalk' but often tended to be much larger and contain any number of 'agronomic sheepwalks'. This is where Welsh terminology can be judged to be more precise since the term *libert* unambiguously referred to the 'tenurial sheepwalk'. A common alternative for *libert* was the term *mynydd* followed by the farm name to which the land was appended. The earliest unambiguous attestation I have found for *mynydd* in this sense is *Mynydh Abergwngi,* collected by Edward Lhuyd in 1700.[33] The mountain lands of Abergwngu at the headwaters of the Elan valley, part of the mountain waste of the crown lordship of Myfenydd, was a vast expanse which can never have approximated a single 'agronomic sheepwalk'. The north Cardiganshire shepherd and oral historian Erwyd Howells gives repeated instances of mountain farms' upland in the Pumlumon area which in the twentieth century were divided into *lots* (sg. *lot*) for separate flocks, with mention of ranges of 5–19 sub-divisions. In the case of Blaenmerin (Devils Bridge) in 1909 the lots were topographical names – namely Banc-mawr, Y Groes, Ffrwd, Bistell, Banc-isa – whereas in other cases some of the lots had proprietorial designations such as Clap Defaid John Hugh, Pant Defaid Lisa, with reference to owners who repeatedly summered their sheep.[34]

The Welsh term for an 'agronomic sheepwalk' was *arhosfa* (pl. *arosfeydd*), composed of *aros* 'staying' + *-ma* 'place'. This term is found all over southern Wales, from Pembrokeshire to Glamorganshire under the reduced forms *rhosfa, rhysfa* and even *(h)osfa, (h)ysfa*. This has led to it being misunderstood as a compound of *rhos* 'moor' by the Welsh dictionaries.[35] The complementary distribution ranges of *libert* and *arhosfa* (not found in Cardiganshire outside the Tywi waters) is of note, though the mention of 'a libert in Nantmawr [Caeo, Carmarthenshire], and a rhosfa to keep the cattle' when discussing the status of sheepwalks on Llanddewi Brefi mountain implies that the two terms were known and probably still distinct.[36] In the same court case a defendant translated *arhosfa* as 'abiding place' in the phrase 'two banks for an abiding place for sheep and cattle that graze there' (the two banks, or hills, being *Lan-fawr* and *Bryndafaden* on Llanddewi Brefi mountain). The term for an 'agronomic sheepwalk' in Merionethshire was *cynefin*. It will be noted that the two words for 'agronomic sheepwalk' are native Welsh whereas the word for 'tenurial sheepwalk' was a loan from English feudal terminology. In northern England and Scotland the technical term which answers to an 'agronomic sheepwalk' is *heaf* (pl. *heaves*) or *heft* and the verbal derivative of the latter has given the name to the practice of *hefting* (i.e. settling) sheep on a particular piece of open land.[37] Hefting was known as *cynefino* in Merionethshire and *rysfeio* (*arosfeio*) on the Epynt mountain of Breconshire where it could be extended to people settling down in a new place *Siwd ŷch chi'n*

rysfeio? which is rather better Welsh than the usual *setlo lawr* (*pers. comm.*). In the 1930s there were three brothers who were employed full-time to heft wethers brought to the mart in Brecon onto the Brecon Beacons, using a rota system between them to complete a task that took anything between two and three weeks working day and night (Gwyn Jones, Tregaron after Glyn Davies, Cwm-duwlas, Llanddewi Brefi, pers. comm.).[38]

CONCLUDING REMARKS ON THE FORMATION OF SHEEPWALKS

Economic considerations dictated that even if many inhabitants throughout a lordship initially had a right to keep livestock on the extensive mountain wastes, it would quickly transpire that in most cases it would prove more economical for those who, living far from the uplands, should come to an arrangement with the mountain dwellers for the latter to guard their animals. Payment for guarding the livestock soon became construed as payment for keeping their animals on a particular stretch of mountain by the shepherd. There are some examples of sheepwalks divided between all the principal farms of a lordship or parish, for example Cellan, south of Llanddewi Brefi, but the preponderant pattern in Cardiganshire by the nineteenth century was that sheepwalks were attached to adjoining farms. In the lordship of Pennardd we have perhaps a fossilisation of an earlier arrangement for the concentration of small agronomic sheepwalks in Blaencaron associated with farms in the townships of Trecefail and Llanio, which stand in contrast to other larger tenurial sheepwalks of farms adjacent to the mountain.

That sheepwalks or *liberts* were not particularly stable before they were mapped on estate plans from the late eighteenth century onwards and especially in the comprehensive great tithe map surveys of the 1830s–1840s can be illustrated by two rather unique documents dating from the first half of the eighteenth century. Written on the reverse of seventeenth-century deeds, they name and describe the circuit boundary of two *liberts*, those of Nantgwyddyl and Brobwll in the Doethïe valley. Besides revealing the toponymical richness of the upland, the boundaries of Nantgwyddyl and Brobwll sheepwalks in the early eighteenth century are shown to be significantly different from the boundaries given at the time of the tithe map surveys around 1840 (continual underlining indicates names whose location is unidentified, broken underlining indicates names whose location is tentative, no underlining indicates names given in my *PNCards* 2004).

Nantgwyddyl (*c.*1700–50 – Neuadd-fawr MS 475, NLW).

> The coṁon belonging to Nant y Gwyddil as follows:

> South by East side oddi-rhwng y dday gae y flaen [ben y Crippelle, ag oddiyno (added)] nant y Cawl, ag oddi-yno y flaen Ffoes y gloch, ag oddi yno y gorse mynach, oddi yno y fryn y garreg Lwyd, oddiyno y ffoyse Coyon, oddyno y pen rhiw r Clochdy, oddyno dros wastad bryn mawr y flaen Nant Ivan Owen. Ag y flaen y draws-ffoes, ag y droed rhiw nwydog, ag y bant y brychwyn, ag y ben rhiw r gwyddil, y flaen y ffoes laes a Ch[n (added)]wch y Gwyddil hyd y rhyd dduy ar lan Dathie.

The boundary continues north of Doethïe-fechan:

> Ar ochor arall ir afon hyd pant yr hên du or ffordd fawr hyd yr afon. Ag o Lydiad y Garreg y fyny y ochor y ddisgwylfa ag oddi yno tya'r hir faen. Ag y lawr tya chyfer Tûy yn y Cornel.

Brobwll and Tyncornel (*c.*1700–50 – Neuadd-fawr MS 459, NLW).

> The Liberty of Common formerly enjoyed by yᵉ occupiers of Browbwll & Tir Jenkin Thoˢ alias Tûy'n-y-Cornel lands.

> Westward Oddiwrth yr afon Dothie gyda Nant y Gwndwn y-ben-y-Cerrig, ag y Esker Wynt, a chyda Nant y Llyn hyd llyn Verwyn. Eastward Ag yn oel y Esker Cerrig hyd ffoês y Gasseg, ag y ddothie Vach y-wared hyd y Nant sydd gyda chae tir Dothie Vach, Ond is-law Dothie Vach y lawr, y Ben y Goyallt, ag y wared yn ben y-ddys-gwylfa, ag oddi-yno y Lydiard y Garreg ag y ddothie.

MS 475 repeats the bounds given in MS 459 with the only significant difference that it is only described as 'Browbwll Comon'.

Despite the difficulty in identifying all the landmarks, the significance of these two documents, among others, is that they provide absolute proof that the *libert* boundaries of these farms in the mid-nineteenth century were radically different from those of their early eighteenth-century counterparts. As well as its own nineteenth-century sheepwalk, Nantgwyddyl seems to include part of Brynambor sheepwalk (Corsmynach), and Coli sheepwalk. As well as its nineteenth-century sheepwalk, Brobwll seems to include part of Blaen-doethïau and Penlan Doethïau sheepwalks, and the presumed earlier sheepwalk of Doethïau-fach, annexed by 1840 to Maesglas in the Camddwr valley. It is not clear if Tyncornel sheepwalk goes with Nantgwyddyl or with Brobwll or with either (despite its association with Brobwll in MS 459).

The correlation of the pre-1750 and the 1840 sheepwalk boundaries seems too complicated to explain in the absence of any other information. However, what does seem clear is that *libert* boundaries were liable to be changed drastically, and we should perhaps not wonder at this as the land was generally neither mapped nor mentioned in deeds (technically not being freehold). Our only hope of information before detailed maps were composed are disputes concerning boundaries. In fact in most cases even such disputes were for the most part never written down to be preserved for the historian's gaze, even if disputes that reached the courts were sometimes reported in nineteenth century newspapers.[39] The commonland status of the uplands, or rather the local law and customs specific to each lordship, tended to shield them from the workings of common law and their actual distance from the centres of often considerably weakened seignorial authorities in the lowlands and allowed a lawless mentality to flourish. Within the living tradition there are anecdotal accounts of shepherds who were fierce and who threatened their meeker neighbours. The absence of authority or interest in law enforcement in what were marginal and unpopulated lands was a recipe for such lawless threatening behaviour, especially when economic motives could come into play.[40] If, on the one hand, we can imagine of the existence of a 'wild-west' mentality, I do not think that we can conclude that all the inhabitants of the Cardiganshire mountains of the eighteenth and nineteenth centuries were lawless, I would hazard a guess that many were honest and neighbourly. Nevertheless, the situation did nothing to discourage a rather rougher society than we have been led to believe by the profusion of Victorian and post-Victorian accounts and parish histories of Wales coloured by Nonconformist pieties and most especially by the understandable natural prudence of local people not to offend neighbours publicly, however justified the reason.

It has been shown that the sheepwalks or *liberts* attached to the farms of the Doethïe valley and elsewhere in the Cardiganshire uplands usually contained more than a single heaf (or 'agronomic sheepwalk'). The *libert* therefore tended to cater for more sheep than were needed for the subsistence of one family and so the practice arose of having lowland sheep let on tack and settled on their particular heaf or arhosfa.[41] We must understand that by the nineteenth century the tacking of lowland sheep and livestock on the mountain 'commonland' during the summer months was not a right that the lowlanders had as 'commoners' of the lordship (in those cases where their farms were indeed within the same lordship) but a commercial agreement between them and the holder of the *libert*. This settling of other people's sheep and other livestock became the economic mainstay of the Cardiganshire mountain farms.

In theory the livestock placed upon the seignorial wastes were supposed to come from within the lordship; any 'foreign' animal was liable to a fine.[42] It is eloquent testimony to the power of commercialism over feudal 'niceties' that by the eighteenth century profits from sheep grazing made seignorial fines little more than an inconvenience to the sheep entrepreneurs. Cledwyn Fychan notes that as early as 1707 Celli-gogau sheep-walk (Perfedd lordship) was stocked by a certain Gruffudd Huw Crowdder of Arwystli lordship in Montgomeryshire, and that it is a measure of the size of his business that he was fined £33-6-8 during the decade 1712–21.[43] Concerning the same lordship in the 1750s, Lewis Morris noted that: 'every man may keep as many sheep as he is able to get and pay a shepherd for the keeping. So that there are some in these parts that have many thousands, even to fifteen or twenty thousand sheep which is more than Job had.'[44] According to Walter Davies the celebrated William Williams (†1773) of Pantsiry (a mountain farm whose *libert* extended into the headwaters of the Doethïe), was nicknamed the 'Job of the West' as he had owned 20,000 sheep, 500 wild horses, and a 'vast number' of wild cattle. To have so many sheep at one time meant of necessity that many if not most of his flocks were set on tack on sheepwalks belonging to others, but his economic clout was so great that in many ways he could proceed with impunity as is suggested by the following anecdote concerning him related by Walter Davies:

> He monopolized the whole range of hills for his numerous flocks; his shepherds kept them during the summer on the summits of the mountains, even in Brecknockshire; . . . He was so purse-proud, that in answer to a landlord, who threatened him with an action for certain damages done to his farm, he is said to have replied – 'You may begin as soon as you please; I will maintain a seven year law-suit with only the breechings of my sheep's wool'.[45]

In the early nineteenth century a certain Ifan Jones, of Nantgraig in a valley adjacent to the Doethïe valley was said to have owned 500 sheep, to which he added a further 600 sheep when he later acquired Nantiwan in the Doethïe valley.[46] Since both places were owned by different landowners in 1840, according to the tithe maps, it is likely that he was only able to have owned so much livestock by renting rather than owning all of the land that was needed. At a later date, the successful sheep grazer Captain Bennett Evans (1887–1972) of Capel Dewi, on the strength of the land that he had rented and had bought to expand his flock in Llangurig parish, came to be nicknamed Syr Watkin Bach 'Little Sir Watkin' with reference to the greatest Welsh landlord of his day, Sir Watkin Williams Wynn who owned most of the land in the parish.[47] These cases are enough to demonstrate that from the eighteenth century onwards it was possible to be economically dominant in the sheep-grazing economy through shrewd rental agreements as much as through owning land. However, since commercial transactions have not been as carefully preserved as deeds to land we are left largely in the dark as concerns the economic details of how land-use actually operated during the nineteenth century.

As we have seen, all aspects of the eighteenth- and nineteenth-century sheep-grazing economy are far from being understood, but what is clear is that it does not seem to correlate much to the cattle-grazing economy that had preceded it in mediaeval times and which had been so different in so many ways. I would like to present one final illustration of the changes. By the late nineteenth century the practice of tillage on mountain farms had come to be neglected by the overweening dominance of sheep 'monoculture', for which phenomenon the owner of Nantmeirch mountain farm in north Cardiganshire stated that the farm owners often found that the ancient enclosure

> will not pay the cost of tillage [so that] ordinary practice [is] . . . to allow it to remain entirely neglected and waste. The land so neglected assumes after some years nearly the same appearance as that of the adjoining sheep walk but with this difference that the herbage on such land is slightly greener and of finer quality than that on the adjoining sheep walk. (1880 Att. Gen. vs. Bonsall: 4).

This abandonment of tillage occurred in degrees and varied from area to area, indeed probably even from farm to farm, but there was some growing of barley in the Doethïe valley even after the 1914–18 war (Gwyn Jones after Glyn Davies, Cwmduwlas *pers. comm.*). Much more could have been said about the practices of transhumance, droving,[48] ponies, geese, mountain hay and the mountain boundary, but I hope that the subjects I have covered here have opened the way for others to study these questions further.

NOTES

1. It will be seen that the river is spelt *Doethïe* in this article with the diaraesis that Welsh orthographical practices demand to aid pronunciation as a trisyllable and not a disyllable. The etymology of the name is uncertain, especially as to the vocalism of the first unstressed syllable pronounced (it is locally pronounced *Dothïe* or *Dythïe* and even sometimes *'Thïe*). I am of the opinion that the form of the name suggests a collective plural in *-au* to a river-name which was originally something like **Doethi* (there are after all two branches Doethïe-fawr and Doethïe-fach). It is otherwise difficult to see what else the final *-e* represents in Doethïe, but as this is not a securely established fact I have preferred the form *Doethïe*, though the spelling *Doethïau* will make an appearance in place-names containing the river-name so that the reader can refer all the easier to the forms in my 2004 *The Place-names of Cardiganshire* (Oxford: Archaeopress), vols. 1–3.

2. In descending order going down the valley the pre-1841 inhabitations are: Magwyr Llethrhafodydd, Lluest Esgair-cerryg, Ffald-y-curnau, Nantgwyddyl, Nant-y-cawl, Cribin Hengwrt, Foelfraith, Lluest-fach, Lluest-fawr, Hendre-boeth, Tŷ-coch, Penrhiwcymer.

3. Neither Penlan nor Brobwll are mentioned in the census, seemingly overlooked.

4. The houses were abandoned in this order: Brobwll, Cnwcheithinog, Cnwchgwyn, 1840s (13 houses in 1861); Nantbenglog 1860s (12 houses in 1871), Cnwchglas, Gurnos, Penlan Doethïau, Tir-bach 1870s (8 houses in 1881); Doethïau-fach 1880s (7 houses in 1891); Dinas, Nantiwan 1890s (5 houses in 1901).

5. Maesbetws was abandoned in 1919.

6. W. J. Lewis, *Ceredigion: Atlas Hanesyddol* (Aberystwyth: Cymdeithas Llyfrau Ceredigion, 1955), pp. 64-65.

7. From pre-OS sources: *Aberdoethïau* 1803, *Cefn Rhiw-cymer* 1815, *Rhiwfelin* 1803, *Rhiwgoch* 1815, *Nant-y-gerwyn* c.1850 (hn). From OS maps: *Cefn Cnwcheithinog* 1834, *Cors Pwllci* 1904, *Craig Pysgotwr* 1834, *Esgair-cerryggllwydon* 1821, *Esgairgwair* 1834, *Pwlluffern* 1904, *Nantcnwch* 1891 (hn), *Nant Cnwchgwyn* 1891 (hn).

8. The local Llanwenog historian David Rees Davies (Cledlyn), born in 1875, remembered being employed as a lad by the OS when surveying the Teifi valley. See D. R. Davies, *Chwedlau ac Odlau* (Aberystwyth: Cymdeithas Llyfrau Ceredigion, 1963).

9. E. Howells, *Good men and True: the Lives and Tales of the Shepherds of Mid Wales* (Capel Madog, 2005), pp. 16-17.

10. However, it was noted that part of Llanddewi Brefi mountain was wire-fenced about 1870 (1915 Cymru: 48.206).

11. G. D. Gadsden, *The Law of Commons* (London, Sweet and Maxwell, 1988).

12. The distinction is discussed in Thomas Edward Scrutton. 1887. *Common Fields or the History and Policy of the Laws relating to Commons and Enclosures in England* (Kitchener: Batoche, 2003 edn), pp. 44-55, who, from the evidence, concludes that the distinction between 'appurtenant' and 'appendant' was not made prior to the late fifteenth century and not established in common law even then.

13. The term 'lordship' and its adjective 'seignorial' are more pertinent to Welsh conditions than the usual 'manor' and 'manorial' pertinent to most of England. Compared to a lordship, a manor's judicial powers were reduced both by being subject to a larger lordship or of a county and by being smaller. The Welsh term for lordship was *arglwydd-iaeth* whereas the sporadic translation of 'manor' as *maenor* – a wholly unrelated term – was basically a homonymous calque whose establishment in Welsh with that meaning is suspect.

14. That such legal distinctions could be poorly understood can be seen from a memorandum that Lord Lisburne of Trawsgoed sent to a London lawyer in 1797, with details concerning the upland commonland of the Crown lordship of Creuddyn, in which he stated that particular tenements claim certain distinct parcels as *appendant or appurtenant* thereto' (Crosswood I MS 1174) (my emphasis).

15. The reference to Foelallt or Faelallt mansion skirting the western boundaries of the mountain commonland in the same context as Fforestresgob no doubt refers to its (? lapsed) status as a deer-park or hunting reserve that existed in its environs, a status recalled by the name *Cae-fforest* for the land immediately east of the mansion.

16. Documents relating to the controversy which surrounded the enclosure of Llanddewi Brefi mountain are found in Ceredigion Archives (1864 onwards, ref. GB 0212 T/TR, ENC/1) as well as in various collections in the National Library of Wales, namely: Ecclesiastical Commissioners for England/Saint Davids (ECE/SD) MSS, NLW: (letters by encroachers 1874–75) MSS 51,188, 51,278, 51,310-12, 51,362; (sporting rights late nineteenth century) 51,697; (Fforestresgob 1890) 71,029. Lucas MSS, NLW: (enclosure and boundaries 1856–57) MS 2,999; (maps of mountain 1882–1903) MSS 2,613-710. Haverfordwest/ Williams and Williams (Hav.WW) MSS, NLW: (legal opinion concerning enclosure 1864–76) MSS 24,081-83, 24,102. This list is just for the purposes of guidance for researchers and has no pretensions of forming an exhaustive list.

17. J. W. Willis Bund (ed.), *The Black Book of St David's: An Extent of 1326* (London. Hon. Soc. Cymmrodorion, 1902), p. 198.

18. There was an increase in sheep as a 'cash-crop' in twelfth- and thirteenth-century Wales spurred on by Cistercian monasteries and their trading networks. The question of the preponderance of sheep against cattle is one that deserves a sustained study, see R. E. Hughes *et al.* 'A review of the density and ratio of sheep and cattle in medieval Gwynedd with particular reference to the uplands', *Journal of the Merioneth Historical and Record Society*, Vol. 7, 1976, pp. 373-83.

19. A. J. L. Winchester, 'Hill farming landscapes of medieval northern England', in Della Hooke (ed.) *Landscape: the*

Richest Historical Record (Amesbury: Society for Landscape Studies, 2000), pp. 76-78.

20. Due to the modern prevalence of sheep on Welsh mountains the Welsh word *bugail* is nowadays translated exclusively as 'shepherd', though etymologically it translates as 'cow-herder'. Until the nineteenth century lowland Wales was not as extensively divided into fields as it is today and late into that century adolescent lads in lowland parts of Cardiganshire were still employed to look after straying cows, their occupation being termed precisely *bugail*.

21. As with much else in this article, I have deliberately kept referencing to a minimum as the details relating to place-name elements will be elaborated in my forthcoming *Welsh Place-name Elements*.

22. NLW, Neuadd-fawr MS 459 *c.*1700–50.

23. L. Morris, 'An Account of the Lead and Silver Mines in the King's Mannor called Cwmmwd y Perveth' in D. Bick & P. W. Davies, *Lewis Morris and the Cardiganshire Mines* (Aberystwyth, NLW, 1994), pp. 16, 26.

24. NLW Coleman MS 147.

25. T. Pennant, *Tours in Wales, 1773* (Caernarfon, Humphreys, 1883), 3.185.

26. Gadsden, op. cit., n. 11, p. 94.

27. Morris, op. cit., n. 23, p. 16.

28. 1875 Eccl. Comm. vs. Griffiths [*The Summing-up of the Lord Chief Justice in an Action of Ejectment: the Ecclesiastical Commissioners for England vs. Griffiths and Others in Crown Lands in Wales*]: 13).

29. (1880 Att. Gen. vs. Bonsall [*Attorney-General vs. J. G. F. Hughes Bonsall* which is 1880 Cymerau MS 218, NLW]: 7).

30. G. Nicholson, *The Cambrian Traveller's Guide* (Stourport, Longman, 2nd edn Hurst, Rees, Orme & Brown), p. 37.

31. Gadsden, op. cit., n. 11, p. 98.

32. Gadsden, op. cit., n. 11, p. 71. In Cardiganshire the arguments for and against the freehold status of sheepwalks in the late nineteenth century were discussed at length in Eccl. Comm. vs. Griffiths (1875) (op. cit.) and Att. Gen. vs. Bonsall (1880) (op. cit.).

33. R. Morris (ed.), *Edward Lhwyd: Parochialia* (London, Cambrian Archaeological Association, 3 vols. 1902-1911), Vol. III, p. 4.

34. Howells, op. cit., n. 9, pp. 7, 15, 84, 116.

35. *Geiriadur Prifysgol Cymru: A Dictionary of the Welsh Language*; s.v. *rhosfa²*, *rhysfa²*, *rhesfa²*, *hysfa ac ysfa*. GPC is needlessly tentative in its assignation of the variants to the headword *arhosfa*, leaving open the temptation of a derivative of *rhos*. H. Meurig Evans & W. O. Thomas, *Y Geiriadur Mawr: the complete Welsh-English English-Welsh Dicitonary* (Llandysul, Gomer, 1971, rev. edn.) s.v. *rhosfa* gives an ambiguous translation 'mountain pasture'.

36. op. cit., Eccl. Comm. vs. Griff. 1875, n. 28, 19.

37. Gadsden, op. cit., n. 11, p. 99.

38. E. Howells (2005, op. cit., n. 9) also gives interesting details on settling cattle and sheep.

39. An account of an argument concerning boundaries between Llethr and Blaendoethïau in *c.*1835 was preserved much later, perhaps based on notes written at the time (>1928 Welsh Folk Museum MS 1793/67).

40. The late Lewis Jones of Cefnresgair, Tregaron, regaled us with stories of robberies and rustling and even murder on the mountain, especially concerning drovers, and wrapping up his account with a conclusion that still reverbates in my mind *Does neb yn gwybod beth ddigwyddodd ar y mynydd!* 'Nobody knows what happened on the mountain!'. But to give one documented example, William Roberts (1842–1936) of Blaenglasffrwd, later Nantnouadd, of whom it was said that: 'There was more that a hint of violence in William Roberts' nature. He was once fined £5 for threatening to kill his neighbour at Tywi Fechan; there are still those living who can point out the desolate spot where he had dug a grave in readiness . . .' (Ruth Bidgood, *Parishes of the Buzzard* (Port Talbot: Alun, 2001), pp. 251-52). E. Howells (2005, op. cit. 57, 208) mentions the regular general exchanges of blows with sticks at the mountain fair of Ffair-rhos and the fact that quarrels over boundaries and other routine matters often led to threats and sometimes fights. If he is generally positive about traditional mountain society as he knew it we are fairly reasonable in positing a more peaceful atmosphere from the mid-nineteenth century onwards. There is no reason to think that deaths were commoner in these mountains than elsewhere, and even if anti-social individuals recur in every generation, this is unlikely to reflect the behaviour of the majority of the peaceful inhabitants. What I am at pains to emphasise is that these mountains of mid Wales prior to the nineteenth century were particularly remote from the land-owning authorities of the time and thus constituted an environment which endorsed anti-social behaviour and taking the law into one's own hands.

41. In Edeirnion (Merionethshire) such tack sheep were termed *defaid troi* (literally. 'turned [out] sheep') (*Bulletin Board Celtic Studies*, Vol. 1, 1923, p. 292).

42. There must have been an invisible boundary between considering such charges as a fine or simply as a payment. Animals from outside the lordship, pasturing on Llanddewi Brefi wastes during the summer, were in the early nineteenth century charged 5s. for a head of cattle, 1s. for a sheep and 4d. for a goose (clearly based on the grazing needs of each animal) (A. Eirug Davies, 'Enclosures in Cardiganshire, 1750–1850', *Ceredigion*, Vol. 8, 1976, p. 102).

43. C. Fychan, *Faner Newydd*, 1996, p. 1.

44. L. Morris, 'The parish of Llanbadarn Fawr BL Ms Add. 14927, fols. 17-36', *Arch Camb.*, Vol. XCIII, 1938, p. 25.

45. W. Davies, *A General View of the Agriculture and Domestic Economy of South Wales* (London, McMillan, 1814), p. 245. For more on William Williams, see >1928 Welsh Folk Museum MS 1793/80:3.

46. This appears to be the Evan Jones of Nantygraig who is noted in the parish registers as living in Nantgraig in the late 1780s. His gravestone dated 1833 is at Soar-y-mynydd (Emyr Lake, Llanddewi Brefi, *pers. comm.*). >1928 Welsh Folk Museum MS 1793/80:3.

47. Howells, op. cit., n. 9, pp. 103-104.

48. Concerning droving, see R. Moore-Colyer, *Welsh Cattle Drovers* (Ashbourne, Landmark, 2002, 2nd. ed.).

The Pothouse:
a Carmarthen Waterfront Building

Terrence James

INTRODUCTION

Potters are believed to have been working in Carmarthen in the thirteenth century because we have personal names like 'Crocker' mentioned in an Extent of 1268.[1] The so-called 'Dyfed Gravel-tempered fabric', which is common in west Wales between the 12th and 17th centuries, may well have been produced at more than one site. As well as pottery, building materials like ridge and floor tiles may have been produced.[2] There is no

evidence for the use of bricks in house building however until very much later, because of the abundance of stone available in the locality (even if it was of poor quality). It is to be expected that clay-firing would have been practised in Carmarthen from at least the early 18th century, when brick began to be used in house building. Many of the early Georgian town houses in Quay and St Mary Street are brick, and ceramic ridge tiles would also have been used. There is evidence for brickyards

Fig. 1: *The Pothouse viewed from the west with the WCA building (now also demolished) just in view (right), photographed by J. F. Jones as demolition was about to begin. Note the hip-roof of the left hand part of the building. The large double doors on the right are 20th century inserts (see Fig. 9).*

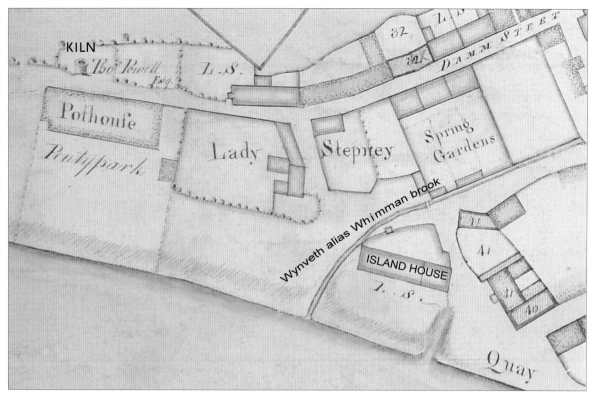

KILN

Tho.ᵒ Powell Es.ᵍ

L. S.

Pothouse

Pentypark

Lady

Stepney

Spring Gardens

Wynveth alias Whimman brook

ISLAND HOUSE

L. S.

DAMM STREET

32

32

L.

41

41

40

Quay

Fig. 2: *Part of Thomas Lewis's map of Carmarthen, 1786; the annotations in the black sans serif typeface are mine.*

using alluvial clays both above the bridge (the Old Station area) and below, about where Pont Lesneven abuts the north bank of the Towy.

A building called 'The Pothouse' is shown on the lower side of the Quay on Thomas Lewis' map of 1786;[3] this may be identified as the building shown on the Buck print of 1747 (*Fig. 4*). The earliest deeds we have for the property are from 1742 and 1766.[4] It was demolished to make way for a new dual carriageway road that links the bottom of Blue Street (and Coracle Way) with the bottom of Morfa Lane and subsequently the Pont Lesneven roundabout, thus effectively divorcing the town from its historic waterfront.

Unfortunately when the building was demolished in the early 1960s no good record was kept, although J. F. Jones, the then curator of Carmarthen Museum, took some photographs. By combining cartographic, photographic and other illustrative evidence, it is clear that the Pothouse had a complex history, going through numerous changes of function, and it is likely that if it was ever a pottery, this must have been during its earlier history.

THE MAP AND PRINT EVIDENCE

To understand the Pothouse we must also look at the adjoining properties, as these allow us to build up a picture of the evolution of this part of the town. Lewis's map of 1786 shows property belonging to Lady Anne Stepney immediately to the east of the Pothouse, bisected by a brook flowing into the R. Towy (*Fig. 2*). The brook was variously known as Wynveth (in the Middle Ages) and Whimman (in the 19th century) heavily used to power mills and supply tanneries from at least the 13th century.

On Lewis' map, the Pothouse is shown as a substantial rectangular building set back some distance from the Towy in an enclosure marked 'Pentypark'. A later extract from this map (*c.*1826)[5] adds 'late Lord Milford' to 'Pentypark' which must relate to his Pembrokeshire estate of that name (*see Fig. 1, p. 284*). Using the scale on Lewis's map, the building measures approximately 1.8 by 0.7 chains (35.9 x 14 m). The next maps of the area do not show a great deal of change apart from a small free-standing building, shown in 1786 on the east side, disappearing to be replaced, by 1826, by a small extension (*Fig. 3*). Wood's map of 1834 also shows a rectangular building marked 'Old Pottery' fronting 'Pothouse Quay'. The Tithe map of 1839 also has it marked as 'Old Pottery'. The dimensions of the building taken from Wood's map of 1834 and also the Tithe map are about 1.9 x 0.7 chains, slightly longer than the 1786 measurements. This may be due to mapping tolerances rather than to any change in the building. The 1850 plan of the town (*Fig. 3*) also shows a rectangular building but with a small square excrescence on its west

elevation. This is useful, for the excrescence is almost certainly a large buttress which was present when the building was demolished. The buttress also indicates that the building began to subside or lean from before 1850, due, as we shall see later, to the outward thrust of internal arches.

These map data tie in with a number of topographical prints which appear to show a double-pile structure. The first of these is the Buck print of 1747 (*Fig. 4*). Cox's view of the Quay about 1830 (*Fig. 5*) shows what

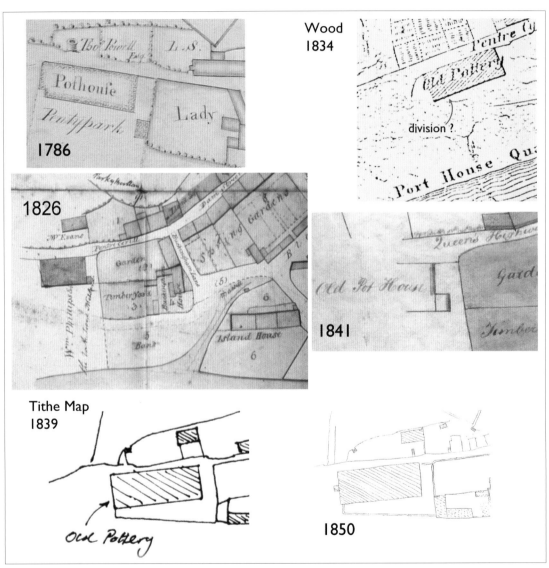

Fig. 3: *The development of the building as depicted in historic maps. Note the possible internal 'division' suggested in Wood's map of 1834, which could be evidence for a functionally different unit at the west end confirmed in other sources. It is clear from all these maps that the building did not originally extend as far as the eastern boundary of the curtilage. This indicates that the growth of the building must post-date 1850.*

Fig. 4: *Enlargement of a part of the Buck brothers' drawing, 1747, that shows the Pothouse on the left edge (see C. & J. Davies, Fig. 2, p. 285, for a full illustration of this view). The building is of three storeys with dormer windows, or louvers for ventilation. A building with a large number of floors of shallow height is what one would expect of a malthouse of this period. The little building to the right may be that shown in the same position in Lewis's map of 1786 (Fig. 2).*

looks like a double-pile building with dormers, but since the foreground is partly obscured by a ship on the stocks we cannot be certain that the building was of two or three storeys. The lesser-known view of Carmarthen with the paddle steamer (*Fig. 6*) is probably at least a decade later than Cox and must be dated to between 1835, when the foundation stone of St David's Church was laid, and 1847, when the second Picton Monument was erected. Despite its apparent naivety, the detail of the buildings is highly accurate. There is no mistaking, for example, the first Picton Monument. The Pothouse has a peculiarity in the roof alignment on the left side of the building. This must be the hipped roof shown in later photographs and will be discussed later.

MID 19th CENTURY DEVELOPMENT

By the late 19th century the building had been enlarged eastwards and southwards so that it now sat hard against the eastern boundary of the property. If one looks at the 1786 and 19th century maps there was space between the eastern wall of the Pothouse and its curtilage that suggests a gateway into the yard from Mill Street (originally named Dam/Dame Street). To the east the adjacent curtilage changed with the construction of Buckingham House and Dame Street/Pentre Cerrig was also growing.

Fig. 5: *Part of an engraving by David Cox, c.1830 of Carmarthen Quay (see Fig. 1, p. 61, for the complete view). The Pothouse is partly obscured by the ship under construction, but appears to be a double pile building possibly with dormer windows.*

Fig. 6: *An undated print, probably executed between 1834-1847. The Pothouse is in the centre of the print showing as a double pile building; the existence of a separate 'wing' on the left is indicated by a different roof alignment and possibly a different window configuration (see enlargement, Fig. 17).*

This was a natural progression once Blue Street had been built around 1800. Blue Street was constructed over the culverted Wynveth Brook, as was Red Street to the north, part of a major late 18th-century re-organisation of the town to permit easier access by traffic from the Quays to the new Market, by-passing the narrow streets of the mediaeval walled town.[6]

The historic use of the open foreshore for ship building was now under threat, with a move towards defined property boundaries within which were timber mills and wood-working shops. However, the Pothouse was set a long way back from the river edge and its curtilage extended all the way down to the waterfront. None the less it is clear from the 1826 map (*Fig. 3*) that a track traversed the property which eventually became Pothouse Road. This now linked the Quay with the river-side downstream (Dam Street was very narrow).

By 1865 the Pothouse had become a larger 'E' shaped building with wings protruding towards the river off the original building. The first evidence we have for this is a print entitled 'A View from Mount Pleasant 1865'. Supporting documentary evidence for these changes has not yet been found.

On the 1888 1:500 scale OS map the buildings are marked as the 'Towy, Tin, Japan and Galvanizing Works' (*Fig. 8*). By this date the building was approaching the limit of its development and the later photographs do not show any subsequent change (apart from the chimney). The whole area had been reorganised with Pothouse Road fronting the building and separating it from Pothouse Wharf. Sawmill Terrace had been built to the east, with, as the name indicates, a Sawmill added on the south side.

Fig. 7: *Extract from a print of 1865 'A View from Mount Pleasant' shows the Pothouse with its protruding wings; St David's Church is in the background.*

288

DOCUMENTARY AND PICTORIAL EVIDENCE FOR USE

Despite the quite remarkable amount of illustrative evidence we have not advanced our knowledge of the building's use. The earliest evidence of use is itself quite late in the building's life and comes from deeds to the property to the east which was being leased to Hector Rees, ship's carpenter, which I will call Buckingham House land. This is the Lady Stepney property shown east of the Pothouse in the 1786 map in Fig. 2. An indenture of 17 May 1766 describes the land to the west as 'lately a Brewhouse now called the Pothouse in the possession of James Phillips, Esq. or his tenants formerly the estate of Walter Middleton'.[7] This Brewhouse is recorded twenty-four years earlier in 1742 when again the adjacent property was described as 'a garden formerly of Walter Middleton, Esq., deceased and now

a Brewhouse in the possession of James Phillips, Esq.'[8] Here then is evidence for a Brewhouse built on open ground in the early 1740s, which was later called a Pothouse. This is not contradicted by the print evidence since the Buck view of 1747 could well show a building newly constructed. The change in names cannot but suggest a change in function. 'Pothouse' surely suggests a pottery.

Edna Dale-Jones has shown that in 1817 Nathaniel Awbery established a pottery adjacent to his brickworks which was further down river. Awbery was also a prominent builder and when he died in 1831 his business was advertised for sale, which included:

> . . . a capital pottery, quite complete, 141 ft long by 23 ft wide with working shed of nearly the same dimensions, a large Pottery kiln, a brick kiln, capable

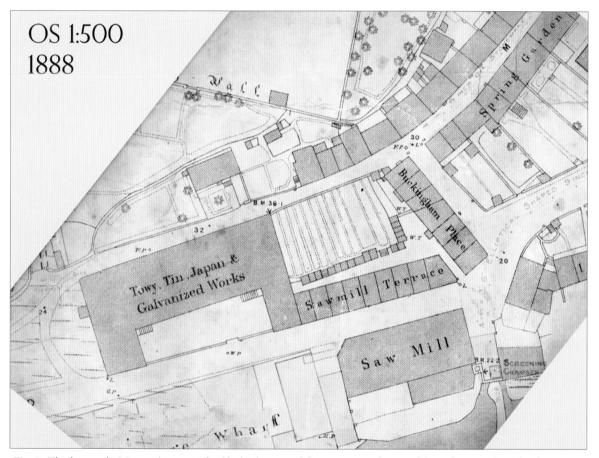

Fig. 8: *This large-scale OS map shows considerable development of the properties to the east of the Pothouse, with Buckingham House replaced by Buckingham Place as well as new housing in Sawmill Terrace. These Victorian single-fronted houses had external privies behind them as well as individual garden strips. Together with Mill Street they became part of Carmarthen's 20th century slums and were finally cleared away after World War II – only Sawmill Terrace remains.*

Fig. 9: *Photograph taken in the late nineteenth century showing the Pothouse; note the hipped roof to the left and the chimney stack to the right.*

Fig. 10: *The 'core' building ('B' on Fig. 15) of the Pothouse after the east wing had been demolished, viewed from the south east. This shows openings in the east pine end for loading and unloading at upper floor levels and these could date from pre-1850 (i.e. before the wings were added). Note the long central window which spans all floors and suggests a central staircase existing at one time.* (Photograph J. F. Jones).

of burning 20,000 Bricks at a time all under cover, together with the brickyard garden and marsh to the Water's edge.[9]

Given that the date of his death (1831) was so close to the date of Wood's map (1834) and the Tithe map (1839) it was not unreasonable to suppose that the pottery advertised was the Pothouse itself because both maps mark it as 'Old Pottery'. Nevertheless, we have seen that the 1826 map (*Fig. 3*) quite clearly marks William Phillips as holding the Pothouse, so Awbery's pottery must have been (as the advertisement suggests) at the Brickworks, marked on the Tithe Map as a quarter of a mile downstream of the Pothouse. It thus remains a frustrating fact that at present there is no evidence for the building's use as a pottery other than the name 'Pothouse' in 1766 and 'Old Pottery' on the maps cited above.

In 1766 the building was being leased to James Phillips, Esq. and in 1826 to a William Phillips. The assumption is that the two were not related. James Phillips was of Pentypark and Picton Castle. Although the evidence is not yet available, I suggest that William Phillips is the well-known Carmarthen shipbuilder and ship owner. If that is so then the building might have been used as a shipwright's yard, stores and lofting house. On 22 February, 1828, the *Carmarthen Journal* advertised the following:

To be let
All those premises being part of the Pothouse. 3 lofts each 95 ft in length [and] 21 ft width; also a cellar 60 ft by 20ft 3 ins. Near R. Towy. Capable of containing a large quantity of grane. Apply Morris Bank.

This is two years after the 1826 map (*Fig. 3*) which shows 'Wm Phillips, Esq' holding it. Given that the Pothouse was at one time used as a malting house, then if the property was split up, this could leave one half of the double-pile structure with either two or three floors ('lofts') capable of use for malting or straight grain storage. The length of the premises (95 ft) is however at variance with the overall length of the Pothouse (112-120 ft). The only way of reconciling this would be if the 'wing' with the hip roof was not included, then the overall lengths would be about the same. If the 1828 advertisement was offering the back part for lease then William Phillips could happily have used the front part, with its extensive yards, for timber storage and ship-

building. The two prints (*Figs. 5 and 6*) of around this date clearly show the riverside area in front of the Pothouse being used for shipbuilding, as was the bank to the east (part of the Buckingham House curtilage). The print reproduced in Fig. 6 shows numerous stacks of timber both in front of and to the side of the Pothouse and the ribs of a ship on the stocks can be seen fronting Island House. So the print evidence confirms the use of this area for shipbuilding. The first half of the 19th century was the premier period for Carmarthen's shipbuilding industry.

LATER NINETEENTH CENTURY USES AND BUILDING DEVELOPMENT

The photographic evidence allows some interpretation of building phases to be attempted. The photograph in Fig. 9, *c.*1890, shows the western of the two wings added to the Pothouse protruding towards the river. One can also see the pine-end of the eastern wing beyond the chimney. These were joined by an enclosing wall (which we cannot see in the photograph) to form an enclosed yard. In the south-east corner of the yard a boilerhouse had been erected with a tall, industrial, square chimney stack (*see Fig. 9*) but this is not shown on the 1:500 scale O.S. map of 1888 (*Fig. 8*). This helps to both date the photograph and the construction of the boilerhouse. The reader's attention is drawn to the hip-roof on the building's left side of the photograph, which must relate to how the building was originally constructed or later modified. On the O.S. map (*Fig. 8*) the dimensions of the Pothouse are approximately 46m x 15m (25m if the two wings are included).

James Davies, the owner of what became Towy Works on Carmarthen Quay, began tin smithing and stamping at his premises in 109 Lammas Street in the 1870s. This enterprise evidently flourished so he needed a new building. In 1878 the Pothouse was vacant and was advertised in the *Carmarthen Journal* on 13th December: 'To be let – Extensive malthouse, stores & premises situated on the Pothouse – vacant through the death of David Edwards'. It was marked as the 'Towy Tin, Japan and Galvanised Works' on the 1888 OS map (*Fig. 8*) clearly part of James Davies's 'Towy Works', a company formed in 1885. The Pothouse apparently was not suitable for the way the company wished to develop, consequently it built new premises on Old Station Road in 1890.[10]

By 1893 the Pothouse and curtilage had been split up and was sold by Thomas Jeremy Thomas, a London

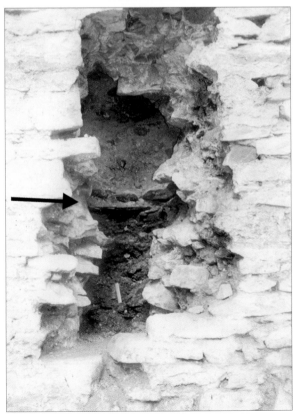

Figs. 11 and 12: *The 'undercroft' is marked '1'*
and this should be used to aid orientation with
Fig. 18. Note the joist holes for the first floor
(arrowed) but also the lack of evidence for more
than one upper floor. The breach in the wall
above the undercroft is shown in greater detail
(right). Unfortunately the slide was very
bleached but still shows a slate and cobble-stone
surface (arrowed) mid way across the gap; below
this is a concentration of what looks like shards
of red tile or pottery, above are concentrations
of mortar. J. F. Jones obviously thought this was
important and placed a one foot ruler in the
opening to allow scaling. The arrowed level
might indicate the ground floor level of
Building A on top of the undercroft arch.

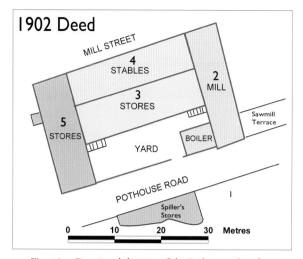

Fig. 13a: *Functional division of the Pothouse taken from information in the 1902 deed.*

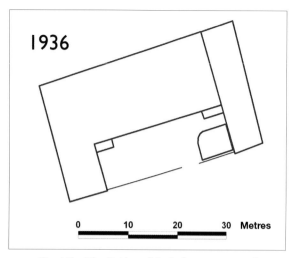

Fig. 13b: *The division of the Pothouse as suggested by the 1936 OS map.*

merchant, to Thomas Jenkins of The Friary, Carmarthen. At that date it was described as:

> All those bark storehouses and timber yard and landing places before the same fronting the Quay and situate on the Pothouse, bounded to the east by the Sawmills [formerly the 'bank' of Buckingham House shown in Fig. 3] on the south by the river Towy and on the north by *malting* premises formerly the property of William Lewis [this must be the Pothouse] and on the west by waste land the property of Lord Cawdor, formerly used as a timber yard.

It should be noted that the term 'Pothouse' is here being used to describe the area. It is evident that the building was used as a malthouse up to 1893. The description goes on to include the Pothouse itself, but without naming it as such:

> And secondly All that *malthouse* and premises with the storeroom underneath [could this be an undercroft?] the same situate on the Pothouse . . . bounded by the lane or road continuing westward from dame Street and known as Pentre Cyril on the south by the said Bark Stores on the east by the property of Alan James Gulston [Buckingham House land] and on the west by the said timber yard.

In 1902 the building was conveyed to Lloyds Bank by Messrs Philipps and Thomas and there is a tortuous description of its components, but fortunately there is also an accompanying plan which I have redrawn (*Fig. 13*). Most usefully the deed is annotated with marginal

notes showing the several tenants of the five blocks into which the complex had been separated:[11]

1. Spiller & Baker, 'Stores' (waterfront grain store).
2. Mr Thomas: Corn Mill and premises with 25 horse power steam engine and boiler, small donkey engine for feeding boiler and hoisting purposes, four pairs of Grind Stones, worn and elevators.
3. Mr Thomas, 'Stores and Yard'.
4. W? H. Thomas, 'Stables and Coachhouse'.
5. Mr Harries, 'stores and premises'.

This gives us evidence for the several units into which the building had been split by the early 20th century. Of particular note is no. 2, the corn mill with its boiler room and 25 h.p. steam engine, which explains the

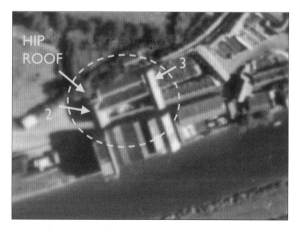

Fig. 14: *RAF vertical air photograph, 1946, enlarged to show the roof configuration of the Pothouse.*

industrial chimney we can see in Fig. 9. The block plan of the building shown in the 1936 25-inch O.S. map (*Fig. 14*) marks a division of the property, which suggests that the Mill wing to the east was a separate unit but also that perhaps the rest of the Pothouse was united under one tenant.

PHASES OF CONSTRUCTION

It is useful to look at the roof configuration with its mixture of hip- and double-pile roofs because this helps untangle the complex structural evolution of the Pothouse. Unfortunately, I could not put my hands on a good low-level oblique photograph, so I have settled for a 1946 RAF high-level vertical photograph (*Fig. 14*) and ground photographs taken in the late 1950s. The documentary evidence suggests a mid-18th-century date for construction of the core of the building but the roof timbers appear to be nineteenth century and belong to the modifications between 1850 and 1865 (*Fig. 19*).

As already noted, the demolition of the building was partly recorded on colour slide film by J. F. Jones, then curator of Carmarthen Museum.[12] He took many photos but only six survived the appalling conditions in which they had been stored. Few photographs have any identification marks and we have no text to accompany them. Jones evidently thought some features were significant, notably a collapse in one of the walls where layers of fill were visible in the space beyond (*Fig. 12*). Regrettably the detail is too bleached to reach firm conclusions. This does not stop us speculating that he might have been looking at kiln slag or even the interior of a kiln, but I doubt this. However, by combining the evidence we can further advance our understanding of the building's construction and functions.

It is fairly clear that the 'back' part of the building ('A' on *Fig. 15*) had a lower roofline than the front part (B)

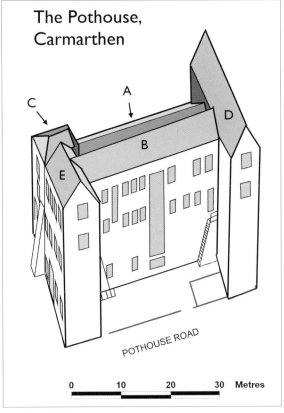

Fig. 15: *Isometric drawing to show the roof configuration of the Pothouse at the time of demolition; the chimney stack and the boiler house are not shown. The lettering refers to the elements of the Pothouse described in the text.*

which was clearly of three storeys in the J. F. Jones photographs. This seems to be confirmed by the print of 1834-47 which shows the same lower roofline (*Fig. 17*). The print also shows a different roofline or wing on the west side, which probably corresponds with the later hip-roofed part of the Pothouse.

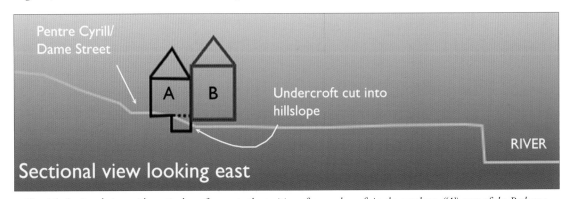

Fig. 16: *Sectional view with particular reference to the position of an undercroft in the northern ('A') part of the Pothouse.*

Because the building was built against a bank it is possible that the original back part was always of two storeys but with an undercroft entered from the front. This was within the front part of the double-pile build-ing (*see Fig. 16*). There is no documentary evidence to support the idea but how else is the 'undercroft' to be interpreted? (*Figs. 11 & 12*). The lack of window open-ings in the wall that separated the front from the back halves argues against a phased development with 'B' being added to 'A'. The 'undercroft' therefore has to be something functionally different – a space for a furnace or access to the base of a kiln are two possibilities. The 18th-century documentary evidence is for a brewhouse and then a pottery. Once again, in 1878, the Pothouse is described as a malthouse. So evidence for malting is what we need to look for in the physical remains recorded before demolition.

The photographs in Figs. 10-12 and Fig. 18 provide the best evidence relating to the 'hip-roofed' part of the building ('C' in *Fig. 15*). By looking at Fig. 11 it can be seen that at ground floor building C had three arched openings into it from building B and the same again on the first floor. Subsequently, some of these openings had been bricked up and concrete lintels inserted. A weak-ness of the design would have been the outward thrust exerted by the arches and it may be that the buttress which is first shown on the 1850 map (*Fig. 3*) was an

Fig. 18: *View looking east after the demolition of the front and side walls of Building 'B' exposing the wall that divided 'A' from 'B'. The undercroft marked '1' can be used to relate to Fig. 11; another undercroft can be seen beyond the road-roller (2). Wall '3' seems to be made up of large brick blocks of an unusual proportion.*

Fig. 19: *The most damaged slide of the surviving six from the J. F. Jones collection of the Pothouse nevertheless shows the roof timbers which appear to be 19th century.*

original feature. In Fig. 18 this wall with its arched openings had been demolished and we can see part of the interior of its rooms (3). It is notable that there are no openings into building A until we get up to the third floor where there is a blocked window, reinforcing the conclusion that the hip-roofed building C was a distinct and functionally separate part of the Pothouse. The walls of the first floor seem to be constructed of bricks of unusual proportions and one wonders whether they could be reused from a malthouse drying floor.

The essentials of a malthouse which could be part of a brewhouse were threefold: a sprouting floor on which the grain was allowed to germinate; a drying floor where the moisture content of the sprouting barley was then reduced; and a steeping tank for the production of malt. The drying floor was floored with tiles with perforated holes to allow warmed air to rise through them and dry out the grain. The undercroft therefore could have housed the furnace for the drying 'kiln' which would have been in the floor or floors above.

The second undercroft (2 in *Fig. 18*) within the eastern end of Building B is more difficult to explain. It clearly took up a great deal of space on the ground floor and provided the foundation for the stone floor of the upper storey – this much is clear from the photograph (*Fig. 18*). It appears to have a structural stone wall on its

west side but it is not clear whether that extended through to the next floor. There are three or four round-headed windows at a level which one might expect to be that of the upper storey, thus suggesting that the east end of building B was open from the first floor to the roof. However, this is contradicted by the doorway (which had a sliding door) that can be seen in the pine-end of building B in Fig. 10. The external staircase which led to the door can be seen in the south elevation in the same photograph (*Fig. 15*). The disposition of the window openings in this photograph suggests a third floor, but on the other hand the lack of floor joist holes (*Fig. 11*) argues against it. Unfortunately, we just do not have enough evidence to fully reconstruct the interior.

The building was substantially remodelled some time between 1850 and 1866 when the two wings were added. The impetus for this work has not been discovered, but whoever undertook it attempted to produce a building with symmetry. For example, matching windows were placed on the pine ends of each wing. The demand for warehousing in such a location may have been the reason and the two wings might have been simply the most logical way of increasing the size of the existing double-pile building. On the basis of the known documentation it is doubtful that it was modified when

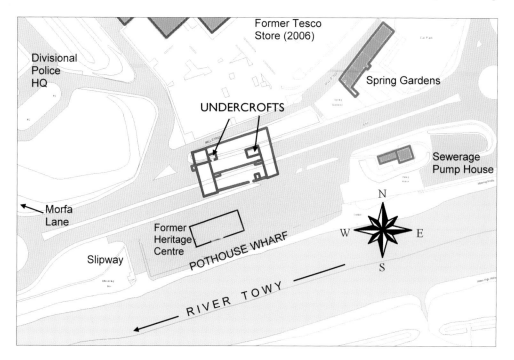

Fig. 20: *The site of the Pothouse in relation to the modern street layout. I have sketched in the approximate position of the undercrofts that can be seen in the J. F. Jones photographs.*

taken over by Towy Works. After that the Pothouse was split up for separate uses for storage and grinding corn.

The Pothouse then was a substantial building with a varied history spanning some two hundred and fifty years. Its use as a pottery still needs to be proved. It is to be hoped that more documentary research in the future will fill out the missing links allowing a more complete history to be written.

ACKNOWLEDGEMENTS

Almost all the historical evidence from deeds was given to me by Edna Dale-Jones, who in the true co-operative spirit of Carmarthenshire Antiquarians helped me patch together the core detail from her own extensive knowledge of Carmarthen's merchant class. We then discussed problems of interpretation on several occasions. The photographs by J. F. Jones form part of his slide collection deposited in Carmarthen Museum. Grateful thanks too go to Carmarthenshire Record Office for allowing me to copy and reproduce here the several historical maps.

NOTES

1. T. A. James, 'Medieval Carmarthen and its Burgesses: a study of town growth and burgess families in the later thirteenth century', *Carms. Antiq.*, Vol. XXV, 1989, pp. 9-26.

2. C. Papazian and E. Campbell, 'Medieval Pottery and Roof Tile in Wales A.D. 1100-1600', *Bulletin of the Welsh Medieval Pottery Research Group*, Vol. 13, 1992, esp. Dyfed Gravel-tempered fabric, pp. 56-59; for ridge tiles see T. A. James, 'Excavations at Carmarthen Greyfriars, 1983-1990', *Med. Archaeol.*, Vol. XLI, 1997, pp. 100-194, esp. 'Ridge-Tile', pp. 181-3; C. O'Mahoney, 'Pottery, Ridge Tile and Water Pipe', Greyfriars Topic Report 2 (available online from Dyfed Archaeological Trust and RCAHMW, Aberystwyth, and in hard copy at local libraries and museums).

3. CRO, Cawdor 219. Map of Carmarthen drawn for John Vaughan of Golden Grove by Thomas Lewis.

4. 1742: CRO Derwydd 563, 1766: CRO Derwydd 562.

5. CRO 219. Map of Carmarthen drawn from John Vaughan of Golden Grove by Thomas Lewis.

6. T. A. James, *Carmarthen: An Archaeological and Topographical Survey* (Carmarthen, 1980), 'Georgian and Regency Development', pp. 52-54.

7. CRO Derwydd D562.

8. CRO Derwydd 563.

9. D. Brennan, G. Evans, H. James and E. Dale-Jones, 'Excavations in Carmarthen, Dyfed, 1976-1990. Finds from the Seventeenth to the Nineteenth Centuries', in *Medieval and Later Pottery in Wales*, No. 14, 1993-4, pp. 15-108.

10. E. Dale-Jones, 'Towy Works (1795-1995): a Celebration', *Carms. Antiq.*, Vol. XXXIV, 1998, pp. 58-9.

11. CRO DX/234/40.

12. T. A. James, 'Saving the photographic slides of J. F. Jones – an exercise in archaeological detection', *Carms. Antiq.*, Vol. XLII, 2006, pp. 104-110.

A Further Study of the Pothouse and its Surroundings

Edna Dale-Jones

Terry James was a brave man, determined to complete as many as possible of his projects. One of these was to update and expand *Carmarthen – an Archaeological and Topographical Survey* (1980).[1] We exchanged information and discussed the 18th and 19th-century development of the town. Terry had managed to assemble the material he had collected on the Pothouse into an article which he regarded as provisional rather than definitive. His article demonstrates his accomplishments as archaeologist and historian, his computer expertise and his knowledge of photography. After his death, I developed his research by exploring at the National Library the Derwydd and Picton Castle Collections, and at the Pembrokeshire Record Office the Pentypark papers in the Lloyd Philipps Collection. My approach in this article is that of a local historian, my intention to complement and compliment Terry's work. To avoid duplication of illustrations, I have referred back to the Figs. in the preceding Pothouse article by Terry.

One objective was to try to establish why the building and area was known as the 'Pothouse' and to find the earliest use of the name. Another was to determine why on Wood's 1834 map, and the tithe map, 1839, and the Carmarthen Town Western Ward Map, 1850, the 'Pothouse', was labelled 'Old Pottery' (*see Fig. 3, p. 286*). In a Derwydd estate lease (1826)[2] it is also described as a 'Pottery' and the *Carmarthen Journal* described the Pothouse Quay as 'Potter's Quay' in 1812. To do this, it was necessary to trace the history of the Pothouse and its curtilage as far back as possible, placing the Pothouse in its context – the marshland and Dam Street. I also wanted to answer Terry's questions about the identity of Walter Middleton, whose name appears on early descriptions, and why, on the 1786 Lewis map

of Carmarthen (*Fig. 2, p. 285*) the Pothouse ground is labelled 'Pentypark', on the Derwydd map of 1826 (*my Fig. 1*) 'The Late Lord Milford' and on a later edition, 'William Philipps'. Some of the answers to these questions emerge as the story of the Pothouse is followed through. Lastly, I wanted to research ship-building on the marshes.

The Pothouse building with its river frontage, stands at the eastern end of the marshlands known as Morfa Moch Issa, aptly called 'fenny lands'. The marshlands belonged to Carmarthen Corporation and were one of its sources of income from leaseholds, mortgages and, eventually, sales. The Court Leet presentation of 1657 states that Morfa Moch Issa, by 'estimation 60 acres more or less', lies 'betwixt the Key on the east side, Towy on the South, Gwayn velyn bach leading to Llanllwch on the west, and the Commons of the said town and certain closes called Arch Deacon's Ground on the north side'.[3] It is probable that in the Middle Ages the Pothouse frontage, the river bank to the east and Island Wharf were part of the Commons, but by the 17th century they had all passed into private ownership.

The two descriptions in 1742 and 1766 of the Pothouse used by Terry, were taken from leases of adjacent properties in the Derwydd collection. I have explored the entire collection further and have thus been able to take the Pothouse back to at least 1703. The 1786 map of Carmarthen drawn to document the holdings of John Vaughan of Golden Grove also defines those belonging to Lady Elizabeth Stepney. It demonstrates the economic power of the Vaughans and Stepneys: they owned nearly all of the lucrative wharves and warehouses by the river. The Stepney estate passed from Richard Vaughan of Derwydd to his niece Bridget Bevan and then to Lady

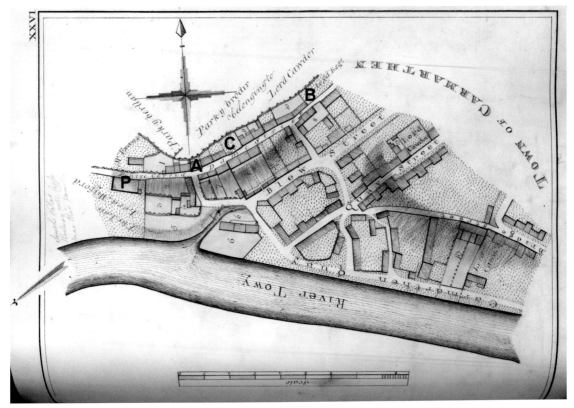

Fig.1: *Map of part of Derwydd Estate properties in Carmarthen, 1826, drawn and described by William Goode for Joseph Gulston (Derwydd, C.A. 52).*

No. 1 = Houses & Garden in Pentre Cerill (sold 1870 as 26, 27, 28, 29 & 30 Dam Street).

No. 2, 3, 4 & 5 = House & Garden, Timber yard & Work Shop, Buckingham Houses & Yard etc., Bank etc. by the river (sold 1870 as The Saw Mill Shed with 13 newly erected Cottages, 2 Cottages adjacent, and large garden).

No. 6 = Island Houses, Garden, Yard etc. (sold in 1870 in 3 lots, The Island Houses, with Yards adjoining, comprising the Custom House, Dwelling-house, and the Sloop; Island Wharf, with Cottage, and Bakehouse, at the pine-end of the Sloop, and the private Road leading to the Quay; Island House, with Four Cottages and Gardens).

No. 12 = House & Yard in Quay Street (sold 1870 as House & premises, No. 27, Quay Street formerly known as the Old Hope & Anchor).

> *A = Pentypark property sold 1825 – 4 houses/14 tenements including The Nelson.*
> *B = Pentypark property leased to George James/George Watkins.*
> *C = Property of John Vaughan, Golden Grove leased to Philip Morgan, ship builder.*
> *P = Pothouse.*

The map has been reproduced with North at the top to allow comparison with others in this and the preceding article, especially that of 1826, Fig. 3.

Stepney and was eventually inherited by Joseph Gulston. A map-book prepared by William Goode in 1826 documents Gulston's properties in Carmarthen. One map (*my Fig. 1*) delineates an area next to the Pothouse (later known as 'Buckingham' after the public house on the site) which Goode describes and numbers 2, 3, 4 and 5. The deeds date back to 1703 and show the development of both 'Buckingham' and the Pothouse:

1703   Lease from Richard Vaughan of Derwith to Morris John, shoemaker: Cottage and garden in Dame Street . . . in a certain place called Pentre Kerrig . . . a garden of Walter Middleton Esq. on the west and a little lane leading to ye Key on the east.

1733   Lease from Arthur Bevan of Laugharne, Esq., and Bridget his wife to William Nicholas, Gent:

Cottage and garden Situate . . . in Dam Street in a place there called Pentrea Kerrig . . . a Garden formerly the estate of Walter Middleton Esq. Deceased and now a Brewhouse in the possession of James Philipps Esq. on the west.

1742   Lease from Arthur Bevan Esq. and Bridget to David Thomas, Glover: Messuage, garden and wast Piece of Ground situate in Dam Street . . . in a Place there called Pentre a Kerrig . . . a Garden formerly the estate of Walter Middleton, Esq. Deceased and then or now a Brewhouse or Storehouse in the possession of James Phillipps Esq. on the west.

1766   Lease from Bridget Bevan, Widow, to Hector Rees, Ship's carpenter. Messuage and dwelling house and Smith's forge, Garden & Coal Yard with all the outhouses . . . a Garden formerly the estate of Walter Middleton Esq. Deceased lately a Brewhouse and now called the Pothouse in the possession of James Phillips. Esq. or his undertenants on the west.

1826   Notes by George Brace, Gulston's agent, on Buckingham House and premises adjoining called Efelfawr & garden & timber yard: Premises consist of dwelling house, stable & yard called Buckingham House otherwise Ship a Ground, a large timber yard walled and sheds, carpenter's shop & bank on the river. Also other houses called Efelfawr much out of repair – occupation of Wm. Morgan Esq., bounded by Buckingham Alley and premises and timber yard belonging to Wm. Phillips Esq. on the west.[4]

The descriptions establish that the Pothouse had been built on a garden, part of the estate of Walter Middleton: first it was described as Brewhouse, then Brewhouse or Storehouse, and, in 1766, for the first time, Pothouse. In 1733 it was owned by James Philipps. The James Philipps named here was of Pentypark in the Parish of Walton East, Pembrokeshire. This is the explanation of why the building is labelled Pentypark on Lewis's map of 1786. The deeds in the Pentypark papers contain specific information about the Pothouse.[5] One of the earliest, dated 3 March 1720, a one-year lease, part of a marriage contract, catalogues their properties in the Borough of Carmarthen. It includes the Pothouse building:

1720   Lease: All that other messuage or pothouse and garden situate lying and being in Damm Street

now or late in the occupation of Thomas Read, Mercer.

The next deed, dated 14 March 1738, is particularly significant as it puts the Pothouse into its context and helps to define its purpose:

1738   Bond between James Philipps and Charles Bowen, of Camrose, Clerk. All that messuage or tenement called the pott house now commonly called the Brewhouse and a Key lately erected on the River Towy near the same with the yard garden and ground thereto belonging and the Buildings thereon built now or late in the possession of the said James Philipps Alexander Gwynn & Rees Davies or some of their undertenants.

This is the first reference to a quay being built on the Pothouse bank. It seems that Philipps had embarked on a large and enterprising commercial venture, building a substantial storehouse (rather confusingly known as a brewhouse or a pothouse) which could be used either by himself or his tenants to store merchandise brought in by ships docking at the quay. The size of this building, by far the largest warehouse along the riverside, is well illustrated on the 1747 Buck brothers preparatory drawing for their engraving (*Fig. 2, p. 42*). The development of the 'Buckingham' site to include a smith's forge, timber yard and workshops, together with more building on Island Wharf, shows an extending industrial area. The Island site would expand into more houses, including a public house, the Customs House, a bakery, and lead and bark yards. The 1786 map clearly shows two limekilns being worked on the marshes, one due north of the Pothouse and the other to the west 'under Friars Park' as the leases describe it. The Corporation Order granting one of the leases has an oblique reference to the Pothouse quay – and now it becomes possible to visualise the nature and extent of this industrial scene. 30 September 1765:

Lease to . . . Morris Howell and George Evans of part of the land which adjoins Fryer's Park for erecting lime kilns where limekilns were before with free liberty of landing stone and culm.[6]

At the same time ship-building was increasing. William Spurrell commented in 1860: 'Ship-building,

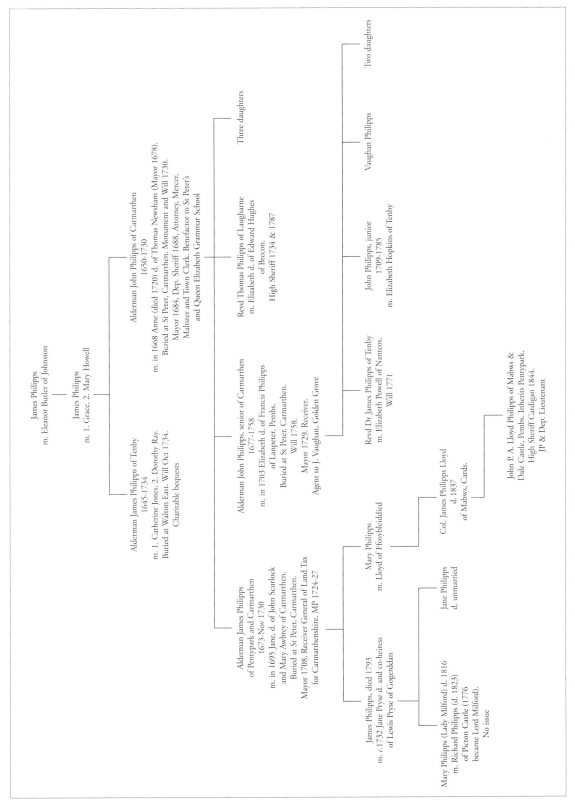

Fig. 2: *Genealogical tree of Philipps Family Pentypark (CRO. DJD/20), drawn by Major Francis Jones, with additional information and dates from Wills.*

too, (was) formerly carried on here to a considerable extent, half-a dozen vessels of different sizes and in different stages of construction being sometimes on the stocks at the same time'. The late Robin Craig recorded, from documents in the Public Record Office, the names of over forty ships built in Carmarthen between 1760 and 1800. These records indicate that at least ten of the ships were owned by Morgan Lewis.[7] Lewis (1733-1812) was the most dominant merchant in Carmarthen during this period, trading in hides, glass, timber and grain. It has always been assumed that the majority of vessels were constructed on the marsh lands although a ship yard worked by Herbert Bedford, of Haverfordwest, was operating on the main quay from circa 1755. There is now both circumstantial and direct evidence to show ships were built on the marsh. Morgan Lewis lived in Gellingham House on the corner of Dark Gate and Dam Street surrounded by his sheds, yards and granaries: circumstantial evidence that he built his ships on or near the Pothouse site. It is important to note that the 1786 map shows only a narrow footbridge connection between the marshes, the Pothouse and the main quay (*see Fig. 2, p. 285*). Dam Street was the vital highway into town until the construction of Blue Street. The direct evidence is contained in his accounts' ledger. In 1797, Lewis supplied timber to Captain David Evans for his new ship and also charged him for the use of 'building ground' on the marshes, which he held by lease from the Corporation. In 1798, Lewis supplied timber to Captain Thomas Morgan for 'his ship on Pothouse'.[8]

Two Corporation Orders relating to the activities of Richard Chitty, a London timber-merchant, contracted by Richard Vaughan, to cull the Golden Grove trees, reveals another commercial use of the marshes. The trees, having been floated down river, were stacked on 'Golden Grove' quay (a section of the main quay which belonged to the Vaughans) until vessels built in Bedford's shipyard could transport them to London, but there remained a huge surplus of timber to accommodate.

> 1757   Whereas Richard Chitty hath this day Petitioned praying to lay down all such timber as may suit his conveniency on part of the Commons leading to & adjacent to Rhyd Gors lands upon paying a yearly rent for such lands . . . It is ordered that seven of the members of the Corporation may go with the said Richard Chitty to the said town lands . . .

> 1758   It is ordered that Council's opinion be taken what methods to take for prosecuting of Richard Chitty & others for several trespasses by them committed on the town lands by laying down great quantity of timber & digging Saw Pitts thereon . . .[9]

These trees must have been loaded and shipped from Pothouse quay or onto barges drawn up on the marshes.

James Philipps, the Pothouse owner, was the grandson of John Philipps of Carmarthen (a younger son of Pentypark). John, an attorney, maltster and merchant, became wealthy and influential. He was active in borough affairs – Town Clerk, Mayor in 1686, and then Alderman. He was also a generous benefactor to the church and town. His will, proved in 1730, gives details of malting houses and kilns in King Street and Spilman Street, but does not mention the Pothouse.[10] He leased from Golden Grove a 'cellar' on the quay for his merchandise. His eldest son, James Philipps, inherited Pentypark from his grandfather. James was appointed Receiver General for Land Tax, was Mayor and Alderman of Carmarthen and M.P. for the County, 1724-27. He also died in 1730 and it is his son, James, whose name appears on the Pentypark deeds. Alderman John Philipps's second son, John, and then his grandson, John Junior, were also active in politics and commerce. There is evidence in a letter written by John Philipps Junior, 21 May 1752, to Sir Thomas Stepney that the family were engaged in building ships on the Pothouse. The context of the letter is difficult; it may relate to the construction of herring busses for Sir Thomas:[11]

> Hon d Sr Thomas
>
> The Dimensions of our New Vessel on the stocks I will insert Below and Hope her size will suit & correspond if it does we will make it worth his while to purchase Her, for those concerned do not know how or where to employ her. If you could help us to Dispose of her it will be a Great addition to favours conferred on
>
> Yr Hon Most obedient humble servant
> John Philipps Junior[12]

John Philipps Senior and Junior both subscribed towards the publication of the Lewis Morris navigational charts in 1748.[13] This certainly indicates that as ship-builders and mercers they had a strong interest in protecting their maritime interests. The will of John Philipps, Junior, proved in 1785, confirms that the family held shares in shipping. He left to his niece, a one half share in the Brig, *The Racehorse*, William Morgan, Master; a one quarter share in the Sloop, *The Racehorse*, Phillips Harries, Master; a one quarter share in the *Lovely Cruiser*, James Morris, Master; a one third share in the Sloop *Industry*, Master Lewis Oriell and a one third share in the Sloop, *Hope*, George Thomas, Master. A bill of sale for the Sloop, *Racehorse*, has survived. John Morgan, the Furnace House iron master, purchased one quarter share in 1781, from a London Merchant. John Vaughan of Golden Grove arranged for his large new stove to be brought from London on this ship. The *Lovely Cruiser* was built, 1776, in Carmarthen for Morgan Lewis (presumably the majority share-holder).[14]

Information on the Pentypark lease of 1720 and from wills revealed more about Walter Middleton. He was the second son of Henry Middleton, High Sheriff in 1644, and builder of Gorse Ddu, their mansion at Llanarthney.[15] He is named in the will of his elder brother, Christopher, who died in 1699, as 'Walter of Tenby friend and trustee'. His previous residence had been Slebech. His own will, proved in 1707, leaves his estates (not defined) to his nephew, Richard Middleton, son of Christopher.[16] Richard himself died in 1733 and this may be when James Philipps bought the Middleton estate, which included two further properties in Dam Street. Both properties are described in the above 'lease for one year', dated 3 March 1720:

> All that house or malthouse in Damm Street with garden in the tenure of Thomas Reid (marked A).

and:

> Also all that messuage house and garden belonging in Damm Street in the occupation of Evan Griffiths (marked B).

These are further described in a later Pentypark document, 1762:

> All that house or malthouse . . . formerly Thomas Rees. Now four houses in the tenure of Wm Higgon widow of Thomas Wood David Morgan and Priscilla Phillip. (A)

and:

> messuage . . . formerly Evan Griffiths now George James. (B)

The two properties in Dam Street can be identified from the leases of the adjacent Derwydd properties and

the 1826 map. They have been numbered A and B and superimposed on the map (*my Fig. 1*).

The Pentypark deeds reveal that the vested interests of Alderman James Philipps and his son lay in the Lower Franchise. They owned Nantyci, Cillefor and 'five fields near Llanllwch' – possibly part of a marriage settlement (1686) between James Philipps and Jane, daughter of John Scurlock. Corporation leases dated 1711, 1730 and 1755 record that the Philippses rented 'Town lands by Pentrehyth & Tawelan' (next to the Scurlock property of Flanders Hill).

A relevant and important discovery was a Corporation Order, dated 8 December 1710:

> George Lewis, Esq. John Scurlock, John Williams & James Philipps Alderman or any three of them to view the encroachments at the Potthouse & ye grounds adjoining thereto and also to see the place where John Read diggs on the Commons and to make the report thereof next Council Day.[17]

This may indicate that James Philipps, perhaps already leasing the Pothouse area from the Middleton estate, was safeguarding his own interests. It is the first known use of the name 'Potthouse'. It is also the first mention of clay being worked on the marshland and there is no other until 1797. This may just possibly indicate that clay had been dug here in the past and there had been a pottery known as the Pothouse. This is the only tentative explanation I can find for the name 'Pothouse'.

Fortunately the Pentypark document, dated 1762, listing their Carmarthen holdings, has information that reveals why the building was called 'Old Pottery', and does answer one of the questions:

> 1762 All that other messuage or pothouse & garden thereto belonging & lying in Dam Street formerly in the tenancy & occupation of John Read Mercer since John Rees now James Stewart Merchant Hector Rees and David Griffiths Potter and undertenants.

There are also two rentals which confirm that a potter worked in the building:

> 1765 Rental: (Identical for the year 1768 but does not name tenants)
> David Griffiths   A vault being part of the
>   potter   B. house £3
>   "   part of   " £4 15
> Mr. James Stewart   " £15

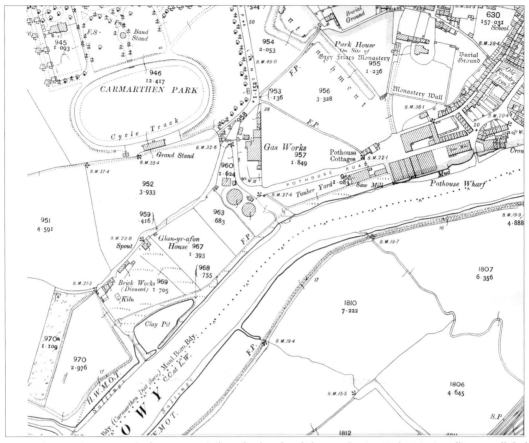

Fig. 3: *CRO, O.S. Map 1906, Sheet XXXIX.6, shows brickyard and clay pit, the Gas Works, Mr. Powell's saw mill shed & timber yard, 1901.*

A significant discovery, but again there is a variation of name for the building, 'Pothouse' 1762 and 'Brewhouse' in 1765. It was satisfying to discover that David Griffiths lived next door to the pottery. He is one of the tenants listed on a Derwydd lease, dated 1774, living in the group of Pentre Cerill houses which are numbered 1 on Goode's 1826 map.

> 1774   And also three cottages or dwellinghouses with gardens thereto adjoining now in several occupation of Benjamin Lewis, Thomas David, John Griffiths and David Griffiths of the Pot house situate at a place called Pentrecerrig . . . the above garden in the occupation of David Griffiths on the west . . .

David Griffiths, probably the man buried in St. Peter's churchyard in 1776, used the building from *c.*1762 to *c.*1776. Unfortunately, there are no Corporation leases to indicate a brickworks (let alone a pottery)

in operation on Morfa Moch Issa at this time. Logically, Griffiths would have used the clay from the marshland. Undoubtedly bricks were being made in Carmarthen in the 17th century and probably much earlier. The 1657 Court Leet presentment refers to 'brick kilns near the Turners'. The 'Turners' (public house, house or guild?) was situated in Upper Water Street, also known as the Backway, and now St. Catherine's Street. There are brief references to brick kilns at the Royal Oak and one to St. Catherine's Chapel 'since a brickyard'. A surviving Corporation lease, 12 September 1786, to Richard Howell, an attorney, is for a 'house, garden and field called the Brickyard, 3 roods & 8 perches, situate in the Backway. A clause forbidding the 'erection of brick kilns and the digging of clay for making brick pantiles' except for use in repairing the gutters and ditches of the house, implies an old site with the clay worked out.[18]

David Griffiths probably made pantiles and crests, pots for 'smokey chimneys', drainpipes and brown-glazed ware. A flourishing brickworks was in operation on the marsh below the Parade from at least 1785. Bills sent to Golden Grove reveal that Mason's brickworks was making crests and flower-pots at that date.[19]

A large brickworks was opened at the western end of Morfa Moch Issa some time before 1796 (recorded on the 1796 Rate Valuation) and was very productive. It was first leased to Morgan Lewis, the merchant, and then, in 1807, to Nathaniel Awbery, a bricklayer and builder. In 1817 he advertised in the *Carmarthen Journal* that he had 'by great expense and study brought to perfection common earthenware' and was able to offer a range of jugs, jars, dishes, washing-pots and milk-pans with different coloured glazes. I had thought, wrongly, when writing an article to celebrate the two hundredth anniversary of Towy Works,[20] that Awbery had used the Pothouse as his pottery and that this accounted for the labelling on Wood's 1834 map. The site of this brickyard, kilns and pottery shed, together with the very large claypit is, in fact, clearly shown on the 1906 O.S. map. The pottery had long ceased to exist by then but the brickyard was still working in the 1890s.

One further important rental (1789) for the Pothouse is in the Picton Castle collection at the National Library:[21]

A Rental of an Estate in the Borough & Town of Carmarthen. Belonging To the Rt. Honble the Lord and Lady Milford.

Tenants' Names	Tenements	Yrly rent
Mr. John Lewis	Old Pothouse	£8
''	1st floor over ''	£8
''	2nd floor over ''	£8
''	3rd floor over ''	£5
Mr. George Watkins	a vault Part of ''	£4
''	Part of the Quay	£3 3
Phillip Morgan	Part of the Quay	£1 1
Mr. Jeremiah Owen	Part of the Pothouse	£15

(N.B. The above was taken from an Old Rental in 1789 excepting Nantykee).

The picture that emerges from the 1789 rental is of a building with two separate functions, consistent with the double pile, hip-roofed building on the 1747 print. The rear is a malthouse, rented in 1765 by James Stewart, and, in 1789, by Jeremiah Owen for the same annual rent of £15. Stewart, described in his will as merchant, died in 1791, and left his estate to his family in London.[22] Jeremiah Owen's obituary, *Cambrian* 7 May 1807, describes him as an 'Eminent Maltster, universally loved and respected, in whom the poor have lost a friend'. He was a prosperous man and Mayor of Carmarthen in 1785. After his death, Walter Bowen another prosperous Maltster, who lived in a fine house in Quay Street leased from Derwydd (No. 12 on map) held the malthouse until his death in 1831, and his firm, Bowen and Thomas, continued in occupation for several more years.

The lessee of 'old pothouse' in 1789 was John Lewis, his total rent £29. The front part comprised a building on three floors and a vault underneath. It appears that John Lewis was the timber merchant employed by John Vaughan to carry out extensive repairs to his pleasure yacht and to build a boat for him at 'Cilsan' Ferry (near Llandeilo). This is supported by a Memorandum for his agent written by Vaughan about 1790 in very truncated language:

> Agreed upon some time since a claim made by the Corporation of Carmarthen of some waste land under Friar's Park where they built the vessel particularly where Mr. Lewis the timber merchant built.[23]

The 1789 rental also shows the Pothouse quay let out in two parts. Philip Morgan, another ship-builder, was also employed by Vaughan to repair his pleasure yacht and by Sir Thomas Kymer to inspect his large lighter being built at Bedford's yard.[24] Morgan leased a house in Dam Street from John Vaughan (*marked C on map*). Here he died in 1793 leaving his possessions to his niece and housekeeper.[25] George Watkins, who rented part of the vault and part of the quay, is named in the will (1771) of George James, a prominent carpenter, as his son-in-law and a joiner.[26] James worked both for the Golden Grove estate and the Corporation. He leased the 'Buckingham' premises for use as a timber yard and lived in one of the Pentypark houses in Dam Street (*marked B in my Fig. 1*). George Watkins may therefore have benefited from Watkins' death and been able to expand from 'joiner' to timber merchant, even ship-builder. This would explain his use of the Pothouse and part of the quay. The 1789 rental records he is now living in James's former house, at a rental of five shillings a year. The other group of Pentypark houses (*marked A in my Fig. 1*) are described now as tenements occupied by fourteen people, yielding a rental of £12 per year.

The title at the top of the 1789 rental states that it has been drawn up for Lord and Lady Milford. James Philipps died in 1793 and left the estate in trust for the lives of his daughters, Jane, a spinster, and Mary, who had married her kinsman, Sir Richard Philipps of Picton Castle, later the first Lord Milford (died 1823). Philipps entailed the estate to his great-nephew, John P. A. Lloyd of Dale Castle, on condition that he took the surname Philipps. This is why the Pothouse is labelled 'late Lord Milford' on the 1826 Derwydd map.

The Carmarthen Rate Survey for the year 1819, a printed and comprehensive survey, records that Lord Milton is the owner of the Pothouse.[27] The storehouse (valued at £16 p.a.) is in the occupation of Messrs. Morris. The malthouse (valued at £20 p.a.) is in the occupation of Walter Bowen. Messrs. Morris were the Carmarthen bankers. David Morris and his two sons who also traded as merchants may have used the warehouse for their own goods but more likely it was underlet, as they leased a large salt warehouse on the quay from Vaughan to store their main import.

Lady Milford died in 1816, Lord Milford in 1823 and the Pentypark estate passed to John P. A. Lloyd Philipps. He apparently decided to sell off the Carmarthen properties as the following advertisement appeared in the *Carmarthen Journal* (5 August 1825):

> Storehouse & Malthouse comprising two malting floors & loft, a kiln, cistern & pump situated on the Quay now in the occupation of Walter Bowen. Annual rent £20. Also adjoining and under the same roof in the foregoing building & of the same extent a capital storehouse, comprising excellent & extensive vaults, a ground floor & two lofts or granaries with timber yard in front & the whole in the occupation of Messrs. Morris & *undertenants*. Lease for 3 lives all now 56, 36 and 33.
>
> These premises are most commodious and most eligibly situated for carrying on an extensive mercantile concern.

William Philipps bought the Pothouse for £1,000. This explains why his name appears on the later Derwydd map and leases. A few years later Messrs. Morris decided to sell off the remaining years of their lease and advertised in the *Carmarthen Journal,* on 15 February 1828:

> *To Dealers in Timber, Bark & Grain Etc.*
> All those premises being part of the Pothouse comprising 3 lofts each 95 ft in length & 21 ft and 20 ft 3 in width or thereabouts conveniently situated near the

River Towy & capable of containing large quantities of bark, grain or any other commodity needing room.

> The premises will be put into repair or an equal sum will be allowed for. Reasonable terms. Apply Morris Bankers.

William Philipps, the new owner of the Pothouse, was a timber-merchant, and the wording of Messrs. Morris's advertisement suggests that he may already have been using the storehouse and yard for his own business. He was already renting the timber yard and newly-built dry dock adjacent to the Pothouse on Morfa Moch Issa. Philipps had been baptised at Henllan Amgoed Independent Chapel in 1772 and would be buried there in 1844, as his will makes clear. Nothing has been discovered of his early career in Carmarthen, but he was certainly a very successful and wealthy man. He owned the whole Red Lion Yard complex, lived in Gwynne House in Quay Street, made enough money to buy the Pothouse, built and lived in Waun Iago House, and served as Mayor of the town and High Sheriff of the County. He was a major ship-owner and ship-builder, using the Pothouse quay for unloading cargoes of Baltic timber and the frontage for storage and ship-building.

In this account of one of his ships, launched 17 April 1829, Philipps receives great credit from the *Carmarthen Journal*:

> A fine schooner, the property of Wm Phillips, Timber Merchant, was launched from building ground near the pothouse. She glided magnificently into the tide, amid the cheers of thousands. She is the finest modelled vessel that has been launched here within our recollection & might from the evidence she exhibited of an improvement in the art of ship building be called *The March of Progress*. She was called *The William* and will sail for the Baltic.

The largest ship ever built in Carmarthen was owned by Philipps (it was actually built by Peter Williams of Pembroke Dock). This was the *Princess Royal*, 332 tons, launched by his niece from Pothouse Wharf in April 1841. It carried emigrants to the New World and brought back timber from Quebec. When he died in 1844 Philipps was rather unkindly described by the *Carmarthen Journal* as 'an old bachelor who made all his money in Carmarthen'.

Bachelors often leave complex wills and William's was no exception.[28] His real estate in Carmarthen was left to John Lewis, son of Benjamin Lewis of Llanboidy, his nephew and partner. Lewis married well and had six children. The timber business at the Pothouse prospered, as did his tannery and slate yard. He lived in Friars Park House, which he rebuilt, sent his sons to the Grammar School, served as Mayor and then Alderman. When William, the eldest son married in 1855, the 'energetic epithalamonial affair' was celebrated with bell-ringing, cannon firing and marching bands, but at the Pothouse a spark fell into a tar barrel, set the timber ablaze and caused £40 worth of damage.

William and John joined the business. The firm, Philipps and Lewis, had offices at 31 Blue Street (next to Bull Lane). They expanded and modernised. This will be the period when Terry suggested that the Pothouse 'building was substantially remodelled and the two wings added' (*p. 296*). The firm built the last ship in Carmarthen, a steam tug called the *William*, launched from the Pothouse in 1847. John Lewis was the owner or part owner of a number of vessels trading between 'neighbouring and foreign parts'. He died in April 1864, aged 66. The *Carmarthen Journal* described him as 'one of the largest tradesmen in the County, timber-merchant, tanner and ship-owner'. His executors immediately sold several of his merchant vessels: *The Emerald Isle, The Triumph, The Pursuit,* the *Elizabeth Cecilia* and *The Acorn*, the latter built in Carmarthen. His will set up Trust Funds for his wife and younger children and it is probable that this, rather than debts, explains why his extensive estate was sold on 25 August 1866.[29] The sale included the Pothouse, sold in two separate lots:

Lot 8:
> Those Storehouses, timber yard & Landing Place with frontage to the Quay, situate on the Pothouse. These premises are very conveniently arranged and well adapted for carrying on a large Timber Trade, now in occupation of Messrs. Philipps and Lewis. The two foregoing lots (the other was a tannery) which hitherto have been successfully worked by Messrs. Philipps and Lewis and are well worth the attention of Timber Merchants and Tanners.

Lot 33:
> Another large and convenient MALTHOUSE & Malting Premises situated on the Pothouse, now in the occupation of John Lewis, Esq.

The two lots, it appears, were bought in twelve shares by the family. 'John Lewis, Esq.', was the second son who lived in Waun Iago House. He appears to have become over-ambitious, for in 1863 he bought the Malting and Hop business of W. G. Thomas of Lammas Street and, at the sale of the Derwydd Estate in 1870, all the houses in Springfield Gardens (*marked 7 & 8 on the map*). William and John Lewis had also expanded the timber business by leasing from Derwydd the 'Buckingham' site in 1865. They had to assign this lease, on the 21 February 1873, to T. J. Thomas for the sum of £1,000. The assignment notes 'the considerable expense which W. & J. Lewis had been put to erecting 13 messuages, two cottages, a steam saw mill with machinery and sheds' on site. John Lewis became bankrupt in 1870 and his part of the Pothouse (the storehouse and yard) was put up for auction. It was bought by T. J. Thomas although Lewis seems to have continued carrying on the timber business from the river frontage. His elder brother, William, however, although continuing as a timber merchant became a railway and building contractor. It is likely that he too became bankrupt as his part of the Pothouse, 'malthouse, premises and storeroom' was conveyed to T. J. Thomas in 1874. His 'modern' house, 7 Picton Place, was sold in 1879. He left Carmarthen to live in Neath and died in 1814 at Merthyr Tydfil. The *Carmarthen Journal* carried a long obituary, describing him as 'one of the greatest contractors Carmarthen ever produced; excelling at grand drainage schemes and the builder of Cwmoernant Reservoir, the Infirmary, and the South Wales Training College'. John Lewis, the younger brother, died in 1887 at 7 Cambrian Place, rather a humble address after Waun Iago House.

The new owner of the Pothouse was Thomas Jeremy Thomas, a merchant whose address is given as Towy House, Beckenham, Kent and London; he was the brother-in-law of William and John Lewis. The building was now leased to David Bonnell Edwards a maltster. He had already bought 31 Blue Street at the 1866 sale. He died in June 1878 at the age of 36. The obituary in *The Welshman* although stating he was 'a good and useful public man' (Mayor in 1876) added he was 'hurried by hot temper into extremes'. The Pothouse was vacant and the following advertisement appeared in the newspapers, 18 September 1879:

To Be Let
Extensive Malthouse Stores & Premises situated on the Pothouse – vacant through he death of the late David Edwards, where a very extensive business was carried on.

The Pothouse lease was taken by James Davies, iron-monger of 109 Lammas Street, who set up a factory for his tinplate-workers. It proved a highly successful enterprise, but Davies soon 'perceived that the place was in various ways unsuitable' and by 1890 he had bought building ground by the old station and set up a modern factory, showrooms and warehouse, and moved out of the Pothouse. Thomas Jeremy Thomas sold the Pothouse in 1893 to Thomas Jenkins, a shipping agent and corn and flour merchant.[30]

The Editor of the *Carmarthen Journal* informed its readers that:

> The late Mayor of Carmarthen moves his flour business from the station to extensive premises bought from James Davies, Ironmonger, known as Towy Works. The premises are to be thoroughly renovated. Mr. Jenkins's present stores close to the river will be considerably enlarged.

All seemed well. The S.S. *Tivyside* arrived three or four times a week bringing cargoes of flour to the Pothouse quay, and advertisements assured the public that business was excellent, but the deeds of the Pothouse reveal a different story. In 1894 Jenkins sold 'all that plot of land and wharf or landing place situate at the Pothouse, amounting to 5,400 sq. ft' to Spillers and Bakers Ltd. Jenkins had become mired in debt and was declared a bankrupt. Jenkins, following in the footsteps of William Philipps and John Lewis, Senior, lived in Friars Park House but was forced to assign the lease. In 1898 he assigned the Pothouse to Lloyds Bank for the sum of £1,225 (only £225 more than William Philipps had paid for it in 1826). The unfortunate Mr. Jenkins and his family left Carmarthen for Harwich, taking with them the good wishes of the people and a presentation silver tea service. This was the beginning of the decline of the Pothouse into the derelict building demolished in the early 1960s.

The industrial development of the marshes and Pothouse frontage in the 18th century had been accelerated by a decision of the Carmarthen Corporation in 1804 to build a dry dock near the Pothouse and to extend the quay eastwards from David Lewis's summer house up to the bridge. The improvements would take time to complete. The quay extension meant the end of the ship-yards on the quay and all ships would now be built on or near Pothouse quay. Fortunately this period of change coincided with the founding of the *Cambrian* in 1804, followed by the *Carmarthen Journal* in 1810.

Both newspapers carried enthusiastic accounts of the dramatic scenes when ships were launched, often by torchlight, to catch the tide.

The money for the dock and other major improvements was raised by a mortgage on certain Corporation lands (including parts of Morfa Moch) and on completion it was to be let out by auction. It was not until October 1809 that a committee met and inspected the plans for the dock and were 'empowered to find and fix a site for building same and to contract with artificers'. The first stone of the dock was laid on 25th October 1809 to commemorate the 50th year of the reign of George III. The exact site of the dry dock was discovered from an advertisement in the *Carmarthen Journal*, 3 June 1811:

> To Be Let:
> A piece of land held from the Corporation by Mr. Nash at the Pothouse Quay to be let by auction on the said 30 July reserving the liberty of making gutters through the same for conveying water to the dry dock that may be deemed proper but the said piece of land to be let subject to the liberty of building vessels thereupon on payment of reasonable compensation for doing so.

This piece of land had been leased to John Nash, October 1787, when it was described as 'part of Morfa Moch Issa together with the lime kiln lately built'; this was the same lime-kiln, under Friars Park garden, leased to Howell and Evans in 1765 and Morgan Lewis in 1785. It is clearly marked on the 1786 map.

Lord Cawdor bought the piece of land containing the dry dock at auction for £114 and leased it to William Philipps, the timber-merchant. The deed between the Corporation and Lord Cawdor was not signed until 1820 and contains the following description:

> All that piece or parcel of land and the dock lately partly erected and built thereon . . . being on the Bank of the River Towy containing by admeasurement 17,334 sq. ft. and also all and singular the gates timber ironstones and other materials heretofore carried and brought to the said piece of land and placed fixed built and deposited for the purpose of erecting such a dock . . .[31]

At the same time Lord Cawdor conveyed to the Corporation land east of Awbery's brickyard so that they could build the gasworks in 1822. The remaining marsh lands were leased out to the Philip Vaughan Foundry in

Fig. 4: *Monument to Philipps family, south wall of St. Peter's Church. The two tablets appear identical but left hand tablet and cherubs is larger; ornaments missing from the top plinths. The wall of the Lady Chapel has a black grave stone inscribed 'Here lie the Bodies of …. Anne, Rachell Bowen, Rachell Lloyd, John Philipps, James Philipps and Thomas Lloyd. Presumably removed from the floor of nave or chancel. Inscription on the Monument (left to right):*

Near this place
And within the arch lyeth the Body of
JOHN PHILLIPS, Esq.,
whose piety and integrity was sincere,
his distribution of justice impartial,
his friendship stedfast, his temper humane,
his charity liberal and his
benevolence universal.
A strenuous asserter of the right and privileges
of the inhabitants of this ancient Corporation,
by whom he was greatly beloved
and deservedly esteemed.
He dyed Augt. 11th 1730 aged 85.

Here also lyeth the Body of
JAMES PHILLIPS, Esq.,
His Eldest Son, who was some time
Member of Parliament for this Corporation.
Died Novemr. The 28th 1730,
In the 59th year of his Age.

Near this place lyeth the Body of
RACHELL LLOYD
only daughter of HUGH LLOYD
and ELIZABETH
his wife, and grand-daughter to
JOHN PHILLIPS, Gent.
She departed this life
the 27th of January
1723 aged 10 years and 6 months.
Her mother caus'd this
in memory of her.

Here lyeth ye Body of
ANNE ye wife of JOHN PHILLIPS of Carmarthen, Gent.
Born A.D. 1646, died Feby, ye 18th 1720.
She possessed in a great degree ye vertues and felicities of her sex
was ye mother of many children of which 6 survived her.
She had ye uncommon happiness to see those 6 well settled
and living all near her, in prosperous circumstances.
The great duties of private life she discharged
with equal prudence & success, & was at once an
affectionate wife and a tender mother.
She had ye comfortable satisfaction of seeing her 6 children
married in ye same order as they were born, viz
James, her eldest son to Jane ye daughter of John Scarlock, Esq.
Rachel, her eldest daughter, to William Bowen of Ness-town, Gent.
John, her 2nd son, to Elizabeth ye daughter
and coheir of Francis Philipps of Lanpeter, Esq.
Elizabeth, her 2d daughter, to Hugh Lloyd of Danyrallt, gent.
Thomas, her 3d son, now Vicar of Laugharne,
to Elizabeth, ye daughter of Edward Hughes of Brecon, Gent.
And Anne ye 3d daughter, to John ye son of Griff. Williams of
Bwlch-y-Gwynt, Esq. Fifty-two years she liv'd in entire mutual
affection with her husband who to ye memory of his deserving
and much lamented wife placed this monument.

*The above named Rachel died on ye 8th of March 1720.
And is interr'd by her mother.*

309

Blue Street. Vaughan presented a petition asking for the river to be embanked to prevent flooding on his marshland. The well-preserved banks flanking the River Towy on the marshlands now bisected by Pont Lesneven, could well be of this date. The Corporation attempted to claim that the river bank below 'Buckingham' (*marked 5 on the map, my Fig. 1*) was their property but the Derwydd agent soon quashed that by producing the deed of 1703, which states the property is bounded by the River Towy on the south side.

David Cox published his engraving of the river banks by the Pothouse *c*.1830 (*Fig. 1*, p. 61 *and detail, Fig. 5*, p. 287). The scene is full of activity and shows shipbuilding at its zenith. The Pothouse, 'Buckingham', Dam Street and the Island had developed into a very busy landscape. These places swarmed with people engaged in ship-building, working in the timber yards, the brickyard and pottery, the malthouses, coal yards and two iron foundries. The river was crowded with vessels loading and unloading and there were boats on the stocks. Dam Street and Blue Street were full of cottages divided into overcrowded tenements and the area was well supplied with public houses with such evocative seafaring names as *Ship A Ground, Ship and*

Bottle, Ship and Castle, Blue Anchor, Hope and Anchor, The Nelson, The Lark, The Albion and The Sloop on Island Wharf. *The Nelson* was one of the 14 tenements in Dam Street owned by Pentypark and sold by Lloyd Philipps in 1825; its landlord, Stephen Phillipps, had been a Master Mariner. The sign of the *Albion Inn* is still in place above a shop at the top of the last remaining vestige of Dam Street. These streets were populated by ship's captains, sail-makers, block-makers, rope-makers, shipwrights, smiths and sailors. The river was polluted, the air fouled by belching chimneys, the streets themselves filthy, and there were disgusting smells from the currier's shed, the two brewhouses and the manure dumps. The menace of the Arms Depot, however, had been removed in 1813.

The history of the Pothouse building, its associated lands and sites is of considerable intrinsic interest, but it is the history of the merchants associated with it which best reflects Carmarthen's maritime and commercial prosperity. The Philipps family of Pentypark have, in St Peter's Church, an elaborate monument symbolic of the wealth and political influence of Carmarthen's merchant class. Although some of the questions concerning the Pothouse have been answered, further research is still needed.

NOTES

The spelling of the surname Philipps of the Pentypark family is completely inconsistent in documents, I have followed the spelling of Major Francis Jones. The spelling of William Philipps surname is also inconsistent. I have used the spelling on his will.

1. Terrence James, *Carmarthen: An Archaeological and Topographical Survey*, Monograph Series, 2, Carmarthenshire Antiquarian Society, 1980.
2. CRO, 2/M34.
3. Ibid, p. 48, Fig. 4.8. Morfa Moch Issa & other lands are shown as part of Lands of New & Old Carmarthen in the later Middle Ages. *TCAS*, Vol. IX, Part 25.
4. I have used the Derwydd leases extensively for Buckingham, The Island and other town properties.
   CRO, Derwydd 178, 27 October 1703.
   Derwydd 566, 10 June 1733
   Derwydd 563, 8 October 1742
   Derwydd 562, 19 May, 1766
   Derwydd 270, 23 February 1841
   Derwydd 206, 21 February 1873/ 8 March 1865
   Derwydd C.A, 19, Valuation & Survey of White House Estate 1826/27.
   Derwydd C.A, 52, Map Book and Rentals, 1748-1914.

   Derwydd Additional 35, refers to Leases of 1766 and 1703.
   NLW, Derwydd 395, 29 August 1752 – quotes 1742 Lease.
   Derwydd 355, 15 April 1776.
5. Pembs Record Office, Lloyd Philipps of Dale Castle Collection.
   D/LP 509-510, 511, 512, 517, 581, 583, 584, 585-6, 463, 482, 490, 497, 498, 725, 726, 829, 1041, 1044, 1077-9, 1087.
6. CRO, Mus. 154, 1764-1835, Corporation Order Book. All following Corporation Orders are from the same.
7. CRO, DB/72/1 transcribed from PRO, BT6/191: AL91: ALl92.
   Private letter from Robin Craig 15/5/2001.
8. NLW, G.E. Owen Collection, No. 152.
   CRO, Mus. 154, Lease dated 12 September 1785 – Corporation to J. Williams & Morgan Lewis, 1 acre. Piece of land where lime-kiln stands.
9. CRO, Mus. 157, 4 July 1757 and 28 April 1758.

10. PRO, 11/641, Will of Alderman John Philipps of Carmarthen, 1730. In his will, he left £300 to his grandson James 'but in case he shall happen to marry Mrs Elizabeth Steele, daughter of Sir Richard Steele, knt., deceased, I give him £2,000'. James courted Elizabeth Steele and addressed letters and verses to her, assuring her 'how entirely he was her faithful slave and martyr'. He fought a duel over her in Bath and a report of their marriage appeared in the *Gentleman's Magazine*, 26 May, 1731. It was false Elizabeth married John Trevor in 1732. James Philipps did manage to marry a co-heiress, Jane Pryse (*TCAS*, Vol. VII, 1911-12, pp. 35-6.

11. 'Buss, a 17th and 18th-century fishing vessel mainly used in the herring industry, broad in the beam with two, and sometimes three, masts with a single square sail on each and usually of from 50 to 70 tons' (P. Kemp (ed.) *The Oxford Companion to Ships and the Sea*, 1979, pp. 122-123; Sir Thomas Stepney secured the contract for the construction of these busses, being built for the Free British Fishery (they were used for net fishing; the crew stayed at sea for long periods sending the catch to the nearest ship). See also M. Mathews, 'In Pursuit of Profit? Local Enterprise in South West Wales in the 18th Century', unpublished Ph.D. thesis, University of Swansea, 1997, esp. Ch. 6.

12. NLW, Cilymaenllwyd Collection, No. 220.

13. Terrence James, 'Carmarthen Bay Subscribers to the Lewis Morris Charts of 1748'. *Carms. Antiq.*, Vol. XLI, 2006, pp. 44-49.

14. PRO, 11/1142, Will of John Philipps of Tenby, 1785.
    CRO, Trant/Yelverton Collection No. 357, Purchase of the *Racehorse*.
    Cawdor/Vaughan 25/1485, Shipped by the *Racehorse*.

15. F. Jones, *Historic Carmarthenshire Homes and their Families* (Carms. Antiq. Soc. and Dyfed County Council, 1987), pp. 132-34; Francis Jones does not mention the name 'Gorse Ddu' for the mansion which I found in the 1699 will.

16. NLW, St. David's Diocese, Will of Christoper Middleton, Llanarthney, 1699/61.

Will of Richard Middleton, Llanarthney, 1733/73.
PRO 11/500, Will of Walter Middleton, Tenby, 24 July 1708.

17. CRO, Mus. 2, Rental of 1765. Mus. 155, 1568-1752 Corporation Order Book.

18. CRO, Trant 208, September 23 1786.

19. CRO, Cawdor/Vaughan 24/1236, 1785.

20. E. Dale-Jones, 'Towy Works (1795-1995): a Celebration', *Carms. Antiq.*, Vol. XXXIV, 1998, pp. 54-66.

21. NLW, Picton Castle Collection, No. 1683, *c.*1790.

22. PRO, 11/1207, Will of James Stewart of Carmarthen, 1791.

23. CRO, Cawdor/Vaughan 21/641.

24. CRO, Cawdor/Vaughan, 24/1185 Bill to John Lewis, 1784; 24/1639 Bill to John Lewis, 1786.
    24/1353 Bill to Phillip Morgan, 1786.

25. CRO, Cawdor/Vaughan 1772. Richard Vaughan to Evan Lewis, formerly Philip Morgan.
    NLW, St. David's Diocese. Will of Philip Morgan, Ship Builder, Carmarthen, 1793/33

26. NLW, St. David's Diocese, Will of James George, Carpenter, Carmarthen, 1771/22.

27. CRO, Mus. 687 (1819).

28. NLW, St. David's Diocese, Will of William Philipps, Carmarthen, 1845/87.

29. CRO, Copy of John Lewis's Will in Trant 283.

30. CRO, DX/234/40.

31. CRO, Cawdor 2/262.

ACKNOWLEDGEMENTS

I would like to thank Muriel Bowen Evans. John Davies and Terry Wells, David Cooke, David Jones (Carmarthen Archives). Diana Bevan, Thomas Lloyd and Mr. Martin Ryder. I am grateful to Tina Carr for photographing the Philipps memorial and preparing the image for publication.

List of Subscribers

Dr D. L. Baker-Jones, F.S.A., Felindre, Llandysul.
Mrs Maureen Barber, Bolton.
Dr Robin Barlow, Myddfai, Llandovery.
Dr & Mrs Mike Benbough-Jackson, Llanybydder.
Diana Bevan, Llansteffan.
Mary Binding, Carmarthen.
Robin Blakely, Sketty, Swansea.
Tim & Betsan Bowen, Ferryside.
Mr A. C. Brueton, London.
Mrs Anne W. N. Chambers, Johnstown, Carmarthen.
Mr D. Conway, Pontyates, Kidwelly.
Mr & Mrs Charles Coughlan, Carmarthen.
Reverend Canon S. Cunnane, Cardigan.
Mr & Mrs D. F. Dale-Jones, Carmarthen.
Mr D. T. Davies, Dryslwyn.
E. K. Davies, Llanybydder.
Mrs Avril Llewellyn Davies, Llandeilo.
Dr Michael Glanmor Davies, Yelverton, Devon.
Dr Philip Davies, Carmarthen & New Jersey, U.S.A.
Richard M. L. Davies, Radyr, Cardiff.
Roy & Susan Davies, Llandeilo.
Ms Wendy Davies, Llanfairpwll, Sir Fôn.
Steve Dubé, Pencader.
Lord Dynevor, Llandeilo.
Dr Huw Edwards, Caerfyrddin.
Mr E. M. Edwards, Carmarthen.
Mrs Mair Evans, Carmarthen.
Muriel Bowen Evans, Trelech, Carmarthen.
Nan Evans, Carmarthen.
Philip Evans, Llangunnor, Carmarthen.
Robert Evans & David Foot, Taliaris, Llandeilo.
The Rt Revd & Mrs J. Wyn Evans, Abergwili.
Mr Peter Francis, Llanelli.
Michael Freeman, Ceredigion Museum.
Mrs Jenny Gammon, Abergwili.
Mr & Mrs D. I. Gealy, Llandovery.
Colonel Richard Gilbertson, Narberth.
David R. Gorman, Preston.

Mr Andrew Green & Ms Carys Evans, Caswell, Swansea.
E. Olwen Griffiths, Pontyberem.
Mr & Mrs Delme Griffiths, Glanaman, Ammanford.
Mrs M. A. Griffiths, St Clears.
Mr & Mrs Martin Hassell, Nantycaws, Carmarthen.
Mr & Mrs Christopher F. W. Heath, Llangynog.
Mr & Mrs Daniel M. E. L. Heath, Llansteffan.
John B. Hilling, Cyncoes, Cardiff.
Prof. & Mrs S. M. Hook, Bristol.
Robert & Wendy Hopkins, Llandybie.
T. Hopkinson, Whitland.
Emyr Hughes, Yeovil.
J. V. Hughes, Port Talbot.
Mr & Mrs P. M. Hughes, Llansteffan.
Byron Huws, Cydweli.
Huw & Ann Iorwerth, Llansteffan.
A. L. & M. A. James, Llanarthne.
David B. James, Bowstreet, Ceredigion.
Mr Peter & Mrs Dorothy James, Carmarthen.
Audrey James, Carmarthen.
Mrs Susan John, Carmarthen.
Dr & Mrs C. G. Jones, Llandeilo.
Brigadier Glynne Jones & Lieut. Colonel Sheila Jones, Glasgow.
D. H. Jones, Rhiwbina, Cardiff.
Dr & Mrs Emyr Wyn Jones, Uzès, France.
Dr Wynne Jones, Carmarthen.
Eric Jones, Carmarthen.
Handel Jones, Rhandir-mwyn.
Howard M. Jones, M.Sc., & Helenor G. Jones, M.A., Hendy.
Mr D. C. Jones, Caerfyrddin.
Mr D. Keith Jones, Ruthin, Bridgend.
Mrs Joan Jones, Carmarthen.
Revd J. Towyn Jones, Carmarthen.
M. et Mme. L. Kerhouant, Plougerneau, Brittany.
Noel & Heather King, Laugharne.

Jeremy K. Knight, Caerphilly .
John & Jacky Knotts, Tauranga, New Zealand.
Emyr Wyn Lake, Lampeter.
J. W. Lewis, Lord of Is-Cennen, Cantref Bychan.
Revd Pamela C. Lewis, Llanelli.
Doctors A. & H. Loxdale, Carmarthen.
Mrs Hazel Martell, Carmarthen.
Miss C. McCann, Llansaint, Kidwelly.
Dr Donald Moore, Penarth.
Edward & Delyth Morgan, Llangain, Carmarthen.
Mrs Eleanor Morgan, Carmarthen.
Hugh Morgan, Clydach, Swansea.
Ian K. Morgan, Pwll, Llanelli.
Miss Emma Morris, Carmarthen.
Miss Kate Morris, Carmarthen.
Mrs Sian Morris, Carmarthen.
Chris Musson, Pisgah, Aberystwyth.
Julian Orbach, Newport, Pembs.
Dr D. Huw Owen, Aberystwyth.
Mr J. G. Owen & Mrs E. D. Owen, Caerphilly.
Menna Owen-Strong, Llangain.
Oliver Padel, St Neot.
Mr & Mrs W. Arwyn Price, Johnstown, Carmarthen.
Robert Protheroe-Jones, Llanelli.
Robert & Carol Pugh, Carmarthen.
Henrietta Quinnell, Exeter.
Alan Randall, Carmarthen.
A. J. Heward Rees, Felinfoel, Llanelli.
Mrs Glenys Rees, Llandybie.
William & Benita Afan Rees, Llanelli.

P. E. & R. Rees, Pontyberem, Llanelli.
Ifan G. Richards, Caerfyrddin.
Mrs Yvonne Salisbury, Allington, Kent.
Mr Robert Scourfield, Cresswell Quay, Pembs.
Beverley & Llinos Smith, Aberystwyth.
Neil & Glenda Speed, Laugharne.
C. E. Spragg, Porthyrhyd.
Revd Coralie M. Steel, Carmarthen.
Jonathon Strong, Llansaint.
Edward Summers, Swansea.
Dr Huw Walters, Aberystwyth.
W. H. S. & M. J. Wanstall, Tauranga, New Zealand.
Mr Jeff Watts, Laugharne.
Mr D. J. Wells, Birchgrove, Cardiff.
D. M. B. White, Carmarthen.
Dr Eileen Wilkes, Hengistbury Head,
   Bournemouth.
Henry & Bronwen Wilkins, Carmarthen.
Mrs Ceri Williams, Llanelli.
Donald & Ira Williams, Bancffosfelen.

Amgueddfa Cymru National Museum of Wales.
Carmarthenshire Archives Service.
Carmarthenshire County Council.
Dyfed Archaeological Trust.
Llyfrgell Ceredigion.
National Waterfront Museum, Swansea.
University of Wales Centre for Advanced Welsh
   & Celtic Studies, Aberystwyth.
University of Wales, Lampeter.

Index

(* = illustration)

Abadam, Edward, of Middleton Hall, 54, 56
abbeys, *see* monasteries
Aberdeunant, Llansadwrn, hall-house, 266
Abergavenny,
    Roman fort, 131
Aberglasney, 40, 104, 200
Abergwili, 193
    Bishops' Palace, 192-201
    College, 181, 192-199*, 225
    mediaeval manor town & market, 151, 194
    parish church, 192*, 193, 197*
    Park & gardens, 192*, 200
Abermarlais, 48, 88-90*, 91, 229
Abernant church, 169-173
Aberteifi, see Cardigan, 214
 Aberystwyth, 46, 212, 216
Ablart, James, of Gloucs., papermaker, 24
Adam the Miller, Cardigan, 219
advowsons, 157, 170-173, 194
aerial archaeology,
    Aerial Archaeology Research Group (AARG), 107
    Cambridge University Committee for Aerial Photography
        (CUCAP), 98, 104, 107, 110
    Carmarthenshire, 98-106
    Committee of the Council for British Archaeology (CBA),
        107
    Devon & Somerset, 107-22
    Research Group (AARG), 107
air photographs, *see* photography
Allen, James, dean of St Davids, 186
Allt Aber-mangoed, Pumsaint, defended enclosure, 101-102*
Allt-y-Cnap road, Roman cremation, 123-134
Allt-y-gog, house, Nantcaredig, garden earthworks 104
Alltyrodin commonplace book, 33
almanacks, 28, 32, 35, 37
Alphington-Exminster parish boundary, Devon, 117-118,
    119*
Allt-y-Cnap road, Roman cremation, 123-134
Alun, river, 174, 175
Aman, river, 255
Ammanford, 99

amphitheatre, Roman, 131
Anglesey, 146, 226
Anian ap Wilym, landowner, mediaeval Cardigan, 216
Annell, river & leat, 144, 146
Annels, Alwyn, mining expert, 138, 145
Appleyard, Fred, artist, 71
Arberth stream, Cardigan, 218
Archaeologia Cambrensis, 138
archaeologists & antiquarians, 137, 140, 143, 146
archaeology
    aerial, *see* photography
    assessments, 174, 195
    church, 172*
    dating, *see* radiocarbon & optical-stimulated luminescence
    environmental, 109, 111, 112, 120, 146
    excavations, 110, 113, 114*, 123-128, 144, 157, 195, 201,
        206, 211, 254
    earthworks, 235
    finds, 127-131, 240, 255
    garden, 104, 201
    industrial, 94-98, 99, 100, 101
    maritime, 99
    military, 99, 105*
    rescue, 112, 115
    sites, 81, 91, 100, 101, 104, 127, 260
    survey, *see also* geophysics, 112, 143, 144
archdeacons & archdeaconries, 158, 181, 183, 184
architects, 90, 136, 181, 188
architecture, Welsh domestic & vernacular, 198, 199, 259,
    260*, 261*, 262*, 266, 267
Argoed/Parcymarles, Cardigan, 204
Arthur, 218
Arthur, J. B., corn & flour merchants, Carmarthen, 86
artists, 40, 41, 42, 43, 44, 45, 50, 61, 62, 67, 70, 73
Arundel, Earl of, 5
Audley, Nicholas, 177
Augmentations, Court of, 160
Augustinian canons & houses, 27, 156, 160
Augustinian College of Steyn, Gouda, 1, 6
Augustinian Priory of St John & St Teulyddog, Carmarthen,
    27, 156, 157, 158, 160, 161, 163, 169, 170, 171*, 172,
    173, 194
    Cartulary, 158, 159, 160, 161, 162*, 169-73

aviation, 107, 112

Awbery, Nathaniel, potter & builder, Carmarthen, 289, 291, 305, 308

Bacon, Thomas, Sir, 184
badges, 240
Badius, Jodocus Badius Ascensius, printer, 1, 2, 3, 6, 7
Banc-y-Warren, Cardigan, 205
banks & banking, 291, 293, 306, 308
Banks, Joseph, Sir, scholar & patron, 44, 140, 143
Banks-Hodgkinson, Robert, of Edwinsford, 44
Barber [-Beaumont], John Thomas (1774-1841), *A Tour through S. Wales & Mon.*, 46, 47*, 48, 54,
Barber, Thomas, 62*
Baring-Gould S. & Fisher, J., authors *Lives of the British Saints*, 157, 158
Barker, William Higgs, Hebrew scholar, 30, 33
barley, 266, 281, 296
Barlow, William, bishop of St Davids, 181, 182, 194, 199, 213, 215
Barrett, Alice, peasant farmer, Llanstephan, 164
Barri de, family of Manorbier, 166
Barrow, Julia, historian, 160
Bartlett, Robert, historian, 166
Baskerville, printers, of Birmingham, 10
Basle, 4, 56
Battle Abbey Chronicle, 153, 156, 163, 166
battles & battle sites, 169, 235
Bauzan, Stephen, 169
Beauties of Cambria, 50
Beauties of England & Wales, The: South Wales, 1815, 36
Bedford, Herbert, ship-builder of Haverfordwest, 302
Bedford, Thomas, architect, 90
beer, breweries & malthouses, 224, 289, 291, 293, 295, 296, 300, 302, 303, 305, 306, 307, 310
Bek, Thomas, bishop of St Davids (1280-1293), 193, 194
Bernard, bishop of St. Davids, 155, 156, 157, 160
Betws-y-Coed artists' colony, 50, 52
Bevan, Arthur & w. Bridget of Laugharne, 298, 300
Bewick, Thomas (1753-1828), wood engraver, 50
Bible and Scriptures, 2, 3, 27
    Book of Common Prayer, Welsh, 225
    catechism, Welsh, 2, 3, 28
    commentators, 33, 37
    creed, 27
    Lord's Prayer, 27
    New Testament, 2, 3, 7, 27
    Patristic scholars & texts, 3, 6, 7
    Peter William's Welsh Bible, 32, 33, 37
    Paul's epistles, 1
    Welsh Bible, 1588, 27, 28, 225
bidding letters, 34, 35*
Bideford, Devon, 62
Bigbury Bay, 115
Biggin, Thomas, papermaker, 18

Bird, Peter, St Davids Cathedral Architect, 188
bishop-houses, 157, 158
Bishop's Forest (*Fforestresgob*), 265, 270, 275*, 276
Black Book of Carmarthen, 27, 71
Black Book of St Davids, 177
Black Death, The, 161
Black Horse rectilinear enclosure, Clyst Honiton, Devon, 112 -115*
Black Mountain, *see* Mynydd Du
Black Prince, the, Prince of Wales, 161, 163
blacksmiths, 300
Blackwell, Beale, ink manufacturers & suppliers of London, 31
Blaendoethïau farmstead, 271, 280
Blakeney, Walter, burgess, Cardigan, 210
Blanche, w. of John of Gaunt, 177, 178, 180
Blessed Virgin Mary, 177
boars, 240
Bodleian Library, Oxford, 135
Boerio, Giovanni Battista, court physician to Henry VII, 2
books,
    early printed, 1-8, 9, 10, 27
    publication & trade, 32, 34, 36, 37
    sale Catalogues, 2*, 4, 5, 8, 35, 36, 37
    travel in Wales, 40,
Book of Llandaff, The, 156, 157, 158
bookbinders, 17, 32, 33, 34, 37
    list of, in Carmarthen, 1720-1820, 38-39
book-plates, 4*, 5*, 37
booksellers, 28, 32, 35
    list of, in Carmarthen 1720-1820, 38-39
    second-hand, 37
Borrow, George, author, 40, 42
boundaries, 249, 265, 280, 281
    commotes, 247
    county, 102, 226, 228
    diocesan, 157
    estate, 161, 162*, 163, 216, 233
    liberts (sheepwalks), 279, 280
    parish, 117, 118, 119*, 200, 233
Bowen, Charles of Camrose, clerk, 300
Bowen, Walter, maltster (Bowen & Thomas), Carmarthen, 305, 306
Boydell, John & Josiah, printers, 49
Brace, George, agent, 300
Bradestone, Thomas de, Constable & Justiciar, 161, 163
Bran, river, 225, 226, 229
Braose, William de, 170
Brecon, 158, 279
    College, 192, 194, 199, 200
Brecon Beacons, 270, 279
Brecon Gaer Roman fort, 131
Breconshire, 193, 226, 246, 266
Breconshire Millboard Company, 23
brewing & brewhouses, 289, 291, 293, 295, 296, 302, 303, 305, 306, 307, 310

Brian, Guy de, Laugharne, 177
bricks, brick kilns & brickyards, 284, 285, 289, 291, 303, 304, 305, 310
Bridgend, 204
bridges, 42*, 43*, 45, 46*, 48, 161
Brigstocke, Owen, 18, 20
Bristol, 16, 36, 46, 215
Bristol Channel, 226
British Museum, 143
Bro Myrddin Housing Association, 18
Brobwll farmstead, Doithïe valley, 271, 279, 28
Bronygaer, Llansadwrn, hillfort, 104
Bronze Age, 110
    barrow cemeteries, 104, 117, 118, 119*
    hut circle, 111
Brunant, 137
Brut y Tywysogyon, 171
Brynaman, 246
Brynambor sheepwalk, 280
Buck, Samuel & Nathaniel, engravers & publishers, 41, 42, 43, 45, 61, 285, 286, 287*, 300
Buisson, W. du, of Glynhir, 50
Bulland enclosure, Staverton, Devon, 118*
Bunyan, John, 28
Burdett, Peter Perez, artist of Liverpool, 45
burials & burial monuments, 119*, 173
    Iron Age rites, 131
    mediaeval, 153
    Romano-British cremations, 123-133
Burgess, Thomas, bishop of St Davids, 30, 48
Burke, J. B., *Visitation, seat & arms of Noblemen*, 1854, 54
Burley, Simon de, Lord of Llanstephan, 160
Burnham, Drs B. & H., Univ. Wales, Lampeter, archaeologists, 144
Butler, Augustus, lithographer, 54
Buzzart Dikes, Glascune, Perthshire, 235

cabinet-makers, 56, 67, 68*, 76
Cadell & Davies, booksellers, 36
Cadw-Welsh Historic Monuments, 172
Caerbwdi stone, 175*, 185, 189
Caerforiog, Whitchurch, 177
Caerleon, 129
    cremations at Abbeyfields, 127
    cremations at Lodge Hill, 128
    legionary fortress baths, 131
    pottery, 128
Caernarfon, 50
    castle, 52
    Roman fort (Segontium), 131
cais, welsh commotal official, 153
Caldey Priory, 194
Calvert, John, geologist, 143
Cambria Archaeologia, see Dyfed Archaeological Trust
Cambrian Archaeological Association, 136, 137, 143

Cambrian, The, 17, 22, 29, 40, 274, 305, 308
Cambrian Magazine, The, 1773, 46
Cambrian Mountains (*Y Mynydd*), 136, 270
Cambrian News, 272
Cambrian Register, 45
Cambridge Univ. Cttee. for Aerial Photography (CUCAP), 98, 104, 107, 110, 218
Camddwr, river & valley, 266, 271, 280
Camden, William,
    Britannia, 1607 edn., 41, 1695 edn, 1, 1722 edn, 1
camera obscura, 45
Camville, William de, Lord of Llanstephan, 164
Canllefaes Uchaf Farm, Cardigan, 218
cantrefi, 158, 225, 276
    Cantref Bychan, 225, 276
    Cantref Gwarthaf, 156, 158
    Cantref Mawr, 225, 276
    Ystrad Tywi, 158, 225
Capel bach, Cardigan, 205*, 213
Capel Dyfddgen, 228
Capel Farm, Cardigan, 209, 213
Capel Gunllo, 228
Capitio, Wolfgang Fabricius, 7
Cardiff, 23, 24, 70
Cardigan, 204*, 205*, 208*, 209, 215
    Banc-y-Warren, 209
    Bartholomew Gate, 209, 210, 212, 216
    Black Lion Mews, 205
    bridges, 206*, 208, 209, 211, 217
    Bridge Street, 206*, 211
    burgages & burgesses, 209, 210, 211, 212, 216, 219
    castle, 90, 205, 206*, 208*, 209, 211, 212, 215, 217
    censars, 212
    Chancery Lane, 206*, 210
    Church Street, 206*
    College, 209
    College Row*, 206
    Commons, 216, 217
    Cross, 209, 210, 215
    Ebens Lane, 205, 206*, 211
    Extents of 1268 & 1301, 209, 210*, 211, 212, 214
    Feidr Fair, 206*, 209
    ferry, 207
    foundation of, 205
    gallows, 209
    Gloster Row, 206*, 207, 208
    Green Street, 206*, 211
    Grosvenor Hill, 211
    Guild of merchants, 215
    High Street, 205, 206*, 210, 211
    Hospital, 204, 207, 209
    markets & fairs, 208, 211, 212, 213, 215
    Market Lane, 206*, 210
    Maudlyn's Hospice, 206*, 209, 210, 213
    Mwldan, 204, 206*, 208, 209, 211, 212, 213, 217, 218

mills, 209, 216, 217
Nature Park, 204*, 207
Netpool, 209, 216
Newgate, 206*, 209, 211, 212
Parc Matheu, 216
Pendre, 206*, 216
port, 211
Priory, of St Mary & lands, 204, 206*, 207, 212, 214, 216, 218
Prison, 206
Pwllhai, 206*, 208, 209, 212, 216
Quay & wharves, 206*, 207
Quay Street, 206*, 210, 211, 215
roads, 207, 208, 216, 217
St Julian's chapel (Capel Sidan), 207
St Mary's Church, 206*, 207, 208, 209
St Mary Street, 206, 207, 209, 210, 211
Sawmill Terrace, 288
Shire Hall, 206*, 215, 216
Shrine of Our Lady of Cardigan, 208, 209, 212, 213, 214, 215, 217
Trinity Church (Llanddwy), 206*, 208, 211, 212, 213, 215
Teifi Gate, 206*, 209, 211
Town walls & towers, 205, 206*, 209
'Vennystretes', 206*, 211, 212
Warrentreehill, 216
William Street, 217
Wolf Gate, 206, 210
Cardigan island, 216
Cardiganshire (Ceredigion), 204, 205, 226, 259, 262, 265, 266, 273, 274, 276, 277
    lead-silver mines, 97, 143
    Quarter Sessions Records, 34
Carew Castle, 45, 224, 231
    deer park, 231
Carlisle, Nicholas, *Topographical Dictionary . . . Wales, 1811*, 54
Carmarthen, 28, 40, 41, 42, * 43*, 48, 49, 52, 54, 200, 224, 225, 228, 229
    Allt-y-Cnap Rd, R-B cremation, 123-133
    Arthur, J. B., Corn & Flour warehouses, 86
    Blue St., 285, 288, 302
    bookbinders, 34, 38-39
    booksellers, 34, 38-9
    Borough charters, 37, 151
    bricks & brickworks, 284, 285, 289, 291, 303, 304, 305, 308, 310
    bridges, 42*, 43*, 48, 49, 61*, 62*, 85, 151, 285, 308
    Buck prints, 42*, 61, 286-7, 289
    Buckingham House, 287, 289, 291, 293
    buildings, 64*
    burgesses, 151, 153, 219
    castle, 42, 61, 62*, 63*, 151, 161, 214, 225, 228
    Catherine Street, 15

Coracle Way, 285
Corporation lands & orders, 298, 300, 302, 303, 308
chapels, 18, 38,
county, mediaeval English, 169
county, mediaeval Welsh of, 153, 169
county court, 158
Dam/Dame street, 287, 294, 299, 300, 302, 303, 305
dry dock, 308
Eisteddfod, 1911
Exchange, 37
felons, 151, 153
Friary, 151, 153, 199, 293
Friar's Park, 42, 300, 305, 307, 308
gasworks, 65, 304, 308
Glannant Road, 15, 18*
Heol Awst Independent Chapel, 18, 38
Honour of, 156
inns & taverns, 300, 304, 310
Infirmary, 307
Insurance agent, 82
Island House, 291
Island Wharf, 61, 64*, 65, 300
John Street, 38
Lammas Street, 69, 291
manure dealer, 62
maps, 61, 150*285-7*, 288-9, 291
markets, 151, 288
Market Street, 37
mayors, 34, 56, 229, 302, 305, 307, 308
mills, 285, 293, 307
Mill St., 287
Millbrook cottages & Crescent, 15
monuments, 86, 287
Morfa Lane, 65, 285
Morley St., 82
motorfactors, 18
Museum, Quay St., 87
Myrtle Hill, 56
New Carmarthen, 150*, 151, 153, 155, 157, 161
Nott Square, 86
Old Carmarthen, 150*, 155, 156, 157, 161
Old Station Road, 291
officials, 19
paper mills, 15-18
Parade, The, 305
Park, 84*, 85
Park Hall, Roman cremation, 124, 127, 128, 129, 131, 133
Pentre Cerrig, 287
Pentre Cyril, 293
Penuel Chapel, Priory Street, 18
Photographers & photographs, 81
Picton Terrace, 81, 82-3
port, 36, 49
Pothouse & Pothouse wharf, 65, 284-297, 298-311
Probate Registry, 81

printers, 27, 28, 29, 30, 31, 32, 33, 34, 38-39 (list of)
Priory, 27, 42, 150, 155, 156, 157, 158, 159, 160, 161, 169-173, 194, 225
Priory Street, 131
quay, 15, 42, 43*, 48, 49, 61-66*, 85, 86*, 285*, 286-7, 291, 293, 300, 308
Quay St., 87, 284, 305, 306
railway & station, 55*, 56, 57, 85
Red St., 288
Red Lion Yard, 306
reservoirs, 307
Roman amphitheatre, 131
Roman fort, 131, 133
Roman Temple, 131
Roman Town (*Moridunum*), 123, 133, 150, 155, 194, 225, 228
St Catherine's Street & chapel, 304
St Mary's chapel, chantry & rood, 153
St Mary Street, 284
St Peter's Church, 19, 40, 41, 42, 49, 78, 150, 152*, 153, 154, 155, 173, 304, 309, 310
Sawmill Terrace, 288
schools, 42
School of Art, 65
sheriffs, 38
ships & ship builders, 291, 300, 302, 303
shops and stores, 37, 69
slaughterhouse, 15
Speed's map, 1610, 61, 228
sporting events, 84, 85
stationers, 34
survey of 1268, 169
tanneries, 15, 285
tinplate works, 49
theatres, 35
Trinity College, 307
town plan, 61, 150*
town walls, 153
Towy Works, 291
warehouses, 86
Water Street, 15, 18, 304
Water St Calvinistic Methodist Chapel, 18
Wynveth brook, 285, 288
Carmarthen Journal, 16, 17, 29, 36, 37, 39, 50, 291, 298, 305, 307, 308
Carmarthenshire, 41, 50, 75, 87, 98, 99, 100, 102, 158, 172, 224, 226, 227*
High Sheriffs, 303, 306
Carmarthenshire Antiquarian Society, 87, 95*, 169, 259
Carmarthenshire Antiquary, The, 98
Carmarthenshire Place-Names Survey
County Council, 123, 124, 125.192
County Museum, 41, 54, 61, 65, 124, 125, 126, 143, 192, 193, 195, 285, 294
County Archives, 56, 81, 247

Carn Goch hillfort, 101
Carnwyllion, commote of, 225
Carreg Cennen castle, 46, 50, 51*, 52, 54, 104, 225, 228
Carter, Harold, Professor, geographer, 208
Carter, Isaac, printer of Trefhedyn & Carmarthen, 28, 29, 30, 37, 38
carucates, *see* ploughs & ploughing
Castle Richard (Castillrichard), Llanstephan, 161
castles, 42, 43, 44*, 45, 46, 47*, 48, 49*, 50, 51*, 52, 53*, 54, 57, 58, 61, 62*, 63*, 73, 74*, 77*, 78*, 83, 90, 99, 104, 151, 155, 156*, 159, 161, 197, 199, 200, 204*, 205, 206*, 208*, 211, 212, 214, 215, 217, 221, 224, 225, 226*, 228, 231, 232, 235
mottes & baileys, 204
cattle, 45, 51, 170, 232, 255, 261, 265, 266, 277, 281
dairying, 51, 52, 265
Dairies & Creameries, 104
milk, cheese & butter, 166
ranches, 276
Cawdor, Earl of, 3, 48, 92, 94, 308
Cawrence Farm, Cardigan, 205
Caxton, William, printer, 10
Cefn bryn-brain, 246
Cefnbrwyn mountain farm, Llangurig, 272
Cellan, Cards., 279
celticism, 70, 71, 73, 76
Cennen, river, 225
Cennen Tower, 88, 89*
Censuses, 256
1831, 17
1841, 17, 22, 248
1851, 18, 22, 23, 248, 267
1861, 23, 248, 267
1871, 23, 248, 267
1881, 23, 248, 267
1891, 23, 248, 251, 267
1901, 24, 248, 267
chapels, mediaeval, 213, 214, 271
Abergwili Palace, 200
Capel Mair, Aberystwyth, 212
Cynwil Elfed, 171, 172
Troed y Rhiw, 172
St Teilo, Pentowyn, 158
Eglwys Trewyn, 158
Chapels, nonconformist,
Calvinistic Methodist, Water St., Carmarthen, 18
Congregational, Maesteg, 68, 69
Heol Awst Independent, Carmarthen, 18, 38
Henllan Amgoed Independent, 306
Moriah, Llanstephan, 83 Penuel, Priory St., Carmarthen, 18
Penuel, Priory St., Carmarthen, 18
Soar-y-Mynydd, Ceredigion, 259, 271
charcoal, 18, 127, 146
charities & charitable works, 182

Charles, Revd. David (1762-1834), ropemaker, papermaker & hymnwriter & family, 15, 16, 17, 18

Charles, David, s. of Revd. D. Charles, 17, 18

Charles-Edwards, T., Prof., 157

charters
latin, 157, 160, 164, 169, 170, 176
celtic, 157, 160

Charter Rolls, 169, 194

Chertsey Abbey, 212, 214

Chester, 36

Chetle, Peter, 18, 19

Childs, George, lithographer, 51*, 52

Chitty, Richard, London timber-merchant, 302

Chivelstone, 115-17, 118

Church House, Llangadog, 93

Church in Wales, Disestablishment and Representative Body, 177, 192

churches, 19, 20, 40, 41, 42, 48, 49, 52, 53*, 78, 99, 150, 151, 152*, 153, 154, 157-160, 169-173, 183, 192*, 193, 194, 197*, 204, 206, *207, 208, 211, 212, 213, 214, 215, 216, 218, 225, 226*, 304, 310
mother, 159, 173
parish, 228
portionary, 170, 172

Church, early mediaeval in Wales, 104, 155, 156, 157, 158, 172, 193, 214
'Early Mediaeval Ecclesiastical Sites' project, 172

Cilgerran, 205, 207, 212

Cill Efwr farm, Carmarthen, 133

Cilsan ferry, Llandeilo, 305

Cilsant, 229

Cilycwm, 102, 103*
church, 183

Cistercians, *see* monasteries

Civil War, the, 181

Clares, de, Norman family, Surrey, 212, 214, 215

Clay, *see* pottery

Clayhanger, Devon, Roman fort, 108*, 109

Clauseen, George, artist, 70

Clearbrook Cottage, 54

Clement VII, anti-pope, 177

Clynnog, Morys, 27

Clwyd, 146

Clyst Honiton, 112

Cnwcheithinog, Doiethïe valley, 271, 274, 275*

Cnwchgwyn, Doiethïe valley, 271

Coalbrook, Pontyberem, 92

coal industry, 68
coalyards, 300, 310
colliers, 248
collieries, 254
miners, 248

Coard, Dr Ros, cremation bone report, 126-127

coats of arms, *see* heraldry

cobblers, 33, 210

Cocks, Mari John, cockle-gatherer, Llanstephan, 72

Coedcanlas garden, 201

Coedmor castle, 205

Coedmor deeds, 209

Coedmor Forest, 210

Coedmor Petty Sessions, 214

Colet, John, 1, 2, 6, 7

Coli, farm & sheepwalk, Doithïe valley, 280

commons, land, pasture & rights, 161, 163, 245, 248, 255, 256, 265, 272, 273, 274, 277, 278, 280, 281, 298, 303

commotes, 153, 156*, 158, 171, 205, 216, 225, 247, 276
officials of, 153

copper-plate engraving & printing, 29, 30, 31

coracles, 85, 86*

Cornwall, 135

Cors Pwllci, 271

Cortner, Thomas, Sir, 184

costume, Welsh, 46, 47*, 48, 49

Cothi, river & leat & valley, 101, 136, 138*, 140, 141, 146, 225, 229

Couling, William, enclosure map, 163

Council for British Archaeology (CBA)
aerial archaeology committee, 107

country houses, 40, 41, 44, 45, 46, 87-93, 104

Courtenay, William de, Archbishop of Canterbury 1381-1396, 178

Cowbridge, 28

Cowin, river, 225, 229

Cox, David (1753-1859), watercolourist, 41, 52, 53*, 54, 56, 61*, 62, 286, 287*, 310

Coyd, Walter, burgess, Cardigan, 210

Craig, Robin, maritime historian, 302

cremation, *see* burials, Roman-Britain & Carmarthen

Cressingham, Hugh de, 216

Crinow, 158

Crompton, T. B., patentee of paper-drying machine, 13

Cromwell, Thomas, 160.181, 182, 199, 213, 215

cropmarks, *see* photography, aerial

Croucher, John le, felon, 153

Crow, Sir Sackville, 232

Crug Llwyn-Llwyd Iron Age 'entrenchment', Cardigan, 217

Crug Mawr/Banc-y-Warren, 217
battle of, 1136, 208

Crymlyn, nant (stream), 161, 162, 163

Cwm Celyn, farm, 162

Cwmagol farmhouse, 57

Cwmau, estate of Carmarthen priory, 160

Cwmbrwyn romanised farmstead, 128

Cwmgwili, 229

Cwmllynfell colliery, 246, 254

Cwmsymlog lead mine, Ceredigion, 97

Cymmrodorion Society, The, 43, 75

Cymerau, battle of 1257, 169

Cwmgwili, 228

Cymro, Welsh periodical writer, 45, 46

Cymru, journal, ed. Owen M. Hughes, 73, 75
Cynwil, St., 173
Cynwyl Elfed church, parish & village, 169, 170, 172, 173
Cynwyl Gaeo, 173
Cyffig parish & deerpark, 231, 232, 233*
Cywin, river, 159

Dale-Jones, Edna, 289, 297
Daniel, John, printer & salesman of Carmarthen, 28, 29, 31, 35, 36, 37, 38
dairying, *see* cattle
Dartmoor, *see* Devon
David I, King of Scotland, 160
David Fitzgerald, bp of St Davids, 160
Davies, Evan, w. Anna & family, papermaker, Carmarthen, 18
Davies, Evan & w. Mary (née Evans), papermaker, Carmarthen, 18
Davies, Iori, Ysbyty-Ystwyth, 277
Davies, James, manufacturer, Carmarthen, 291, 308
Davies, John, papermaker, 17, 18
Davies, Mansel, motorcycle racer, 85
Davies, Oliver, archaeologist, Roman mines in Europe, 144
Davies, R. R., Professor, 155, 161
Davies, Reuben, historian, 157-8
Davies, Richard, bishop of St Davids (1561-90), 181, 200
Davies, Samuel, w. Mary & family, papermaker, 18
Davies, William, & w. Hannah, Llangain, bookseller of Cadell & Davies, London, 36
Davies, Walter, agriculturalist, 281
Davies, Walter, motorcycle mechanic, Coventry, 85
Davies, William, bookseller of Cadell & Davies, 36
Davies, Wendy, Professor, 157, 160
Davis, John, cabinet-maker, 56
Daviston, Robert, Prior of St John's, Carmarthen, 151
Davys, Miss Campbell, 90
deans & deaneries, 158, 184, 193
deer & deer parks, 45, 229, 231-234, 235-243, 274
Deheubarth, kingdom of, 159, 225
Derbyshire, 135
Derllys, commote & royal demesne, 153, 159, 169, 172
Derwydd estate, 298, 299*, 304, 305, 306, 307, 310
Deulwyn, Ieuan, bard, 229
Devil's Bridge (Blaenmerin), 279
Devon, 135
    Aerial archaeology, 107-22
    Aerial Reconnaissance Project, 110, 120
    County Council, 107
    Dartmoor, 109, 110
    excavations, 110
    Historic Landscape Characterisation, 112
    lowlands, 109, 120
    Post-Reconnaissance Fieldwork Project, 111
    Prehistoric sites, 109
    Roman forts, 108*
    Sherford new town, 115

Dewisland, 177
Dickinson, John, patentee of cylinder papermaking machine, 13
dictionaries,
    Welsh, 28
Diderot, D., *Encyclopédie*, 11
Din Gereint (Old Castle), Cardigan, 204*, 205*, 214
Dinas, Cwm Doithïe, deserted farmstead, 259-268*, 271
Dinefwr Castle & Park, 43*, 44*, 45, 48, 50, 53, 54, 225, 228
    historic gardens, 104
    Newton, 224, 225, 229
    Roman forts, 104, 131
Dineley, Thomas, *Duke of Beaufort's progress through Wales*, 212, 213
Dingwall, Christopher, 235
Directories,
    Craig's Paper Mills, 1876, 23
    Pigot's, 1830 & 1835, 22
    Slater's, 1880, 23
    Universal British, 1791, 22
    Worrall's, 23*
dogs, hunting, 238, 239
Doithïau-fach farmstead, 271, 280
Doithïe Fawr, 259
Doithïe, river & valley, 259*, 263*, 265, 268, 270-283, 273, 274, 276, 277
Doithïe/Camddwr township, 259-269
Dolaucothi, *see also* Pumsaint, 100
    Allt Cmwhenog opencast, 138*
    Cwrt-y-cilion trenches, 138, 141, 142, 147
    Carreg Pumsaint, 140, 143
    Estate, 136
    leats, rivers Annell & Cothi, 144
    Melin-y-Milwyr, 141*, 144
    Ogofau opencast, 139
    Penlanwen Farm, 138, 140*
    Roman & later gold & metal mines, 101, 135-147
    Ynyssau, 142
Dolauhirion bridge, Llandovery, 48
Dolerwydd, 231
Doomsday Book, 112
Don, Sir Edward of Horsenden, Bucks., 224, 229
Donkin, Bryan, engineer & builder of Fourdrinier papermaking machine, 13
Donovan, Edward, artist, naturalist & writer, *Descriptive Excursions . . . S. Wales & Mon.*, 47, 48
Dorwen, deserted farm, Twrch valley, 246
Dover, 1
dower houses, *see* farmsteads
Down, The, Down & Ffynnon Down farms, Llanstephan, 160, 163
drawings, 41, 42*, 73*, 75*, 77*, 128*, 130*, 152*, 188*, 198*, 287*, 294*
Drayton, Michael, *Poly-Olbion*, 1612, 41
drovers & droving, 271, 281
Drygarn-fawr (mynydd), Brecs., 270

Dryslwyn, 193
    castle, 49*, 53*, 54, 57, 58, 73, 74*, 225, 228
    bridge, ford & ferry, 49
Dublin, 205
Dulais, river, 56, 225
Duncan I, Earl of Fife, 236
Dürer, Albrecht, 2, 4*, 5*
Dwnn, David, of Kidwelly, 229
Dwnn, Lewys, herald, 229
Dyer, John, poet, *Grongar Hill*, 57
Dyfed, 81, 157, 266
    Irish dynasty of, 157
Dyfed Archaeological Trust, 100, 104, 111, 124, 145, 132, 193, 217
Dynevor, Lord, 48, 50

earthworks, 104, 109, 111, 117, 140, 235, 236*, 237*, 239*
East India Company, 56
Edrych, Istrigge, Pdrych, John, Prior, Carmarthen Priory, 170
Edward I, King, 154, 161, 169, 170, 171
Edward VI, King of England, 182, 183, 185, 199
Edwards, bridgebuilder, 48
Edwards, David Bonnell, maltster, Carmarthen, 307
Edwards, Morgan, 266
Edwards, Owen M., 73
Edwards, Thomas Charles, 157
Edwinsford, 44, 45
Eglwys gymun, 228
Egyptology, 135
Eisteddfodau, National & local, 70, 71, 73, 75, 205, 214
Elan, river & Elenydd, district, 270
Eldridge, John, Prior of St John's, Carmarthen, 154
Elfed, commote of, 153, 169, 171, 172, 173
Elizabeth I, Queen of England, 199, 226
Enclosure (of common land), 245, 265
enclosures, 256
    concentric antenna, 99
    defended, 99, 101*, 102, 103*, 104, 132*, 133, 172*, 217
    Devon & Somerset, 107-122
    Wales Defended Enclosures project, 104, 115, 132
Endeavour, voyage of, 44
engine houses, 97
England, 41, 156, 178
englishries, 159
engravers, 3, 40, 41, 42, 43, 44, 45, 46, 49, 50, 51, 52, 54, 56, 181, 182, 226
Epynt mountain, Brecs., 279
Erasmus, 1-8
Esgairwen, Caron Uwch-Clawdd, 272
European Regional Development Fund, 177
Evan, David Thomas ap, 255
Evans, Alcwyn, Carmarthen historian, 169
Evans, Anne, w. Revd. John Evans, 21, 22
Evans, Bennet, captain (*Sir Watkin Bach*), 281
Evans, David, ship's captain, 302

Evans, David Oliver, paper merchant of Cardiff, 23, 24
Evans, Gavin, Carmarthenshire Museums archaeologist, 124
Evans, George, limeburner, 300, 308
Evans, George Eyre, 151
Evans, Gwenogfryn, 158
Evans, John, printer of Carmarthen, 29, 30, 32, 33, 35-6, 37, 38, 50
Evans, J.Wyn, the Very Revd., Dean St Davids, 185, 189
Evans, Margaret, shopkeeper, Carmarthen, 69
Evans, P. C. C., historian, 213
Evans, William, printer, 17
Excise List, 1816, 22, 24
Exeter, 112

Fabon, manor, 247
Falkland, Fife, 236*
    Palace & hunting park, 236
    Parish*, 236
farms & farmers, 47, 50, 57, 77*, 111, 112, 133, 137, 160, 163-166, 218, 231, 232, 266, 267
    deserted & ruined, 94, 245-258*, 259-69
    hill, 245
    Iron Age/Romano-British, 99, 104, 128, 133
    lluestau, 259
    upland & pastoral, 259-269, 281
Felindre, Ceredigion, 216
Ferrar, Robert, bishop St Davids, 86, 198, 199
Ferrier, Robert of Haverfordwest, gent., 21
ferries, *see* rivers
feudal rights & dues, 277, 281
Ferryside, 49, 72, 85
Ffrwd, Llangyndeyrn, 90, 91*
Ffrwdwenith Farm, Aberporth, 219.
Ffynnon Drindod/Trinity Well, Llanfihangel-y-Creuddyn, 213
Ffynnon Las farm, Dolaucothi, 142
Ffynnonwen Farm, Cardigan, 218
field boundaries & systems, 115, 117, 120, 133, 157, 163, 166, 264
    medieval open fields, 133, 158, 159, 160, 163-166, 218
    field names, 109, 118, 158, 163-165*, 196, 197, 200, 238, 248, 263, 264
    meadows, 163, 192*, 197*, 200, 262, 263*, 264, 265, 281
Fife, Scotland, 235*
fires & fire insurance, 16, 17, 22, 48, 307
fish, shellfish & fishing, 49, 62, 72, 159, 163
    fishtraps/fishweirs, 99, 163, 164*, 207, 224
Fisher, John, bishop of Rochester, 7, 8
Fishguard, 177
Fitzgerald, Maurice, steward of Bishops of St Davids, 160
flax-dressers, 16
Flemings, 155, 159, 166, 208, 217, 219
Flintshire, 43
Flints, *see* Neolithic & Bronze Age
Foley, Thomas, Sir, admiral, of Abermarlais, 48, 90

folklore, Welsh,
  Mari Lwyd, 87
fords, *see* rivers
Forestry Commission & plantations, 270, 112, 165, 166
Forster, Thomas Campbell, newspaper correspondent, 57
Forth, paddle-steamer, 85
Fox, Cyril, Sir, archaeologist, 67, 266
France, 176, 182
  paper imported from, 10, 31
Frances, John & w. Alice, peasant farmers, Llanstephan, 164
Francis, Benjamin, 29
Francis, May, Carmarthen, 77
friendly societies, 34
Froben, Johann, printer of Basle, 1, 3, 6-8
Frongoch lead mine, Ceredigion, 97
funerals, 48, 83*
Fychan, Cledwyn, 281
Fychan, Ednyfed, 229
Fychan, Maredudd, 170

Gadsden, G. D., lawyer, 273, 278
Gardde, St Clears, 92*
gardens, *see* parks & gardens
Garw, river & valley, 245, 254
gas, 115
  Liquified Natural Gas Pipeline, 104
Gastineau, Henry, artist & engraver, 52, 53*, 62*
Gaunt, John of & w. Blanche, 177, 178
geese, 163, 281
Gelling, Dr. Margaret, place-name scholar, 118
Genealogy, 301
gentry & aristocracy, Welsh, 3, 5, 21, 27, 28, 42, 43, 45, 47,
  48, 49, 50, 54, 71, 90, 92, 136, 160, 169, 177, 207, 214,
  219, 229, 231-2, 233, 262, 281, 285, 289, 291, 298, 299-
  302, 303, 306, 308, 309, 310
gentry & aristocracy, English, 1, 23, 44, 45, 48, 54, 170, 177,
  178, 180, 213, 224, 231, 232
gentry houses, 40, 44, 88, 90*, 91*, 224, 228, 229
geology & geologists, 137, 109, 126, 143, 145, 175*185, 246,
  249
  soils, 112, 117, 125, 126
geophysical survey, 112, 115, 116*, 144, 193, 195, 201
Gerald of Wales (Gerallt Gymro, Giraldus Cambrensis), 150,
  151, 166, 207, 217
Gerald of Windsor, 160
Gerardston/Trerefe, royal manor, 216, 217, 218
Germany, 4, 6
Gerrard, Sandy, 111
Gibson, John, sculptor, 50, 75, 76
Giffard, Richard, 169
Gilpin, Revd. William, *author*, 42
Glamorganshire, 68, 226
Glanareth (Pontbren Arath), Llandeilo, 91*, 92
Glanbrân mansion, 228
Glanllynan, Cardigan, 205
glass, mediaeval, 189

Gloucestershire, 24
Glyn Cothi, forest, 229
Glyn Cothi, Lewis, brad, 229
Glyndŵr, Owain, 163, 217
Glynhir waterfall, 46, 50, 51*
Glynn Vivian Art Gallery, Swansea, 78
Goerio, Giovanni Battista, court physician to Henry VII, 2
Gold Park, 110
Golden Grove (Gelli Aur) 40, 41, 51, 54, 228, 302, 305
  Estate archives, 245, 247, 248
Goode, William, map-maker, 299
Goodman, John, *Maddeuant i'r edifairiol*, 1725-6, 30
Gorseinon Miners' Welfare Institute Library, 8
Gough, Thomas, 22
Gough, William, of Prendergast, & d. Anne, merchant, 21, 22
gold, 135, 136, 143, 144, 146
Gove, Dawkin, mayor of Carmarthen & bookseller, 34
Gower, 159, 160, 226
Gower, Henry, Bishop of St Davids, 194, 197
Graf, Urs, 7*
granges, *see* monasteries
Gravelot, H. F. B., French artist, 41, 42
Greek language and literature, 1, 2, 3, 30
  scholars, 2, 3
  type, 3, 8, 30
Green Castle, 49
Green, Stephen, 182, 183, 184
Greville, Charles, the Hon., 44
Griffiths, Ralph A., Professor, 151, 212, 214, 216
Griffiths, David, potter, Carmarthen, 303, 304
Griffiths, Vaughan, bookseller in London, 36
Gruffudd ap Nicholas of Dinefwr, 229
Gruffydd, Huw Crowdder, of Arwystli, 281
Gron Gaer hillfort, 101
Grongar Hill, 52, 53*, 57*, 58
Gulston, Alan James, 293
Gulston, Joseph, 299, 300
guns, culverin, 237
Gurnos farmstead, Doithïe valley, 271
Gwarthaf, cantref, 158
Gwendraeth fach river, 15, 19*, 163, 225, 229
Gwendraeth fawr, river, 225, 226*, 228, 229
Gwendraeth estuary, 163, 224
Gwenllian, d. of Rhys ap Gruffudd (The Lord Rhys), 229
Gwenno's well, Dolaucothi, 139
Gwidigada, *see* Widigada
Gwili, river, 41, 229
Gwilym, Dafydd ap, poet, 268
Gwynfe, manor, 247
Gwynn, Rhydderch of Glanbrân, 229
Gwynne, H. L. E., of Rhyd-y-Gors, 50
Gwynedd, 170, 229

hafod, *hafotai* (summer dwellings), 162, 277
Hafod Farm, defended enclosure, 103*, 104

Hall-houses, mediaeval, 26

Hampton, John, air photographer, 107, 120

Haroldston, John de, 177

Haroldstone, St Issels parish, Pembs., 25, 183, 20

Harries, Des, mason, St Davids cathedral, 174, 175*

Harries, Esther, Pilroath, Llanstephan, d. 1911, 83

Harris, John, almanacker of Carmarthen, 35

Harris, John, printer of Carmarthen, 35, 37

Harris, Jonathan, printer of Carmarthen, 29, 31, 34, 35, 36

Harris, Morgan & Jones, tinplate works owners, Carmarthen, 49

Harvey, Benjamin, & Sons, papermaker, Haverfordwest, 22, 23, 25

Haverfield, Francis, Prof., Roman archaeologist, 144, 145

Haverfordwest, 16
    airport, 102
    paper mills, 15, 20-25*, 31
    St. Martin's parish, 21, 24
    St Mary's Church, 16
    St Philip Out parish, 24

Havering, John de, justice of West Wales, 170

Hayne Lane enclosure, Devon, 111, 113*, 114

Hebrew, 7, 30, 33
    type, 29, 30*

Hendre farm, Llanstephan, 68, 69*, 70, 71*, 77

Henfaes, Fforestresgob, 274

henges & cursus, *see* neolithic

Henry of Lancaster, 178, 180

Henry, earl of Northumberland, 160

Henry I, King, 155, 156

Henry II, King of England, 205

Henry III, King of England, 169

Henry VIII, King of England, 160, 182, 183, 199, 210, 213

heraldry & heralds, 41, 229

Herbert, Lord, 229

Heritage Lottery Fund, 177

Herkomer, Hubert, artist, 70

Heywood, Thomas, *The Life of Merlin*, 1812, 35

hillforts, 101-104*, 109, 110*, 111, 117*, 131, 132, 133, 159, 172

Hinds, John, Liberal MP, west Carms., 1910-1923, 76

Hirwern, Afon, 205
    Ponthirwaun, 205

Historic Scotland, 235

Hole, William, engraver, 41

Holland, *see* Netherlands

Hooper & Sparrow, print-makers, 181, 182*

Hore, Thomas, Prior, Cardigan priory, 215

Horner, Bill Devon archaeologist & air photographer, 110, 120

horses, ponies, 163, 232, 255, 266, 281

Horwood, Devon, enclosure complex, 118, 120*

hospitals, 177, 182

Houghton, Adam, Bishop of St Davids, 175, 176, 177, 178, 179, 180, 183, 185, 186

Howell, David, Dean of St Davids, 1897-1903, 186

Howell, Morris, limeburner, 300, 308

Howells, Dai, mason, St Davids cathedral, 174

Howells, Erwyd, shepherd, 272, 279

Howells, John, of Haverfordwest, 21

Howells, Walter Rice, of Maesgwyne, Carmarthen, 21

Huett, Thomas, Precentor, St Davids cathedral, 181

Hughes, Hugh (1790-1863), artist & engraver, *The Beauties of Cambria*, 38, 50, 51*, 52, 88, 89

Hughes, Lewis & w. Frances, attorney & town clerk, Carmarthen, 19

Hughes, Owen, Welsh author, 31

Hughes, Stephen, nonconformist, 28

Hughes, W. J., major, of Middleton Hall, 54

Hughes, Worthington Poole, Canon & warden, Llandovery College, 76

hunting, *see* deer & dogs

Hywel, Ieuan ap, beadle of Widigada, 153

Ice Age, 207, 219

Illustrated London News, 55, 56

ink, 10, 31, 37, 57

insurance agents, 37

Iolo Morganwg, *see* Williams, Edward

Ireland, 146, 160

Iron Age, 98, 101, 102, 104, 112, 217
    burials, 131, 132
    pottery, 128
    round houses, 110, 111, 115

iron forges, 15, 18, 19, 20

ironworks & foundries, 68, 310

Iscennen, commote, 225

Iscoed Ishirwen half commote, 205*, 216

Italy, 2, 3, 4, 6, 9, 43, 71, 72, 75, 128

James, George, carpenter, Carmarthen, 305

James, Heather, 100, 107, 259

James, Terry, 81, 87, 92, 93, 94, 95*, 96*, 135, 150, 151, 154, 175, 259, 298
    aerial photography, 94, 98, 99, 100, 104, 105, 107, 109, 132
    excavations, 157
    photography, 81, 87, 92, 93, 95*, 96*
    printing, 1

James, Thomas, 293

James I, King of Scotland, 237

James II (1437-1460), King of Scotland, 237

James IV, King of Scotland, 237
    natural son of, 6

Jeakes, Joseph, aquatint engraver, 46, 47*

Jenkins, Thomas, The Friary, Carmarthen, 293, 308

Jenkinson, bishop of St Davids, 187

Jerome, St., 3, 6, 7

John, Augustus, artist, 67

John, Morris, shoemaker, Carmarthen, 299

Johnes, John Sir & w. Betha, of Dolaucothi, 136, 137, 143
Johnstown, 132
Jones, Andrew, *Llyfr du y gydwybod*, 33
Jones, Chrispianus, bookbinder & bookseller, 32, 33, 37
Jones & Co., publishers, *Wales Illustrated . . . Henry Gastineau*, 52
Jones, David, apprentice printer, Carmarthen, 29
Jones, Francis, Major, Wales Herald, *Historic Carmarthenshire Homes*, 90, 92, 197
Jones, G. B. D., Professor, archaeologist, 140, 142, 144
Jones, Glanville, Professor, 166
Jones, Griffith, Llanddowror, 37, 271
Jones, Gwyn, Tregaron, 279, 281
Jones, Harry, of Llanstephan, 76, 77
Jones, Henry, Sir, of Abermarlais, 229
Jones, Henry, Hendre Farm, Llanstephan, 77*
Jones, Huw, shepherd, 268
Jones, Ifan, Nantgraig farm, 281
Jones J. F., museum curator & photographer, 87-93*, 284*, 285, 290, 292*, 294, 296*, 297
Jones, John, M.P. of Ystrad, 50, 133
Jones, John, Hendre Farm, Llanstephan & w. Anna, 67, 68
Jones, Nathaniel & family, of Dinas, 267
Jones, Richard & w. Elizabeth of Cwmgwili, 229
Jones, Richard, Dyfed Archaeological Trust, 124
Jones, Robert Protheroe, National Industrial & Maritime Museum of Wales, 143
Jones, Sam, Glanrafon-isa, Blaencaron, 278
Jones, Thomas, tailor, bookseller & printer, 28
Jones, Thomas (1742-1803), artist, *Six Views in S. Wales*, 43*
Jones, William, engraver, Principal Carm. School of Art, 64, 65
Jones, W. B. & Freeman E. A., *The History & Antiquities of St Davids*, 181, 185
Joseph, J. K. S. St., Professor & air photographer, 98, 107, 120
Julius II, Pope, 214
Justiciars, royal officials in South Wales, 153

Keene, Alfred (1821-1893), artist, 62, 63
Kerr, F. J., artist & teacher, Neath, 70
Kidwelly, 19, 52, 100, 156*, 200, 225, 226, 229
    Borough Council, 1, 19, 20
    castle, 50, 52, 228
    church, 19, 20
    lordship, 224
    paper mill, 15, 18-20
    forge, 15, 18, 19, 20
Kifts, mediaeval Flemish family of Cardigan & Carmarthen, 219
King's Court, Talley, hall-house, 266
King's Printer's, London, 28, 29
Kip, William, engraver, 41
Knights Hospitaller, Slebech Commandery, 159, 160, 163, 209, 216

Koops, Mathias, 13
Kymer, Sir Thomas, 305
Kyng, John, prisoner mediaeval Carmarthen, 153

Lampeter College Founders' Library, 3
Lampeter, University College of Wales, 144
Lamphey, Bishop's Palace, 197, 198, 199, 200
Lancaster, Henry, Duke of, 178, 179
landscape, Welsh, 40, 41, 42, 43, 44, 45, 58, 98, 272
Landseer, John, artist, 45, 52, 70
Landshipping garden, 201
Lane-Fox, Augustus, 143
Laques & Laques Fawr farms, Llanstephan, 163
Laporte, 40
Latin language and literature, 1, 2, 3, 5, 6, 7, 27, 181, 226
Laud, William, Bishop of St Davids (1621-27), 200, 201
Laugharne, 90, 155, 156*, 226*, 228
    Castle, 52, 73*, 225, 228, 231, 232
    Lordship, 156, 158, 231
Laundry, mediaeval family of Llandeilo Abercowin, 158
Laurence, William, Sir, 184
law, lawyers & courts, 19, 20, 210, 214, 273, 277, 278, 280, 281
    Chancery, 199
    Court of Great Sessions, 265
    Star Chamber, 231, 232
    Welsh, 157, 214, 274
lead, *see also* mines, 94-7, 184
Leighton, Lord, artist, 70, 76
Leland, John, Tudor antiquary, 157, 198, 224, 225, 229
Lewis, Benjamin Archibald (1857-1946), artist, 62, 63*, 64*, 65*
Lewis, David, Carmarthen, 308
Lewis, Edward Morland (1903-1943), artist, 65, 66*
Lewis, George of Carmarthen, 303
Lewis, Jim, of Troedrhiwruddwen, 271
Lewis, John, timber merchant, Carmarthen, 305, 308
Lewis, John s.Benjamin Lewis, Llanboidy (Phillips & Lewis), 306, 307
Lewis, Morgan, Carmarthen merchant & ship-builder, 302, 303, 305, 308
Lewis, P. R., archaeologist, Dolaucothi, 140, 142, 144
Lewis, Philip, sir, 184
Lewis, Samuel, printer, Carmarthen, 30
Lewis, Thomas, Carmarthen mapmaker, 285, 298, 300, 302, 308
Lewis, Thomas, Revd., Llangadog, 247, 256
Lewis, W. J., *Cardiganshire Historical Atlas*, 271
Lewis, William, w. Mary & family, papermaker, Waindew, 18
Lhuyd, Edward, antiquary, 1, 143
libraries, 3, 4, 5, 8, 28, 37, 38, 181
lime & lime kilns, 45, 300, 308
Linnaeus & Linnaean Society, 43, 48
Lipscomb, George, *Journey in S. Wales*, 1801, 54
Litelking, Letard, 159

Liverpool, 23, 40, 45, 50, 70

Llainau hillfort, Abernant, 172

Llanarthney, 229

Llanbadarn, 214

Llanddowror, 156, 158, 228

Llanddew Brecs, manor house, 198, 212

Llanddewi (Gower) Bishop's house, 197, 198, 199

Llanddewi Brefi, parish & lordship, 271, 273, 274, 276, 278, 279
 Collegiate church of, 183, 193, 194, 199

Llanddwy church, Ceredigion, 213

Llandeilo Abercowin, 156, 158, 228*

Llandeilo Fawr, 40, 48, 88, 90, 157, 172, 229, 255, 305
 bridge, 45, 46*
 church, 48, 49, 225
 Roman forts, *see* Dynevor park

Llandovery, 28, 52, 67, 76, 94, 100, 104, 226, 229
 bridge, 48
 castle, 52, 53*, 225, 228
 College, 76
 Roman cremations, 131
 Roman fort, 103, 131
 Roman roads, 131

Llandingat Church, 52, 53*

Llandow, Glam., 212

Llandybie, 71, 228

Llandyfaelog, 172

Llandygwydd (Ceredigion) Bishop's house, 197, 198, 199, 200

Llanedi, 228, 229

Llanegwad, 229

Llanelli, 56, 99, 104, 225, 228, 229
 Art School, 75

Llanerchaeron, 216

Llanfaes Dominican Friary, 199

Llanfihangel Abercowin, 15

Llanfihangel Aberbythych, 228

Llanfynydd, 146, 194

Llangadog, 93, 224, 226, 229, 247
 College, 193, 194

Llangain (*Maenor Gain*), 67, 156, 158, 228*

Llangan church, 99

Llangennech, 228

Llangoedmor, 205, 209, 213, 214, 216, 218

Llangrannog, 105

Llangunnor, 86, 88-9

Llangyndeyrn, 19, 90
 Church, 19

Llangynog, 133, 158, 159, 228*

Llanllwch, Carms., 226, 303
 mill, 67, 68

Llannon, 228

Llanreith, 183

Llansadwrn, 88-9, 104

Llansadwrnen, 228

Llansanffraed church, 183

Llansawell, 102

Llanstephan, 52, 62, 85, 133, 158
 castle, 45, 46, 47*, 49, 50, 52, 77*, 78*, 83, 159, 225, 226*, 228
 church, 157-160
 fairs & markets, 163
 ferry to Ferryside, 49, 62, 72, 159, 224
 ferry to Laugharne, 155
 fields, 163, 165
 lordship of, 155, 158, 160, 164, 165
 Moriah Chapel, 83
 Plas Llanstephan, 71, 160, 162
 Tithe map & schedule, 165

Llanstinan church, Pembs., 183

Llanteulyddog, see Carmarthen Priory

Llanwrtyd Wells, 102, 271

Llanybri (Morabri) 159, 161, 163, 164, 165, 166

Llawhaden, Bishop's castle, 197, 199, 200

Llethr farmstead, Doithïe valley, 271

Llethrllwyd, libert (sheepwalk), 278

Llewelin, Lewis, 247

Lloyd, David, owner of *Alltyrodin Commonplace Book*, 33

Lloyd, Fanny Letitia, 23

Lloyd family of Plas, Llanstephan, 160

Lloyd, George, of Brunant, 137

Lloyd, Herbert, Clerk of the Peace, 34

Lloyd, Herbert, Sir, of Peterwell, 92

Lloyd, J. F., Carmarthen, photographer, 72*, 81- 86

Lloyd, Joseph & Sons, papermakers, 17

Lloyd, Richard, of Haverfordwest, gent., 22

Lloyd, Thomas ap Morgan ap Jevan, of Llangadog, 255

Lloyd, Thomas, *Lost Houses of Wales*, 89, 90, 133, 177

Lloyd, Thomas, miller & papermaker of Haverfordwest, 22, 24, 25, 31

Lloyd-Philipps records, Pembs Record Office, 298

Llwyd, Humphrey, cartographer, 209, 224, 225, 226, 228, 229

Llwyn-rhys, Llanbadarn Odwyn, cruck-framed house, 266

Llwyd, Morgan, Welsh author, 28

Llwyncwnstabl, 246, 247

Llwynhywel mansion, 228, 229

Llyfni Ironworks Co., 68

Llŷn peninsula, 226

Llywelyn, Dafydd ab, Prince of Gwynedd, 276

London, 29, 36, 44, 48, 50, 52, 66, 70, 71, 291, 302, 303, 305
 University, 48

longhouse, *see* architecture, Welsh domestic & vernacular

Lord, Joseph, 184-5

Lord's park farm, Llanstephan, 163

Loughor (Llwchwr) river, 5, 46, 50, 225, 226*, 228, 229
 Roman fort, 128

Lucas, Caroline, w. Sir John Gardner Wilkinson, 135, 136

Ludlow, Neil, archaeologist & artist, 152*, 172

Luntley, John, Master of St Mary's College, St Davids, 177*, 183

Luther, Martin, 7

Mabinogion, The, 71

Macbeth (Mac Bethad), thane, of Scotland, 236

maenor, 166

Maenor Gain, see Llangain

Maesbetws farmstead & chapel, Doithïe valley, 271

Maesteg, 75
    shop, Commercial Street, 68

Malcolm IV, King of Scotland, 236

Malkin, B. H., *Tours . . . South Wales*, 1804, 40

Mallaen, 171

malting, *see* brewing

Manchester, 8, 40

Manorafon, Cardigan, 204, 213

Manorbier, 166

Manorowen church, Pembs., 183

manors, 157, 183, 193, 217, 247, 262
    manor-house, 198

manuscripts,
    Account Rolls, Principality of West Wales, 170
    Calendar of Patent Rolls, 193
    Court of Kings Bench, 171
    Cronica Walliae, 225
    Cymerau MSS, 274
    Liber A, 170
    Peniarth 401D, 160

Manutius, Aldus, printer of Venice, 1, 2, 3-6

maps and plans, *see also* Ordnance Survey, 16*, 19*, 20*, 21*, 40, 41*, 117, 125*, 136, 150*, 156*, 162*, 165*, 171*, 172*, 179*, 184*, 192*, 195*, 197*, 204*, 205*, 208*, 224, 225, 226*, 227*, 228*, 233*, 235*, 236*, 237*, 239*, 245, 246*, 251*, 252*, 253*, 261*, 267*, 285*, 286*, 291, 302, 308
    distribution, 100*, 110*, 111*, 272*, 273*
    Enclosure, 163
    estate, 137, 196*, 245, 248*, 256
    excavation & survey, 114*, 125*, 238*
    maritime charts, 302
    St Davids mapbook, 1796, 196
    Tithe, 109, 118, 137, 163, 249*, 251, 278, 279, 286, 291
    Wales, 226*

March, the, Marcher lords, 155
    Council of the Marches, 232

Maredudd ap Richard, 169, 172

Maredudd ap Richard ap Maredudd, of Elfed, 170, 172

Maredudd Fychan, 170

markets & fairs, 225

Marlais, river, 225

Marloes church, Pembs., 183, 218

Marmion, Geoffrey de, Lord of Llanstephan, 159

Marros, 228

marsh, saltmarsh, 163, 165*, 207, 298, 302, 303, 305, 308, 310

Martin, John, Prior, Carmarthen Priory, 161

Martin, Bishop of St Davids, 197

Martinsgrove, Llangynog, 162

masons, 174, 210

Mathews, Thomas, writer & Welsh language propagandist, 71, 73, 75, 76

Matilda, Queen, 156

Mawddach, river, 146

Maxwell, Gordon, Scottish archaeologist, 107

meadows, *see* fields

Meares family of Plas, Llanstephan, 160

medicine, medical profession & doctors, 37, 70, 71

Merioneth, 146, 267, 279

Merlin's Hill, hillfort, 86, 101, 133

Merlin, 226
    Life of, 1812, 35

Merthyr, church, 173

Methodists, 50

Meylett, Morgan, & w. Anne, of Lawrenny, esq., 21

Meyrick, Samuel, sir, 207

Middleton, Christopher & s. Richard, 303

Middleton Hall, 41, 48, 54, 104

Middleton, Henry of Gorse Ddu, Llanarthne, 303

Middleton, Marmaduke, Bishop of St Davids (1581-90), 200, 201

Middleton, Walter, 289, 298, 300, 303

Midgley, J. C., artist, Principal, Carmarthen School of Art, 65-6

midwife, 68

Milbourne, Bishop of St Davids (1615-1621), 200, 201

Miles family, Cardigan, 216

Milford, Lord, of Pentypark, Pembs., 285, 298, 305, 306

Milford Haven, 226

Millennium Appeal, 185, 188

mills, 67, 209, 216
    cotton, 22, 23
    corn or grist, 21, 22, 24, 68, 161, 163, 217, 293
    paper, 15, 18, 19, 20, 21, 22, 24, 31
    snuff, 21
    stamp, 144
    woollen, 18, 217, 218

mines & mining, 265
    copper, 143, 145
    lead, 48, 94-97
    lead-silver, 97, 145
    Roman, 101
    zinc, 94, 95

Mining Journal, The, 144

mining techniques, 143, 145, 147

moats, 177

monasteries, 1, 6, 155, 159, 172, 179, 194, 212
    chronicles, 153, 155, 166

Cistercian, 160, 276
   Dissolution of, 27, 160, 225
   granges, 157, 158, 160
   in west Wales, 157
Montgomery, Roger of, 204
Montrose's Camp, Fyvie, Aberdeenshire, 239
More, Sir Thomas, 2, 6, 8
Morgan, David, architect, 90
Morgan, John, bishop of St Davids, 180, 184
Morgan, John, ironmaster, Carmarthen, 303
Morgan, John, Rhosmaen, 247
Morgan, Mrs, *A Tour to Milford Haven*, 40
Morgan, Philip, shipbuilder, Carmarthen, 305
Morgan, Robert & w. Frances, ironmaster, Carmarthen, 19, 20
Morgan, Thomas, ship's captain, 302
Morgan, William, bishop of Llandaff, 27
Morganwg, Iolo, see Williams, Edward, 38
Moridunum, see Carmarthen, Roman Town
Morley, David, 50
Morris, David & sons, bankers, Carmarthen, 306
Morris, David, bookbinder, 17, 34
Morris, David, corn & paper miller, 24
Morris, John, shoemaker, Carmarthen, 299
Morris, Lewis, maritime cartographer, 277, 278, 281, 302
Morris, William, mayor of Carmarthen 1852, 56
Mortimer, Nest, widow of Roger, 216
Mortmain, Stautes of, 161
Motorbicycle races, 84*, 85
motorfactors, Carmarthen, 18
Mount Folly, Bigbury Bay, Iron-Age/Romano-British enclosure, 115
Mount Pleasant, Carmarthen, 288
Mountjoy, Lord William, 1, 2, 3
Murchison, Roderick, Sir, geologist, 143
Murdoch, earl of Fife & Duke of Albany, 236
Murphy, Ken, 111, 132
Murray, William Grant, 78
music & musical instruments, 131, 133, 178, 179, 180, 186
Mwche farm & bridge, 161, 162, 163, 165*
Myddfai, 100
   church, 193
Mwnt (Eglwys y Grog), Ceredigion, 205*, 209, 218
Mynydd-bach, Ceredigion, 270
Mynydd Crwbin, 98
Mynydd Du (The Black Mountain), 99, 100, 225, 245, 246*, 248, 255, 256
Mynydd Llangyndeyrn, 98
Mynydd Pumlumon, 270, 277
Myrtle Hill, Carmarthen, railway station, 56
Mysmead, Cardigan, 204, 217

Nantgaredig, 104
Nant-y-bai valley, 94

Nant-y-ci, Carms., 303
Nant-y-Mwyn lead mine, 48, 94-97*
Nantiwan farmstead, Doithïe valley, 271, 281
Nantllwyd, farm, Doithïe/Camddwr, 267, 271
Nantgwyddel farmstead, Doithïe valley, 271, 279, 280
Nantmawr libert, Caeo, Carms., 279
Nantmeirch mountain farm, Ponterwyd, 278, 281
Napoleonic wars, 267
Nash, John, architect, 136, 181, 185, 188, 308
National Library of Wales, 33, 52, 71, 88, 89, 224, 226, 262, 274, 298, 305
National Monuments Record, England, 110
National Monuments Record of Wales, 104
National Museum of Wales, 65, 67, 70
National Trust, 135, 136, 140, 145
navigation,
   Global Positioning System (GPS), 109
nawdd, see sanctuary
Neath Technical Institute, 70
Neele, S. J., map engraver, 40
Neolithic, 109
   flints, 109
   henge & cursus, 109, 111
Nelson, Lord Viscount, 90
   Nelson's Tower, 49, 50, 53*, 54*
Nest, d. Rhys ap Tewdwr, 160
Netherlands, The, 2, 31, 75
Netpool, Cardigan, 204
Nevern church, 183
Newarke College, Leicester, 180
Newcastle Emlyn, 28, 224, 225, 226, 228
Newchurch, 173
Newgale, 177
newspapers, 29
Newport, National Eisteddfod, 1897, 70, 71
Newton House, *see* Dinefwr, 40
Nicholas, Thomas, yeoman & family of Dinas, 262, 263
Nicholas, William, gent., 299
Nicholson, G., *Cambrian Traveller's Guide*, 1808, 40, 278
Nicolas, Owain ap Gruffudd ap, 229
Nonconformity (Welsh), 28, 37, 50, 68
Norman, Richard, 123
Normans, 155, 156, 158, 159, 160, 166, 179, 208, 214, 218
North Africa, 75
North Tawton, 118, 119*
Northumberland, Countess of & Earl of, 231, 232
North Wales Gazette, The, 29
Nott, general, 86
Nuthill, estate, Fife, 237

oats, 266
Ogofau mines, *see* Dolaucothi
Optically-stimulated luminescence, 146
Ordnance Survey maps, 133, 138, 143, 233, 249*, 251, 258, 263, 271, 272, 288, 291, 294, 304*, 305
   Archaeology Division, 132

Ortelius, Abraham, of Antwerp, 225
Oswestry, 70
Ottley, Adam, bishop of St Davids, 200
Owen, Geraint Dyfnallt, historian, 157
Owen, H. (ed.) G. Owen's *Pembrokeshire*, 158, 159
Owen, Jeremiah, maltster, 305
Oystermouth Castle & Bay, 52
Oxford, 27
    University, 1, 176, 200
Oystermouth castle, 52

Paintings, 64*, 65*, 66*, 68*, 69*, 71*, 72*, 74*, 77*, 78*
Pale, Great, Old, Little & Pale Gate farms, 231
Pant-y-Cendy, Roman cremation & defended enclosure, 172*
paper, 9-26, 31
    carta damascena, 9
    Chinese invention of, 9
    'Cox paper', 54
    fibres, 14*, 15
    hand-made, 11*, 15
    laid, 10
    machine-made, 12, 13,
    rope brown, 23
    spread to Asia & Europe, 9-10
    watermarks, 31
    wove, 10
papermakers, 13, 17, 18-25,
    papermaking machinery, 10, 11, 12, 13
    West Wales, 15-25
paper mills
    Carmarthen, Felinganol, 15, 16*, 17
    Cleddau Mill, Haverfordwest, 23
    early illustration of, 10*
    Frogmore, Herts., 13
    Gun's Mills, Gloucester, 17
    Halghton, Flint, 18
    Haverfordwest (St Martin, Hartsore, Harford), 21, 22, 23, 24, 31
    Home Park Mill, Hemel Hempstead, 13
    Kidwelly, 18, 19*, 20
    Melin Mynach, Swansea, 19
    Neckinger Mill, Bermondsey, 13
    numbers in UK by 1800, 13
    Peterhof, Russia, 22
    Prendergast Mills (Millbank, Cleddau), Haverfordwest, 22-24, 31
    Priory Mills (St Thomas), Haverfordwest, 22, 23, 24
    Tate's, John, Hertford, 10
Parc y Marles/Argoed, Cardigan, 218, 219
Parc y Spitt, 158
Paris, 2, 6
    University of, 1
parishes, 158, 172, 172, 177, 179, 182, 183, 213, 214, 218, 272
    parish boundaries, 117, 118, 153, 156*, 158, 200, 236*

Park Glas farm, Llanstephan, 77
Park y Rhun (Parkreame), 228, 229
Park-y-Vicar Farm, Llanstephan, 163
parks & gardens, historic, 104, 133, 137, 143, 236, 237, 238
Parliament, Acts of, 182, 225
    Chantries & Colleges Act, 1546, 182, 183, 199
    Copyright Act, 42
    Emancipation Bill, 50
    House of Commons Papers, 18, 52
    Licensing Act, 1695, 28
    Llanddewi Brefi Enclosure Act 1888, 273, 274
    Statutes of Mortmain, 161
    Union of England & Wales, 225
Parry, Medwyn, 105*
Parys Mountain, Anglesey, 97
pastoralism, 165, 166
Pavy, Hugh, Bishop of St David's (1485-1495), 198
Payne, Archdeacon, 181
Paxton, Sir William of Middleton Hall, 48, 49
    Paxton's Tower, *see* Nelson's Tower
Peate, Iorwerth, 260, 261
Pebidiog, cantref, 160
Pederton, Walter de, Justiciar, 210
Peel, William & s. Mary, of Taliaris Park, 56
Pembrey, 225, 228
Pembrokeshire, 41, 46, 85, 205, 207, 208, 224, 226, 228
    County Record Office, 298
Penallt, 224
Penally, 157
Pendeggy (Mondegu) mill, 161, 162* 163
Pendine, 99, 105, 158, 228
    races, 85
Pengam, Mon., school, 71
Penhouët, Comte de (1764-1839, Breton antiquarian, 45, 46
Penley, Aaron (1806-1870), watercolourist, 55*, 56
Penlanwen Farm, 138, 140, 141
Pennant, Thomas (1726-1798), writer, *Tours in Wales*, 43-44, 50
Pennardd, lordship, 279
Penparc, battle of, 205, 218
Penres (Penrees) Stephen & family Lords of Llanstephan, 160, 161
Penrhiwyruchain, Cilycwm, hillfort, 102, 103*
Penrhyn Deuddwr (commote) 156, 158, 159, 161, 165
Pentowyn grange & farm, 155-168, 171
Pentrewyn, 158
Pentypark estate, pembs., 299, 300, 303, 305
Pen-y-Coed defended enclosure, 133
Pen-y-Ddinas, Llansawel, lost hillfort, 102
Pen-y-Graig farm, 233
Perfedd, commote & lordship, 247, 255, 256
    courts leet, 255
Perfedd, Cardiganshire, lordship, 278, 281
Perot, Stephen, 160
Perrot, John, Sir 231, 232

Peterwell Estate, 37
Peuliniog (commote), 156
'Pevsner' – Buildings of Wales series, 173
Picton Castle, 305
Picton, General, portrait of, 56
Peterwell Estate, 37
Philcus, burgess of Cardigan, 210
Phillimore, Egerton, antiquarian, 158
Philip, John ap & Philip ap Maredudd ap Philip of Cilsant, 229
Philipps, John P. A. Lloyd, Dale Castle, 306
Philipps, William, timber merchant, Carmarthen, 306, 308
Phillips, Evan Owen, Dean of St Davids, 1895-1897, 186
Phillips, Eynon, 232
Phillips, James, esq. of Pentypark & Picton Castle, 289, 291, 300, 302, 303, 306
    family tree, 301*
    monument, St Peter's church, 309*, 310
Phillips, James, mayor of Carmarthen, 302, 303
Phillips, James, papermaker, 23
Phillips, John, of Haverfordwest, 21, 24
Philipps, John, attorney, maltster & merchant, Carmarthen, 302
Phillips, John, draper, 22
Phillips, Morgan of Picton, 231, 232
Phillips, Richard, editor, *Carm. Jnl*, 36
Phillips, Richard, Sir, Picton Castle, 306
Phillips, Samuel Levi, banker of Haverfordwest, 16
Phillips, Sarah, wife of Revd. D. Charles & d. Samuel Levi Phillips, 16
Phillipps, Stephen, landlord, *The Nelson*, 310
Phillips, Thomas, *Natur cyfammod eglwys*, 33*
Phillips, William, ship-builder of Carmarthen, 291, 308
Phillips family of Tregibby & Cardigan Priory, 214
photographs & photography, 10*, 12*, 18*, 23*, 50, 56, 72, 73, 81-86*, 82*, 87-93, 94-97*, 124*129* 175*, 177*, 187*, 188*, 189*, 240*, 250*, 254*, 260*, 262*, 284*, 288, 290*, 291, 292*, 295*, 296*, 309
    air photographers, 94, 98, 100, 107, 132, 176
    air photographs, 94*, 99*, 101*, 102*, 103* 105*, 108, 112*, 113*, 116*, 146 117*, 118*, 119*120*, 132*, 133, 163, 164*, 176*, 218, 248, 253*, 263*, 264*, 275*, 293
    digital, 109
    dry collodion process, 81
Pibwr Wen, Llangunnor, 88, 89*, 90
Pickering, Jim, air photographer, 107
Picton Castle estate, pembs., 298, 305
pilgrims & pilgrimage 175, 185, 189, 209, 210, 213, 214
Pill priory, 194
pillow mounds, 140
Pilroath, Llanstephan, 83
Pipe Rolls, 156
pipelines, 104
Piper, John (1903-1992) artists & writer, 57*, 58

Pirckheimer, Willibald, 4, 5
Pistyllgwion, 105*
Pitt-Rivers, General, archaeologist, 143
place-names, 117, 133, 137, 158, 207, 217, 218, 235, 262, 263, 270-283*
    arhosfa, 279, 280
    berry, burh, beorg, 109, 118
    betws, 217
    Carmarthenshire, 224-229
    clun (hayground), 265
    Dinas, 259
    eglwys, 158
    gaer, 104
    lak, 161
    maendy, 199
    mynydd, 279
    pale, 231, 233, 236
    park (Scots), 239
    sinshill, Saints' hill, 164
planning process, 174
ploughs & ploughing, 104, 159, 160, 209, 214, 218, 232, 264, 281
Plymouth, 115
Pontbren Arath, 91*
Ponthenry iron forge, 19
Pontyberem, 92
potatoes, 266
pottery, 304, 305
    kilns, 289, 303
    mediaeval, 144, 284
    Roman, 87, 123, 127-128*, 133, 144
    tiles, 284, 304
Powell, David, of Ystradwallter, H. S., 229
Powell, Evan, printer, Carmarthen, 30
Powell, George, of Ystradwallter, 229
Powell, William, of Glanarth, 92
Powis, Earl of, library, 5
Powys, 102, 266
Prehistory & prehistoric sites, *see also* Neolithic, Bronze Age, Iron Age, 100, 115
Prehistoric ritual & funerary monuments & practices, 117
prehistoric settlements, 101, 109,
Price, Arthur, 19
Price, Edward, gent., of Dinas, 262
Price, John, Sir, 27, 28
Price, Uvedale Sir (1747-1829), 42
Prichard, Rees, author of *Canwyll y Cymry*, 27
Pridham, Dr, builder Cennen Tower, 88
Prince of Wales, Investiture, 1911, 76
St Davids Cloisters opening, 174
Printers
    Carmarthen, 37-39
    Europe, 1-8
    London, 36
Printing
    block printing by Japanese, 9

copper-plate, 29, 30, 31, 40, 41, 43
corrections, 31, 32
devices, 2*, 3, 4*, 6
jobbing, 34-5, 37
lithography, 54, 56
in London, 27, 28
in Oxford & Cambridge, 27
in Shrewsbury, 28
ornaments, 5, 30
type, 29
Printing Presses, 6
    Aldine Press, Venice, 1, 3-6, 4*, 5*, 8
    Bala Press, N. Wales, 31
    Curwen Press, 58
    cylinder, 29
    clandestine Roman Catholic, 28
    Plantin-Moretus Press, Antwerp, 1
    Rampart Press, Carmarthen, 1
    rolling, 29
    Stourton Press, 57
    wooden presses, 29*
printing types, 29-30
Prints, topographical, 40, 181*, 288*, 295*
    aquatints, 40, 44*, 45, 46, 47*, 49
    chromolithographs, 55*, 56
    copper engraving, 29, 40, 41*, 42, 43*
    etchings, 40, 45, 46*, 48, 49*, 64*, 182*
    lithographs, 40, 51*, 52, 54, 57*
    steel engraving, 40, 52, 53*, 54, 61*, 62*, 288*
    woodcuts, wood engravings, 5*, 7, 10*, 30, 31, 40, 50,
        51*, 55*, 56
priories, *see* monasteries
Prichard, Rees, *Canwyll y Cymry*, 27
Pritchard, Emily, Cardigan historian, 212
Protestantism, 27, 28
Protheroe-Jones, Robert, 143
Pryse family of Gogerddan, 214
Ptolemy, 4
Pumsaint, *see also* Dolaucothi, 100, 101, 135, 138
    Roman baths & cremation urn, 128, 129
    Roman fort, 131, 136, 144
    Roman roads, 131
Purdue, John, archaeologist, 124
Pwll-y-gwichiaid farm, Llandudno, 50
Pysgotwr, river & valley, 270, 271

Quarter Sessions Records, Cardiganshire, 34

Rabagliati family, 53, 54, 68, 69, 74, 78
Radclyffe, William (1783-1855), engraver, of Birmingham,
    53*, 54
Radyr, Richard, Master, St Mary's College, 184
radiocarbon dates, 144, 146, 254
Radnorshire, 193, 226
railways, 40,

South Wales Railway, 55, 56
    Heart of Wales line, 102
Ramsay, R., 132
Randolf, Philip & Walter, peasant farmers, Llanstephan, 164
Read, John, mercer, Carmarthen, 303
Read, Joseph John, 23
Read, Samuel, of Airdrie, Lanarkshire, papermaker, 22, 23, 24
Rebecca Riots, 1843, 57
Rees, Eiluned, Llanstephan, 158, 161, 162, 166
Rees, Hector, ship's carpenter, 289, 300, 303
Rees, John, miller of Haverfordwest, 24, 25
Rees, Owen, partner, Longmans, 36
Rees, Samuel, lessee Prendergast mills, 22
Rees, Thomas, bookseller, Unitarian minister & author, 36, 50
Rees, William, *Map of S. Wales in XIV century*, 158, 213
Reeve, Thomas, Gloucs., papermaker, 24
Rhenanus, Beatus, printer, 3, 6, 7
Rhode, John & w. Anne, 24
Rhos-Llangeler, WWII stop-line, 105*
Rhyd-y-fuwch, Cardigan, 204, 212
Rhydderch, Hywel ap & w. Gwenllian, of Ystradwallter, 229
Rhydderch, John, printer of Shrewsbury, 28
Rhydygors castle, 155
Rhys ap Aron, *cais* of Widigada, 153
Rhys ap Maredudd, insurrection of, 170, 171
Rhys ab Owain, 169
Rhys ap Griffith, deputy Justiciar, 153
Rhys ap Gruffydd (The Lord Rhys), 159, 205, 212, 214, 215,
    218
Rhys ap Gruffud, sir of Dinefwr, 229
Rhys ap Gweirydd, *Hanes y Brytaniad a'r Cymry*, 1872, 54
Rhys ap Maredudd, 170, 171
Rhys ap Tewdwr, 160
Rhys, John David, 27
Richard II, King of England, 160, 176, 177
Richard, Jonah & w. Mary, papermaker, Carmarthen, 18
Richard ab Owain, 169
Richard ap Maredudd ap Richard, 169
Riley, Derrick, air photographer, 107
Rio Tinto Zinc Corporation, smelter at Hartlepool, 95
rivers & streams, 15, 19, 41*, 42, *43*, 46, 48, 49, 56, 58, 61-
    66, 85*94,, 99, 101, 136, 138, 140, 141, 144, 146, 147,
    155, 158, 159, 161, 162, 163, 165*, 192*, 197*, 200, 204,
    206, 208, 209, 211-18, 217, 218, 224, 225, 226*, 228,
    229, 231, 237*, 245, 246, 251, 254, 256, 259, 263, 266,
    270, 271, 280, 297, 298, 308,
    ferries, 49, 72, 155, 159, 165*
    fords, 49, 162
    waterfalls, 50
roads & trackways, 102, 104, 112, 237*
    mediaeval, 165*, 193, 194, 197*, 216, 217, 218
    Roman, 99, 100, 104, 132, 157, 194, 197*
Robert, Gruffydd, 27
Robinson, John Henry (1796-1871), artist & engraver, 50,
    51*, 52

Rogers, John, printer of Shrewsbury, 28
Rome, 6, 42
Roman Britain,
 amphitheatre, 131
 baths, 128
 battles, 235
 bone objects, 130*-131
 clothing, 130, 131
 barrows, mortuary enclosures, 133
 cemeteries, 157
 cremations, 123-134*, 172
 forts, 103, 104, 108*, 109, 111, 131, 143, 144
 gold mine, 136
 jewellery, 143
 lamps, 128-129*, 133
 legionary fortresses, 133
 mines, 101, 135-49
 musical instrument, 130*, 131, 133
 pottery, 87, 123, 127-128*, 133, 144
 farms, 99
 glass, 129, 133
 ironwork, 129-130, 133
 roads, 99, 100, 104, 123*, 131, 132, 143, 157, 194
 temple, 131
 tile, 129
 towns, 123, 133, 150, 155
 town walls, 157
 villas, 110
Roman mining sites in Europe, 143, 144
Roman Trenches, Parkmill, Ayrshire, 239*
rope-makers, 15, 16
Roscoe, Thomas, *Wanderings & Excursions in N. Wales, & S. Wales,* 52, 54
Rosehill Farm, Cardigan, 204
Ross, John, Scotsman, printer in London & Carmarthen, 28, 29, 32, 34, 36, 37, 38
Rowly-Williams, Lucy, 124
Royal, General, military surveyor, 143
Royal Academy, The, 44, 45, 46, 52, 56, 70, 71, 76
Royal Cambrian Academy, 71
Royal College of Art, 57, 70
Royal Commission on the Historical Monuments of England (RCHME), 107
Royal Commission on the Historical Monuments of Scotland (RCHMS), 107
Royal Commission on Ancient & Historical Monuments, Wales (RCAHMW), 88, 100, 104, 135, 144, 169, 176
 Carmarthenshire volume, 144, 195
Royal Institution, The, 48
Royal Military Academy, 56
Rudd, Anthony, Bishop of St Davids (1594-1614), 200
rugby, 83*, 85

saddlers & saddlery, 255
saints, 173
 Latin, 156, 157, 173
 Welsh, 155, 156, 157, 158, 173
St Bride's Bay, 226
St. Clears, 18, 92, 156, 158, 226, 228
 castle, 225, 228
St Celynnin, 271
St David, shrine & relics, 181, 182, 213
St Lucy, 173
St Maurice, 193
St Thomas the Martyr, 193
St. Davids, Bishops of, 27, 30, 48, 86, 151, 155, 156, 157, 159, 160, 174, 175-180, 181, 182, 183, 184, 185, 186, 187, 193, 194, 197, 198, 199, 200, 201, 213, 215, 274, 278
St Davids cathedral, 157, 174-189, 176*, 179*, 182*, 209
 architect, 175
 Bishops' Palace, 176*, 185, 186, 188, 197, 198, 200
 choir & choristers, 177, 178, 179, 180, 181, 183, 185, 186, 187
 Close, 176*, 177, 185
 Cloisters, 174, 175, 176, 185, 186, 187*, 188*, 189*
 Deans & chapters, 174, 175, 177, 178, 184, 185
 fabric, 175, 180, 181, 183, 185, 186
 Fabric Advisory Committee, 175
 Friends of the Cathedral, 177, 186
 library, 181, 183, 186, 187
 North Porch, 174
 St Mary's College, 175-185, 184*, 193, 194, 195*
 school, 177, 181, 183
 Statute Book, 197
 Treasury, 187
St Davids diocese, 199
St Davids estates, 160, 183, 193, 197
St Davids, parish of, 184
St Dogmael's Abbey, 194, 204, 205
St Ishmaels, chapel & church, 183, 226*
St Joseph, J. K. S., Professor, 98, 107, 120
St Lucy, 173
St Peter's Abbey, Gloucester, 212, 214, 215
sale catalogues (property), 37, 133
Salesbury, William, 1, 27
sanctuary, 151, 153, 176
Sandby, Paul (1731-1809), artist, *XII Views of Wales,* 44*, 45
Sandby, Thomas Paul, 44
Sannau, river, 146
Sarn Faen farm, Twrch valley, 245-258 *
Sarum Use, 180
Sathanas, Thomas, felon, 151, 154
Savory, H. N., National Museum of Wales, archaeologist, 132
saxons, 118
Saxton, Christopher, cartographer, 209, 224, 225, 226, 227*, 228, 229
Schaffer, Jacob Christian, 13

schools, 69, 70, 71
    circulating schools of Griffith Jones, 37
Scotland, 43, 44, 143, 146
    The Hebrides, 44
    Scottish Place-name Database, 235
Scott, Ann, publisher, Carmarthen, 35
Scott, Lady Frances, amateur artist, 45
Scott, Walter, market gardener, & w. Ann, 35
Scriptures, *see* Bible
Scurlock, John & d. Jane, Flanders Hill, 303
seals, 177*
Selman, Francis & family, of Kidwelly, papermaker, 18, 19, 20
Selman, Thomas & w. Anna Philips, papermaker, 19
Seren Gomer, 50
Sergeant, John Singer, artist, 70
settlements,
    deserted, 100, 245-258
    Iron Age, 102
    Romano-British, 104
    prehistoric, 101
sheep, 133, 219, 232, 255, 265, 266, 279
    shearers & woolpickers, 271, 274
    shepherds, 248, 268, 271, 272, 277, 279, 280
    sheepwalks, 265, 273*, 274, 276, 277, 278
Sheridan, 46
ships & shipping, 19, 31, 43*, 44, 49, 61*, 62*, 63, 65, 85*, 226, 287*, 288*, 300, 301, 303, 305, 306, 307, 308
    shipwrecks, 99
shops & shopping, 68, 69
Shrewsbury, 28, 36
silver, *see also* mines, 187
Simon, Benjamin, of Abergwili, bookbinder, copyist & poet, 33
Simpson, Doug, 98
skeletons, human, 126
Skrine, Henry, *Tours through Wales*, 1798, 54
Smith, James Allen, Dean of St Davids (1903-1918), 186
Smith, J. Beverley, professor, 169
Smith, Peter, 259, 266
smiths & smithies, 300
Smythe, Warington, geologist, 143
Snowdon (mt.), 40
Soar-y-Mynydd chapel, 259, 271
Society for Promoting Christian Knowledge (SPCK), 28, 37
    in diocese of St Davids, 37
soils, *see* geology
Soil Survey, The, Trawscoed, 219
Somerset,
    air photography in, 110
    County Council, 110
Spain, 72, 75
Speed, John, map-maker, 61, 206, 208*, 210, 224, 225, 229
    Theatre of the Empire of Great Britain, 208*, 209, 228
springs & wells, 139, 213
Spurrell, printers, Carmarthen, 38

Spurrell, William, 300
Stadler, J. C., aquatintist, 49
Stationers & stationery, 34, 37
Steele, Sir Richard, 47*, 48
Stepney, Lady Anne, 285, 289
Stepney, Lady Elizabeth, 298, 299
Stepney, Sir Thomas, 302
Stevyns, William, Sir, 184
Stewart, James, merchant, Carmarthen, 303, 305
Stoke Rivers hillfort, Devon, 117*
stone & stone quarries, 102, 104, 267
    Caerbwdi, 175*, 185
    flints, 109
    limestone, 56, 100, 165*
Strange, William, Revd., 161
Stuart, Ninian, of Falkland, 235
Sugar Loaf hillfort, 102
swans, 240
Swansea, 46, 225
    Glynn Vivian Art Galley, 78
Symond, Richard, peasant farmer, Llanstephan, 164
Symond, Brother William, Prior, Carmarthen Priory, 164

Tadema, Sir Lawrence Alma, artist, 76
Taf, river & estuary, 99, 155, 158, 159, 161, 163, 165*, 224, 225, 229, 231
tai-unnos (squatters' houses), 271
Talbenny, Pembs., 22
Talbot, Gilbert, Justiciar, 153, 154
Talhardd, Ffairfach hall-house, 266
Taliaris park, 55*, 56
Tallacharn, *see* Laugharne
Talley
    Abbey, 100, 225
    lakes, 99*
Tate, John, papermaker, d. 1507, 9, 10
Taverner, David, felon, 151, 153
Teifi, Afon & estuary, 204*, 205*, 206, 209, 213, 217, 226, 229
Teifi valley, 100
Teigncombe, 111
Teilo, St., 49, 157, 158, 159, 172, 173
Teulyddog, St., 156, 157
Thomas, David, glover, Carmarthen, 300
Thomas, Edgar, artist, 73
Thomas, Evan, compositor, of Shrewsbury, Chester & Carmarthen, 32
Thomas, Jeremy Thomas, merchant, London & Carmarthen 291, 293, 307
Thomas, Nicholas, printer of Carmarthen, 28, 29, 30, 31, 32, 33, 38
Thomas, Rhys, printer of Carmarthen, Llandovery & Cowbridge, 28, 31
Thomas, Rhys ap, Sir 75*, 224, 229
Thomas, Roger, 105*

Thomas, W. G., maltster, Carmarthen, 307

Thompson, Michael, archaeologist, 197

Thornberry, Chivelstone, Devon, defended emclosure, 115, 116*, 117, 118

Tibetot, Robert, justiciar, 169, 170

Tillotson's *Picturesque Scenery in Wales* (1860), 52

Times, The, 57

timber, 207, 288, 291, 293, 300, 302, 304, 306, 307, 310
    charcoal, 18
    cordwood, 19

tinplate works, 49

Tir Griffith ap Rees Llewelyn Du, 264

tithes, 157, 159, 160, 171, 172

Toller, Hugh, fieldworker, Roman roads, 104

Tomas, Morgan & Harry ap, 220

Topham, Mathew, cotton miller, 22

towns, 226, 229
    mediaeval, 99, 204-223
    plans, 166, 204, 228

tourists and travellers, 40, 42, 43, 52, 54, 175, 185, 189

Townsend, Chauncey, mining entrepreneur, 143

Towy, river, *see* Tywi

Towy Works, Carmarthen, 291, 305, 308

Towyn Farm, Gwbert, 219

transhumance, 245, 254, 277, 281

transport, 85, 104
    carts, 72
    sledge (*car llusg*), 46

Trecifft, Cardigan, 204, 219

Tredgolde, John, felon, 151, 153

Tree, R. J., 186

Trefhedyn, 28

Tremain, 216, 217

Trenches, The, Falkland, 237*, 238*

Treprior Farm, Cardigan, 218

Trerefe/Gerardston, Cardigan, 205*

Trevine, Bishop's lodgings, 197, 200

Tregib mansion, Llandeilo, 88*

Tregibby, Cardigan, 205

Trelech a'r Betws, 158, 173

Treschel, Jean, 2

Troedrhiwcymer farmstead & mountain, Doithïe valley, 271, 272

Trimsaran, 228

Troedyrhiw, Cardigan, 207

Troedrhiwcymer farm, Doithïe/Camddwr, 266

Troedrhiwruddwen farm,, Doithïe/Camddwr, 271, 274

Tro'r Derlwyn, Garw valley, 254, 255

turbary, 255, 274

Turner, J. M. W., artist, 40, 45, 52, 54, 58

Turnpike roads & Trusts, 36, 192*, 194,

Twrch, river & valley, 245, 246, 251, 254, 256

Tŷ Gwyn farm, Llangunnor, 47*

Tyncornel farm, Doithïe/Camddwr, 259, 271, 271, 280

Tyddyn Nant Ieuan, 263

Tywi (Towy), river & estuary, 41, 42*, 43*, 48, 49, 58, 61-66, 85*, 94, 99, 155, 159, 163, 192*, 197*, 200, 224, 225, 226*, 229, 285, 297, 298, 308

Tywi (Towy), valley, 40, 42, 45, 46, 48, 50, 52, 53*, 54, 56, 58, 73, 86, 99, 100, 104, 136, 151

Tywyn Farm, Gwbert, 205*

University of Wales,
    Cardiff, 144
    Lampeter, 144

Urban, Bishop of Llandaff, 157, 158

Valla, Lorenzo, 2, 7, 8

Valor Ecclesiasticus, 160, 183, 184, 193, 195, 199, 200, 215

Vaughan, Philip, foundry, Carmarthen, 308

Vaughan, Richard of Derwydd, 298, 299

Vaughans of Golden Grove, 229, 255
    Vaughan, John, 247, 298, 303, 305
    Vaughan, Richard, 247, 302
    Vaughan, Walter, 229

vicars, 172

Victoria, Queen & family, 56, 71

Vitruvian waterwheel, 144, 146

Vincent, Thomas, Welsh author, 31

Waleran, Robert, 206, 208

Wales, maps of, 209, 224

Wales, principality of, 158

Walsingham, shrine & Slipper Chapel, 213

Walter, Hubert, archbishop of Canterbury, 170

Walters, Dr, of Llangadog, 93

Warham, William, Archbishop of Canterbury, 3, 184

watercolours, 44*, 45*, 52*, 54*, 56*, 62*, 63*65, 70, 135

Watkins, George, joiner, Carmarthen, 305

Watts, G. F., artist, 70, 73

Watts, William (1742-1851), engraver, 44

Webster, Peter, archaeologist, 144

wells, *see* springs

Welsh Art, 73, 75, 76, 78

Welsh books, 27, 28

Welsh counties, 225, 226, 228

Welsh folklore (Mari Llwyd), 87

Welsh genealogy & genealogists, 224

Welsh language & literature, 27, 28, 29, 30, 31, 32, 35, 36, 37, 42, 45, 49, 50, 54, 70, 71, 73, 76, 158, 219, 224, 226, 268, 271

Welsh Laws, 157, 214, 274

Welsh Kings & Princes, 155, 159, 169, 171, 205, 208, 229, 274, 276

Welsh Trust, interdenominational, 28

Welshman, The, newspaper, 307

Welshpool, 36

Welshries, 159, 165, 166, 169, 205

Wenallt, 231, 232

Westmead Estate, 232

Whatman, James, the elder, papermaker, 10
Whitchurch, 177
Whitchurch, Edward, printer of London, *Yny lhyvyr hwnn*, 27
White, Hannah, bookseller, of Carmarthen, 38
White Hall deserted farmstead, Nant-y-Bai valley, 94
Whitland Abbey, 160, 196, 225
Whitland iron forge, 19
Whitwell mediaeval hospital, St Davids, 177, 183, 184, 185
Widigada, commote of, 153, 154, 169, 172
Wilfred, Bishop of St. Davids, 159
Wilkes, Eileen, archaeologist, 115, 116*
Wilkinson, Gardner John, Sir, Egyptologist and archaeologist, 135-147
William, Prior, Carmarthen Priory, 161
Williams, Christopher, artist, 67-78
Williams, David (1809-1896), farmer, Llangain, w. Rachel & family, 67
Williams, Emily, w. of Christopher, 67, 71
Williams, Evan (1845-1915), 67 (father, Christopher Williams), & w. Mary, 67, 68
Williams, Evan, cabinet-maker, Llandovery, & family, 67, 68*
Williams, Evan & Thomas, London booksellers, 36
Williams, Edward (Iolo Morganwg) 38
Williams, Evan & Thomas, London booksellers, 36
Williams, Glanmor, historian, 197
Williams, Ifor, son Christopher Williams, 72
Williams, James, Sir, 137
Williams, John of Carmarthen, 303
Williams, John, printer of Carmarthen, 28
Williams, John, Sir, physician, 71, 72*
Williams, Christopher & w. Margaret, Llyfni Ironworks Co., 68
Williams, Margaret Lindsey, artist, 67, 73
Williams, Mathew, engraver, 40
Williams, Morgan, theologian, 33*, 36
Williams, Penry, 73
Williams, Peter, Revd., Bible commentator, 31, 32, 33, 37
Williams, Peter, shipbuilder, Pembroke Dock, 306
Williams, Rowland (*Hwfa Môn*), Archdruid, 71
Williams, Thomas, & d. Bridget, *of Edwinsford*, 44
Williams, Thomas & Penry, artists, 73
Williams, William & bros. cabinet-makers, Llandovery, 68*, 76
Williams, William, Dean of St Davids 1919-1930, 186
Williams, William, sheep farmer, Pantsiry, 281
Wilson, David, Cambridge, air-photographer, 107, 120
Wilson, Richard (1713-82), artist, 42, 43
Winchester, Angus, 276

Winchester, King Alfred's College, 110
Windsor castle, 45
Windsor, Gerald de & w. Nest, Constable of Pembroke Castle, 160
wine, 224
Wizo of Wiston, 159
woods, forests & plantations, 112, 133, 138, 171, 210, 226, 229, 232, 236, 264, 265, 266
    see also timber & Forestry Commission
Wood, map of Carmarthen 1834, 286, 291, 298, 305
Wood, John George (1768-1838), FSA, *Principal rivers of Wales*, 48, 49, 50, 56
Woodward's *History of Wales* (1853), 52
Wolfscastle, Bishop's house, 197, 200
wolves, 210
World War I, 75, 266, 267
World War II, 175, 248
    defences in west Wales, 105*
Wmffre, Iwan, 213, 217, 218, 219, 265
Wye, river, 225
Wyndham, H. P., author & tourist, 40
Wynn, Sir Watkin Williams, 45, 50, 281
Wynter, Walter, bailiff, Llanstephan, 164

Y Ferwig, Cardigan, 205*, 214, 216, 219
Yardley, E., *Menevia Sacra*, 184*, 185, 194, 195, 200
Yarford enclosures, Devon, 112
Yates, Bert, Humber motorcycle works rider, 85
Yonge, Thomas, felon, 151, 153
Younge, William le, agent of the Black Prince, 161
Youngs, mediaeval Carmarthen burgess family, 151
York, University of, 111
Ynys Enlli (Bardsey Island), 209
Ysbyty Ystradmeurig, lordship & commons, 277
Ysbyty-Ystwyth, 278
Ystlwyf (Oysterlowe) commote, 156
Ystrad Ffin, upper Tywi valley, 48
Ystrad estate, hill & woods, Carmarthen, 123, 132, 133
Ystrad Wallter, 228, 229
Ystradfflur (Strata Florida) Cistercian monastery, 276
Ystradgynlais, 247
Ystradmarchell Cistercian monastery, 276
Ystradowen, 246
Ystwyth, river & valley, 146
Ystyffan, St., 159

Zinc, *see* mines, zinc